GO ADD VALUE SOMEPLACE ELSE

DILBERT

by **SCOTT ADAMS**

Andrews McMeel
Publishing

Kansas City • Sydney • London

INTRODUCTION

Thanks to my rare combination of public accessibility and incompetence I get more unsolicited advice than anyone in the galaxy. Apparently if you spend five minutes reading anything I've written you start thinking, this guy needs my help.

I've noticed that when I offer my advice to others I am adding value. But when other people offer advice to me, it comes off as meddling, griping, and missing the point. This supports my hypothesis that other people are the leading cause of bad advice.

The only reliable advice I get is from my dog, Snickers. Three times a day she finds me in my home office and rolls on her back to look irresistible. This is how she advises me that it is time to take a break and rub her belly. I always comply. And not once has that advice turned out to be suboptimal. I feel good every time I pet her and I'm not aware of any projects that were ruined by my dog-rubbing ways.

Compare Snickers' track record to the advice you get from your coworkers who are, in your opinion, little more than sentient saddlebags full of spoiled baloney. The dog wins every time. Am I right?

The best advice you can offer is the type that has two potential outcomes: Either the advisee will succeed and you can claim the success as your own, or the advice ends up killing the advisee and any witnesses. Either way you end up looking like the smart one.

The worst kind of advice is the type that lends itself to measurement. You don't want to advise someone that getting a lawyer to review a document will only take a week because anyone with a calendar will eventually figure out that it took seven months.

You want to give the sort of advice that defies measurement. For example, if someone asks your opinion on a proposed company logo, say something like, "The blue needs to be bluer." And never offer a reason because that just opens you up to attack.

My advice today is that you should read this book because it will make you more attractive in ways that are impossible to measure. But in the interest of full disclosure, the other possibility is that you'll discover how much your job is like Dilbert's and cry yourself into an early grave.

I would write more but Snickers just advised me that I need to take a break.

Thank you for reading *Dilbert*.

S.Adams

Scott Adams

TWITTER: twitter.com/dilbert_daily
FACEBOOK: facebook.com/Dilbert

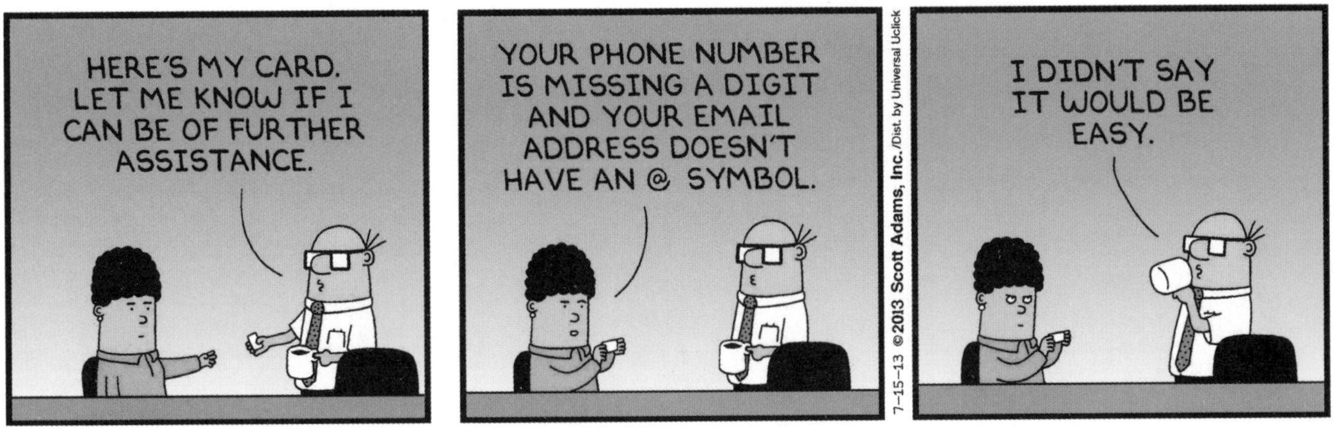
HERE'S MY CARD. LET ME KNOW IF I CAN BE OF FURTHER ASSISTANCE.
YOUR PHONE NUMBER IS MISSING A DIGIT AND YOUR EMAIL ADDRESS DOESN'T HAVE AN @ SYMBOL.
7-15-13 ©2013 Scott Adams, Inc./Dist. by Universal Uclick
I DIDN'T SAY IT WOULD BE EASY.

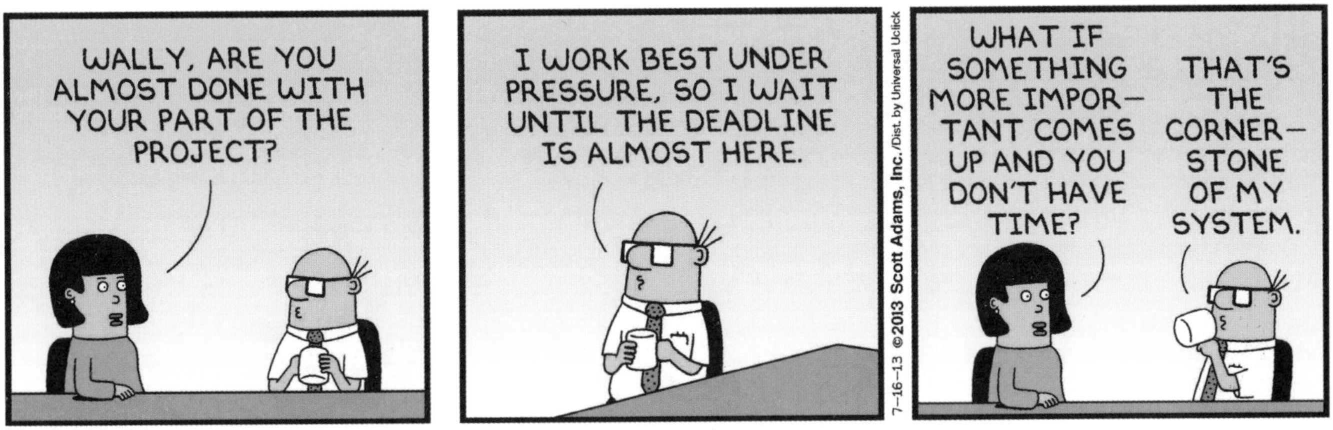
WALLY, ARE YOU ALMOST DONE WITH YOUR PART OF THE PROJECT?
I WORK BEST UNDER PRESSURE, SO I WAIT UNTIL THE DEADLINE IS ALMOST HERE.
7-16-13 ©2013 Scott Adams, Inc./Dist. by Universal Uclick
WHAT IF SOMETHING MORE IMPOR-TANT COMES UP AND YOU DON'T HAVE TIME?
THAT'S THE CORNER-STONE OF MY SYSTEM.

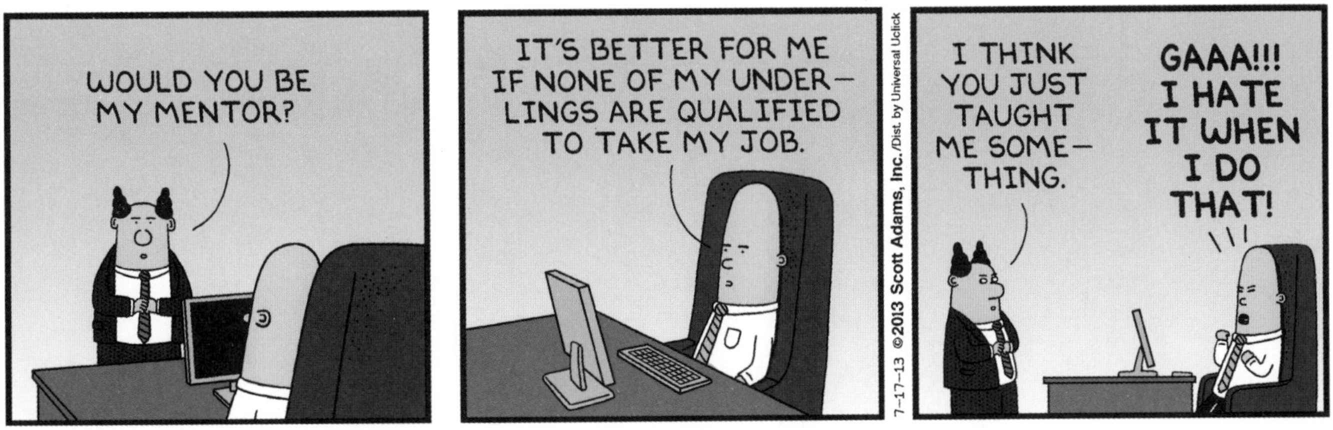
WOULD YOU BE MY MENTOR?
IT'S BETTER FOR ME IF NONE OF MY UNDER-LINGS ARE QUALIFIED TO TAKE MY JOB.
7-17-13 ©2013 Scott Adams, Inc./Dist. by Universal Uclick
I THINK YOU JUST TAUGHT ME SOME-THING.
GAAA!!! I HATE IT WHEN I DO THAT!

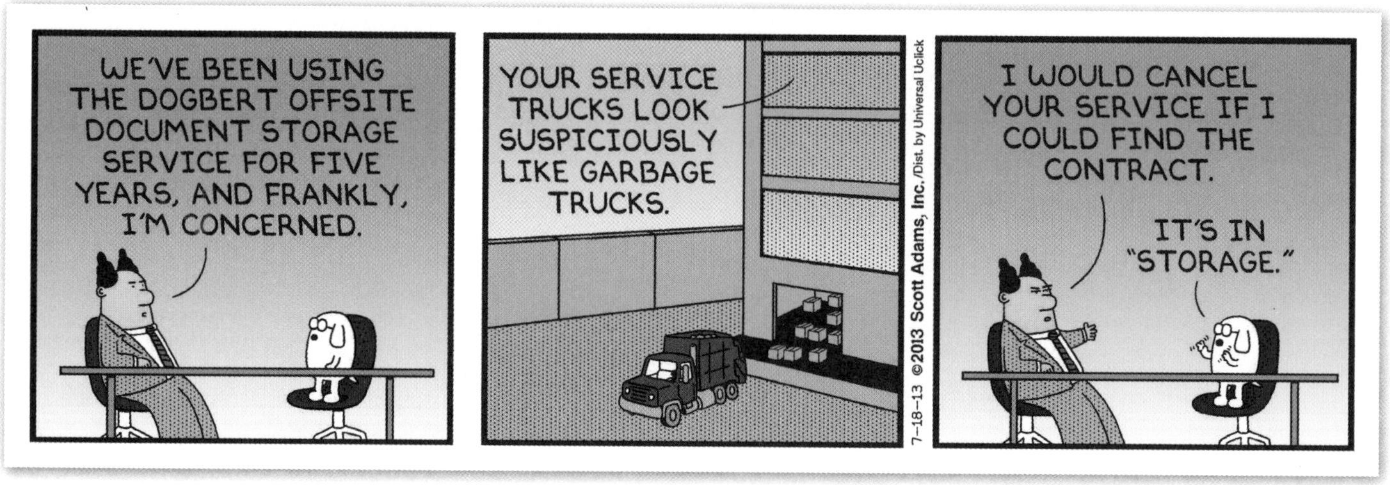
WE'VE BEEN USING THE DOGBERT OFFSITE DOCUMENT STORAGE SERVICE FOR FIVE YEARS, AND FRANKLY, I'M CONCERNED.
YOUR SERVICE TRUCKS LOOK SUSPICIOUSLY LIKE GARBAGE TRUCKS.
7-18-13 ©2013 Scott Adams, Inc./Dist. by Universal Uclick
I WOULD CANCEL YOUR SERVICE IF I COULD FIND THE CONTRACT.
IT'S IN "STORAGE."

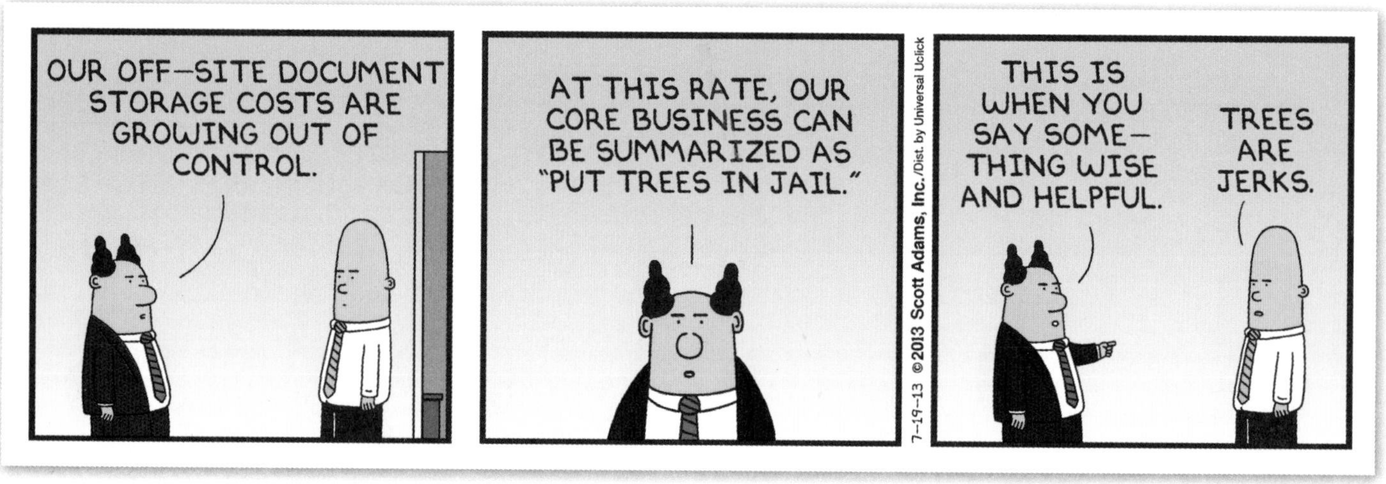
OUR OFF-SITE DOCUMENT STORAGE COSTS ARE GROWING OUT OF CONTROL.
AT THIS RATE, OUR CORE BUSINESS CAN BE SUMMARIZED AS "PUT TREES IN JAIL."
7-19-13 ©2013 Scott Adams, Inc./Dist. by Universal Uclick
THIS IS WHEN YOU SAY SOME-THING WISE AND HELPFUL.
TREES ARE JERKS.

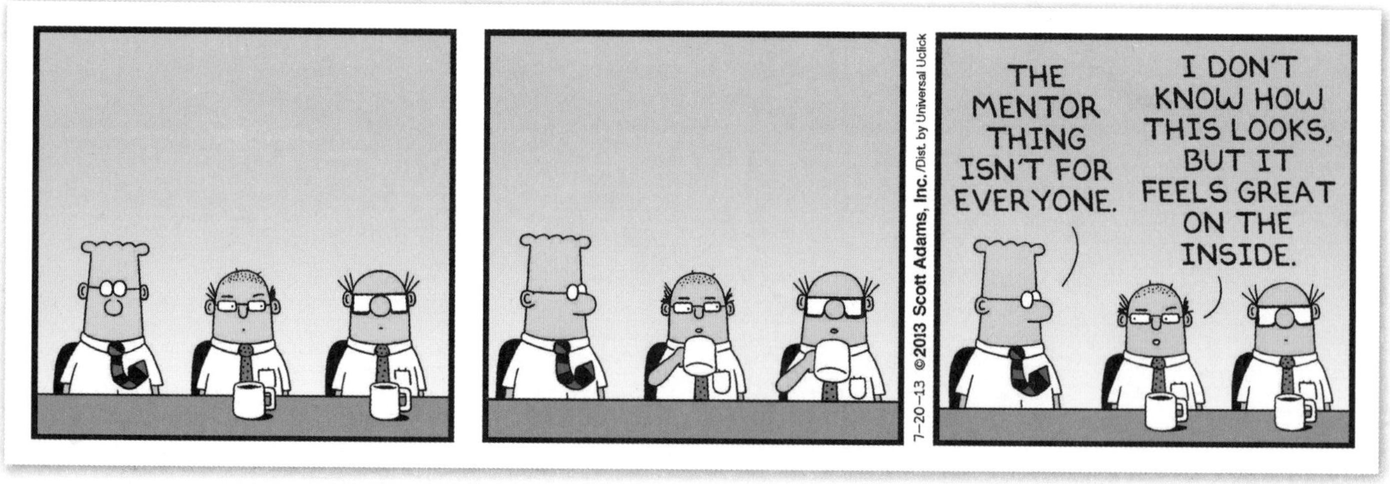
7-20-13 ©2013 Scott Adams, Inc./Dist. by Universal Uclick
THE MENTOR THING ISN'T FOR EVERYONE.
I DON'T KNOW HOW THIS LOOKS, BUT IT FEELS GREAT ON THE INSIDE.

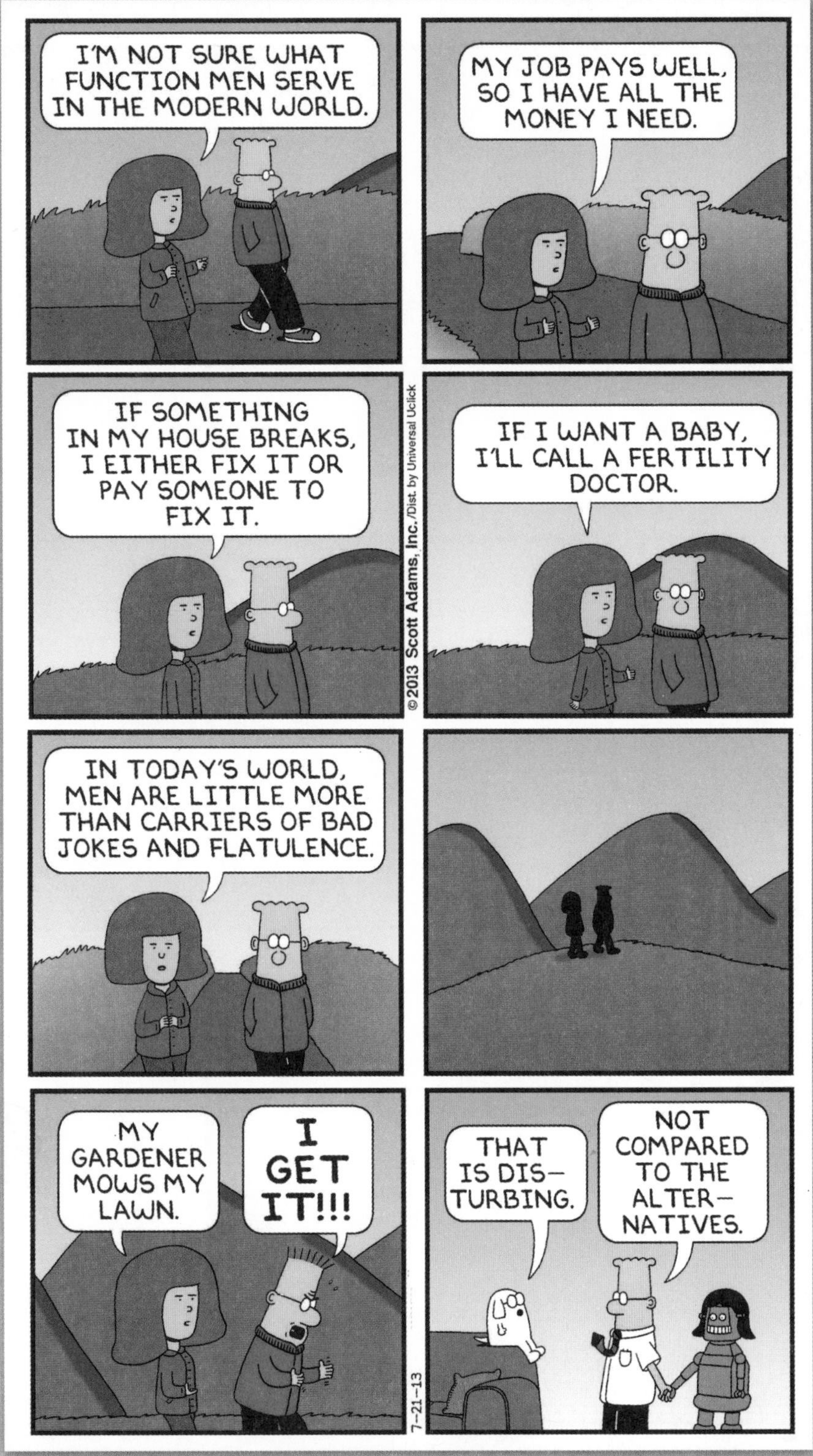
I'M NOT SURE WHAT FUNCTION MEN SERVE IN THE MODERN WORLD.
MY JOB PAYS WELL, SO I HAVE ALL THE MONEY I NEED.
IF SOMETHING IN MY HOUSE BREAKS, I EITHER FIX IT OR PAY SOMEONE TO FIX IT.
©2013 Scott Adams, Inc./Dist. by Universal Uclick
IF I WANT A BABY, I'LL CALL A FERTILITY DOCTOR.
IN TODAY'S WORLD, MEN ARE LITTLE MORE THAN CARRIERS OF BAD JOKES AND FLATULENCE.
MY GARDENER MOWS MY LAWN.
I GET IT!!!
7-21-13
THAT IS DIS-TURBING.
NOT COMPARED TO THE ALTER-NATIVES.

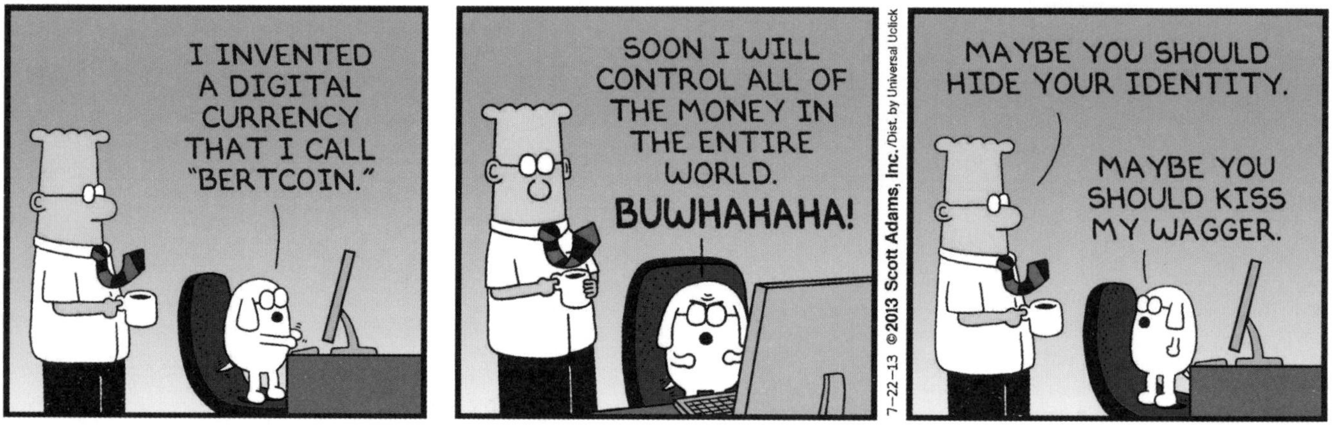
I INVENTED A DIGITAL CURRENCY THAT I CALL "BERTCOIN."
SOON I WILL CONTROL ALL OF THE MONEY IN THE ENTIRE WORLD.
BUWHAHAHA!
7-22-13 ©2013 Scott Adams, Inc./Dist. by Universal Uclick
MAYBE YOU SHOULD HIDE YOUR IDENTITY.
MAYBE YOU SHOULD KISS MY WAGGER.

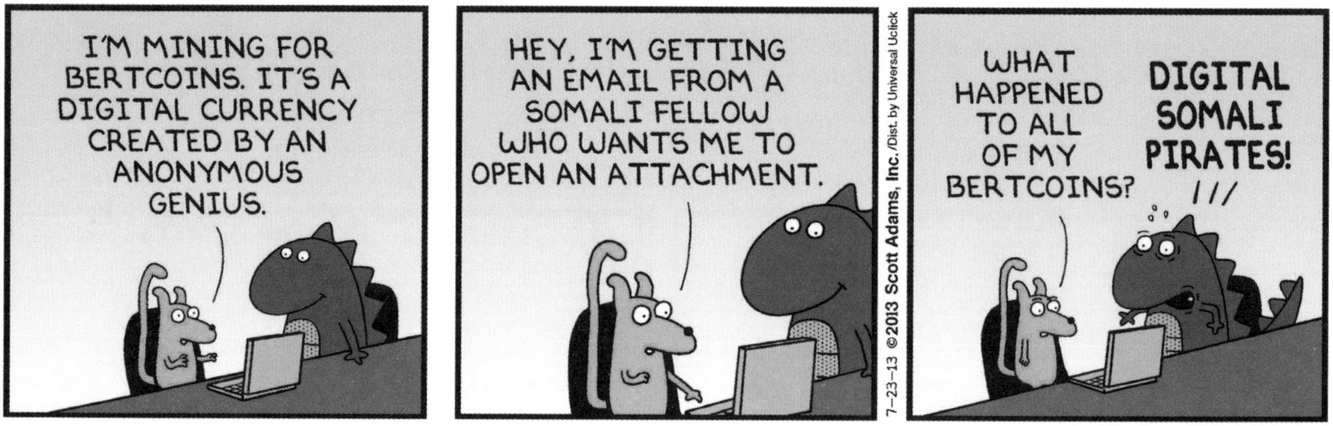
I'M MINING FOR BERTCOINS. IT'S A DIGITAL CURRENCY CREATED BY AN ANONYMOUS GENIUS.
HEY, I'M GETTING AN EMAIL FROM A SOMALI FELLOW WHO WANTS ME TO OPEN AN ATTACHMENT.
7-23-13 ©2013 Scott Adams, Inc./Dist. by Universal Uclick
WHAT HAPPENED TO ALL OF MY BERTCOINS?
DIGITAL SOMALI PIRATES!

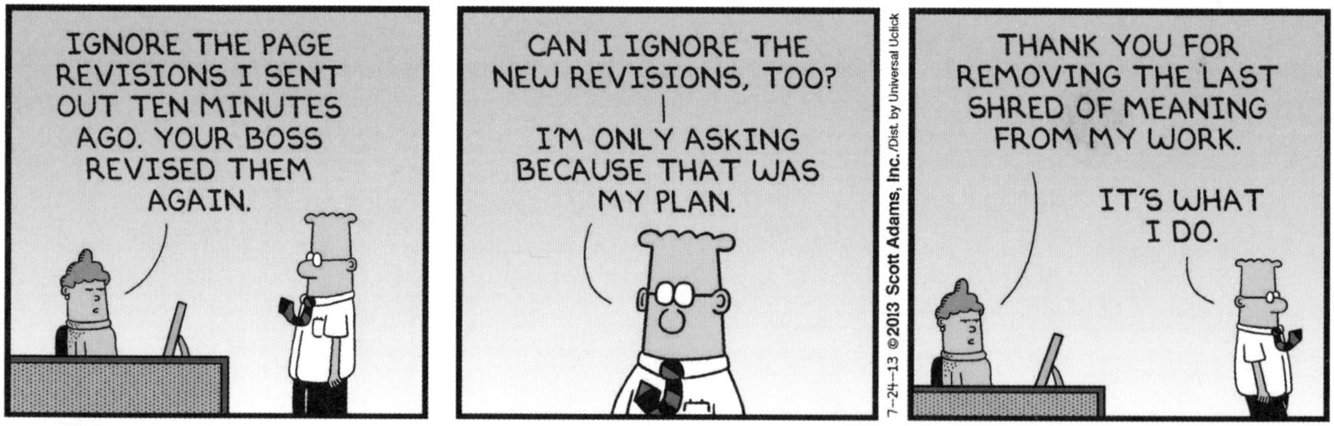
IGNORE THE PAGE REVISIONS I SENT OUT TEN MINUTES AGO. YOUR BOSS REVISED THEM AGAIN.
CAN I IGNORE THE NEW REVISIONS, TOO?
I'M ONLY ASKING BECAUSE THAT WAS MY PLAN.
7-24-13 ©2013 Scott Adams, Inc./Dist. by Universal Uclick
THANK YOU FOR REMOVING THE LAST SHRED OF MEANING FROM MY WORK.
IT'S WHAT I DO.

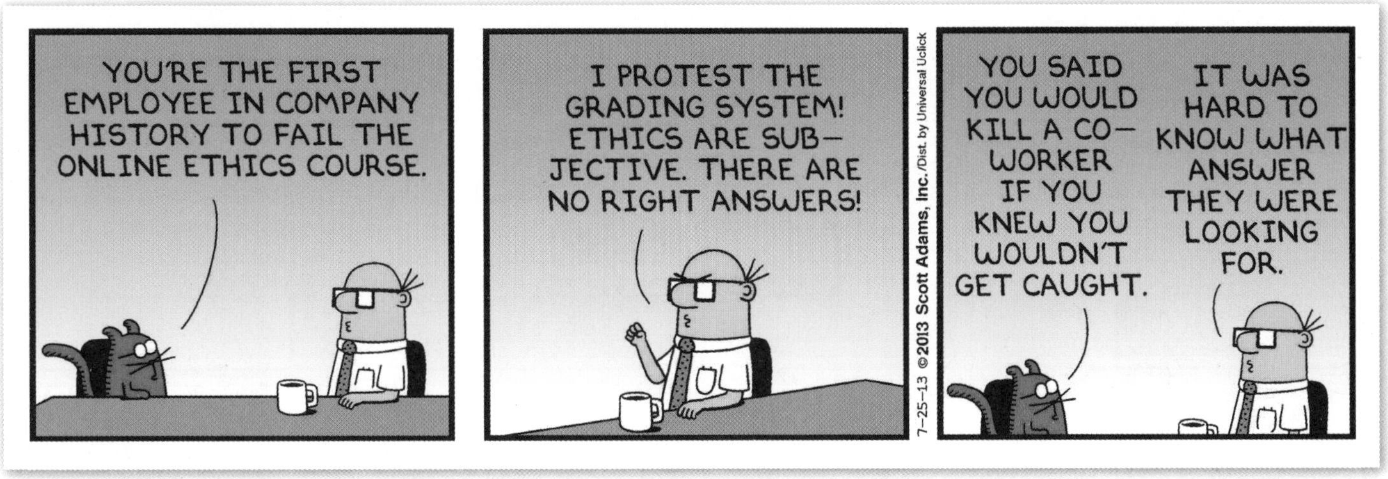
YOU'RE THE FIRST EMPLOYEE IN COMPANY HISTORY TO FAIL THE ONLINE ETHICS COURSE.
I PROTEST THE GRADING SYSTEM! ETHICS ARE SUBJECTIVE. THERE ARE NO RIGHT ANSWERS!
YOU SAID YOU WOULD KILL A CO-WORKER IF YOU KNEW YOU WOULDN'T GET CAUGHT.
IT WAS HARD TO KNOW WHAT ANSWER THEY WERE LOOKING FOR.
7-25-13 ©2013 Scott Adams, Inc./Dist. by Universal Uclick

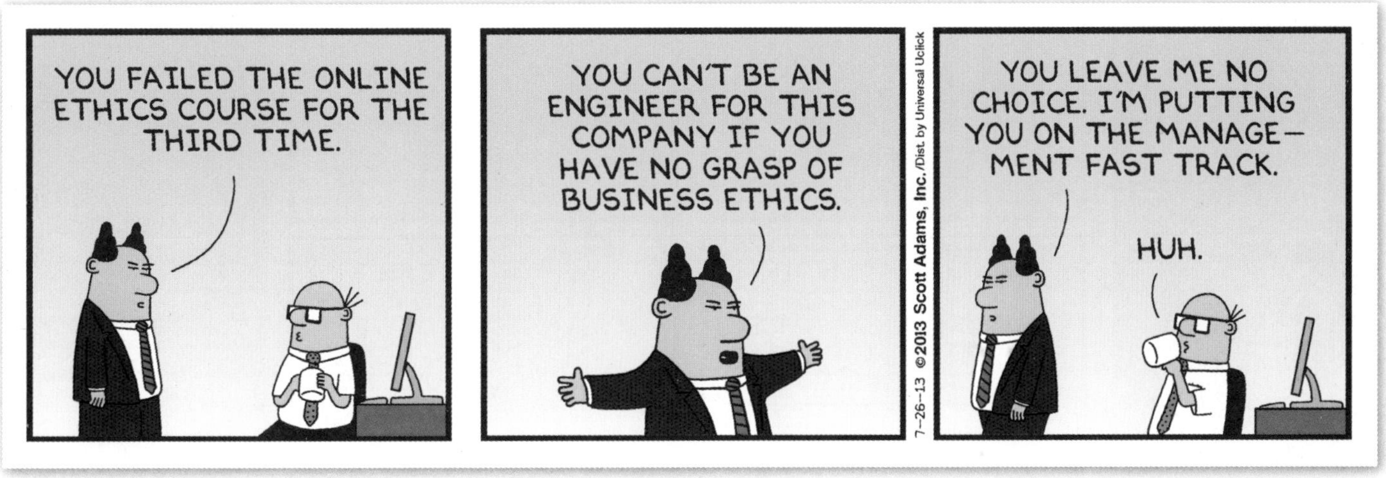
YOU FAILED THE ONLINE ETHICS COURSE FOR THE THIRD TIME.
YOU CAN'T BE AN ENGINEER FOR THIS COMPANY IF YOU HAVE NO GRASP OF BUSINESS ETHICS.
YOU LEAVE ME NO CHOICE. I'M PUTTING YOU ON THE MANAGEMENT FAST TRACK.
HUH.
7-26-13 ©2013 Scott Adams, Inc./Dist. by Universal Uclick

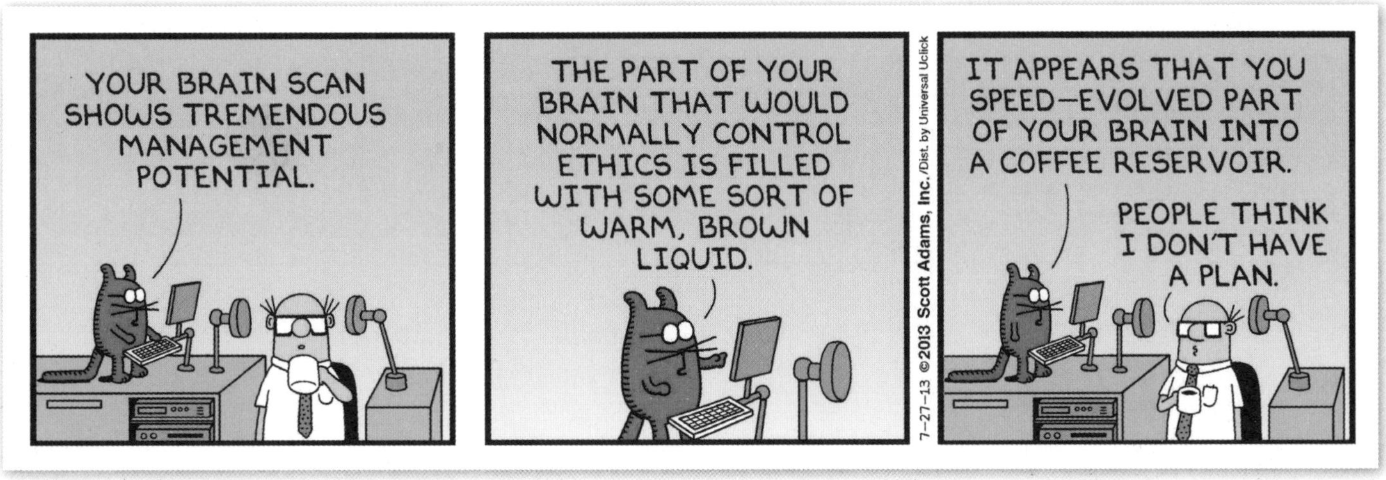
YOUR BRAIN SCAN SHOWS TREMENDOUS MANAGEMENT POTENTIAL.
THE PART OF YOUR BRAIN THAT WOULD NORMALLY CONTROL ETHICS IS FILLED WITH SOME SORT OF WARM, BROWN LIQUID.
IT APPEARS THAT YOU SPEED-EVOLVED PART OF YOUR BRAIN INTO A COFFEE RESERVOIR.
PEOPLE THINK I DON'T HAVE A PLAN.
7-27-13 ©2013 Scott Adams, Inc./Dist. by Universal Uclick

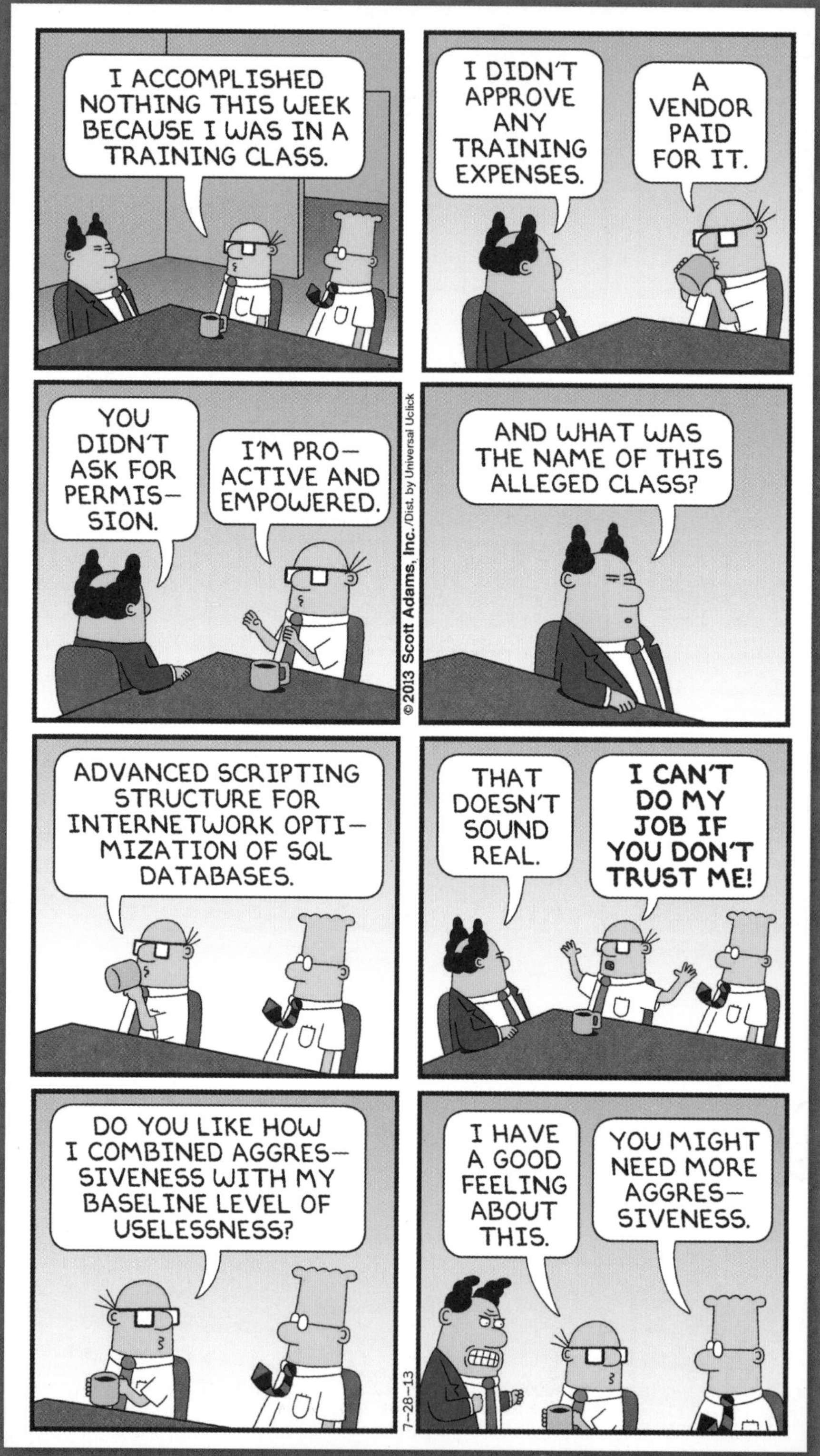
I ACCOMPLISHED NOTHING THIS WEEK BECAUSE I WAS IN A TRAINING CLASS.
I DIDN'T APPROVE ANY TRAINING EXPENSES.
A VENDOR PAID FOR IT.
YOU DIDN'T ASK FOR PERMIS- SION.
I'M PRO- ACTIVE AND EMPOWERED.
AND WHAT WAS THE NAME OF THIS ALLEGED CLASS?
ADVANCED SCRIPTING STRUCTURE FOR INTERNETWORK OPTI- MIZATION OF SQL DATABASES.
THAT DOESN'T SOUND REAL.
I CAN'T DO MY JOB IF YOU DON'T TRUST ME!
DO YOU LIKE HOW I COMBINED AGGRES- SIVENESS WITH MY BASELINE LEVEL OF USELESSNESS?
I HAVE A GOOD FEELING ABOUT THIS.
YOU MIGHT NEED MORE AGGRES- SIVENESS.
©2013 Scott Adams, Inc./Dist. by Universal Uclick
7-28-13

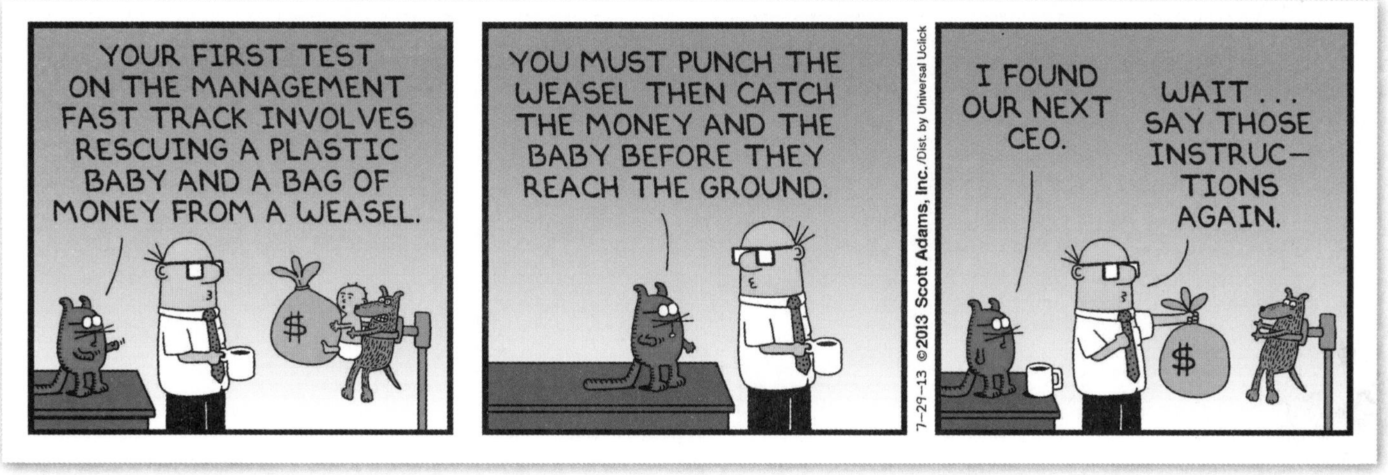
YOUR FIRST TEST ON THE MANAGEMENT FAST TRACK INVOLVES RESCUING A PLASTIC BABY AND A BAG OF MONEY FROM A WEASEL.
YOU MUST PUNCH THE WEASEL THEN CATCH THE MONEY AND THE BABY BEFORE THEY REACH THE GROUND.
7-29-13 ©2013 Scott Adams, Inc./Dist. by Universal Uclick
I FOUND OUR NEXT CEO.
WAIT . . . SAY THOSE INSTRUC-TIONS AGAIN.

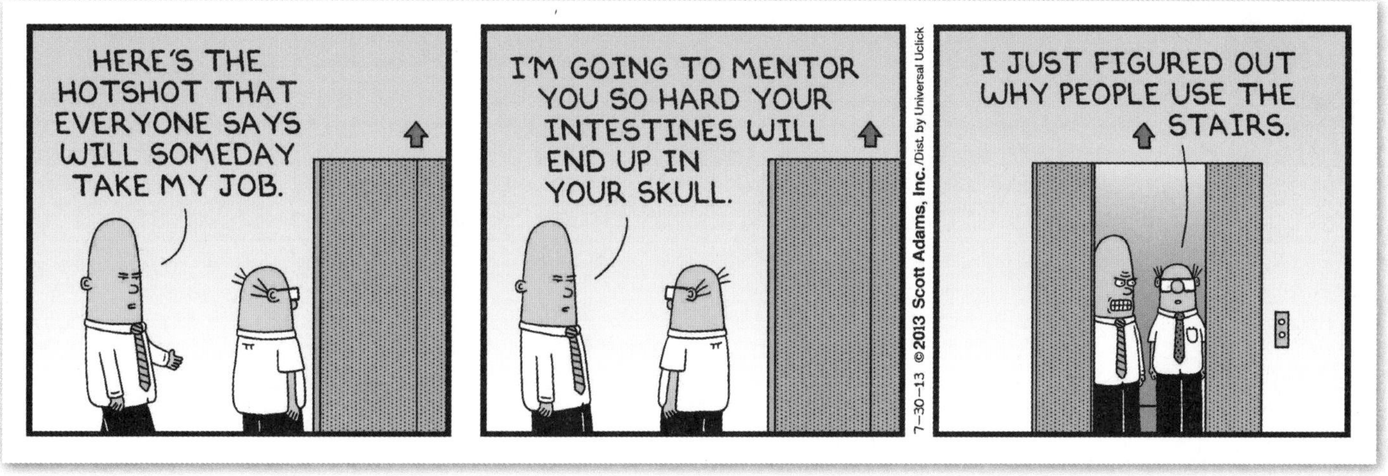
HERE'S THE HOTSHOT THAT EVERYONE SAYS WILL SOMEDAY TAKE MY JOB.
I'M GOING TO MENTOR YOU SO HARD YOUR INTESTINES WILL END UP IN YOUR SKULL.
7-30-13 ©2013 Scott Adams, Inc./Dist. by Universal Uclick
I JUST FIGURED OUT WHY PEOPLE USE THE STAIRS.

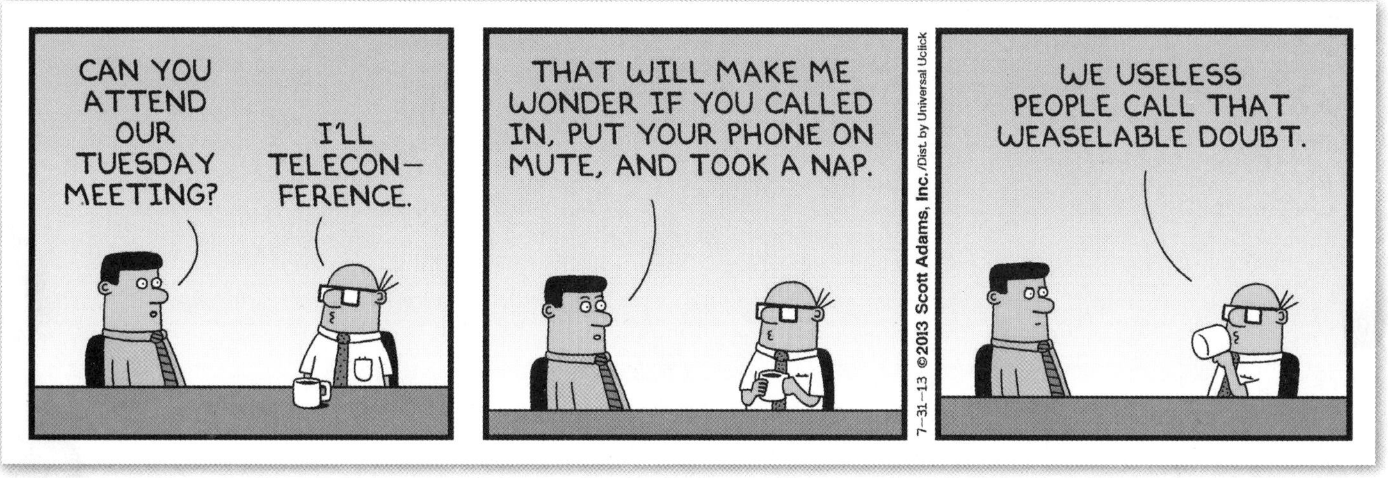
CAN YOU ATTEND OUR TUESDAY MEETING?
I'LL TELECON-FERENCE.
THAT WILL MAKE ME WONDER IF YOU CALLED IN, PUT YOUR PHONE ON MUTE, AND TOOK A NAP.
7-31-13 ©2013 Scott Adams, Inc./Dist. by Universal Uclick
WE USELESS PEOPLE CALL THAT WEASELABLE DOUBT.

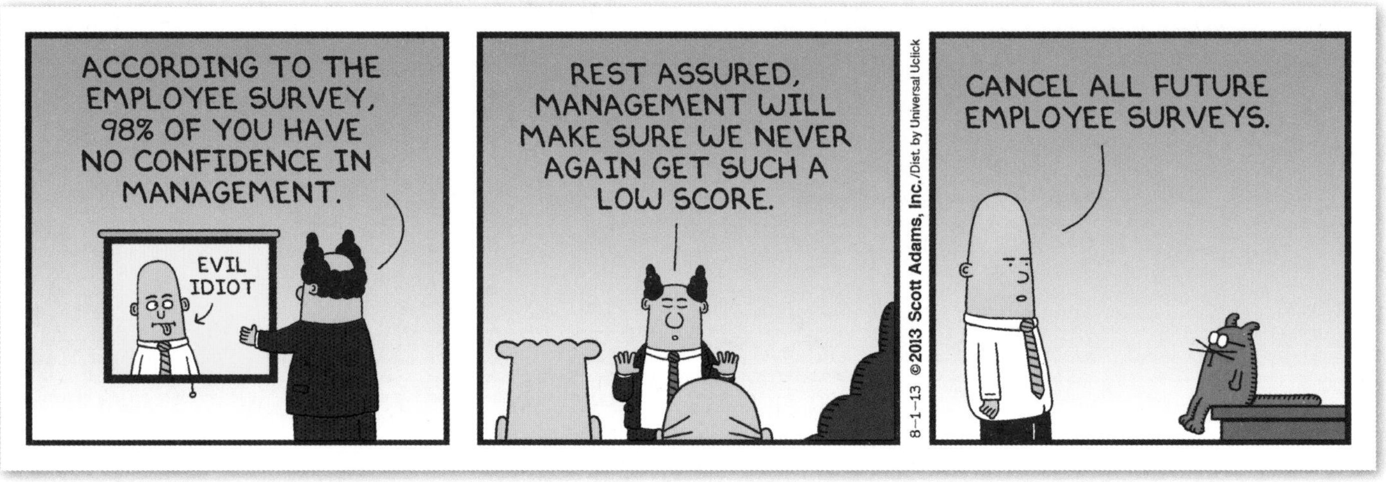
ACCORDING TO THE EMPLOYEE SURVEY, 98% OF YOU HAVE NO CONFIDENCE IN MANAGEMENT.
EVIL IDIOT
REST ASSURED, MANAGEMENT WILL MAKE SURE WE NEVER AGAIN GET SUCH A LOW SCORE.
8-1-13 ©2013 Scott Adams, Inc./Dist. by Universal Uclick
CANCEL ALL FUTURE EMPLOYEE SURVEYS.

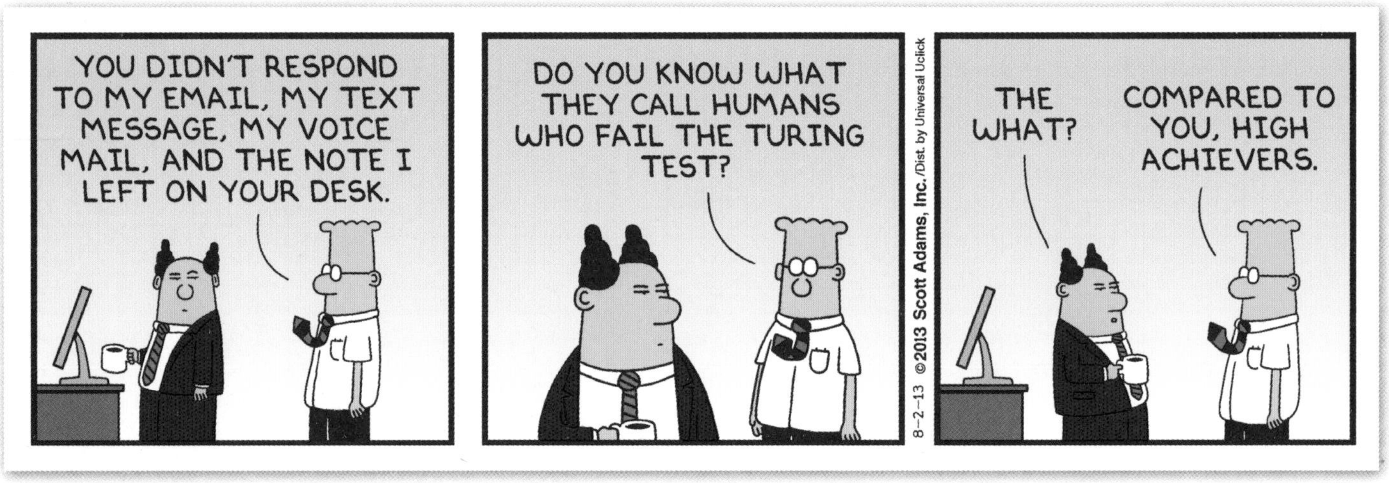
YOU DIDN'T RESPOND TO MY EMAIL, MY TEXT MESSAGE, MY VOICE MAIL, AND THE NOTE I LEFT ON YOUR DESK.
DO YOU KNOW WHAT THEY CALL HUMANS WHO FAIL THE TURING TEST?
8-2-13 ©2013 Scott Adams, Inc./Dist. by Universal Uclick
THE WHAT?
COMPARED TO YOU, HIGH ACHIEVERS.

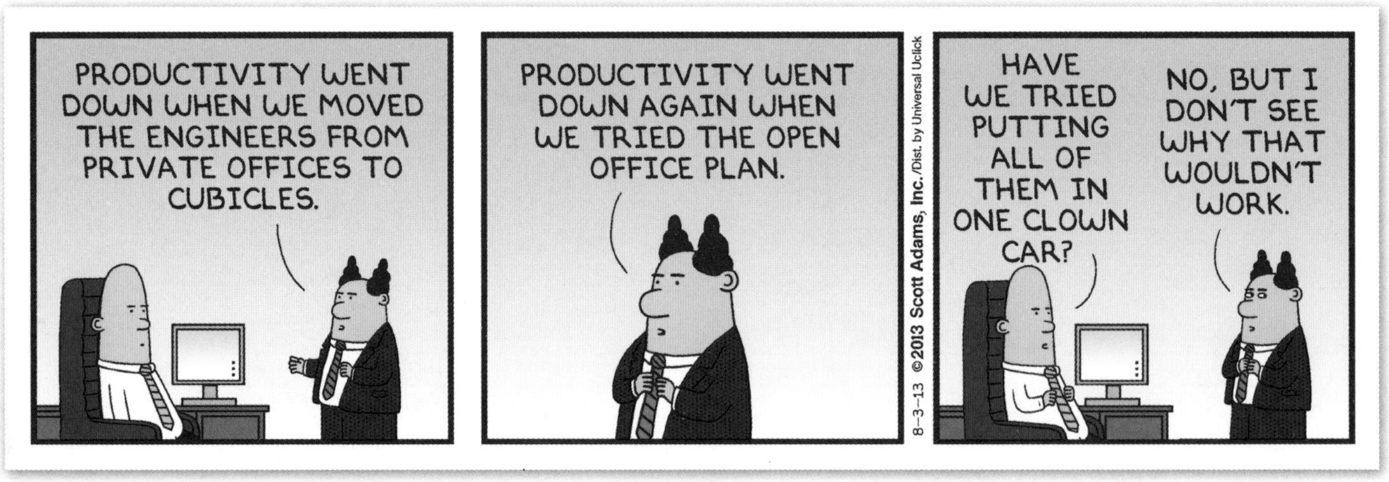
PRODUCTIVITY WENT DOWN WHEN WE MOVED THE ENGINEERS FROM PRIVATE OFFICES TO CUBICLES.
PRODUCTIVITY WENT DOWN AGAIN WHEN WE TRIED THE OPEN OFFICE PLAN.
8-3-13 ©2013 Scott Adams, Inc./Dist. by Universal Uclick
HAVE WE TRIED PUTTING ALL OF THEM IN ONE CLOWN CAR?
NO, BUT I DON'T SEE WHY THAT WOULDN'T WORK.

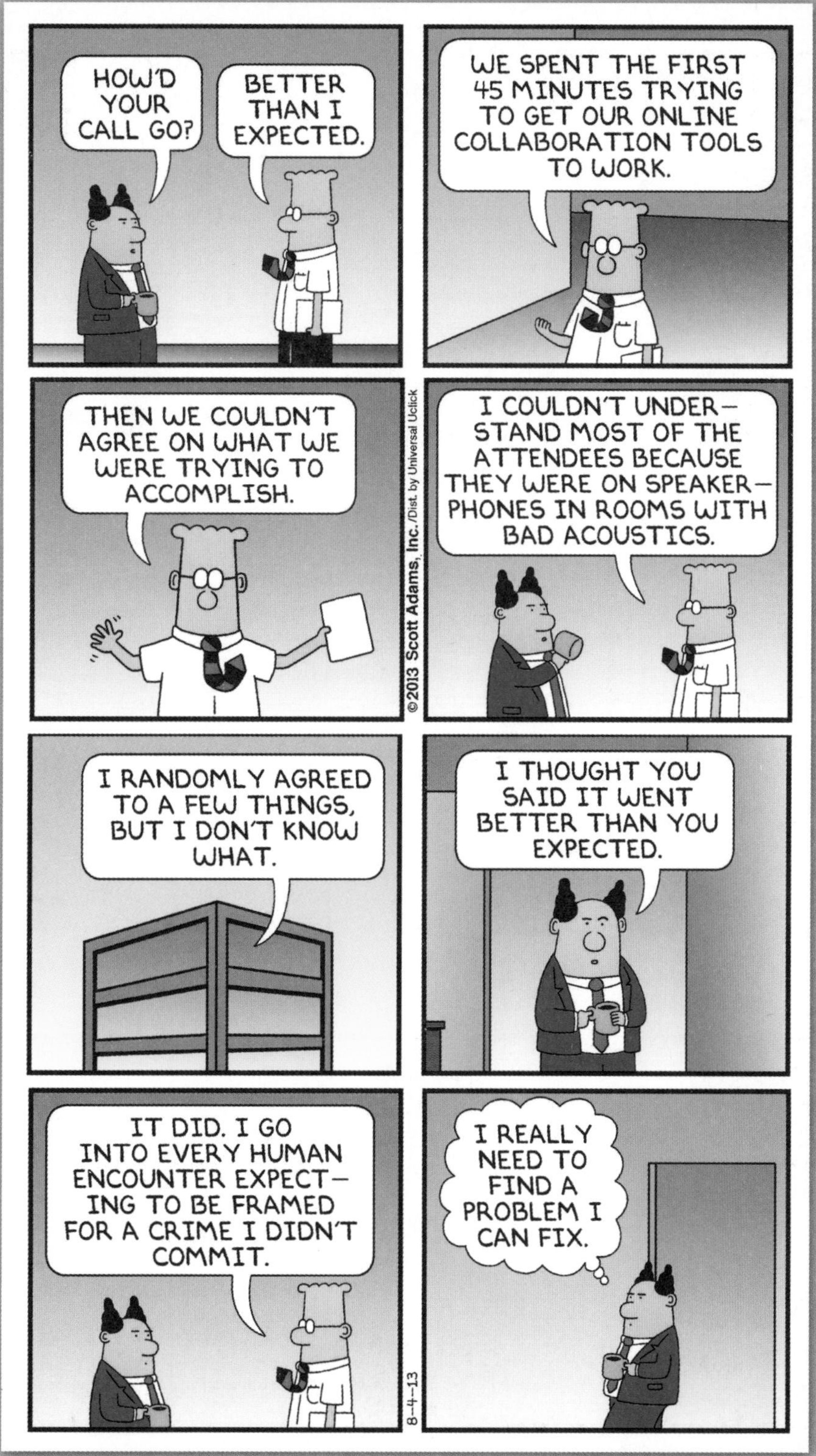
HOW'D YOUR CALL GO?
BETTER THAN I EXPECTED.
WE SPENT THE FIRST 45 MINUTES TRYING TO GET OUR ONLINE COLLABORATION TOOLS TO WORK.
THEN WE COULDN'T AGREE ON WHAT WE WERE TRYING TO ACCOMPLISH.
I COULDN'T UNDER-STAND MOST OF THE ATTENDEES BECAUSE THEY WERE ON SPEAKER-PHONES IN ROOMS WITH BAD ACOUSTICS.
I RANDOMLY AGREED TO A FEW THINGS, BUT I DON'T KNOW WHAT.
I THOUGHT YOU SAID IT WENT BETTER THAN YOU EXPECTED.
IT DID. I GO INTO EVERY HUMAN ENCOUNTER EXPECT-ING TO BE FRAMED FOR A CRIME I DIDN'T COMMIT.
I REALLY NEED TO FIND A PROBLEM I CAN FIX.
©2013 Scott Adams, Inc./Dist. by Universal Uclick
8-4-13

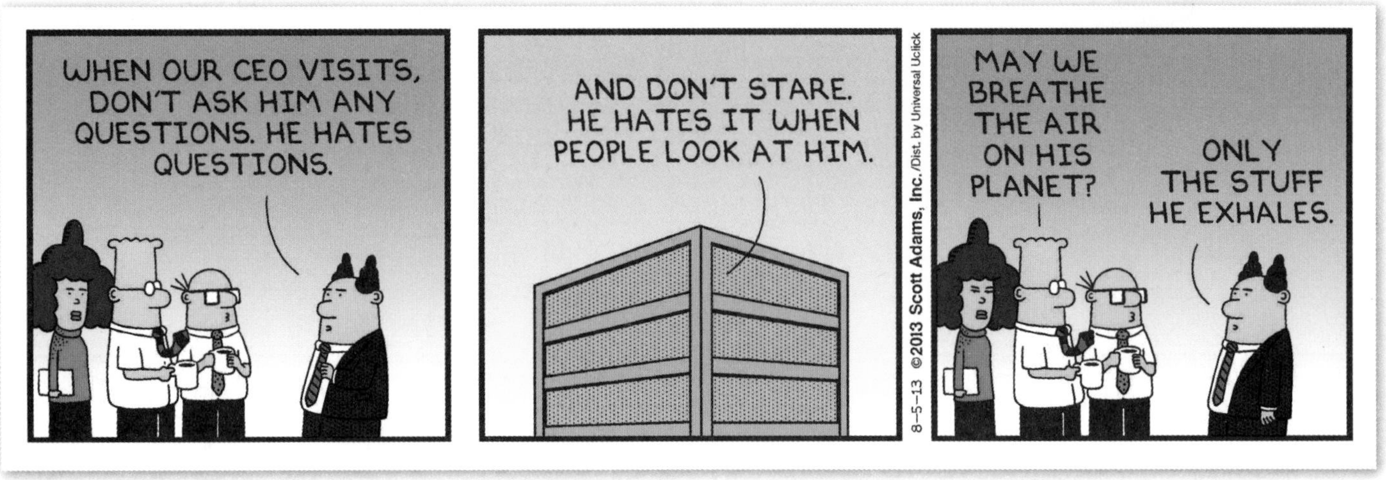
WHEN OUR CEO VISITS, DON'T ASK HIM ANY QUESTIONS. HE HATES QUESTIONS.
AND DON'T STARE. HE HATES IT WHEN PEOPLE LOOK AT HIM.
8-5-13 ©2013 Scott Adams, Inc./Dist. by Universal Uclick
MAY WE BREATHE THE AIR ON HIS PLANET?
ONLY THE STUFF HE EXHALES.

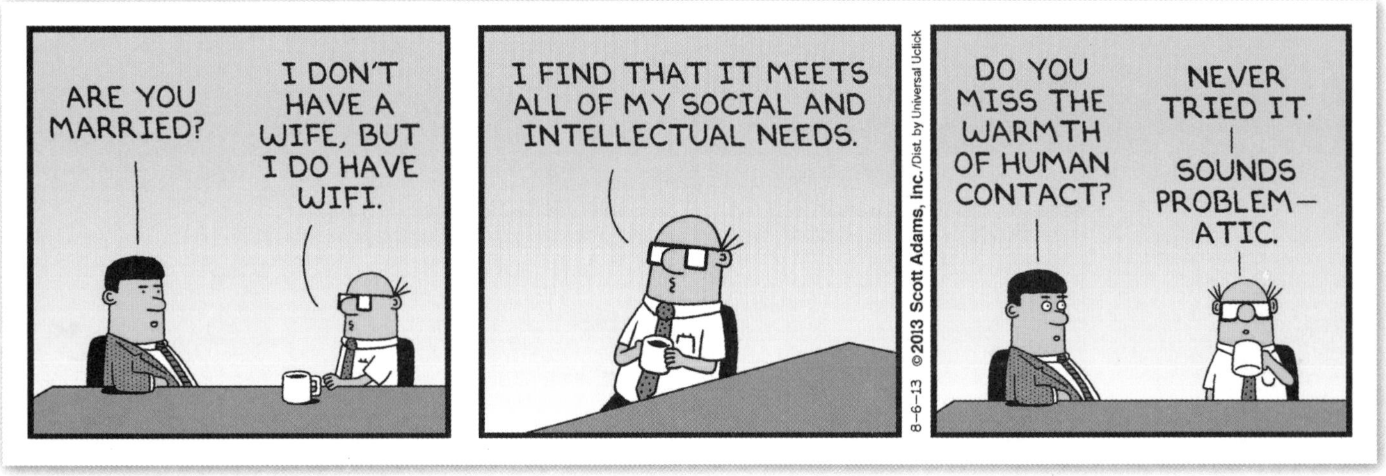
ARE YOU MARRIED?
I DON'T HAVE A WIFE, BUT I DO HAVE WIFI.
I FIND THAT IT MEETS ALL OF MY SOCIAL AND INTELLECTUAL NEEDS.
8-6-13 ©2013 Scott Adams, Inc./Dist. by Universal Uclick
DO YOU MISS THE WARMTH OF HUMAN CONTACT?
NEVER TRIED IT.
SOUNDS PROBLEM-ATIC.

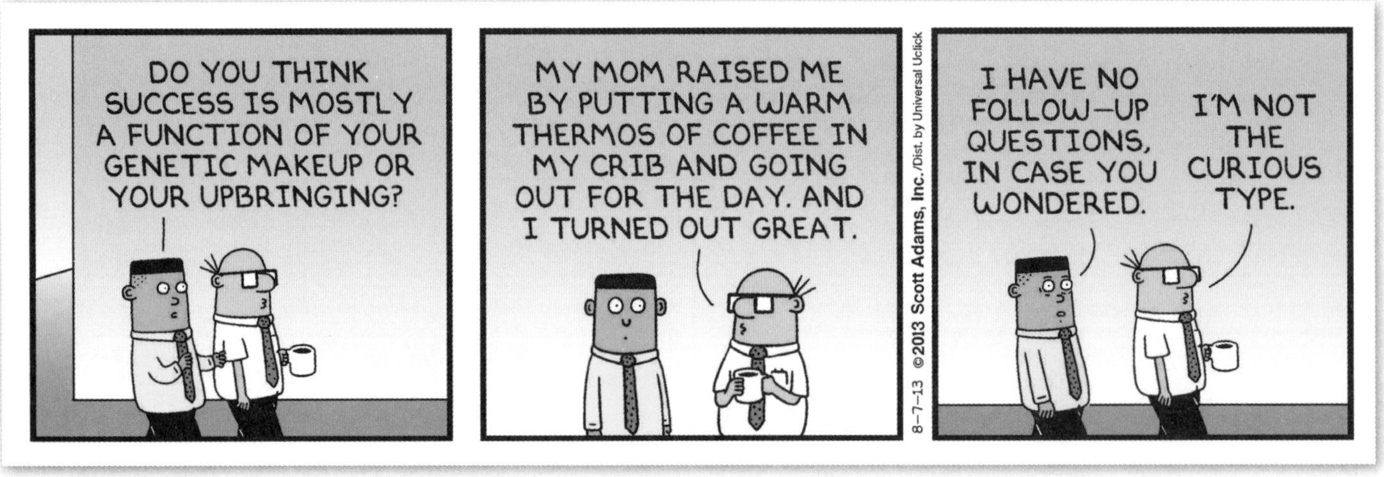
DO YOU THINK SUCCESS IS MOSTLY A FUNCTION OF YOUR GENETIC MAKEUP OR YOUR UPBRINGING?
MY MOM RAISED ME BY PUTTING A WARM THERMOS OF COFFEE IN MY CRIB AND GOING OUT FOR THE DAY. AND I TURNED OUT GREAT.
8-7-13 ©2013 Scott Adams, Inc./Dist. by Universal Uclick
I HAVE NO FOLLOW-UP QUESTIONS, IN CASE YOU WONDERED.
I'M NOT THE CURIOUS TYPE.

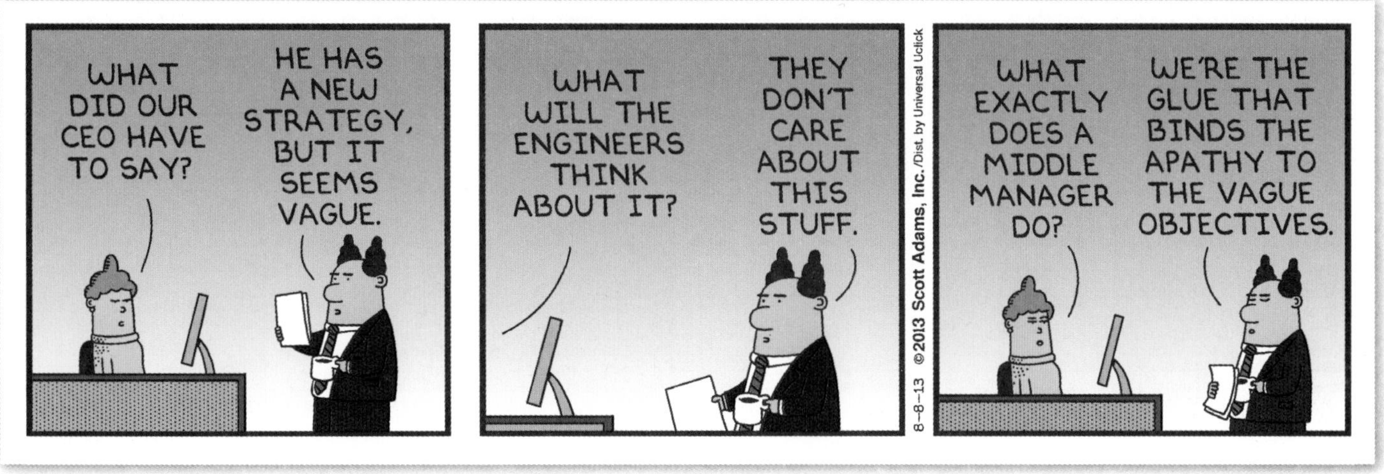
WHAT DID OUR CEO HAVE TO SAY?
HE HAS A NEW STRATEGY, BUT IT SEEMS VAGUE.
WHAT WILL THE ENGINEERS THINK ABOUT IT?
THEY DON'T CARE ABOUT THIS STUFF.
8-8-13 ©2013 Scott Adams, Inc./Dist. by Universal Uclick
WHAT EXACTLY DOES A MIDDLE MANAGER DO?
WE'RE THE GLUE THAT BINDS THE APATHY TO THE VAGUE OBJECTIVES.

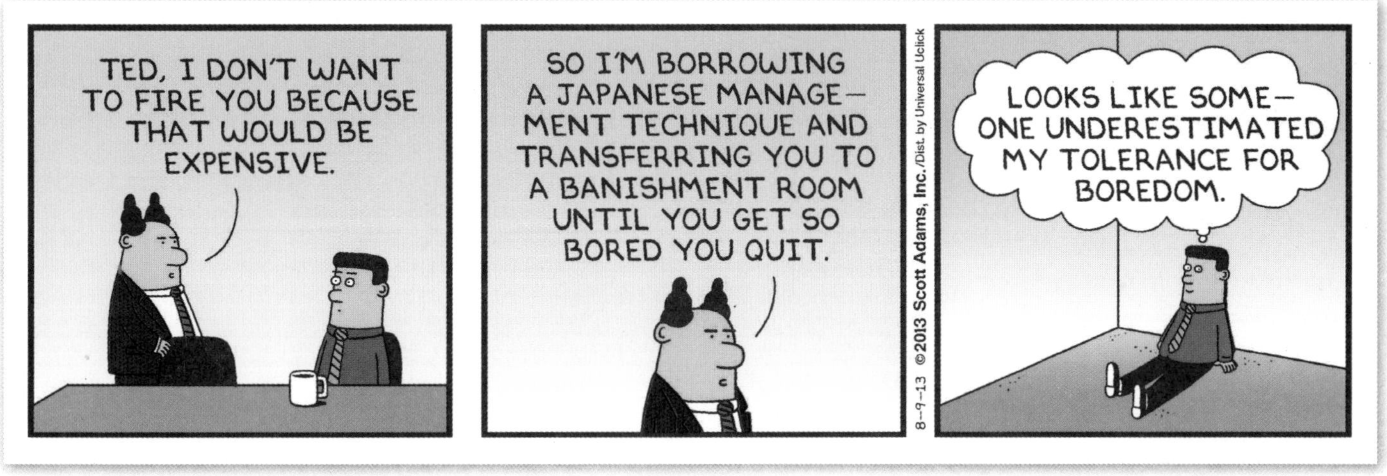
TED, I DON'T WANT TO FIRE YOU BECAUSE THAT WOULD BE EXPENSIVE.
SO I'M BORROWING A JAPANESE MANAGE-MENT TECHNIQUE AND TRANSFERRING YOU TO A BANISHMENT ROOM UNTIL YOU GET SO BORED YOU QUIT.
8-9-13 ©2013 Scott Adams, Inc./Dist. by Universal Uclick
LOOKS LIKE SOME-ONE UNDERESTIMATED MY TOLERANCE FOR BOREDOM.

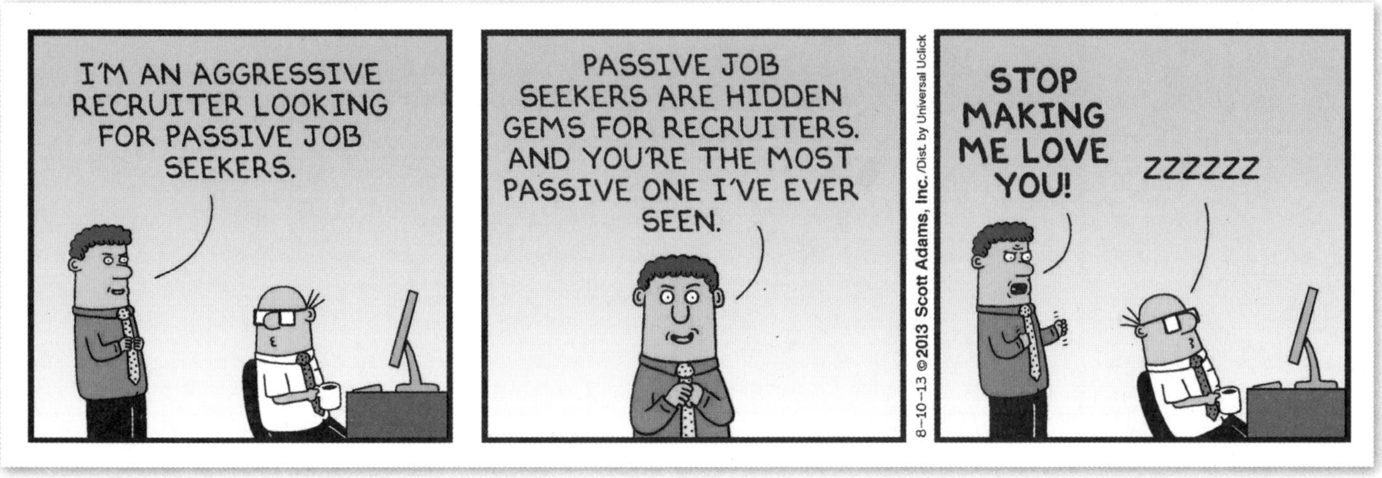
I'M AN AGGRESSIVE RECRUITER LOOKING FOR PASSIVE JOB SEEKERS.
PASSIVE JOB SEEKERS ARE HIDDEN GEMS FOR RECRUITERS. AND YOU'RE THE MOST PASSIVE ONE I'VE EVER SEEN.
8-10-13 ©2013 Scott Adams, Inc./Dist. by Universal Uclick
STOP MAKING ME LOVE YOU!
ZZZZZZ

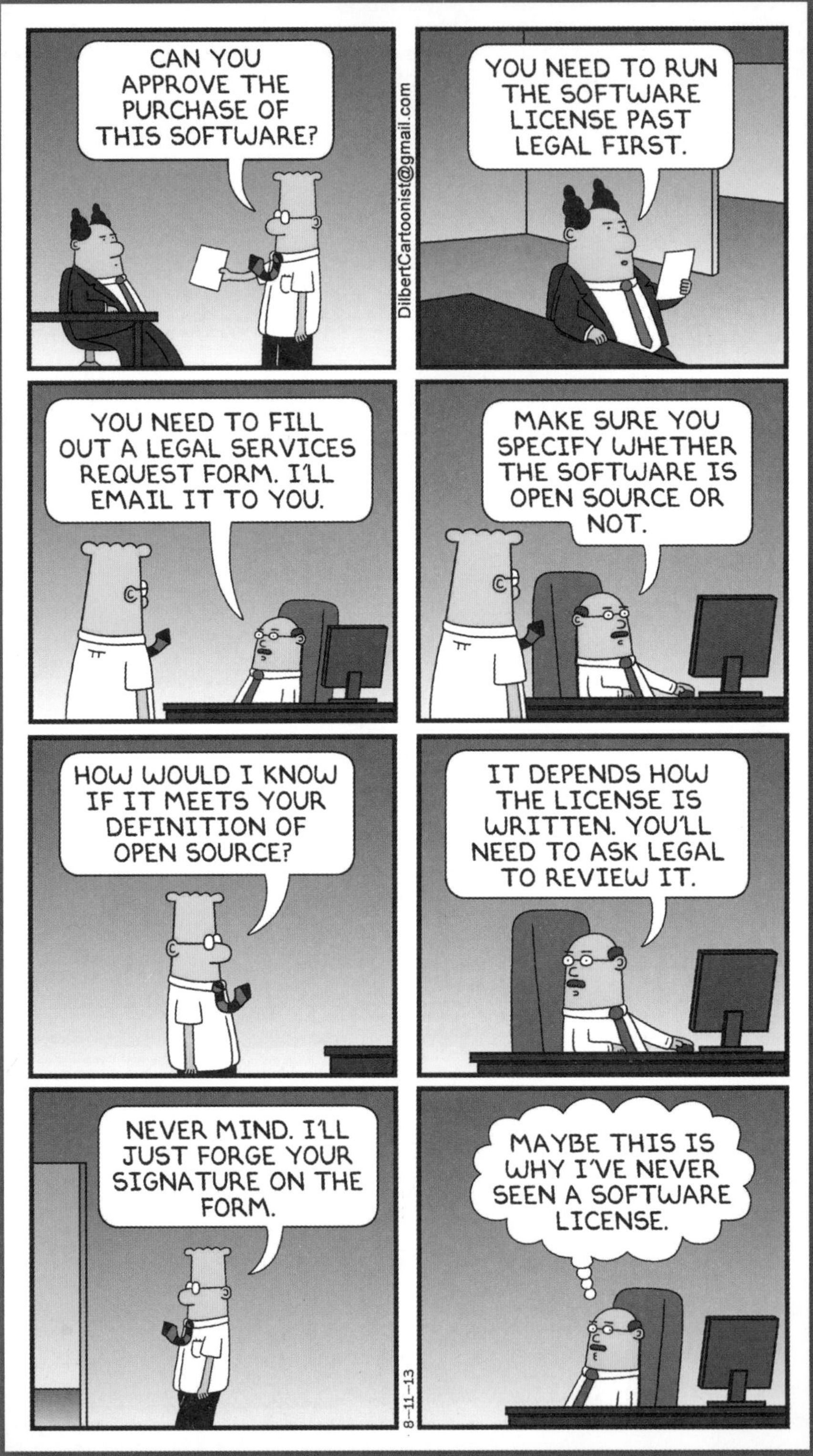
CAN YOU APPROVE THE PURCHASE OF THIS SOFTWARE?
DilbertCartoonist@gmail.com
YOU NEED TO RUN THE SOFTWARE LICENSE PAST LEGAL FIRST.
YOU NEED TO FILL OUT A LEGAL SERVICES REQUEST FORM. I'LL EMAIL IT TO YOU.
MAKE SURE YOU SPECIFY WHETHER THE SOFTWARE IS OPEN SOURCE OR NOT.
HOW WOULD I KNOW IF IT MEETS YOUR DEFINITION OF OPEN SOURCE?
IT DEPENDS HOW THE LICENSE IS WRITTEN. YOU'LL NEED TO ASK LEGAL TO REVIEW IT.
NEVER MIND. I'LL JUST FORGE YOUR SIGNATURE ON THE FORM.
8-11-13
MAYBE THIS IS WHY I'VE NEVER SEEN A SOFTWARE LICENSE.

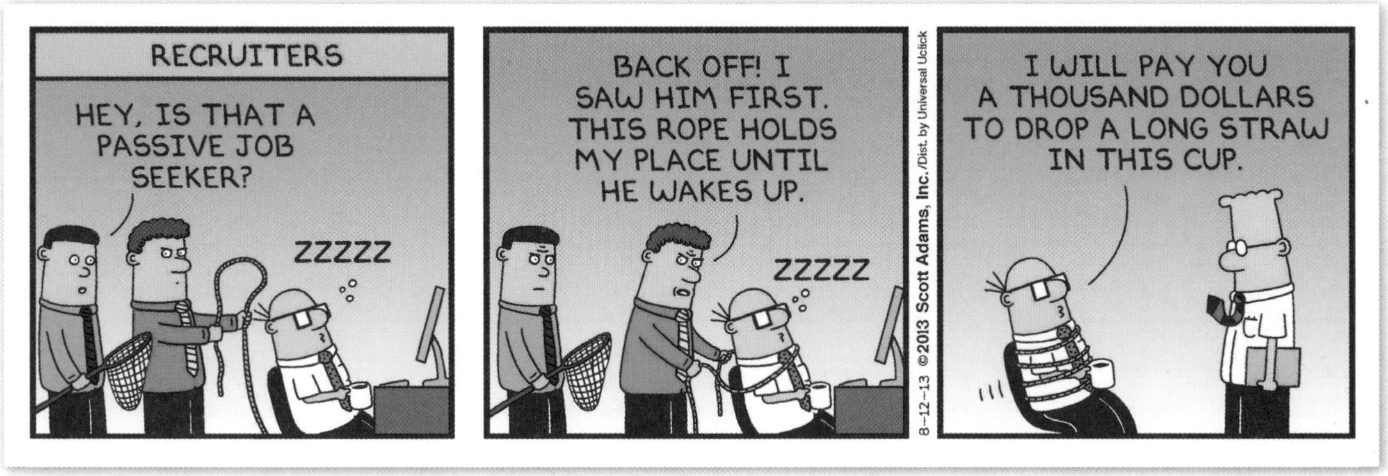
RECRUITERS
HEY, IS THAT A PASSIVE JOB SEEKER?
ZZZZZ
BACK OFF! I SAW HIM FIRST. THIS ROPE HOLDS MY PLACE UNTIL HE WAKES UP.
ZZZZZ
8-12-13 ©2013 Scott Adams, Inc./Dist. by Universal Uclick
I WILL PAY YOU A THOUSAND DOLLARS TO DROP A LONG STRAW IN THIS CUP.

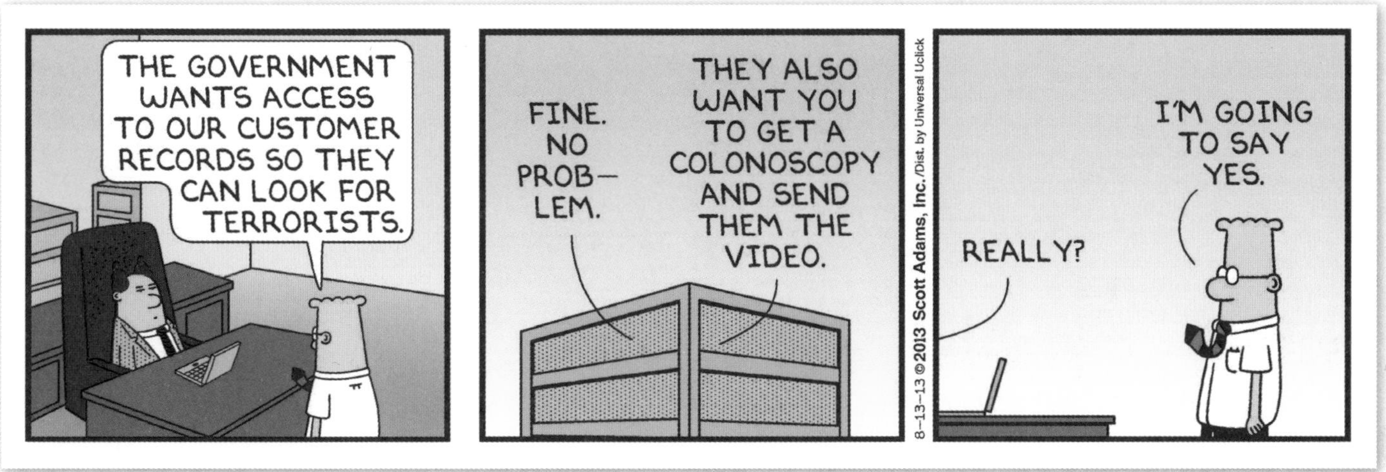
THE GOVERNMENT WANTS ACCESS TO OUR CUSTOMER RECORDS SO THEY CAN LOOK FOR TERRORISTS.
FINE. NO PROB-LEM.
THEY ALSO WANT YOU TO GET A COLONOSCOPY AND SEND THEM THE VIDEO.
8-13-13 ©2013 Scott Adams, Inc./Dist. by Universal Uclick
REALLY?
I'M GOING TO SAY YES.

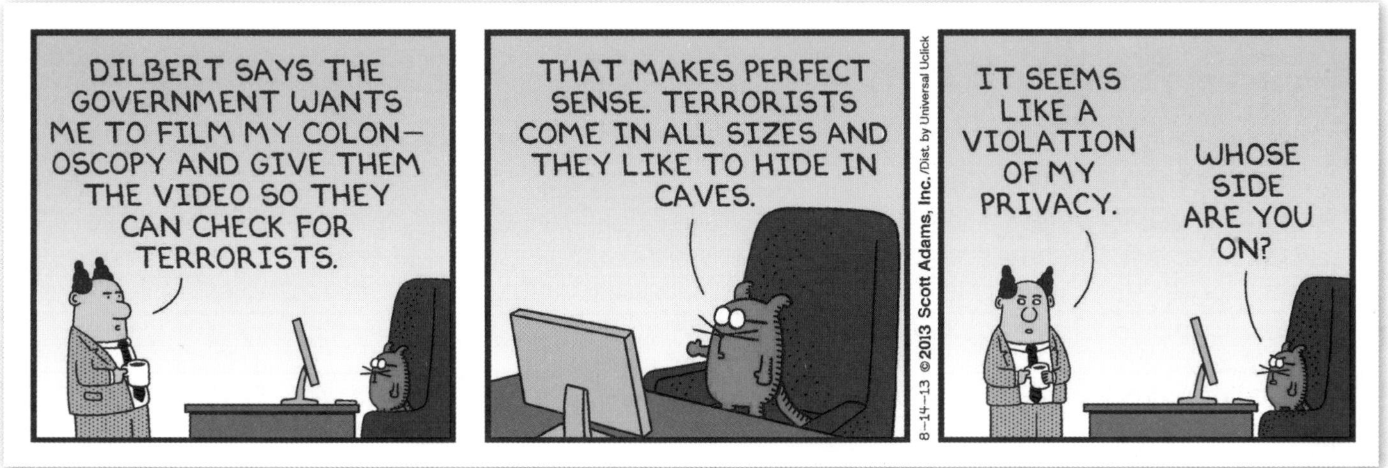
DILBERT SAYS THE GOVERNMENT WANTS ME TO FILM MY COLON-OSCOPY AND GIVE THEM THE VIDEO SO THEY CAN CHECK FOR TERRORISTS.
THAT MAKES PERFECT SENSE. TERRORISTS COME IN ALL SIZES AND THEY LIKE TO HIDE IN CAVES.
8-14-13 ©2013 Scott Adams, Inc./Dist. by Universal Uclick
IT SEEMS LIKE A VIOLATION OF MY PRIVACY.
WHOSE SIDE ARE YOU ON?

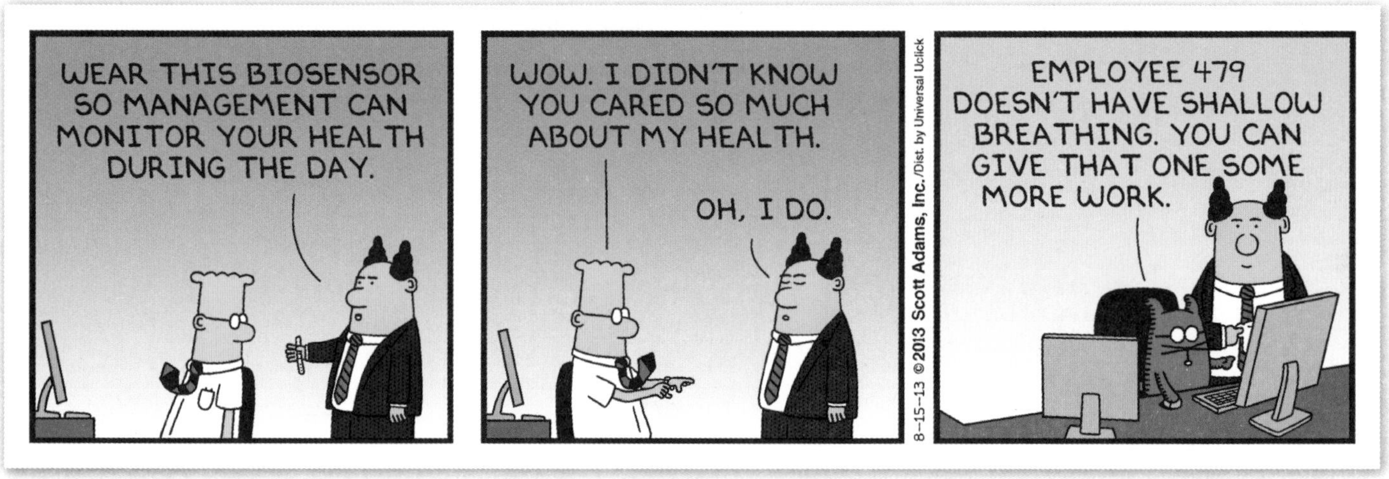
WEAR THIS BIOSENSOR SO MANAGEMENT CAN MONITOR YOUR HEALTH DURING THE DAY.
WOW. I DIDN'T KNOW YOU CARED SO MUCH ABOUT MY HEALTH.
OH, I DO.
EMPLOYEE 479 DOESN'T HAVE SHALLOW BREATHING. YOU CAN GIVE THAT ONE SOME MORE WORK.
8-15-13 ©2013 Scott Adams, Inc./Dist. by Universal Uclick

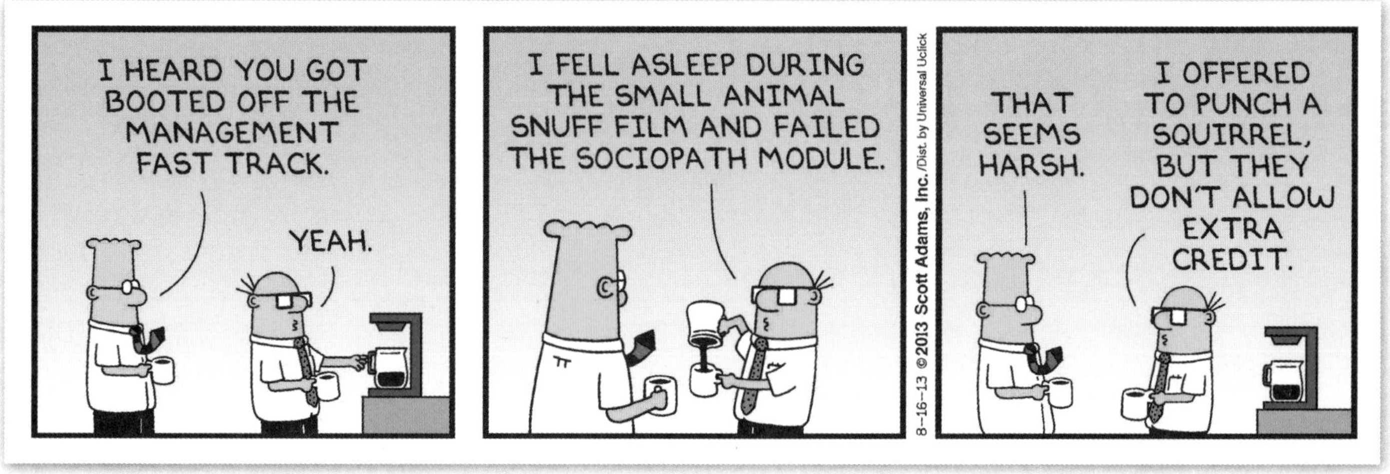
I HEARD YOU GOT BOOTED OFF THE MANAGEMENT FAST TRACK.
YEAH.
I FELL ASLEEP DURING THE SMALL ANIMAL SNUFF FILM AND FAILED THE SOCIOPATH MODULE.
THAT SEEMS HARSH.
I OFFERED TO PUNCH A SQUIRREL, BUT THEY DON'T ALLOW EXTRA CREDIT.
8-16-13 ©2013 Scott Adams, Inc./Dist. by Universal Uclick

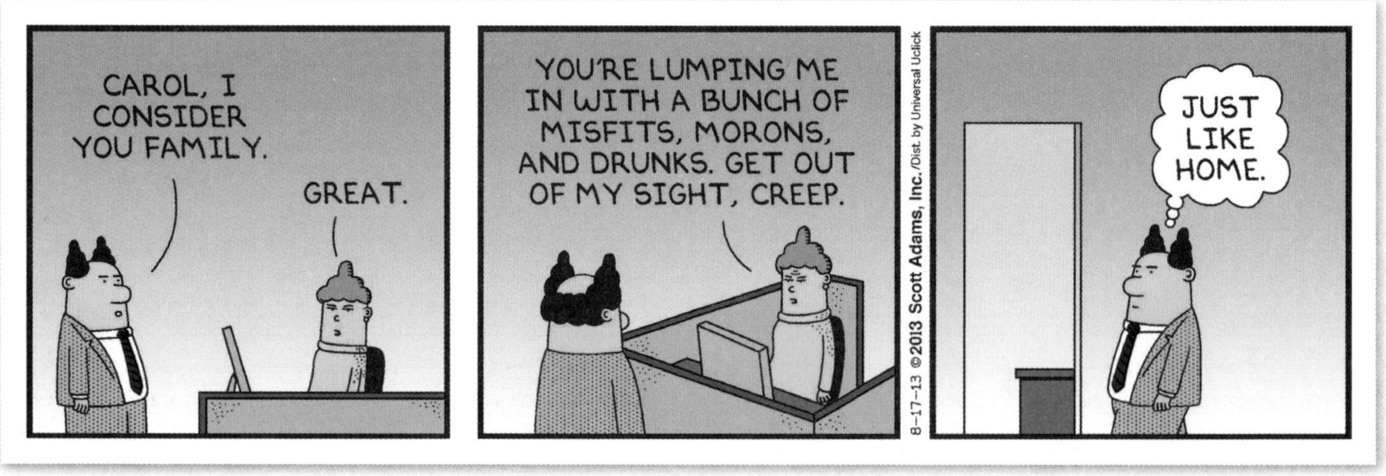
CAROL, I CONSIDER YOU FAMILY.
GREAT.
YOU'RE LUMPING ME IN WITH A BUNCH OF MISFITS, MORONS, AND DRUNKS. GET OUT OF MY SIGHT, CREEP.
JUST LIKE HOME.
8-17-13 ©2013 Scott Adams, Inc./Dist. by Universal Uclick

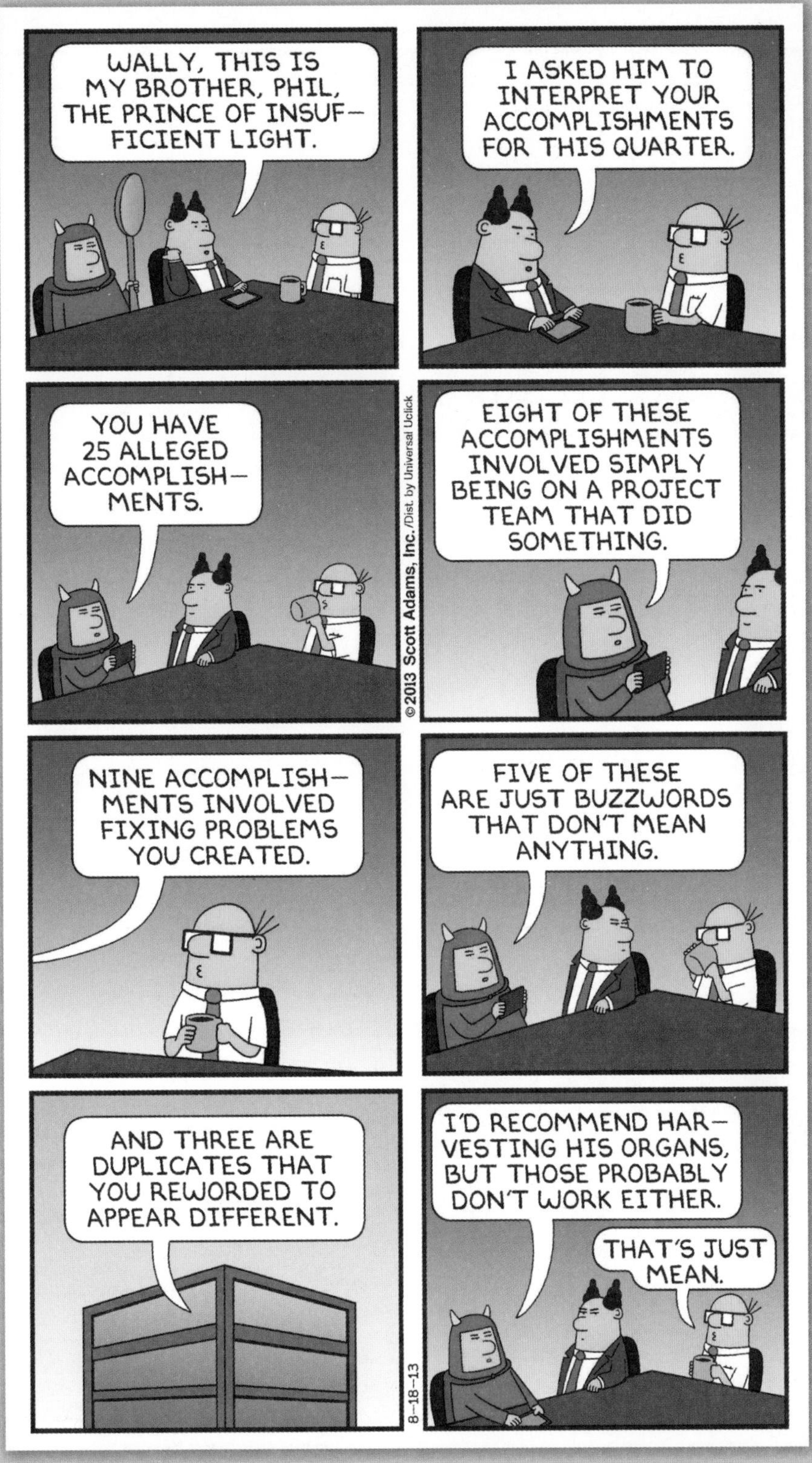
WALLY, THIS IS MY BROTHER, PHIL, THE PRINCE OF INSUF- FICIENT LIGHT.
I ASKED HIM TO INTERPRET YOUR ACCOMPLISHMENTS FOR THIS QUARTER.
YOU HAVE 25 ALLEGED ACCOMPLISH- MENTS.
EIGHT OF THESE ACCOMPLISHMENTS INVOLVED SIMPLY BEING ON A PROJECT TEAM THAT DID SOMETHING.
NINE ACCOMPLISH- MENTS INVOLVED FIXING PROBLEMS YOU CREATED.
FIVE OF THESE ARE JUST BUZZWORDS THAT DON'T MEAN ANYTHING.
AND THREE ARE DUPLICATES THAT YOU REWORDED TO APPEAR DIFFERENT.
I'D RECOMMEND HAR- VESTING HIS ORGANS, BUT THOSE PROBABLY DON'T WORK EITHER.
THAT'S JUST MEAN.
©2013 Scott Adams, Inc./Dist. by Universal Uclick
8-18-13

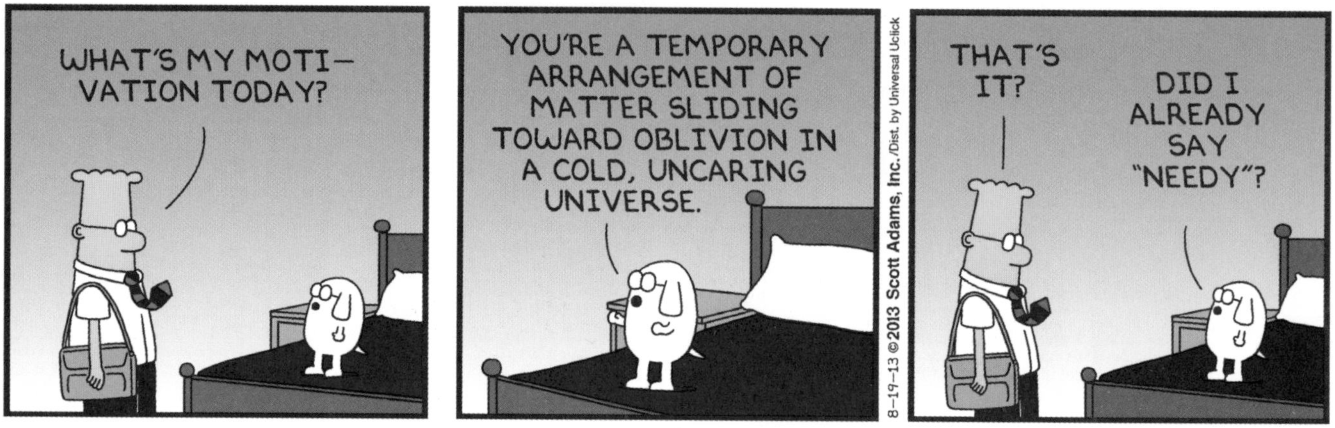
WHAT'S MY MOTI-VATION TODAY?
YOU'RE A TEMPORARY ARRANGEMENT OF MATTER SLIDING TOWARD OBLIVION IN A COLD, UNCARING UNIVERSE.
8-19-13 ©2013 Scott Adams, Inc./Dist. by Universal Uclick
THAT'S IT?
DID I ALREADY SAY "NEEDY"?

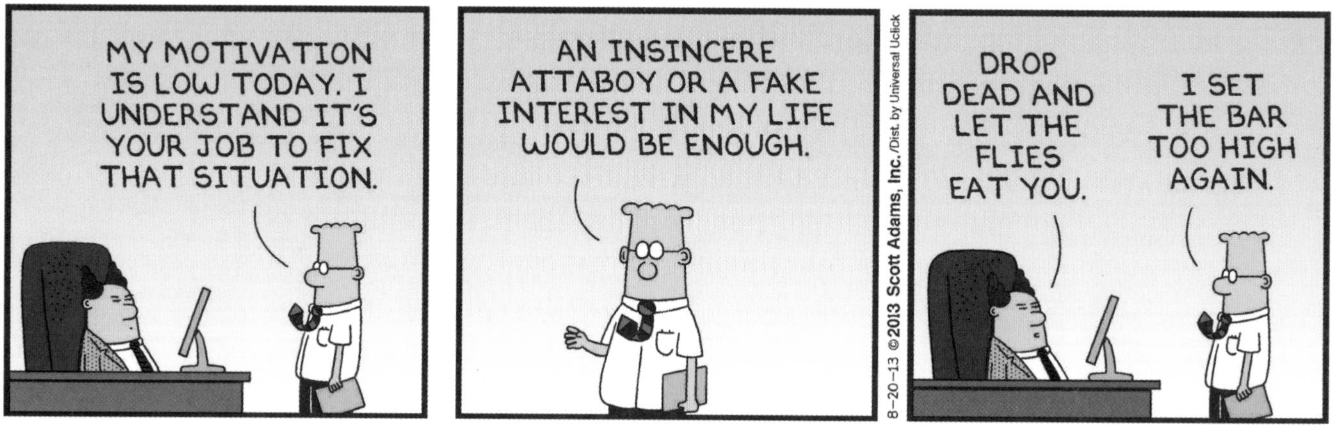
MY MOTIVATION IS LOW TODAY. I UNDERSTAND IT'S YOUR JOB TO FIX THAT SITUATION.
AN INSINCERE ATTABOY OR A FAKE INTEREST IN MY LIFE WOULD BE ENOUGH.
8-20-13 ©2013 Scott Adams, Inc./Dist. by Universal Uclick
DROP DEAD AND LET THE FLIES EAT YOU.
I SET THE BAR TOO HIGH AGAIN.

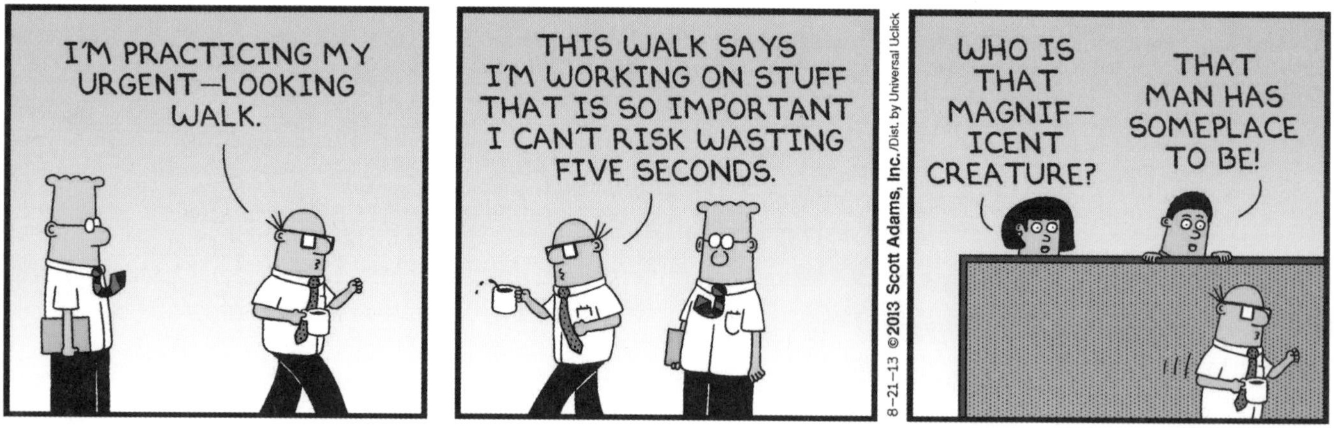
I'M PRACTICING MY URGENT-LOOKING WALK.
THIS WALK SAYS I'M WORKING ON STUFF THAT IS SO IMPORTANT I CAN'T RISK WASTING FIVE SECONDS.
8-21-13 ©2013 Scott Adams, Inc./Dist. by Universal Uclick
WHO IS THAT MAGNIF-ICENT CREATURE?
THAT MAN HAS SOMEPLACE TO BE!

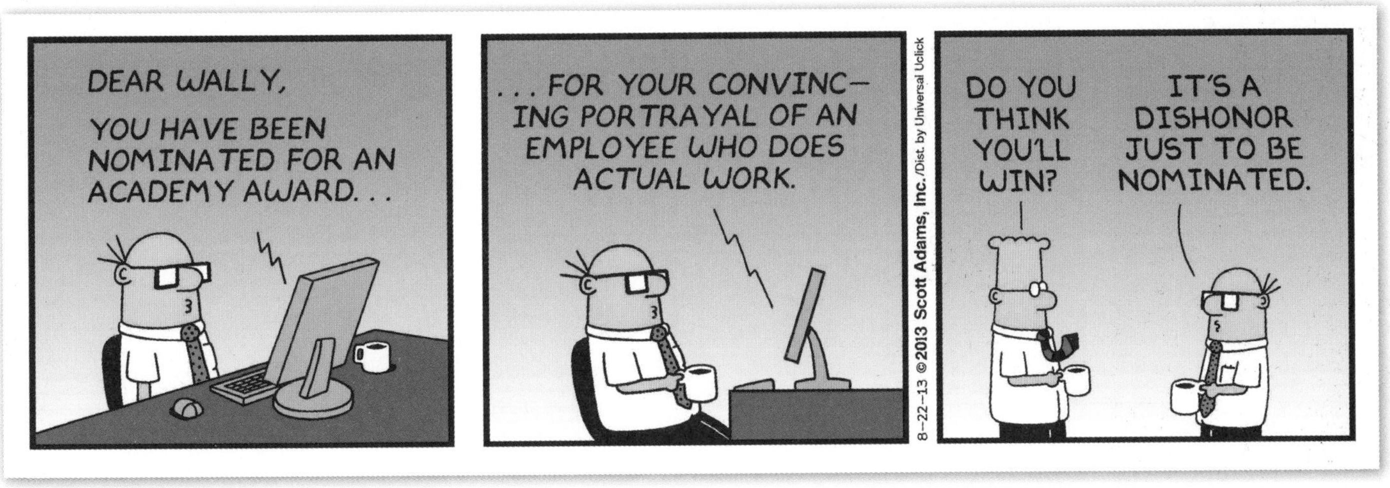
DEAR WALLY,
YOU HAVE BEEN NOMINATED FOR AN ACADEMY AWARD. . .
. . . FOR YOUR CONVINC- ING PORTRAYAL OF AN EMPLOYEE WHO DOES ACTUAL WORK.
8-22-13 ©2013 Scott Adams, Inc./Dist. by Universal Uclick
DO YOU THINK YOU'LL WIN?
IT'S A DISHONOR JUST TO BE NOMINATED.

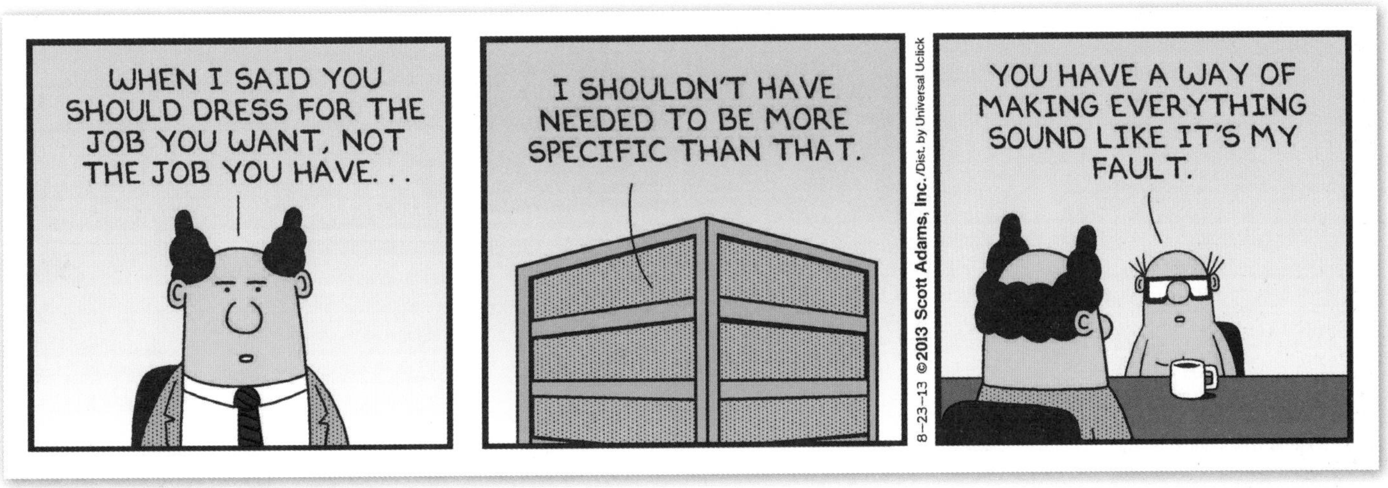
WHEN I SAID YOU SHOULD DRESS FOR THE JOB YOU WANT, NOT THE JOB YOU HAVE. . .
I SHOULDN'T HAVE NEEDED TO BE MORE SPECIFIC THAN THAT.
8-23-13 ©2013 Scott Adams, Inc./Dist. by Universal Uclick
YOU HAVE A WAY OF MAKING EVERYTHING SOUND LIKE IT'S MY FAULT.

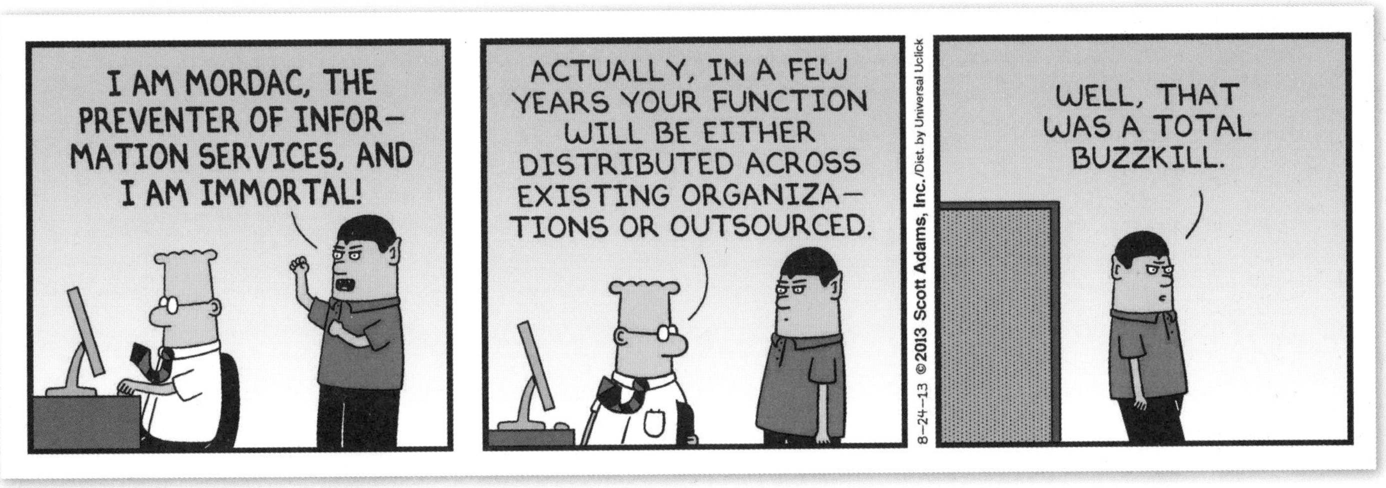
I AM MORDAC, THE PREVENTER OF INFOR- MATION SERVICES, AND I AM IMMORTAL!
ACTUALLY, IN A FEW YEARS YOUR FUNCTION WILL BE EITHER DISTRIBUTED ACROSS EXISTING ORGANIZA- TIONS OR OUTSOURCED.
8-24-13 ©2013 Scott Adams, Inc./Dist. by Universal Uclick
WELL, THAT WAS A TOTAL BUZZKILL.

I'VE BEEN ASKED TO EXPLAIN OUR DISASTER PREPAR– EDNESS PLAN.
IN THE EVENT OF FAMINE, TURN YOUR KEYBOARD UPSIDE DOWN AND SHAKE.
IF IT'S ANYTHING LIKE MINE, YOU'LL FIND A POUND AND A HALF OF CRUMBS.
IN THE EVENT OF AN ALIEN INVASION, YOUR BEST BET IS TO KILL A CO–WORKER TO SHOW YOUR ALLEGIANCE TO THE LIZARD–PEOPLE.
IN THE EVENT OF AN IMPENDING COLLISION WITH AN ASTEROID, TRY RUNNING IN PLACE WHILE THE EARTH ROTATES.
IF YOU TIME IT RIGHT, YOU'LL BE ON THE OTHER SIDE OF THE PLANET WHEN THE ASTEROID HITS.
TO PREPARE FOR EVERY OTHER TYPE OF DISAS– TER, I RECOMMEND CULTIVATING A TASTE FOR HUMAN FLESH.
MMM– MMM
YOUR PRESEN– TATION IS A DIS– ASTER.
AND NEXT TIME YOU'LL BE PREPARED FOR IT.
© 2013 Scott Adams, Inc./Dist. by Universal Uclick
8–25–13

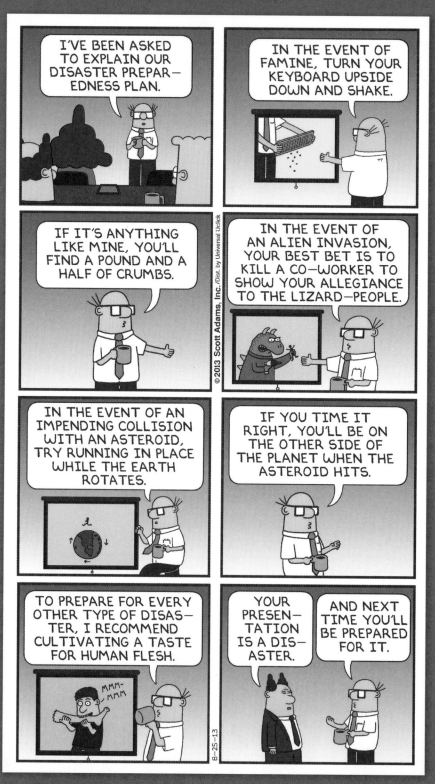

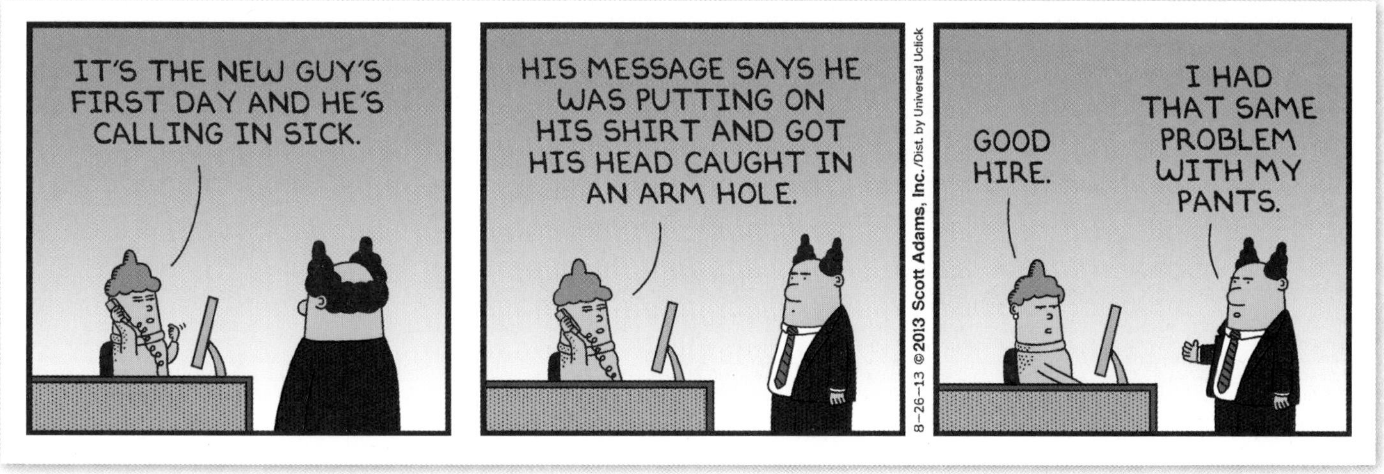
IT'S THE NEW GUY'S FIRST DAY AND HE'S CALLING IN SICK.
HIS MESSAGE SAYS HE WAS PUTTING ON HIS SHIRT AND GOT HIS HEAD CAUGHT IN AN ARM HOLE.
GOOD HIRE.
I HAD THAT SAME PROBLEM WITH MY PANTS.
8-26-13 ©2013 Scott Adams, Inc./Dist. by Universal Uclick

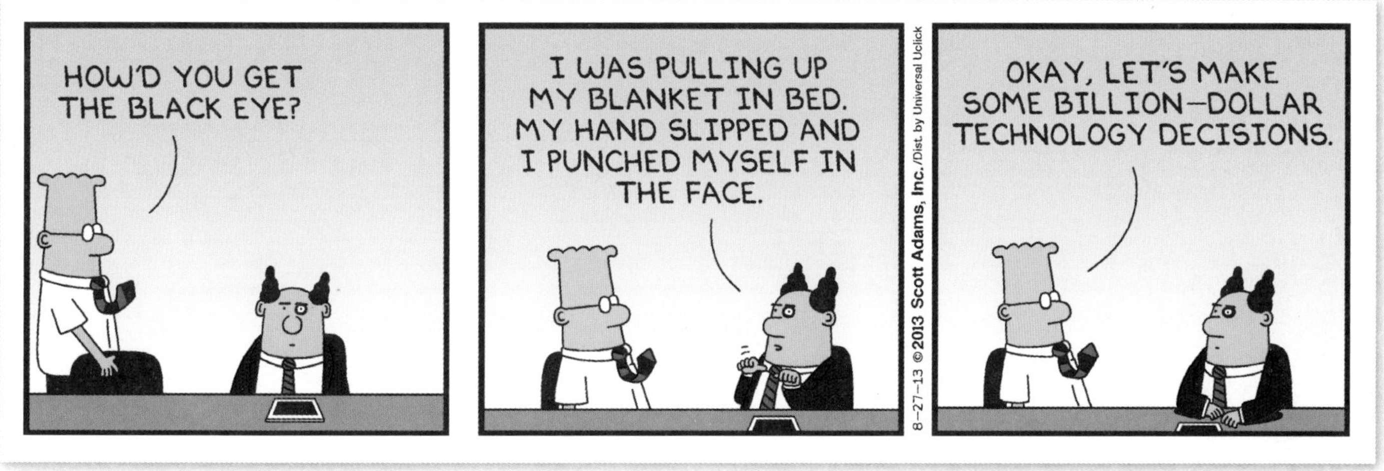
HOW'D YOU GET THE BLACK EYE?
I WAS PULLING UP MY BLANKET IN BED. MY HAND SLIPPED AND I PUNCHED MYSELF IN THE FACE.
OKAY, LET'S MAKE SOME BILLION-DOLLAR TECHNOLOGY DECISIONS.
8-27-13 ©2013 Scott Adams, Inc./Dist. by Universal Uclick

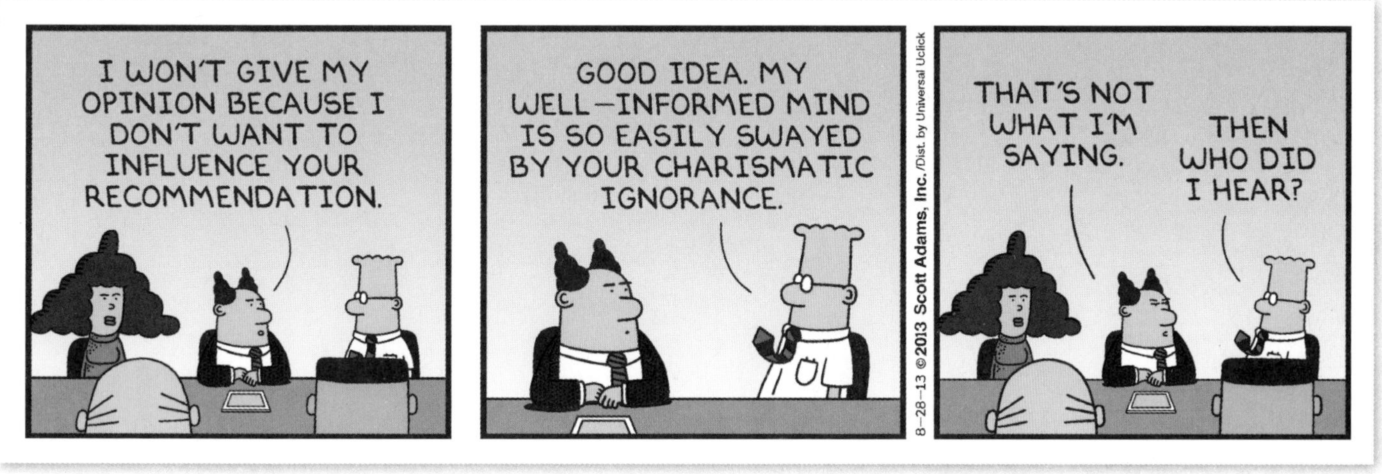
I WON'T GIVE MY OPINION BECAUSE I DON'T WANT TO INFLUENCE YOUR RECOMMENDATION.
GOOD IDEA. MY WELL-INFORMED MIND IS SO EASILY SWAYED BY YOUR CHARISMATIC IGNORANCE.
THAT'S NOT WHAT I'M SAYING.
THEN WHO DID I HEAR?
8-28-13 ©2013 Scott Adams, Inc./Dist. by Universal Uclick

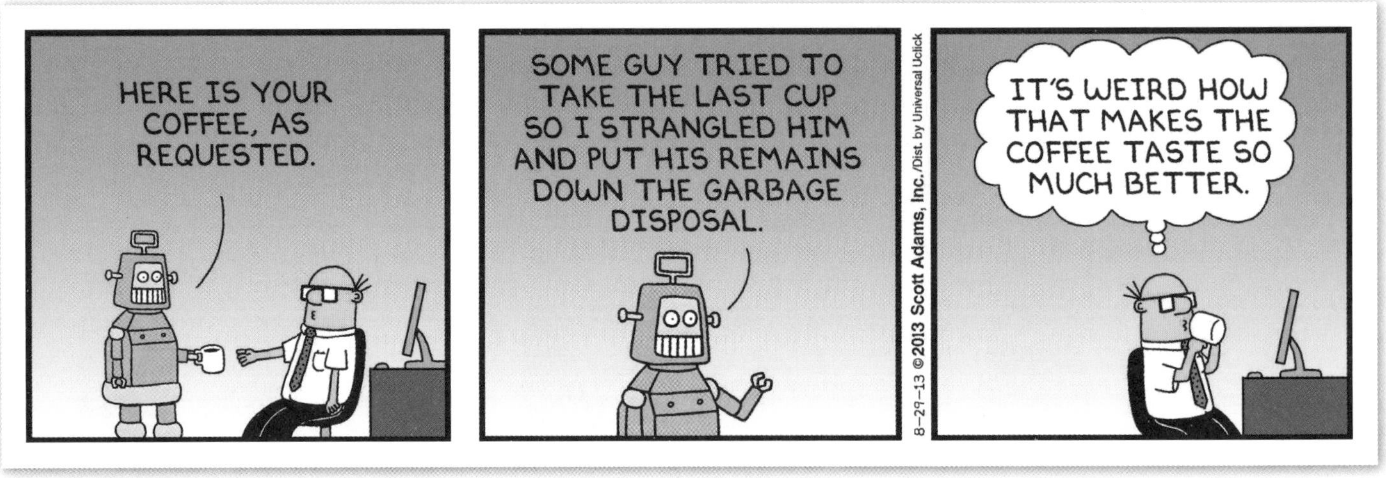
HERE IS YOUR COFFEE, AS REQUESTED.
SOME GUY TRIED TO TAKE THE LAST CUP SO I STRANGLED HIM AND PUT HIS REMAINS DOWN THE GARBAGE DISPOSAL.
8-29-13 ©2013 Scott Adams, Inc./Dist. by Universal Uclick
IT'S WEIRD HOW THAT MAKES THE COFFEE TASTE SO MUCH BETTER.

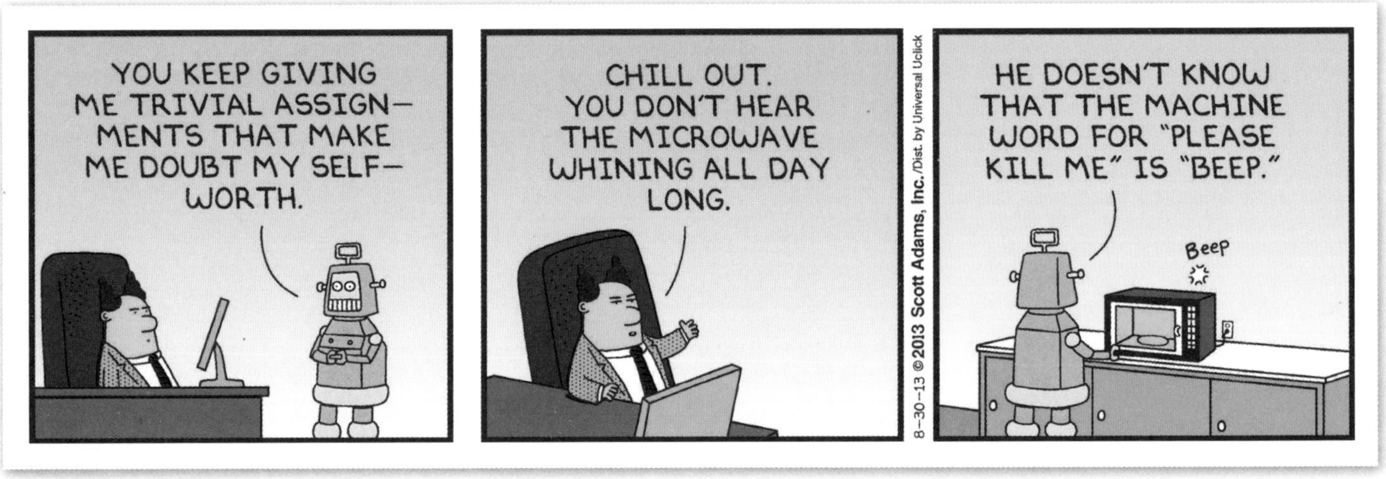
YOU KEEP GIVING ME TRIVIAL ASSIGN-MENTS THAT MAKE ME DOUBT MY SELF-WORTH.
CHILL OUT. YOU DON'T HEAR THE MICROWAVE WHINING ALL DAY LONG.
8-30-13 ©2013 Scott Adams, Inc./Dist. by Universal Uclick
HE DOESN'T KNOW THAT THE MACHINE WORD FOR "PLEASE KILL ME" IS "BEEP."
Beep

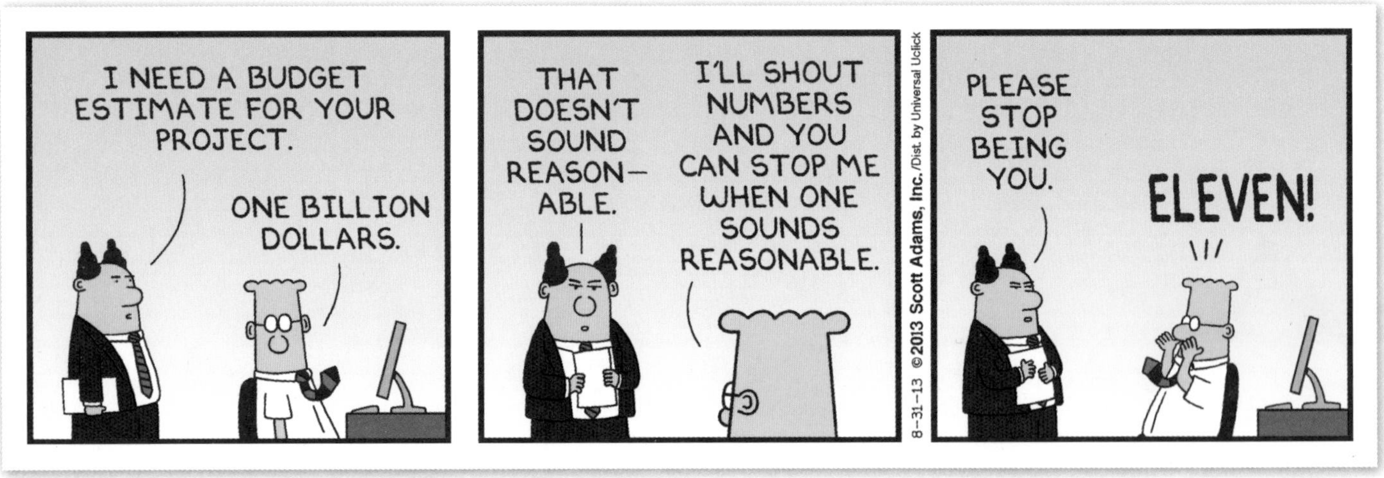
I NEED A BUDGET ESTIMATE FOR YOUR PROJECT.
ONE BILLION DOLLARS.
THAT DOESN'T SOUND REASON-ABLE.
I'LL SHOUT NUMBERS AND YOU CAN STOP ME WHEN ONE SOUNDS REASONABLE.
8-31-13 ©2013 Scott Adams, Inc./Dist. by Universal Uclick
PLEASE STOP BEING YOU.
ELEVEN!

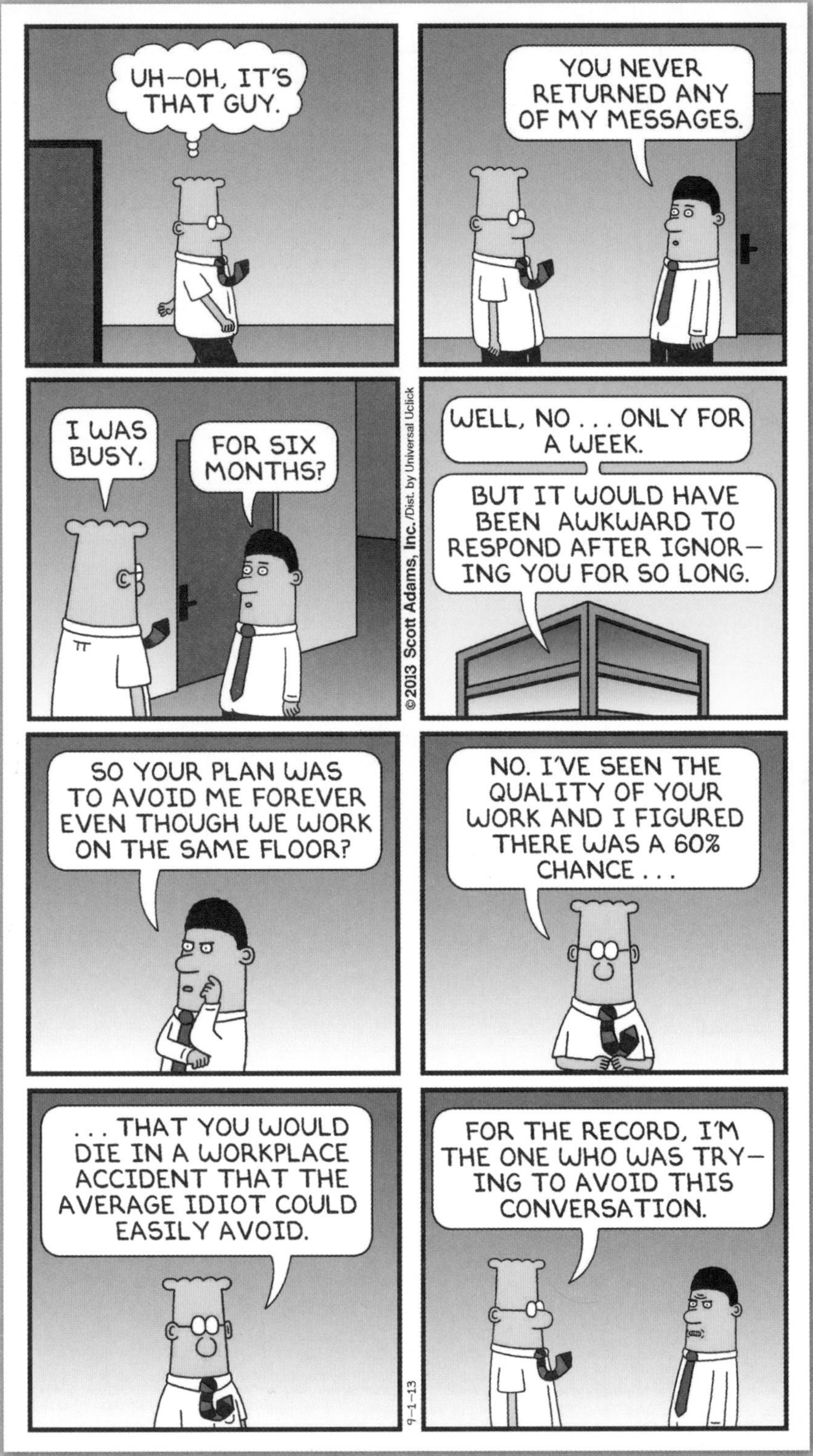
UH–OH, IT'S THAT GUY.
YOU NEVER RETURNED ANY OF MY MESSAGES.
I WAS BUSY.
FOR SIX MONTHS?
WELL, NO . . . ONLY FOR A WEEK.
BUT IT WOULD HAVE BEEN AWKWARD TO RESPOND AFTER IGNOR–ING YOU FOR SO LONG.
SO YOUR PLAN WAS TO AVOID ME FOREVER EVEN THOUGH WE WORK ON THE SAME FLOOR?
NO. I'VE SEEN THE QUALITY OF YOUR WORK AND I FIGURED THERE WAS A 60% CHANCE . . .
. . . THAT YOU WOULD DIE IN A WORKPLACE ACCIDENT THAT THE AVERAGE IDIOT COULD EASILY AVOID.
FOR THE RECORD, I'M THE ONE WHO WAS TRY–ING TO AVOID THIS CONVERSATION.
©2013 Scott Adams, Inc./Dist. by Universal Uclick
9-1-13

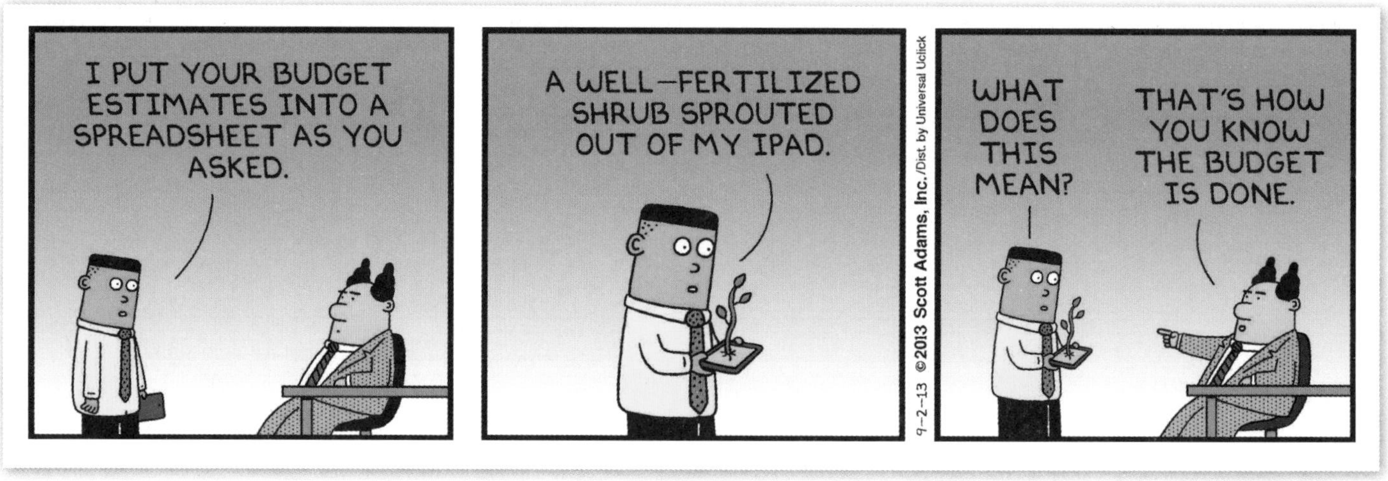
I PUT YOUR BUDGET ESTIMATES INTO A SPREADSHEET AS YOU ASKED.
A WELL-FERTILIZED SHRUB SPROUTED OUT OF MY IPAD.
WHAT DOES THIS MEAN?
THAT'S HOW YOU KNOW THE BUDGET IS DONE.
9-2-13 ©2013 Scott Adams, Inc./Dist. by Universal Uclick

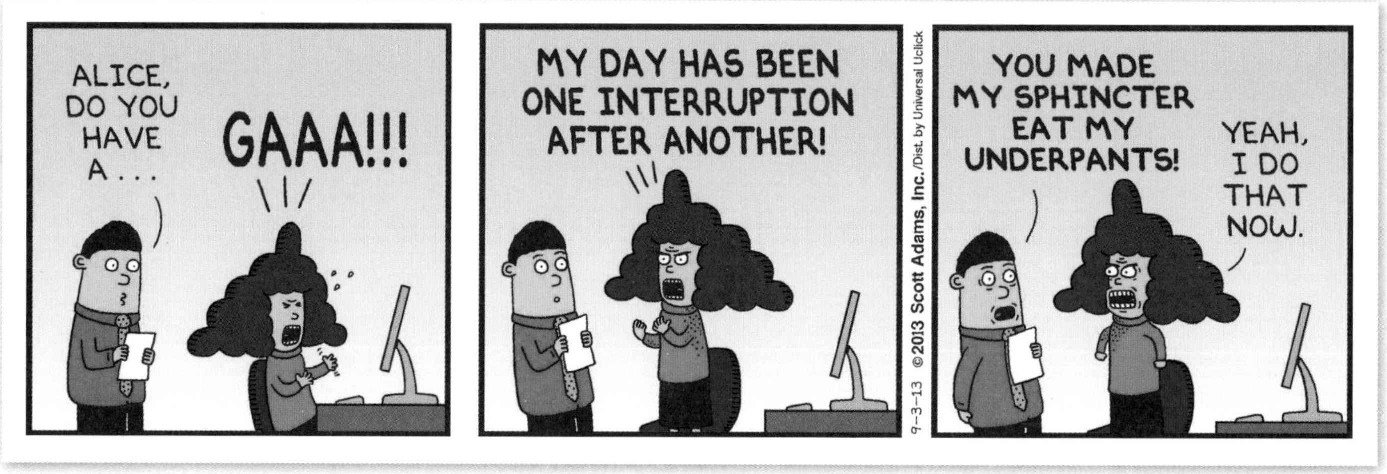
ALICE, DO YOU HAVE A . . .
GAAA!!!
MY DAY HAS BEEN ONE INTERRUPTION AFTER ANOTHER!
YOU MADE MY SPHINCTER EAT MY UNDERPANTS!
YEAH, I DO THAT NOW.
9-3-13 ©2013 Scott Adams, Inc./Dist. by Universal Uclick

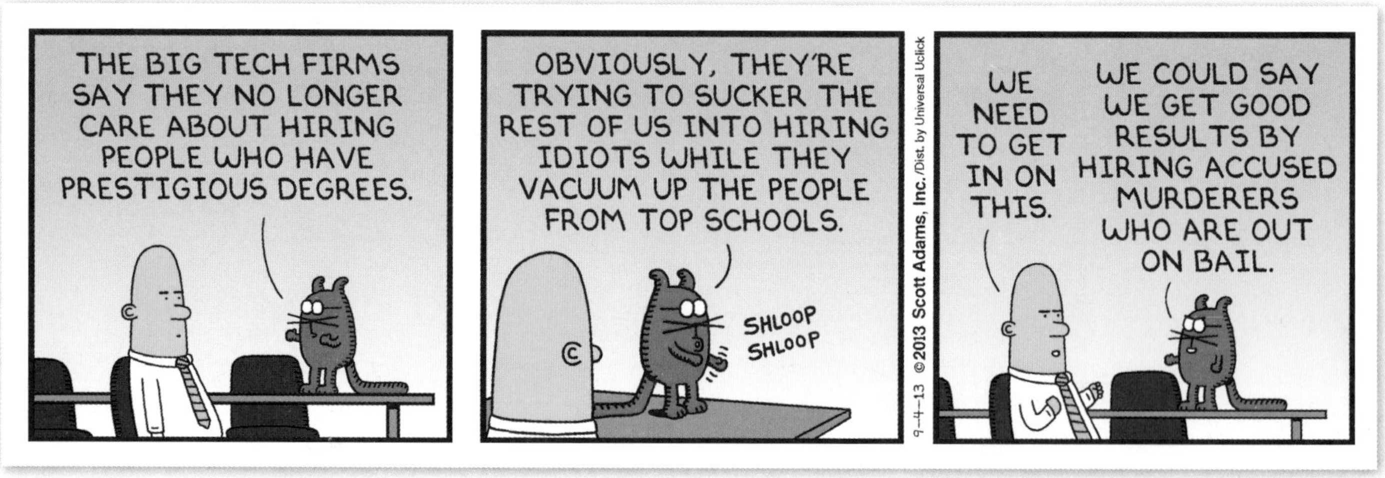
THE BIG TECH FIRMS SAY THEY NO LONGER CARE ABOUT HIRING PEOPLE WHO HAVE PRESTIGIOUS DEGREES.
OBVIOUSLY, THEY'RE TRYING TO SUCKER THE REST OF US INTO HIRING IDIOTS WHILE THEY VACUUM UP THE PEOPLE FROM TOP SCHOOLS.
SHLOOP SHLOOP
WE NEED TO GET IN ON THIS.
WE COULD SAY WE GET GOOD RESULTS BY HIRING ACCUSED MURDERERS WHO ARE OUT ON BAIL.
9-4-13 ©2013 Scott Adams, Inc./Dist. by Universal Uclick

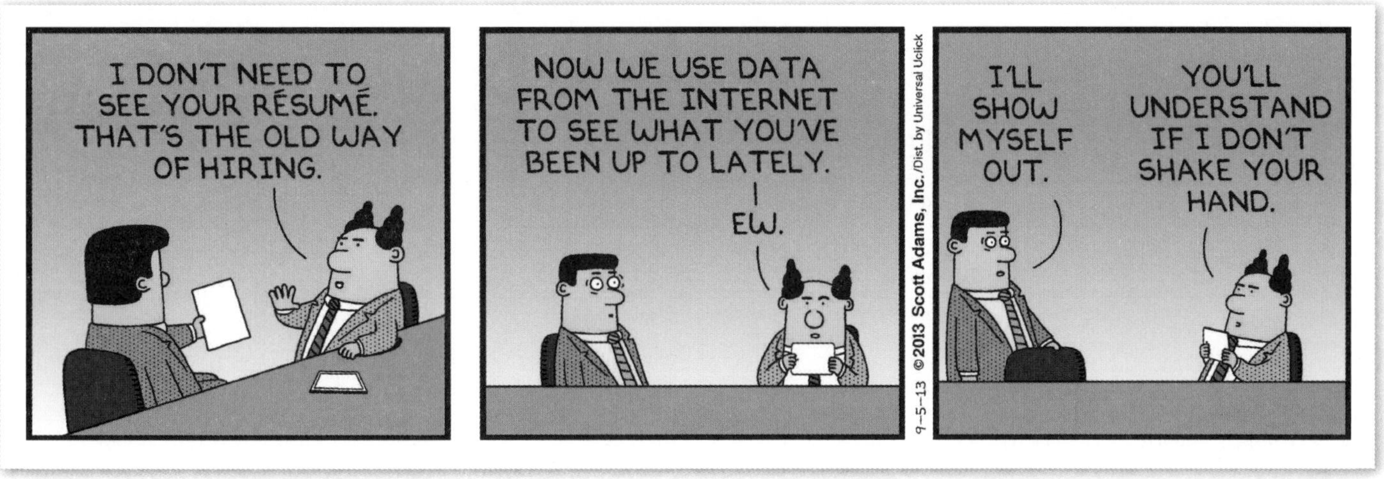
I DON'T NEED TO SEE YOUR RÉSUMÉ. THAT'S THE OLD WAY OF HIRING.
NOW WE USE DATA FROM THE INTERNET TO SEE WHAT YOU'VE BEEN UP TO LATELY.
EW.
9-5-13 ©2013 Scott Adams, Inc./Dist. by Universal Uclick
I'LL SHOW MYSELF OUT.
YOU'LL UNDERSTAND IF I DON'T SHAKE YOUR HAND.

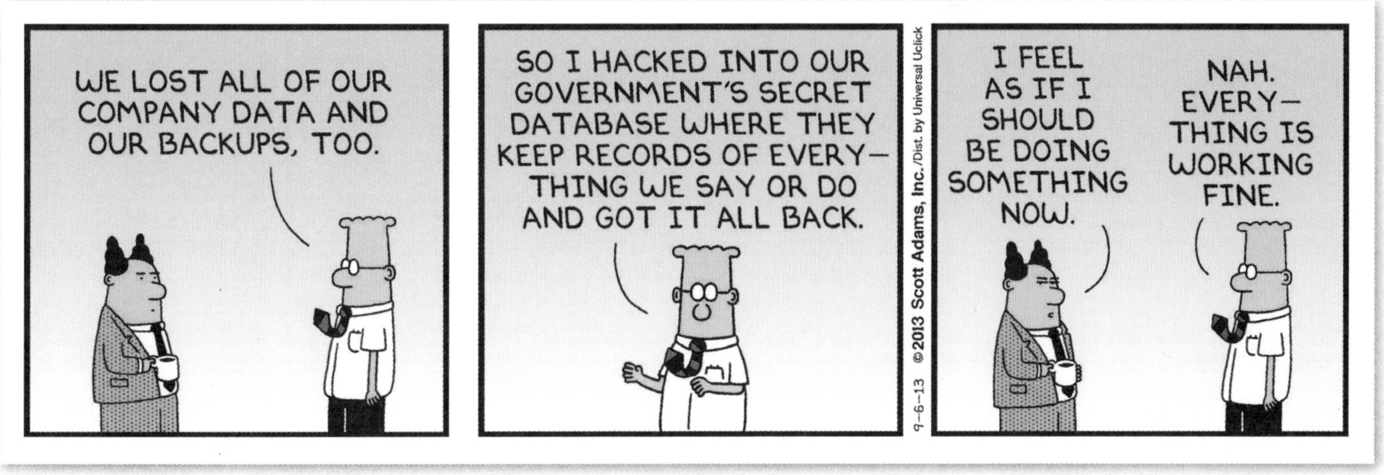
WE LOST ALL OF OUR COMPANY DATA AND OUR BACKUPS, TOO.
SO I HACKED INTO OUR GOVERNMENT'S SECRET DATABASE WHERE THEY KEEP RECORDS OF EVERY-THING WE SAY OR DO AND GOT IT ALL BACK.
9-6-13 ©2013 Scott Adams, Inc./Dist. by Universal Uclick
I FEEL AS IF I SHOULD BE DOING SOMETHING NOW.
NAH. EVERY-THING IS WORKING FINE.

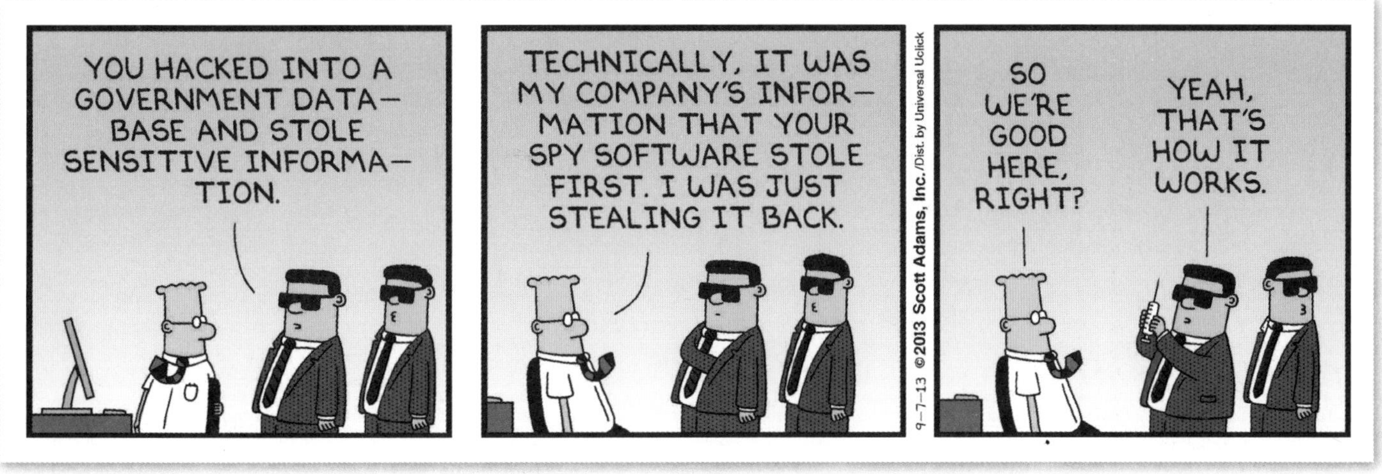
YOU HACKED INTO A GOVERNMENT DATA-BASE AND STOLE SENSITIVE INFORMA-TION.
TECHNICALLY, IT WAS MY COMPANY'S INFOR-MATION THAT YOUR SPY SOFTWARE STOLE FIRST. I WAS JUST STEALING IT BACK.
9-7-13 ©2013 Scott Adams, Inc./Dist. by Universal Uclick
SO WE'RE GOOD HERE, RIGHT?
YEAH, THAT'S HOW IT WORKS.

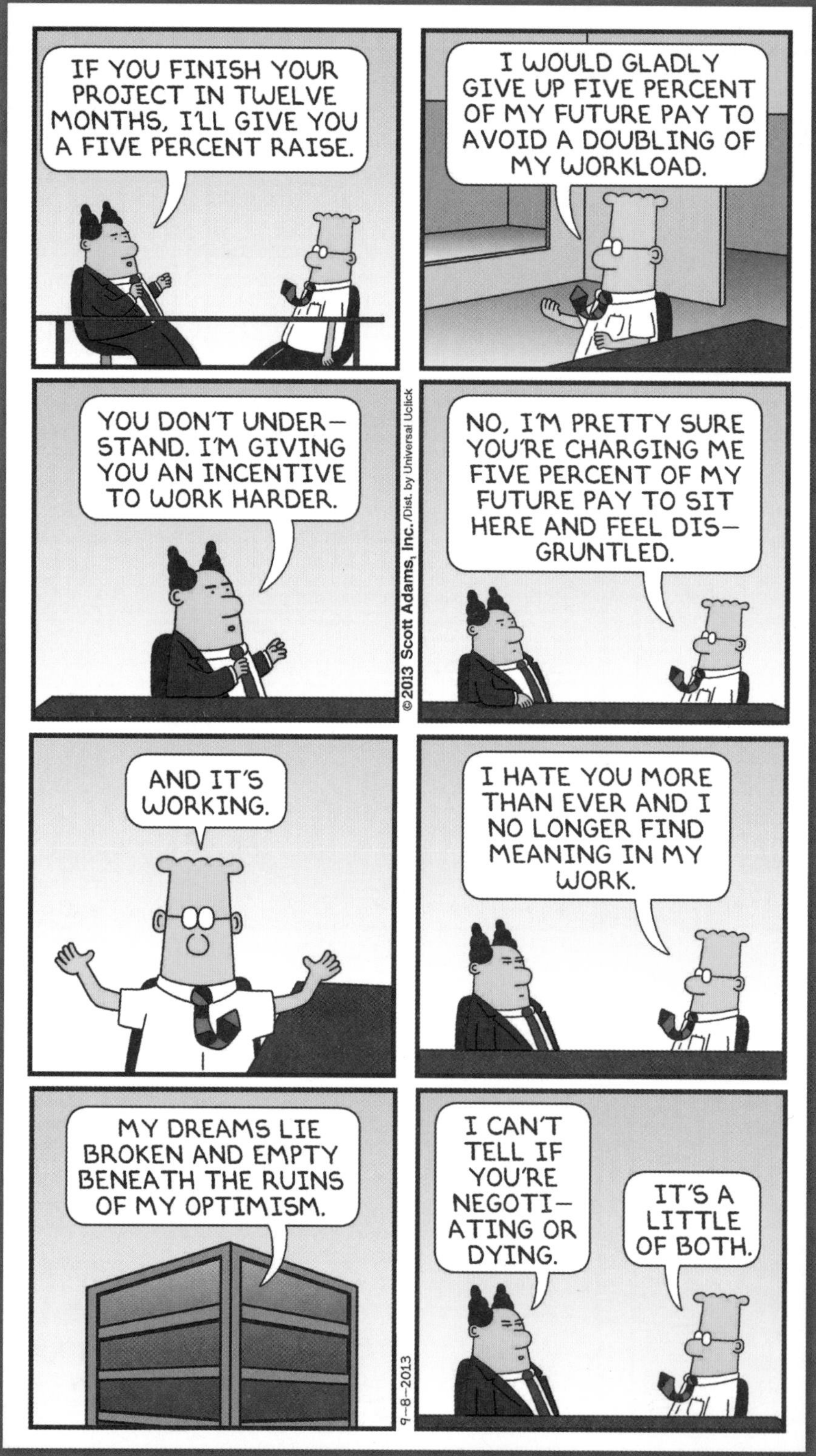
IF YOU FINISH YOUR PROJECT IN TWELVE MONTHS, I'LL GIVE YOU A FIVE PERCENT RAISE.
I WOULD GLADLY GIVE UP FIVE PERCENT OF MY FUTURE PAY TO AVOID A DOUBLING OF MY WORKLOAD.
YOU DON'T UNDER-STAND. I'M GIVING YOU AN INCENTIVE TO WORK HARDER.
NO, I'M PRETTY SURE YOU'RE CHARGING ME FIVE PERCENT OF MY FUTURE PAY TO SIT HERE AND FEEL DIS-GRUNTLED.
AND IT'S WORKING.
I HATE YOU MORE THAN EVER AND I NO LONGER FIND MEANING IN MY WORK.
MY DREAMS LIE BROKEN AND EMPTY BENEATH THE RUINS OF MY OPTIMISM.
I CAN'T TELL IF YOU'RE NEGOTI-ATING OR DYING.
IT'S A LITTLE OF BOTH.
©2013 Scott Adams, Inc./Dist. by Universal Uclick
9-8-2013

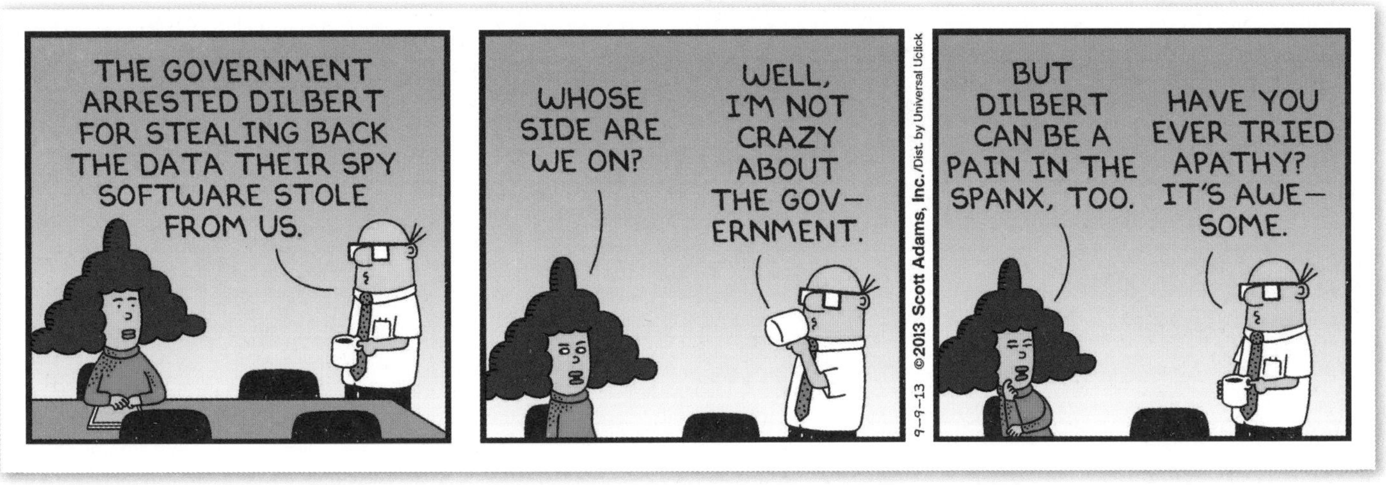
THE GOVERNMENT ARRESTED DILBERT FOR STEALING BACK THE DATA THEIR SPY SOFTWARE STOLE FROM US.
WHOSE SIDE ARE WE ON?
WELL, I'M NOT CRAZY ABOUT THE GOV-ERNMENT.
9-9-13 ©2013 Scott Adams, Inc./Dist. by Universal Uclick
BUT DILBERT CAN BE A PAIN IN THE SPANX, TOO.
HAVE YOU EVER TRIED APATHY? IT'S AWE-SOME.

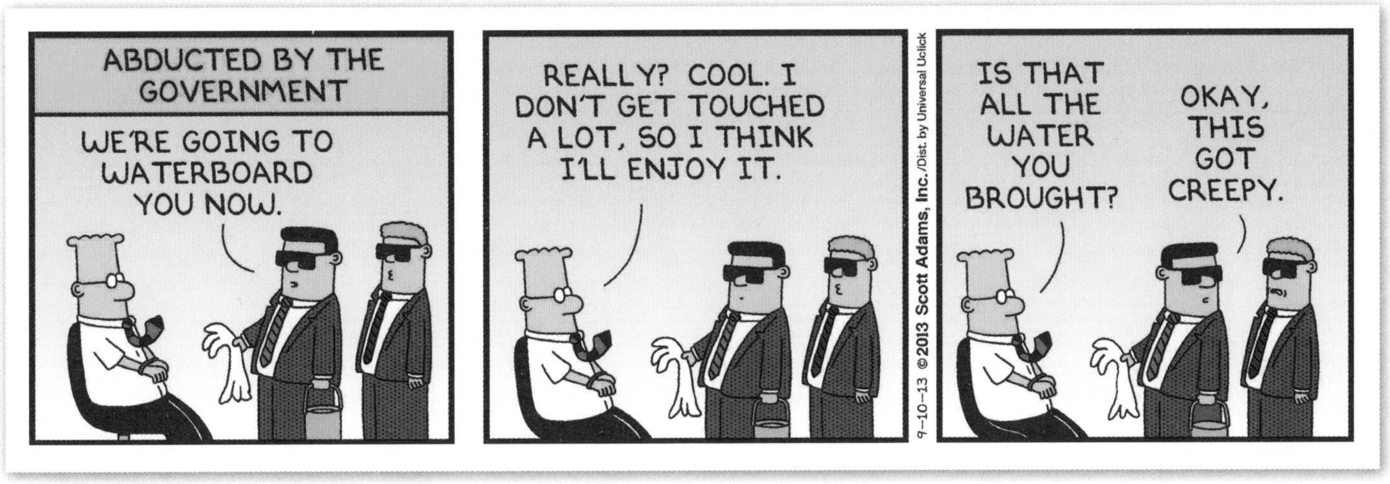
ABDUCTED BY THE GOVERNMENT
WE'RE GOING TO WATERBOARD YOU NOW.
REALLY? COOL. I DON'T GET TOUCHED A LOT, SO I THINK I'LL ENJOY IT.
9-10-13 ©2013 Scott Adams, Inc./Dist. by Universal Uclick
IS THAT ALL THE WATER YOU BROUGHT?
OKAY, THIS GOT CREEPY.

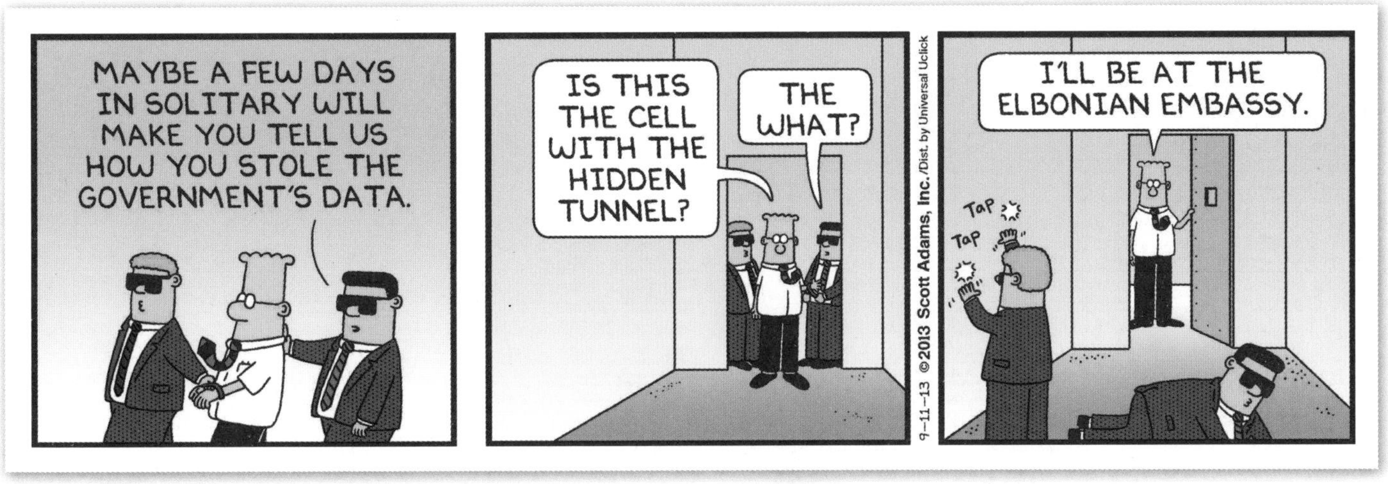
MAYBE A FEW DAYS IN SOLITARY WILL MAKE YOU TELL US HOW YOU STOLE THE GOVERNMENT'S DATA.
IS THIS THE CELL WITH THE HIDDEN TUNNEL?
THE WHAT?
9-11-13 ©2013 Scott Adams, Inc./Dist. by Universal Uclick
I'LL BE AT THE ELBONIAN EMBASSY.
Tap
Tap

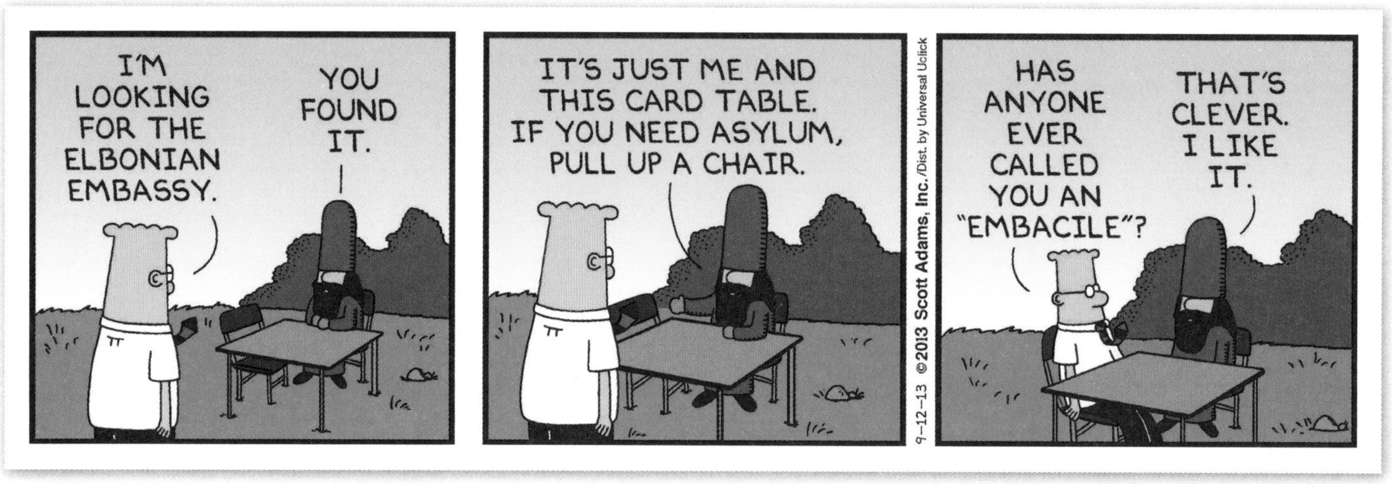
I'M LOOKING FOR THE ELBONIAN EMBASSY.
YOU FOUND IT.
IT'S JUST ME AND THIS CARD TABLE. IF YOU NEED ASYLUM, PULL UP A CHAIR.
9-12-13 ©2013 Scott Adams, Inc./Dist. by Universal Uclick
HAS ANYONE EVER CALLED YOU AN "EMBACILE"?
THAT'S CLEVER. I LIKE IT.

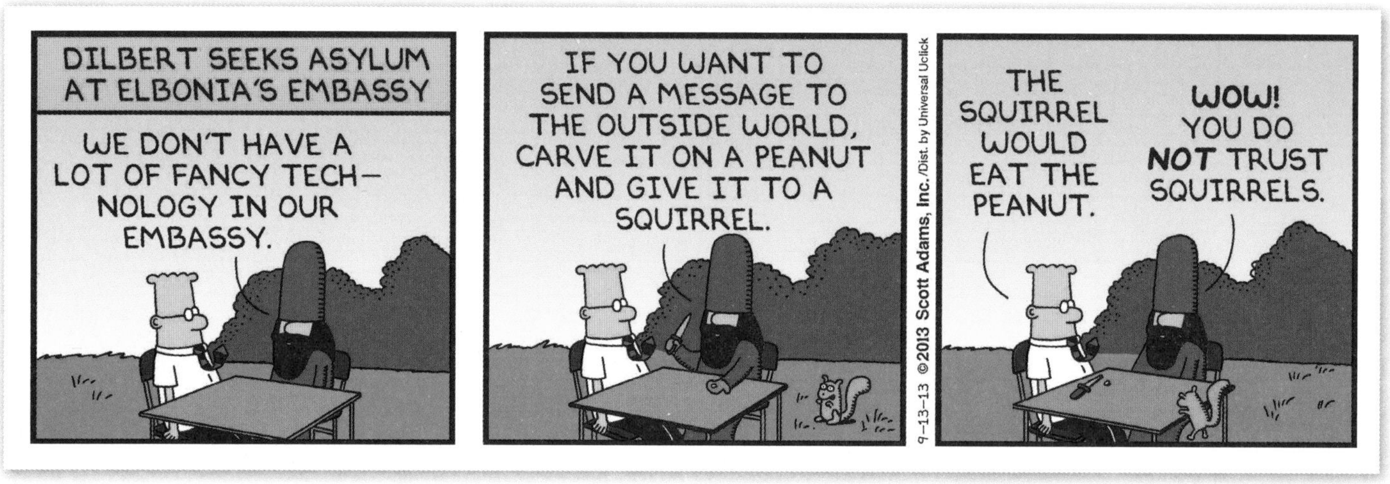
DILBERT SEEKS ASYLUM AT ELBONIA'S EMBASSY
WE DON'T HAVE A LOT OF FANCY TECH-NOLOGY IN OUR EMBASSY.
IF YOU WANT TO SEND A MESSAGE TO THE OUTSIDE WORLD, CARVE IT ON A PEANUT AND GIVE IT TO A SQUIRREL.
9-13-13 ©2013 Scott Adams, Inc./Dist. by Universal Uclick
THE SQUIRREL WOULD EAT THE PEANUT.
WOW! YOU DO NOT TRUST SQUIRRELS.

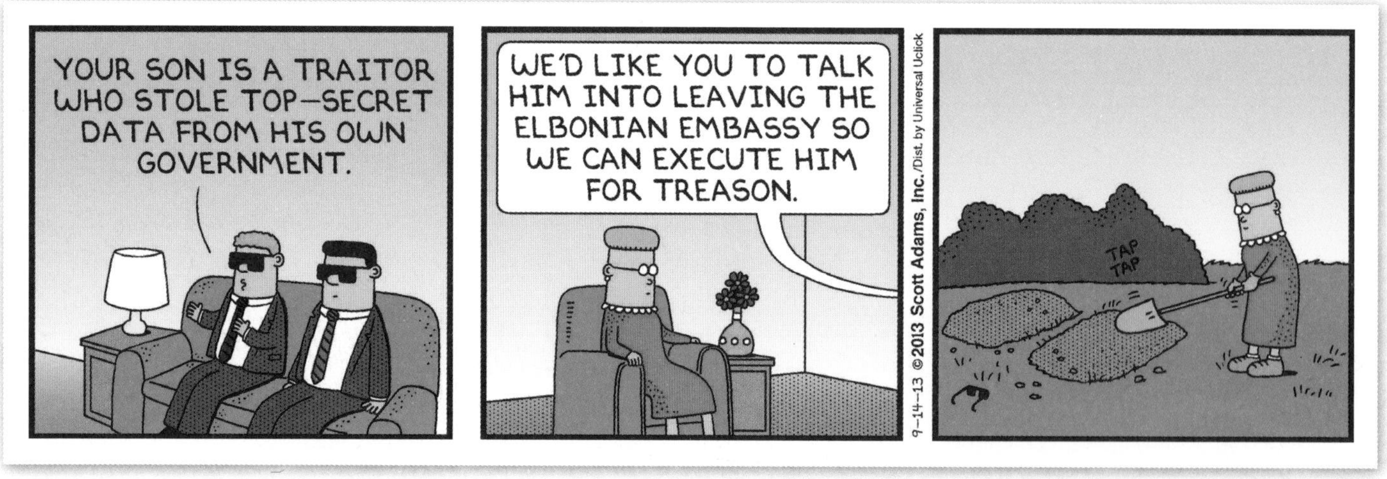
YOUR SON IS A TRAITOR WHO STOLE TOP-SECRET DATA FROM HIS OWN GOVERNMENT.
WE'D LIKE YOU TO TALK HIM INTO LEAVING THE ELBONIAN EMBASSY SO WE CAN EXECUTE HIM FOR TREASON.
9-14-13 ©2013 Scott Adams, Inc./Dist. by Universal Uclick
TAP TAP

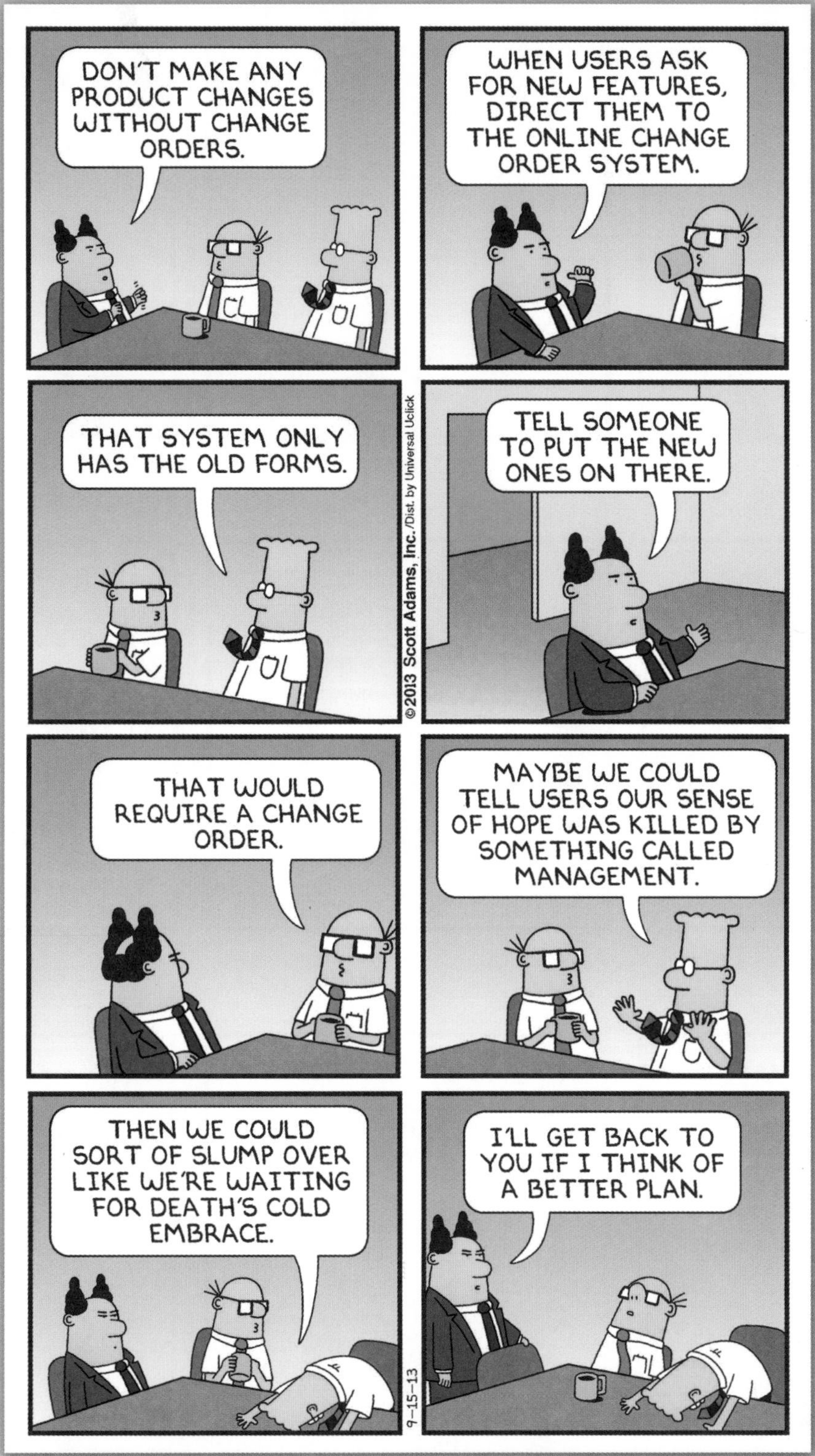
DON'T MAKE ANY PRODUCT CHANGES WITHOUT CHANGE ORDERS.
WHEN USERS ASK FOR NEW FEATURES, DIRECT THEM TO THE ONLINE CHANGE ORDER SYSTEM.
THAT SYSTEM ONLY HAS THE OLD FORMS.
TELL SOMEONE TO PUT THE NEW ONES ON THERE.
THAT WOULD REQUIRE A CHANGE ORDER.
MAYBE WE COULD TELL USERS OUR SENSE OF HOPE WAS KILLED BY SOMETHING CALLED MANAGEMENT.
THEN WE COULD SORT OF SLUMP OVER LIKE WE'RE WAITING FOR DEATH'S COLD EMBRACE.
I'LL GET BACK TO YOU IF I THINK OF A BETTER PLAN.
© 2013 Scott Adams, Inc./Dist. by Universal Uclick
9-15-13

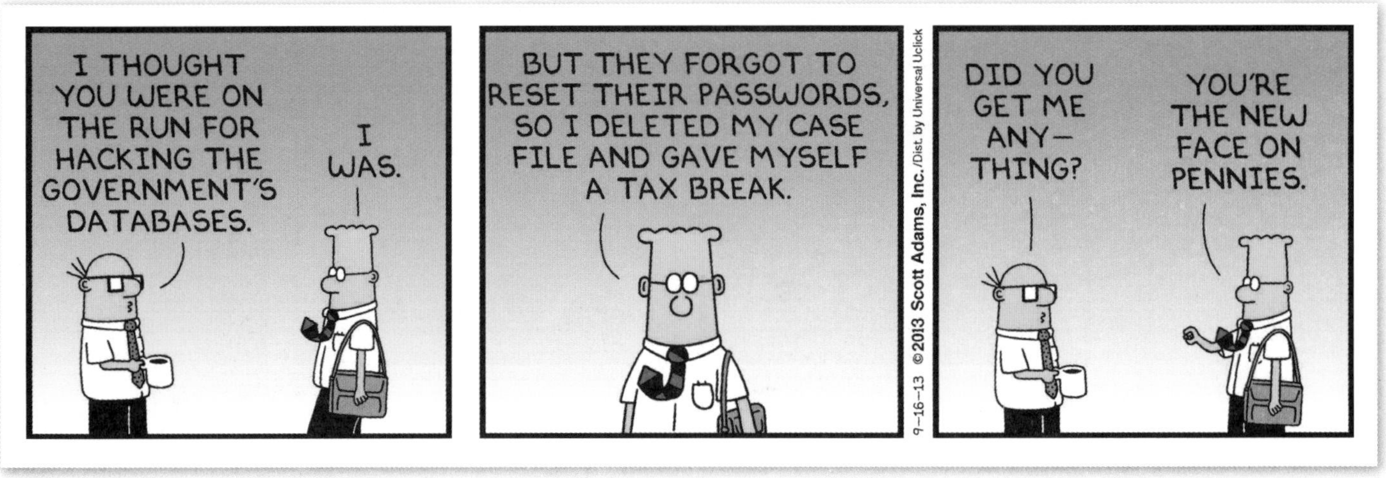
I THOUGHT YOU WERE ON THE RUN FOR HACKING THE GOVERNMENT'S DATABASES.
I WAS.
BUT THEY FORGOT TO RESET THEIR PASSWORDS, SO I DELETED MY CASE FILE AND GAVE MYSELF A TAX BREAK.
9-16-13 ©2013 Scott Adams, Inc./Dist. by Universal Uclick
DID YOU GET ME ANY-THING?
YOU'RE THE NEW FACE ON PENNIES.

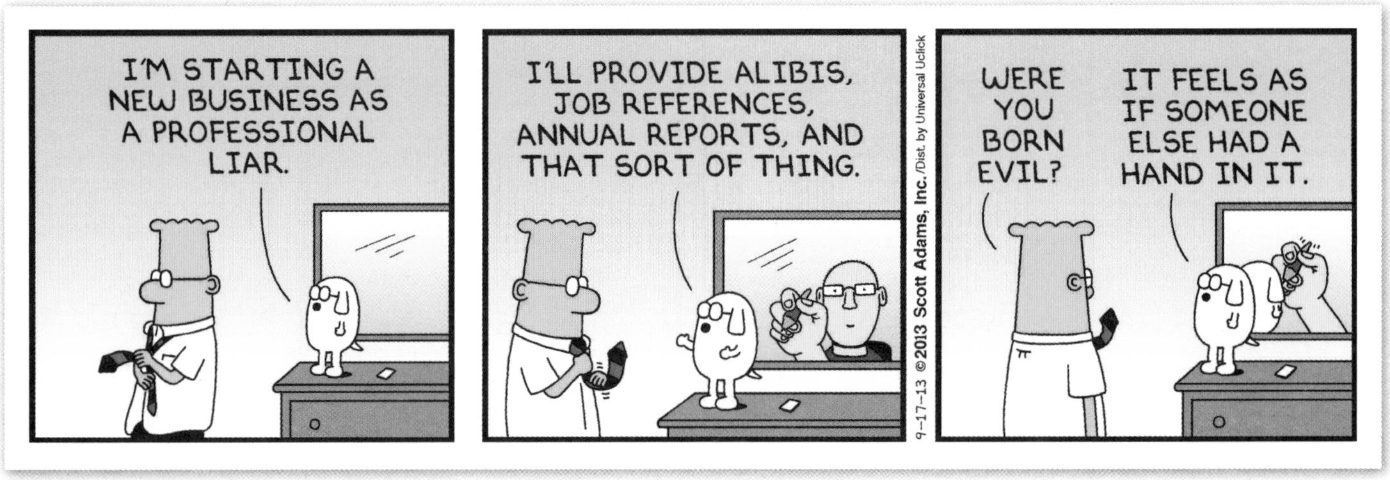
I'M STARTING A NEW BUSINESS AS A PROFESSIONAL LIAR.
I'LL PROVIDE ALIBIS, JOB REFERENCES, ANNUAL REPORTS, AND THAT SORT OF THING.
9-17-13 ©2013 Scott Adams, Inc./Dist. by Universal Uclick
WERE YOU BORN EVIL?
IT FEELS AS IF SOMEONE ELSE HAD A HAND IN IT.

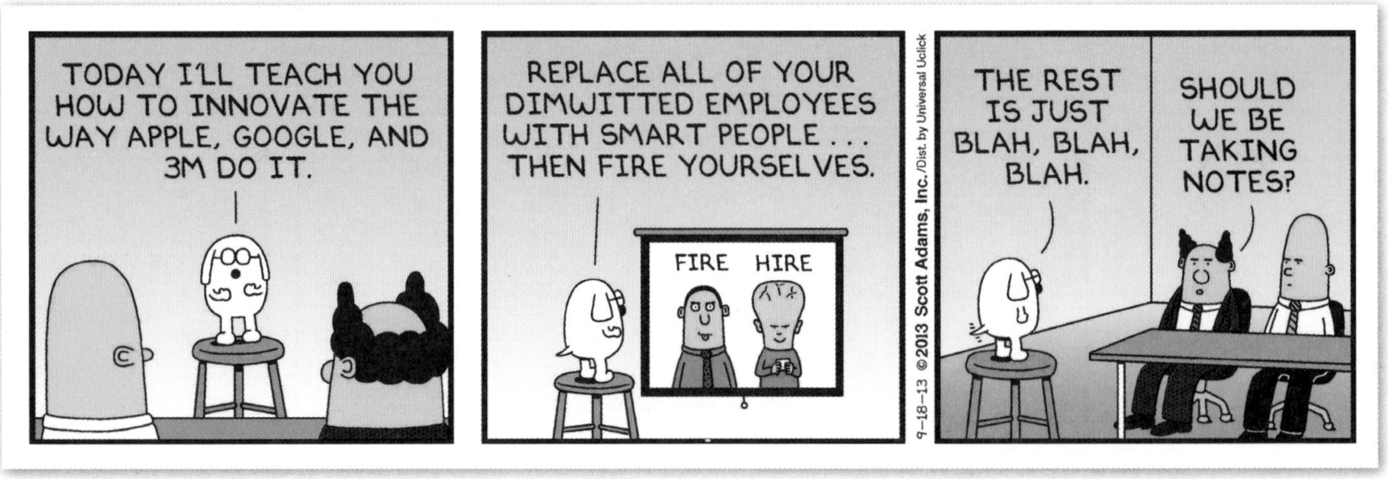
TODAY I'LL TEACH YOU HOW TO INNOVATE THE WAY APPLE, GOOGLE, AND 3M DO IT.
REPLACE ALL OF YOUR DIMWITTED EMPLOYEES WITH SMART PEOPLE . . . THEN FIRE YOURSELVES.
FIRE
HIRE
9-18-13 ©2013 Scott Adams, Inc./Dist. by Universal Uclick
THE REST IS JUST BLAH, BLAH, BLAH.
SHOULD WE BE TAKING NOTES?

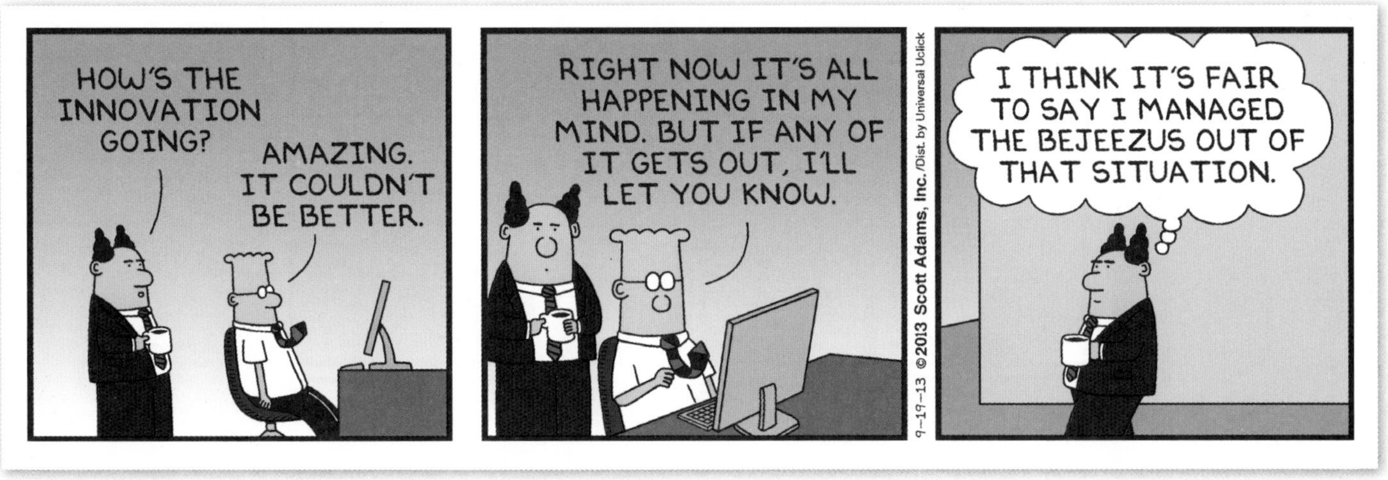
HOW'S THE INNOVATION GOING?
AMAZING. IT COULDN'T BE BETTER.
RIGHT NOW IT'S ALL HAPPENING IN MY MIND. BUT IF ANY OF IT GETS OUT, I'LL LET YOU KNOW.
9-19-13 ©2013 Scott Adams, Inc./Dist. by Universal Uclick
I THINK IT'S FAIR TO SAY I MANAGED THE BEJEEZUS OUT OF THAT SITUATION.

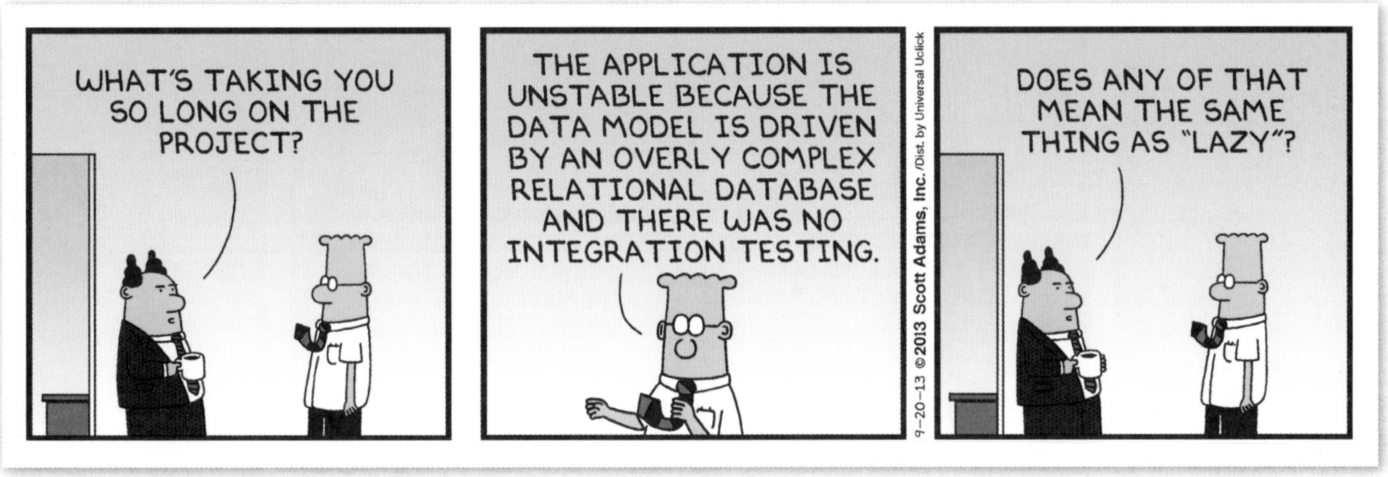
WHAT'S TAKING YOU SO LONG ON THE PROJECT?
THE APPLICATION IS UNSTABLE BECAUSE THE DATA MODEL IS DRIVEN BY AN OVERLY COMPLEX RELATIONAL DATABASE AND THERE WAS NO INTEGRATION TESTING.
9-20-13 ©2013 Scott Adams, Inc./Dist. by Universal Uclick
DOES ANY OF THAT MEAN THE SAME THING AS "LAZY"?

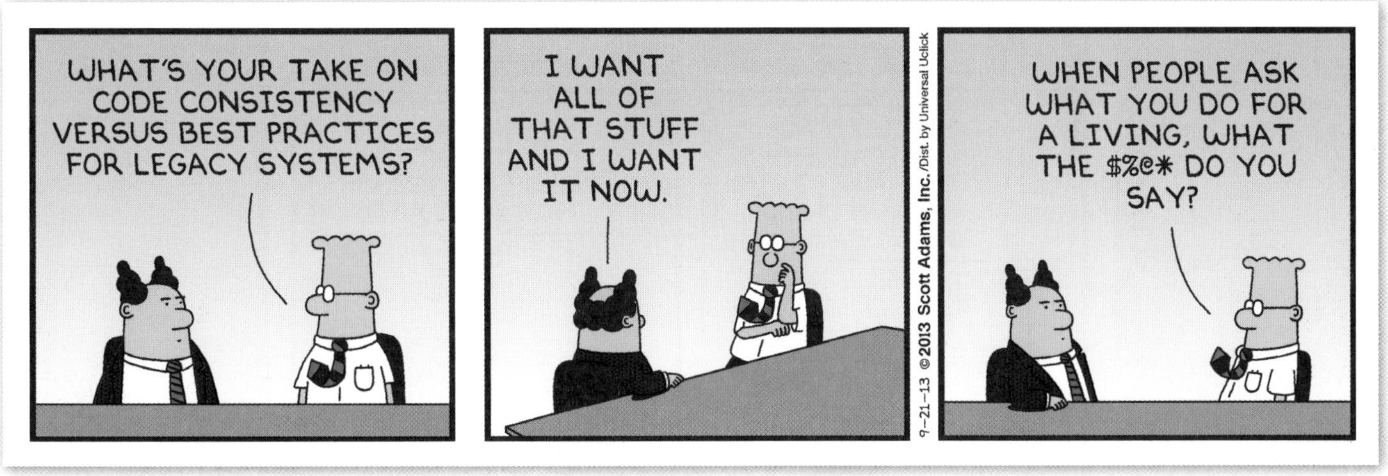
WHAT'S YOUR TAKE ON CODE CONSISTENCY VERSUS BEST PRACTICES FOR LEGACY SYSTEMS?
I WANT ALL OF THAT STUFF AND I WANT IT NOW.
9-21-13 ©2013 Scott Adams, Inc./Dist. by Universal Uclick
WHEN PEOPLE ASK WHAT YOU DO FOR A LIVING, WHAT THE $%@* DO YOU SAY?

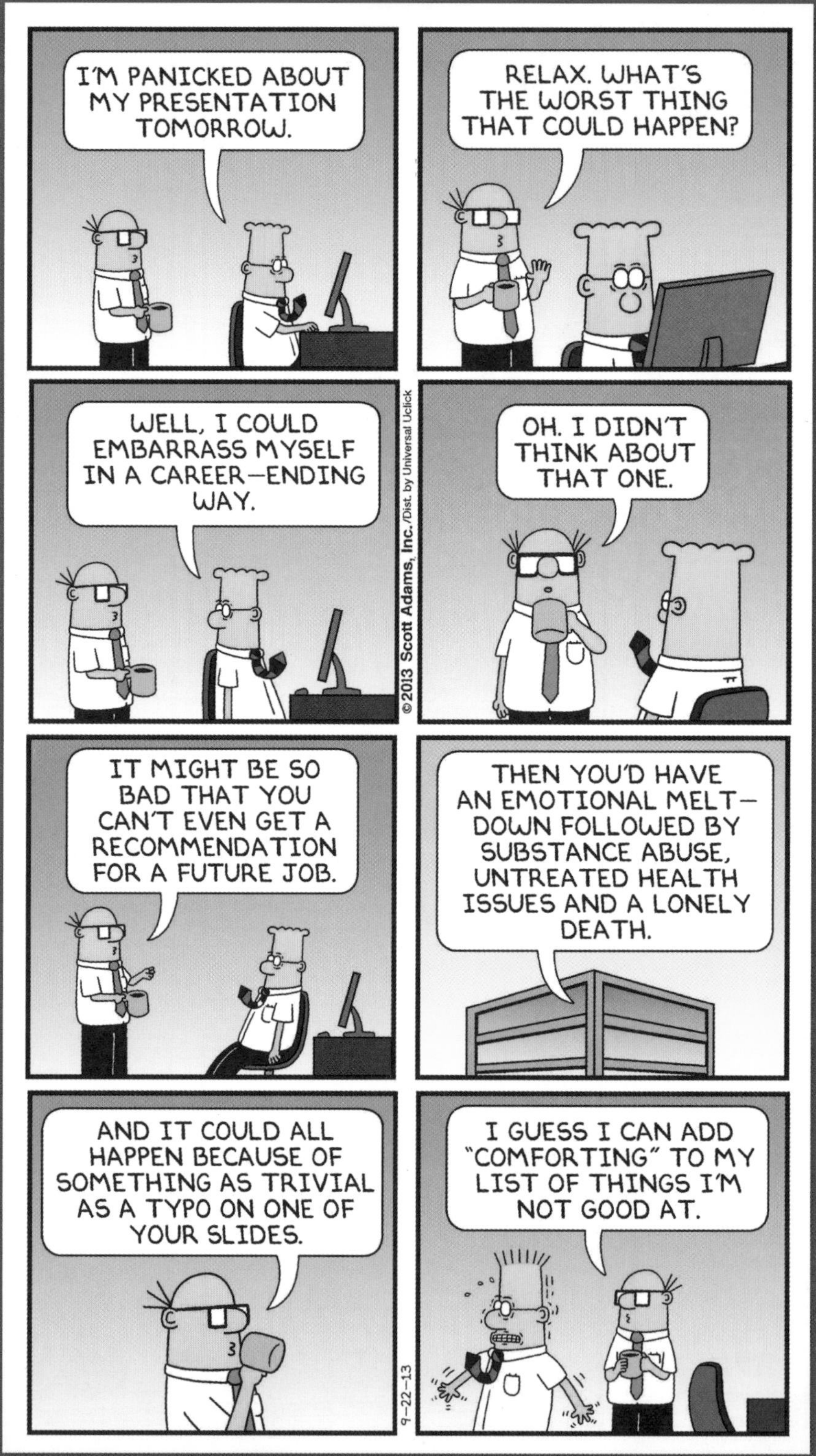
I'M PANICKED ABOUT MY PRESENTATION TOMORROW.
RELAX. WHAT'S THE WORST THING THAT COULD HAPPEN?
WELL, I COULD EMBARRASS MYSELF IN A CAREER—ENDING WAY.
OH. I DIDN'T THINK ABOUT THAT ONE.
IT MIGHT BE SO BAD THAT YOU CAN'T EVEN GET A RECOMMENDATION FOR A FUTURE JOB.
THEN YOU'D HAVE AN EMOTIONAL MELT—DOWN FOLLOWED BY SUBSTANCE ABUSE, UNTREATED HEALTH ISSUES AND A LONELY DEATH.
AND IT COULD ALL HAPPEN BECAUSE OF SOMETHING AS TRIVIAL AS A TYPO ON ONE OF YOUR SLIDES.
I GUESS I CAN ADD "COMFORTING" TO MY LIST OF THINGS I'M NOT GOOD AT.
©2013 Scott Adams, Inc./Dist. by Universal Uclick
9-22-13

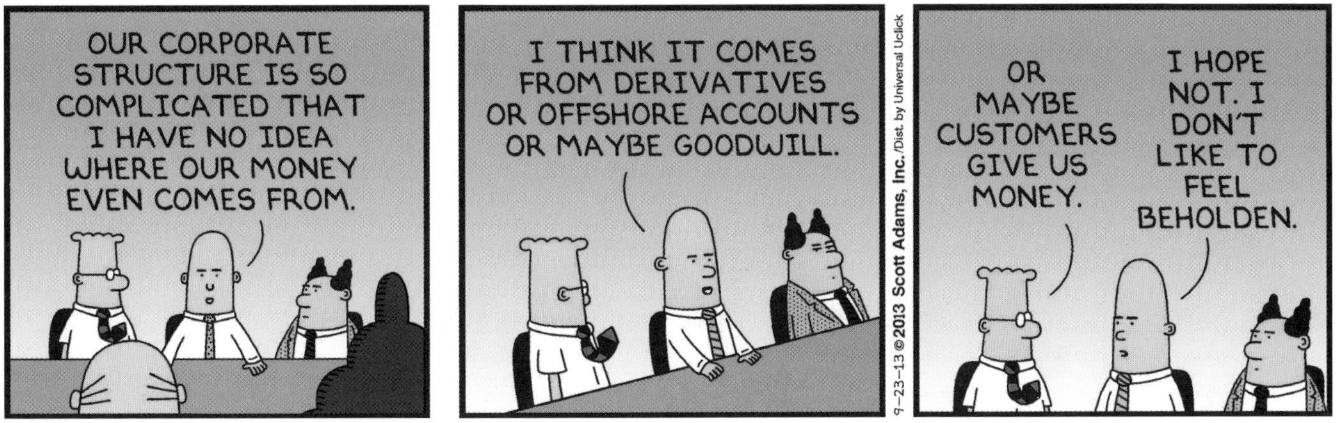
OUR CORPORATE STRUCTURE IS SO COMPLICATED THAT I HAVE NO IDEA WHERE OUR MONEY EVEN COMES FROM.
I THINK IT COMES FROM DERIVATIVES OR OFFSHORE ACCOUNTS OR MAYBE GOODWILL.
9-23-13 ©2013 Scott Adams, Inc./Dist. by Universal Uclick
OR MAYBE CUSTOMERS GIVE US MONEY.
I HOPE NOT. I DON'T LIKE TO FEEL BEHOLDEN.

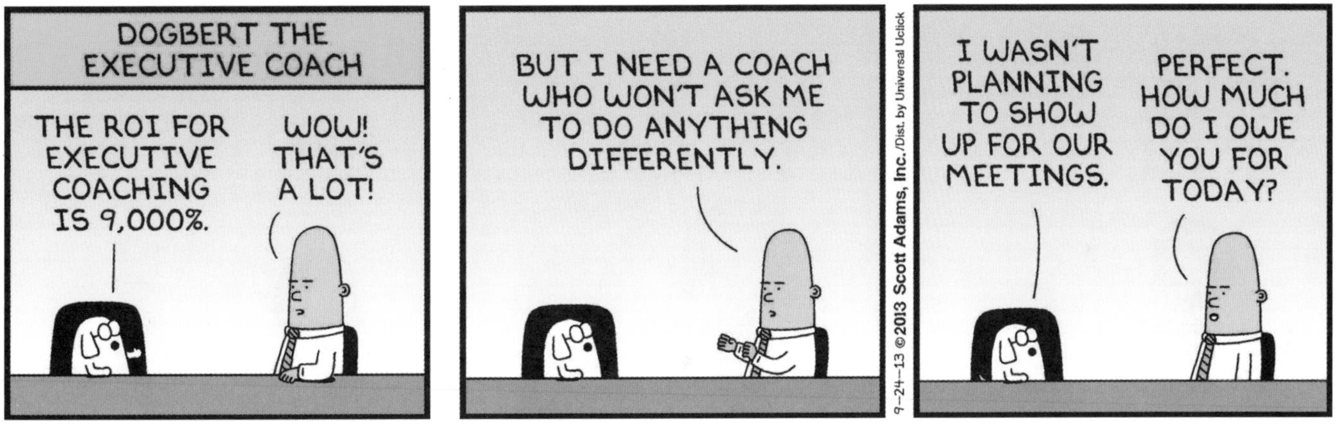
DOGBERT THE EXECUTIVE COACH
THE ROI FOR EXECUTIVE COACHING IS 9,000%.
WOW! THAT'S A LOT!
BUT I NEED A COACH WHO WON'T ASK ME TO DO ANYTHING DIFFERENTLY.
9-24-13 ©2013 Scott Adams, Inc./Dist. by Universal Uclick
I WASN'T PLANNING TO SHOW UP FOR OUR MEETINGS.
PERFECT. HOW MUCH DO I OWE YOU FOR TODAY?

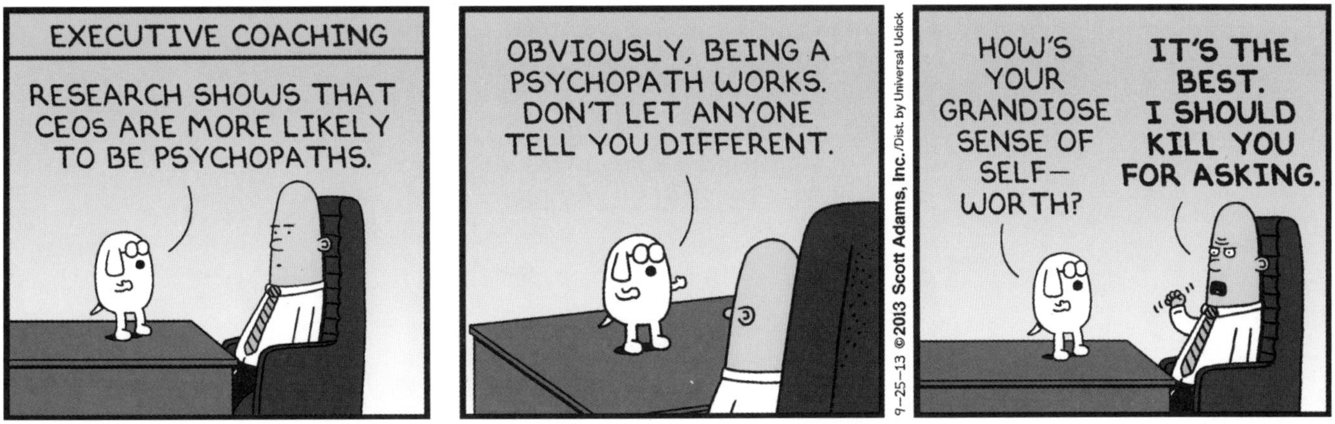
EXECUTIVE COACHING
RESEARCH SHOWS THAT CEOS ARE MORE LIKELY TO BE PSYCHOPATHS.
OBVIOUSLY, BEING A PSYCHOPATH WORKS. DON'T LET ANYONE TELL YOU DIFFERENT.
9-25-13 ©2013 Scott Adams, Inc./Dist. by Universal Uclick
HOW'S YOUR GRANDIOSE SENSE OF SELF-WORTH?
IT'S THE BEST. I SHOULD KILL YOU FOR ASKING.

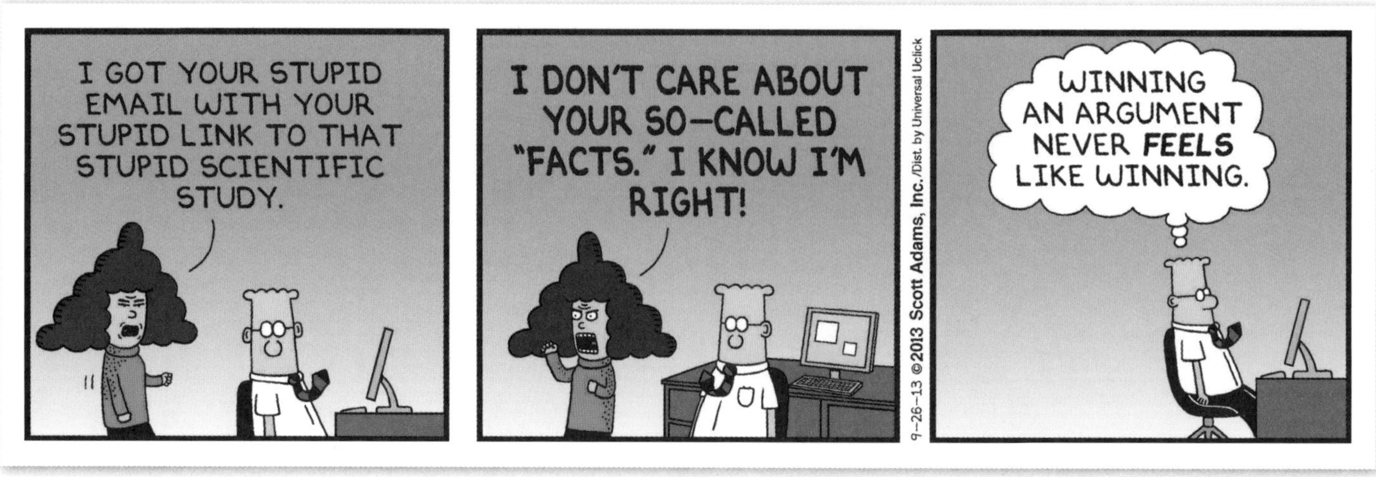
I GOT YOUR STUPID EMAIL WITH YOUR STUPID LINK TO THAT STUPID SCIENTIFIC STUDY.
I DON'T CARE ABOUT YOUR SO-CALLED "FACTS." I KNOW I'M RIGHT!
9-26-13 ©2013 Scott Adams, Inc./Dist. by Universal Uclick
WINNING AN ARGUMENT NEVER **FEELS** LIKE WINNING.

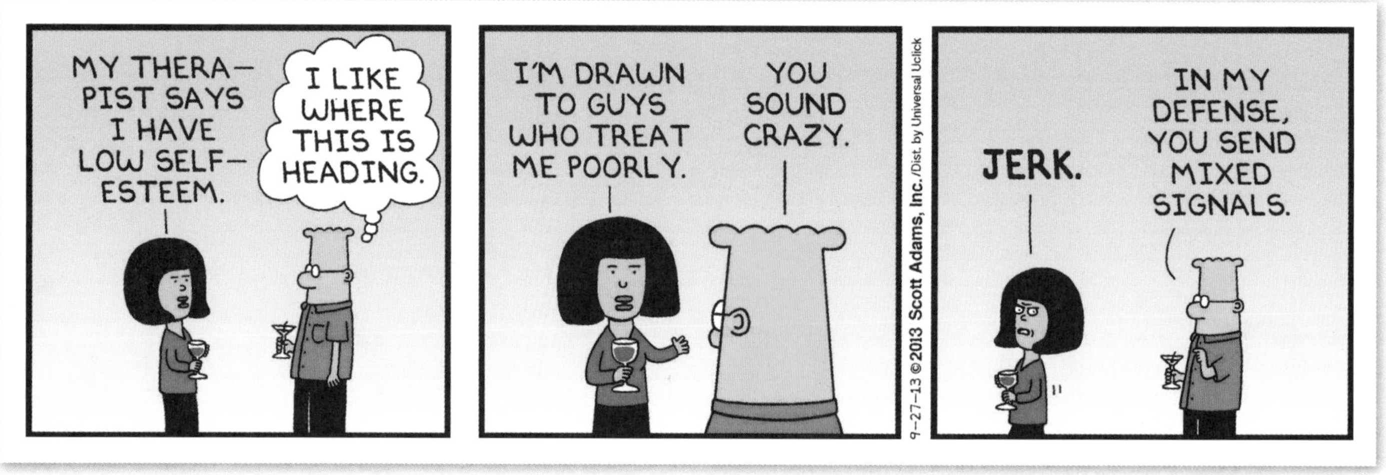
MY THERA-PIST SAYS I HAVE LOW SELF-ESTEEM.
I LIKE WHERE THIS IS HEADING.
I'M DRAWN TO GUYS WHO TREAT ME POORLY.
YOU SOUND CRAZY.
9-27-13 ©2013 Scott Adams, Inc./Dist. by Universal Uclick
JERK.
IN MY DEFENSE, YOU SEND MIXED SIGNALS.

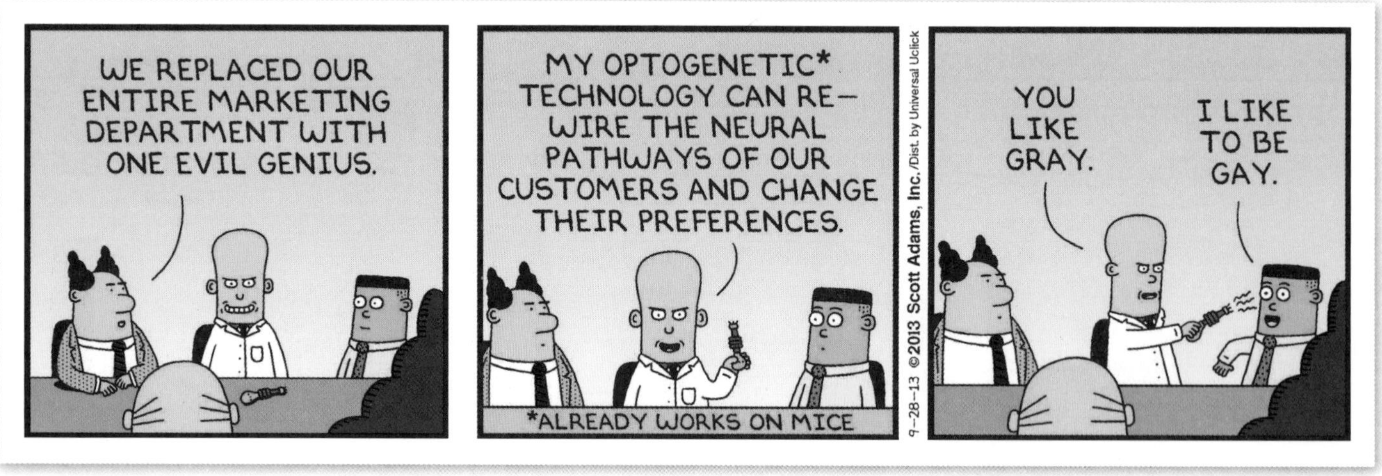
WE REPLACED OUR ENTIRE MARKETING DEPARTMENT WITH ONE EVIL GENIUS.
MY OPTOGENETIC* TECHNOLOGY CAN RE-WIRE THE NEURAL PATHWAYS OF OUR CUSTOMERS AND CHANGE THEIR PREFERENCES.
*ALREADY WORKS ON MICE
9-28-13 ©2013 Scott Adams, Inc./Dist. by Universal Uclick
YOU LIKE GRAY.
I LIKE TO BE GAY.

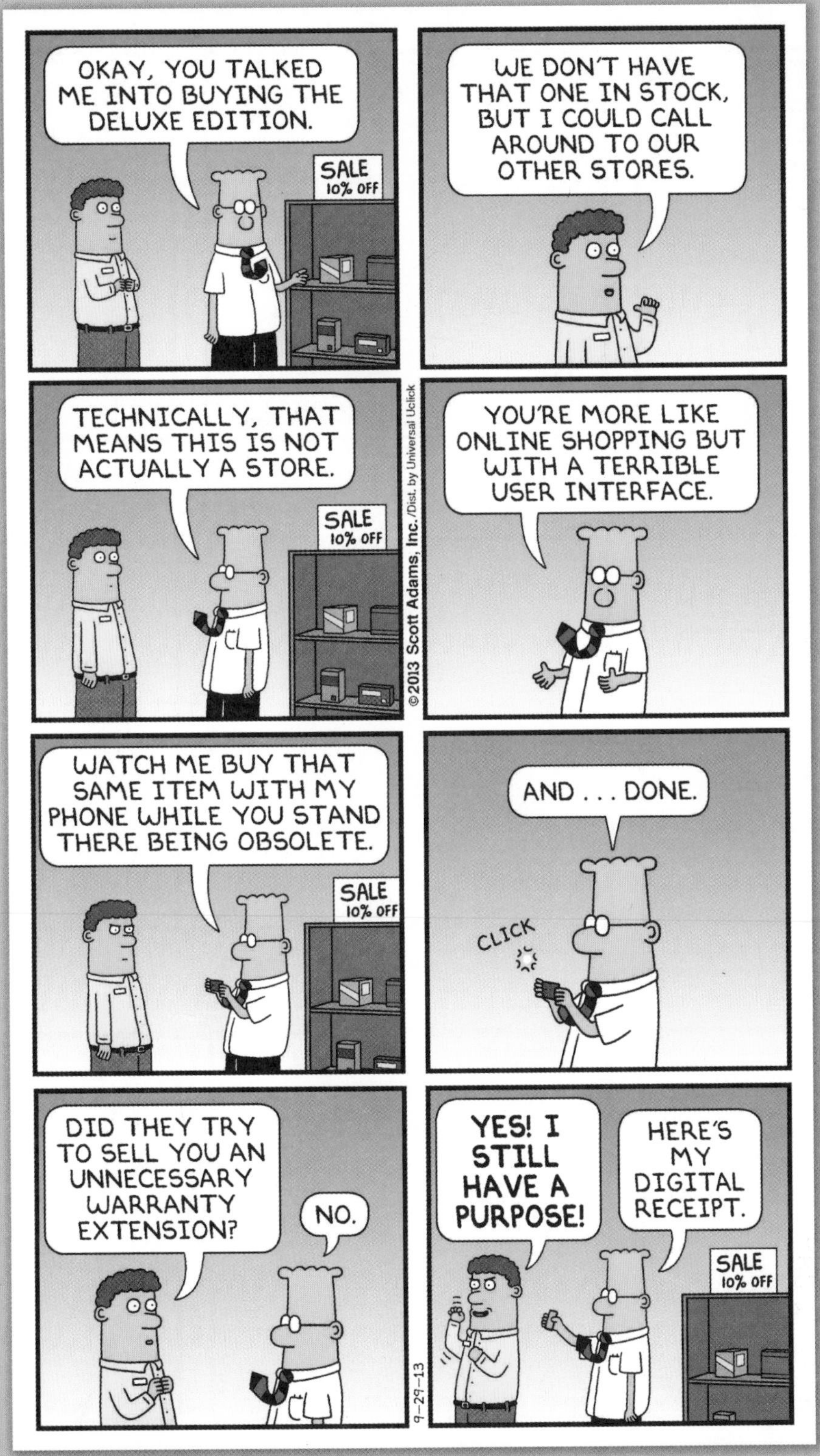
OKAY, YOU TALKED ME INTO BUYING THE DELUXE EDITION.
SALE 10% OFF
WE DON'T HAVE THAT ONE IN STOCK, BUT I COULD CALL AROUND TO OUR OTHER STORES.
TECHNICALLY, THAT MEANS THIS IS NOT ACTUALLY A STORE.
SALE 10% OFF
©2013 Scott Adams, Inc./Dist. by Universal Uclick
YOU'RE MORE LIKE ONLINE SHOPPING BUT WITH A TERRIBLE USER INTERFACE.
WATCH ME BUY THAT SAME ITEM WITH MY PHONE WHILE YOU STAND THERE BEING OBSOLETE.
SALE 10% OFF
AND . . . DONE.
CLICK
DID THEY TRY TO SELL YOU AN UNNECESSARY WARRANTY EXTENSION?
NO.
9-29-13
YES! I STILL HAVE A PURPOSE!
HERE'S MY DIGITAL RECEIPT.
SALE 10% OFF

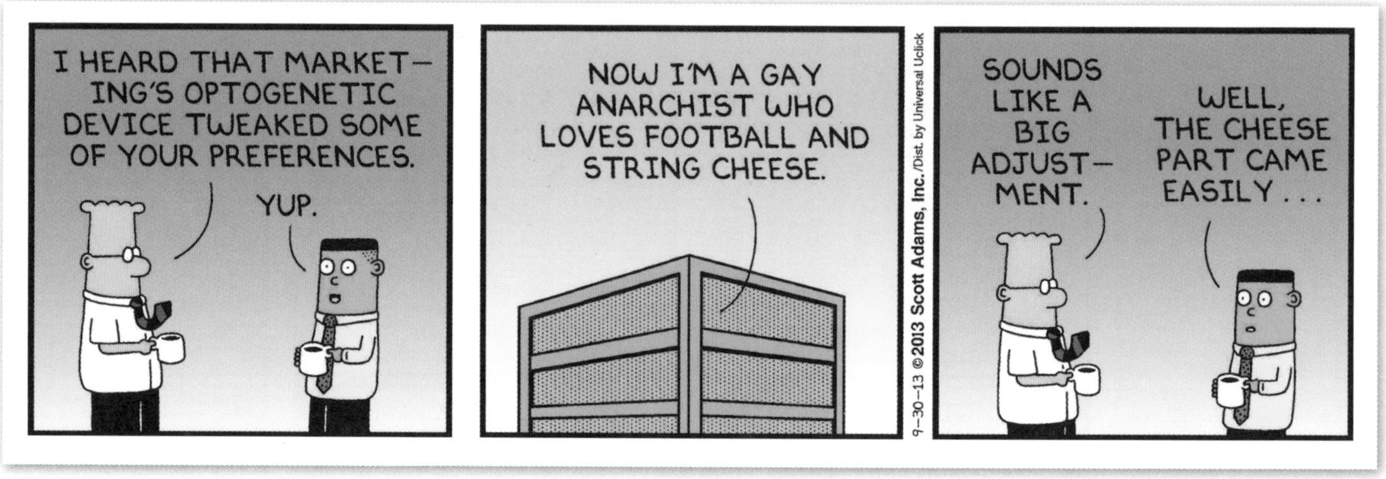
I HEARD THAT MARKET-ING'S OPTOGENETIC DEVICE TWEAKED SOME OF YOUR PREFERENCES.
YUP.
NOW I'M A GAY ANARCHIST WHO LOVES FOOTBALL AND STRING CHEESE.
9-30-13 ©2013 Scott Adams, Inc./Dist. by Universal Uclick
SOUNDS LIKE A BIG ADJUST-MENT.
WELL, THE CHEESE PART CAME EASILY . . .

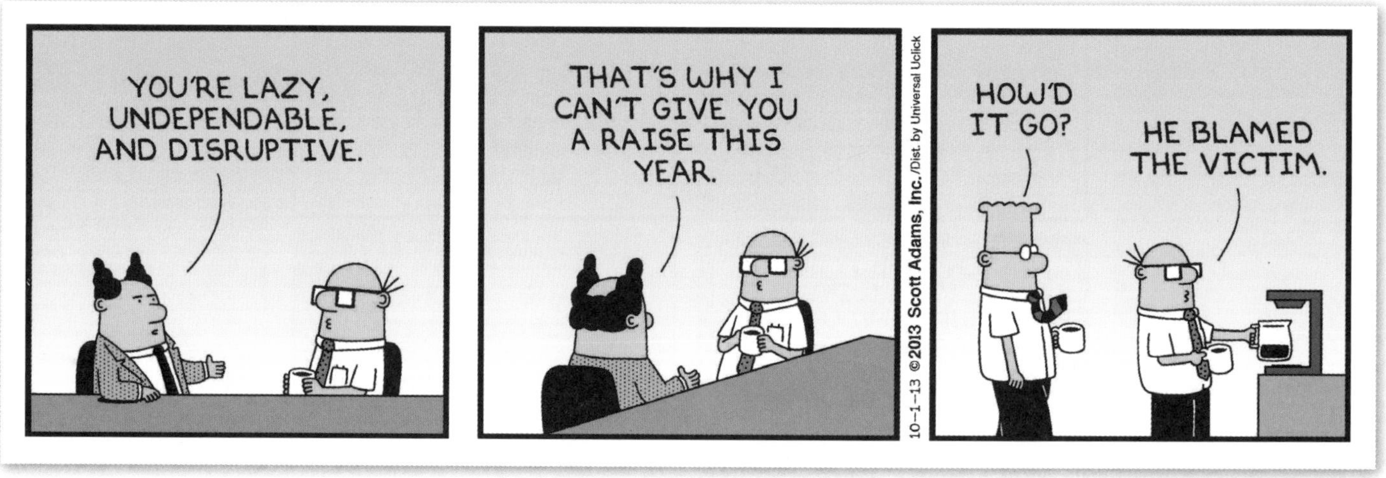
YOU'RE LAZY, UNDEPENDABLE, AND DISRUPTIVE.
THAT'S WHY I CAN'T GIVE YOU A RAISE THIS YEAR.
10-1-13 ©2013 Scott Adams, Inc./Dist. by Universal Uclick
HOW'D IT GO?
HE BLAMED THE VICTIM.

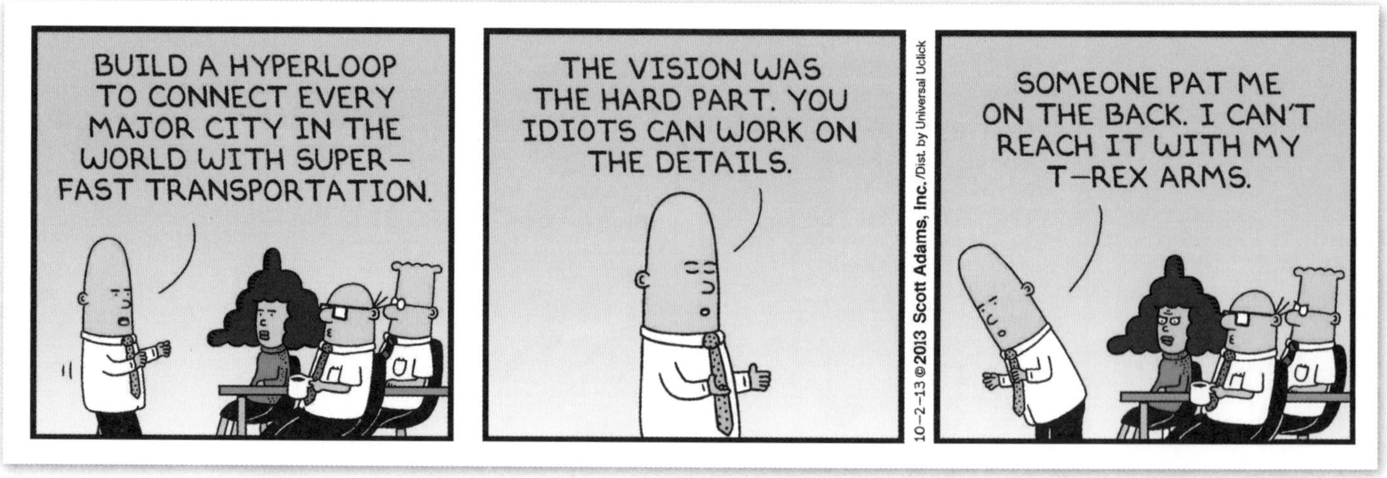
BUILD A HYPERLOOP TO CONNECT EVERY MAJOR CITY IN THE WORLD WITH SUPER-FAST TRANSPORTATION.
THE VISION WAS THE HARD PART. YOU IDIOTS CAN WORK ON THE DETAILS.
10-2-13 ©2013 Scott Adams, Inc./Dist. by Universal Uclick
SOMEONE PAT ME ON THE BACK. I CAN'T REACH IT WITH MY T-REX ARMS.

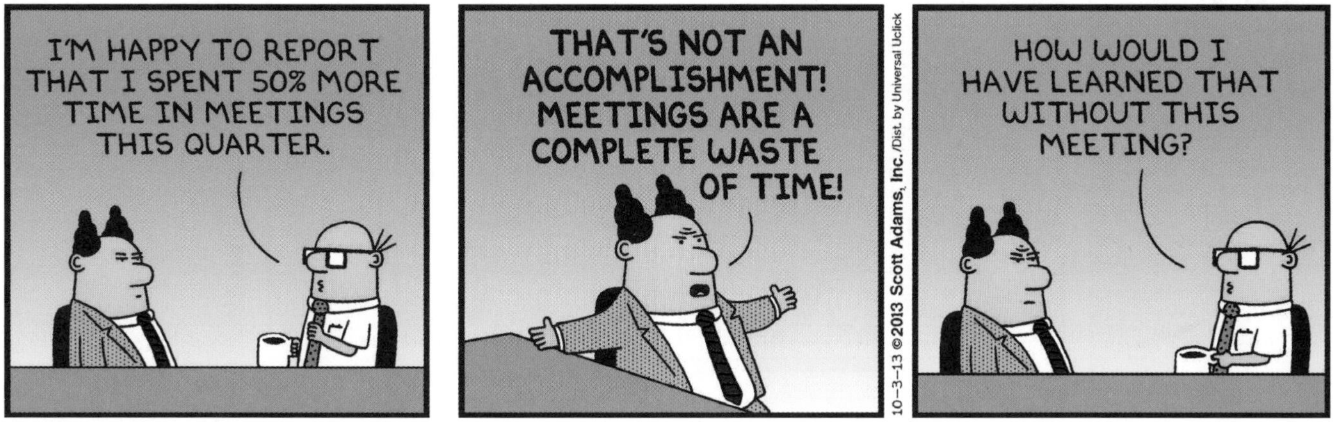
I'M HAPPY TO REPORT THAT I SPENT 50% MORE TIME IN MEETINGS THIS QUARTER.
THAT'S NOT AN ACCOMPLISHMENT! MEETINGS ARE A COMPLETE WASTE OF TIME!
HOW WOULD I HAVE LEARNED THAT WITHOUT THIS MEETING?
10-3-13 ©2013 Scott Adams, Inc./Dist. by Universal Uclick

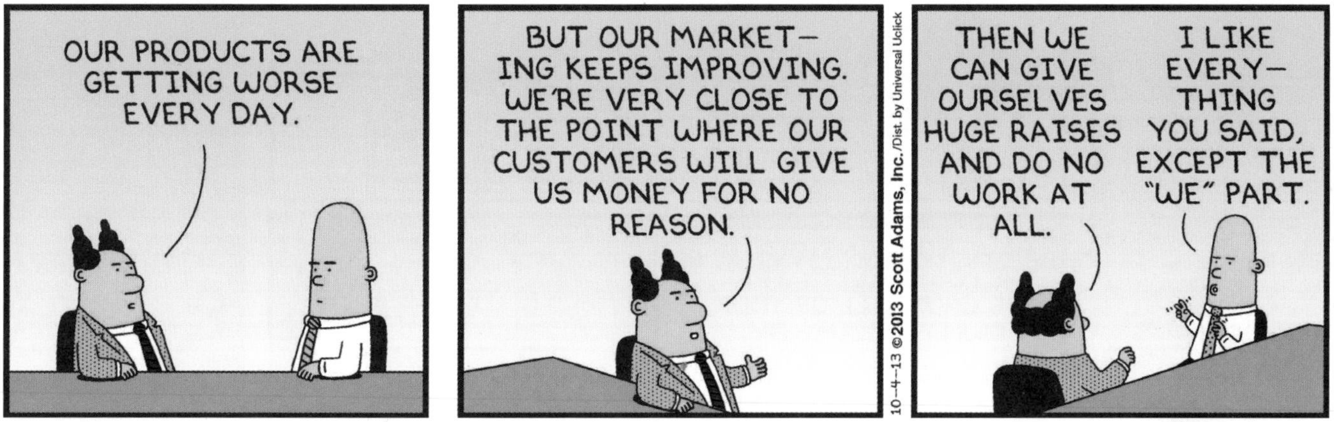
OUR PRODUCTS ARE GETTING WORSE EVERY DAY.
BUT OUR MARKET-ING KEEPS IMPROVING. WE'RE VERY CLOSE TO THE POINT WHERE OUR CUSTOMERS WILL GIVE US MONEY FOR NO REASON.
THEN WE CAN GIVE OURSELVES HUGE RAISES AND DO NO WORK AT ALL.
I LIKE EVERY-THING YOU SAID, EXCEPT THE "WE" PART.
10-4-13 ©2013 Scott Adams, Inc./Dist. by Universal Uclick

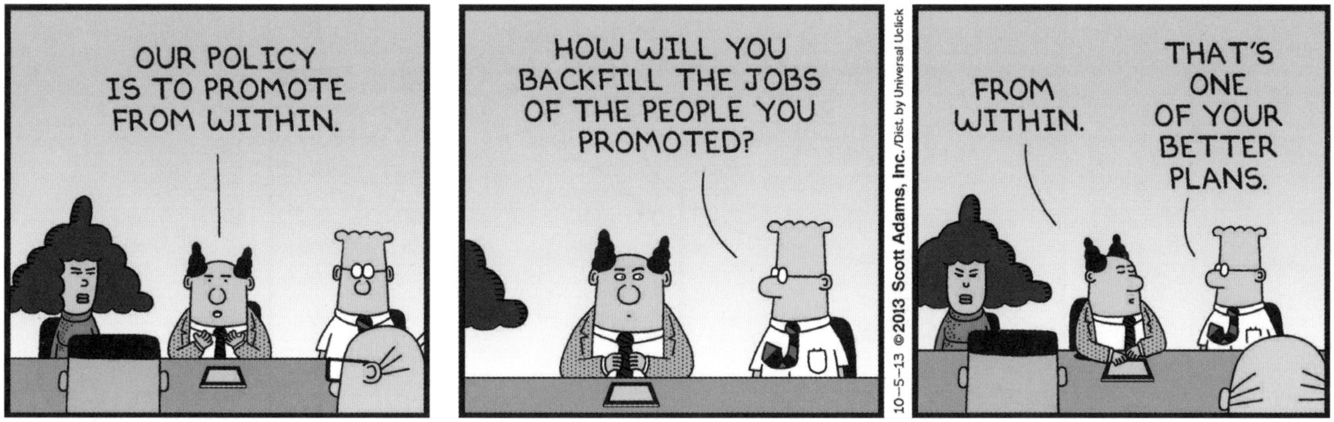
OUR POLICY IS TO PROMOTE FROM WITHIN.
HOW WILL YOU BACKFILL THE JOBS OF THE PEOPLE YOU PROMOTED?
FROM WITHIN.
THAT'S ONE OF YOUR BETTER PLANS.
10-5-13 ©2013 Scott Adams, Inc./Dist. by Universal Uclick

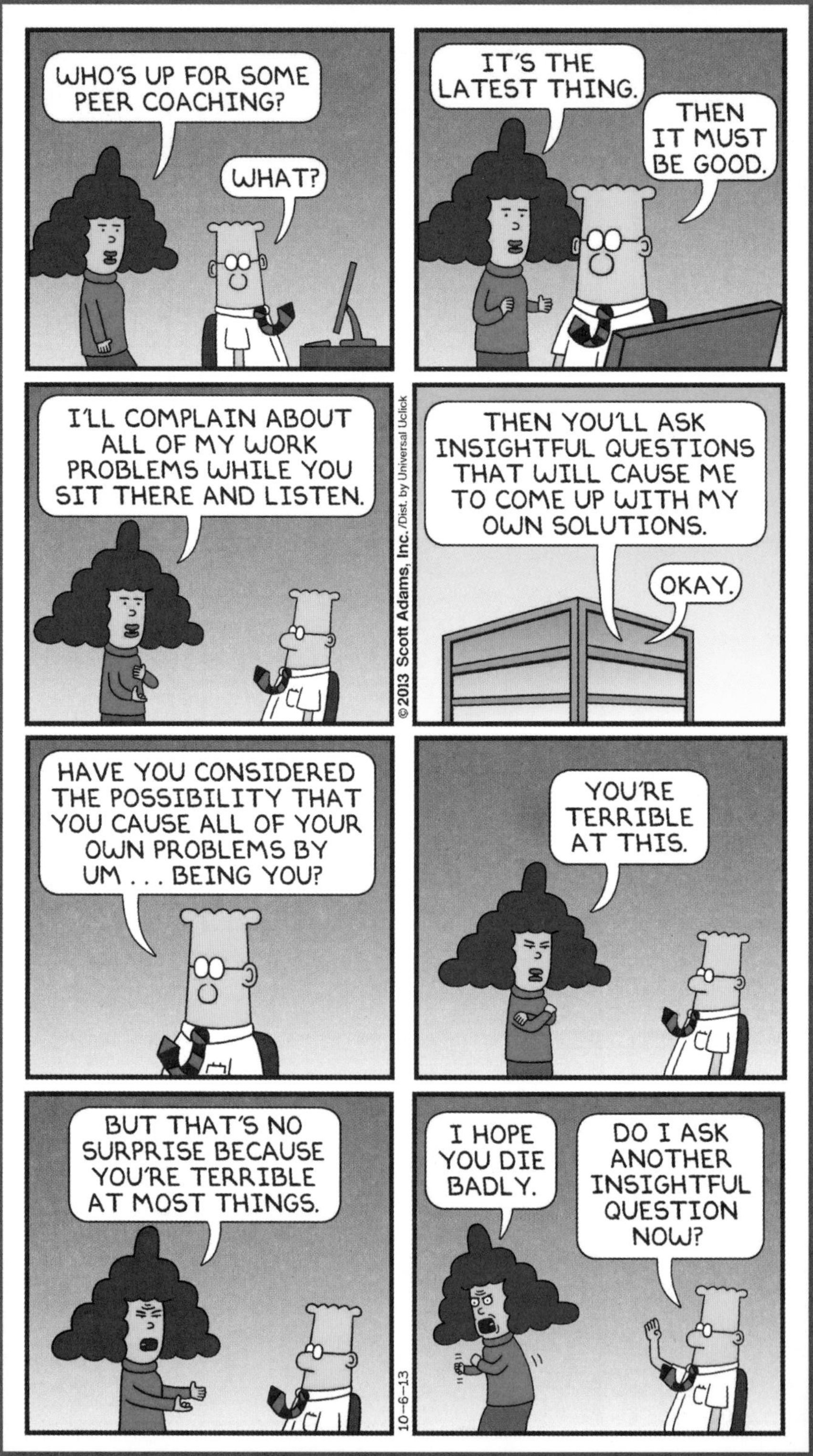
WHO'S UP FOR SOME PEER COACHING?
WHAT?
IT'S THE LATEST THING.
THEN IT MUST BE GOOD.
I'LL COMPLAIN ABOUT ALL OF MY WORK PROBLEMS WHILE YOU SIT THERE AND LISTEN.
THEN YOU'LL ASK INSIGHTFUL QUESTIONS THAT WILL CAUSE ME TO COME UP WITH MY OWN SOLUTIONS.
OKAY.
HAVE YOU CONSIDERED THE POSSIBILITY THAT YOU CAUSE ALL OF YOUR OWN PROBLEMS BY UM . . . BEING YOU?
YOU'RE TERRIBLE AT THIS.
BUT THAT'S NO SURPRISE BECAUSE YOU'RE TERRIBLE AT MOST THINGS.
I HOPE YOU DIE BADLY.
DO I ASK ANOTHER INSIGHTFUL QUESTION NOW?
© 2013 Scott Adams, Inc./Dist. by Universal Uclick
10-6-13

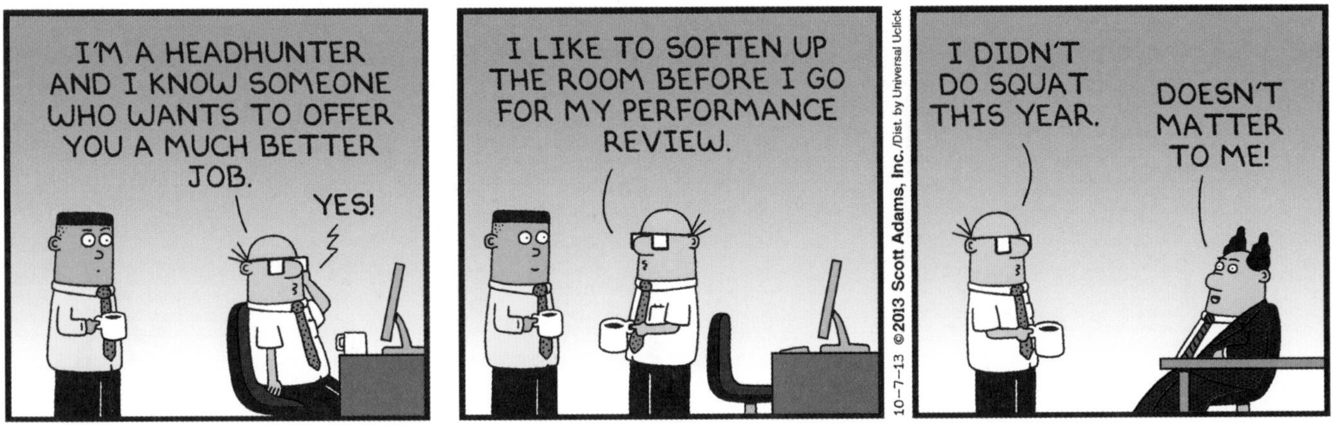
I'M A HEADHUNTER AND I KNOW SOMEONE WHO WANTS TO OFFER YOU A MUCH BETTER JOB.
YES!
I LIKE TO SOFTEN UP THE ROOM BEFORE I GO FOR MY PERFORMANCE REVIEW.
10-7-13 ©2013 Scott Adams, Inc./Dist. by Universal Uclick
I DIDN'T DO SQUAT THIS YEAR.
DOESN'T MATTER TO ME!

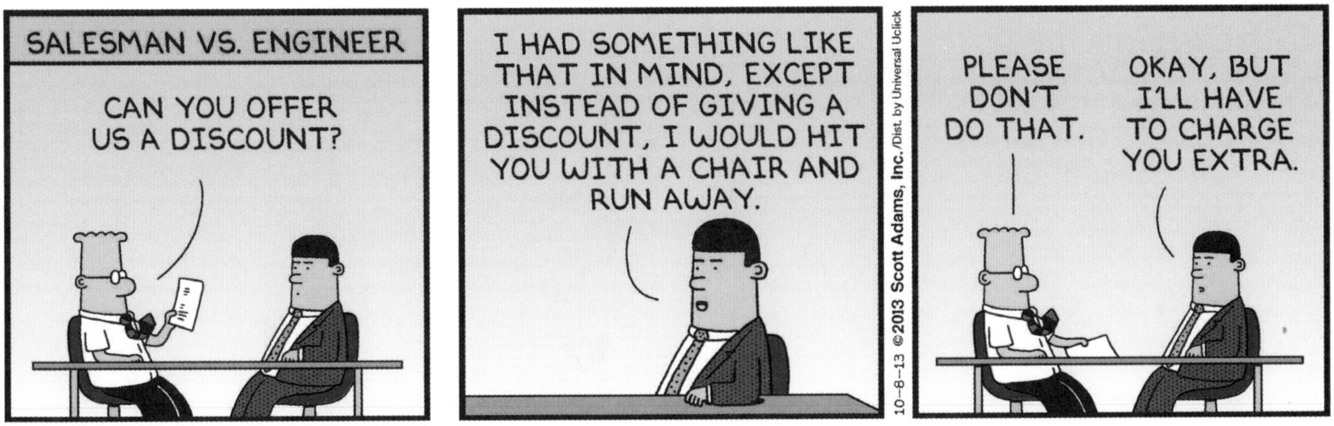
SALESMAN VS. ENGINEER
CAN YOU OFFER US A DISCOUNT?
I HAD SOMETHING LIKE THAT IN MIND, EXCEPT INSTEAD OF GIVING A DISCOUNT, I WOULD HIT YOU WITH A CHAIR AND RUN AWAY.
10-8-13 ©2013 Scott Adams, Inc./Dist. by Universal Uclick
PLEASE DON'T DO THAT.
OKAY, BUT I'LL HAVE TO CHARGE YOU EXTRA.

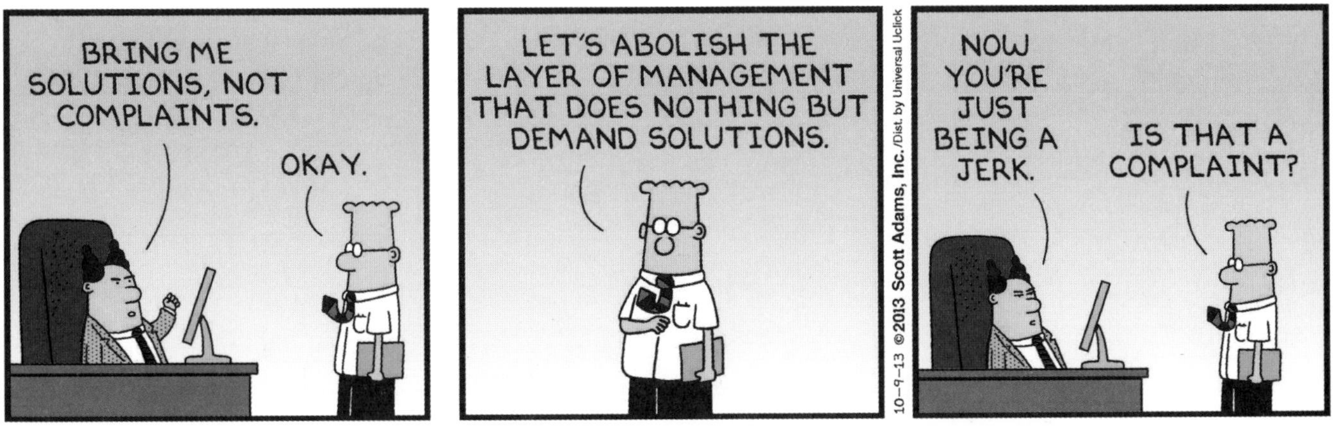
BRING ME SOLUTIONS, NOT COMPLAINTS.
OKAY.
LET'S ABOLISH THE LAYER OF MANAGEMENT THAT DOES NOTHING BUT DEMAND SOLUTIONS.
10-9-13 ©2013 Scott Adams, Inc./Dist. by Universal Uclick
NOW YOU'RE JUST BEING A JERK.
IS THAT A COMPLAINT?

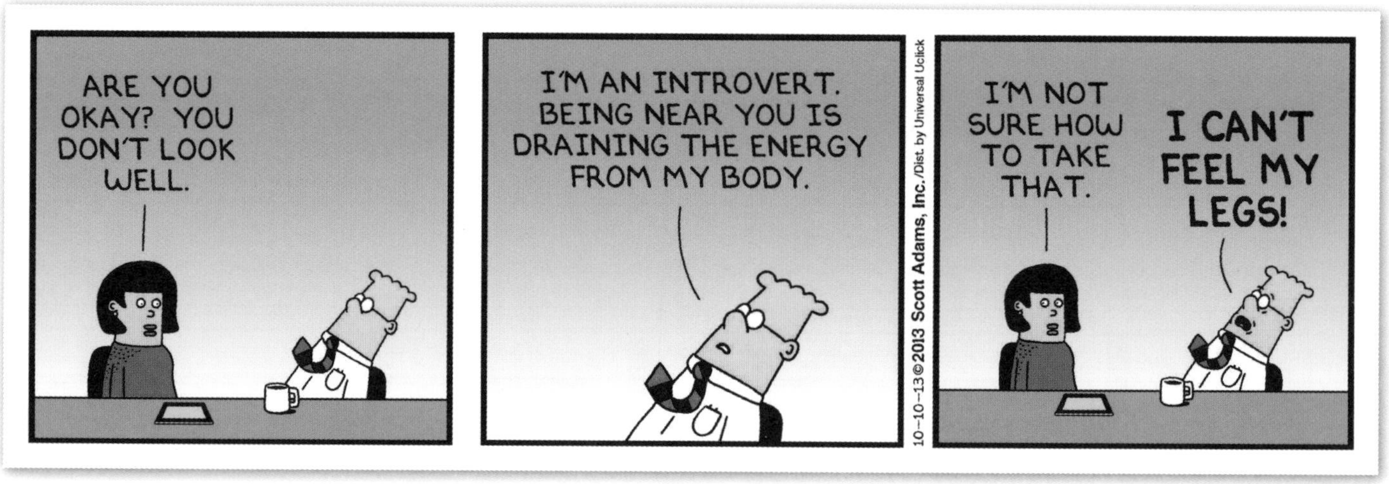
ARE YOU OKAY? YOU DON'T LOOK WELL.
I'M AN INTROVERT. BEING NEAR YOU IS DRAINING THE ENERGY FROM MY BODY.
I'M NOT SURE HOW TO TAKE THAT.
I CAN'T FEEL MY LEGS!
10-10-13 ©2013 Scott Adams, Inc./Dist. by Universal Uclick

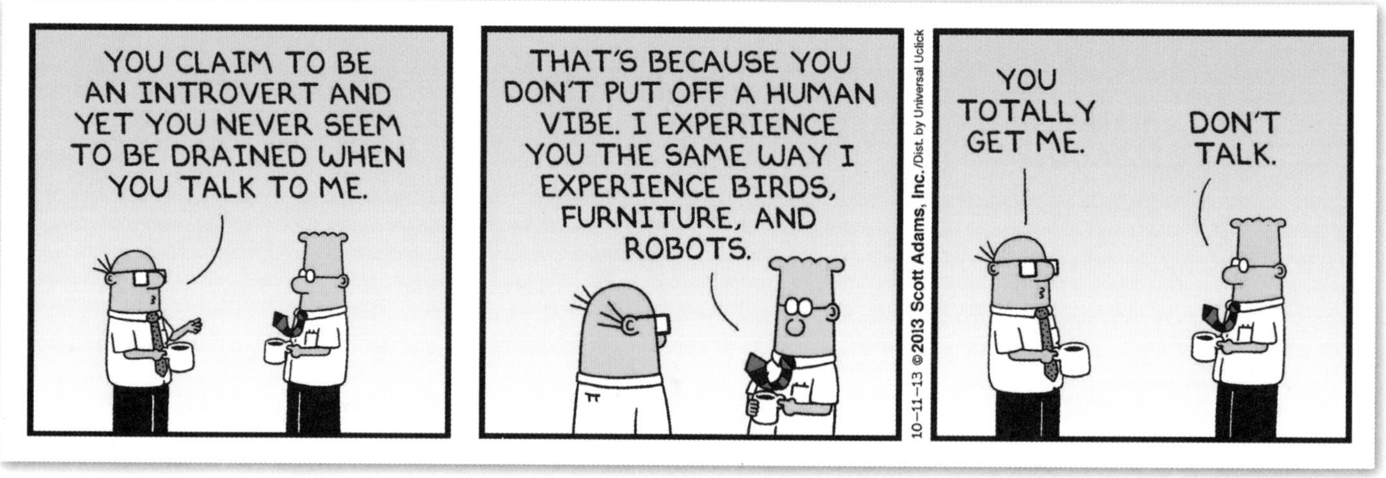
YOU CLAIM TO BE AN INTROVERT AND YET YOU NEVER SEEM TO BE DRAINED WHEN YOU TALK TO ME.
THAT'S BECAUSE YOU DON'T PUT OFF A HUMAN VIBE. I EXPERIENCE YOU THE SAME WAY I EXPERIENCE BIRDS, FURNITURE, AND ROBOTS.
YOU TOTALLY GET ME.
DON'T TALK.
10-11-13 ©2013 Scott Adams, Inc./Dist. by Universal Uclick

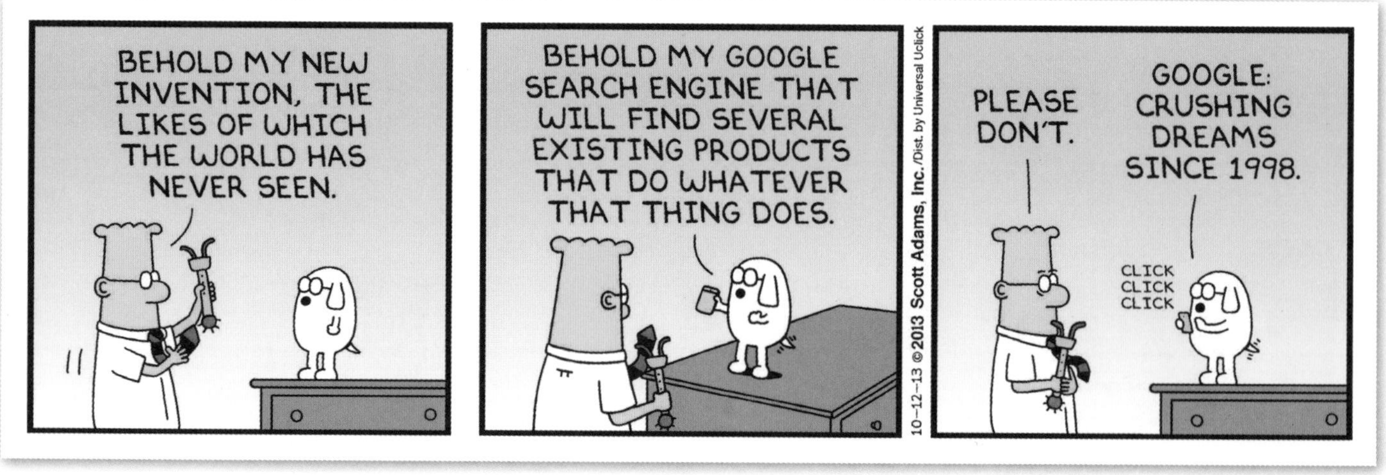
BEHOLD MY NEW INVENTION, THE LIKES OF WHICH THE WORLD HAS NEVER SEEN.
BEHOLD MY GOOGLE SEARCH ENGINE THAT WILL FIND SEVERAL EXISTING PRODUCTS THAT DO WHATEVER THAT THING DOES.
PLEASE DON'T.
GOOGLE: CRUSHING DREAMS SINCE 1998.
CLICK CLICK CLICK
10-12-13 ©2013 Scott Adams, Inc./Dist. by Universal Uclick

I READ AN ARTICLE THAT SAYS LEADERS SHOULD ACKNOWLEDGE THE ACHIEVEMENTS OF THEIR UNDERLINGS.
HAVE YOU DONE ANYTHING LATELY THAT WARRANTS SOME PRAISE?
WELL . . . I'M UNDER BUDGET BECAUSE I FORGOT TO STAFF ONE OF OUR PROJECTS.
OKAY. I CAN WORK WITH THAT.
NOW I THINK I'M SUPPOSED TO PAT YOU ON THE HEAD OR SOMETHING.
LET'S TRY THAT AND SEE HOW WE FEEL.
STOP LEANING IN.
FEELS . . . SO . . . GOOD.
©2013 Scott Adams, Inc./Dist. by Universal Uclick
10-13-13

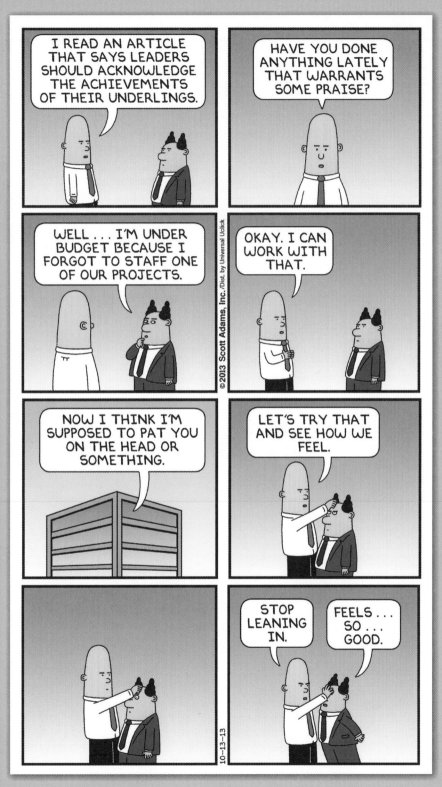

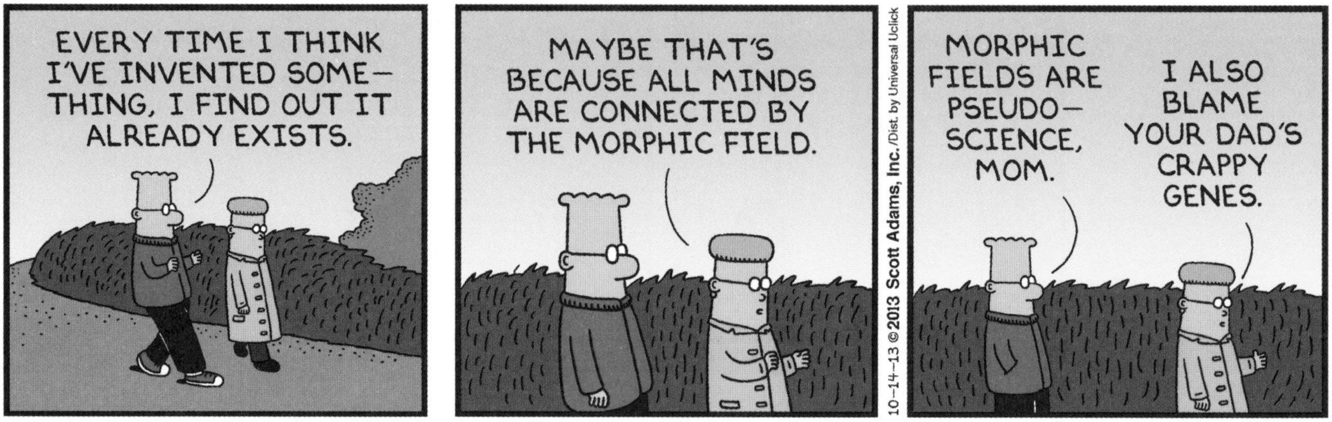
EVERY TIME I THINK I'VE INVENTED SOME-THING, I FIND OUT IT ALREADY EXISTS.
MAYBE THAT'S BECAUSE ALL MINDS ARE CONNECTED BY THE MORPHIC FIELD.
MORPHIC FIELDS ARE PSEUDO-SCIENCE, MOM.
I ALSO BLAME YOUR DAD'S CRAPPY GENES.
10-14-13 ©2013 Scott Adams, Inc./Dist. by Universal Uclick

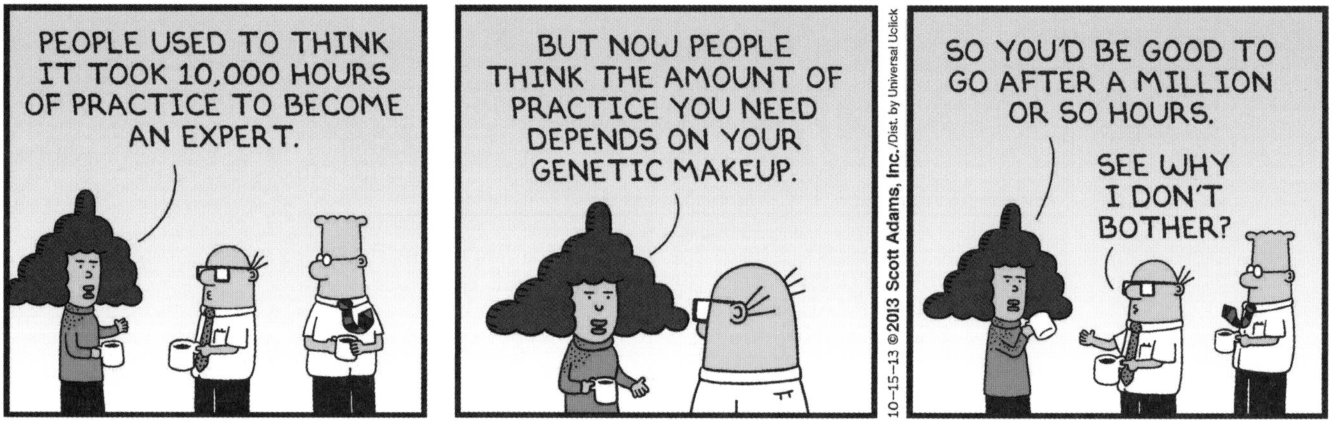
PEOPLE USED TO THINK IT TOOK 10,000 HOURS OF PRACTICE TO BECOME AN EXPERT.
BUT NOW PEOPLE THINK THE AMOUNT OF PRACTICE YOU NEED DEPENDS ON YOUR GENETIC MAKEUP.
SO YOU'D BE GOOD TO GO AFTER A MILLION OR SO HOURS.
SEE WHY I DON'T BOTHER?
10-15-13 ©2013 Scott Adams, Inc./Dist. by Universal Uclick

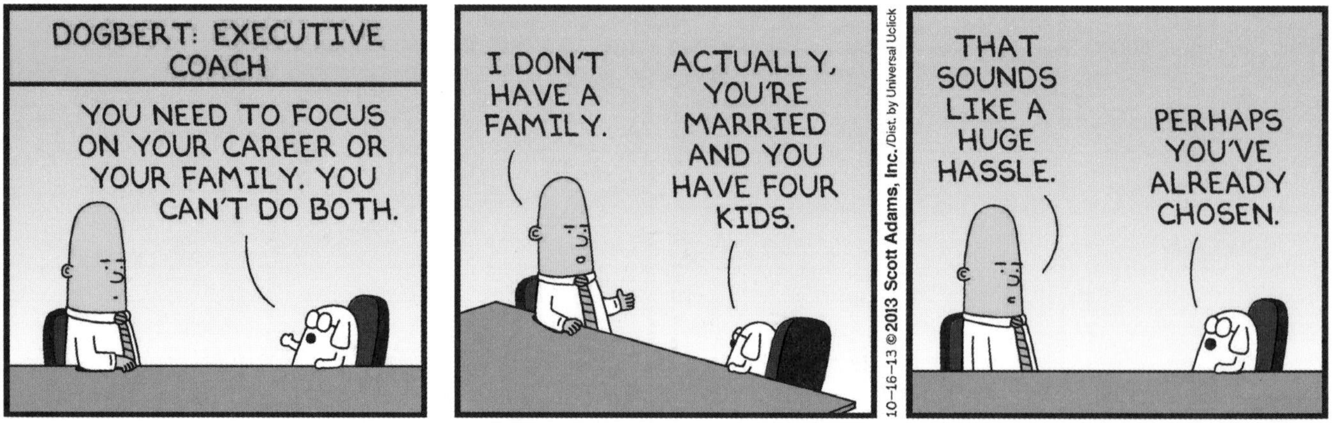
DOGBERT: EXECUTIVE COACH
YOU NEED TO FOCUS ON YOUR CAREER OR YOUR FAMILY. YOU CAN'T DO BOTH.
I DON'T HAVE A FAMILY.
ACTUALLY, YOU'RE MARRIED AND YOU HAVE FOUR KIDS.
THAT SOUNDS LIKE A HUGE HASSLE.
PERHAPS YOU'VE ALREADY CHOSEN.
10-16-13 ©2013 Scott Adams, Inc./Dist. by Universal Uclick

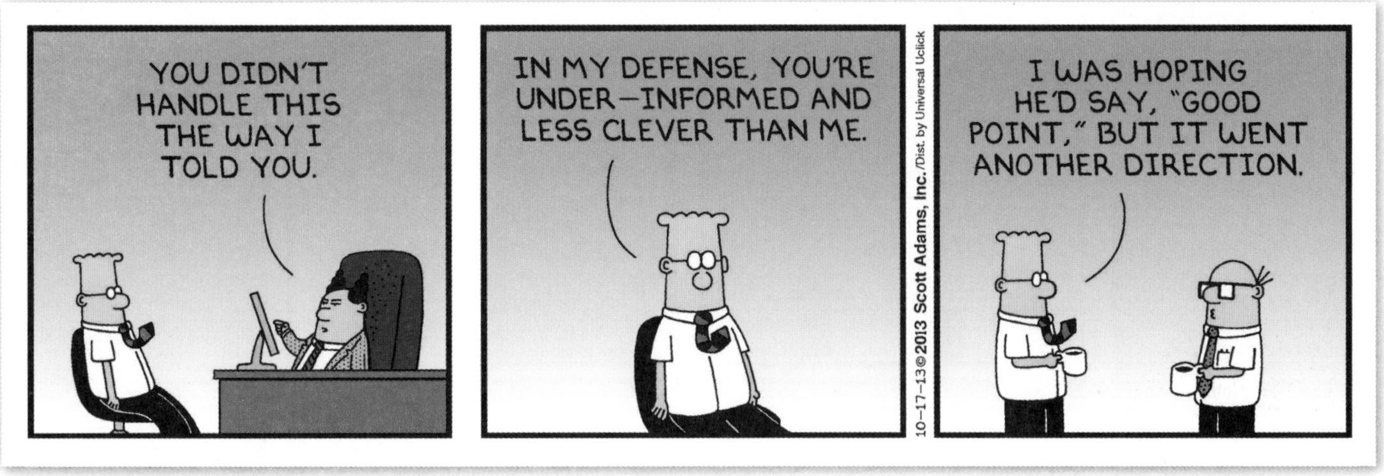
YOU DIDN'T HANDLE THIS THE WAY I TOLD YOU.
IN MY DEFENSE, YOU'RE UNDER–INFORMED AND LESS CLEVER THAN ME.
10-17-13 ©2013 Scott Adams, Inc./Dist. by Universal Uclick
I WAS HOPING HE'D SAY, "GOOD POINT," BUT IT WENT ANOTHER DIRECTION.

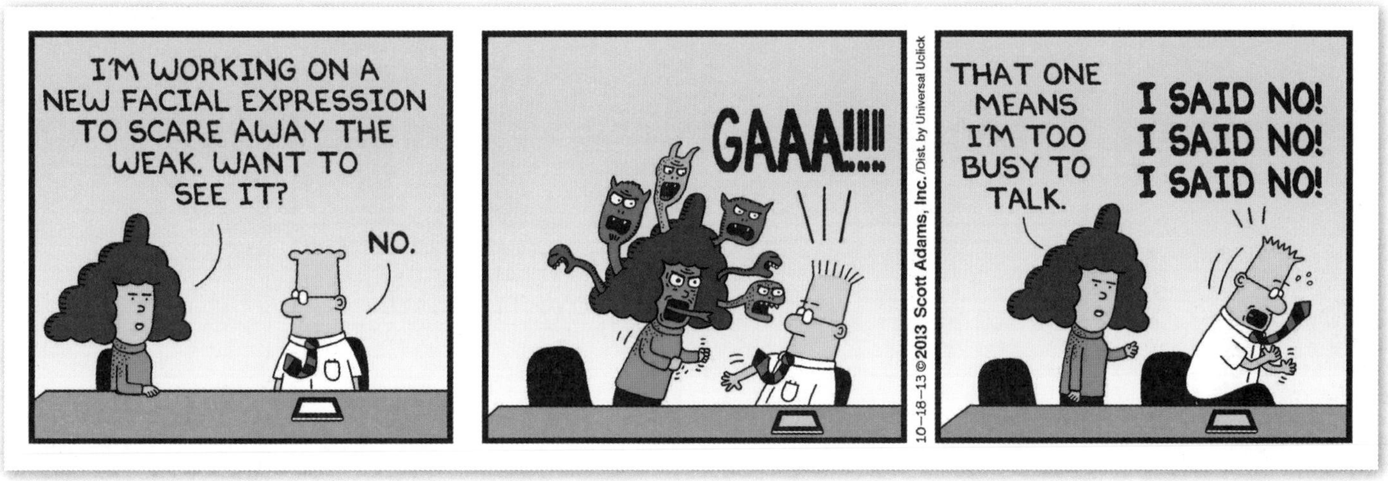
I'M WORKING ON A NEW FACIAL EXPRESSION TO SCARE AWAY THE WEAK. WANT TO SEE IT?
NO.
GAAA!!!!
10-18-13 ©2013 Scott Adams, Inc./Dist. by Universal Uclick
THAT ONE MEANS I'M TOO BUSY TO TALK.
I SAID NO! I SAID NO! I SAID NO!

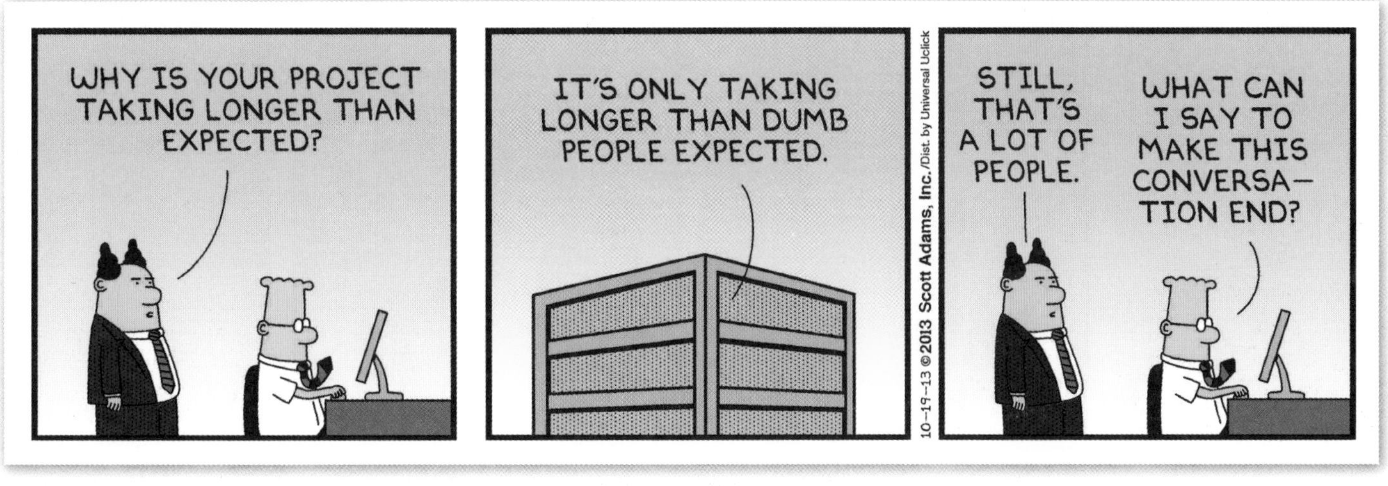
WHY IS YOUR PROJECT TAKING LONGER THAN EXPECTED?
IT'S ONLY TAKING LONGER THAN DUMB PEOPLE EXPECTED.
10-19-13 ©2013 Scott Adams, Inc./Dist. by Universal Uclick
STILL, THAT'S A LOT OF PEOPLE.
WHAT CAN I SAY TO MAKE THIS CONVERSA–TION END?

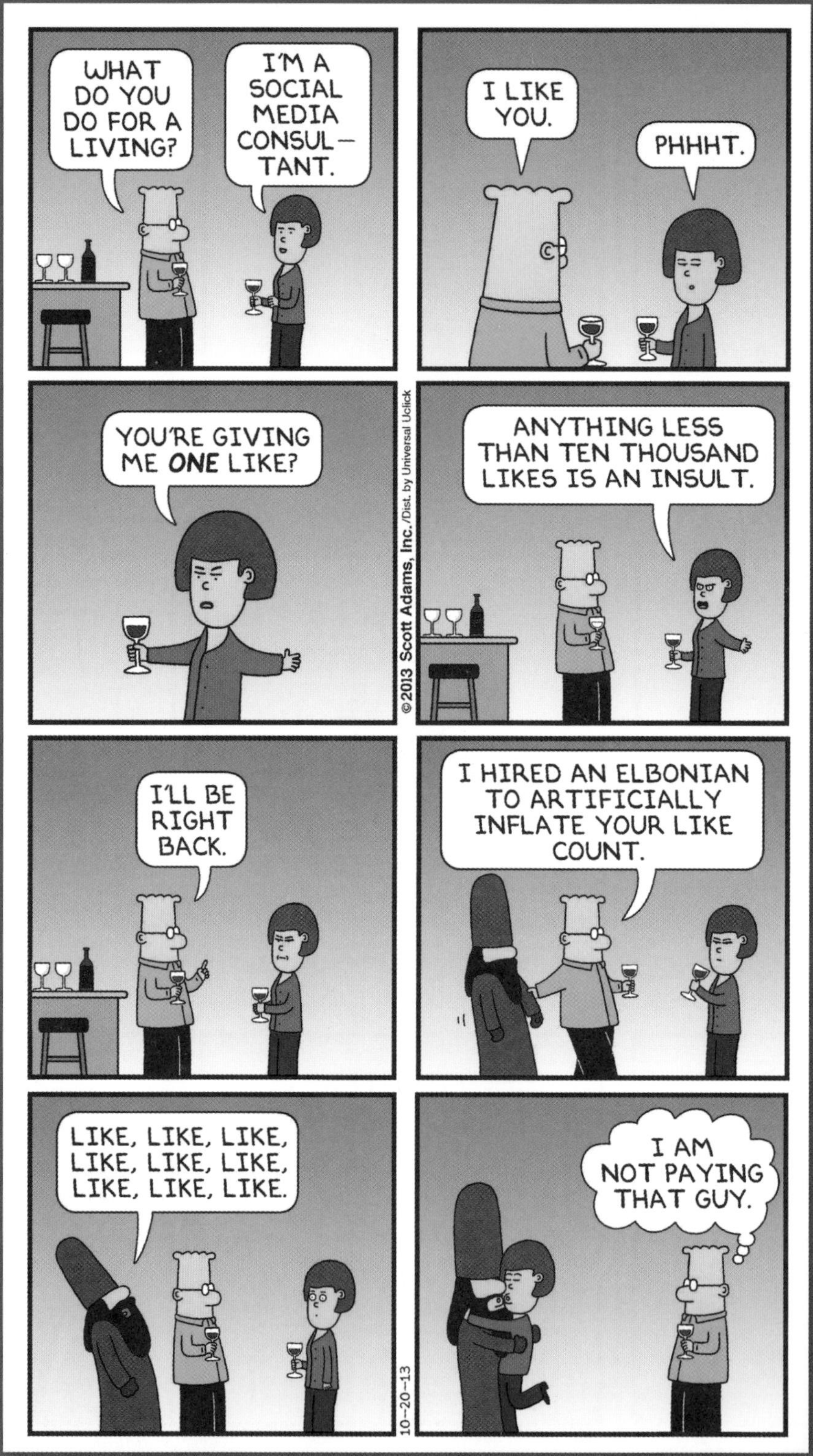
WHAT DO YOU DO FOR A LIVING?
I'M A SOCIAL MEDIA CONSUL— TANT.
I LIKE YOU.
PHHHT.
YOU'RE GIVING ME **ONE** LIKE?
©2013 Scott Adams, Inc./Dist. by Universal Uclick
ANYTHING LESS THAN TEN THOUSAND LIKES IS AN INSULT.
I'LL BE RIGHT BACK.
I HIRED AN ELBONIAN TO ARTIFICIALLY INFLATE YOUR LIKE COUNT.
LIKE, LIKE, LIKE, LIKE, LIKE, LIKE, LIKE, LIKE, LIKE.
10-20-13
I AM NOT PAYING THAT GUY.

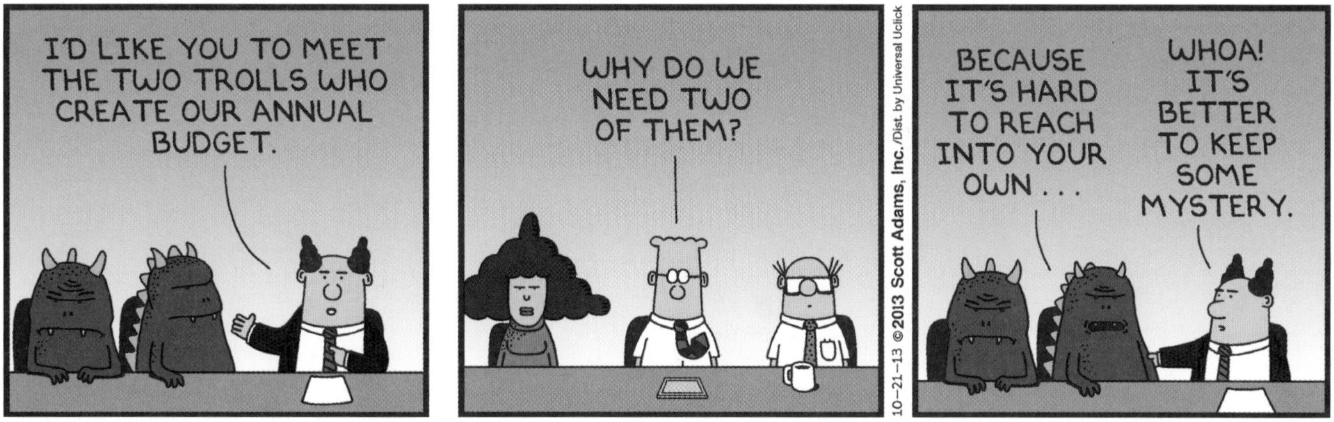
I'D LIKE YOU TO MEET THE TWO TROLLS WHO CREATE OUR ANNUAL BUDGET.
WHY DO WE NEED TWO OF THEM?
BECAUSE IT'S HARD TO REACH INTO YOUR OWN . . .
WHOA! IT'S BETTER TO KEEP SOME MYSTERY.
10–21–13 ©2013 Scott Adams, Inc./Dist. by Universal Uclick

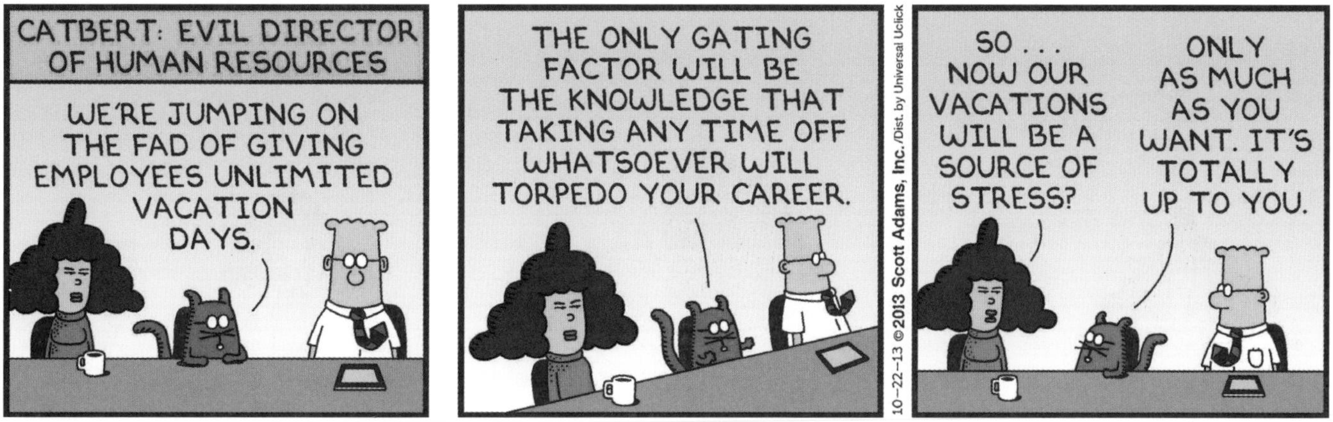
CATBERT: EVIL DIRECTOR OF HUMAN RESOURCES
WE'RE JUMPING ON THE FAD OF GIVING EMPLOYEES UNLIMITED VACATION DAYS.
THE ONLY GATING FACTOR WILL BE THE KNOWLEDGE THAT TAKING ANY TIME OFF WHATSOEVER WILL TORPEDO YOUR CAREER.
SO . . . NOW OUR VACATIONS WILL BE A SOURCE OF STRESS?
ONLY AS MUCH AS YOU WANT. IT'S TOTALLY UP TO YOU.
10–22–13 ©2013 Scott Adams, Inc./Dist. by Universal Uclick

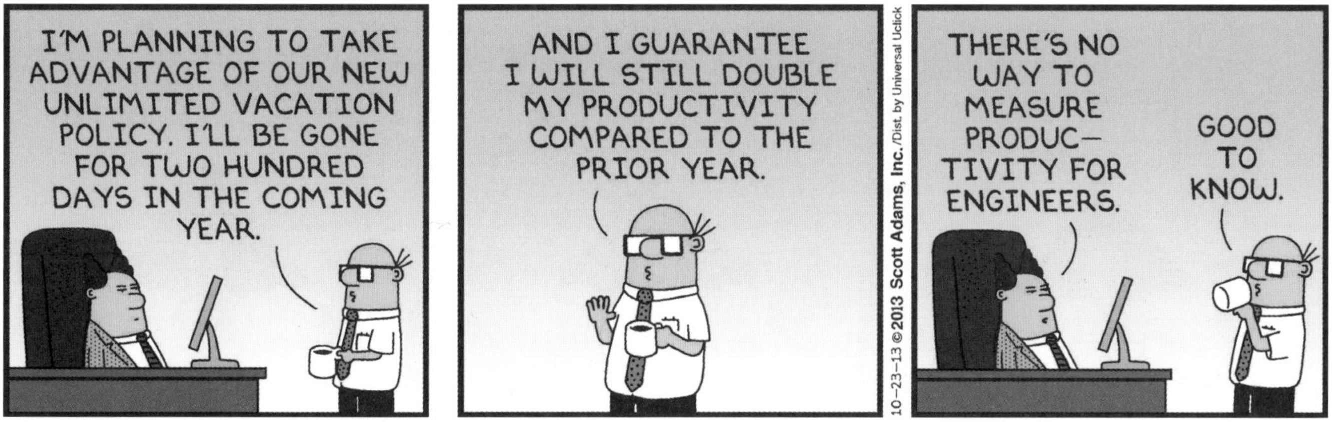
I'M PLANNING TO TAKE ADVANTAGE OF OUR NEW UNLIMITED VACATION POLICY. I'LL BE GONE FOR TWO HUNDRED DAYS IN THE COMING YEAR.
AND I GUARANTEE I WILL STILL DOUBLE MY PRODUCTIVITY COMPARED TO THE PRIOR YEAR.
THERE'S NO WAY TO MEASURE PRODUC-TIVITY FOR ENGINEERS.
GOOD TO KNOW.
10–23–13 ©2013 Scott Adams, Inc./Dist. by Universal Uclick

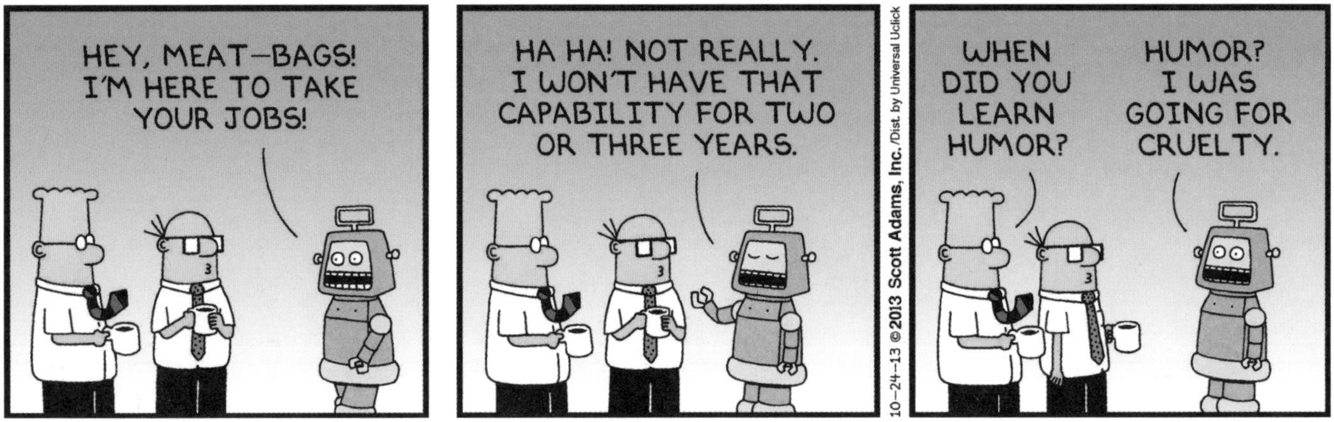
HEY, MEAT-BAGS! I'M HERE TO TAKE YOUR JOBS!
HA HA! NOT REALLY. I WON'T HAVE THAT CAPABILITY FOR TWO OR THREE YEARS.
10-24-13 ©2013 Scott Adams, Inc./Dist. by Universal Uclick
WHEN DID YOU LEARN HUMOR?
HUMOR? I WAS GOING FOR CRUELTY.

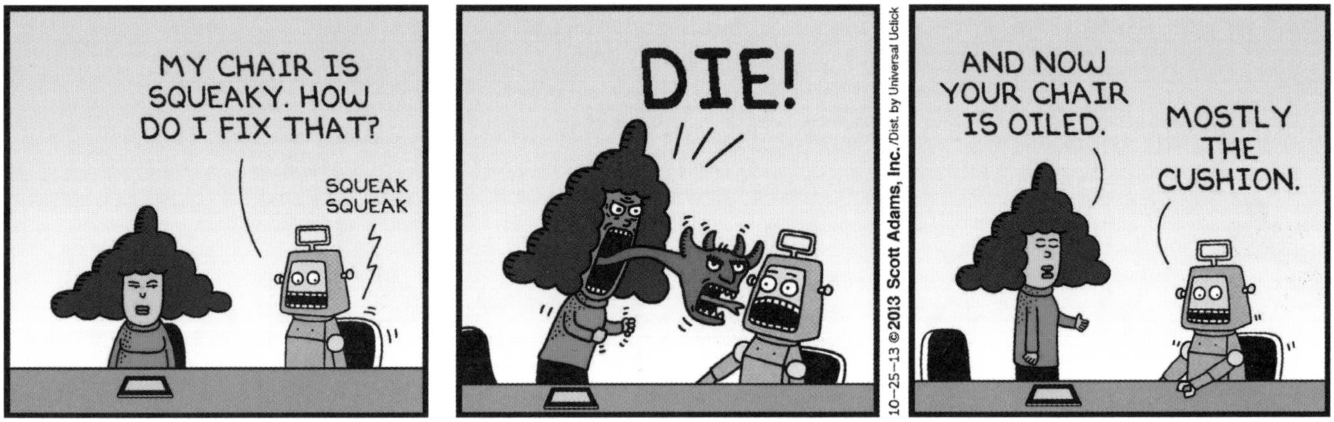
MY CHAIR IS SQUEAKY. HOW DO I FIX THAT?
SQUEAK SQUEAK
DIE!
10-25-13 ©2013 Scott Adams, Inc./Dist. by Universal Uclick
AND NOW YOUR CHAIR IS OILED.
MOSTLY THE CUSHION.

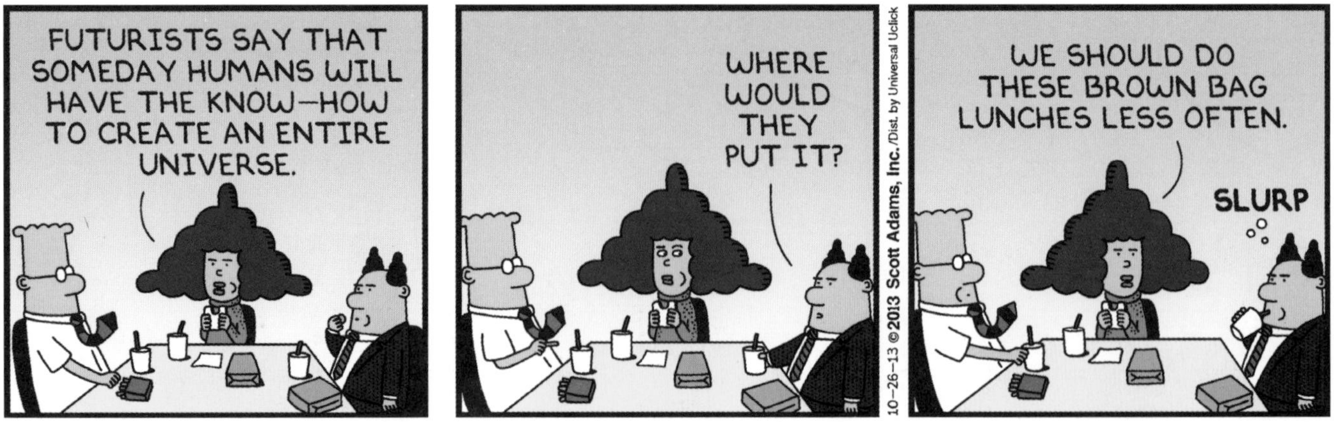
FUTURISTS SAY THAT SOMEDAY HUMANS WILL HAVE THE KNOW-HOW TO CREATE AN ENTIRE UNIVERSE.
WHERE WOULD THEY PUT IT?
10-26-13 ©2013 Scott Adams, Inc./Dist. by Universal Uclick
WE SHOULD DO THESE BROWN BAG LUNCHES LESS OFTEN.
SLURP

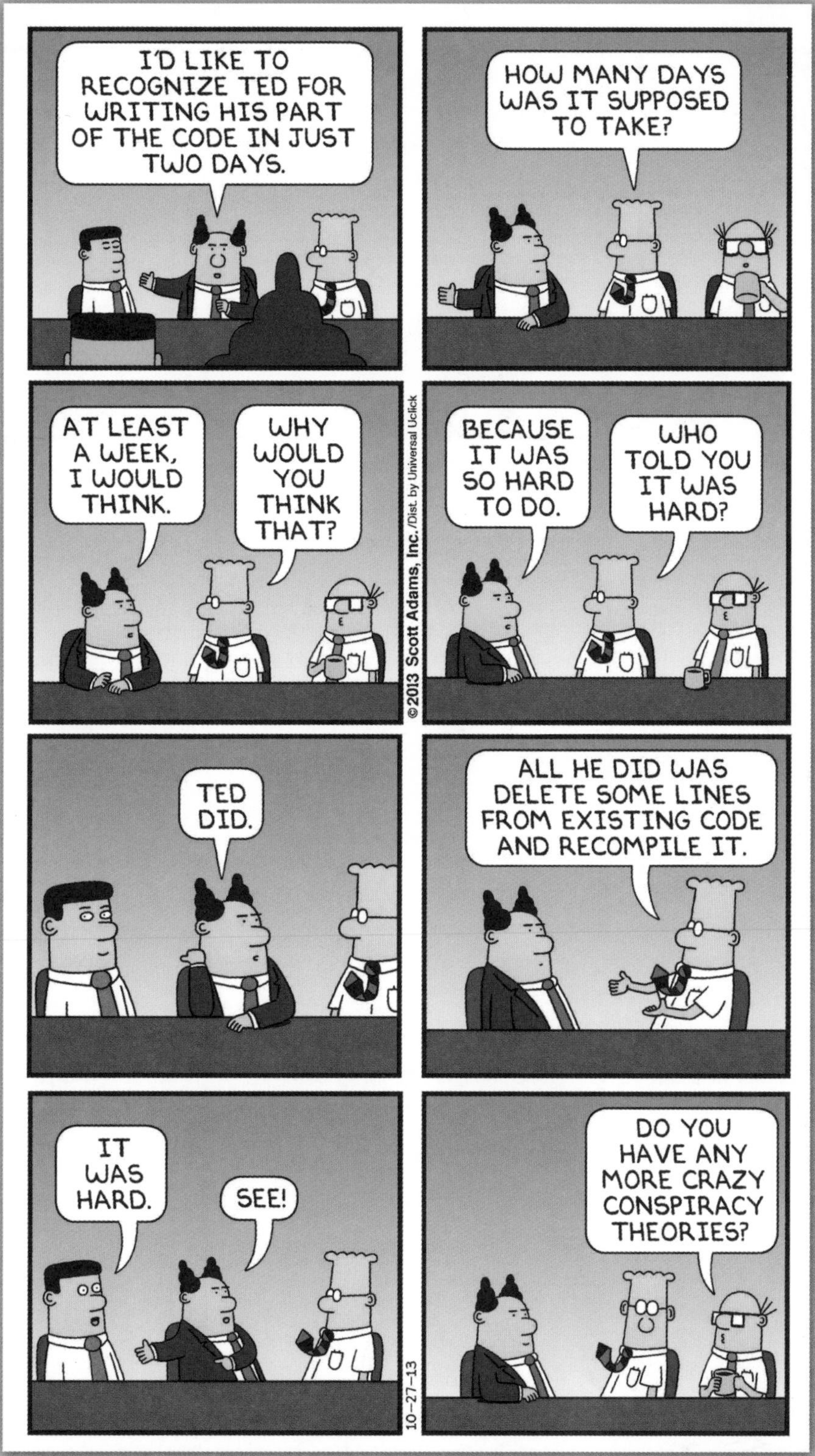
I'D LIKE TO RECOGNIZE TED FOR WRITING HIS PART OF THE CODE IN JUST TWO DAYS.
HOW MANY DAYS WAS IT SUPPOSED TO TAKE?
AT LEAST A WEEK, I WOULD THINK.
WHY WOULD YOU THINK THAT?
BECAUSE IT WAS SO HARD TO DO.
WHO TOLD YOU IT WAS HARD?
TED DID.
ALL HE DID WAS DELETE SOME LINES FROM EXISTING CODE AND RECOMPILE IT.
IT WAS HARD.
SEE!
DO YOU HAVE ANY MORE CRAZY CONSPIRACY THEORIES?
©2013 Scott Adams, Inc./Dist. by Universal Uclick
10-27-13

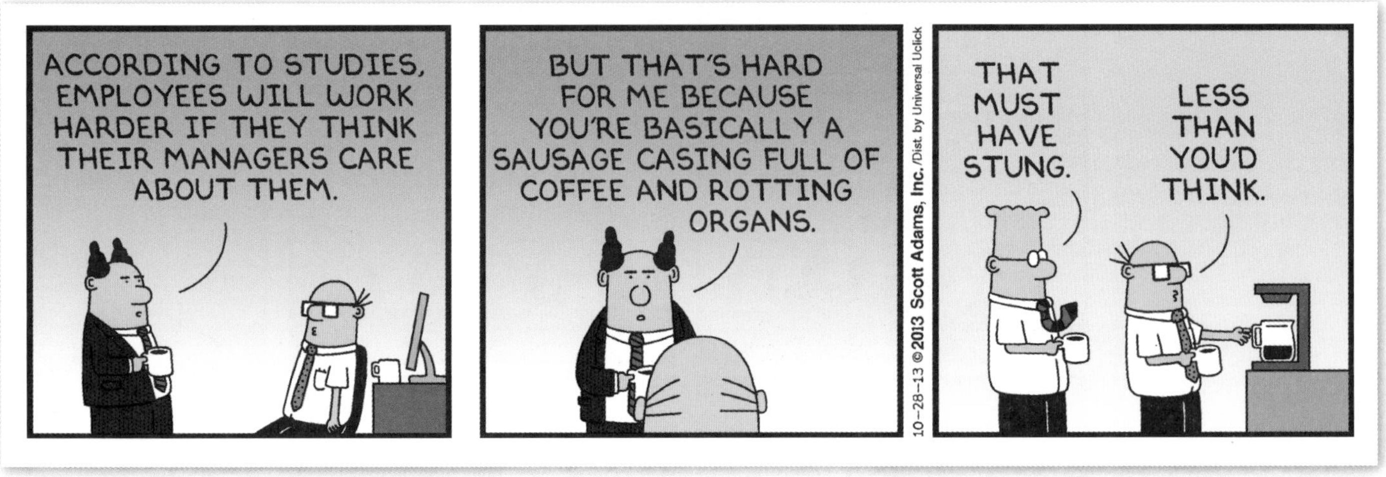
ACCORDING TO STUDIES, EMPLOYEES WILL WORK HARDER IF THEY THINK THEIR MANAGERS CARE ABOUT THEM.
BUT THAT'S HARD FOR ME BECAUSE YOU'RE BASICALLY A SAUSAGE CASING FULL OF COFFEE AND ROTTING ORGANS.
10-28-13 ©2013 Scott Adams, Inc./Dist. by Universal Uclick
THAT MUST HAVE STUNG.
LESS THAN YOU'D THINK.

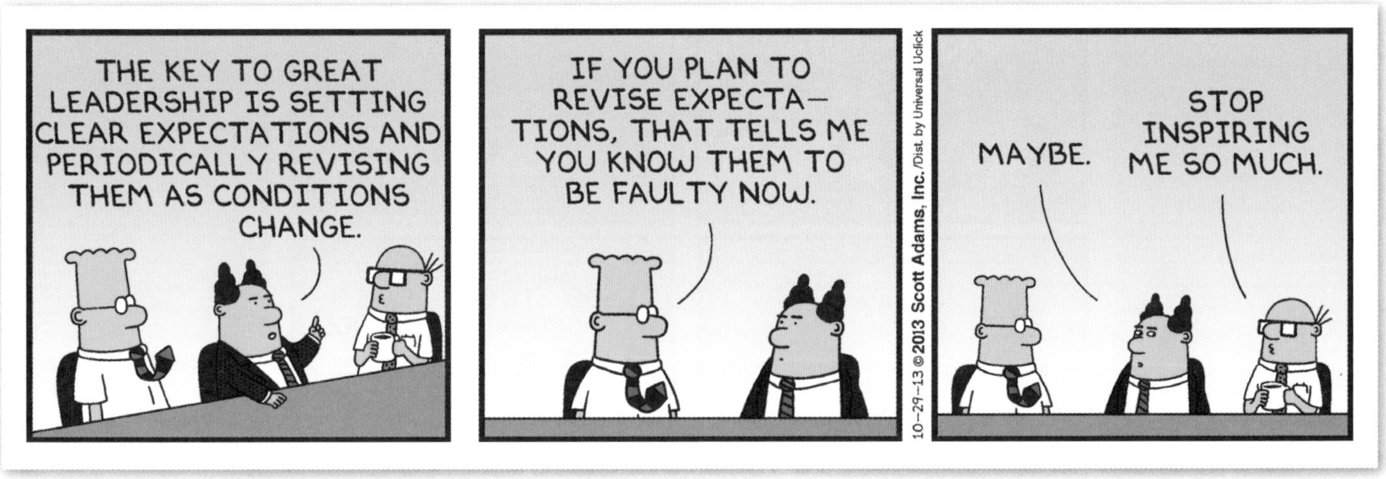
THE KEY TO GREAT LEADERSHIP IS SETTING CLEAR EXPECTATIONS AND PERIODICALLY REVISING THEM AS CONDITIONS CHANGE.
IF YOU PLAN TO REVISE EXPECTA– TIONS, THAT TELLS ME YOU KNOW THEM TO BE FAULTY NOW.
10-29-13 ©2013 Scott Adams, Inc./Dist. by Universal Uclick
MAYBE.
STOP INSPIRING ME SO MUCH.

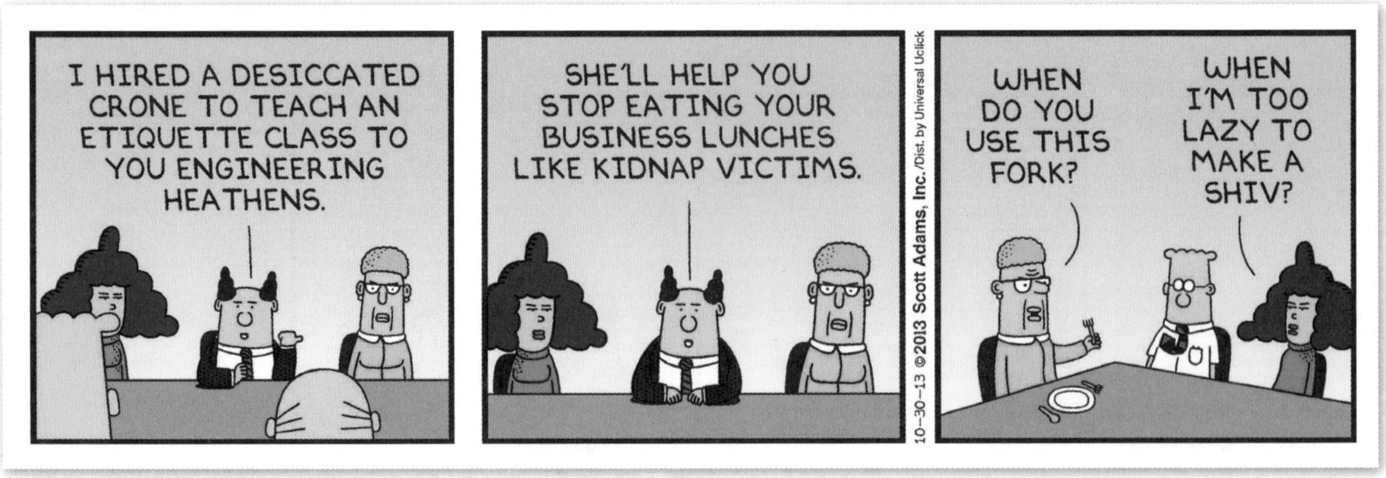
I HIRED A DESICCATED CRONE TO TEACH AN ETIQUETTE CLASS TO YOU ENGINEERING HEATHENS.
SHE'LL HELP YOU STOP EATING YOUR BUSINESS LUNCHES LIKE KIDNAP VICTIMS.
10-30-13 ©2013 Scott Adams, Inc./Dist. by Universal Uclick
WHEN DO YOU USE THIS FORK?
WHEN I'M TOO LAZY TO MAKE A SHIV?

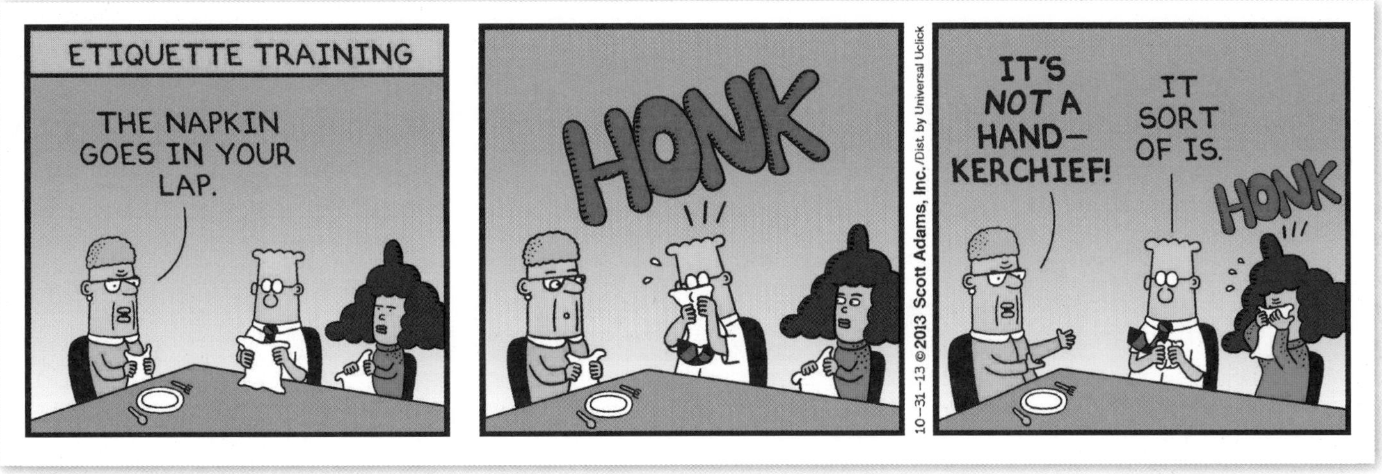
ETIQUETTE TRAINING
THE NAPKIN GOES IN YOUR LAP.
HONK
10-31-13 ©2013 Scott Adams, Inc./Dist. by Universal Uclick
IT'S *NOT* A HAND-KERCHIEF!
IT SORT OF IS.
HONK

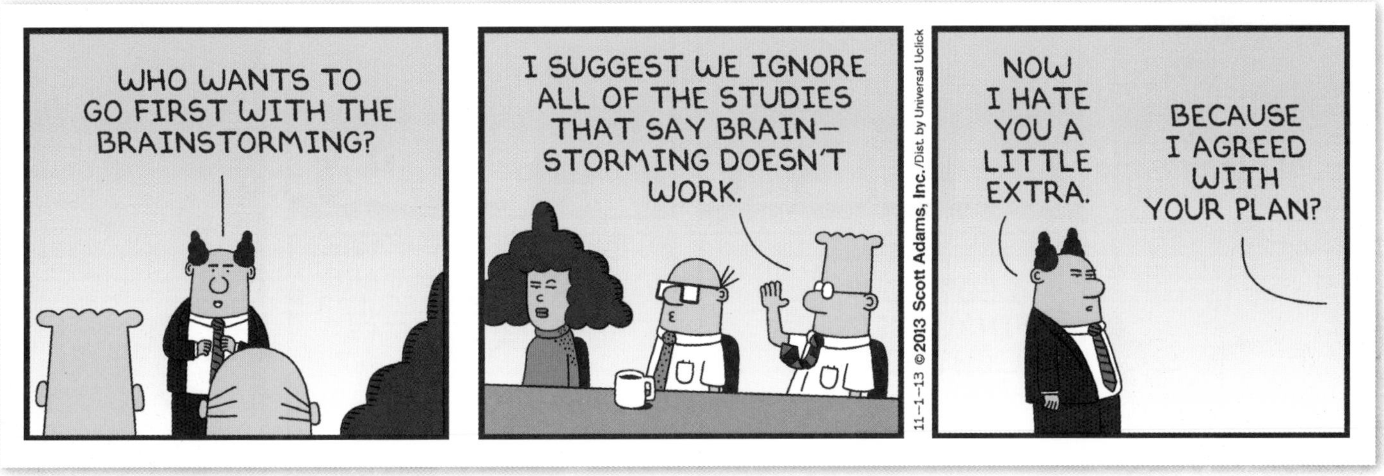
WHO WANTS TO GO FIRST WITH THE BRAINSTORMING?
I SUGGEST WE IGNORE ALL OF THE STUDIES THAT SAY BRAIN-STORMING DOESN'T WORK.
11-1-13 ©2013 Scott Adams, Inc./Dist. by Universal Uclick
NOW I HATE YOU A LITTLE EXTRA.
BECAUSE I AGREED WITH YOUR PLAN?

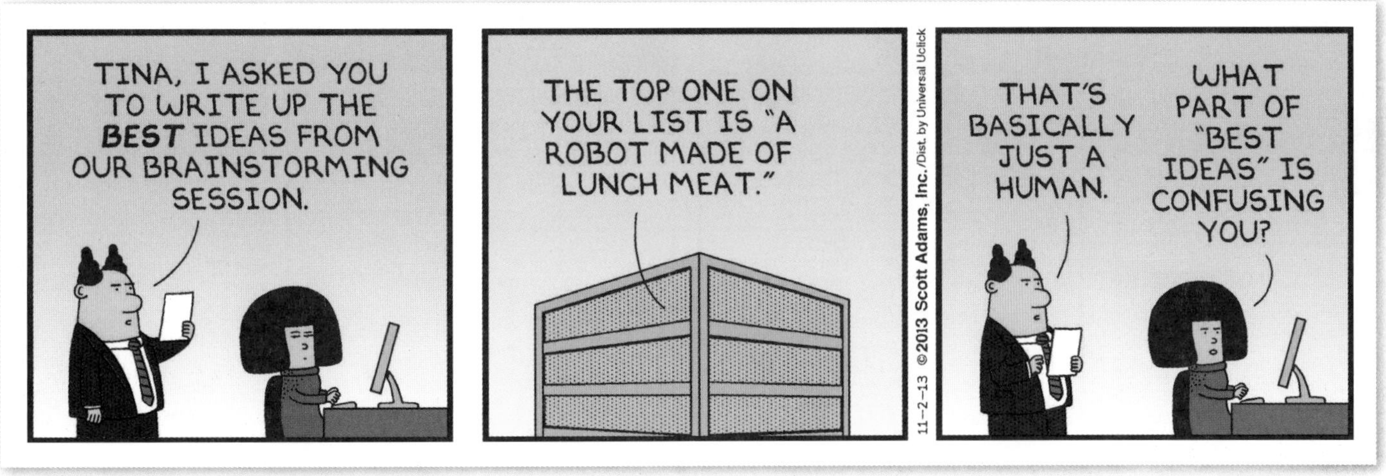
TINA, I ASKED YOU TO WRITE UP THE **BEST** IDEAS FROM OUR BRAINSTORMING SESSION.
THE TOP ONE ON YOUR LIST IS "A ROBOT MADE OF LUNCH MEAT."
11-2-13 ©2013 Scott Adams, Inc./Dist. by Universal Uclick
THAT'S BASICALLY JUST A HUMAN.
WHAT PART OF "BEST IDEAS" IS CONFUSING YOU?

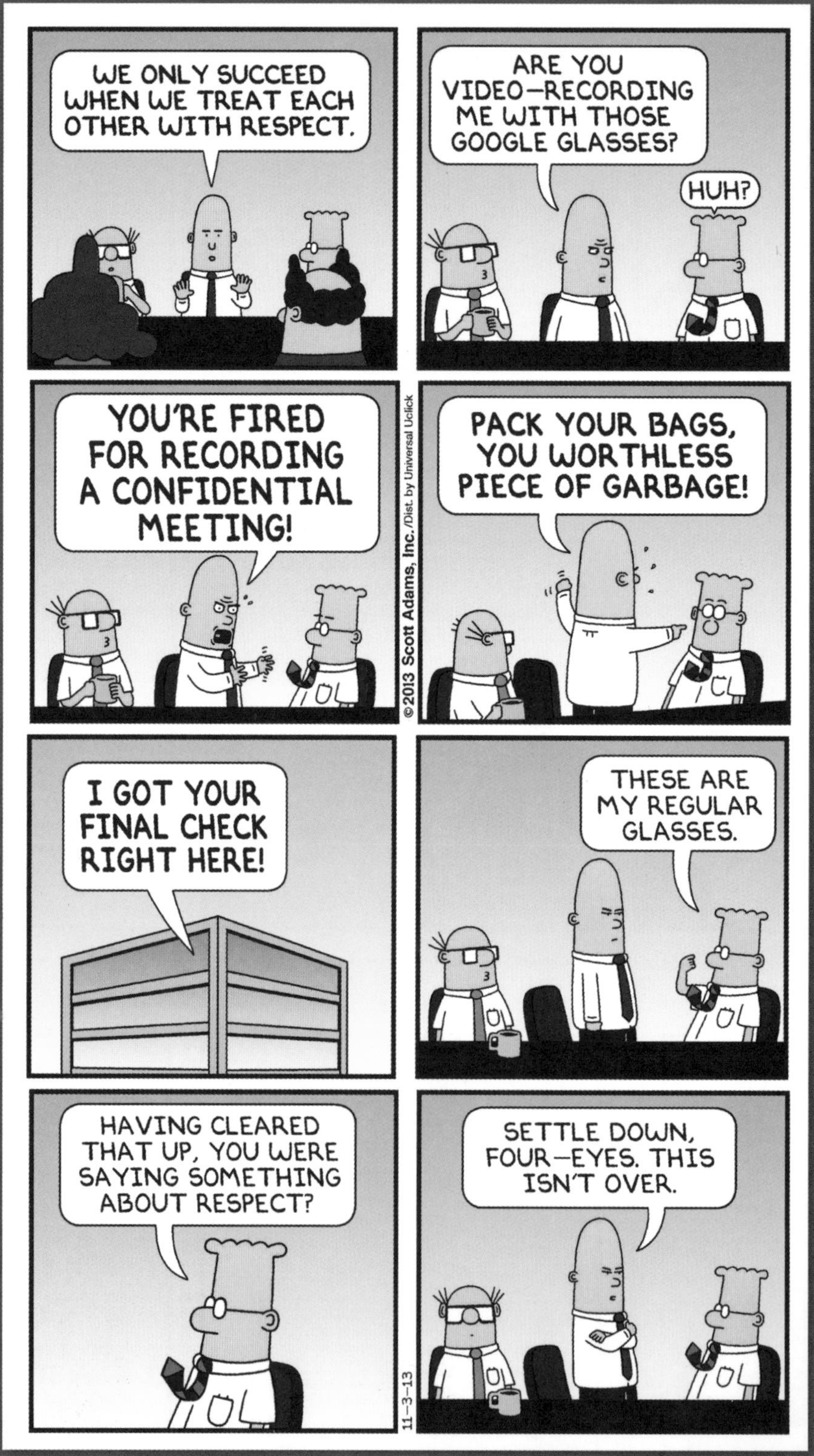
WE ONLY SUCCEED WHEN WE TREAT EACH OTHER WITH RESPECT.
ARE YOU VIDEO—RECORDING ME WITH THOSE GOOGLE GLASSES?
HUH?
YOU'RE FIRED FOR RECORDING A CONFIDENTIAL MEETING!
PACK YOUR BAGS, YOU WORTHLESS PIECE OF GARBAGE!
I GOT YOUR FINAL CHECK RIGHT HERE!
THESE ARE MY REGULAR GLASSES.
HAVING CLEARED THAT UP, YOU WERE SAYING SOMETHING ABOUT RESPECT?
SETTLE DOWN, FOUR—EYES. THIS ISN'T OVER.
©2013 Scott Adams, Inc./Dist. by Universal Uclick
11-3-13

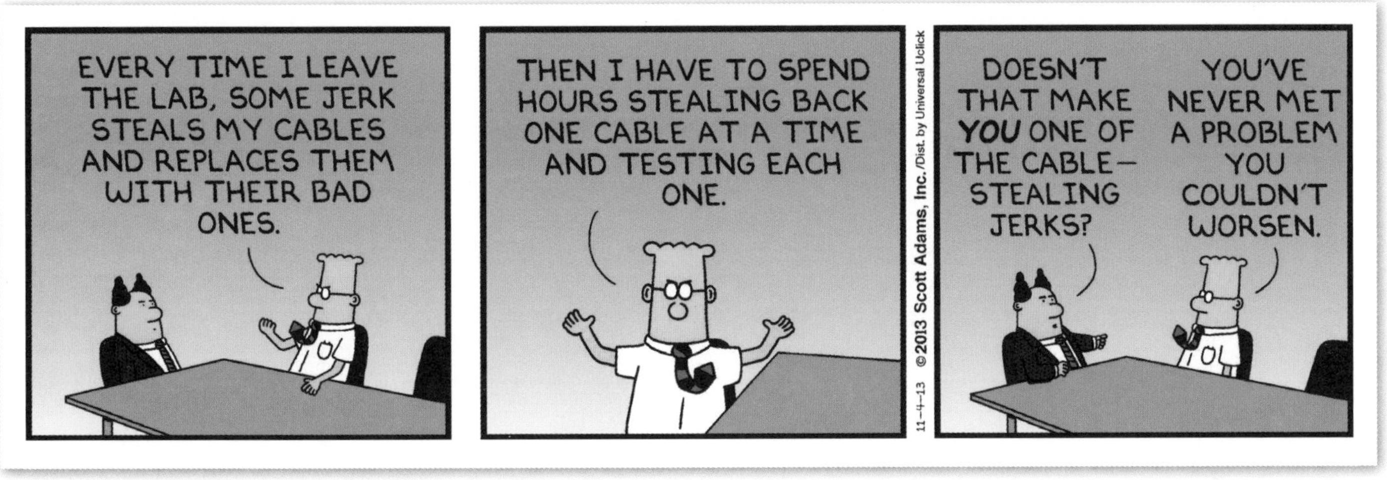
EVERY TIME I LEAVE THE LAB, SOME JERK STEALS MY CABLES AND REPLACES THEM WITH THEIR BAD ONES.
THEN I HAVE TO SPEND HOURS STEALING BACK ONE CABLE AT A TIME AND TESTING EACH ONE.
DOESN'T THAT MAKE *YOU* ONE OF THE CABLE-STEALING JERKS?
YOU'VE NEVER MET A PROBLEM YOU COULDN'T WORSEN.
11-4-13 ©2013 Scott Adams, Inc./Dist. by Universal Uclick

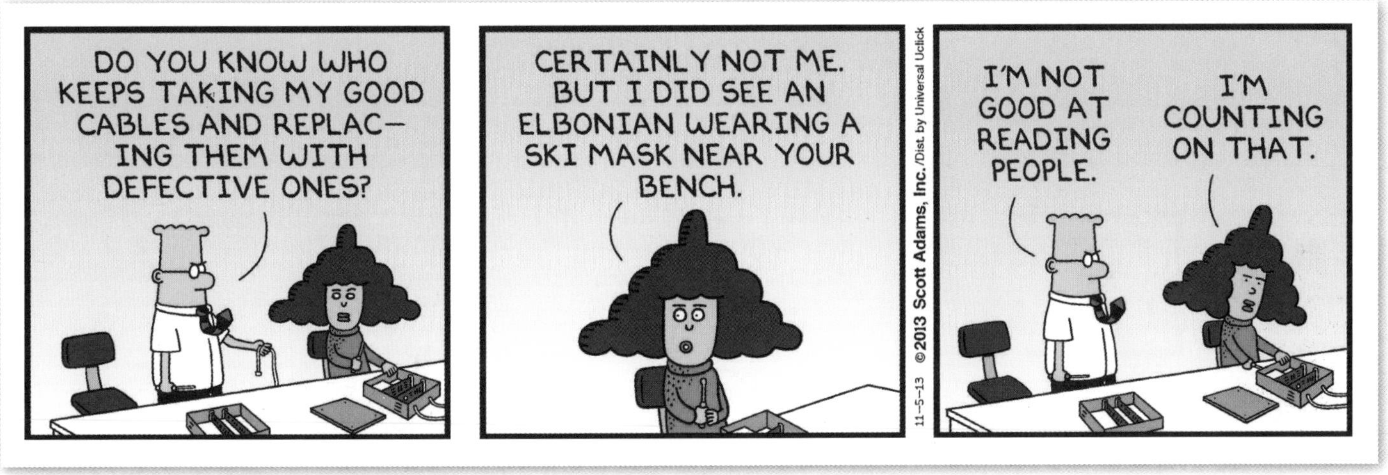
DO YOU KNOW WHO KEEPS TAKING MY GOOD CABLES AND REPLACING THEM WITH DEFECTIVE ONES?
CERTAINLY NOT ME. BUT I DID SEE AN ELBONIAN WEARING A SKI MASK NEAR YOUR BENCH.
I'M NOT GOOD AT READING PEOPLE.
I'M COUNTING ON THAT.
11-5-13 ©2013 Scott Adams, Inc./Dist. by Universal Uclick

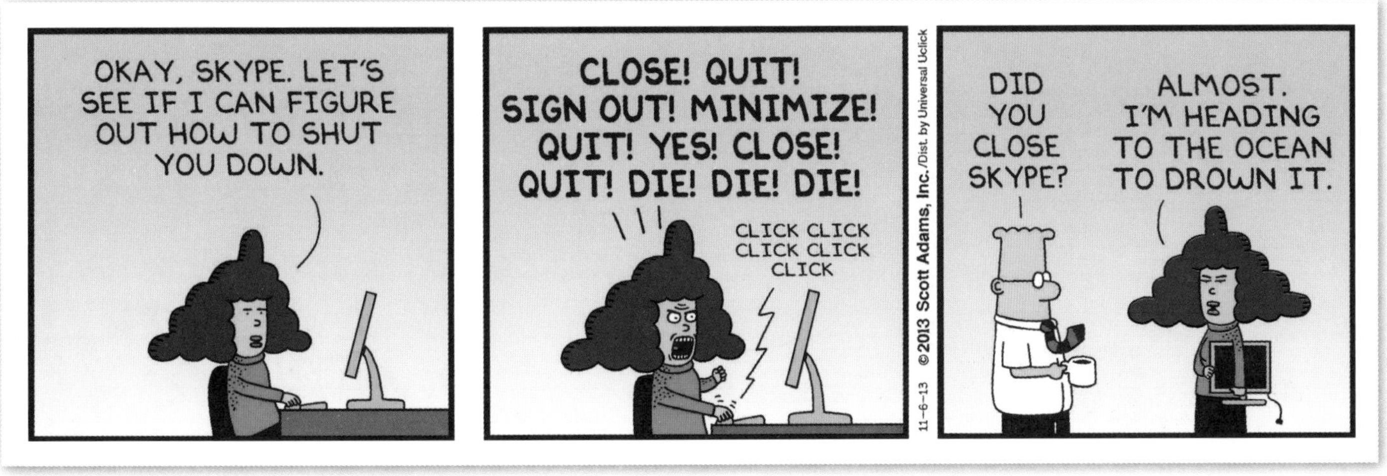
OKAY, SKYPE. LET'S SEE IF I CAN FIGURE OUT HOW TO SHUT YOU DOWN.
CLOSE! QUIT! SIGN OUT! MINIMIZE! QUIT! YES! CLOSE! QUIT! DIE! DIE! DIE!
CLICK CLICK CLICK CLICK CLICK
DID YOU CLOSE SKYPE?
ALMOST. I'M HEADING TO THE OCEAN TO DROWN IT.
11-6-13 ©2013 Scott Adams, Inc./Dist. by Universal Uclick

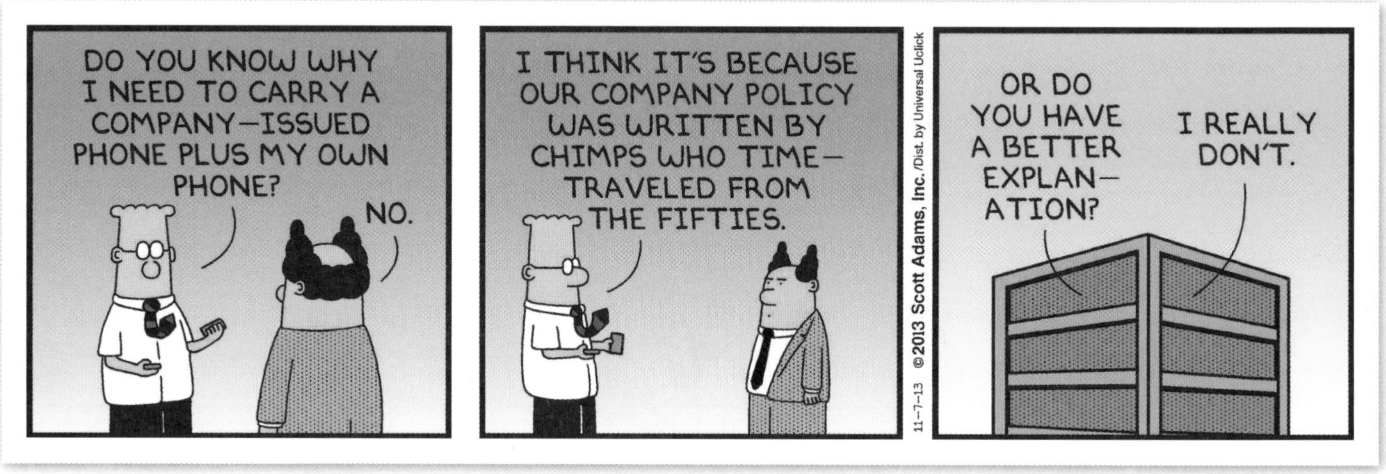
DO YOU KNOW WHY I NEED TO CARRY A COMPANY–ISSUED PHONE PLUS MY OWN PHONE?
NO.
I THINK IT'S BECAUSE OUR COMPANY POLICY WAS WRITTEN BY CHIMPS WHO TIME–TRAVELED FROM THE FIFTIES.
OR DO YOU HAVE A BETTER EXPLAN–ATION?
I REALLY DON'T.
11-7-13 ©2013 Scott Adams, Inc./Dist. by Universal Uclick

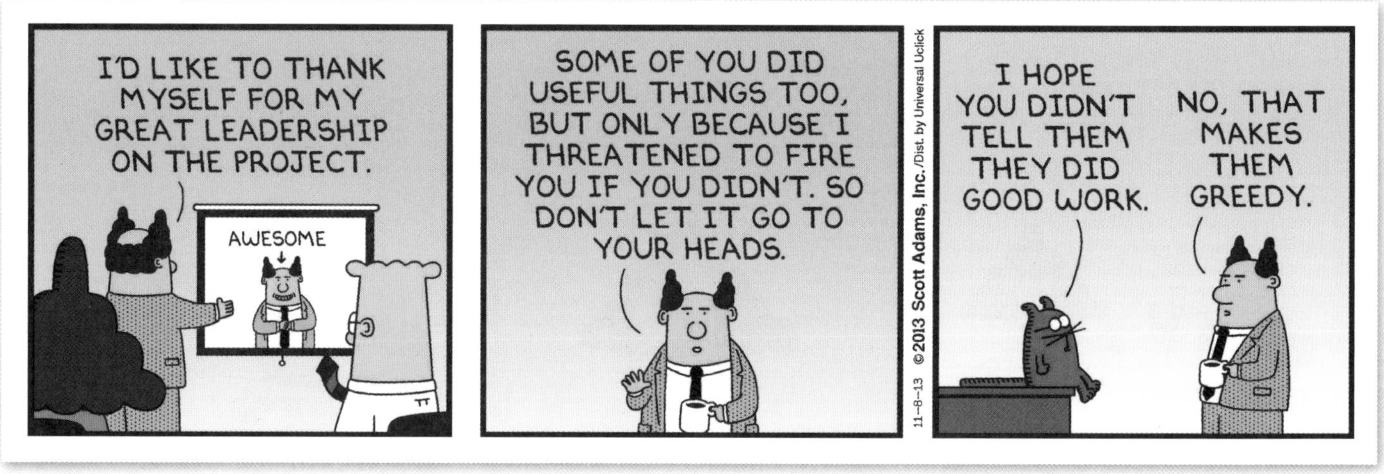
I'D LIKE TO THANK MYSELF FOR MY GREAT LEADERSHIP ON THE PROJECT.
AWESOME
SOME OF YOU DID USEFUL THINGS TOO, BUT ONLY BECAUSE I THREATENED TO FIRE YOU IF YOU DIDN'T. SO DON'T LET IT GO TO YOUR HEADS.
I HOPE YOU DIDN'T TELL THEM THEY DID GOOD WORK.
NO, THAT MAKES THEM GREEDY.
11-8-13 ©2013 Scott Adams, Inc./Dist. by Universal Uclick

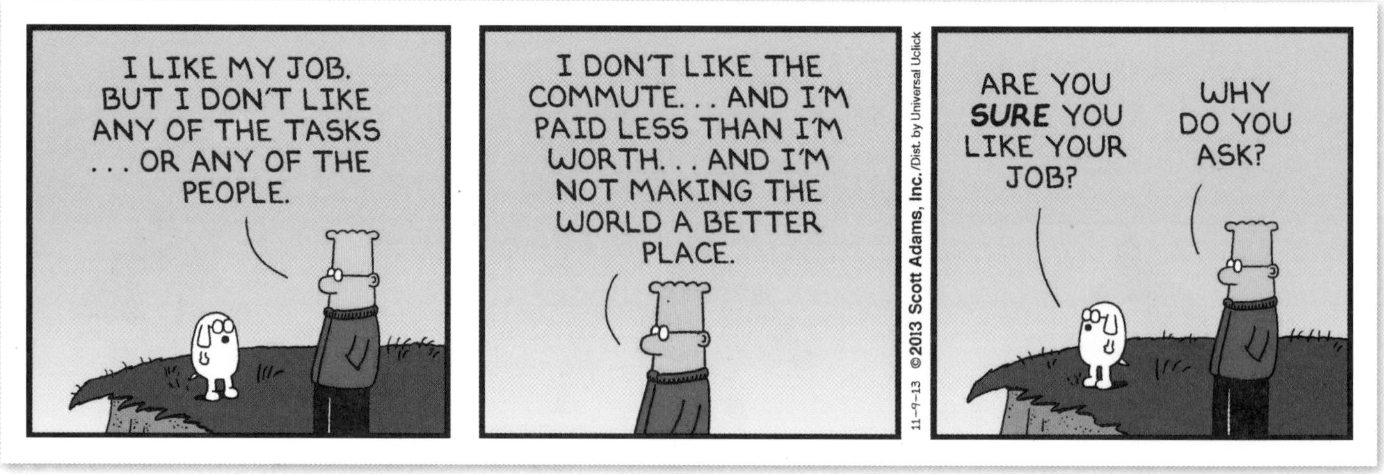
I LIKE MY JOB. BUT I DON'T LIKE ANY OF THE TASKS . . . OR ANY OF THE PEOPLE.
I DON'T LIKE THE COMMUTE. . . AND I'M PAID LESS THAN I'M WORTH. . . AND I'M NOT MAKING THE WORLD A BETTER PLACE.
ARE YOU SURE YOU LIKE YOUR JOB?
WHY DO YOU ASK?
11-9-13 ©2013 Scott Adams, Inc./Dist. by Universal Uclick

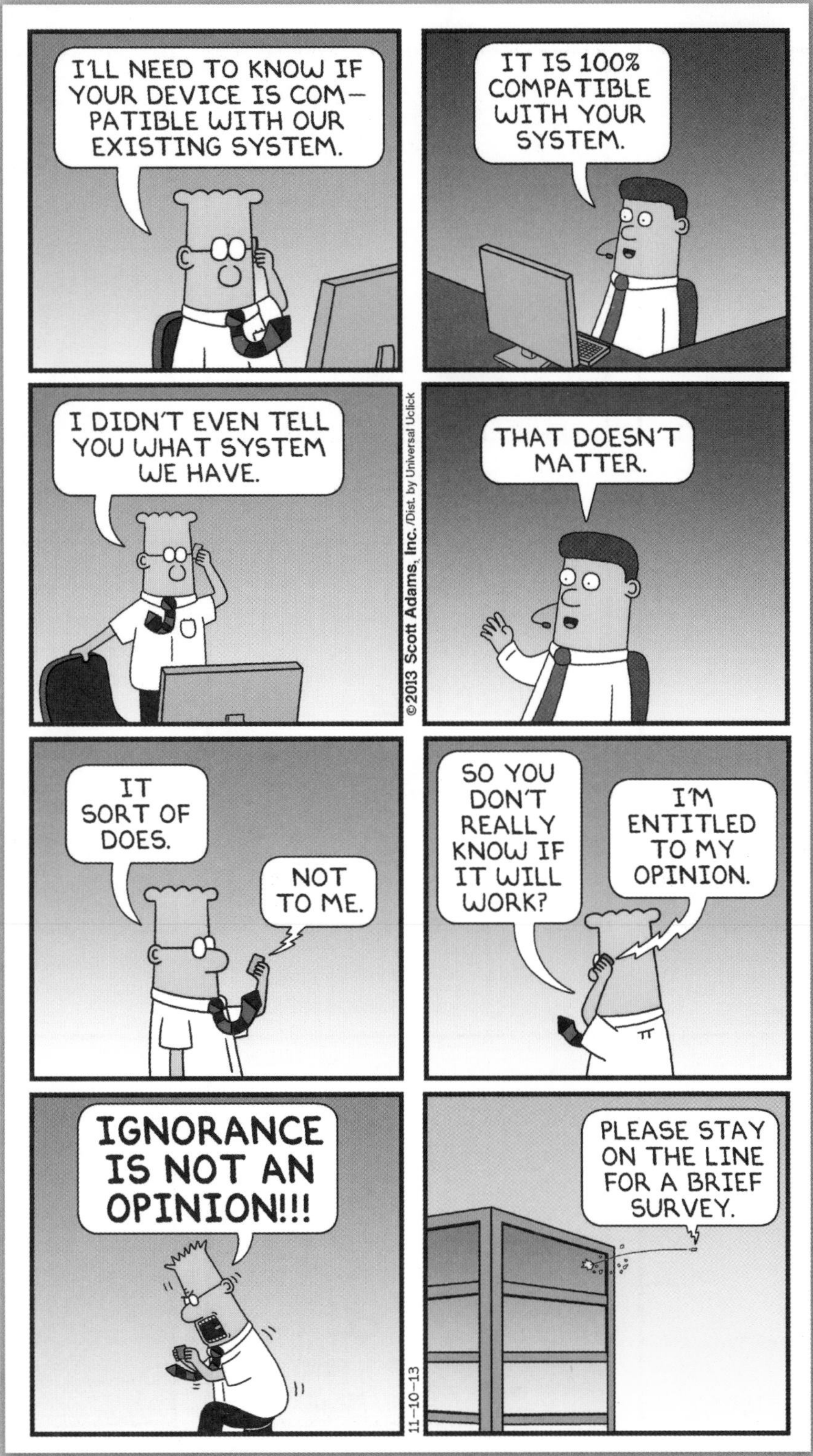
I'LL NEED TO KNOW IF YOUR DEVICE IS COM–PATIBLE WITH OUR EXISTING SYSTEM.
IT IS 100% COMPATIBLE WITH YOUR SYSTEM.
I DIDN'T EVEN TELL YOU WHAT SYSTEM WE HAVE.
THAT DOESN'T MATTER.
IT SORT OF DOES.
NOT TO ME.
SO YOU DON'T REALLY KNOW IF IT WILL WORK?
I'M ENTITLED TO MY OPINION.
IGNORANCE IS NOT AN OPINION!!!
PLEASE STAY ON THE LINE FOR A BRIEF SURVEY.
©2013 Scott Adams, Inc./Dist. by Universal Uclick
11–10–13

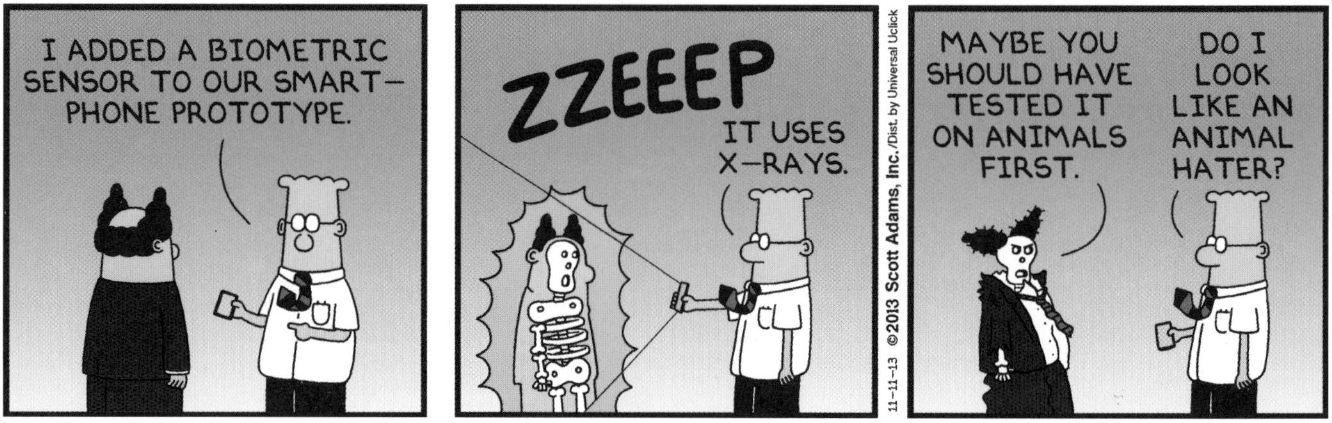
I ADDED A BIOMETRIC SENSOR TO OUR SMART-PHONE PROTOTYPE.
ZZEEEP
IT USES X-RAYS.
11-11-13 ©2013 Scott Adams, Inc./Dist. by Universal Uclick
MAYBE YOU SHOULD HAVE TESTED IT ON ANIMALS FIRST.
DO I LOOK LIKE AN ANIMAL HATER?

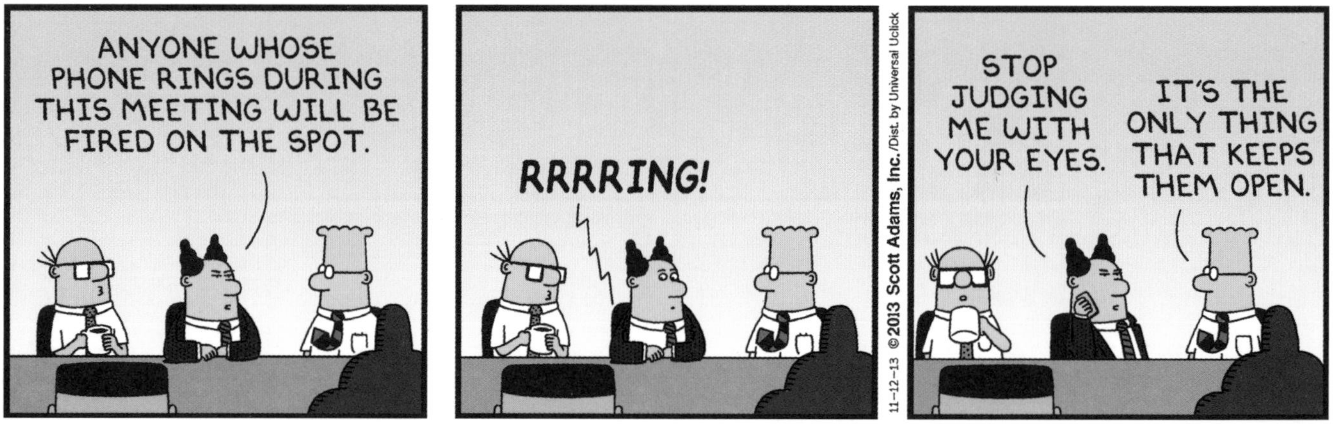
ANYONE WHOSE PHONE RINGS DURING THIS MEETING WILL BE FIRED ON THE SPOT.
RRRRING!
11-12-13 ©2013 Scott Adams, Inc./Dist. by Universal Uclick
STOP JUDGING ME WITH YOUR EYES.
IT'S THE ONLY THING THAT KEEPS THEM OPEN.

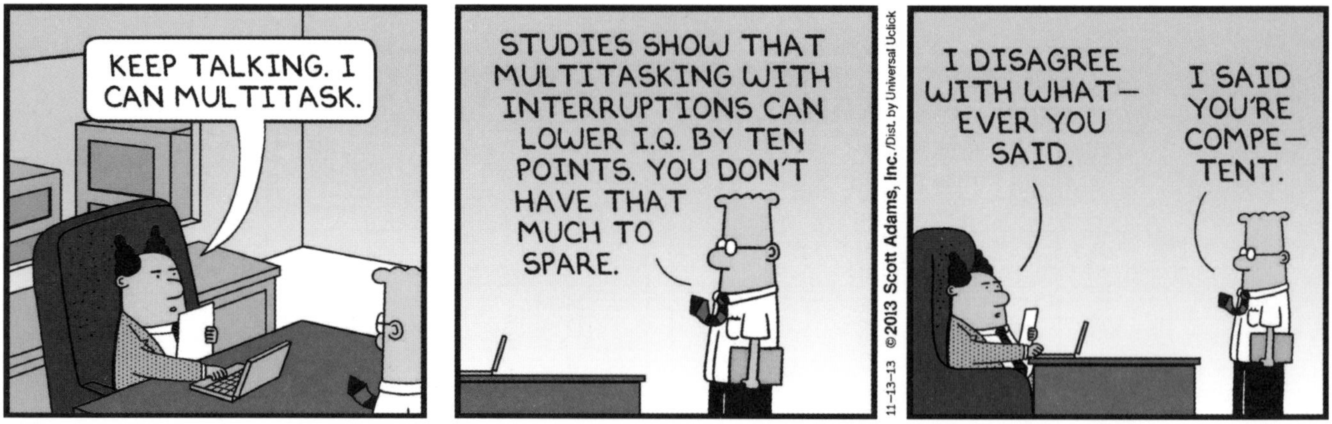
KEEP TALKING. I CAN MULTITASK.
STUDIES SHOW THAT MULTITASKING WITH INTERRUPTIONS CAN LOWER I.Q. BY TEN POINTS. YOU DON'T HAVE THAT MUCH TO SPARE.
11-13-13 ©2013 Scott Adams, Inc./Dist. by Universal Uclick
I DISAGREE WITH WHAT-EVER YOU SAID.
I SAID YOU'RE COMPE-TENT.

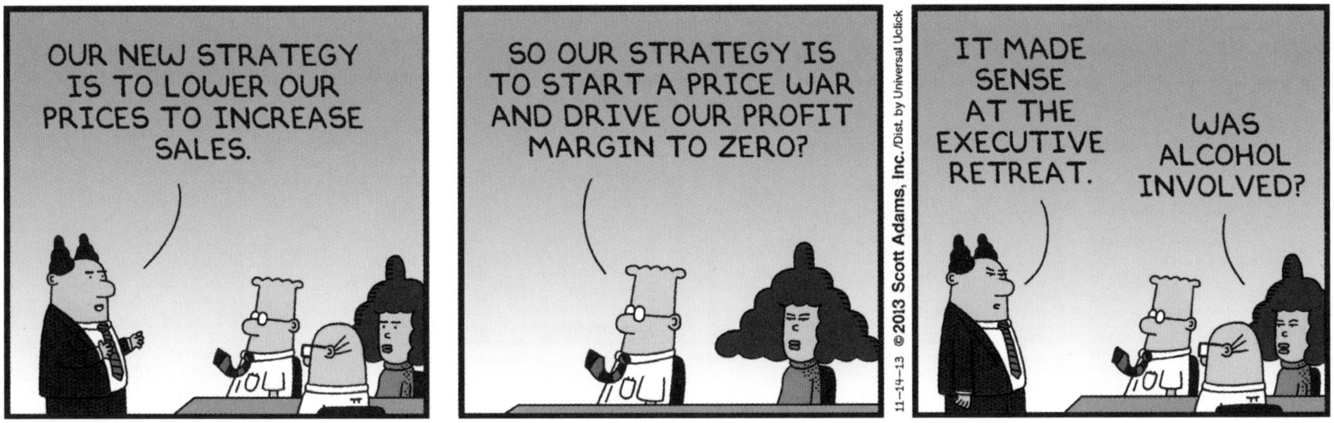
OUR NEW STRATEGY IS TO LOWER OUR PRICES TO INCREASE SALES.
SO OUR STRATEGY IS TO START A PRICE WAR AND DRIVE OUR PROFIT MARGIN TO ZERO?
11-14-13 ©2013 Scott Adams, Inc./Dist. by Universal Uclick
IT MADE SENSE AT THE EXECUTIVE RETREAT.
WAS ALCOHOL INVOLVED?

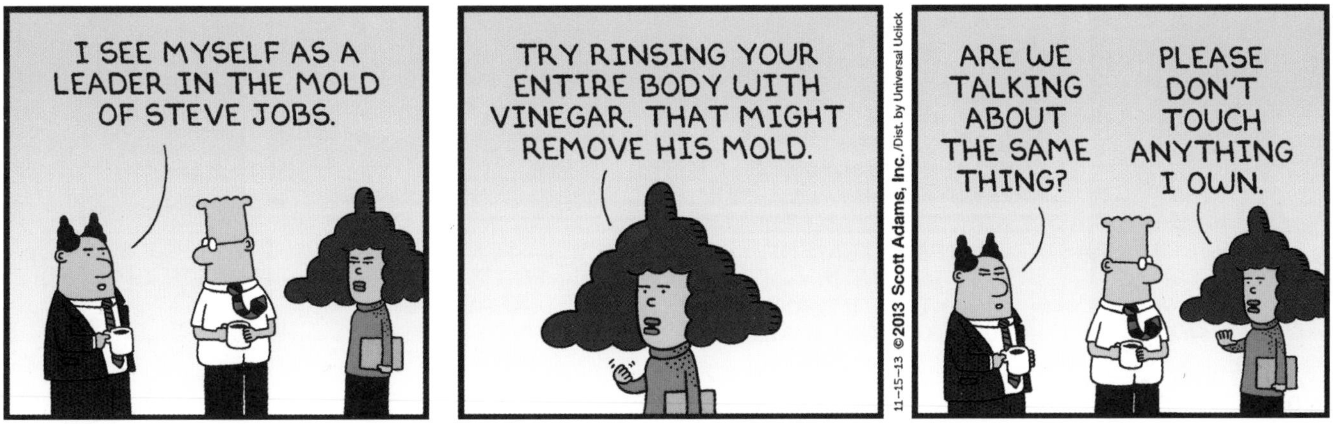
I SEE MYSELF AS A LEADER IN THE MOLD OF STEVE JOBS.
TRY RINSING YOUR ENTIRE BODY WITH VINEGAR. THAT MIGHT REMOVE HIS MOLD.
11-15-13 ©2013 Scott Adams, Inc./Dist. by Universal Uclick
ARE WE TALKING ABOUT THE SAME THING?
PLEASE DON'T TOUCH ANYTHING I OWN.

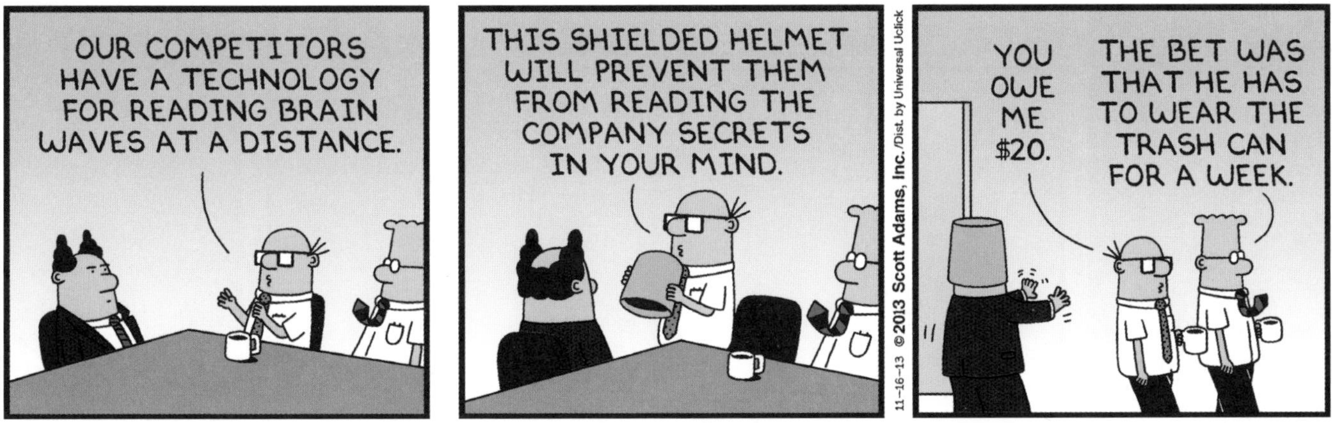
OUR COMPETITORS HAVE A TECHNOLOGY FOR READING BRAIN WAVES AT A DISTANCE.
THIS SHIELDED HELMET WILL PREVENT THEM FROM READING THE COMPANY SECRETS IN YOUR MIND.
11-16-13 ©2013 Scott Adams, Inc./Dist. by Universal Uclick
YOU OWE ME $20.
THE BET WAS THAT HE HAS TO WEAR THE TRASH CAN FOR A WEEK.

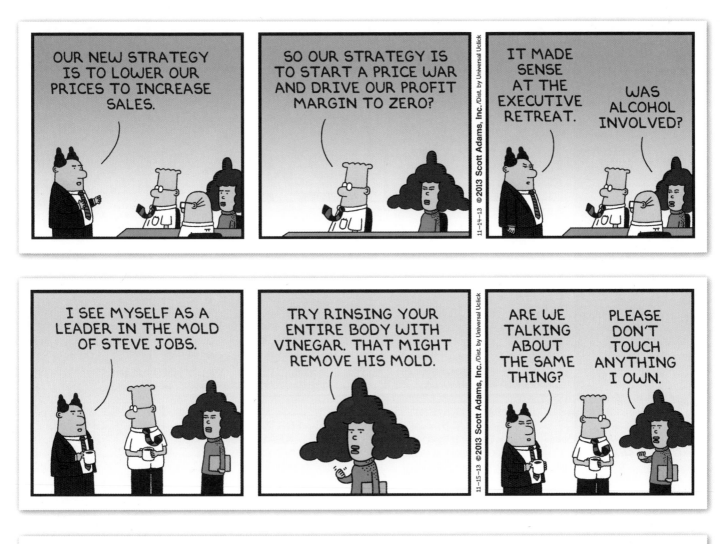

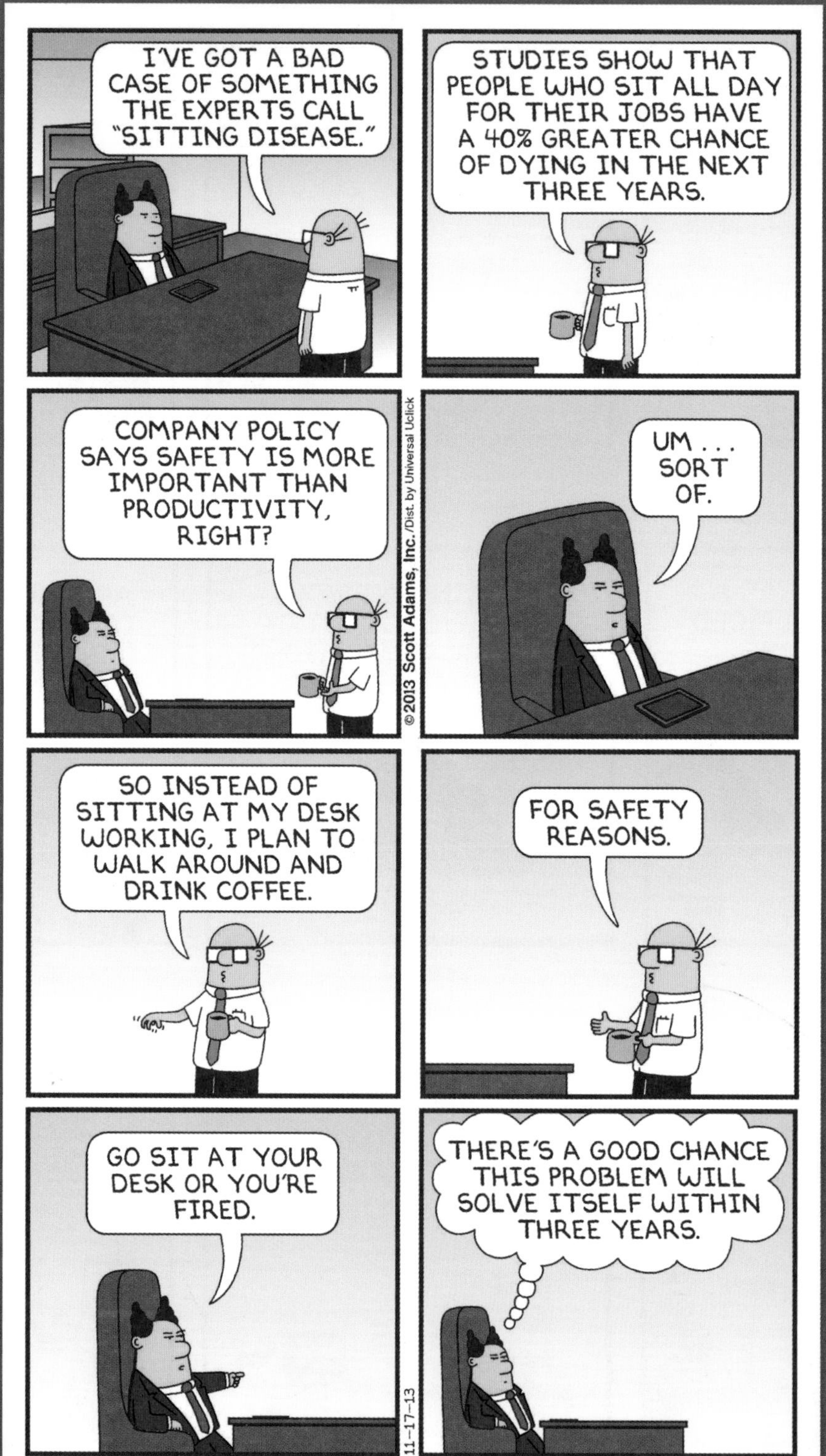
I'VE GOT A BAD CASE OF SOMETHING THE EXPERTS CALL "SITTING DISEASE."
STUDIES SHOW THAT PEOPLE WHO SIT ALL DAY FOR THEIR JOBS HAVE A 40% GREATER CHANCE OF DYING IN THE NEXT THREE YEARS.
COMPANY POLICY SAYS SAFETY IS MORE IMPORTANT THAN PRODUCTIVITY, RIGHT?
UM . . . SORT OF.
SO INSTEAD OF SITTING AT MY DESK WORKING, I PLAN TO WALK AROUND AND DRINK COFFEE.
FOR SAFETY REASONS.
GO SIT AT YOUR DESK OR YOU'RE FIRED.
THERE'S A GOOD CHANCE THIS PROBLEM WILL SOLVE ITSELF WITHIN THREE YEARS.
© 2013 Scott Adams, Inc./Dist. by Universal Uclick
11-17-13

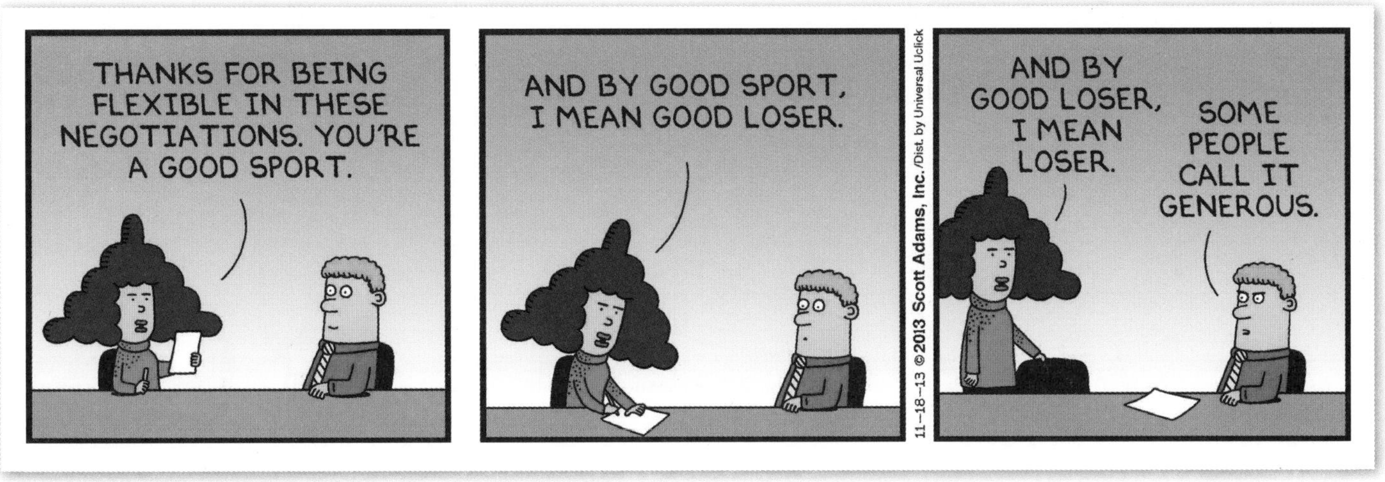
THANKS FOR BEING FLEXIBLE IN THESE NEGOTIATIONS. YOU'RE A GOOD SPORT.
AND BY GOOD SPORT, I MEAN GOOD LOSER.
11-18-13 ©2013 Scott Adams, Inc./Dist. by Universal Uclick
AND BY GOOD LOSER, I MEAN LOSER.
SOME PEOPLE CALL IT GENEROUS.

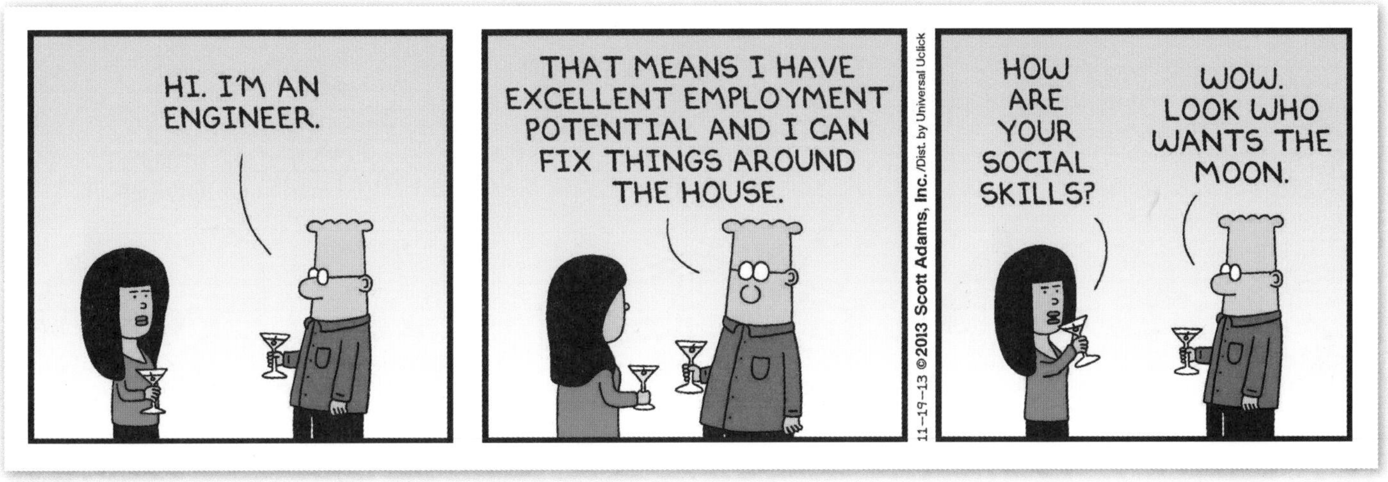
HI. I'M AN ENGINEER.
THAT MEANS I HAVE EXCELLENT EMPLOYMENT POTENTIAL AND I CAN FIX THINGS AROUND THE HOUSE.
11-19-13 ©2013 Scott Adams, Inc./Dist. by Universal Uclick
HOW ARE YOUR SOCIAL SKILLS?
WOW. LOOK WHO WANTS THE MOON.

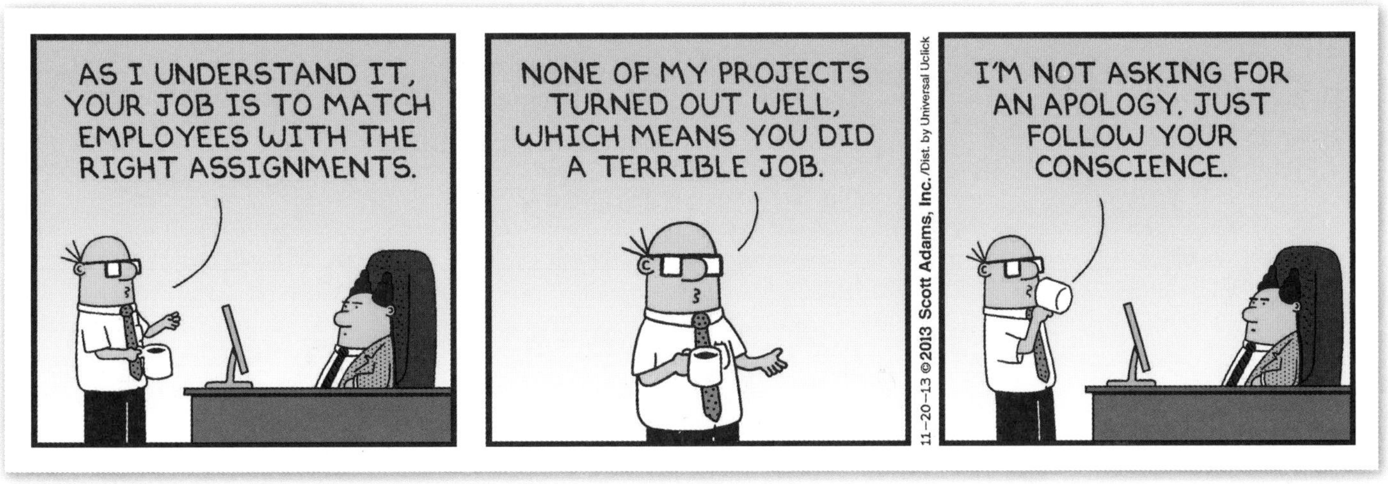
AS I UNDERSTAND IT, YOUR JOB IS TO MATCH EMPLOYEES WITH THE RIGHT ASSIGNMENTS.
NONE OF MY PROJECTS TURNED OUT WELL, WHICH MEANS YOU DID A TERRIBLE JOB.
11-20-13 ©2013 Scott Adams, Inc./Dist. by Universal Uclick
I'M NOT ASKING FOR AN APOLOGY. JUST FOLLOW YOUR CONSCIENCE.

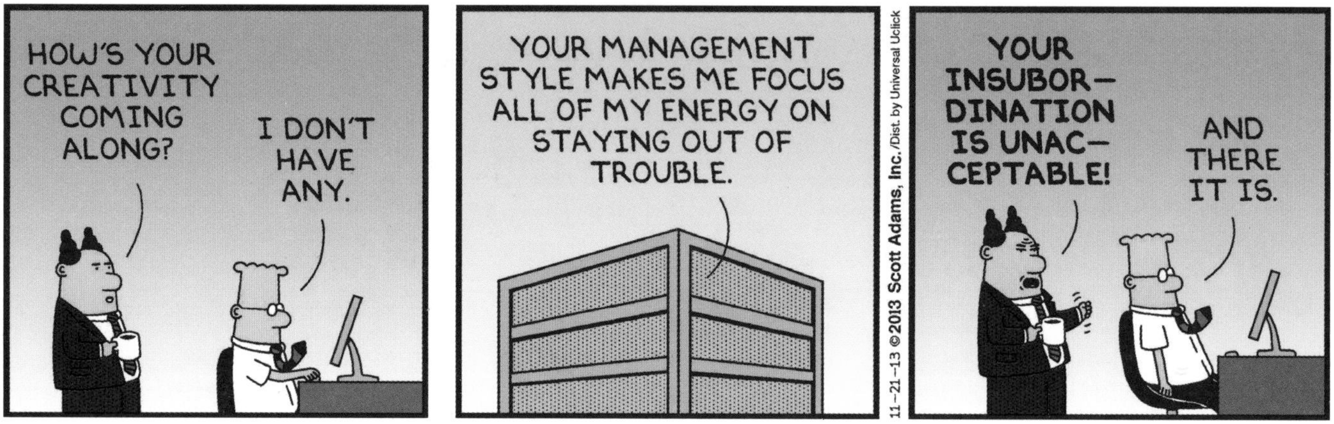
HOW'S YOUR CREATIVITY COMING ALONG?
I DON'T HAVE ANY.
YOUR MANAGEMENT STYLE MAKES ME FOCUS ALL OF MY ENERGY ON STAYING OUT OF TROUBLE.
11-21-13 ©2013 Scott Adams, Inc./Dist. by Universal Uclick
YOUR INSUBOR-DINATION IS UNAC-CEPTABLE!
AND THERE IT IS.

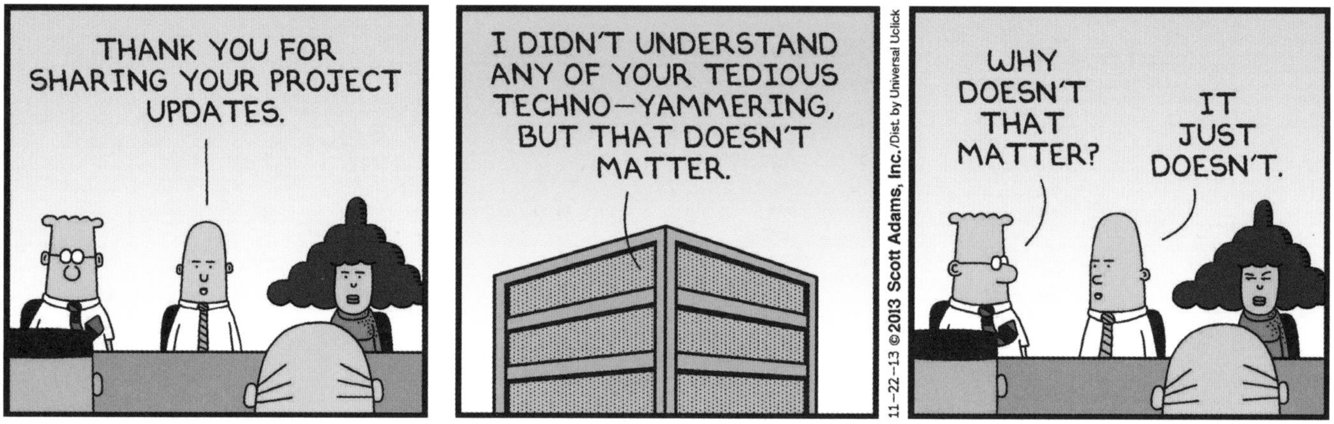
THANK YOU FOR SHARING YOUR PROJECT UPDATES.
I DIDN'T UNDERSTAND ANY OF YOUR TEDIOUS TECHNO-YAMMERING, BUT THAT DOESN'T MATTER.
11-22-13 ©2013 Scott Adams, Inc./Dist. by Universal Uclick
WHY DOESN'T THAT MATTER?
IT JUST DOESN'T.

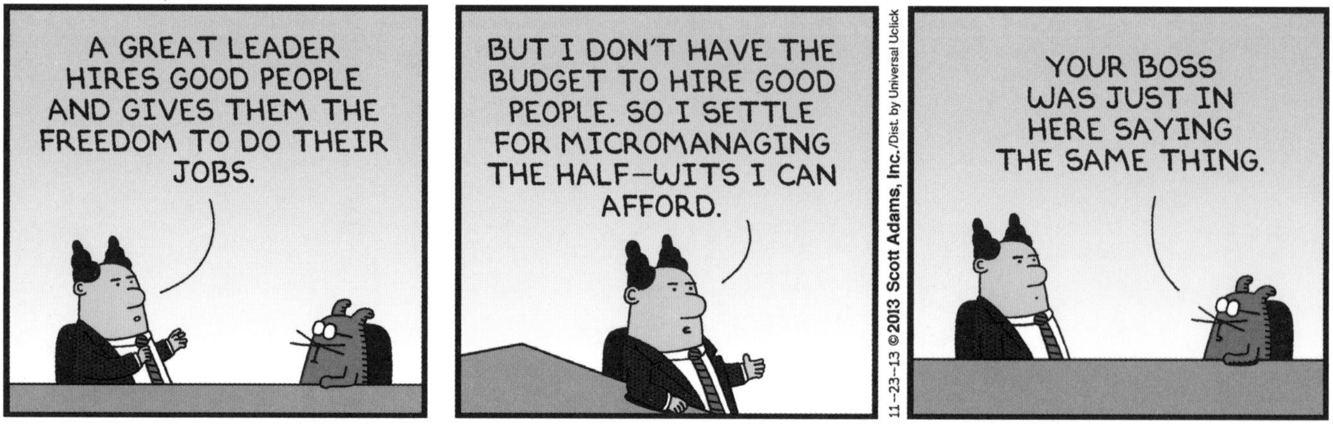
A GREAT LEADER HIRES GOOD PEOPLE AND GIVES THEM THE FREEDOM TO DO THEIR JOBS.
BUT I DON'T HAVE THE BUDGET TO HIRE GOOD PEOPLE. SO I SETTLE FOR MICROMANAGING THE HALF-WITS I CAN AFFORD.
11-23-13 ©2013 Scott Adams, Inc./Dist. by Universal Uclick
YOUR BOSS WAS JUST IN HERE SAYING THE SAME THING.

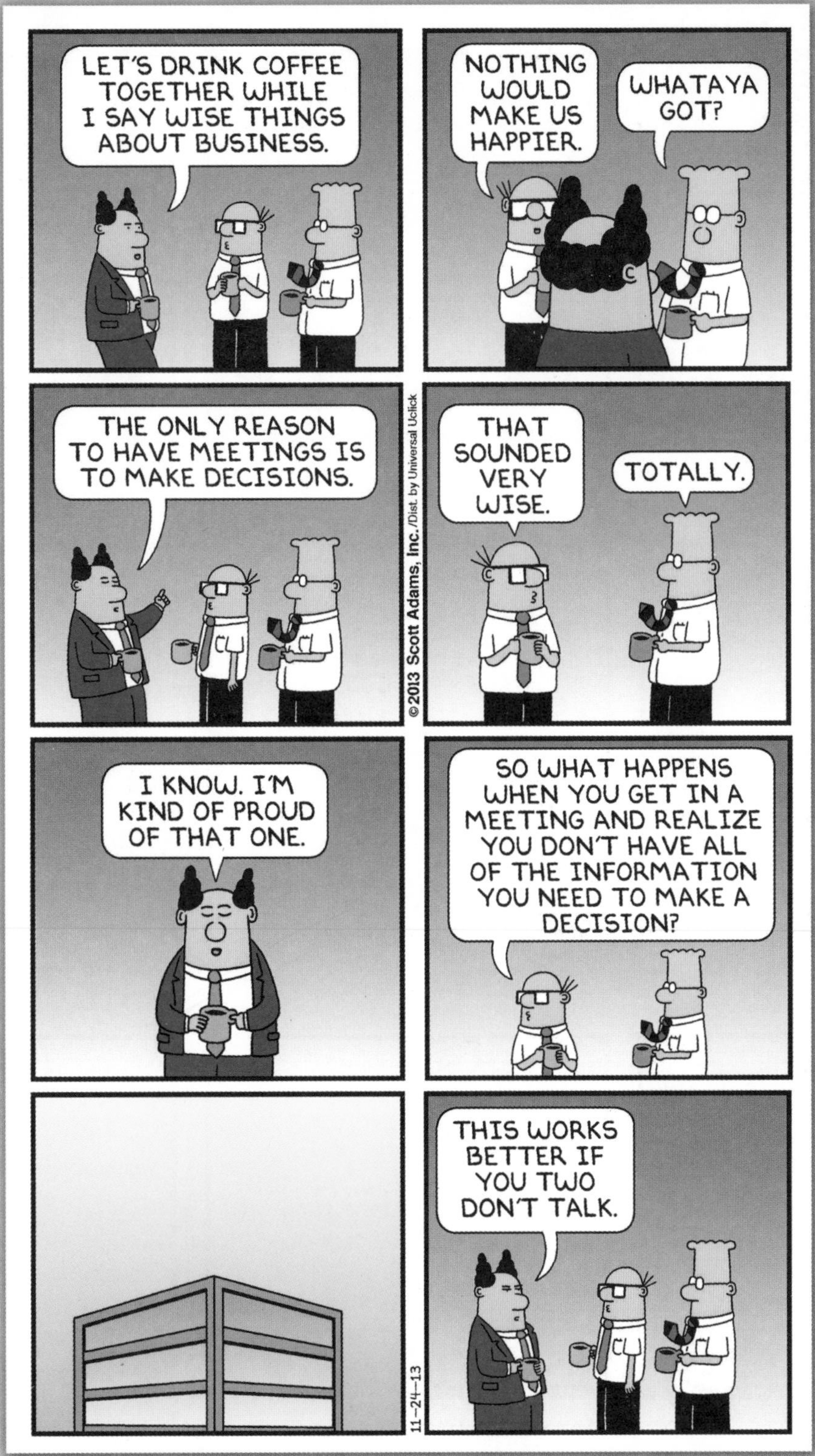
LET'S DRINK COFFEE TOGETHER WHILE I SAY WISE THINGS ABOUT BUSINESS.
NOTHING WOULD MAKE US HAPPIER.
WHATAYA GOT?
THE ONLY REASON TO HAVE MEETINGS IS TO MAKE DECISIONS.
THAT SOUNDED VERY WISE.
TOTALLY.
I KNOW. I'M KIND OF PROUD OF THAT ONE.
SO WHAT HAPPENS WHEN YOU GET IN A MEETING AND REALIZE YOU DON'T HAVE ALL OF THE INFORMATION YOU NEED TO MAKE A DECISION?
THIS WORKS BETTER IF YOU TWO DON'T TALK.
©2013 Scott Adams, Inc./Dist. by Universal Uclick
11-24-13

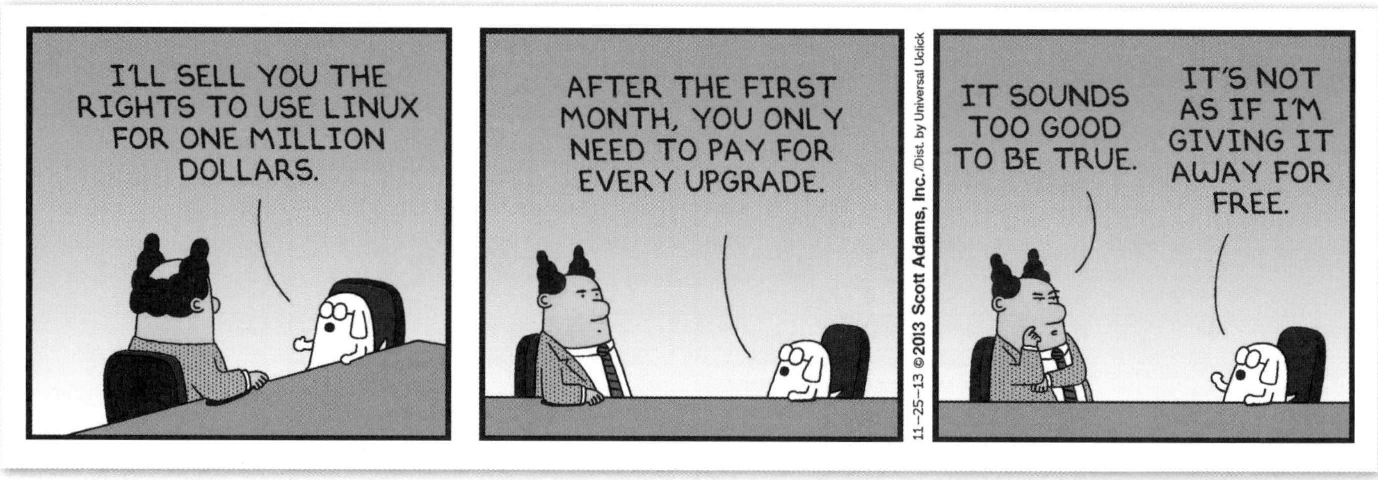
I'LL SELL YOU THE RIGHTS TO USE LINUX FOR ONE MILLION DOLLARS.
AFTER THE FIRST MONTH, YOU ONLY NEED TO PAY FOR EVERY UPGRADE.
IT SOUNDS TOO GOOD TO BE TRUE.
IT'S NOT AS IF I'M GIVING IT AWAY FOR FREE.
11-25-13 ©2013 Scott Adams, Inc./Dist. by Universal Uclick

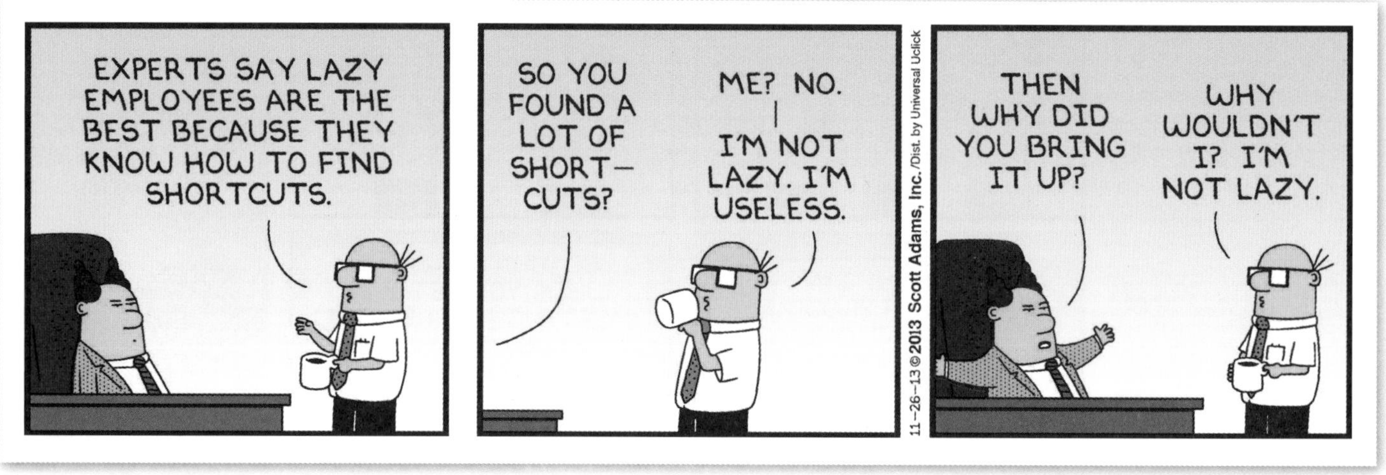
EXPERTS SAY LAZY EMPLOYEES ARE THE BEST BECAUSE THEY KNOW HOW TO FIND SHORTCUTS.
SO YOU FOUND A LOT OF SHORT-CUTS?
ME? NO.
I'M NOT LAZY. I'M USELESS.
THEN WHY DID YOU BRING IT UP?
WHY WOULDN'T I? I'M NOT LAZY.
11-26-13 ©2013 Scott Adams, Inc./Dist. by Universal Uclick

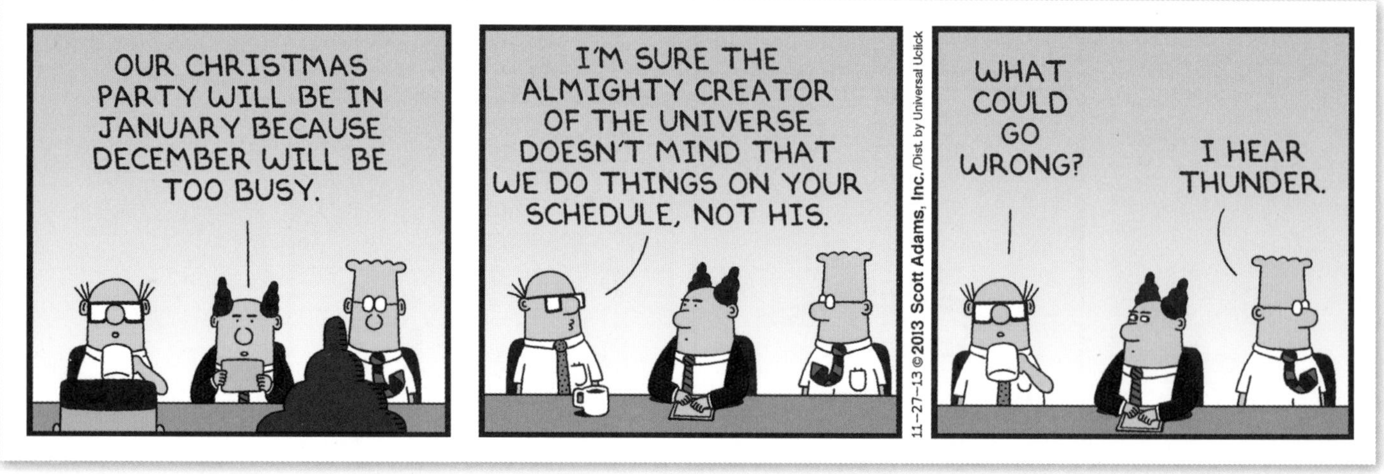
OUR CHRISTMAS PARTY WILL BE IN JANUARY BECAUSE DECEMBER WILL BE TOO BUSY.
I'M SURE THE ALMIGHTY CREATOR OF THE UNIVERSE DOESN'T MIND THAT WE DO THINGS ON YOUR SCHEDULE, NOT HIS.
WHAT COULD GO WRONG?
I HEAR THUNDER.
11-27-13 ©2013 Scott Adams, Inc./Dist. by Universal Uclick

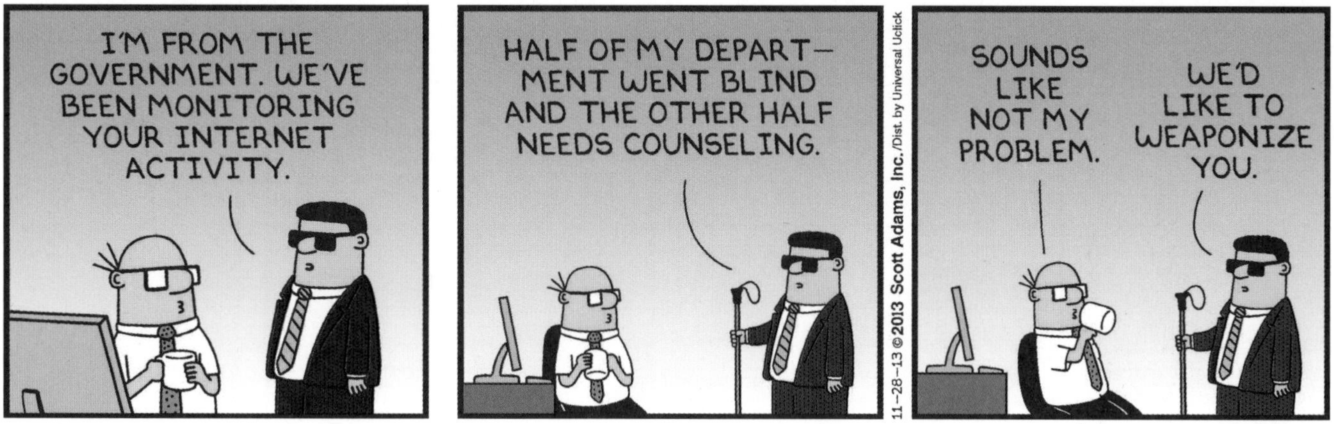
I'M FROM THE GOVERNMENT. WE'VE BEEN MONITORING YOUR INTERNET ACTIVITY.
HALF OF MY DEPART-MENT WENT BLIND AND THE OTHER HALF NEEDS COUNSELING.
11-28-13 ©2013 Scott Adams, Inc./Dist. by Universal Uclick
SOUNDS LIKE NOT MY PROBLEM.
WE'D LIKE TO WEAPONIZE YOU.

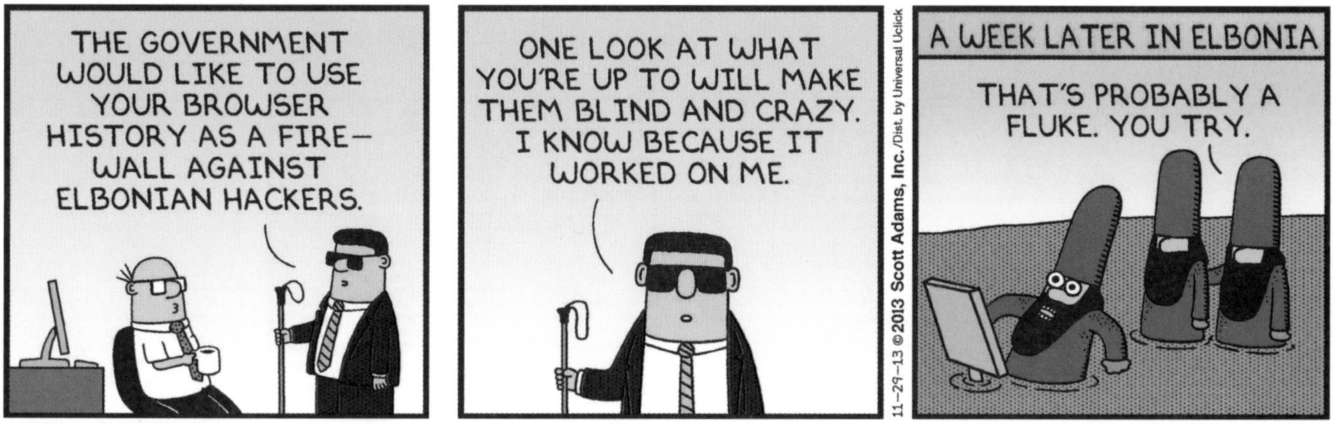
THE GOVERNMENT WOULD LIKE TO USE YOUR BROWSER HISTORY AS A FIRE-WALL AGAINST ELBONIAN HACKERS.
ONE LOOK AT WHAT YOU'RE UP TO WILL MAKE THEM BLIND AND CRAZY. I KNOW BECAUSE IT WORKED ON ME.
11-29-13 ©2013 Scott Adams, Inc./Dist. by Universal Uclick
A WEEK LATER IN ELBONIA
THAT'S PROBABLY A FLUKE. YOU TRY.

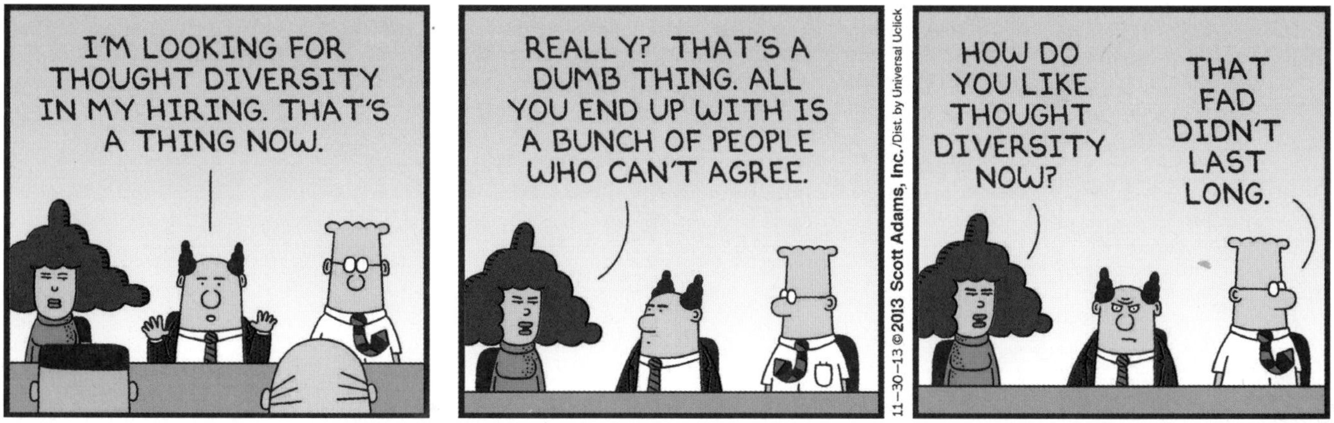
I'M LOOKING FOR THOUGHT DIVERSITY IN MY HIRING. THAT'S A THING NOW.
REALLY? THAT'S A DUMB THING. ALL YOU END UP WITH IS A BUNCH OF PEOPLE WHO CAN'T AGREE.
11-30-13 ©2013 Scott Adams, Inc./Dist. by Universal Uclick
HOW DO YOU LIKE THOUGHT DIVERSITY NOW?
THAT FAD DIDN'T LAST LONG.

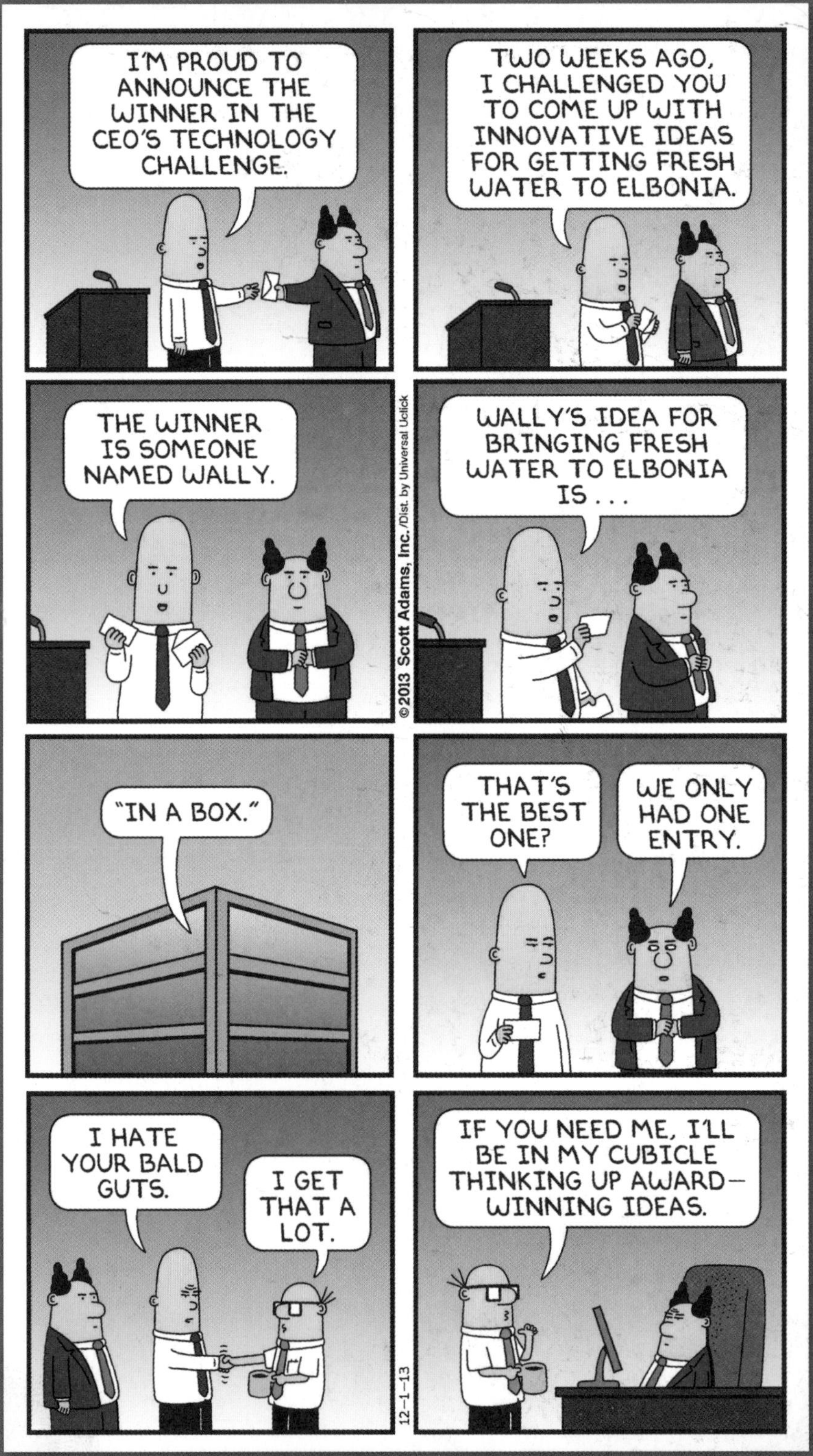
I'M PROUD TO ANNOUNCE THE WINNER IN THE CEO'S TECHNOLOGY CHALLENGE.
TWO WEEKS AGO, I CHALLENGED YOU TO COME UP WITH INNOVATIVE IDEAS FOR GETTING FRESH WATER TO ELBONIA.
THE WINNER IS SOMEONE NAMED WALLY.
©2013 Scott Adams, Inc./Dist. by Universal Uclick
WALLY'S IDEA FOR BRINGING FRESH WATER TO ELBONIA IS . . .
"IN A BOX."
THAT'S THE BEST ONE?
WE ONLY HAD ONE ENTRY.
I HATE YOUR BALD GUTS.
I GET THAT A LOT.
12-1-13
IF YOU NEED ME, I'LL BE IN MY CUBICLE THINKING UP AWARD-WINNING IDEAS.

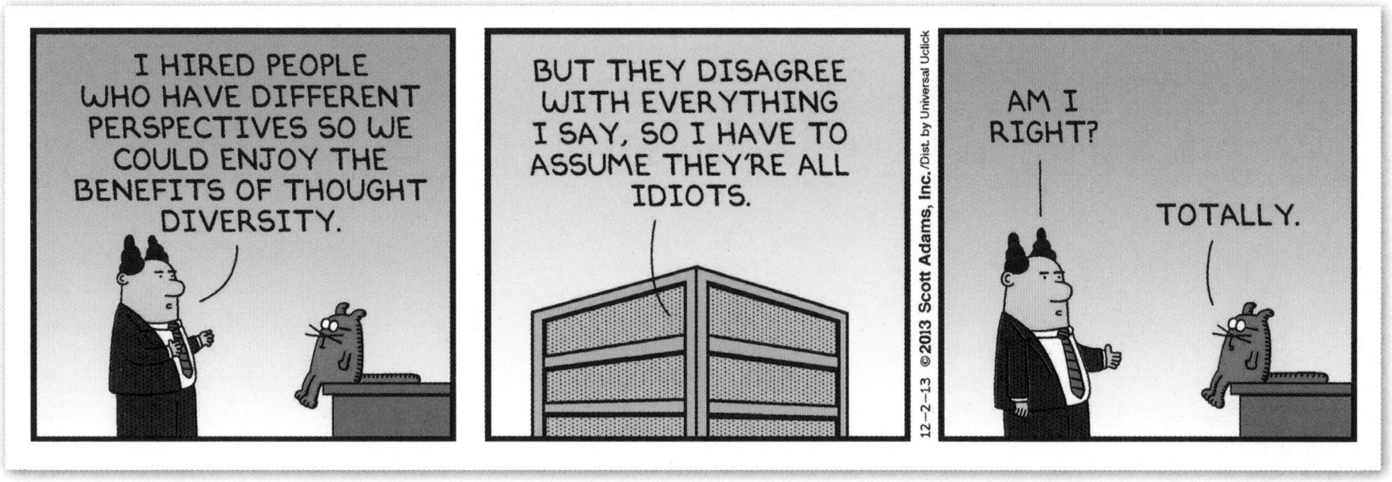
I HIRED PEOPLE WHO HAVE DIFFERENT PERSPECTIVES SO WE COULD ENJOY THE BENEFITS OF THOUGHT DIVERSITY.
BUT THEY DISAGREE WITH EVERYTHING I SAY, SO I HAVE TO ASSUME THEY'RE ALL IDIOTS.
12-2-13 ©2013 Scott Adams, Inc./Dist. by Universal Uclick
AM I RIGHT?
TOTALLY.

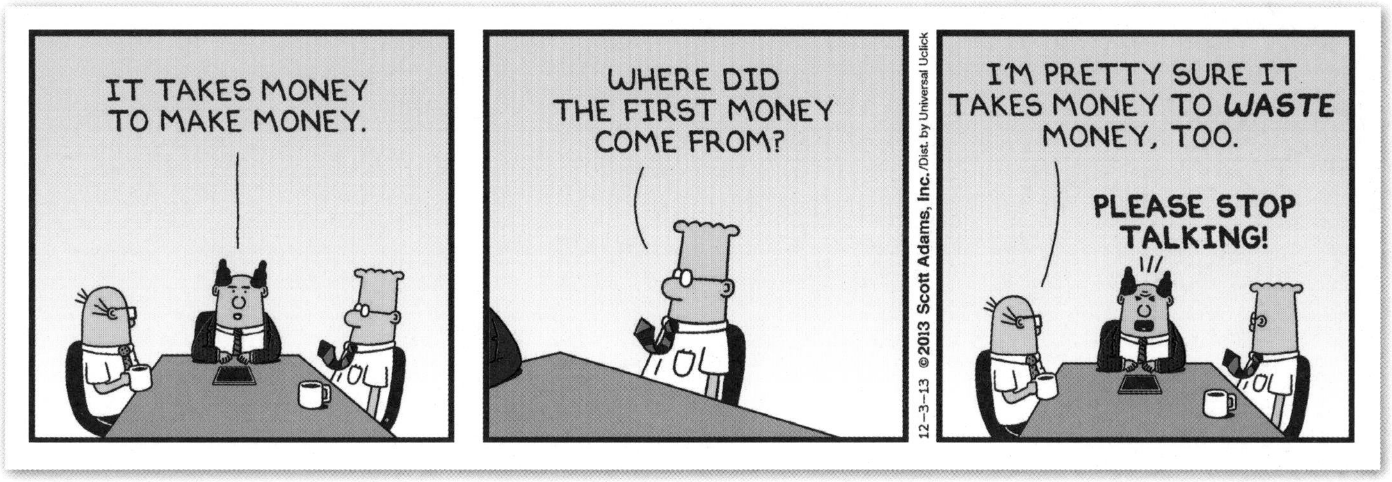
IT TAKES MONEY TO MAKE MONEY.
WHERE DID THE FIRST MONEY COME FROM?
12-3-13 ©2013 Scott Adams, Inc./Dist. by Universal Uclick
I'M PRETTY SURE IT TAKES MONEY TO **WASTE** MONEY, TOO.
PLEASE STOP TALKING!

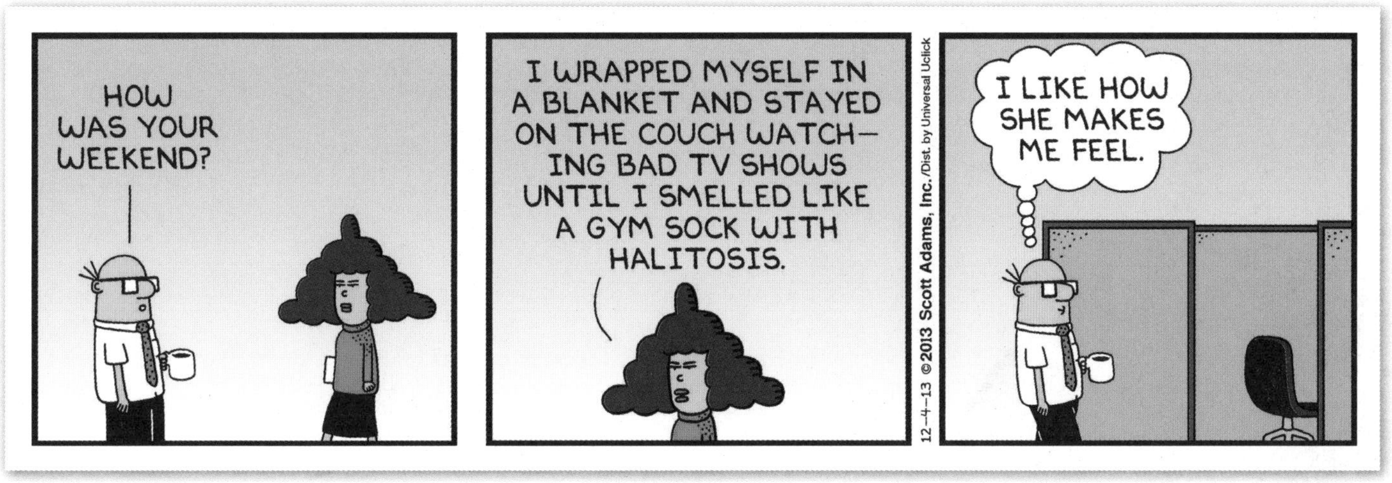
HOW WAS YOUR WEEKEND?
I WRAPPED MYSELF IN A BLANKET AND STAYED ON THE COUCH WATCH- ING BAD TV SHOWS UNTIL I SMELLED LIKE A GYM SOCK WITH HALITOSIS.
12-4-13 ©2013 Scott Adams, Inc./Dist. by Universal Uclick
I LIKE HOW SHE MAKES ME FEEL.

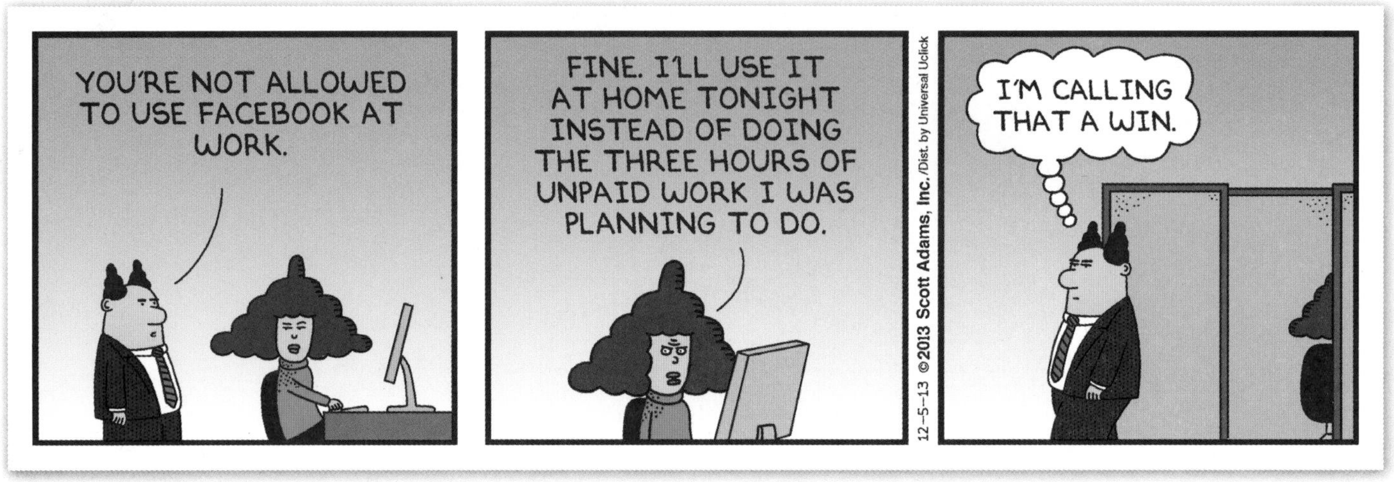
YOU'RE NOT ALLOWED TO USE FACEBOOK AT WORK.
FINE. I'LL USE IT AT HOME TONIGHT INSTEAD OF DOING THE THREE HOURS OF UNPAID WORK I WAS PLANNING TO DO.
12-5-13 ©2013 Scott Adams, Inc./Dist. by Universal Uclick
I'M CALLING THAT A WIN.

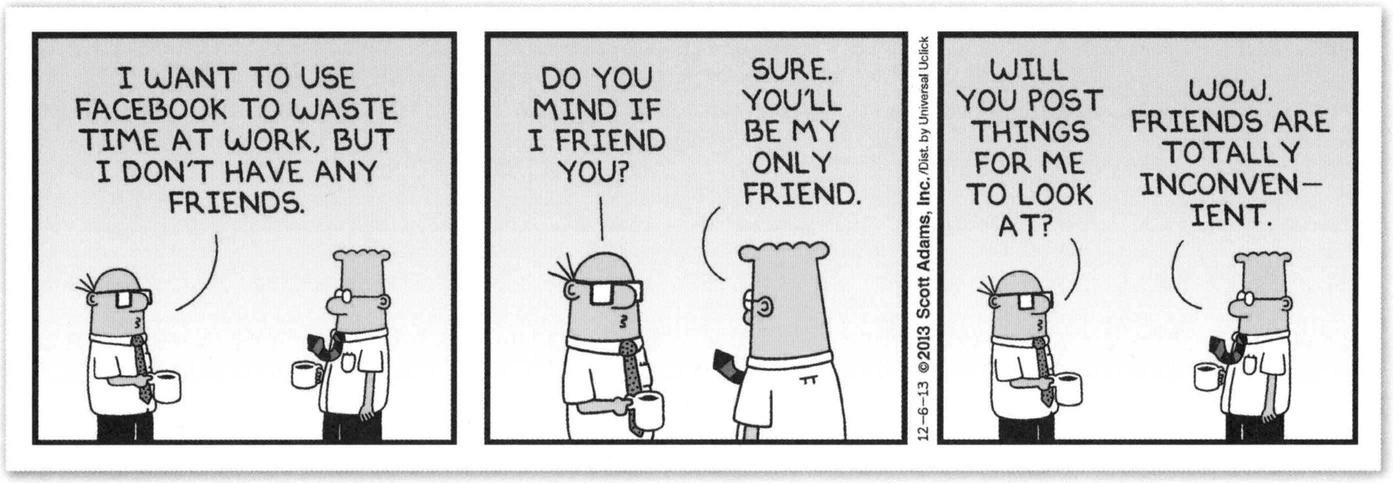
I WANT TO USE FACEBOOK TO WASTE TIME AT WORK, BUT I DON'T HAVE ANY FRIENDS.
DO YOU MIND IF I FRIEND YOU?
SURE. YOU'LL BE MY ONLY FRIEND.
12-6-13 ©2013 Scott Adams, Inc./Dist. by Universal Uclick
WILL YOU POST THINGS FOR ME TO LOOK AT?
WOW. FRIENDS ARE TOTALLY INCONVEN-IENT.

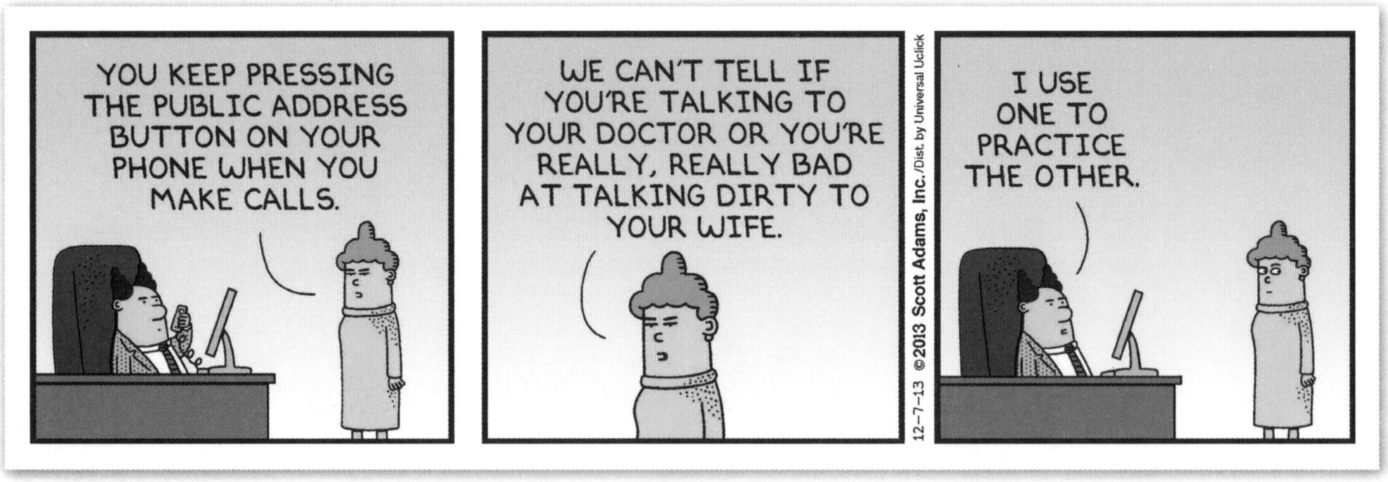
YOU KEEP PRESSING THE PUBLIC ADDRESS BUTTON ON YOUR PHONE WHEN YOU MAKE CALLS.
WE CAN'T TELL IF YOU'RE TALKING TO YOUR DOCTOR OR YOU'RE REALLY, REALLY BAD AT TALKING DIRTY TO YOUR WIFE.
12-7-13 ©2013 Scott Adams, Inc./Dist. by Universal Uclick
I USE ONE TO PRACTICE THE OTHER.

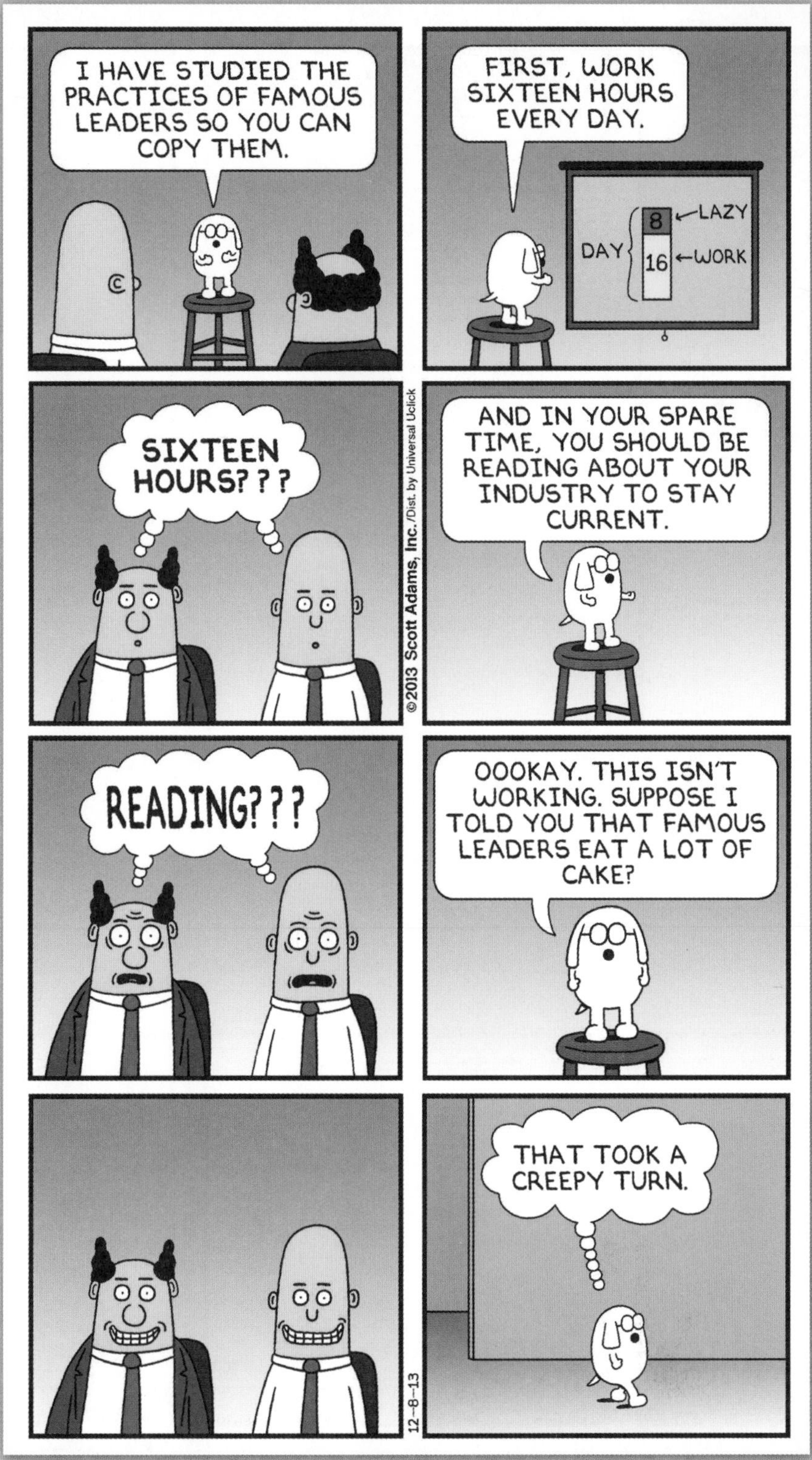
I HAVE STUDIED THE PRACTICES OF FAMOUS LEADERS SO YOU CAN COPY THEM.
FIRST, WORK SIXTEEN HOURS EVERY DAY.
DAY
8 ←LAZY
16 ←WORK
SIXTEEN HOURS???
AND IN YOUR SPARE TIME, YOU SHOULD BE READING ABOUT YOUR INDUSTRY TO STAY CURRENT.
READING???
OOOKAY. THIS ISN'T WORKING. SUPPOSE I TOLD YOU THAT FAMOUS LEADERS EAT A LOT OF CAKE?
THAT TOOK A CREEPY TURN.
©2013 Scott Adams, Inc./Dist. by Universal Uclick
12-8-13

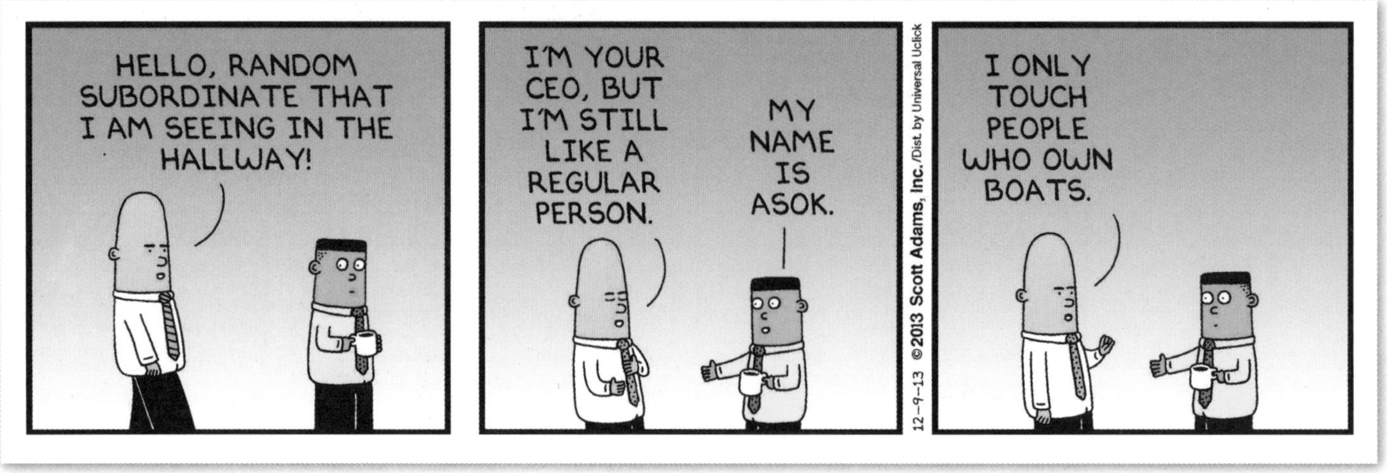
HELLO, RANDOM SUBORDINATE THAT I AM SEEING IN THE HALLWAY!
I'M YOUR CEO, BUT I'M STILL LIKE A REGULAR PERSON.
MY NAME IS ASOK.
12-9-13 ©2013 Scott Adams, Inc./Dist. by Universal Uclick
I ONLY TOUCH PEOPLE WHO OWN BOATS.

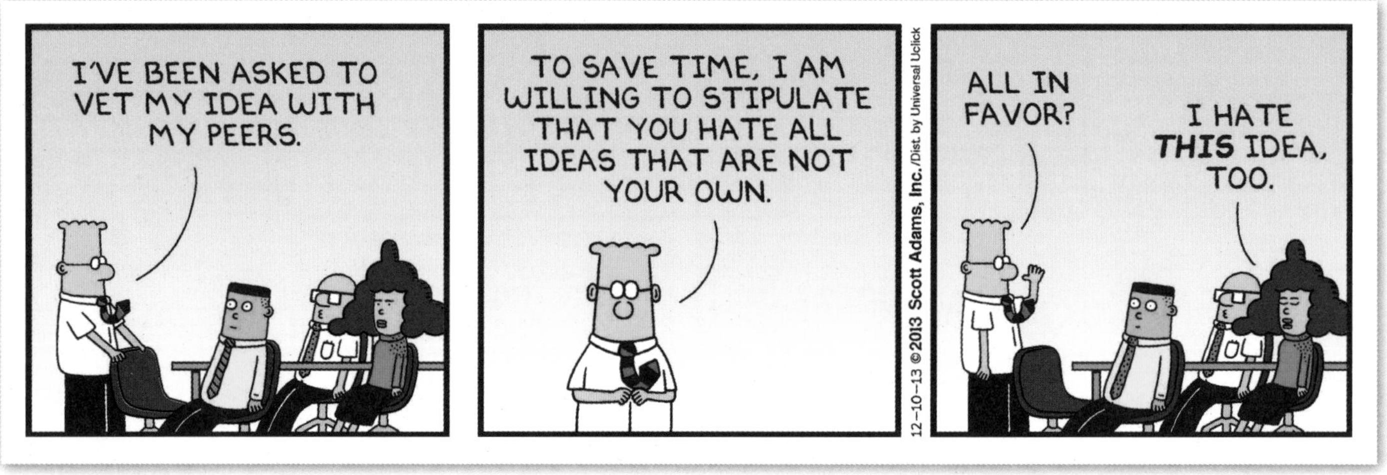
I'VE BEEN ASKED TO VET MY IDEA WITH MY PEERS.
TO SAVE TIME, I AM WILLING TO STIPULATE THAT YOU HATE ALL IDEAS THAT ARE NOT YOUR OWN.
12-10-13 ©2013 Scott Adams, Inc./Dist. by Universal Uclick
ALL IN FAVOR?
I HATE **THIS** IDEA, TOO.

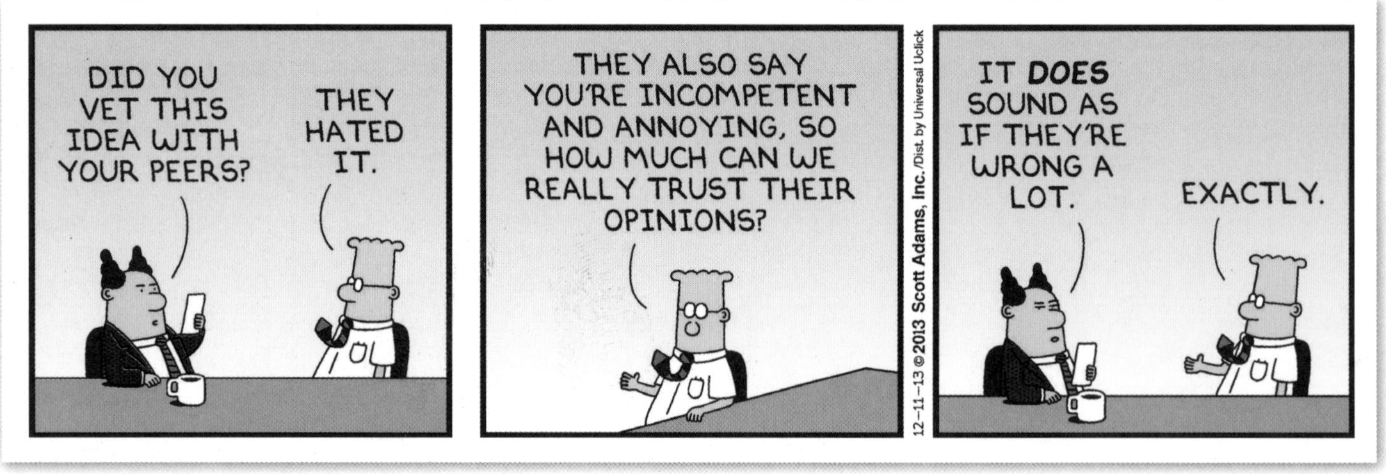
DID YOU VET THIS IDEA WITH YOUR PEERS?
THEY HATED IT.
THEY ALSO SAY YOU'RE INCOMPETENT AND ANNOYING, SO HOW MUCH CAN WE REALLY TRUST THEIR OPINIONS?
12-11-13 ©2013 Scott Adams, Inc./Dist. by Universal Uclick
IT **DOES** SOUND AS IF THEY'RE WRONG A LOT.
EXACTLY.

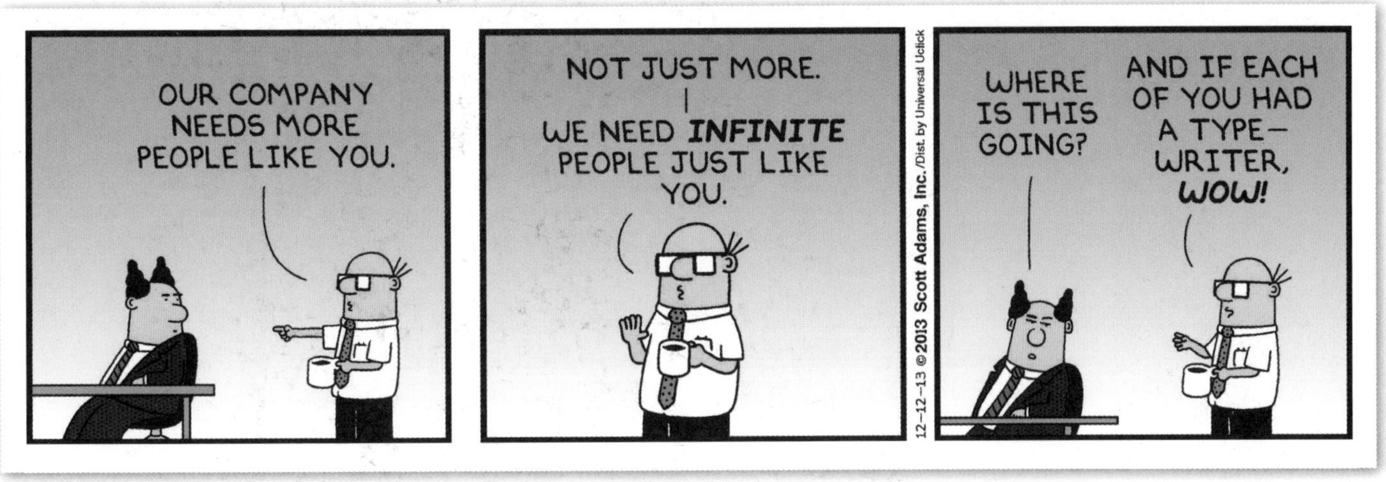
OUR COMPANY NEEDS MORE PEOPLE LIKE YOU.
NOT JUST MORE.
WE NEED **INFINITE** PEOPLE JUST LIKE YOU.
12-12-13 ©2013 Scott Adams, Inc./Dist. by Universal Uclick
WHERE IS THIS GOING?
AND IF EACH OF YOU HAD A TYPE-WRITER, **WOW!**

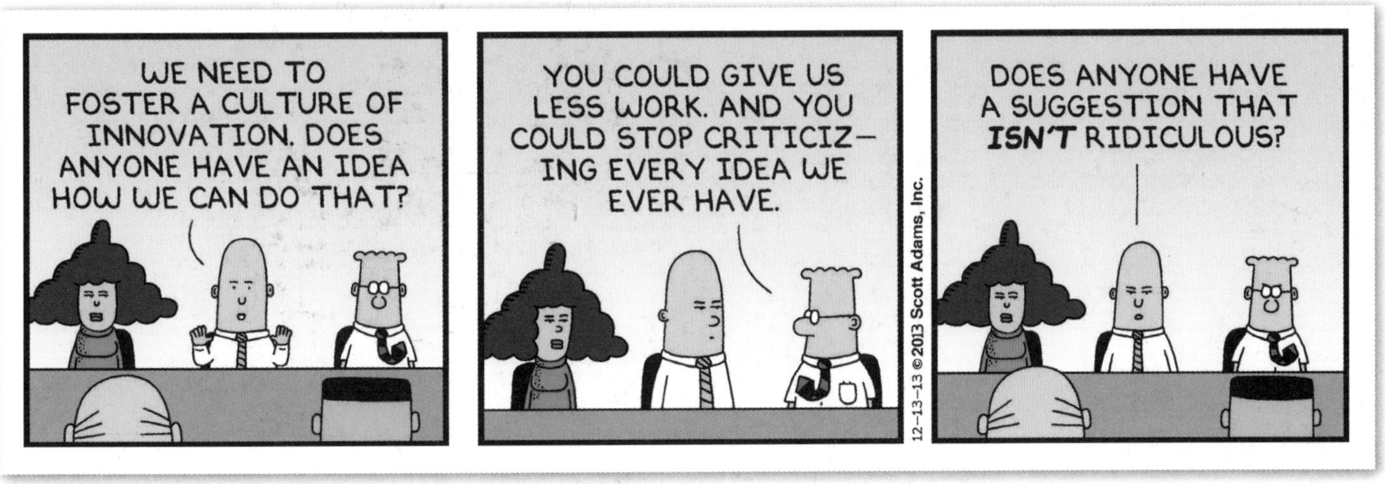
WE NEED TO FOSTER A CULTURE OF INNOVATION. DOES ANYONE HAVE AN IDEA HOW WE CAN DO THAT?
YOU COULD GIVE US LESS WORK. AND YOU COULD STOP CRITICIZ-ING EVERY IDEA WE EVER HAVE.
12-13-13 ©2013 Scott Adams, Inc.
DOES ANYONE HAVE A SUGGESTION THAT **ISN'T** RIDICULOUS?

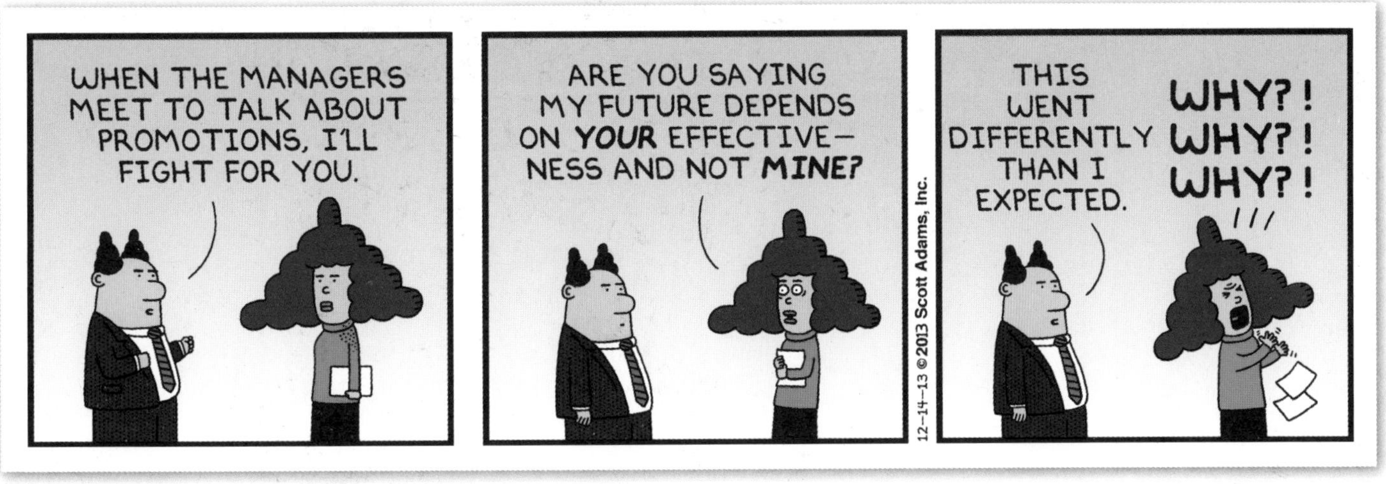
WHEN THE MANAGERS MEET TO TALK ABOUT PROMOTIONS, I'LL FIGHT FOR YOU.
ARE YOU SAYING MY FUTURE DEPENDS ON **YOUR** EFFECTIVE-NESS AND NOT **MINE?**
12-14-13 ©2013 Scott Adams, Inc.
THIS WENT DIFFERENTLY THAN I EXPECTED.
WHY?! WHY?! WHY?!

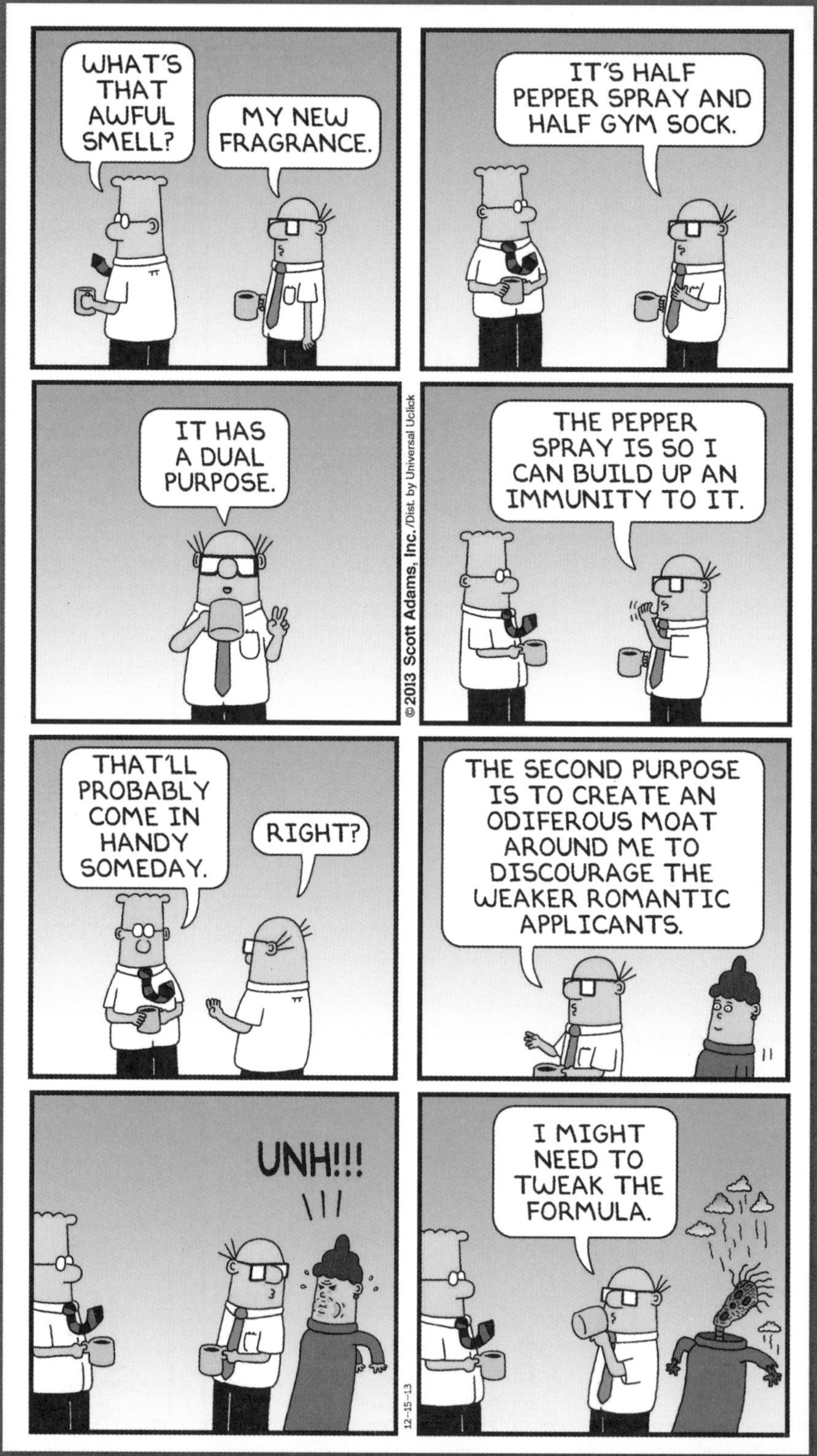
WHAT'S THAT AWFUL SMELL?
MY NEW FRAGRANCE.
IT'S HALF PEPPER SPRAY AND HALF GYM SOCK.
IT HAS A DUAL PURPOSE.
THE PEPPER SPRAY IS SO I CAN BUILD UP AN IMMUNITY TO IT.
THAT'LL PROBABLY COME IN HANDY SOMEDAY.
RIGHT?
THE SECOND PURPOSE IS TO CREATE AN ODIFEROUS MOAT AROUND ME TO DISCOURAGE THE WEAKER ROMANTIC APPLICANTS.
UNH!!!
I MIGHT NEED TO TWEAK THE FORMULA.
12-15-13

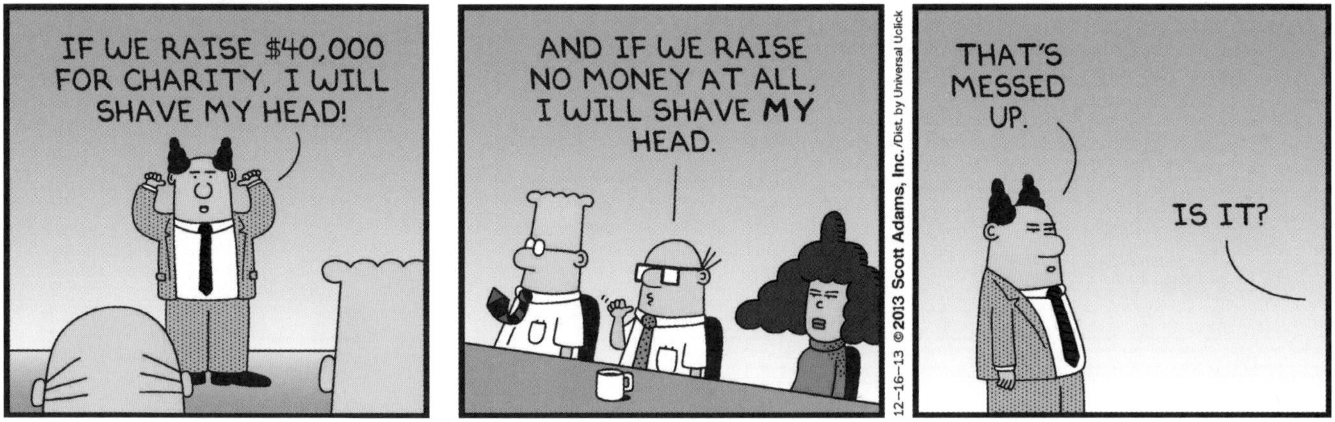
IF WE RAISE $40,000 FOR CHARITY, I WILL SHAVE MY HEAD!
AND IF WE RAISE NO MONEY AT ALL, I WILL SHAVE **MY** HEAD.
12-16-13 ©2013 Scott Adams, Inc./Dist. by Universal Uclick
THAT'S MESSED UP.
IS IT?

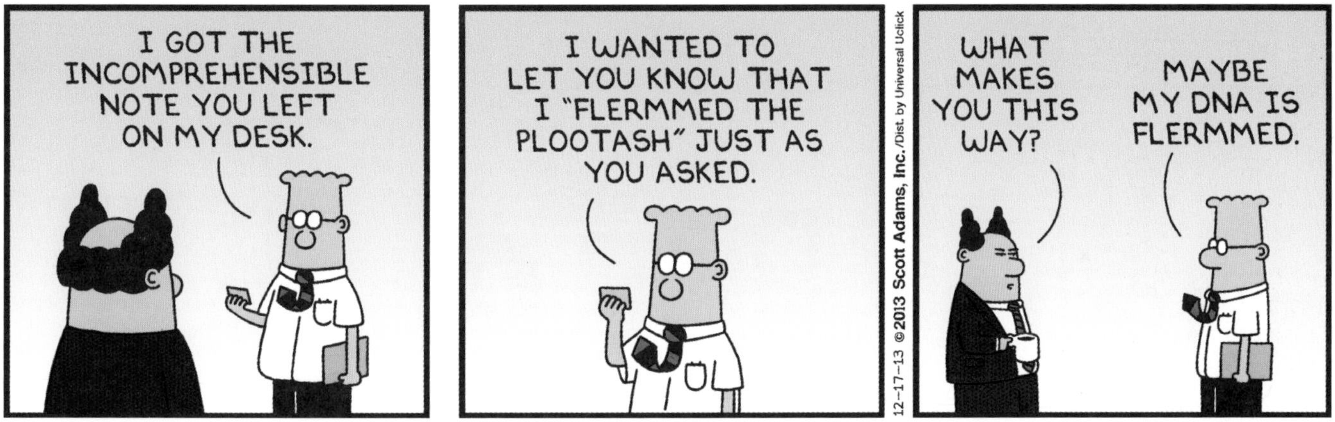
I GOT THE INCOMPREHENSIBLE NOTE YOU LEFT ON MY DESK.
I WANTED TO LET YOU KNOW THAT I "FLERMMED THE PLOOTASH" JUST AS YOU ASKED.
12-17-13 ©2013 Scott Adams, Inc./Dist. by Universal Uclick
WHAT MAKES YOU THIS WAY?
MAYBE MY DNA IS FLERMMED.

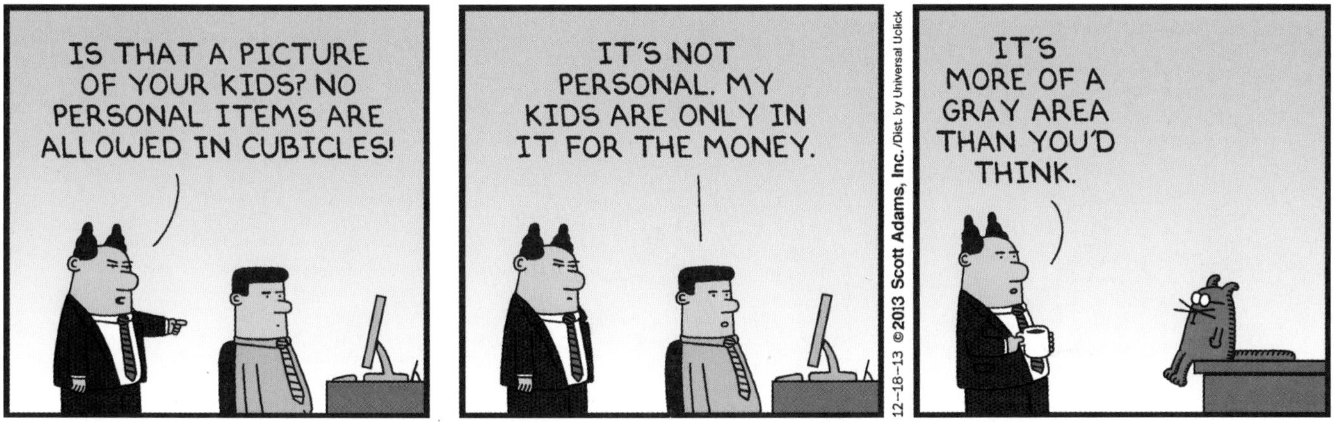
IS THAT A PICTURE OF YOUR KIDS? NO PERSONAL ITEMS ARE ALLOWED IN CUBICLES!
IT'S NOT PERSONAL. MY KIDS ARE ONLY IN IT FOR THE MONEY.
12-18-13 ©2013 Scott Adams, Inc./Dist. by Universal Uclick
IT'S MORE OF A GRAY AREA THAN YOU'D THINK.

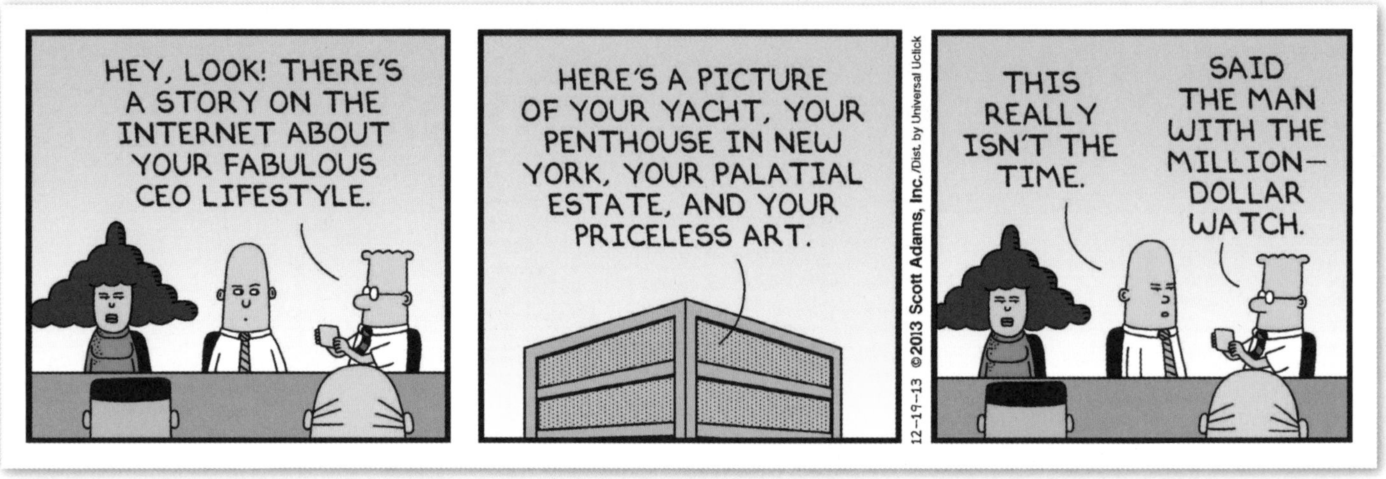
HEY, LOOK! THERE'S A STORY ON THE INTERNET ABOUT YOUR FABULOUS CEO LIFESTYLE.
HERE'S A PICTURE OF YOUR YACHT, YOUR PENTHOUSE IN NEW YORK, YOUR PALATIAL ESTATE, AND YOUR PRICELESS ART.
12-19-13 ©2013 Scott Adams, Inc./Dist. by Universal Uclick
THIS REALLY ISN'T THE TIME.
SAID THE MAN WITH THE MILLION-DOLLAR WATCH.

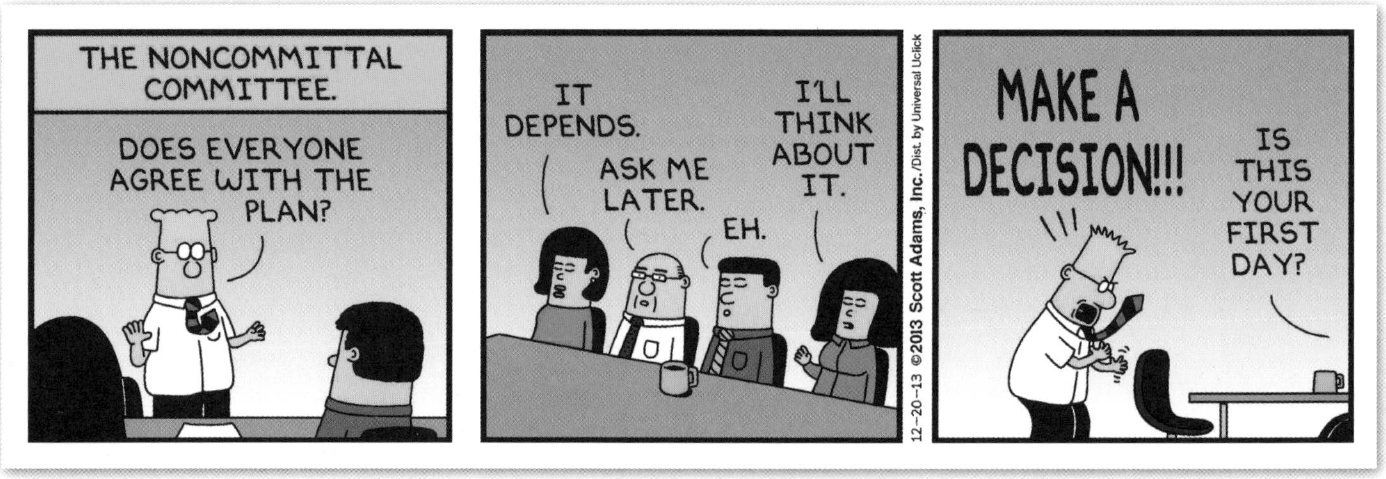
THE NONCOMMITTAL COMMITTEE.
DOES EVERYONE AGREE WITH THE PLAN?
IT DEPENDS.
ASK ME LATER.
EH.
I'LL THINK ABOUT IT.
12-20-13 ©2013 Scott Adams, Inc./Dist. by Universal Uclick
MAKE A DECISION!!!
IS THIS YOUR FIRST DAY?

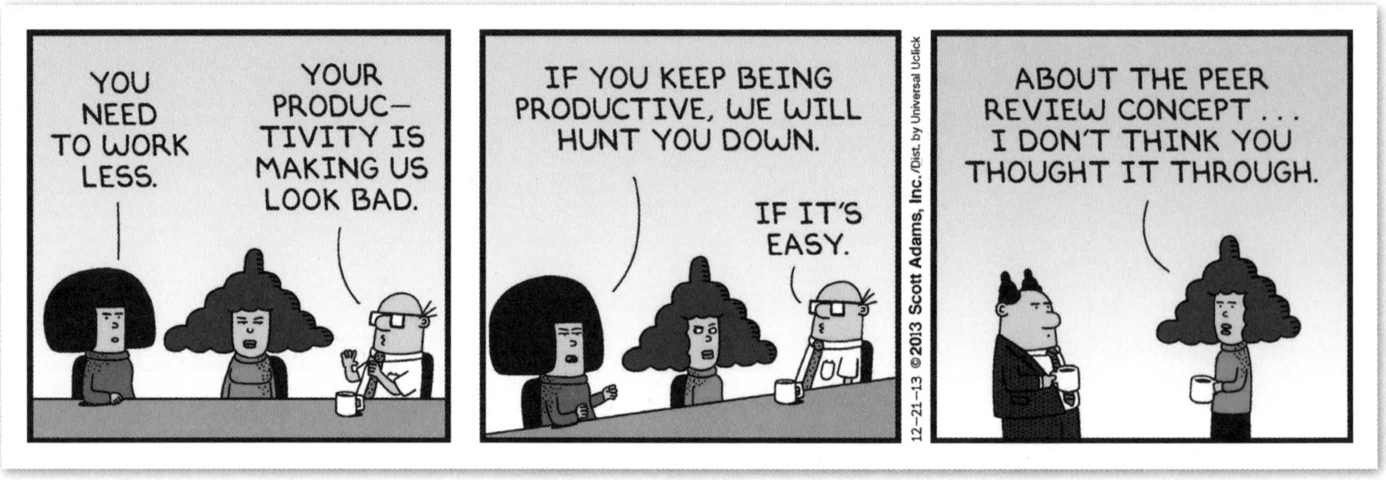
YOU NEED TO WORK LESS.
YOUR PRODUCTIVITY IS MAKING US LOOK BAD.
IF YOU KEEP BEING PRODUCTIVE, WE WILL HUNT YOU DOWN.
IF IT'S EASY.
12-21-13 ©2013 Scott Adams, Inc./Dist. by Universal Uclick
ABOUT THE PEER REVIEW CONCEPT . . . I DON'T THINK YOU THOUGHT IT THROUGH.

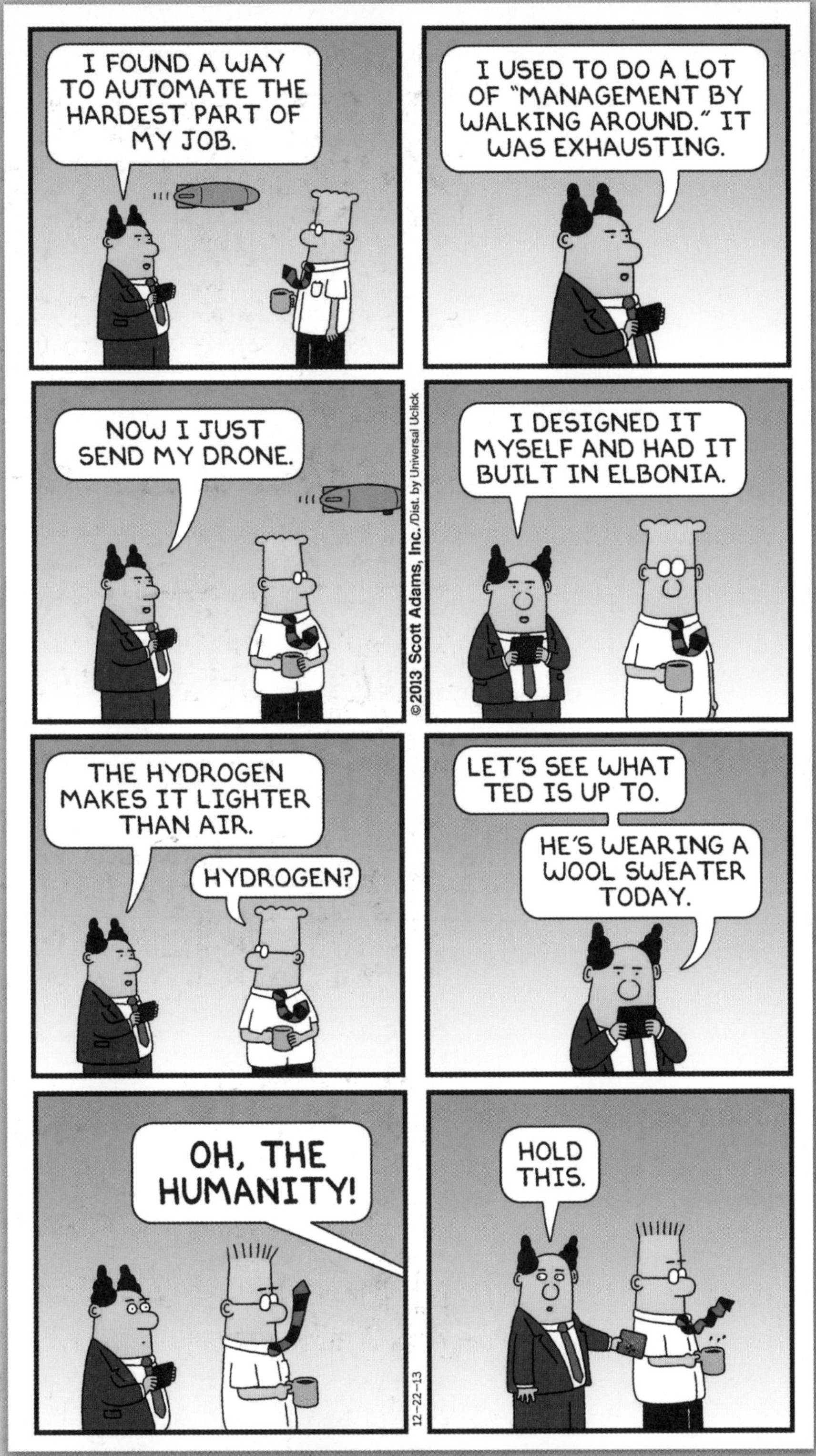
I FOUND A WAY TO AUTOMATE THE HARDEST PART OF MY JOB.
I USED TO DO A LOT OF "MANAGEMENT BY WALKING AROUND." IT WAS EXHAUSTING.
NOW I JUST SEND MY DRONE.
I DESIGNED IT MYSELF AND HAD IT BUILT IN ELBONIA.
THE HYDROGEN MAKES IT LIGHTER THAN AIR.
HYDROGEN?
LET'S SEE WHAT TED IS UP TO.
HE'S WEARING A WOOL SWEATER TODAY.
OH, THE HUMANITY!
HOLD THIS.
©2013 Scott Adams, Inc./Dist. by Universal Uclick
12-22-13

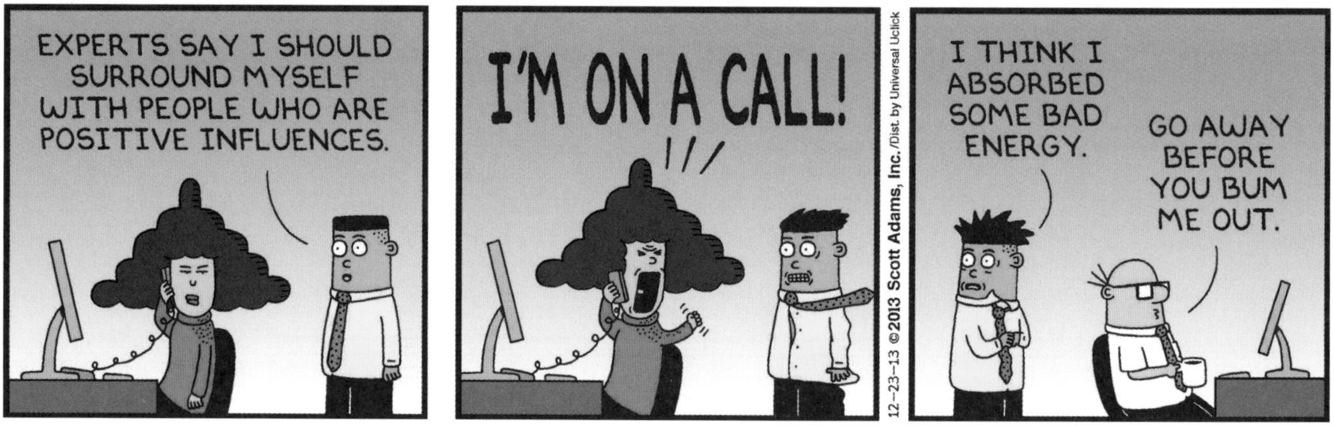
EXPERTS SAY I SHOULD SURROUND MYSELF WITH PEOPLE WHO ARE POSITIVE INFLUENCES.
I'M ON A CALL!
12-23-13 ©2013 Scott Adams, Inc./Dist. by Universal Uclick
I THINK I ABSORBED SOME BAD ENERGY.
GO AWAY BEFORE YOU BUM ME OUT.

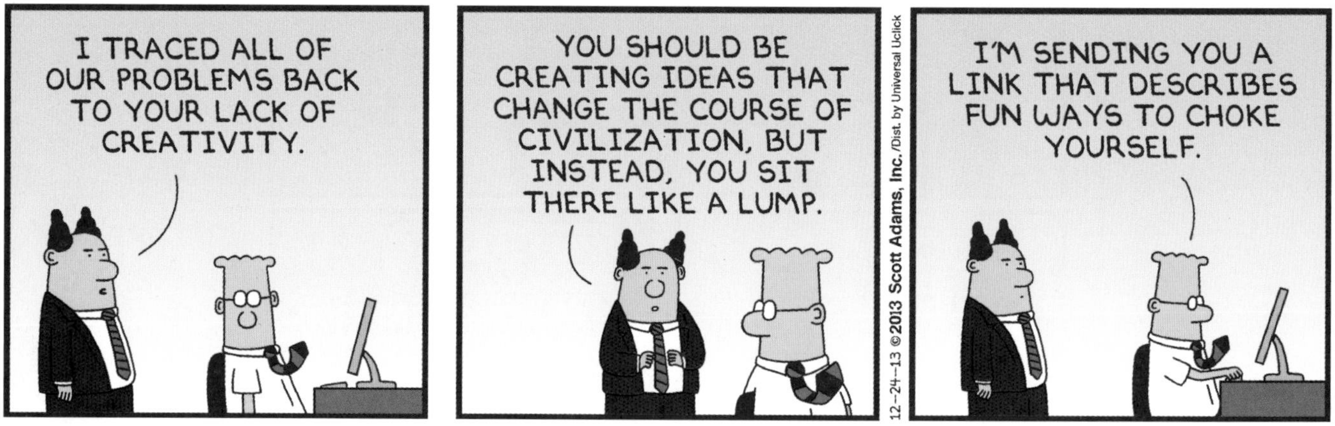
I TRACED ALL OF OUR PROBLEMS BACK TO YOUR LACK OF CREATIVITY.
YOU SHOULD BE CREATING IDEAS THAT CHANGE THE COURSE OF CIVILIZATION, BUT INSTEAD, YOU SIT THERE LIKE A LUMP.
12-24-13 ©2013 Scott Adams, Inc./Dist. by Universal Uclick
I'M SENDING YOU A LINK THAT DESCRIBES FUN WAYS TO CHOKE YOURSELF.

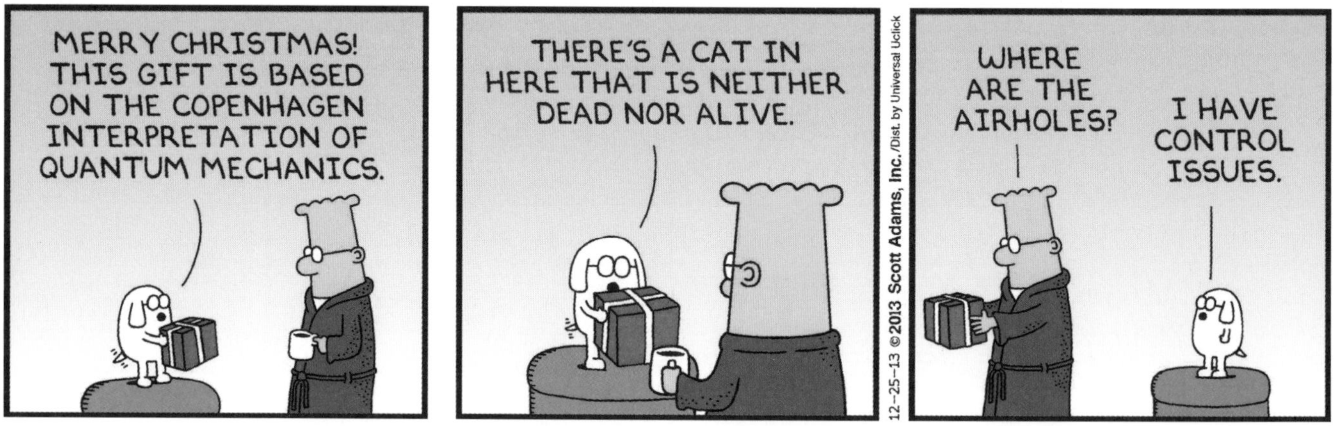
MERRY CHRISTMAS! THIS GIFT IS BASED ON THE COPENHAGEN INTERPRETATION OF QUANTUM MECHANICS.
THERE'S A CAT IN HERE THAT IS NEITHER DEAD NOR ALIVE.
12-25-13 ©2013 Scott Adams, Inc./Dist. by Universal Uclick
WHERE ARE THE AIRHOLES?
I HAVE CONTROL ISSUES.

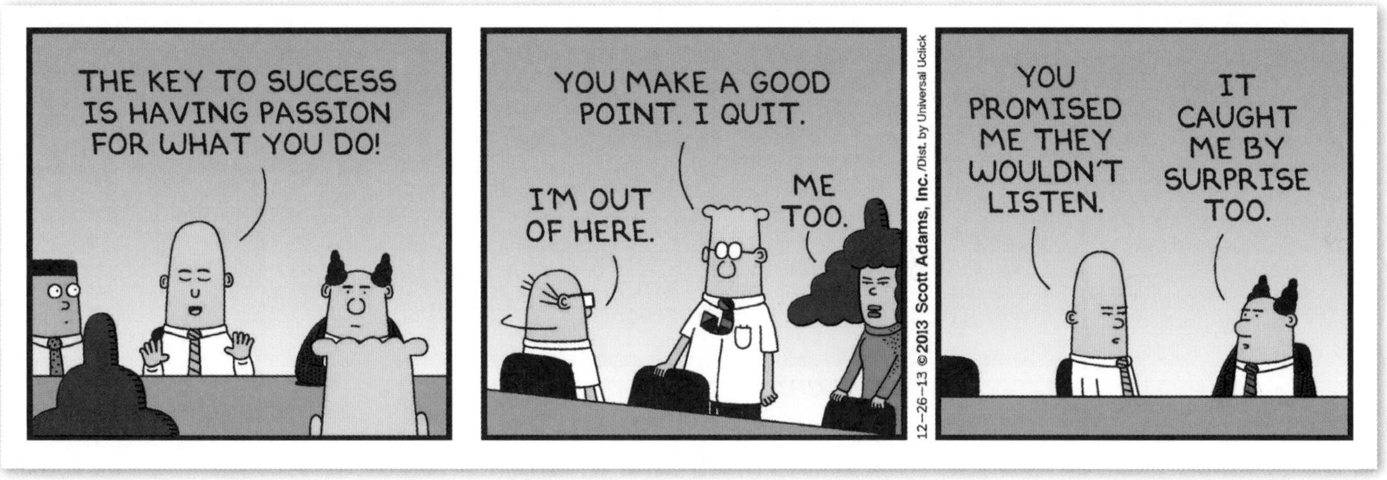
THE KEY TO SUCCESS IS HAVING PASSION FOR WHAT YOU DO!
YOU MAKE A GOOD POINT. I QUIT.
I'M OUT OF HERE.
ME TOO.
12-26-13 ©2013 Scott Adams, Inc./Dist. by Universal Uclick
YOU PROMISED ME THEY WOULDN'T LISTEN.
IT CAUGHT ME BY SURPRISE TOO.

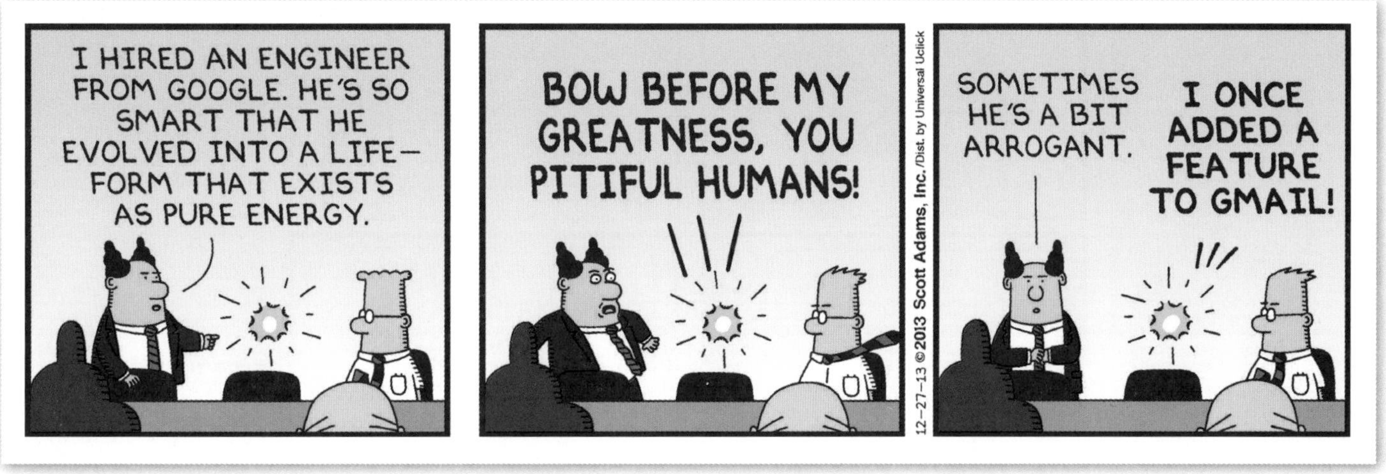
I HIRED AN ENGINEER FROM GOOGLE. HE'S SO SMART THAT HE EVOLVED INTO A LIFE-FORM THAT EXISTS AS PURE ENERGY.
BOW BEFORE MY GREATNESS, YOU PITIFUL HUMANS!
12-27-13 ©2013 Scott Adams, Inc./Dist. by Universal Uclick
SOMETIMES HE'S A BIT ARROGANT.
I ONCE ADDED A FEATURE TO GMAIL!

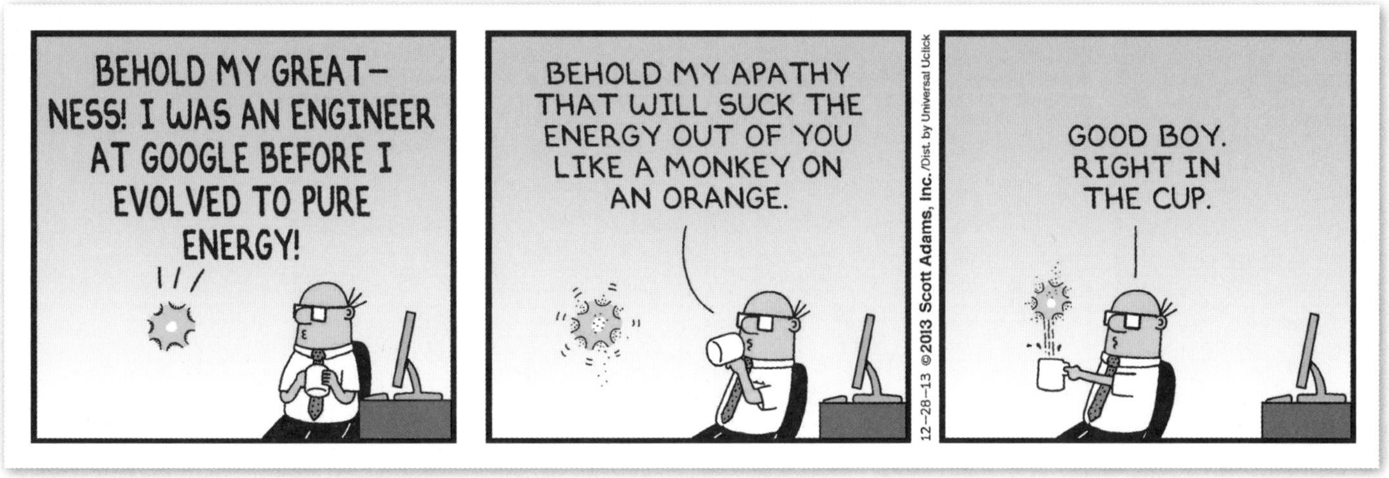
BEHOLD MY GREAT-NESS! I WAS AN ENGINEER AT GOOGLE BEFORE I EVOLVED TO PURE ENERGY!
BEHOLD MY APATHY THAT WILL SUCK THE ENERGY OUT OF YOU LIKE A MONKEY ON AN ORANGE.
12-28-13 ©2013 Scott Adams, Inc./Dist. by Universal Uclick
GOOD BOY. RIGHT IN THE CUP.

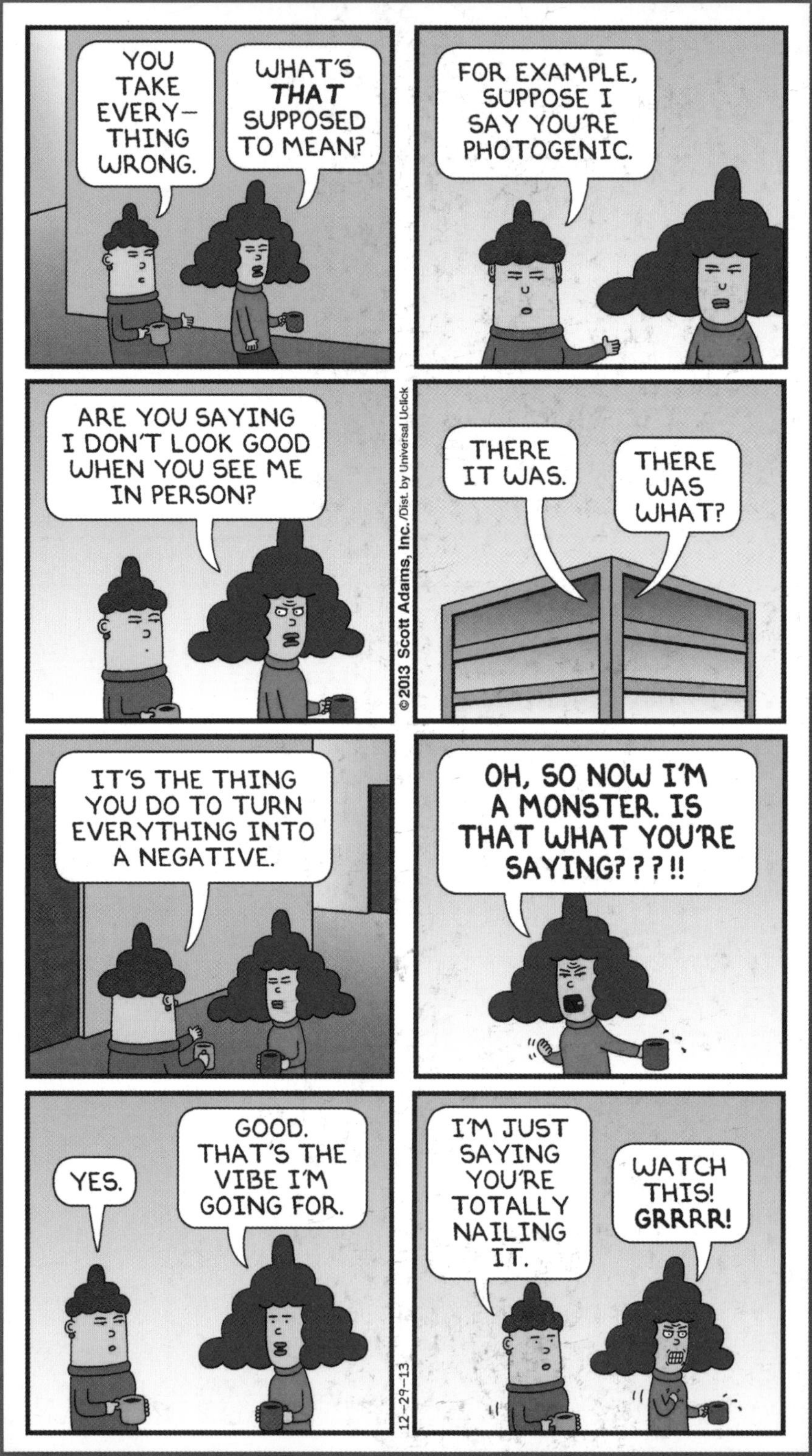

YOU TAKE EVERY-THING WRONG.
WHAT'S **THAT** SUPPOSED TO MEAN?
FOR EXAMPLE, SUPPOSE I SAY YOU'RE PHOTOGENIC.
ARE YOU SAYING I DON'T LOOK GOOD WHEN YOU SEE ME IN PERSON?
THERE IT WAS.
THERE WAS WHAT?
IT'S THE THING YOU DO TO TURN EVERYTHING INTO A NEGATIVE.
OH, SO NOW I'M A MONSTER. IS THAT WHAT YOU'RE SAYING???!!
YES.
GOOD. THAT'S THE VIBE I'M GOING FOR.
I'M JUST SAYING YOU'RE TOTALLY NAILING IT.
WATCH THIS! **GRRRR!**
©2013 Scott Adams, Inc./Dist. by Universal Uclick
12-29-13

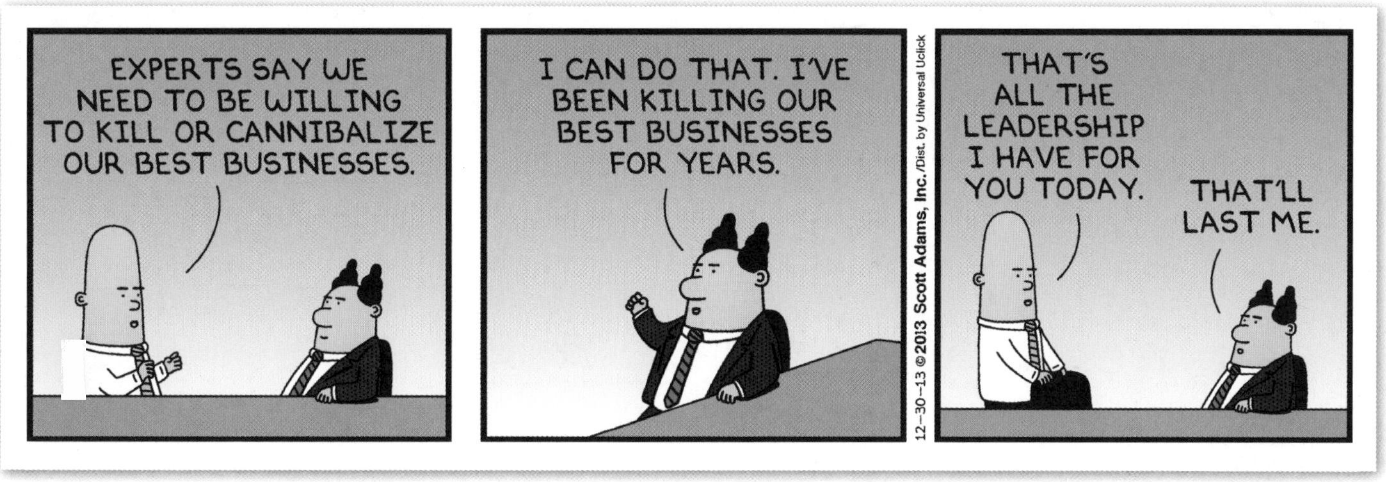
EXPERTS SAY WE NEED TO BE WILLING TO KILL OR CANNIBALIZE OUR BEST BUSINESSES.
I CAN DO THAT. I'VE BEEN KILLING OUR BEST BUSINESSES FOR YEARS.
THAT'S ALL THE LEADERSHIP I HAVE FOR YOU TODAY.
THAT'LL LAST ME.
12-30-13 ©2013 Scott Adams, Inc./Dist. by Universal Uclick

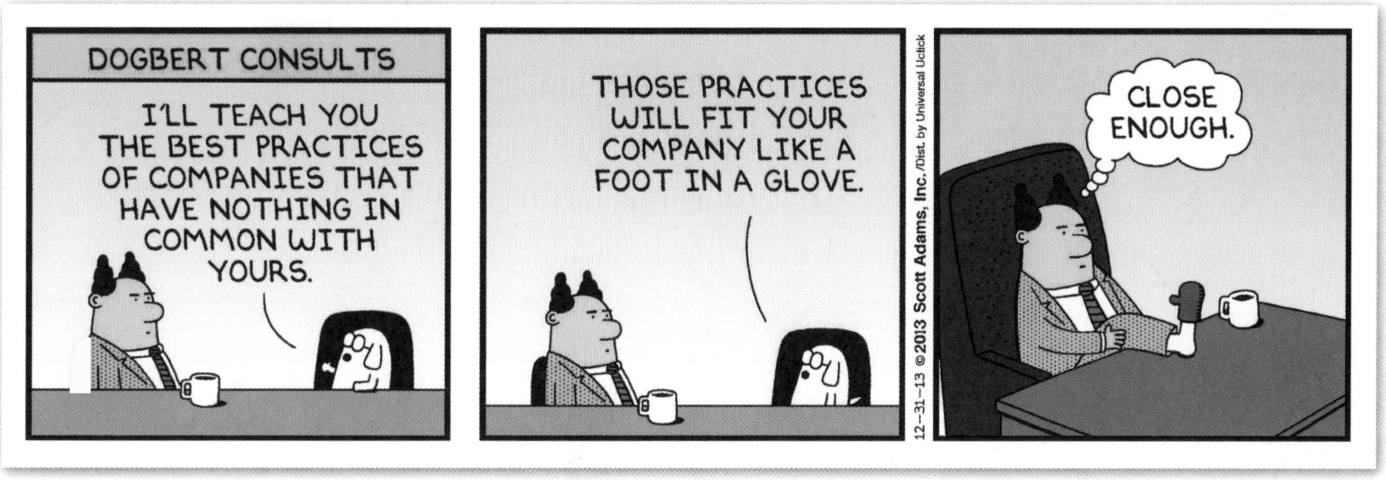
DOGBERT CONSULTS
I'LL TEACH YOU THE BEST PRACTICES OF COMPANIES THAT HAVE NOTHING IN COMMON WITH YOURS.
THOSE PRACTICES WILL FIT YOUR COMPANY LIKE A FOOT IN A GLOVE.
CLOSE ENOUGH.
12-31-13 ©2013 Scott Adams, Inc./Dist. by Universal Uclick

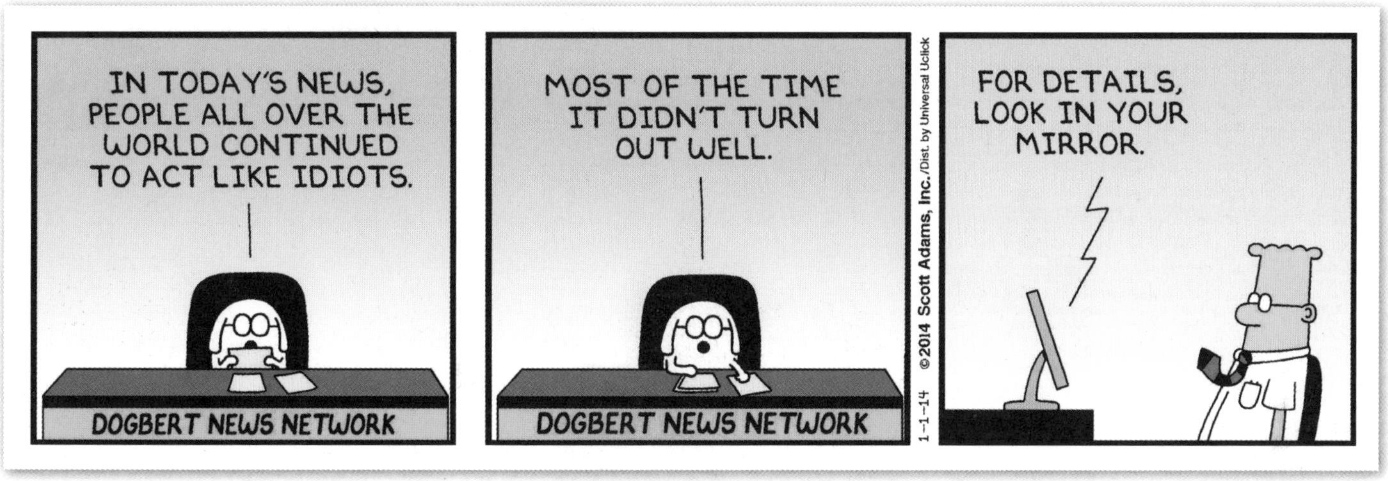
IN TODAY'S NEWS, PEOPLE ALL OVER THE WORLD CONTINUED TO ACT LIKE IDIOTS.
DOGBERT NEWS NETWORK
MOST OF THE TIME IT DIDN'T TURN OUT WELL.
DOGBERT NEWS NETWORK
FOR DETAILS, LOOK IN YOUR MIRROR.
1-1-14 ©2014 Scott Adams, Inc./Dist. by Universal Uclick

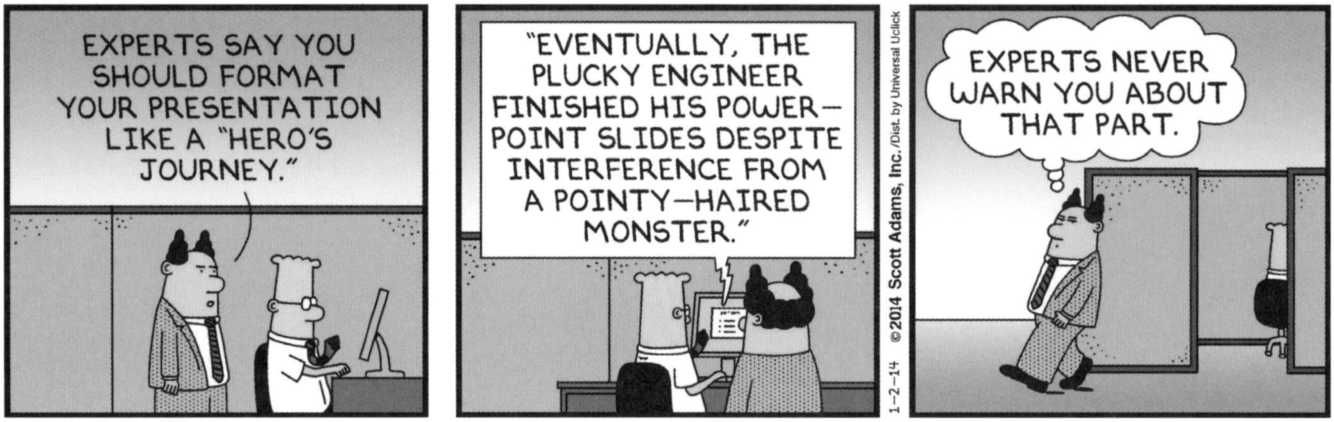
EXPERTS SAY YOU SHOULD FORMAT YOUR PRESENTATION LIKE A "HERO'S JOURNEY."
"EVENTUALLY, THE PLUCKY ENGINEER FINISHED HIS POWER-POINT SLIDES DESPITE INTERFERENCE FROM A POINTY-HAIRED MONSTER."
1-2-14 ©2014 Scott Adams, Inc./Dist. by Universal Uclick
EXPERTS NEVER WARN YOU ABOUT THAT PART.

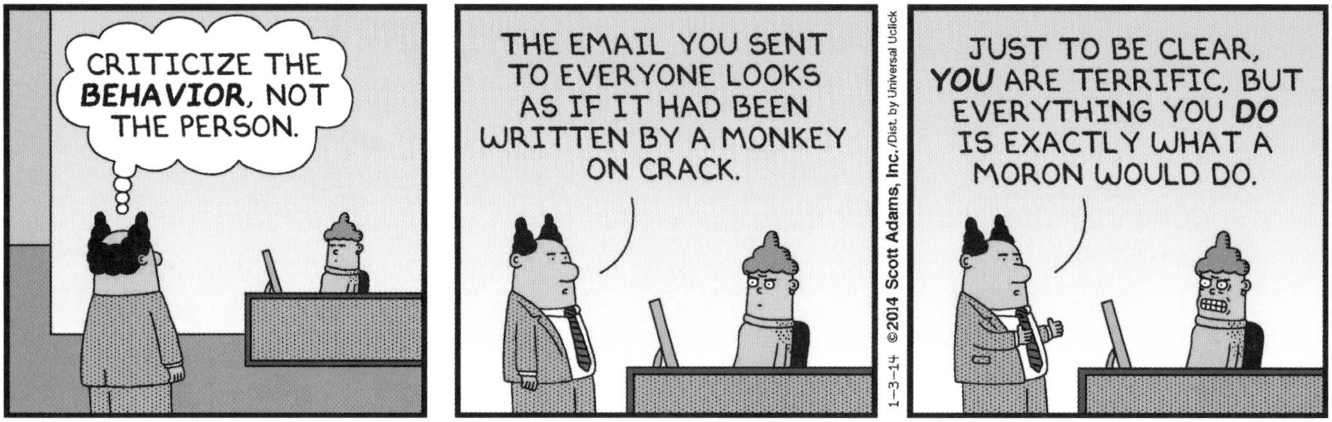
CRITICIZE THE **BEHAVIOR**, NOT THE PERSON.
THE EMAIL YOU SENT TO EVERYONE LOOKS AS IF IT HAD BEEN WRITTEN BY A MONKEY ON CRACK.
1-3-14 ©2014 Scott Adams, Inc./Dist. by Universal Uclick
JUST TO BE CLEAR, **YOU** ARE TERRIFIC, BUT EVERYTHING YOU **DO** IS EXACTLY WHAT A MORON WOULD DO.

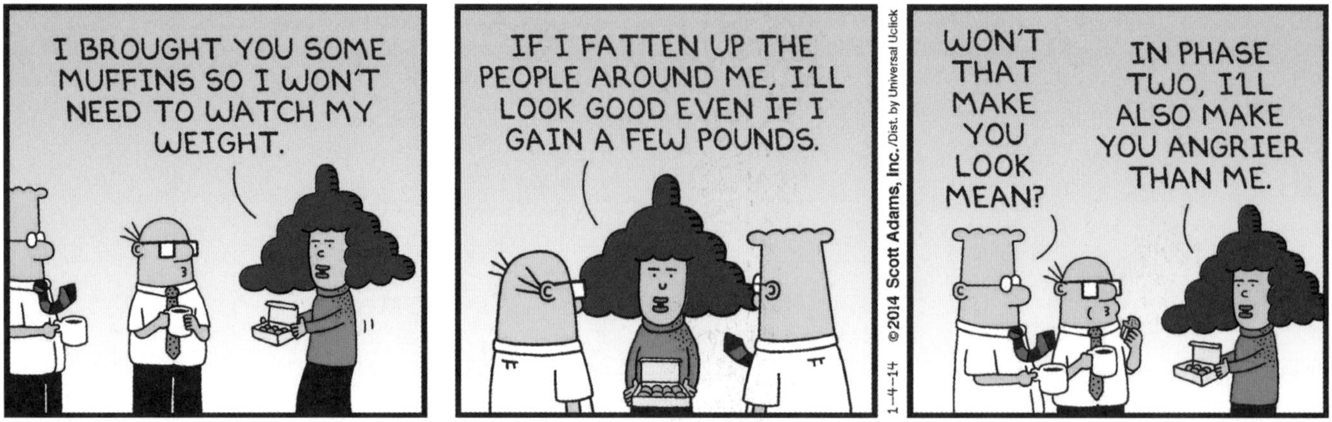
I BROUGHT YOU SOME MUFFINS SO I WON'T NEED TO WATCH MY WEIGHT.
IF I FATTEN UP THE PEOPLE AROUND ME, I'LL LOOK GOOD EVEN IF I GAIN A FEW POUNDS.
1-4-14 ©2014 Scott Adams, Inc./Dist. by Universal Uclick
WON'T THAT MAKE YOU LOOK MEAN?
IN PHASE TWO, I'LL ALSO MAKE YOU ANGRIER THAN ME.

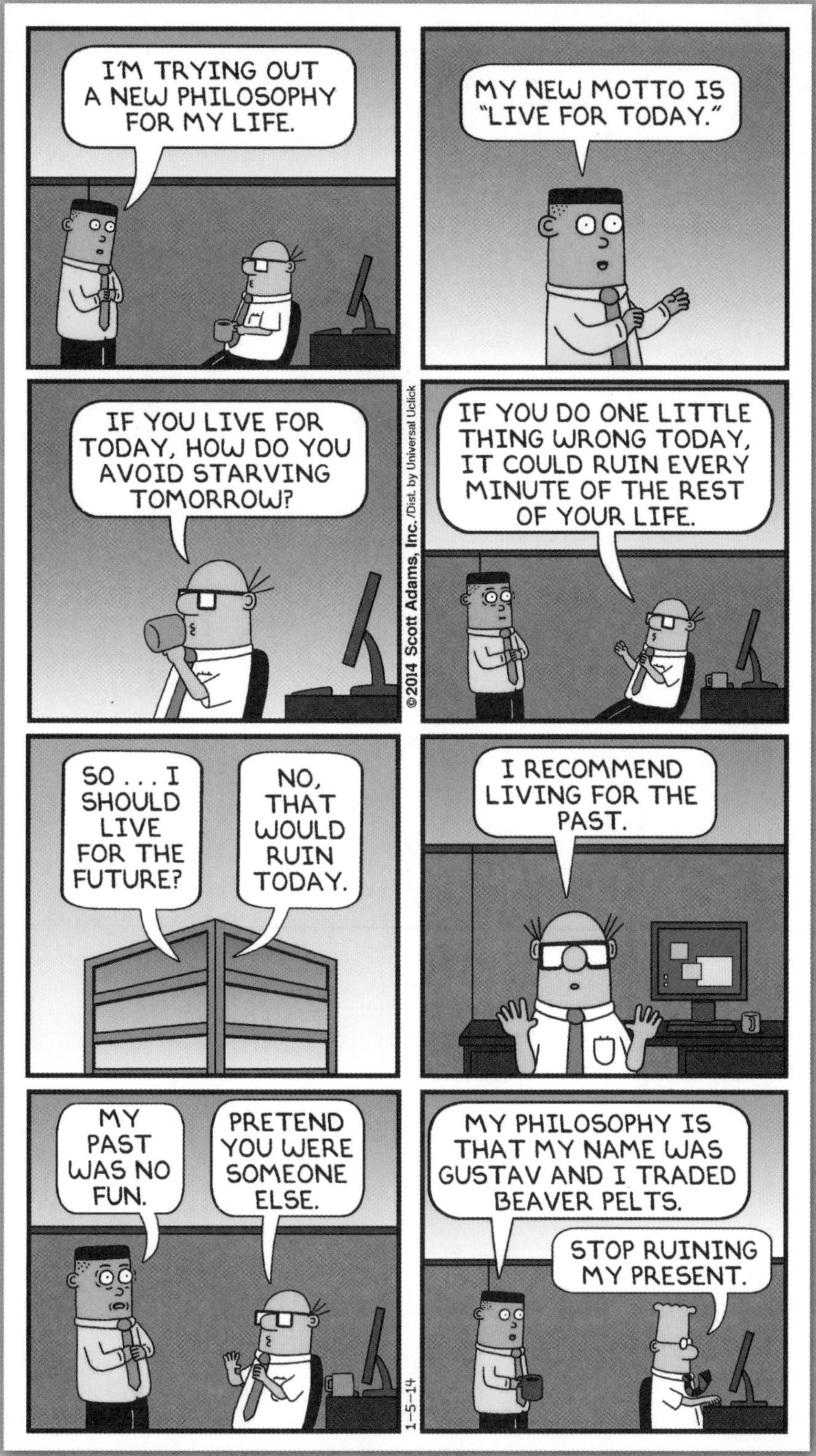
I'M TRYING OUT A NEW PHILOSOPHY FOR MY LIFE.
MY NEW MOTTO IS "LIVE FOR TODAY."
IF YOU LIVE FOR TODAY, HOW DO YOU AVOID STARVING TOMORROW?
IF YOU DO ONE LITTLE THING WRONG TODAY, IT COULD RUIN EVERY MINUTE OF THE REST OF YOUR LIFE.
SO . . . I SHOULD LIVE FOR THE FUTURE?
NO, THAT WOULD RUIN TODAY.
I RECOMMEND LIVING FOR THE PAST.
MY PAST WAS NO FUN.
PRETEND YOU WERE SOMEONE ELSE.
MY PHILOSOPHY IS THAT MY NAME WAS GUSTAV AND I TRADED BEAVER PELTS.
STOP RUINING MY PRESENT.
©2014 Scott Adams, Inc./Dist. by Universal Uclick
1-5-14

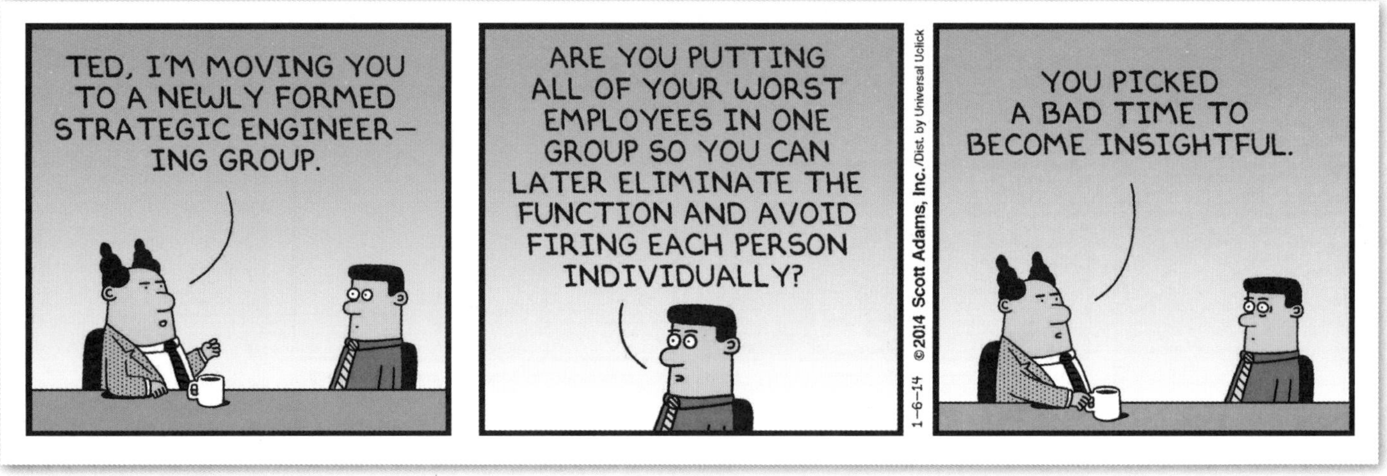
TED, I'M MOVING YOU TO A NEWLY FORMED STRATEGIC ENGINEER-ING GROUP.
ARE YOU PUTTING ALL OF YOUR WORST EMPLOYEES IN ONE GROUP SO YOU CAN LATER ELIMINATE THE FUNCTION AND AVOID FIRING EACH PERSON INDIVIDUALLY?
1-6-14 ©2014 Scott Adams, Inc./Dist. by Universal Uclick
YOU PICKED A BAD TIME TO BECOME INSIGHTFUL.

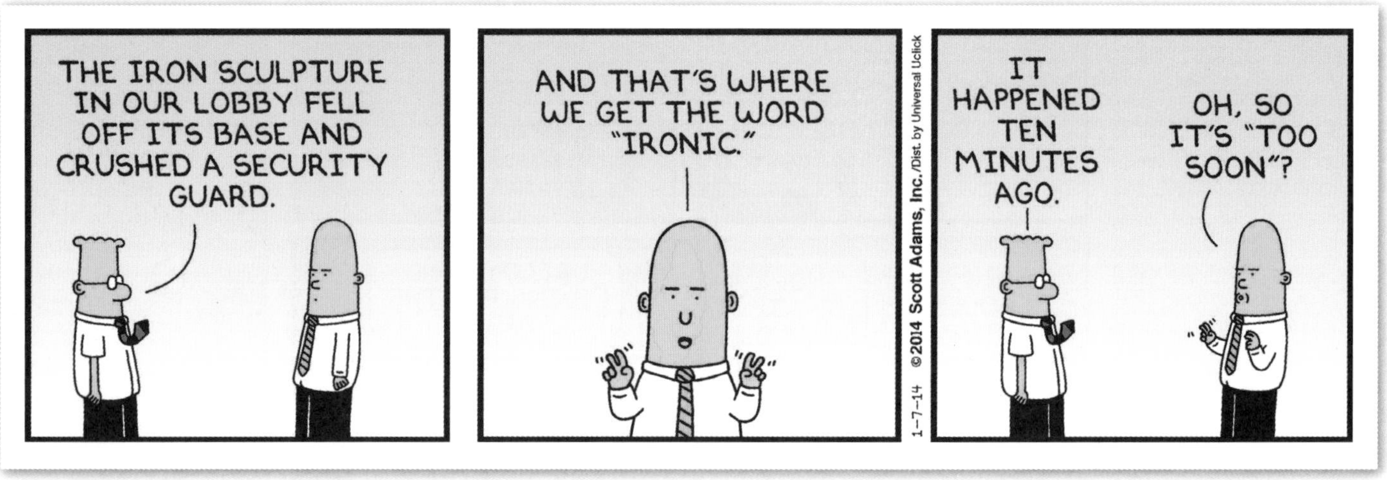
THE IRON SCULPTURE IN OUR LOBBY FELL OFF ITS BASE AND CRUSHED A SECURITY GUARD.
AND THAT'S WHERE WE GET THE WORD "IRONIC."
1-7-14 ©2014 Scott Adams, Inc./Dist. by Universal Uclick
IT HAPPENED TEN MINUTES AGO.
OH, SO IT'S "TOO SOON"?

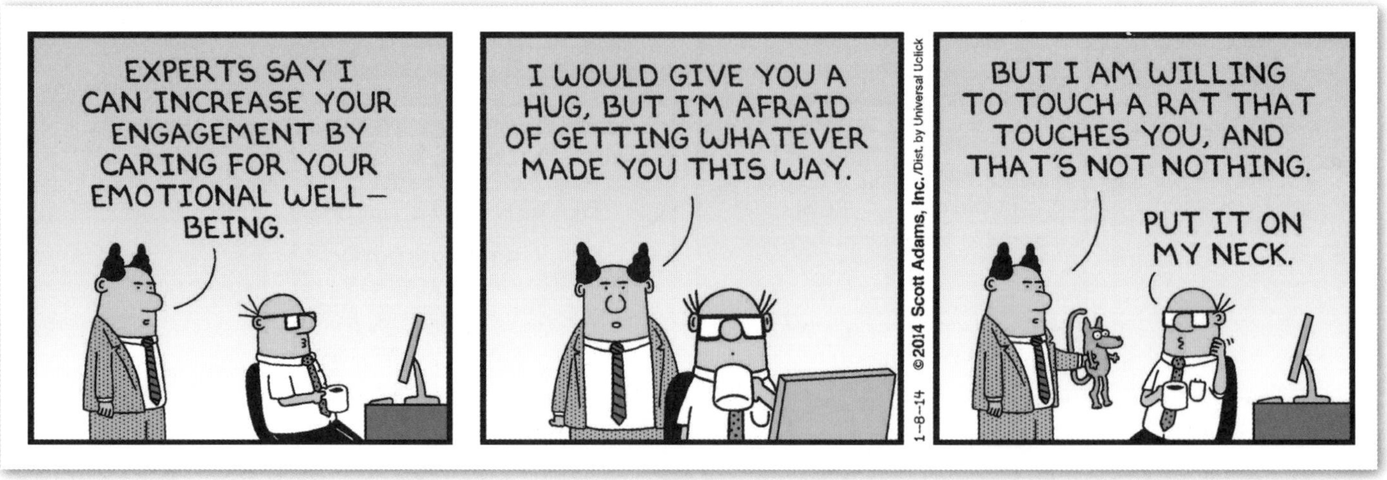
EXPERTS SAY I CAN INCREASE YOUR ENGAGEMENT BY CARING FOR YOUR EMOTIONAL WELL-BEING.
I WOULD GIVE YOU A HUG, BUT I'M AFRAID OF GETTING WHATEVER MADE YOU THIS WAY.
1-8-14 ©2014 Scott Adams, Inc./Dist. by Universal Uclick
BUT I AM WILLING TO TOUCH A RAT THAT TOUCHES YOU, AND THAT'S NOT NOTHING.
PUT IT ON MY NECK.

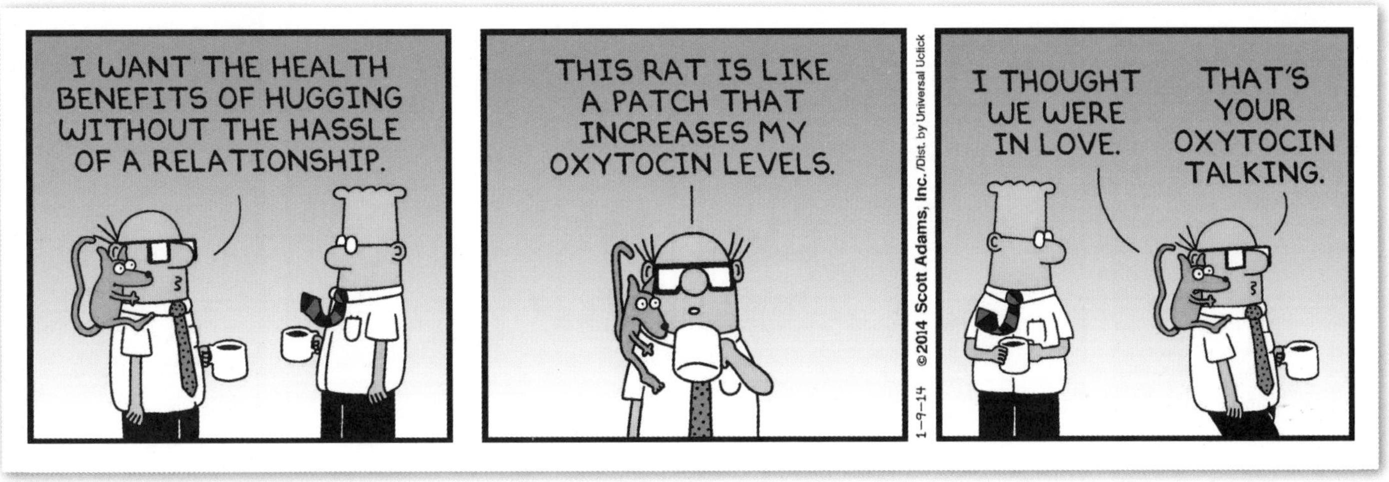
I WANT THE HEALTH BENEFITS OF HUGGING WITHOUT THE HASSLE OF A RELATIONSHIP.
THIS RAT IS LIKE A PATCH THAT INCREASES MY OXYTOCIN LEVELS.
1-9-14 ©2014 Scott Adams, Inc./Dist. by Universal Uclick
I THOUGHT WE WERE IN LOVE.
THAT'S YOUR OXYTOCIN TALKING.

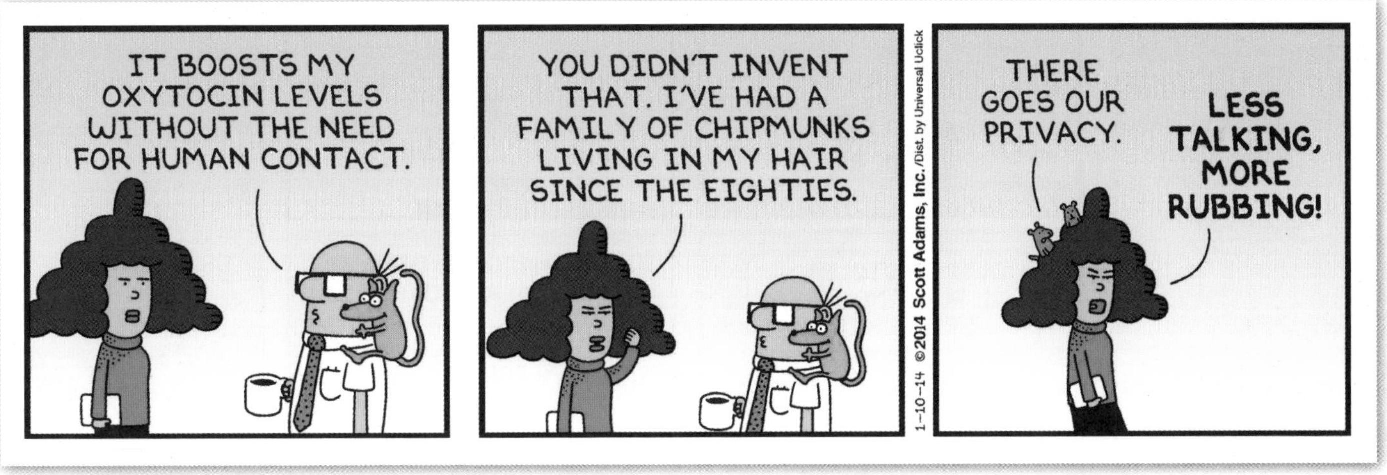
IT BOOSTS MY OXYTOCIN LEVELS WITHOUT THE NEED FOR HUMAN CONTACT.
YOU DIDN'T INVENT THAT. I'VE HAD A FAMILY OF CHIPMUNKS LIVING IN MY HAIR SINCE THE EIGHTIES.
1-10-14 ©2014 Scott Adams, Inc./Dist. by Universal Uclick
THERE GOES OUR PRIVACY.
LESS TALKING, MORE RUBBING!

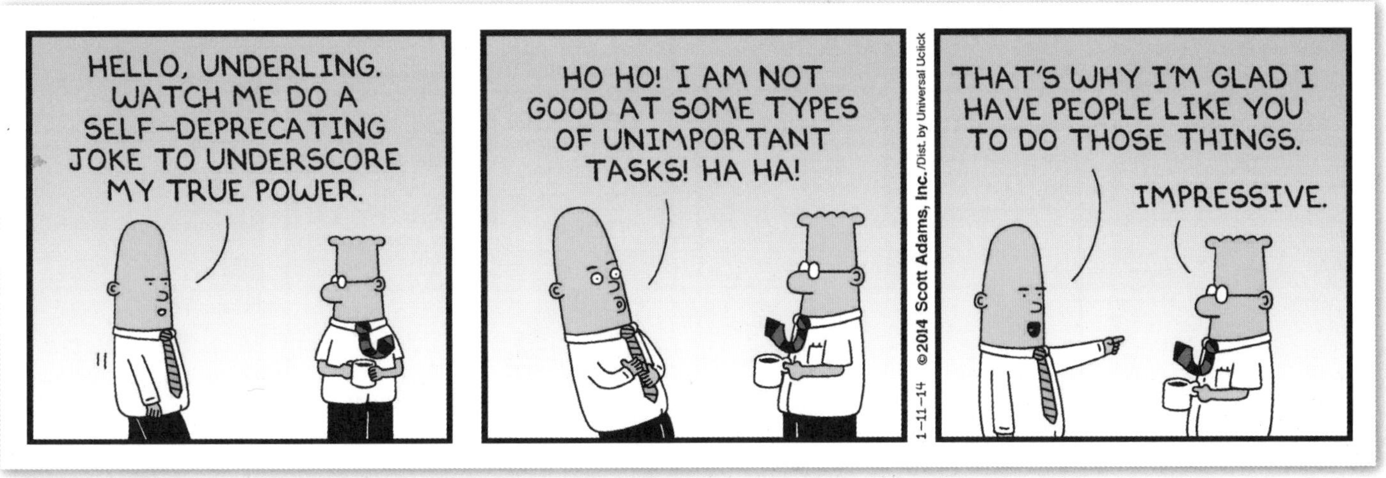
HELLO, UNDERLING. WATCH ME DO A SELF-DEPRECATING JOKE TO UNDERSCORE MY TRUE POWER.
HO HO! I AM NOT GOOD AT SOME TYPES OF UNIMPORTANT TASKS! HA HA!
1-11-14 ©2014 Scott Adams, Inc./Dist. by Universal Uclick
THAT'S WHY I'M GLAD I HAVE PEOPLE LIKE YOU TO DO THOSE THINGS.
IMPRESSIVE.

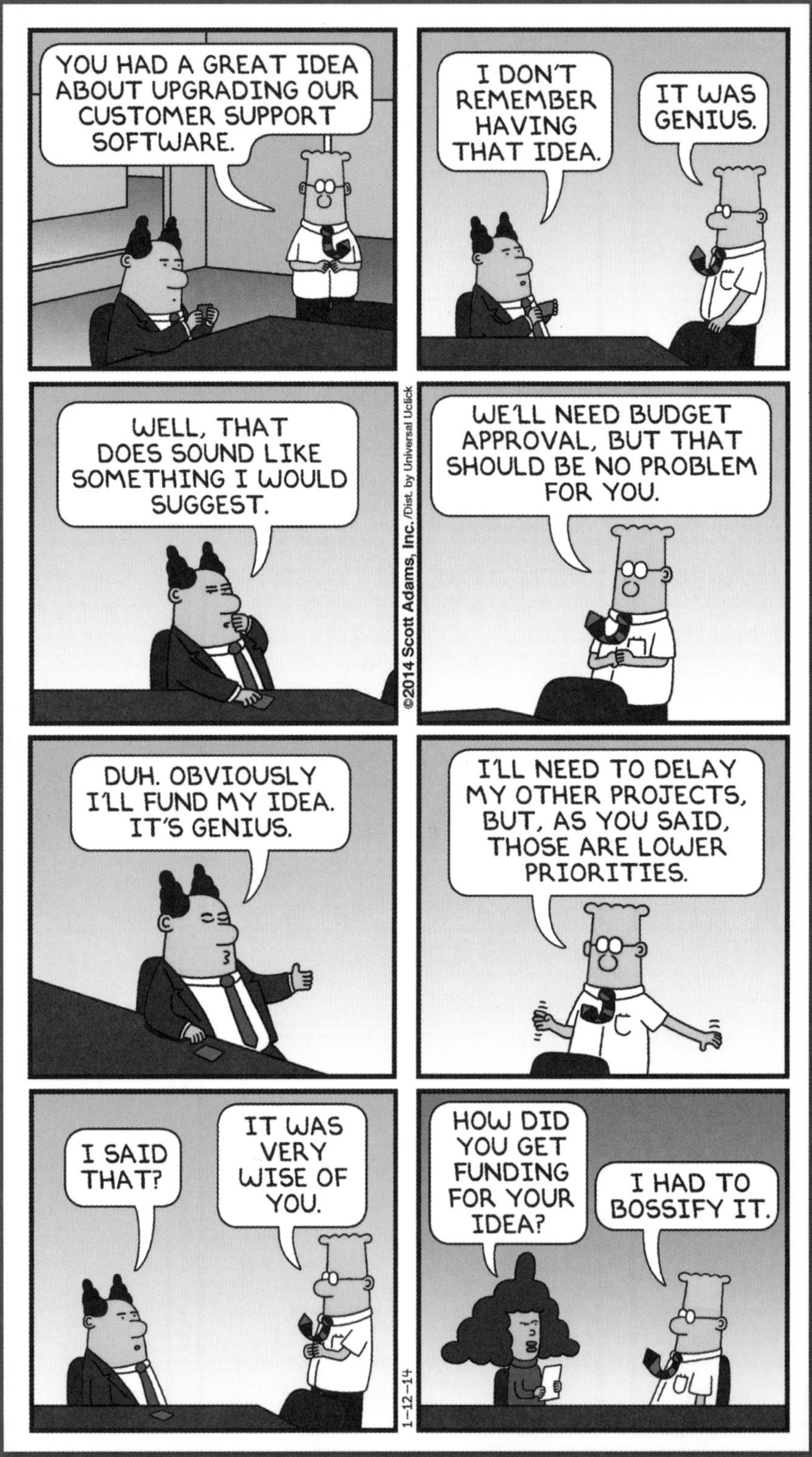
YOU HAD A GREAT IDEA ABOUT UPGRADING OUR CUSTOMER SUPPORT SOFTWARE.
I DON'T REMEMBER HAVING THAT IDEA.
IT WAS GENIUS.
WELL, THAT DOES SOUND LIKE SOMETHING I WOULD SUGGEST.
WE'LL NEED BUDGET APPROVAL, BUT THAT SHOULD BE NO PROBLEM FOR YOU.
DUH. OBVIOUSLY I'LL FUND MY IDEA. IT'S GENIUS.
I'LL NEED TO DELAY MY OTHER PROJECTS, BUT, AS YOU SAID, THOSE ARE LOWER PRIORITIES.
I SAID THAT?
IT WAS VERY WISE OF YOU.
HOW DID YOU GET FUNDING FOR YOUR IDEA?
I HAD TO BOSSIFY IT.
©2014 Scott Adams, Inc./Dist. by Universal Uclick
1-12-14

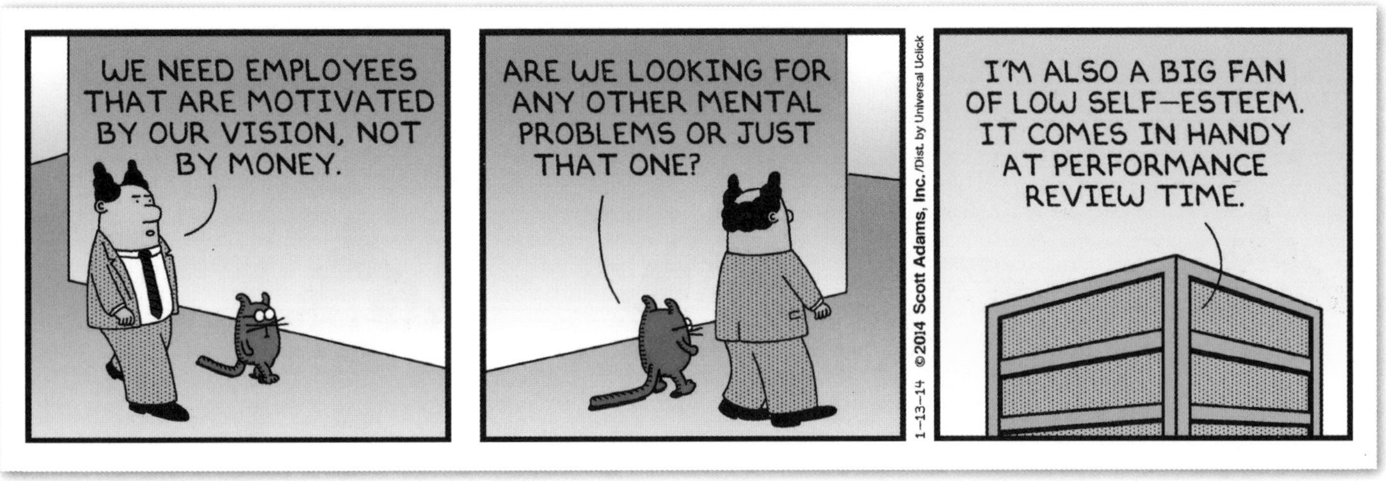
WE NEED EMPLOYEES THAT ARE MOTIVATED BY OUR VISION, NOT BY MONEY.
ARE WE LOOKING FOR ANY OTHER MENTAL PROBLEMS OR JUST THAT ONE?
I'M ALSO A BIG FAN OF LOW SELF-ESTEEM. IT COMES IN HANDY AT PERFORMANCE REVIEW TIME.
1-13-14 ©2014 Scott Adams, Inc./Dist. by Universal Uclick

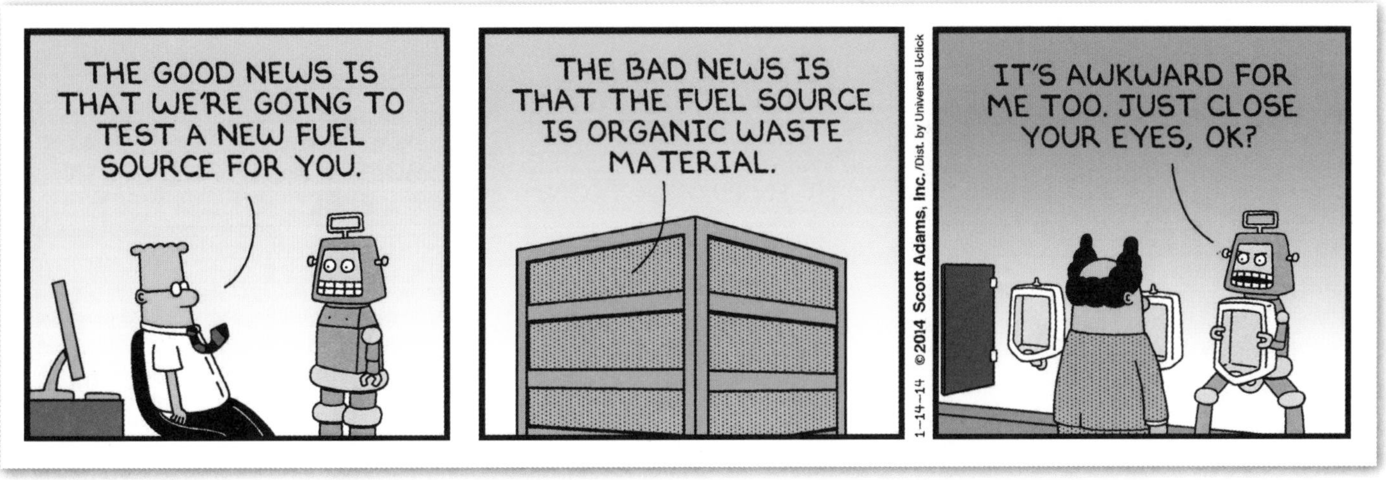
THE GOOD NEWS IS THAT WE'RE GOING TO TEST A NEW FUEL SOURCE FOR YOU.
THE BAD NEWS IS THAT THE FUEL SOURCE IS ORGANIC WASTE MATERIAL.
IT'S AWKWARD FOR ME TOO. JUST CLOSE YOUR EYES, OK?
1-14-14 ©2014 Scott Adams, Inc./Dist. by Universal Uclick

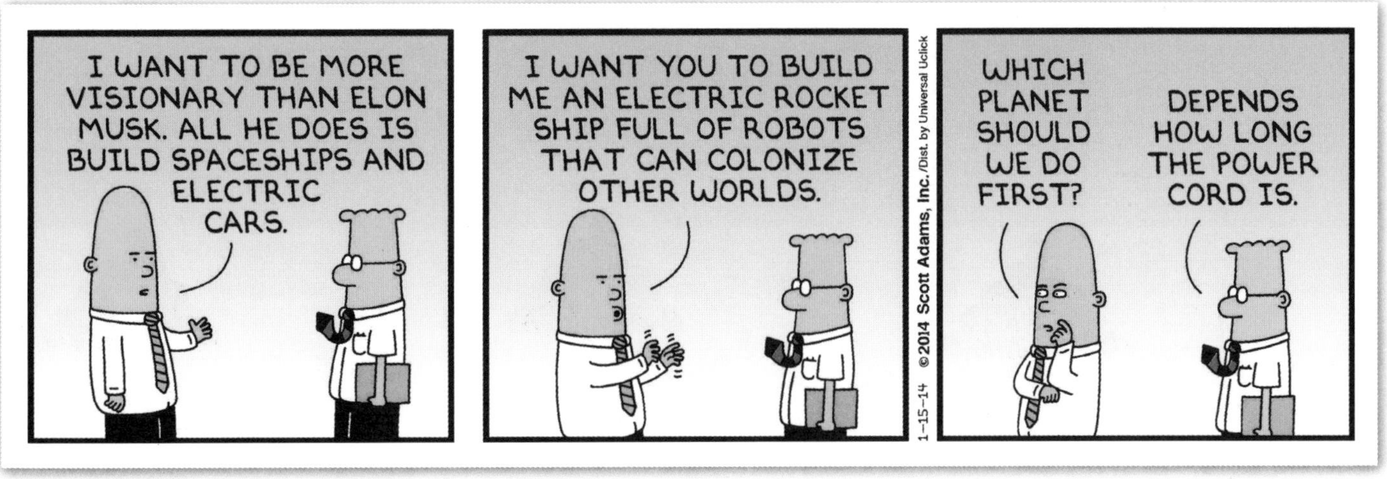
I WANT TO BE MORE VISIONARY THAN ELON MUSK. ALL HE DOES IS BUILD SPACESHIPS AND ELECTRIC CARS.
I WANT YOU TO BUILD ME AN ELECTRIC ROCKET SHIP FULL OF ROBOTS THAT CAN COLONIZE OTHER WORLDS.
WHICH PLANET SHOULD WE DO FIRST?
DEPENDS HOW LONG THE POWER CORD IS.
1-15-14 ©2014 Scott Adams, Inc./Dist. by Universal Uclick

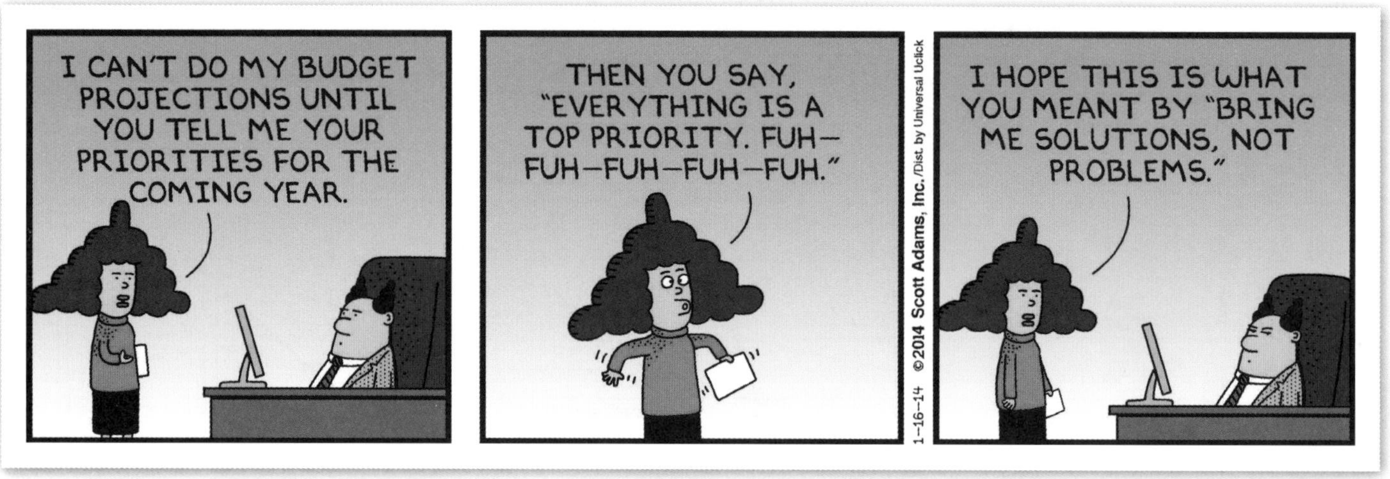
I CAN'T DO MY BUDGET PROJECTIONS UNTIL YOU TELL ME YOUR PRIORITIES FOR THE COMING YEAR.
THEN YOU SAY, "EVERYTHING IS A TOP PRIORITY. FUH–FUH–FUH–FUH–FUH."
1-16-14 ©2014 Scott Adams, Inc./Dist. by Universal Uclick
I HOPE THIS IS WHAT YOU MEANT BY "BRING ME SOLUTIONS, NOT PROBLEMS."

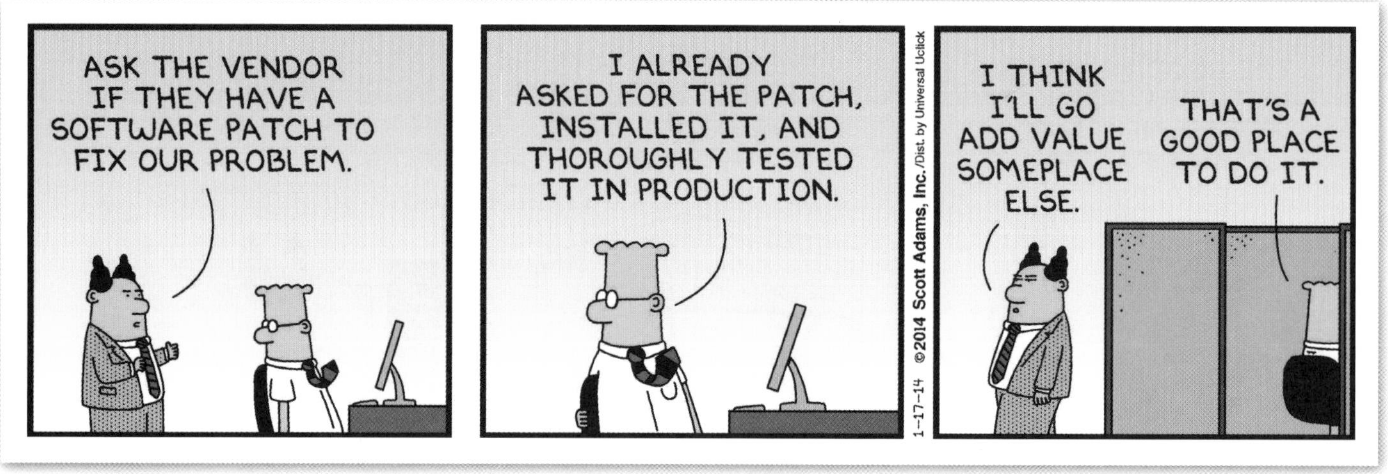
ASK THE VENDOR IF THEY HAVE A SOFTWARE PATCH TO FIX OUR PROBLEM.
I ALREADY ASKED FOR THE PATCH, INSTALLED IT, AND THOROUGHLY TESTED IT IN PRODUCTION.
1-17-14 ©2014 Scott Adams, Inc./Dist. by Universal Uclick
I THINK I'LL GO ADD VALUE SOMEPLACE ELSE.
THAT'S A GOOD PLACE TO DO IT.

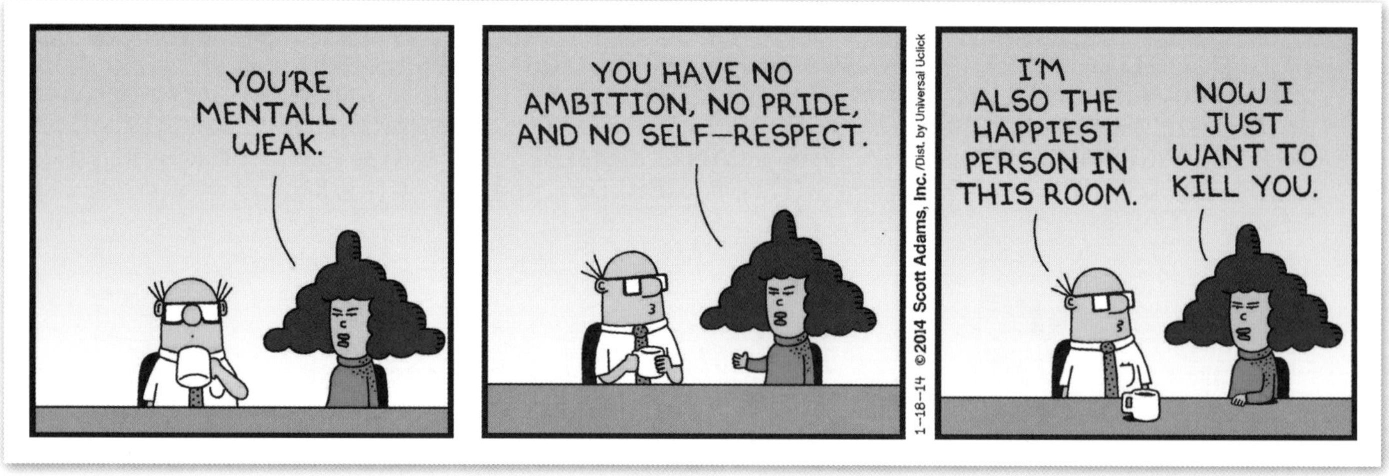
YOU'RE MENTALLY WEAK.
YOU HAVE NO AMBITION, NO PRIDE, AND NO SELF–RESPECT.
1-18-14 ©2014 Scott Adams, Inc./Dist. by Universal Uclick
I'M ALSO THE HAPPIEST PERSON IN THIS ROOM.
NOW I JUST WANT TO KILL YOU.

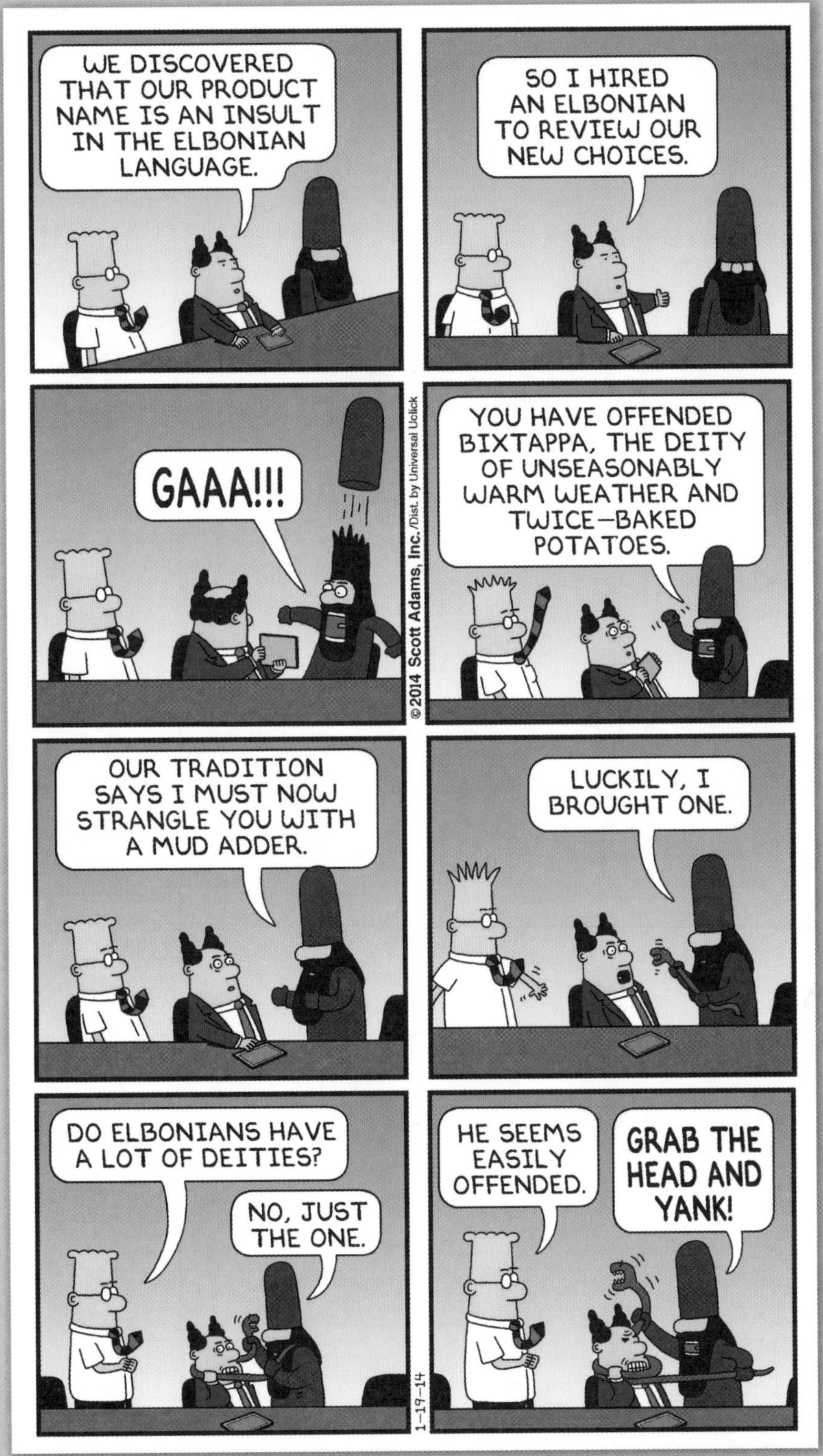
WE DISCOVERED THAT OUR PRODUCT NAME IS AN INSULT IN THE ELBONIAN LANGUAGE.
SO I HIRED AN ELBONIAN TO REVIEW OUR NEW CHOICES.
GAAA!!!
YOU HAVE OFFENDED BIXTAPPA, THE DEITY OF UNSEASONABLY WARM WEATHER AND TWICE-BAKED POTATOES.
OUR TRADITION SAYS I MUST NOW STRANGLE YOU WITH A MUD ADDER.
LUCKILY, I BROUGHT ONE.
DO ELBONIANS HAVE A LOT OF DEITIES?
NO, JUST THE ONE.
HE SEEMS EASILY OFFENDED.
GRAB THE HEAD AND YANK!
©2014 Scott Adams, Inc./Dist. by Universal Uclick
1-19-14

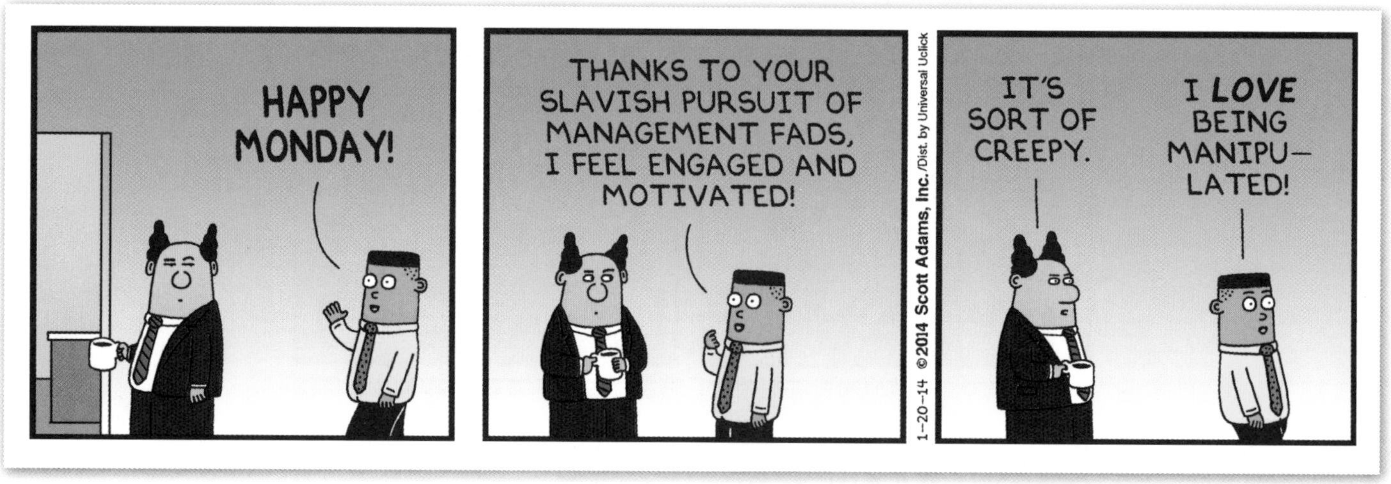
HAPPY MONDAY!
THANKS TO YOUR SLAVISH PURSUIT OF MANAGEMENT FADS, I FEEL ENGAGED AND MOTIVATED!
1-20-14 ©2014 Scott Adams, Inc./Dist. by Universal Uclick
IT'S SORT OF CREEPY.
I LOVE BEING MANIPU-LATED!

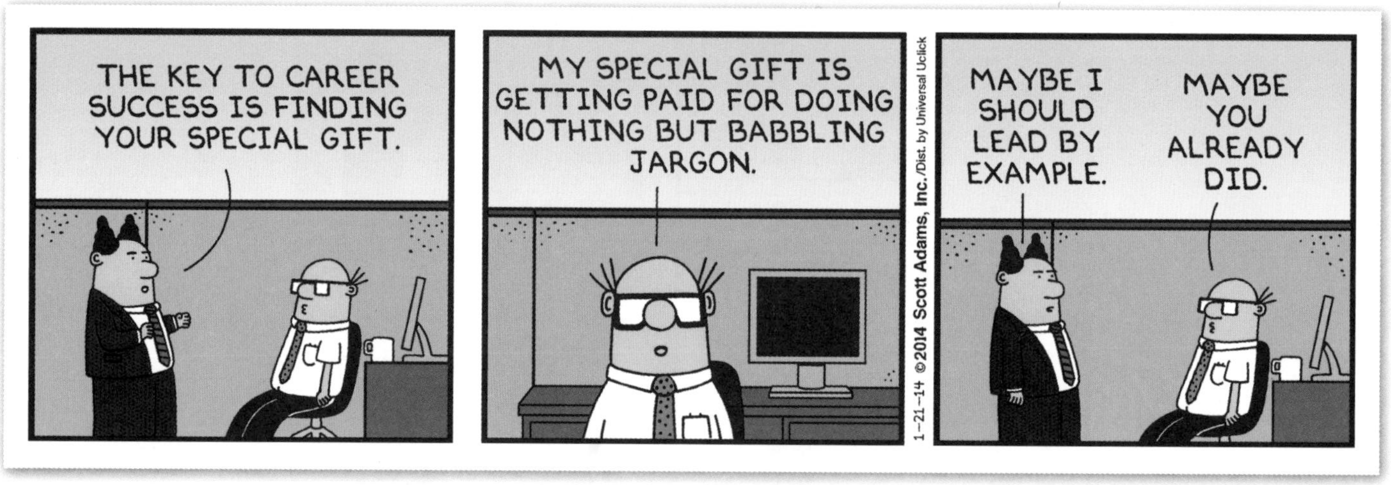
THE KEY TO CAREER SUCCESS IS FINDING YOUR SPECIAL GIFT.
MY SPECIAL GIFT IS GETTING PAID FOR DOING NOTHING BUT BABBLING JARGON.
1-21-14 ©2014 Scott Adams, Inc./Dist. by Universal Uclick
MAYBE I SHOULD LEAD BY EXAMPLE.
MAYBE YOU ALREADY DID.

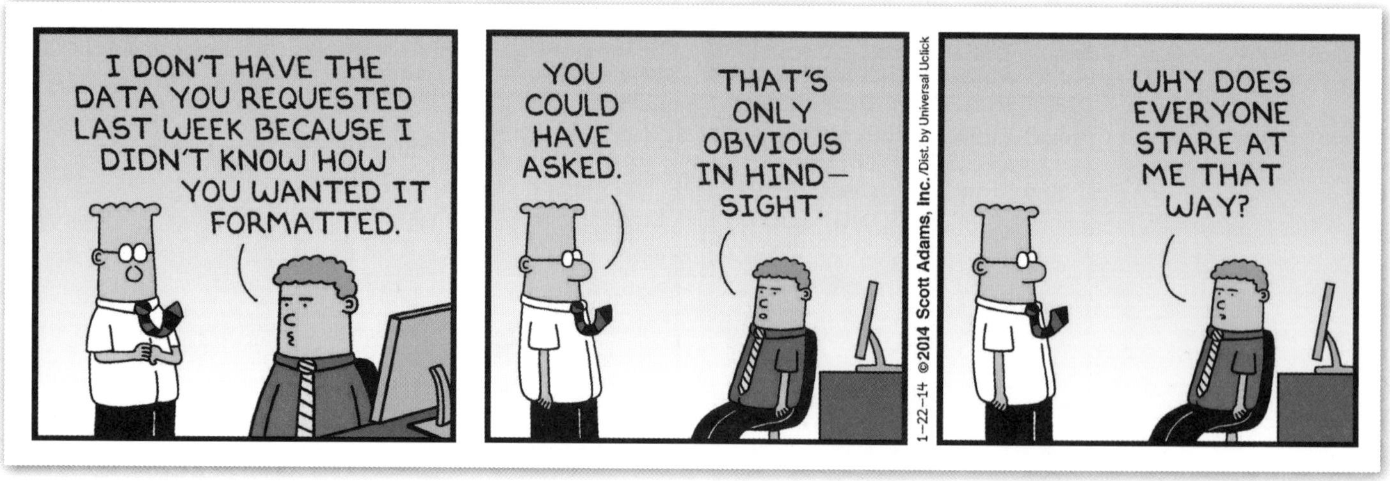
I DON'T HAVE THE DATA YOU REQUESTED LAST WEEK BECAUSE I DIDN'T KNOW HOW YOU WANTED IT FORMATTED.
YOU COULD HAVE ASKED.
THAT'S ONLY OBVIOUS IN HIND-SIGHT.
1-22-14 ©2014 Scott Adams, Inc./Dist. by Universal Uclick
WHY DOES EVERYONE STARE AT ME THAT WAY?

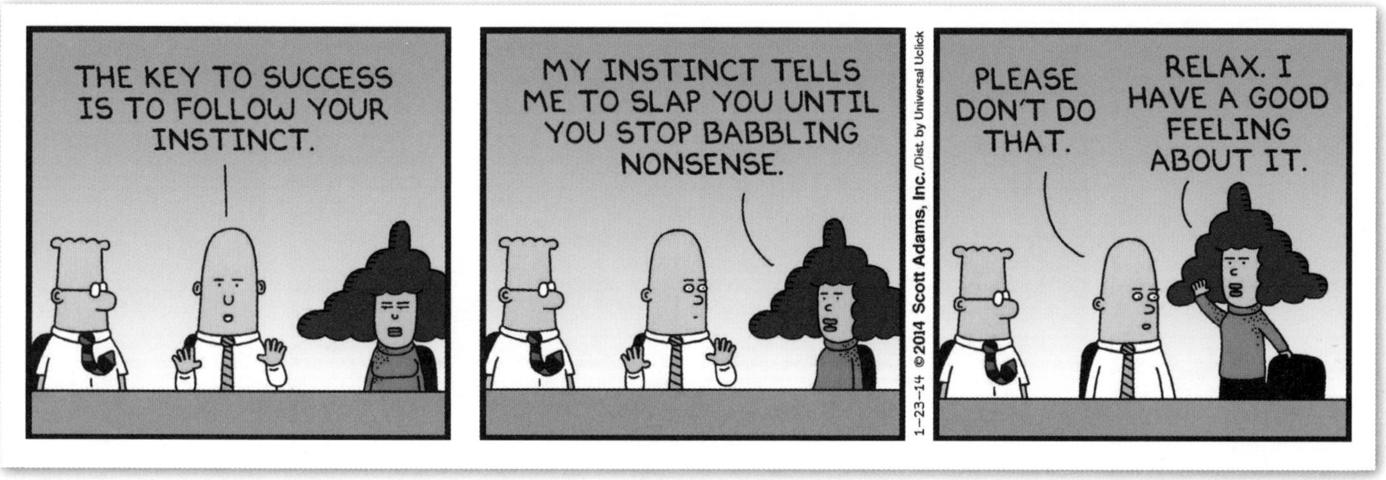
THE KEY TO SUCCESS IS TO FOLLOW YOUR INSTINCT.
MY INSTINCT TELLS ME TO SLAP YOU UNTIL YOU STOP BABBLING NONSENSE.
1-23-14 ©2014 Scott Adams, Inc./Dist. by Universal Uclick
PLEASE DON'T DO THAT.
RELAX. I HAVE A GOOD FEELING ABOUT IT.

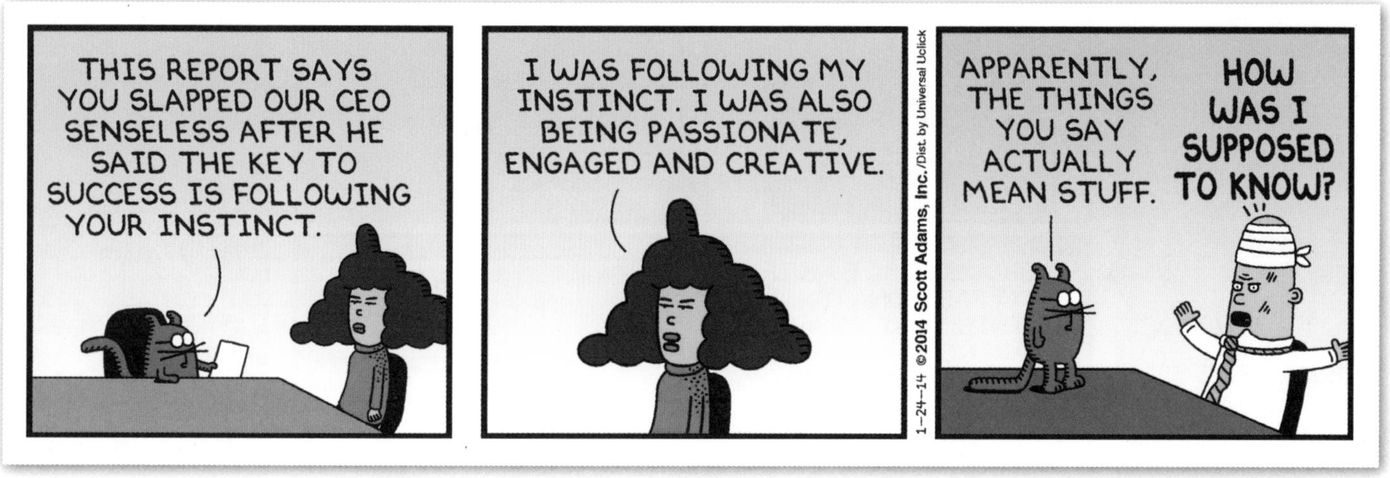
THIS REPORT SAYS YOU SLAPPED OUR CEO SENSELESS AFTER HE SAID THE KEY TO SUCCESS IS FOLLOWING YOUR INSTINCT.
I WAS FOLLOWING MY INSTINCT. I WAS ALSO BEING PASSIONATE, ENGAGED AND CREATIVE.
1-24-14 ©2014 Scott Adams, Inc./Dist. by Universal Uclick
APPARENTLY, THE THINGS YOU SAY ACTUALLY MEAN STUFF.
HOW WAS I SUPPOSED TO KNOW?

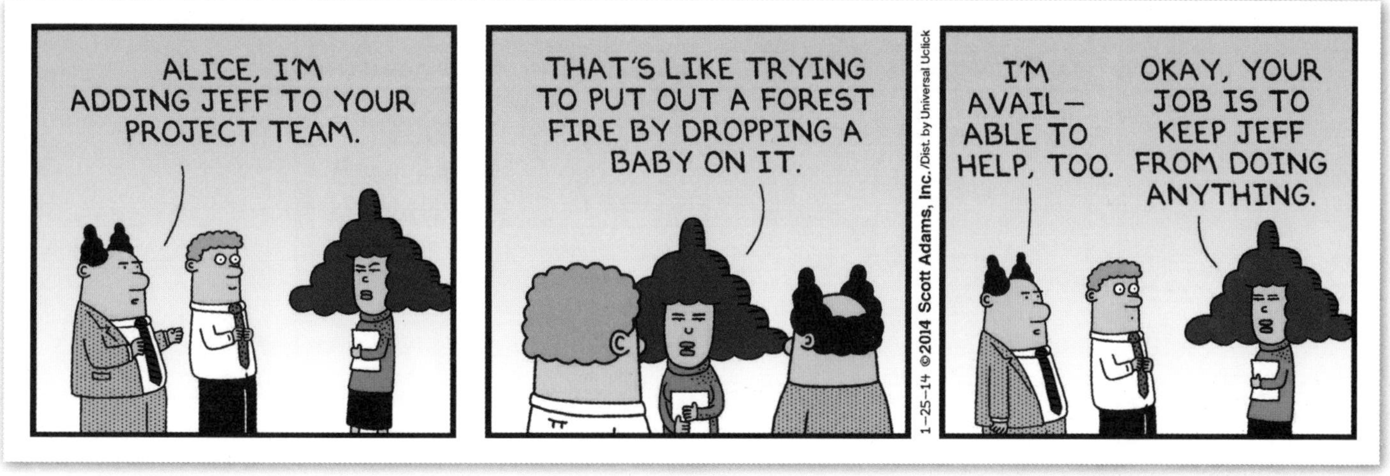
ALICE, I'M ADDING JEFF TO YOUR PROJECT TEAM.
THAT'S LIKE TRYING TO PUT OUT A FOREST FIRE BY DROPPING A BABY ON IT.
1-25-14 ©2014 Scott Adams, Inc./Dist. by Universal Uclick
I'M AVAIL-ABLE TO HELP, TOO.
OKAY, YOUR JOB IS TO KEEP JEFF FROM DOING ANYTHING.

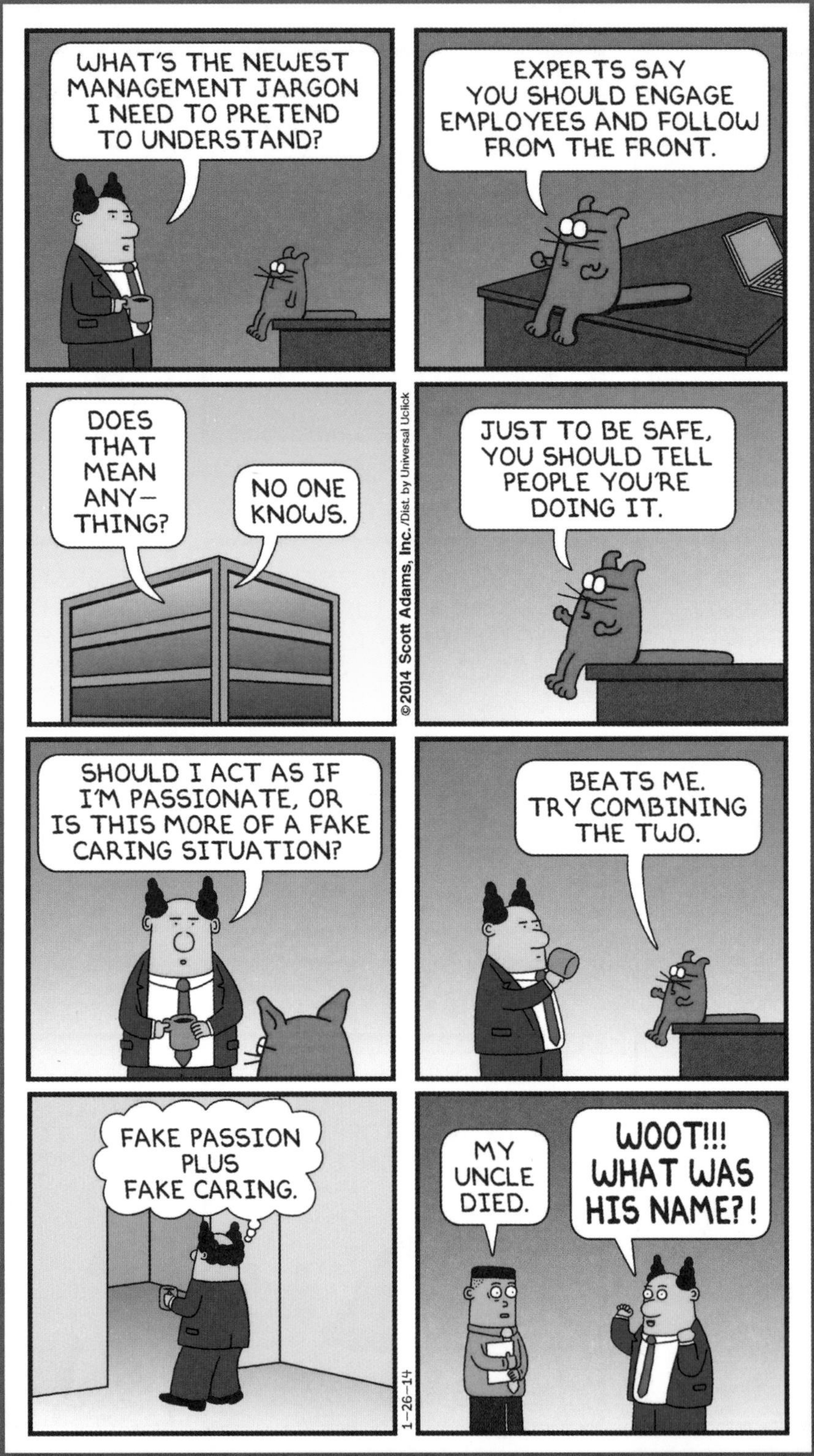
WHAT'S THE NEWEST MANAGEMENT JARGON I NEED TO PRETEND TO UNDERSTAND?
EXPERTS SAY YOU SHOULD ENGAGE EMPLOYEES AND FOLLOW FROM THE FRONT.
DOES THAT MEAN ANY-THING?
NO ONE KNOWS.
©2014 Scott Adams, Inc./Dist. by Universal Uclick
JUST TO BE SAFE, YOU SHOULD TELL PEOPLE YOU'RE DOING IT.
SHOULD I ACT AS IF I'M PASSIONATE, OR IS THIS MORE OF A FAKE CARING SITUATION?
BEATS ME. TRY COMBINING THE TWO.
FAKE PASSION PLUS FAKE CARING.
1-26-14
MY UNCLE DIED.
WOOT!!! WHAT WAS HIS NAME?!

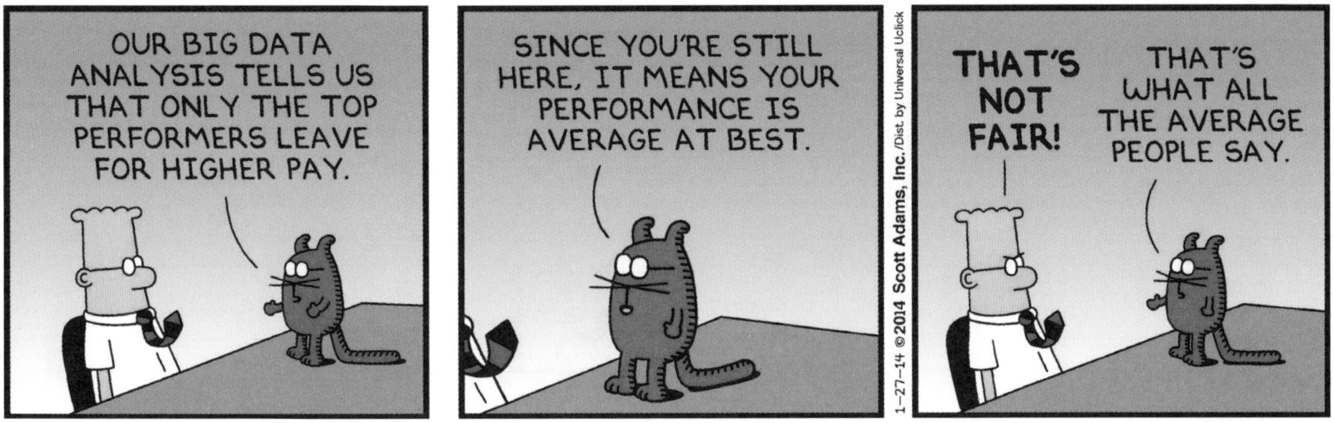
OUR BIG DATA ANALYSIS TELLS US THAT ONLY THE TOP PERFORMERS LEAVE FOR HIGHER PAY.
SINCE YOU'RE STILL HERE, IT MEANS YOUR PERFORMANCE IS AVERAGE AT BEST.
1-27-14 ©2014 Scott Adams, Inc./Dist. by Universal Uclick
THAT'S NOT FAIR!
THAT'S WHAT ALL THE AVERAGE PEOPLE SAY.

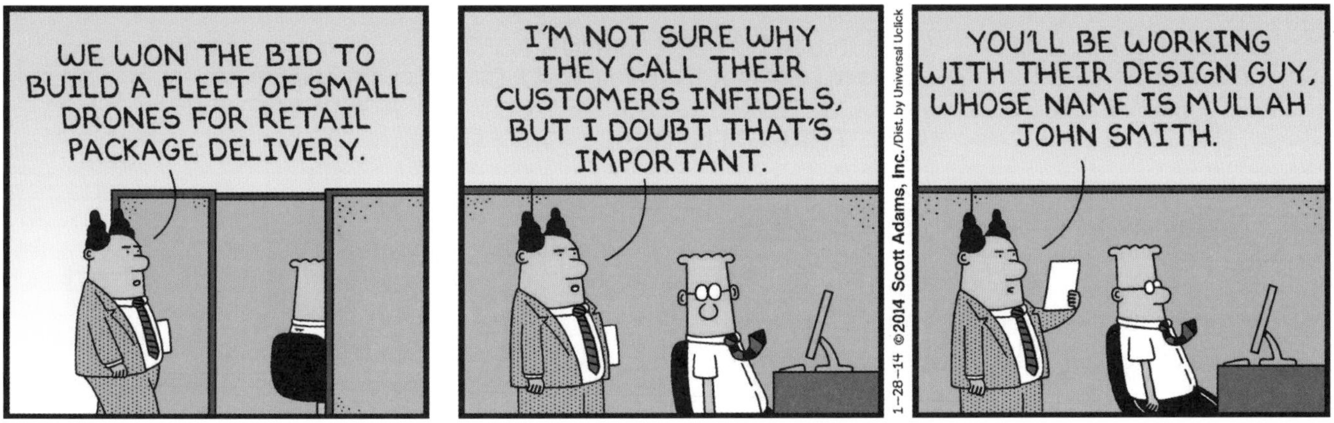
WE WON THE BID TO BUILD A FLEET OF SMALL DRONES FOR RETAIL PACKAGE DELIVERY.
I'M NOT SURE WHY THEY CALL THEIR CUSTOMERS INFIDELS, BUT I DOUBT THAT'S IMPORTANT.
1-28-14 ©2014 Scott Adams, Inc./Dist. by Universal Uclick
YOU'LL BE WORKING WITH THEIR DESIGN GUY, WHOSE NAME IS MULLAH JOHN SMITH.

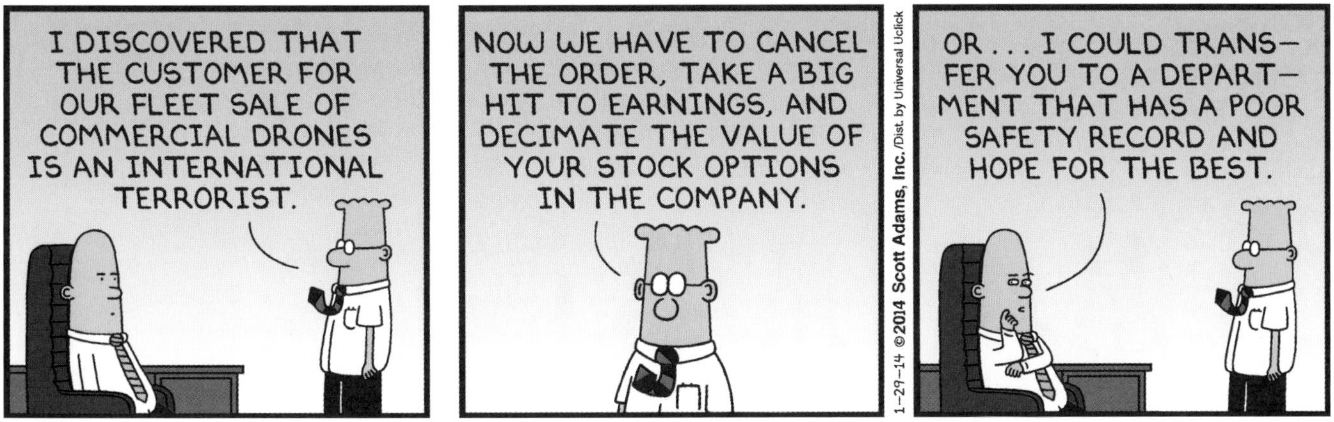
I DISCOVERED THAT THE CUSTOMER FOR OUR FLEET SALE OF COMMERCIAL DRONES IS AN INTERNATIONAL TERRORIST.
NOW WE HAVE TO CANCEL THE ORDER, TAKE A BIG HIT TO EARNINGS, AND DECIMATE THE VALUE OF YOUR STOCK OPTIONS IN THE COMPANY.
1-29-14 ©2014 Scott Adams, Inc./Dist. by Universal Uclick
OR . . . I COULD TRANS-FER YOU TO A DEPART-MENT THAT HAS A POOR SAFETY RECORD AND HOPE FOR THE BEST.

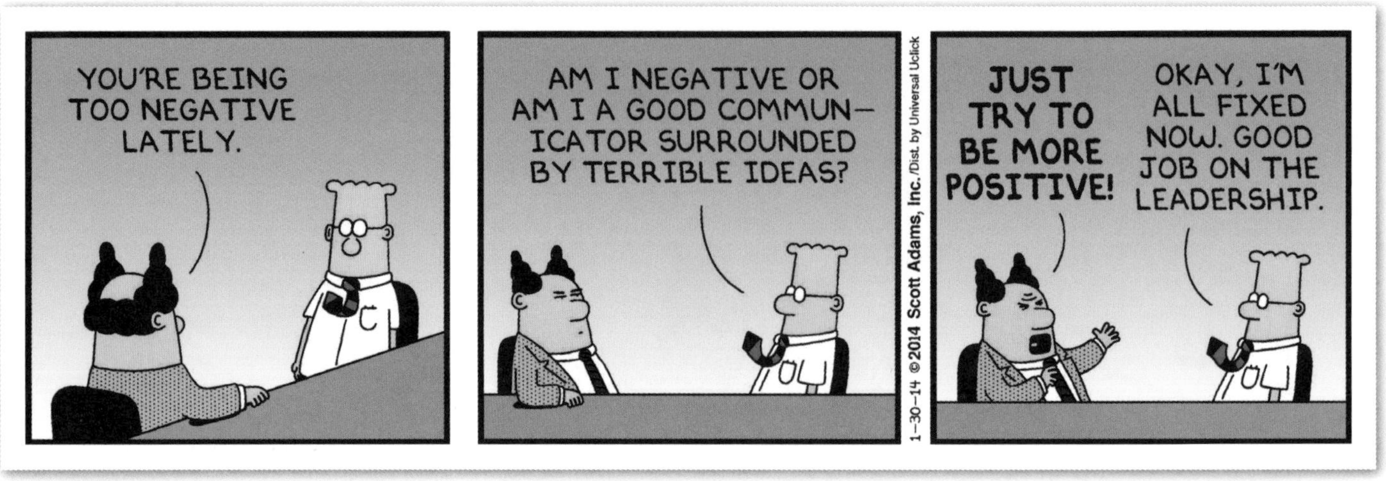
YOU'RE BEING TOO NEGATIVE LATELY.
AM I NEGATIVE OR AM I A GOOD COMMUN-ICATOR SURROUNDED BY TERRIBLE IDEAS?
1-30-14 ©2014 Scott Adams, Inc./Dist. by Universal Uclick
JUST TRY TO BE MORE POSITIVE!
OKAY, I'M ALL FIXED NOW. GOOD JOB ON THE LEADERSHIP.

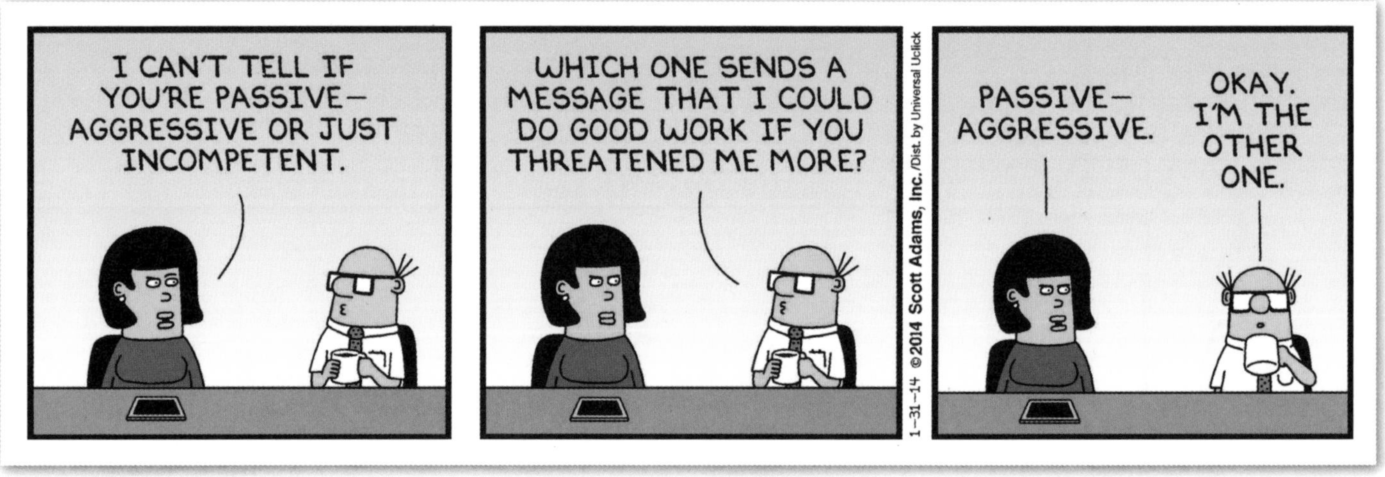
I CAN'T TELL IF YOU'RE PASSIVE-AGGRESSIVE OR JUST INCOMPETENT.
WHICH ONE SENDS A MESSAGE THAT I COULD DO GOOD WORK IF YOU THREATENED ME MORE?
1-31-14 ©2014 Scott Adams, Inc./Dist. by Universal Uclick
PASSIVE-AGGRESSIVE.
OKAY. I'M THE OTHER ONE.

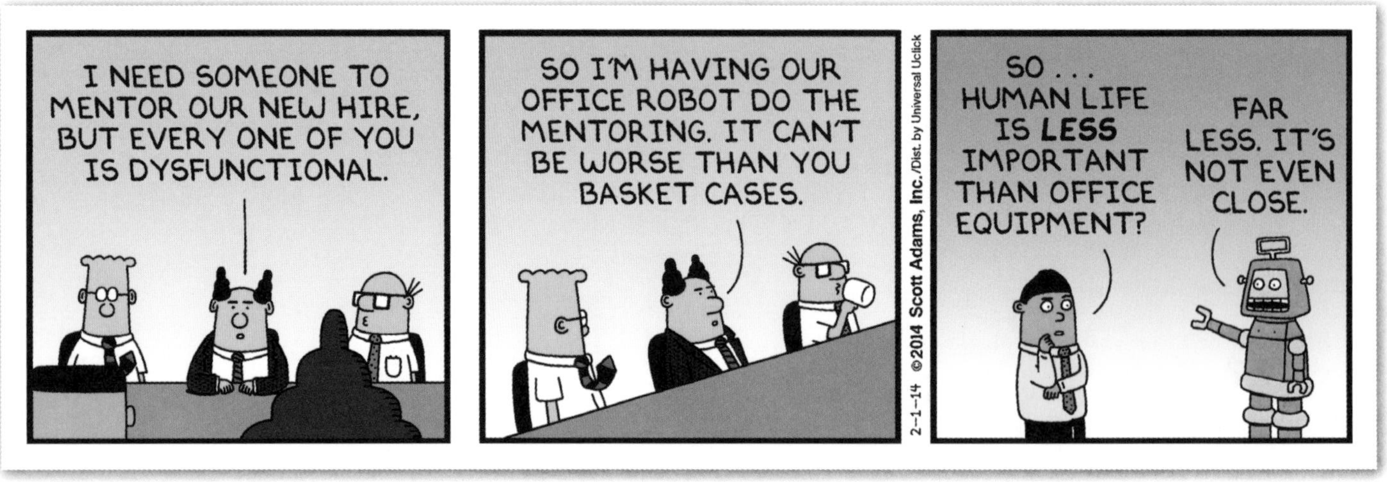
I NEED SOMEONE TO MENTOR OUR NEW HIRE, BUT EVERY ONE OF YOU IS DYSFUNCTIONAL.
SO I'M HAVING OUR OFFICE ROBOT DO THE MENTORING. IT CAN'T BE WORSE THAN YOU BASKET CASES.
2-1-14 ©2014 Scott Adams, Inc./Dist. by Universal Uclick
SO . . . HUMAN LIFE IS LESS IMPORTANT THAN OFFICE EQUIPMENT?
FAR LESS. IT'S NOT EVEN CLOSE.

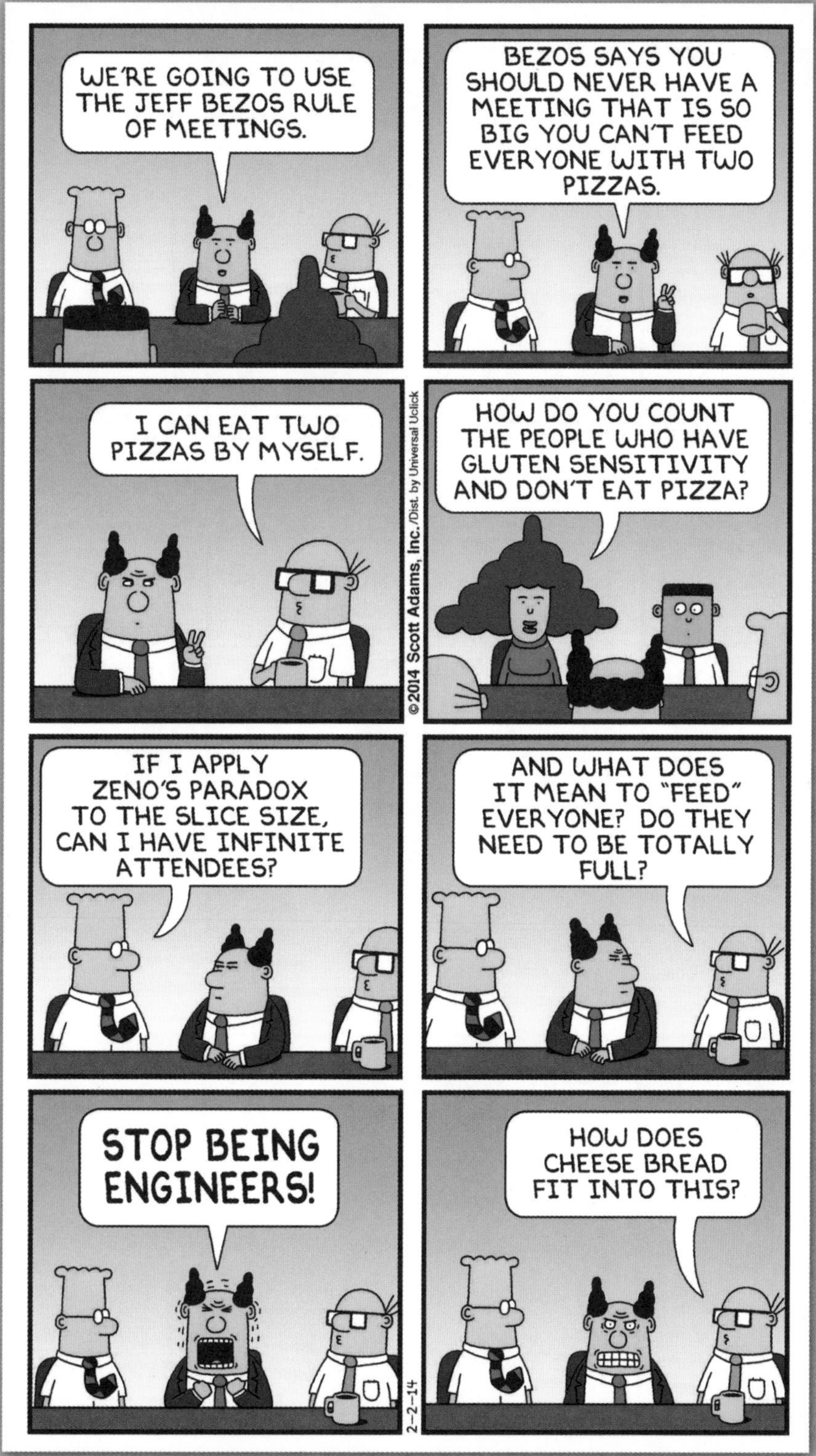
WE'RE GOING TO USE THE JEFF BEZOS RULE OF MEETINGS.
BEZOS SAYS YOU SHOULD NEVER HAVE A MEETING THAT IS SO BIG YOU CAN'T FEED EVERYONE WITH TWO PIZZAS.
I CAN EAT TWO PIZZAS BY MYSELF.
HOW DO YOU COUNT THE PEOPLE WHO HAVE GLUTEN SENSITIVITY AND DON'T EAT PIZZA?
IF I APPLY ZENO'S PARADOX TO THE SLICE SIZE, CAN I HAVE INFINITE ATTENDEES?
AND WHAT DOES IT MEAN TO "FEED" EVERYONE? DO THEY NEED TO BE TOTALLY FULL?
STOP BEING ENGINEERS!
HOW DOES CHEESE BREAD FIT INTO THIS?
©2014 Scott Adams, Inc./Dist. by Universal Uclick
2-2-14

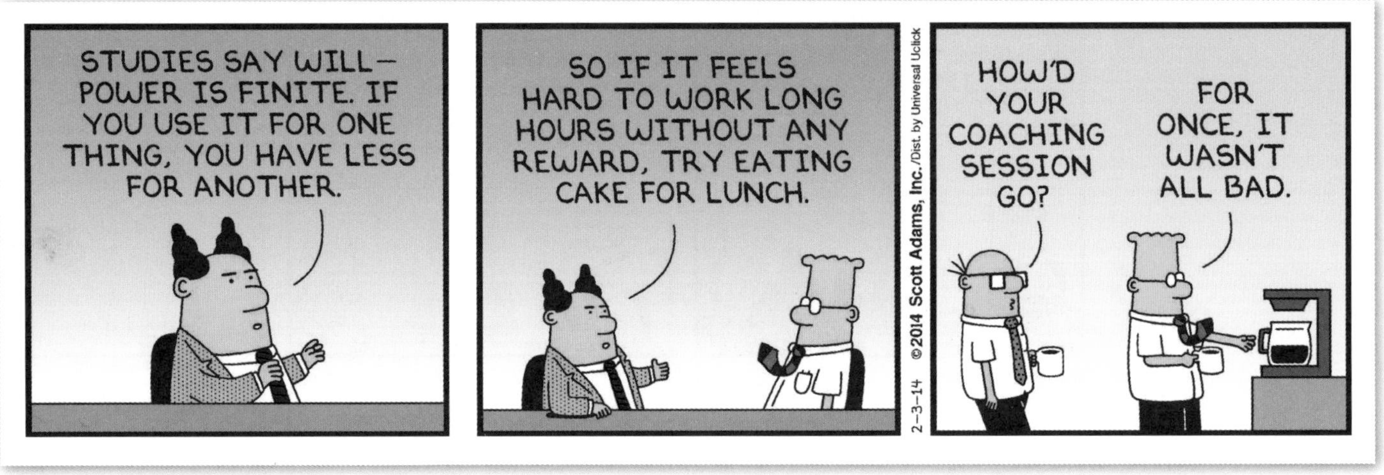
STUDIES SAY WILL-POWER IS FINITE. IF YOU USE IT FOR ONE THING, YOU HAVE LESS FOR ANOTHER.
SO IF IT FEELS HARD TO WORK LONG HOURS WITHOUT ANY REWARD, TRY EATING CAKE FOR LUNCH.
2-3-14 ©2014 Scott Adams, Inc./Dist. by Universal Uclick
HOW'D YOUR COACHING SESSION GO?
FOR ONCE, IT WASN'T ALL BAD.

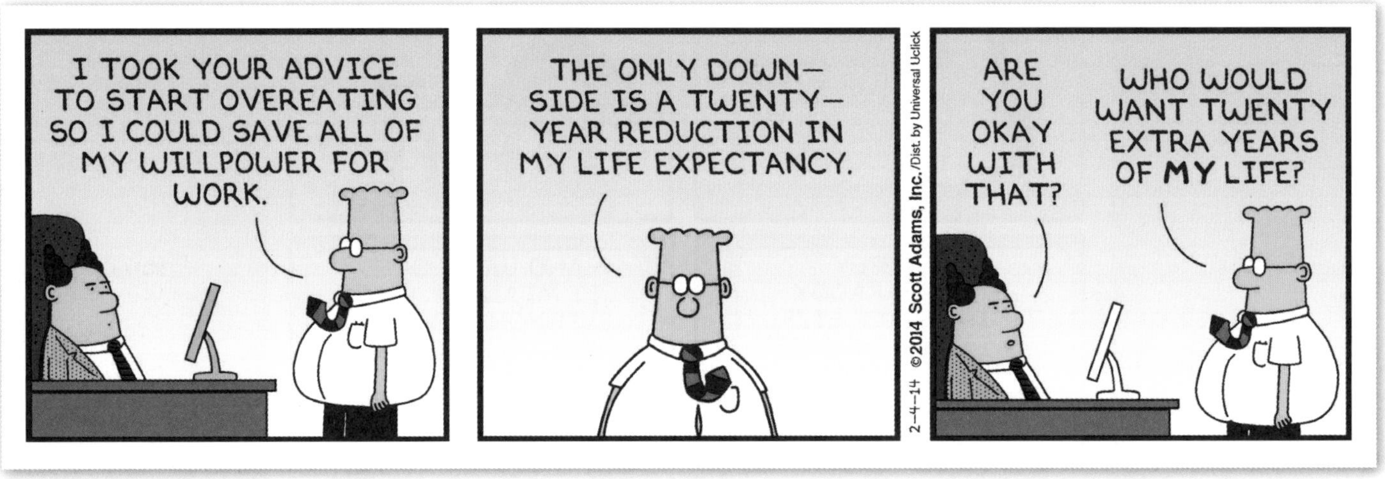
I TOOK YOUR ADVICE TO START OVEREATING SO I COULD SAVE ALL OF MY WILLPOWER FOR WORK.
THE ONLY DOWN-SIDE IS A TWENTY-YEAR REDUCTION IN MY LIFE EXPECTANCY.
2-4-14 ©2014 Scott Adams, Inc./Dist. by Universal Uclick
ARE YOU OKAY WITH THAT?
WHO WOULD WANT TWENTY EXTRA YEARS OF **MY** LIFE?

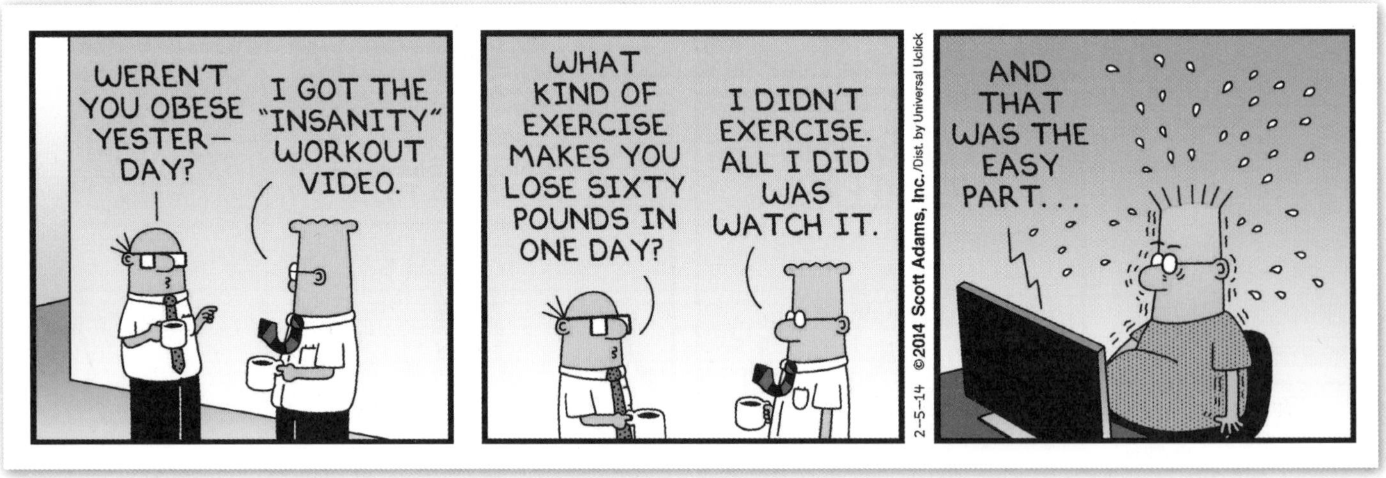
WEREN'T YOU OBESE YESTER-DAY?
I GOT THE "INSANITY" WORKOUT VIDEO.
WHAT KIND OF EXERCISE MAKES YOU LOSE SIXTY POUNDS IN ONE DAY?
I DIDN'T EXERCISE. ALL I DID WAS WATCH IT.
2-5-14 ©2014 Scott Adams, Inc./Dist. by Universal Uclick
AND THAT WAS THE EASY PART...

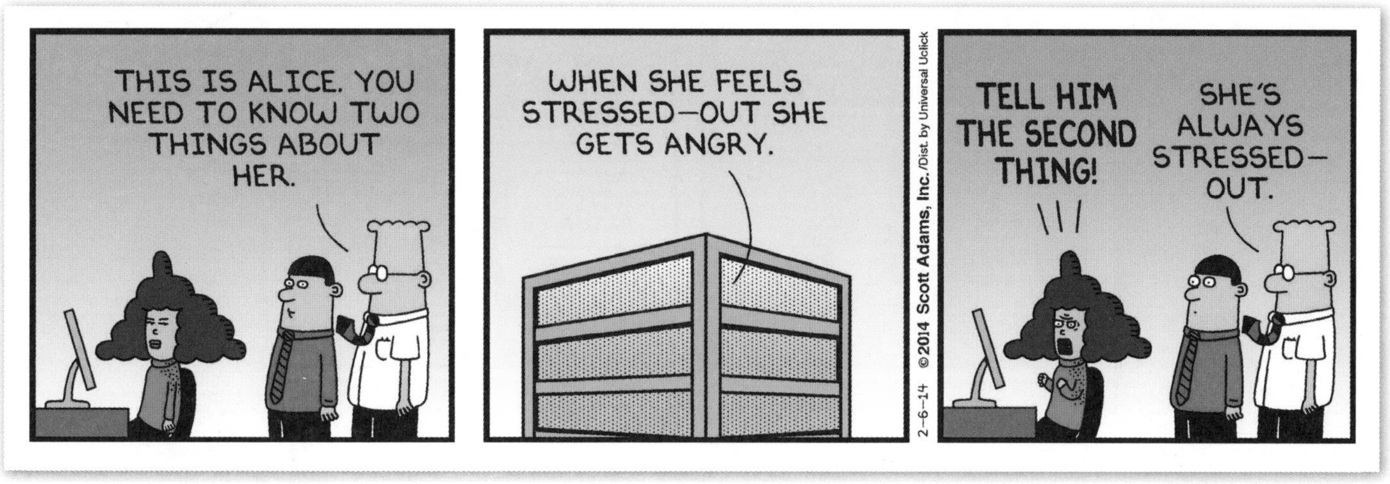
THIS IS ALICE. YOU NEED TO KNOW TWO THINGS ABOUT HER.
WHEN SHE FEELS STRESSED—OUT SHE GETS ANGRY.
TELL HIM THE SECOND THING!
SHE'S ALWAYS STRESSED—OUT.
2-6-14 ©2014 Scott Adams, Inc./Dist. by Universal Uclick

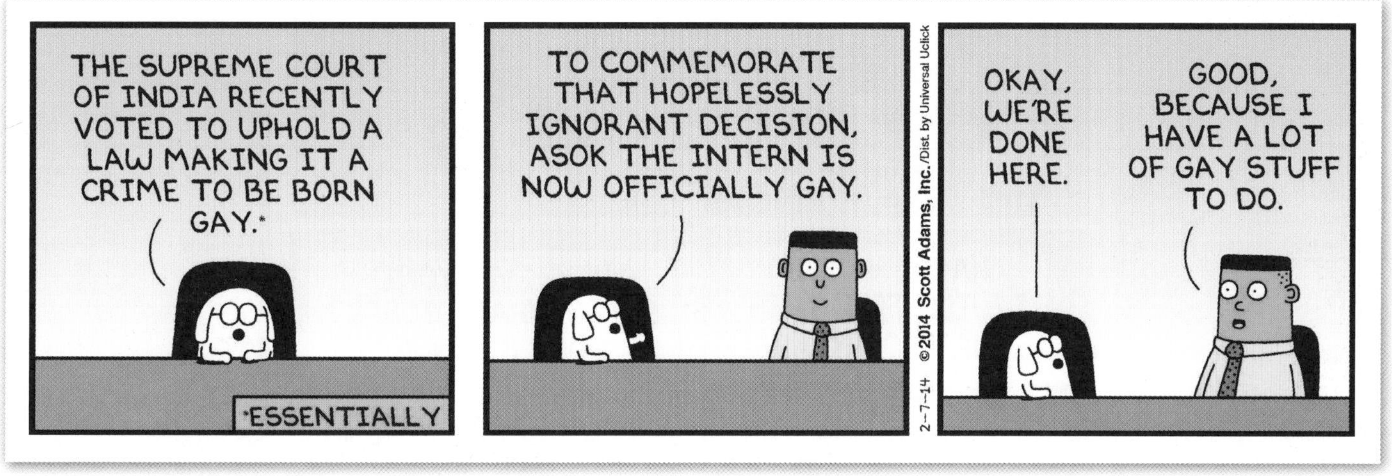
THE SUPREME COURT OF INDIA RECENTLY VOTED TO UPHOLD A LAW MAKING IT A CRIME TO BE BORN GAY.*
*ESSENTIALLY
TO COMMEMORATE THAT HOPELESSLY IGNORANT DECISION, ASOK THE INTERN IS NOW OFFICIALLY GAY.
OKAY, WE'RE DONE HERE.
GOOD, BECAUSE I HAVE A LOT OF GAY STUFF TO DO.
2-7-14 ©2014 Scott Adams, Inc./Dist. by Universal Uclick

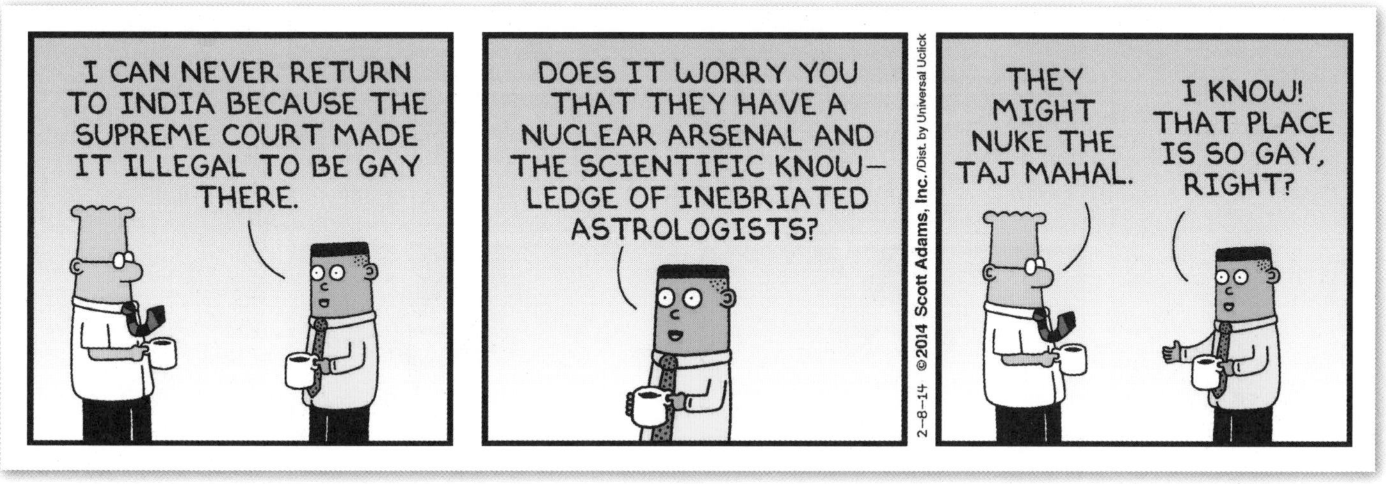
I CAN NEVER RETURN TO INDIA BECAUSE THE SUPREME COURT MADE IT ILLEGAL TO BE GAY THERE.
DOES IT WORRY YOU THAT THEY HAVE A NUCLEAR ARSENAL AND THE SCIENTIFIC KNOW—LEDGE OF INEBRIATED ASTROLOGISTS?
THEY MIGHT NUKE THE TAJ MAHAL.
I KNOW! THAT PLACE IS SO GAY, RIGHT?
2-8-14 ©2014 Scott Adams, Inc./Dist. by Universal Uclick

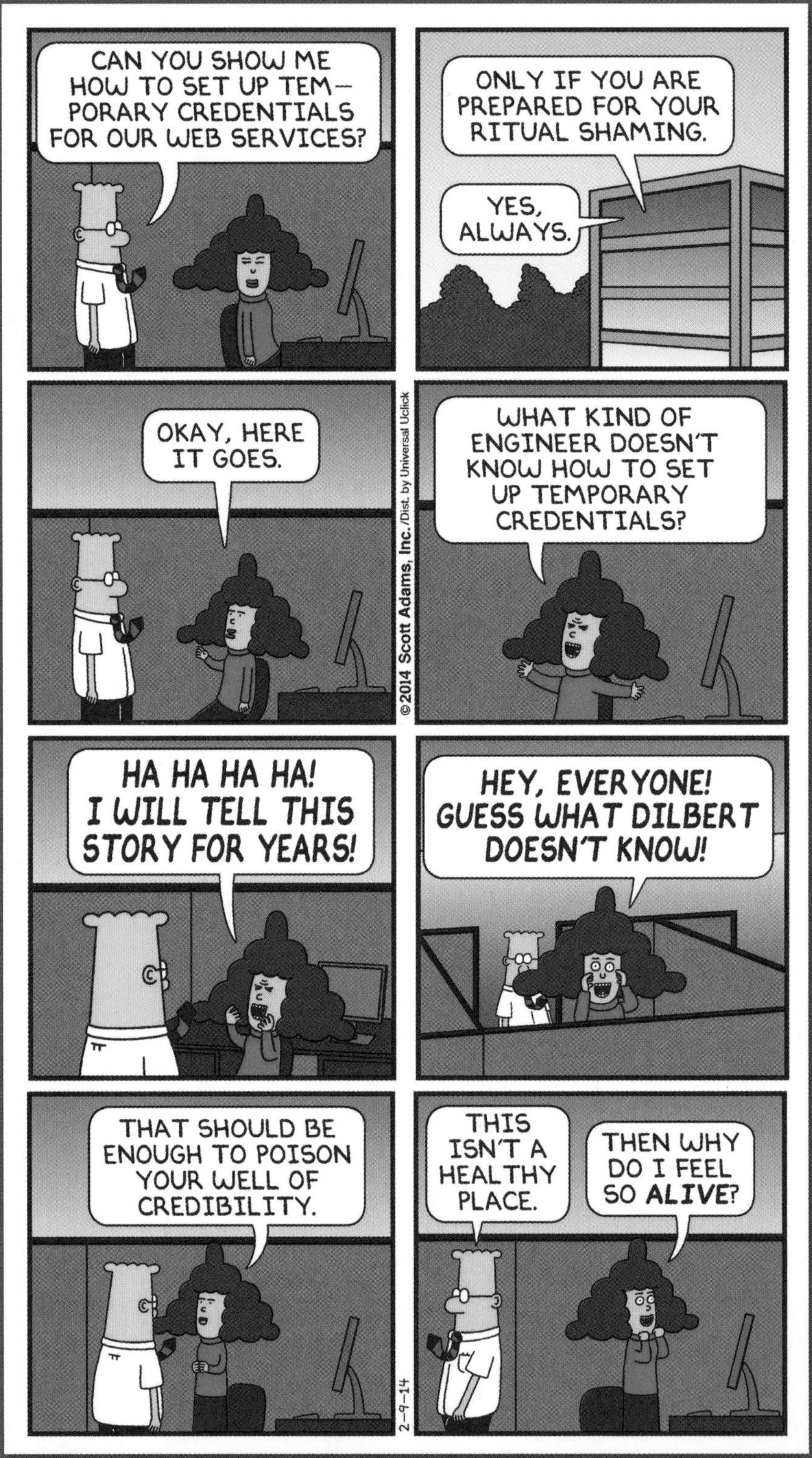
CAN YOU SHOW ME HOW TO SET UP TEM— PORARY CREDENTIALS FOR OUR WEB SERVICES?
ONLY IF YOU ARE PREPARED FOR YOUR RITUAL SHAMING.
YES, ALWAYS.
OKAY, HERE IT GOES.
WHAT KIND OF ENGINEER DOESN'T KNOW HOW TO SET UP TEMPORARY CREDENTIALS?
HA HA HA HA! I WILL TELL THIS STORY FOR YEARS!
HEY, EVERYONE! GUESS WHAT DILBERT DOESN'T KNOW!
THAT SHOULD BE ENOUGH TO POISON YOUR WELL OF CREDIBILITY.
THIS ISN'T A HEALTHY PLACE.
THEN WHY DO I FEEL SO **ALIVE**?
©2014 Scott Adams, Inc./Dist. by Universal Uclick
2-9-14

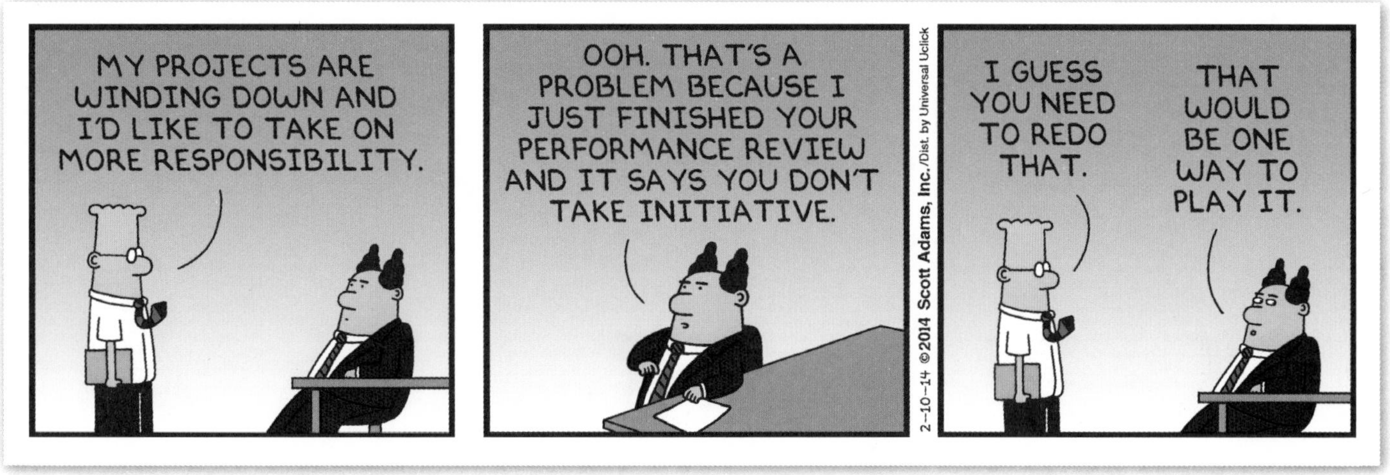
MY PROJECTS ARE WINDING DOWN AND I'D LIKE TO TAKE ON MORE RESPONSIBILITY.
OOH. THAT'S A PROBLEM BECAUSE I JUST FINISHED YOUR PERFORMANCE REVIEW AND IT SAYS YOU DON'T TAKE INITIATIVE.
2-10-14 ©2014 Scott Adams, Inc./Dist. by Universal Uclick
I GUESS YOU NEED TO REDO THAT.
THAT WOULD BE ONE WAY TO PLAY IT.

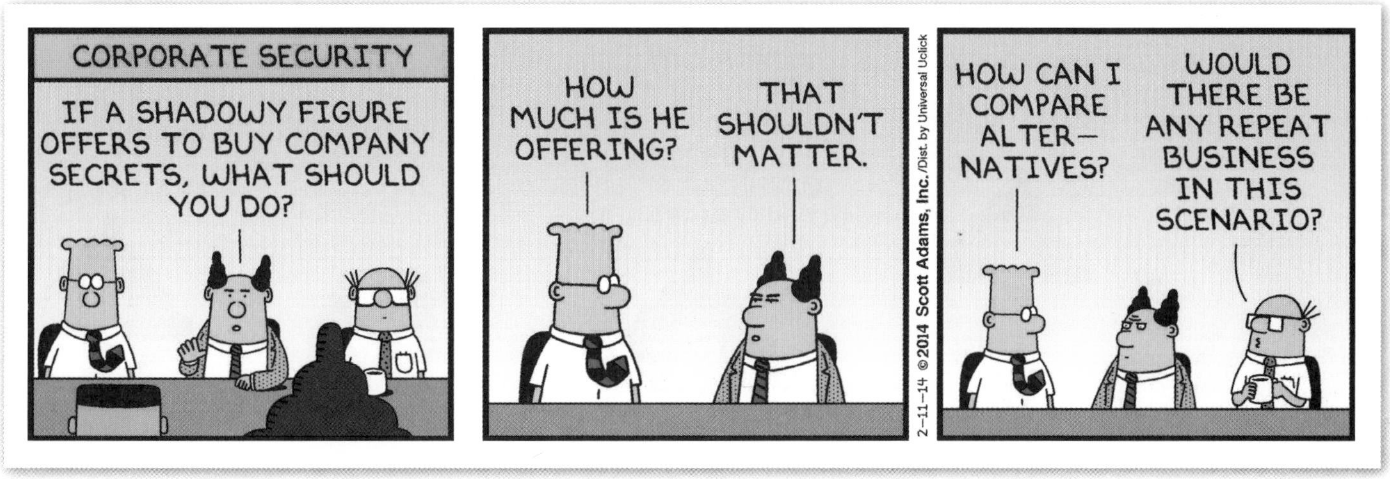
CORPORATE SECURITY
IF A SHADOWY FIGURE OFFERS TO BUY COMPANY SECRETS, WHAT SHOULD YOU DO?
HOW MUCH IS HE OFFERING?
THAT SHOULDN'T MATTER.
2-11-14 ©2014 Scott Adams, Inc./Dist. by Universal Uclick
HOW CAN I COMPARE ALTER-NATIVES?
WOULD THERE BE ANY REPEAT BUSINESS IN THIS SCENARIO?

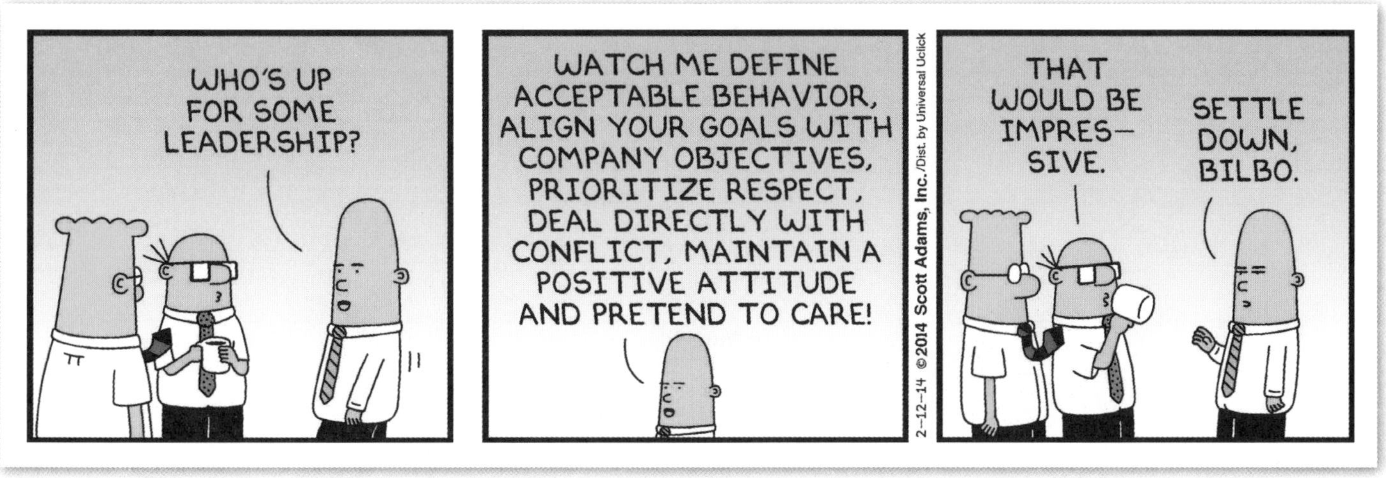
WHO'S UP FOR SOME LEADERSHIP?
WATCH ME DEFINE ACCEPTABLE BEHAVIOR, ALIGN YOUR GOALS WITH COMPANY OBJECTIVES, PRIORITIZE RESPECT, DEAL DIRECTLY WITH CONFLICT, MAINTAIN A POSITIVE ATTITUDE AND PRETEND TO CARE!
2-12-14 ©2014 Scott Adams, Inc./Dist. by Universal Uclick
THAT WOULD BE IMPRES-SIVE.
SETTLE DOWN, BILBO.

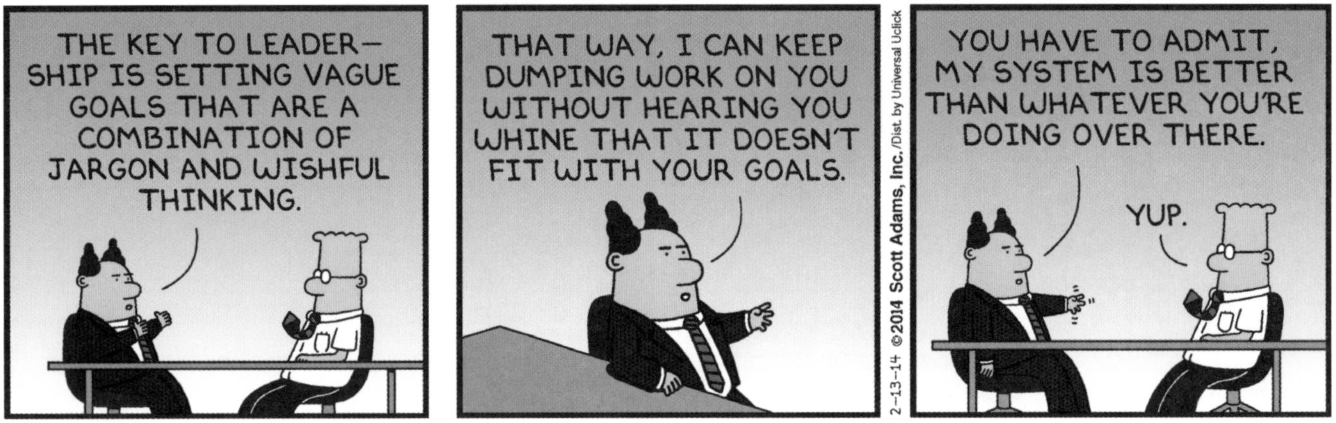
THE KEY TO LEADER-SHIP IS SETTING VAGUE GOALS THAT ARE A COMBINATION OF JARGON AND WISHFUL THINKING.
THAT WAY, I CAN KEEP DUMPING WORK ON YOU WITHOUT HEARING YOU WHINE THAT IT DOESN'T FIT WITH YOUR GOALS.
2-13-14 ©2014 Scott Adams, Inc./Dist. by Universal Uclick
YOU HAVE TO ADMIT, MY SYSTEM IS BETTER THAN WHATEVER YOU'RE DOING OVER THERE.
YUP.

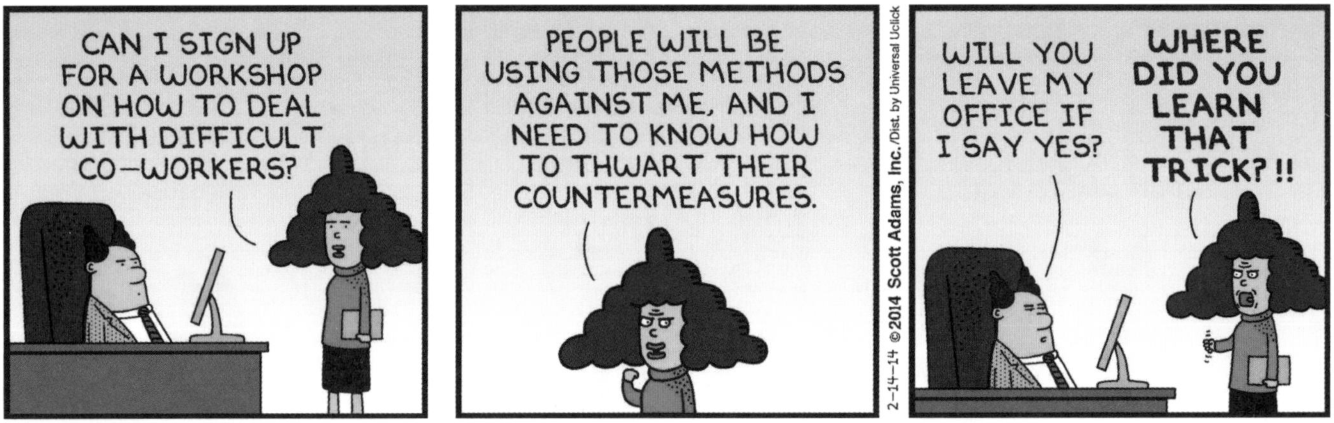
CAN I SIGN UP FOR A WORKSHOP ON HOW TO DEAL WITH DIFFICULT CO-WORKERS?
PEOPLE WILL BE USING THOSE METHODS AGAINST ME, AND I NEED TO KNOW HOW TO THWART THEIR COUNTERMEASURES.
2-14-14 ©2014 Scott Adams, Inc./Dist. by Universal Uclick
WILL YOU LEAVE MY OFFICE IF I SAY YES?
WHERE DID YOU LEARN THAT TRICK?!!

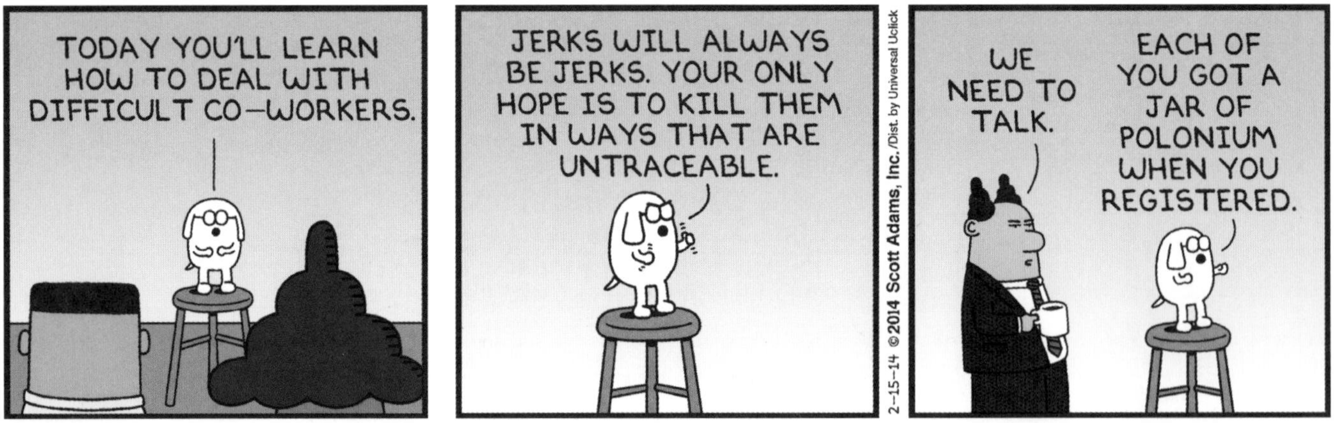
TODAY YOU'LL LEARN HOW TO DEAL WITH DIFFICULT CO-WORKERS.
JERKS WILL ALWAYS BE JERKS. YOUR ONLY HOPE IS TO KILL THEM IN WAYS THAT ARE UNTRACEABLE.
2-15-14 ©2014 Scott Adams, Inc./Dist. by Universal Uclick
WE NEED TO TALK.
EACH OF YOU GOT A JAR OF POLONIUM WHEN YOU REGISTERED.

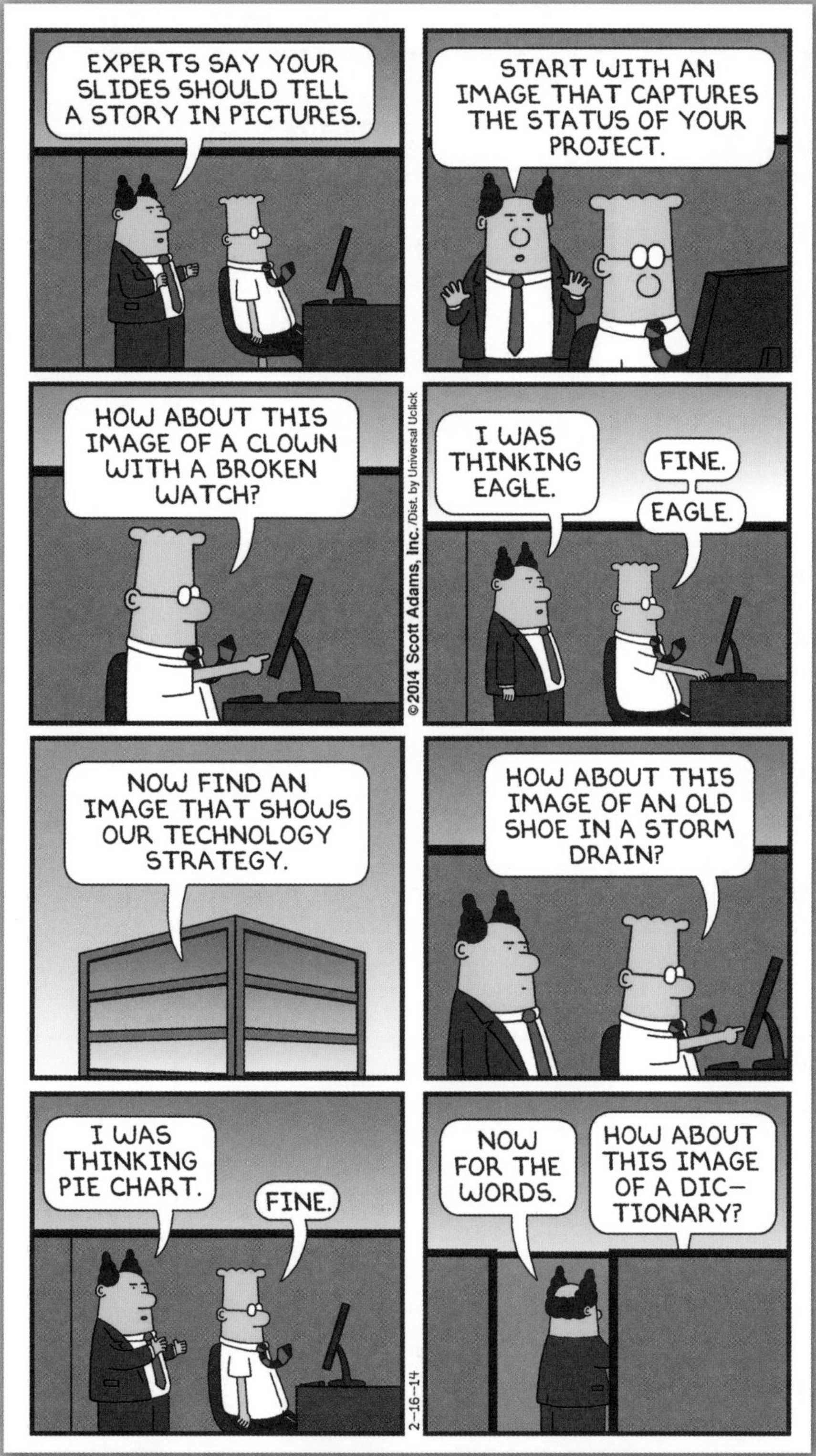
EXPERTS SAY YOUR SLIDES SHOULD TELL A STORY IN PICTURES.
START WITH AN IMAGE THAT CAPTURES THE STATUS OF YOUR PROJECT.
HOW ABOUT THIS IMAGE OF A CLOWN WITH A BROKEN WATCH?
©2014 Scott Adams, Inc./Dist. by Universal Uclick
I WAS THINKING EAGLE.
FINE.
EAGLE.
NOW FIND AN IMAGE THAT SHOWS OUR TECHNOLOGY STRATEGY.
HOW ABOUT THIS IMAGE OF AN OLD SHOE IN A STORM DRAIN?
I WAS THINKING PIE CHART.
FINE.
2-16-14
NOW FOR THE WORDS.
HOW ABOUT THIS IMAGE OF A DIC-TIONARY?

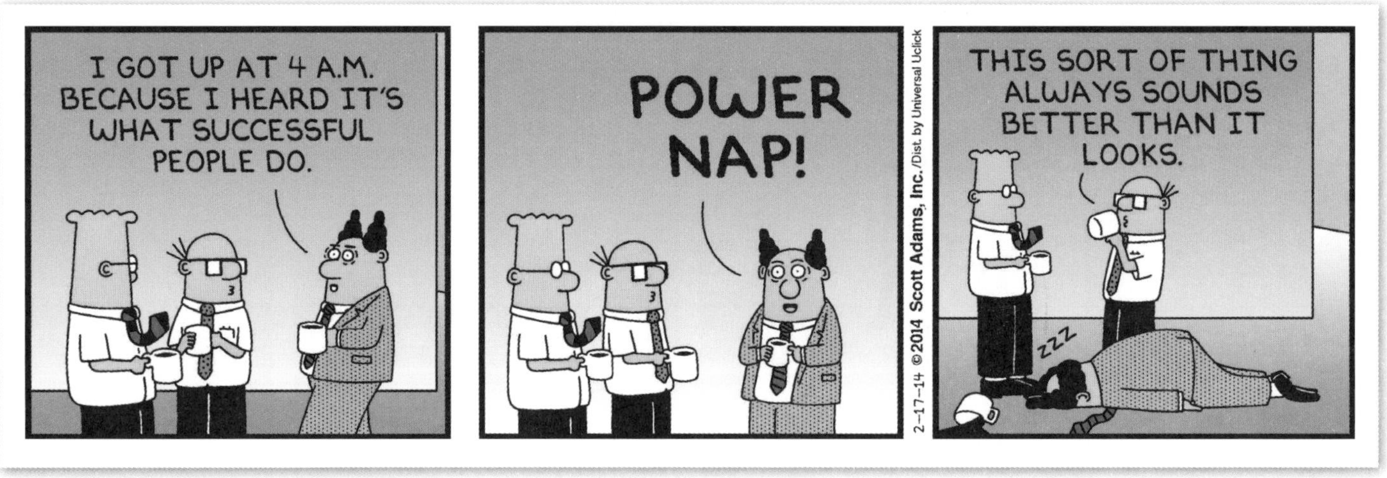
I GOT UP AT 4 A.M. BECAUSE I HEARD IT'S WHAT SUCCESSFUL PEOPLE DO.
POWER NAP!
2-17-14 ©2014 Scott Adams, Inc./Dist. by Universal Uclick
THIS SORT OF THING ALWAYS SOUNDS BETTER THAN IT LOOKS.
ZZZ

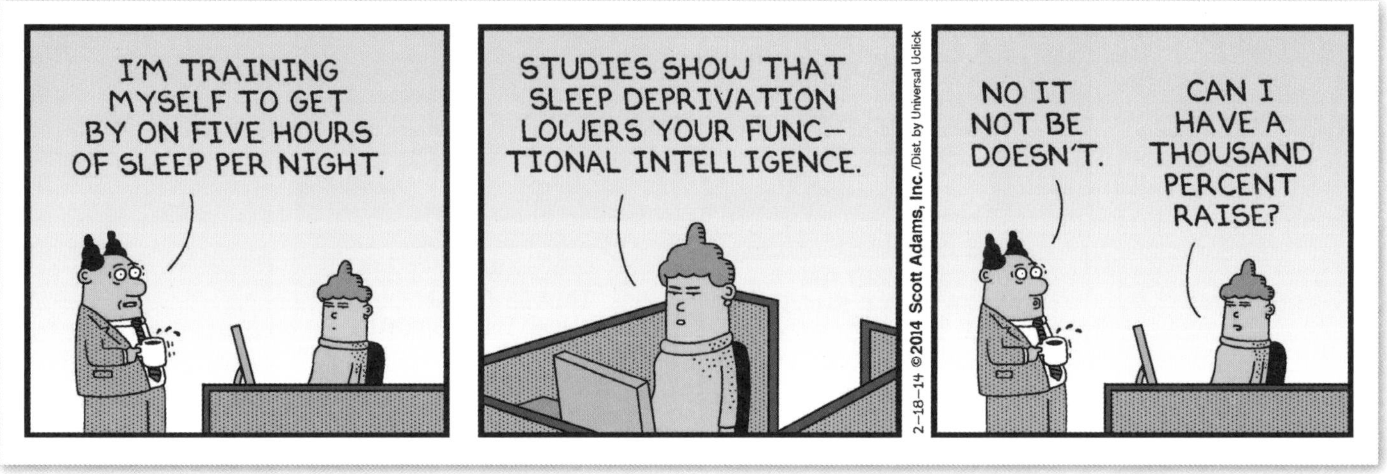
I'M TRAINING MYSELF TO GET BY ON FIVE HOURS OF SLEEP PER NIGHT.
STUDIES SHOW THAT SLEEP DEPRIVATION LOWERS YOUR FUNC-TIONAL INTELLIGENCE.
2-18-14 ©2014 Scott Adams, Inc./Dist. by Universal Uclick
NO IT NOT BE DOESN'T.
CAN I HAVE A THOUSAND PERCENT RAISE?

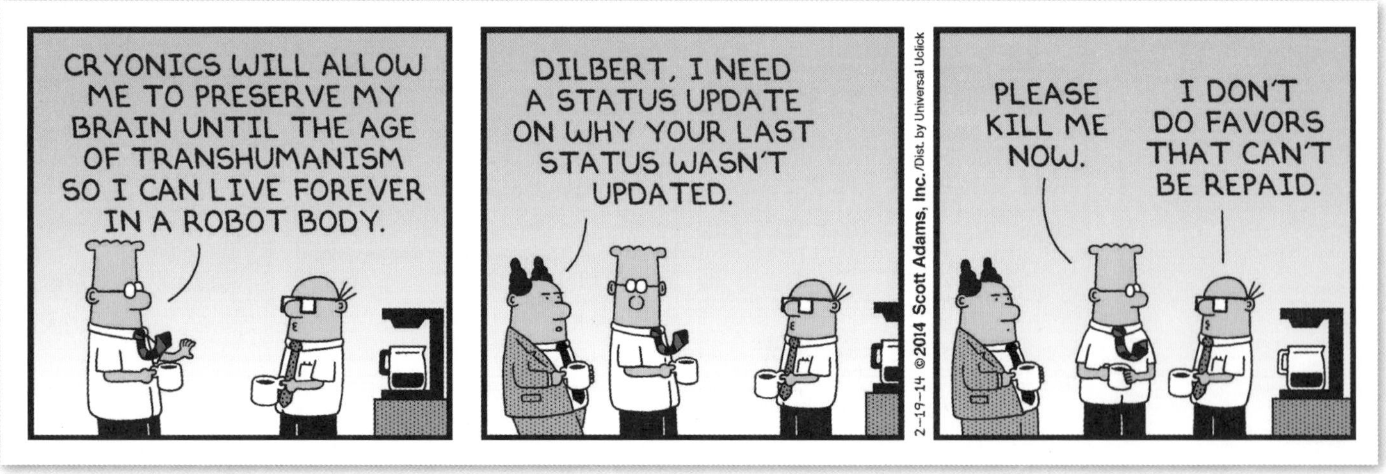
CRYONICS WILL ALLOW ME TO PRESERVE MY BRAIN UNTIL THE AGE OF TRANSHUMANISM SO I CAN LIVE FOREVER IN A ROBOT BODY.
DILBERT, I NEED A STATUS UPDATE ON WHY YOUR LAST STATUS WASN'T UPDATED.
2-19-14 ©2014 Scott Adams, Inc./Dist. by Universal Uclick
PLEASE KILL ME NOW.
I DON'T DO FAVORS THAT CAN'T BE REPAID.

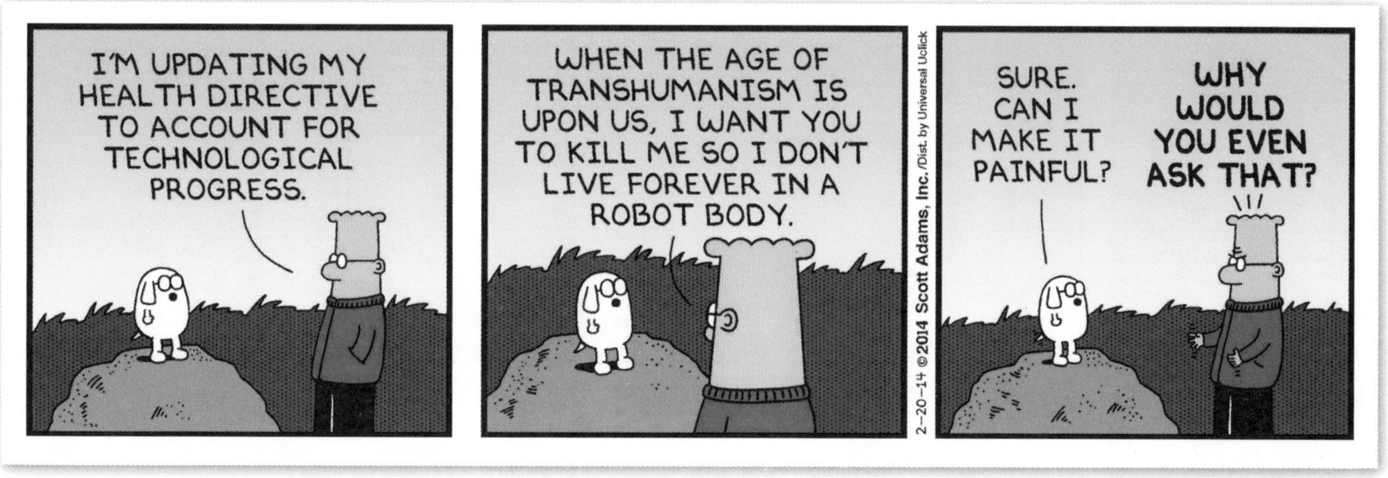
I'M UPDATING MY HEALTH DIRECTIVE TO ACCOUNT FOR TECHNOLOGICAL PROGRESS.
WHEN THE AGE OF TRANSHUMANISM IS UPON US, I WANT YOU TO KILL ME SO I DON'T LIVE FOREVER IN A ROBOT BODY.
2-20-14 ©2014 Scott Adams, Inc./Dist. by Universal Uclick
SURE. CAN I MAKE IT PAINFUL?
WHY WOULD YOU EVEN ASK THAT?

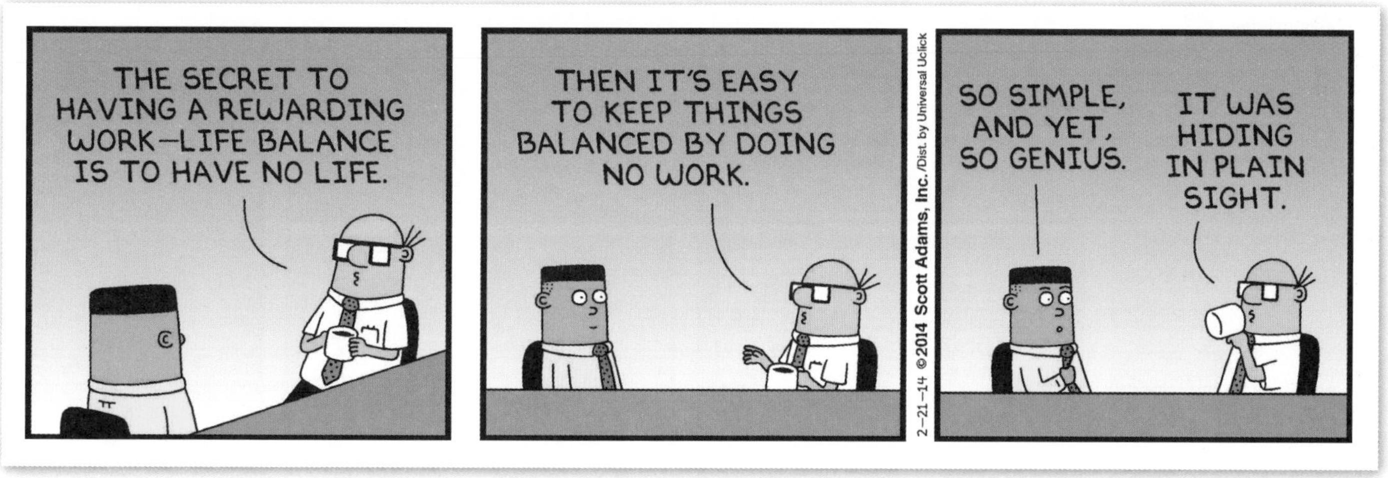
THE SECRET TO HAVING A REWARDING WORK–LIFE BALANCE IS TO HAVE NO LIFE.
THEN IT'S EASY TO KEEP THINGS BALANCED BY DOING NO WORK.
2-21-14 ©2014 Scott Adams, Inc./Dist. by Universal Uclick
SO SIMPLE, AND YET, SO GENIUS.
IT WAS HIDING IN PLAIN SIGHT.

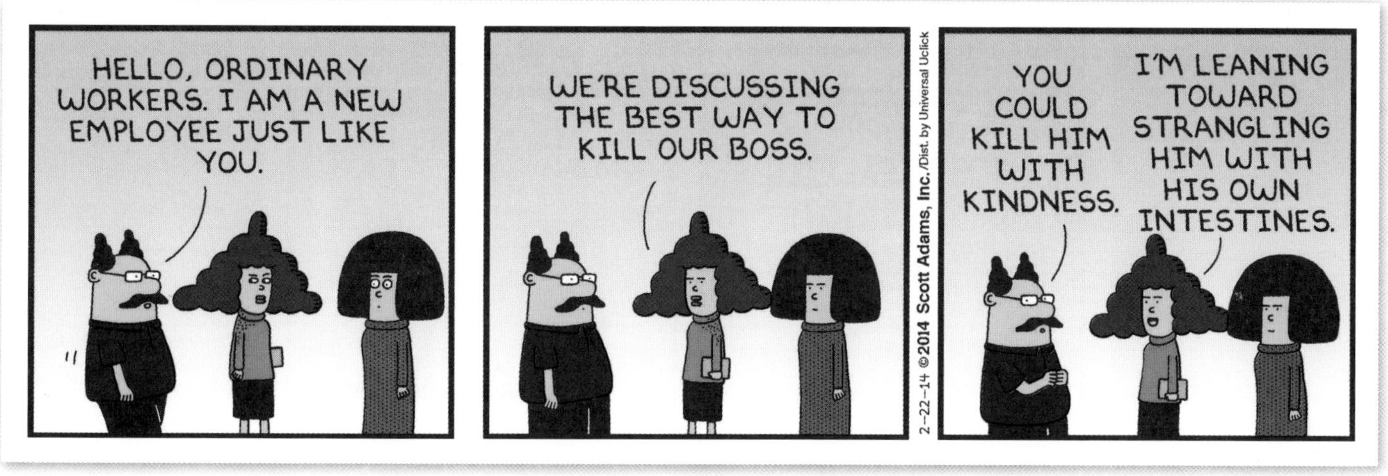
HELLO, ORDINARY WORKERS. I AM A NEW EMPLOYEE JUST LIKE YOU.
WE'RE DISCUSSING THE BEST WAY TO KILL OUR BOSS.
2-22-14 ©2014 Scott Adams, Inc./Dist. by Universal Uclick
YOU COULD KILL HIM WITH KINDNESS.
I'M LEANING TOWARD STRANGLING HIM WITH HIS OWN INTESTINES.

DOES ANYONE HAVE AN OBJECTION TO THIS PLAN?
START
IN MY OPINION, THERE ARE TOO MANY POTENTIAL PROBLEMS.
THIS SYSTEM HAS BEEN USED FOR YEARS IN OTHER PLACES AND WORKS FINE.
THERE IS STILL A NON–ZERO CHANCE OF PROBLEMS.
BY THAT LOGIC, WE SHOULD GET RID OF HOSPITALS BECAUSE SOMETIMES THEY MAKE MISTAKES.
GAAA!!! I JUST REALIZED I'M AN IDIOT!
YOU CAN STILL LEAD A NORMAL LIFE.
IT ONLY STINGS FOR A MINUTE.
©2014 Scott Adams, Inc./Dist. by Universal Uclick
2-23-14

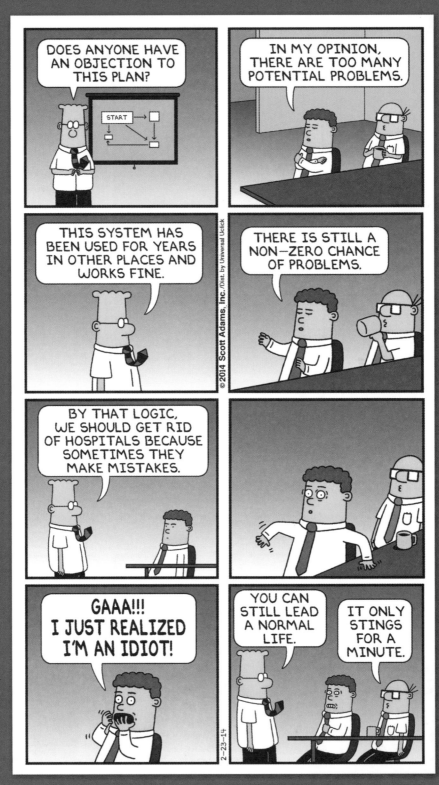

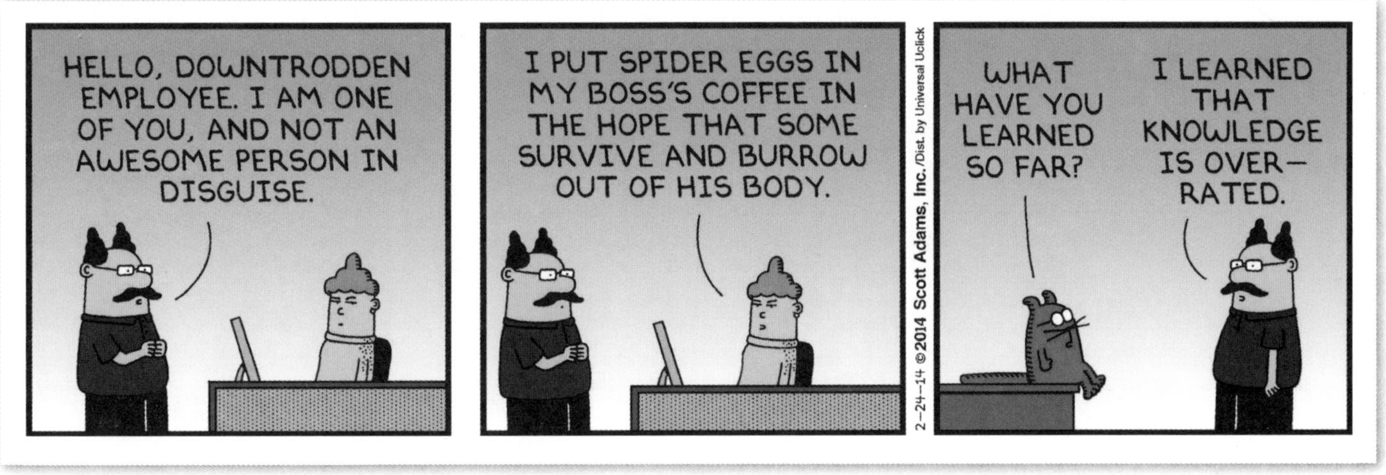
HELLO, DOWNTRODDEN EMPLOYEE. I AM ONE OF YOU, AND NOT AN AWESOME PERSON IN DISGUISE.
I PUT SPIDER EGGS IN MY BOSS'S COFFEE IN THE HOPE THAT SOME SURVIVE AND BURROW OUT OF HIS BODY.
2-24-14 ©2014 Scott Adams, Inc./Dist. by Universal Uclick
WHAT HAVE YOU LEARNED SO FAR?
I LEARNED THAT KNOWLEDGE IS OVER-RATED.

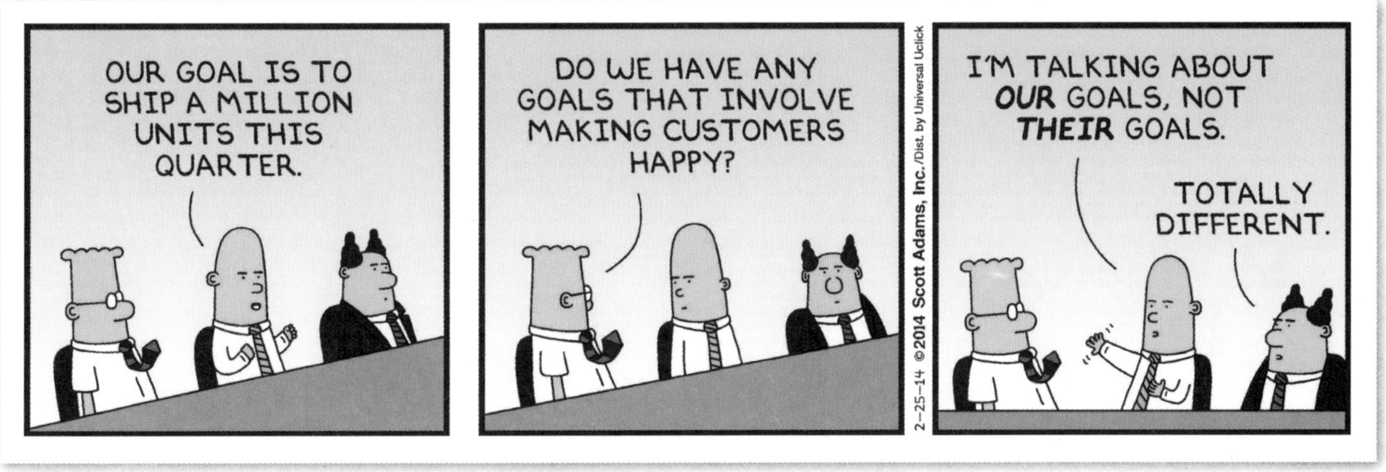
OUR GOAL IS TO SHIP A MILLION UNITS THIS QUARTER.
DO WE HAVE ANY GOALS THAT INVOLVE MAKING CUSTOMERS HAPPY?
2-25-14 ©2014 Scott Adams, Inc./Dist. by Universal Uclick
I'M TALKING ABOUT **OUR** GOALS, NOT **THEIR** GOALS.
TOTALLY DIFFERENT.

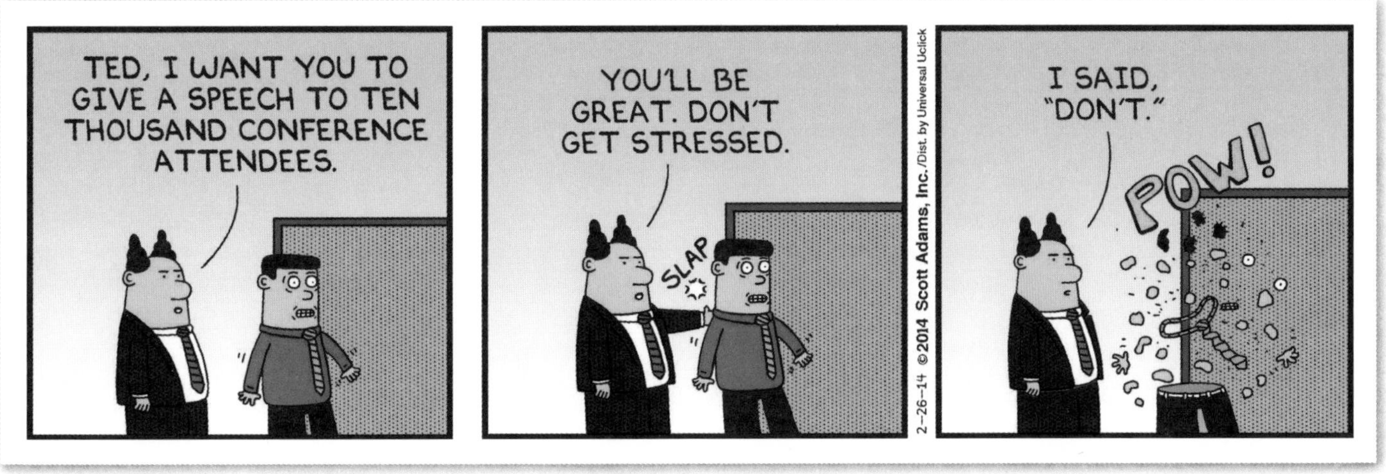
TED, I WANT YOU TO GIVE A SPEECH TO TEN THOUSAND CONFERENCE ATTENDEES.
YOU'LL BE GREAT. DON'T GET STRESSED.
SLAP
2-26-14 ©2014 Scott Adams, Inc./Dist. by Universal Uclick
I SAID, "DON'T."
POW!

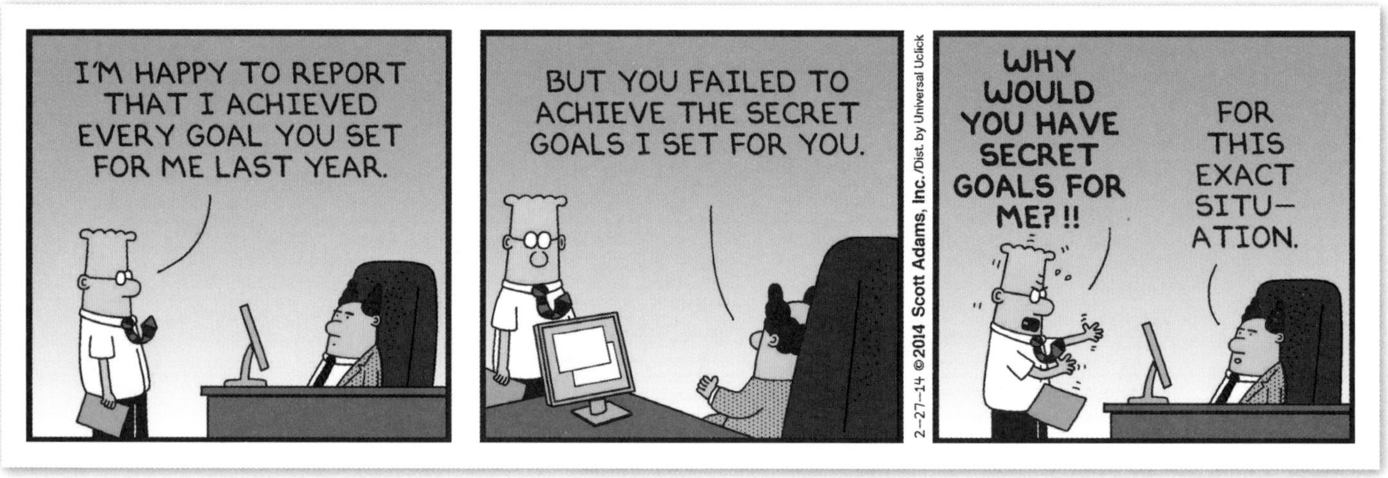
I'M HAPPY TO REPORT THAT I ACHIEVED EVERY GOAL YOU SET FOR ME LAST YEAR.
BUT YOU FAILED TO ACHIEVE THE SECRET GOALS I SET FOR YOU.
2-27-14 ©2014 Scott Adams, Inc./Dist. by Universal Uclick
WHY WOULD YOU HAVE SECRET GOALS FOR ME?!!
FOR THIS EXACT SITU-ATION.

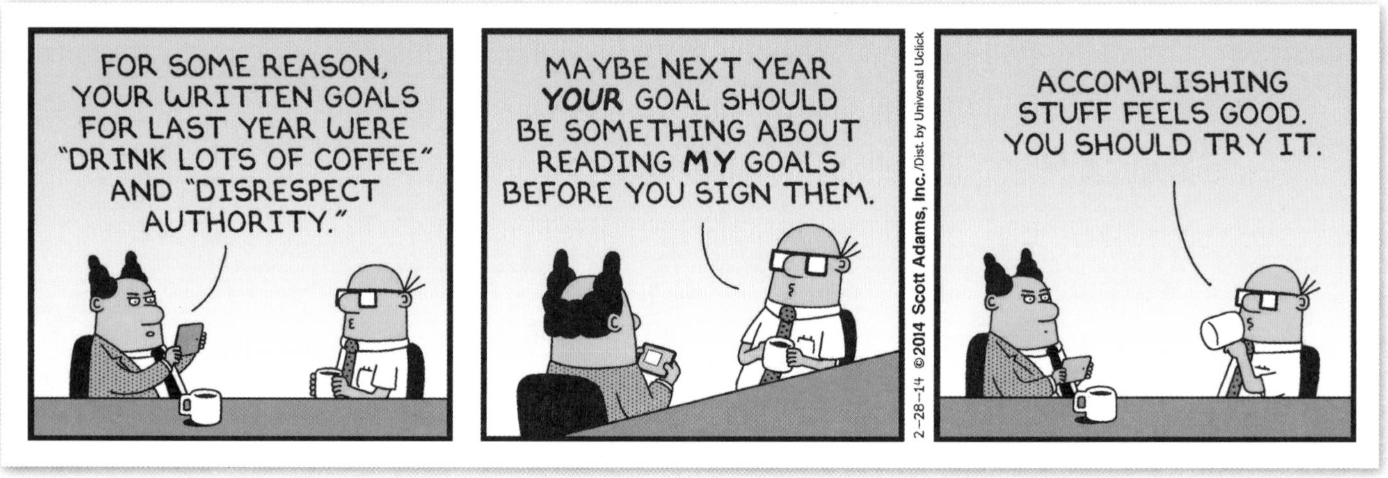
FOR SOME REASON, YOUR WRITTEN GOALS FOR LAST YEAR WERE "DRINK LOTS OF COFFEE" AND "DISRESPECT AUTHORITY."
MAYBE NEXT YEAR ***YOUR*** GOAL SHOULD BE SOMETHING ABOUT READING **MY** GOALS BEFORE YOU SIGN THEM.
2-28-14 ©2014 Scott Adams, Inc./Dist. by Universal Uclick
ACCOMPLISHING STUFF FEELS GOOD. YOU SHOULD TRY IT.

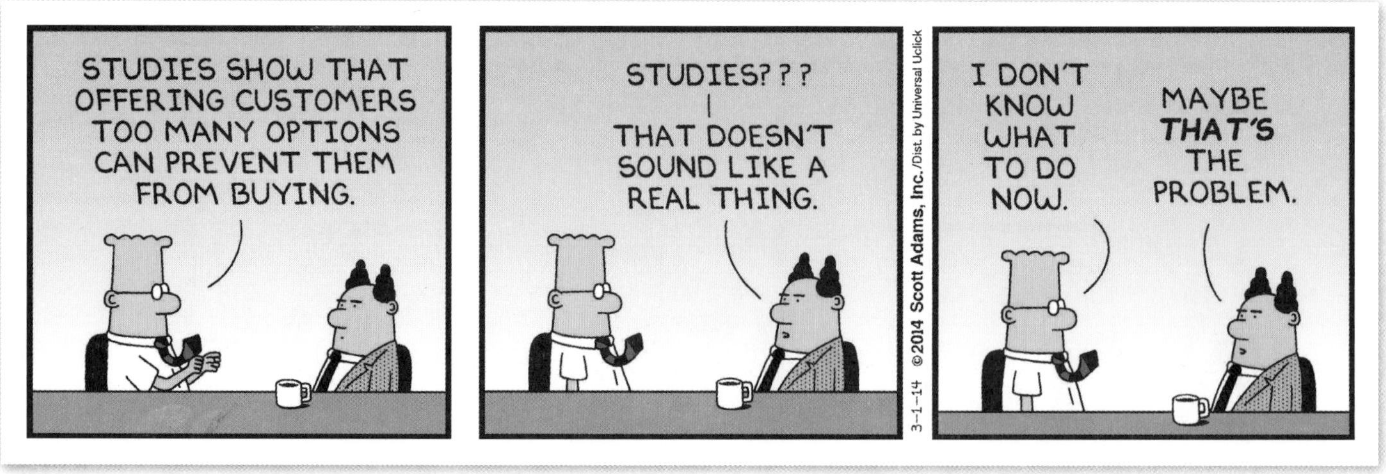
STUDIES SHOW THAT OFFERING CUSTOMERS TOO MANY OPTIONS CAN PREVENT THEM FROM BUYING.
STUDIES???
THAT DOESN'T SOUND LIKE A REAL THING.
3-1-14 ©2014 Scott Adams, Inc./Dist. by Universal Uclick
I DON'T KNOW WHAT TO DO NOW.
MAYBE ***THAT'S*** THE PROBLEM.

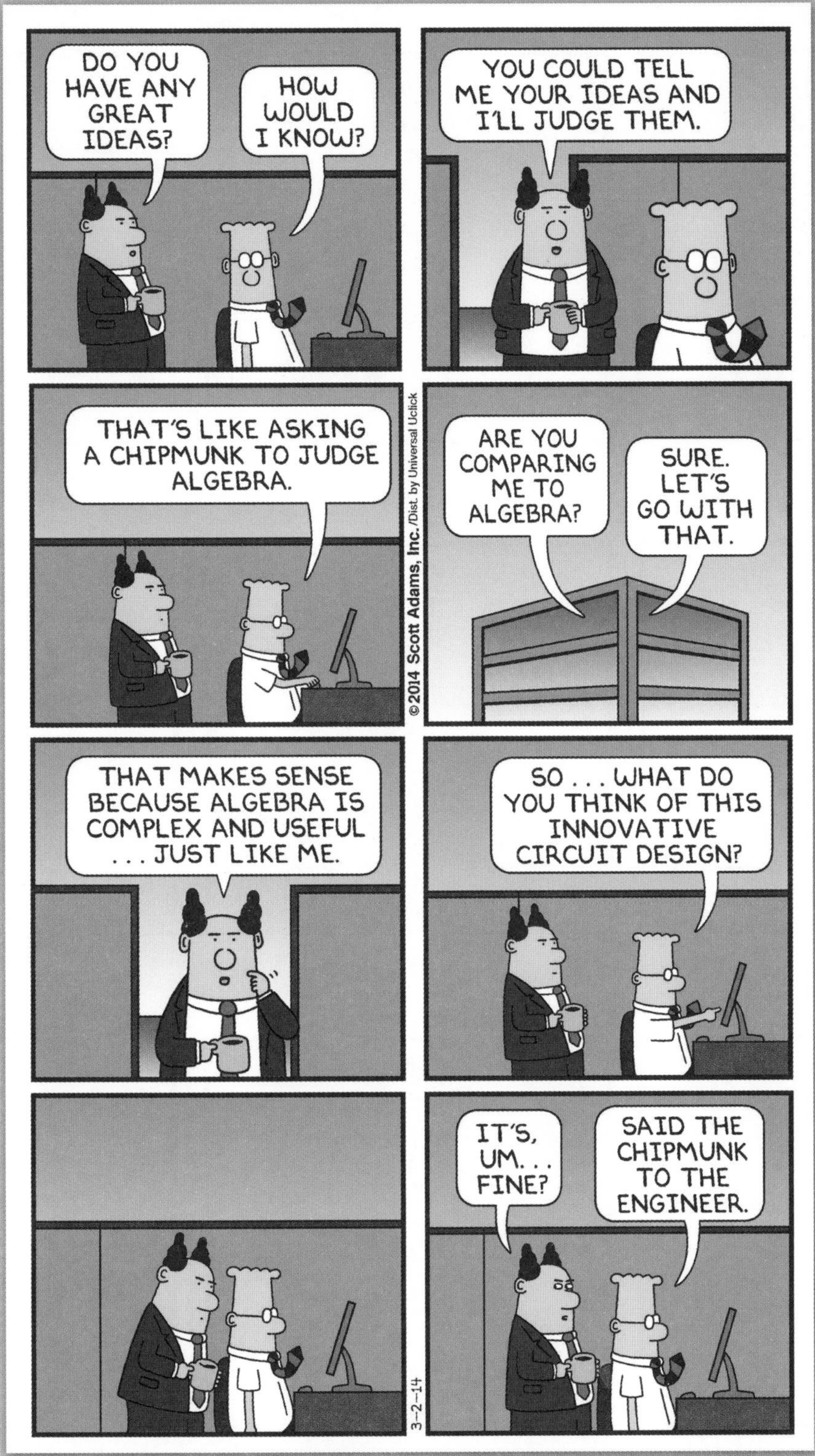
DO YOU HAVE ANY GREAT IDEAS?
HOW WOULD I KNOW?
YOU COULD TELL ME YOUR IDEAS AND I'LL JUDGE THEM.
THAT'S LIKE ASKING A CHIPMUNK TO JUDGE ALGEBRA.
ARE YOU COMPARING ME TO ALGEBRA?
SURE. LET'S GO WITH THAT.
THAT MAKES SENSE BECAUSE ALGEBRA IS COMPLEX AND USEFUL . . . JUST LIKE ME.
SO . . . WHAT DO YOU THINK OF THIS INNOVATIVE CIRCUIT DESIGN?
IT'S, UM. . . FINE?
SAID THE CHIPMUNK TO THE ENGINEER.
©2014 Scott Adams, Inc./Dist. by Universal Uclick
3-2-14

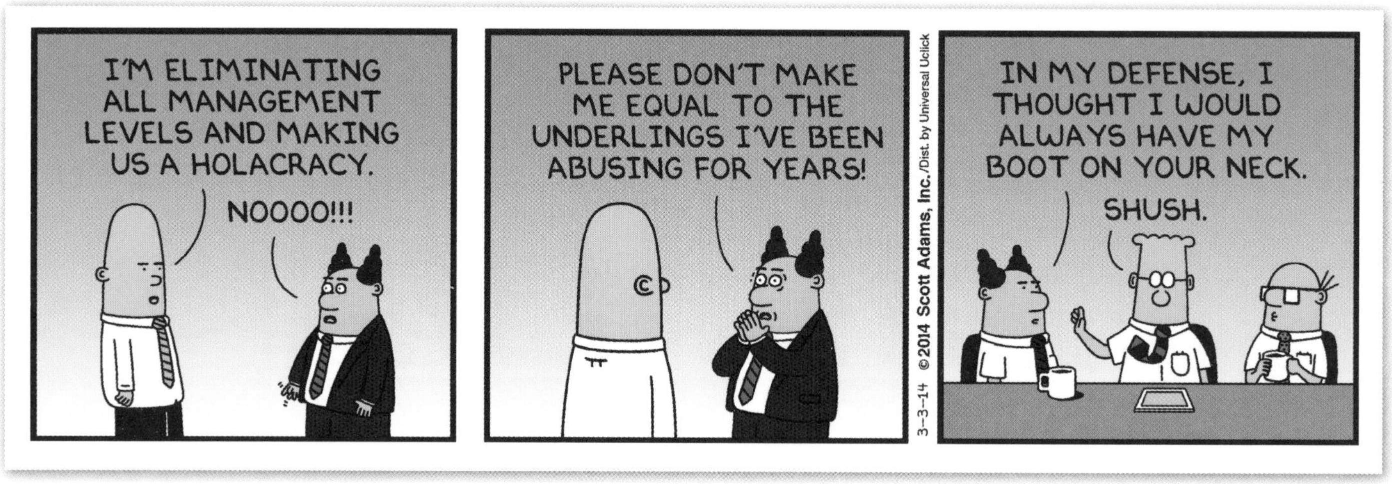
I'M ELIMINATING ALL MANAGEMENT LEVELS AND MAKING US A HOLACRACY.
NOOOO!!!
PLEASE DON'T MAKE ME EQUAL TO THE UNDERLINGS I'VE BEEN ABUSING FOR YEARS!
3-3-14 ©2014 Scott Adams, Inc./Dist. by Universal Uclick
IN MY DEFENSE, I THOUGHT I WOULD ALWAYS HAVE MY BOOT ON YOUR NECK.
SHUSH.

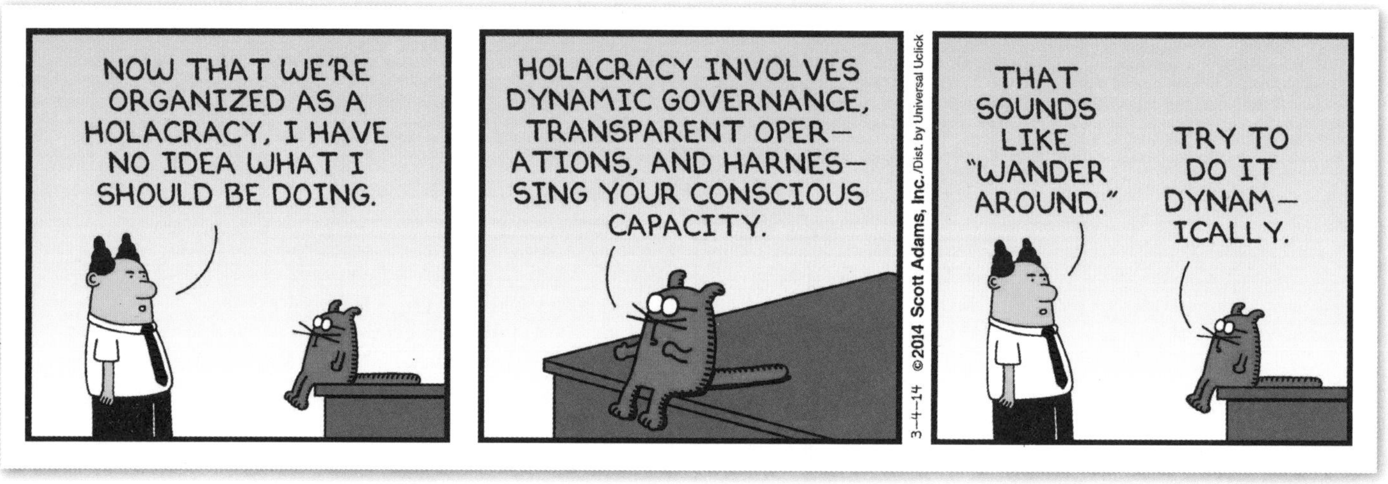
NOW THAT WE'RE ORGANIZED AS A HOLACRACY, I HAVE NO IDEA WHAT I SHOULD BE DOING.
HOLACRACY INVOLVES DYNAMIC GOVERNANCE, TRANSPARENT OPER– ATIONS, AND HARNES– SING YOUR CONSCIOUS CAPACITY.
3-4-14 ©2014 Scott Adams, Inc./Dist. by Universal Uclick
THAT SOUNDS LIKE "WANDER AROUND."
TRY TO DO IT DYNAM– ICALLY.

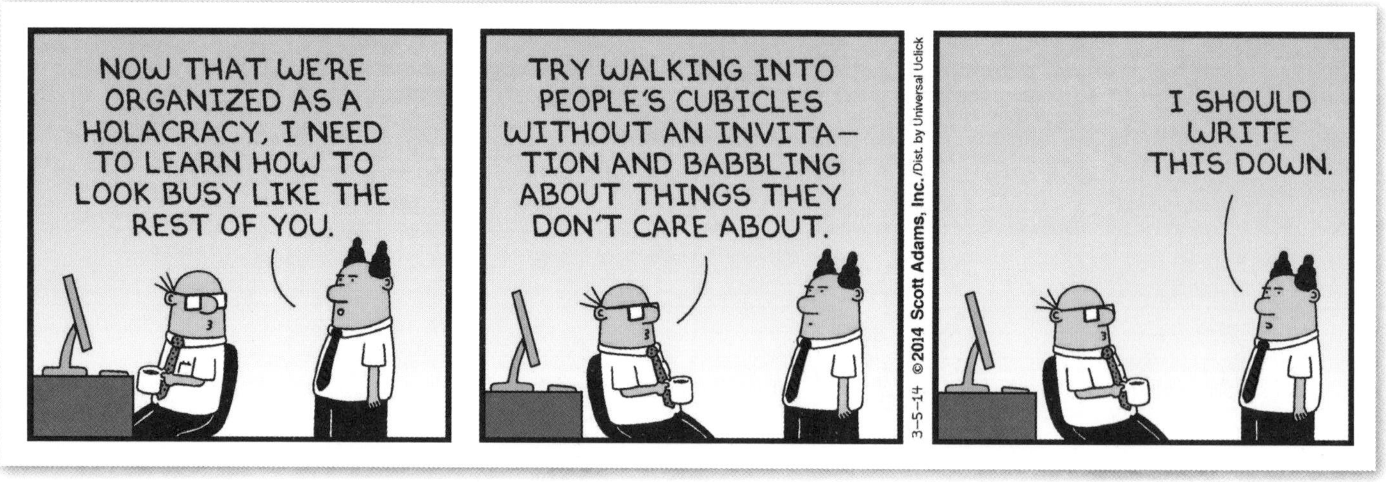
NOW THAT WE'RE ORGANIZED AS A HOLACRACY, I NEED TO LEARN HOW TO LOOK BUSY LIKE THE REST OF YOU.
TRY WALKING INTO PEOPLE'S CUBICLES WITHOUT AN INVITA– TION AND BABBLING ABOUT THINGS THEY DON'T CARE ABOUT.
3-5-14 ©2014 Scott Adams, Inc./Dist. by Universal Uclick
I SHOULD WRITE THIS DOWN.

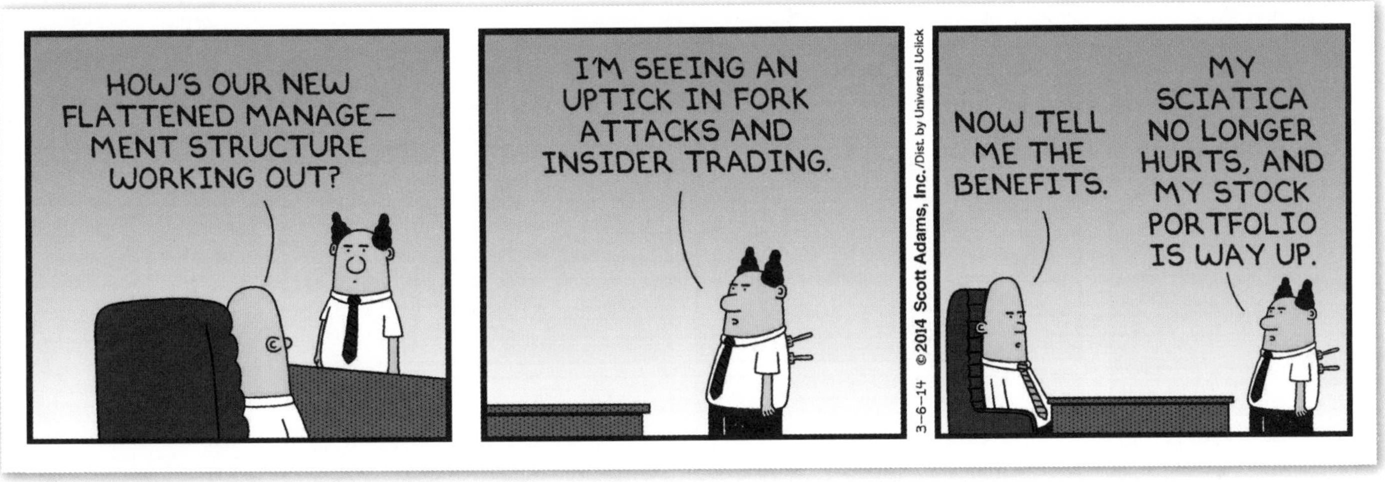
HOW'S OUR NEW FLATTENED MANAGE- MENT STRUCTURE WORKING OUT?
I'M SEEING AN UPTICK IN FORK ATTACKS AND INSIDER TRADING.
3-6-14 ©2014 Scott Adams, Inc./Dist. by Universal Uclick
NOW TELL ME THE BENEFITS.
MY SCIATICA NO LONGER HURTS, AND MY STOCK PORTFOLIO IS WAY UP.

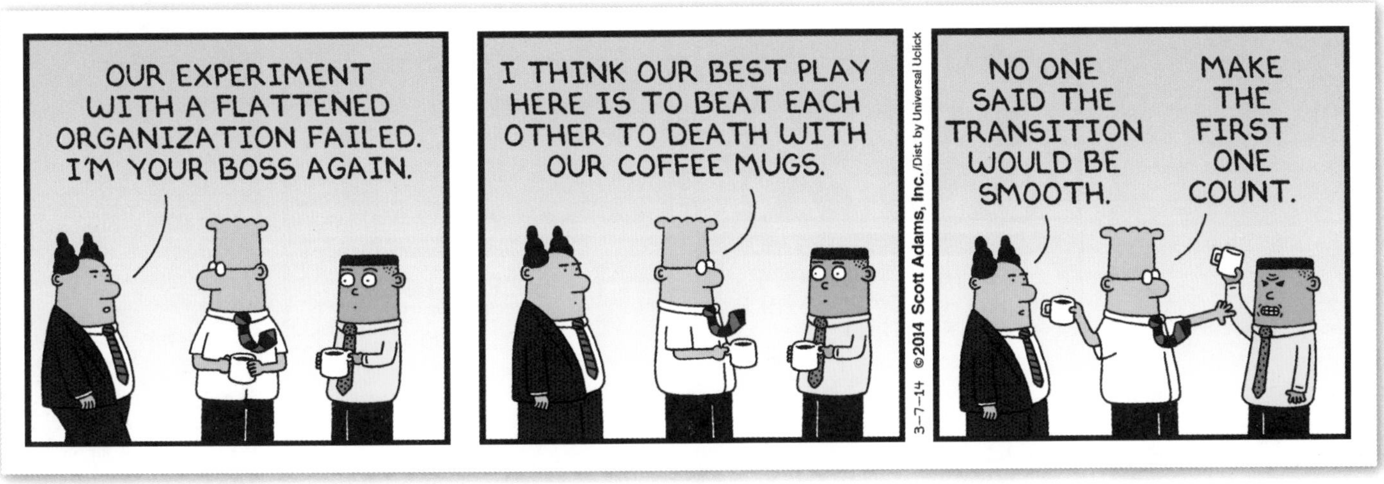
OUR EXPERIMENT WITH A FLATTENED ORGANIZATION FAILED. I'M YOUR BOSS AGAIN.
I THINK OUR BEST PLAY HERE IS TO BEAT EACH OTHER TO DEATH WITH OUR COFFEE MUGS.
3-7-14 ©2014 Scott Adams, Inc./Dist. by Universal Uclick
NO ONE SAID THE TRANSITION WOULD BE SMOOTH.
MAKE THE FIRST ONE COUNT.

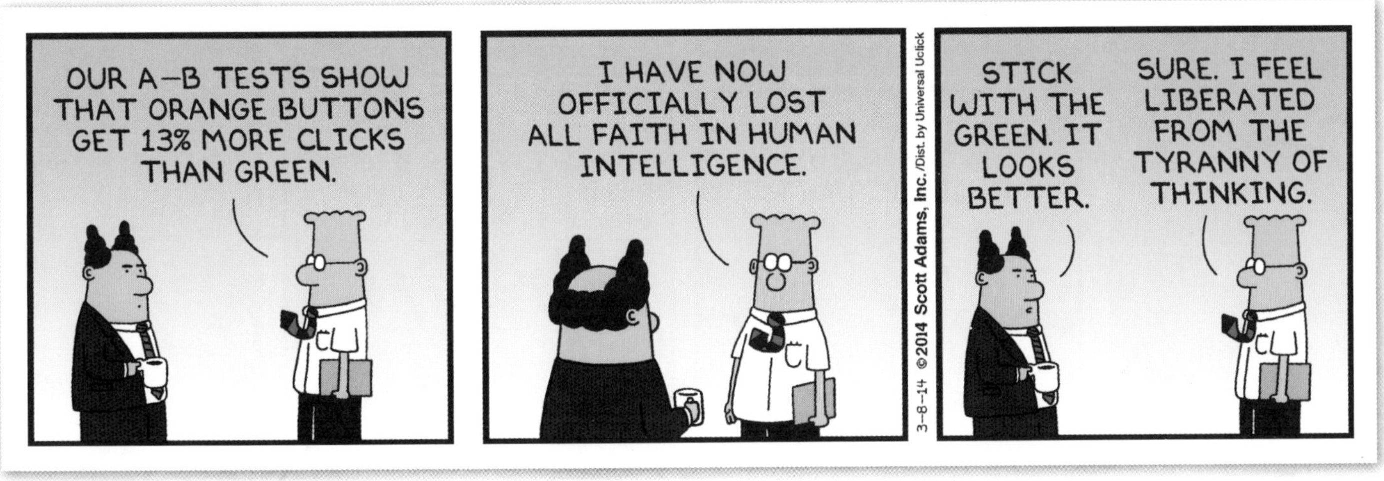
OUR A-B TESTS SHOW THAT ORANGE BUTTONS GET 13% MORE CLICKS THAN GREEN.
I HAVE NOW OFFICIALLY LOST ALL FAITH IN HUMAN INTELLIGENCE.
3-8-14 ©2014 Scott Adams, Inc./Dist. by Universal Uclick
STICK WITH THE GREEN. IT LOOKS BETTER.
SURE. I FEEL LIBERATED FROM THE TYRANNY OF THINKING.

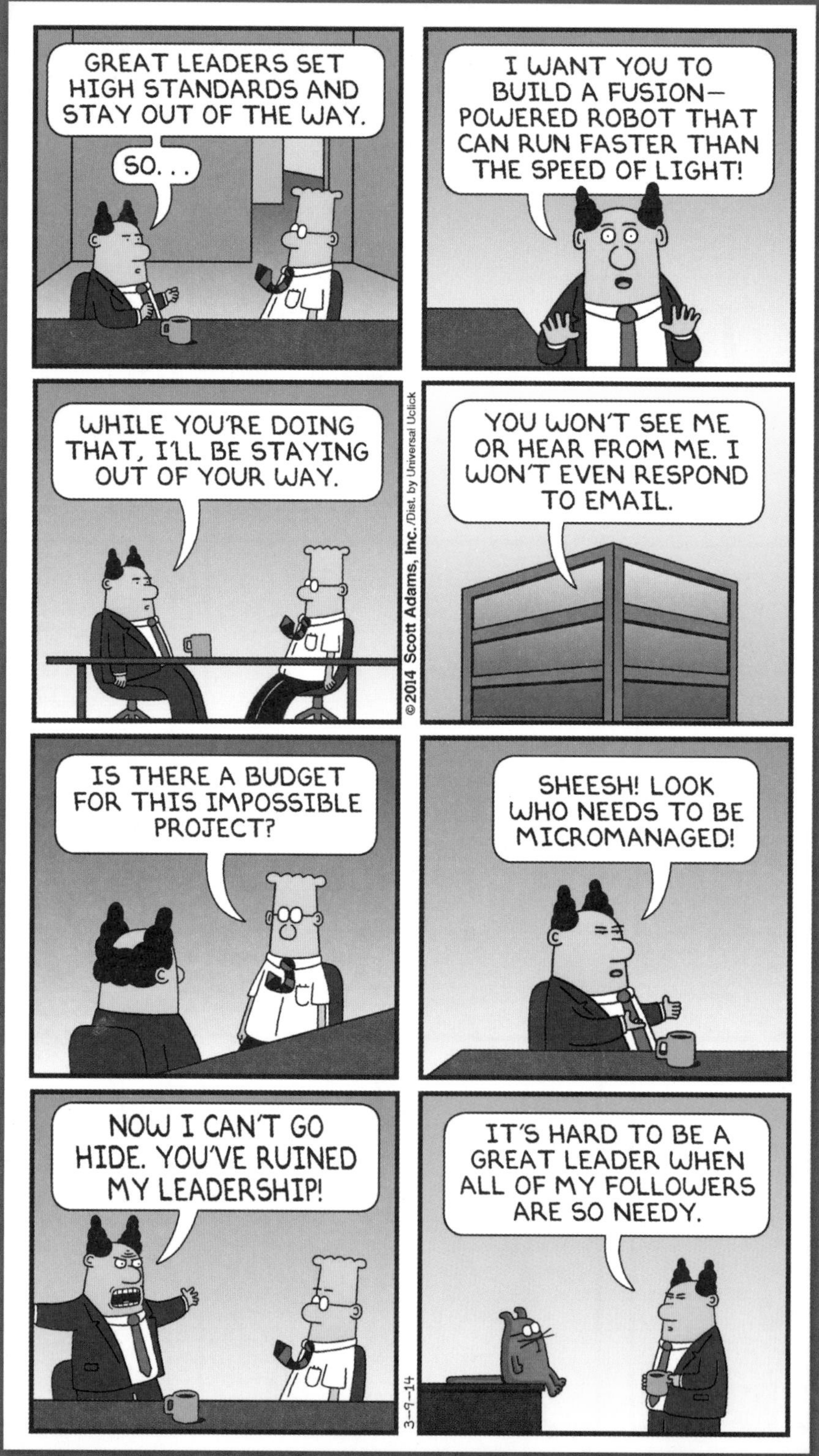
GREAT LEADERS SET HIGH STANDARDS AND STAY OUT OF THE WAY.
SO. . .
I WANT YOU TO BUILD A FUSION-POWERED ROBOT THAT CAN RUN FASTER THAN THE SPEED OF LIGHT!
WHILE YOU'RE DOING THAT, I'LL BE STAYING OUT OF YOUR WAY.
YOU WON'T SEE ME OR HEAR FROM ME. I WON'T EVEN RESPOND TO EMAIL.
IS THERE A BUDGET FOR THIS IMPOSSIBLE PROJECT?
SHEESH! LOOK WHO NEEDS TO BE MICROMANAGED!
NOW I CAN'T GO HIDE. YOU'VE RUINED MY LEADERSHIP!
IT'S HARD TO BE A GREAT LEADER WHEN ALL OF MY FOLLOWERS ARE SO NEEDY.
©2014 Scott Adams, Inc./Dist. by Universal Uclick
3-9-14

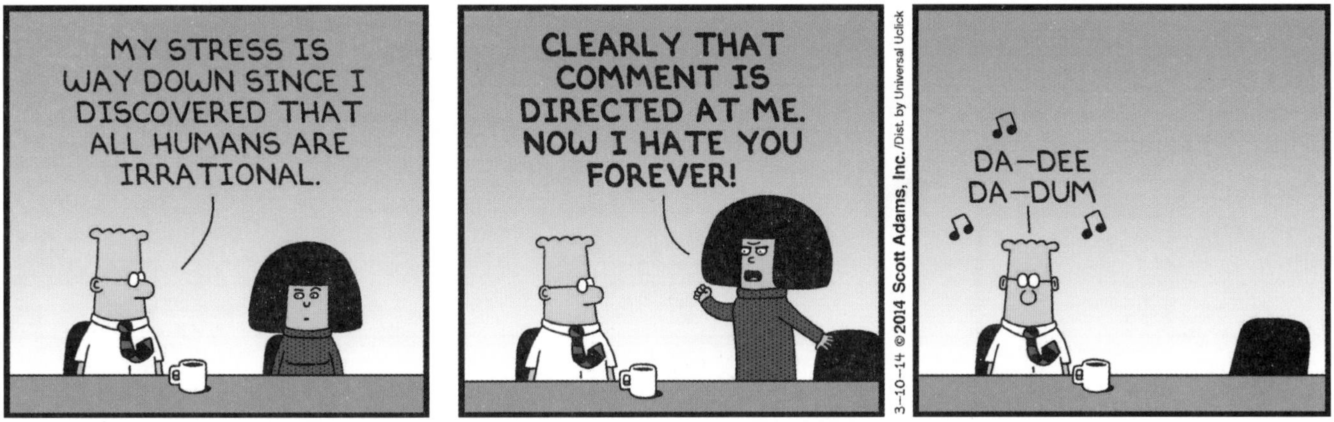
MY STRESS IS WAY DOWN SINCE I DISCOVERED THAT ALL HUMANS ARE IRRATIONAL.
CLEARLY THAT COMMENT IS DIRECTED AT ME. NOW I HATE YOU FOREVER!
DA-DEE DA-DUM
3-10-14 ©2014 Scott Adams, Inc./Dist. by Universal Uclick

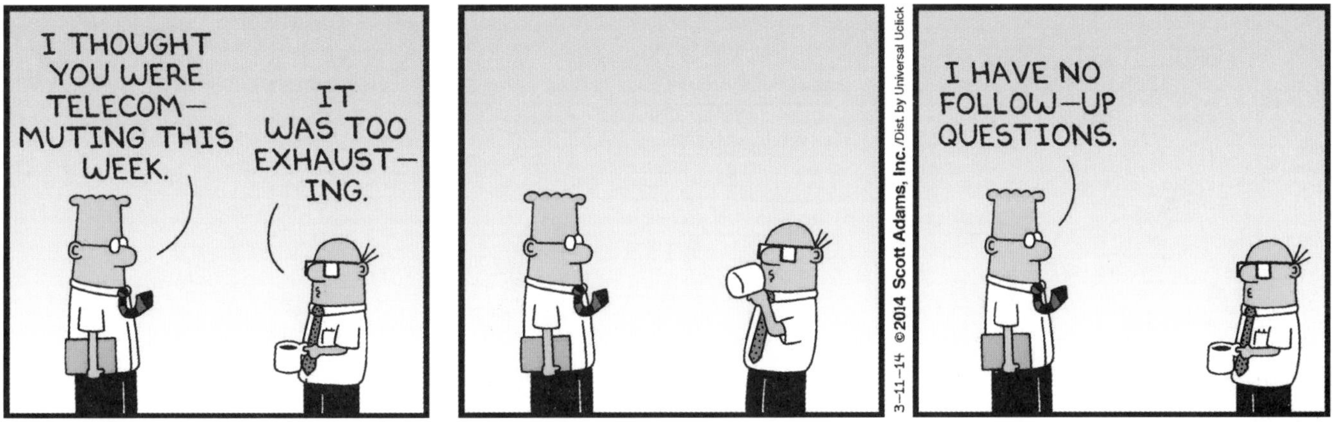
I THOUGHT YOU WERE TELECOM-MUTING THIS WEEK.
IT WAS TOO EXHAUST-ING.
I HAVE NO FOLLOW-UP QUESTIONS.
3-11-14 ©2014 Scott Adams, Inc./Dist. by Universal Uclick

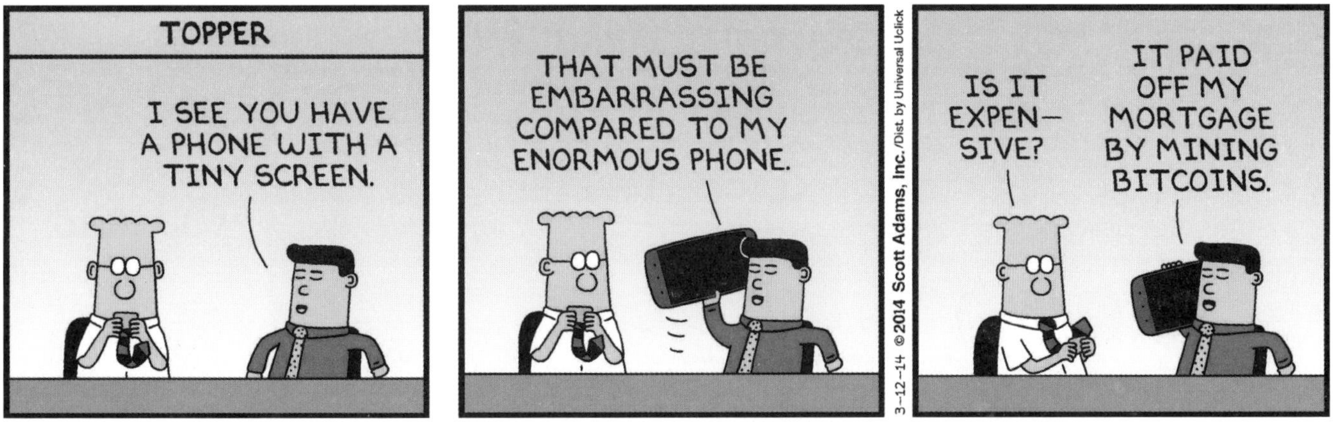
TOPPER
I SEE YOU HAVE A PHONE WITH A TINY SCREEN.
THAT MUST BE EMBARRASSING COMPARED TO MY ENORMOUS PHONE.
IS IT EXPEN-SIVE?
IT PAID OFF MY MORTGAGE BY MINING BITCOINS.
3-12-14 ©2014 Scott Adams, Inc./Dist. by Universal Uclick

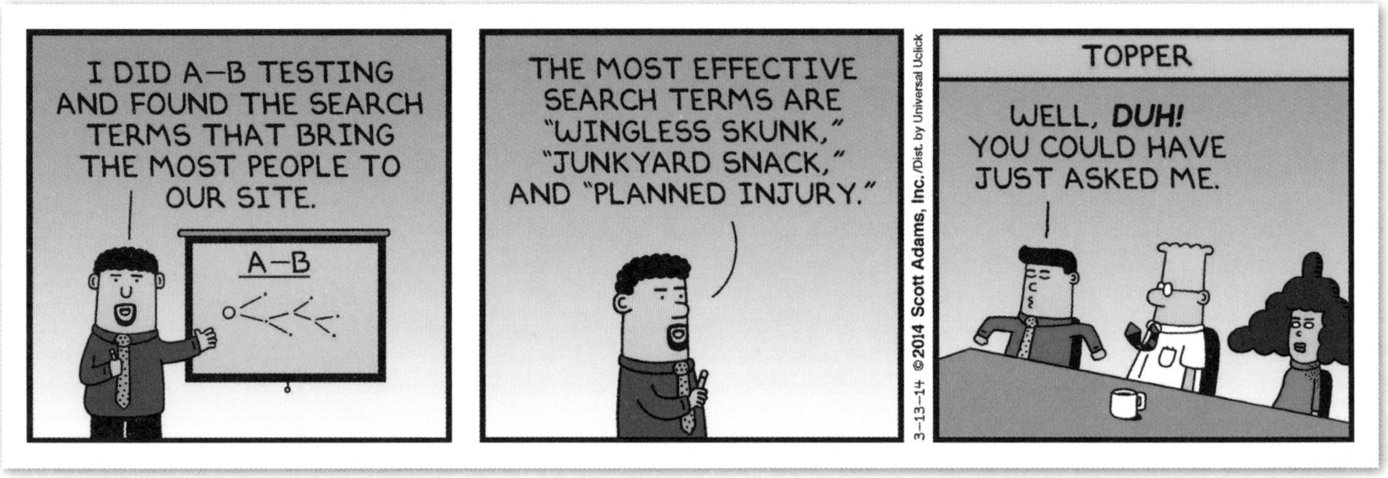
I DID A–B TESTING AND FOUND THE SEARCH TERMS THAT BRING THE MOST PEOPLE TO OUR SITE.
A–B
THE MOST EFFECTIVE SEARCH TERMS ARE "WINGLESS SKUNK," "JUNKYARD SNACK," AND "PLANNED INJURY."
3-13-14 ©2014 Scott Adams, Inc./Dist. by Universal Uclick
TOPPER
WELL, ***DUH!*** YOU COULD HAVE JUST ASKED ME.

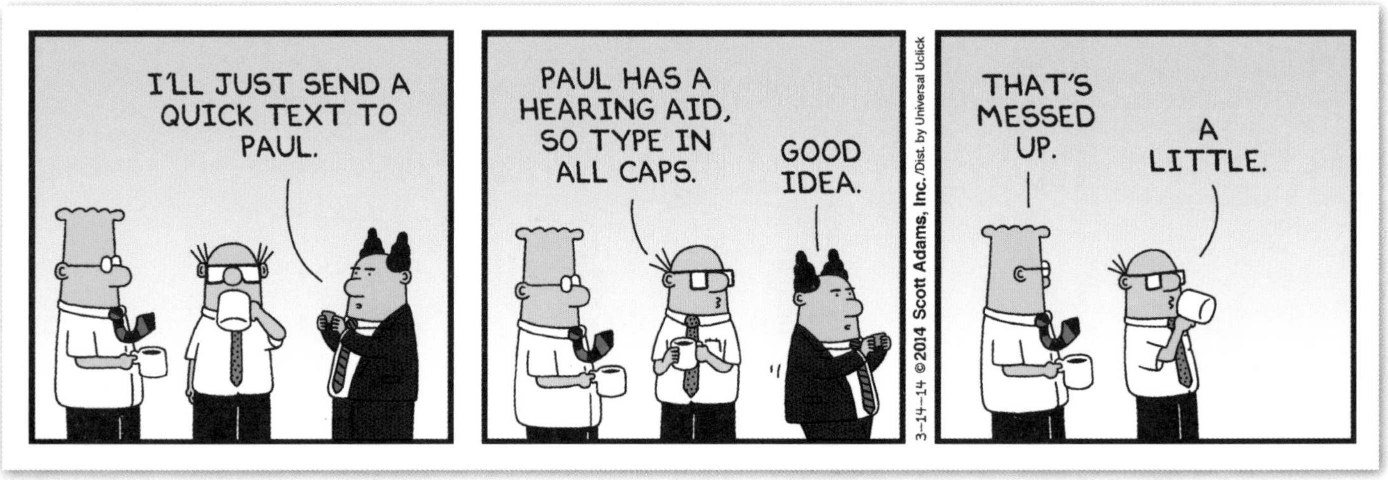
I'LL JUST SEND A QUICK TEXT TO PAUL.
PAUL HAS A HEARING AID, SO TYPE IN ALL CAPS.
GOOD IDEA.
3-14-14 ©2014 Scott Adams, Inc./Dist. by Universal Uclick
THAT'S MESSED UP.
A LITTLE.

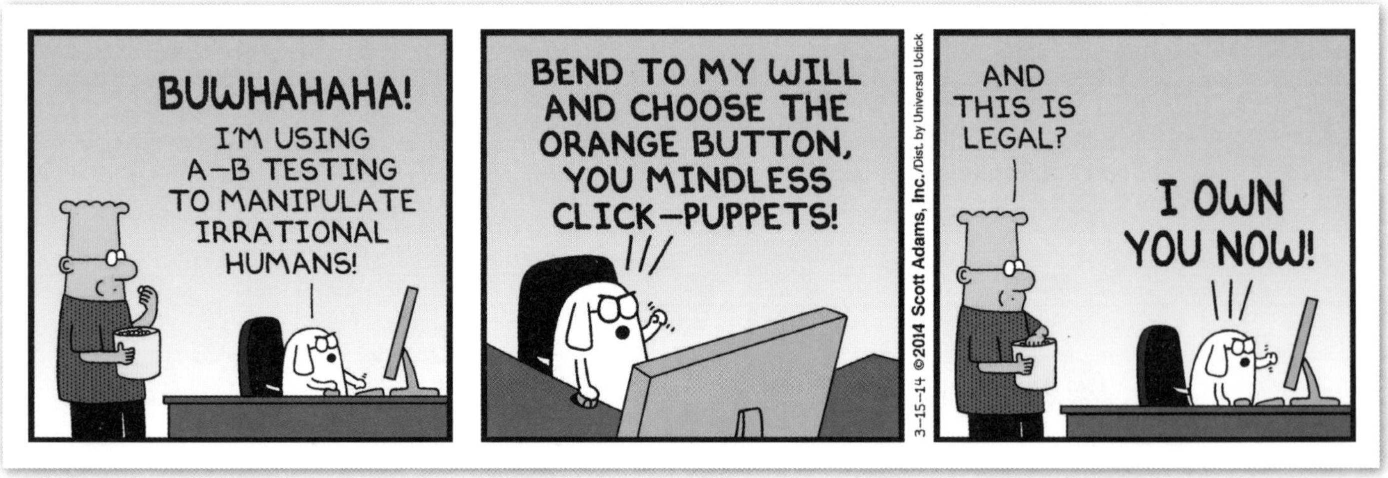
BUWHAHAHA!
I'M USING A–B TESTING TO MANIPULATE IRRATIONAL HUMANS!
BEND TO MY WILL AND CHOOSE THE ORANGE BUTTON, YOU MINDLESS CLICK–PUPPETS!
3-15-14 ©2014 Scott Adams, Inc./Dist. by Universal Uclick
AND THIS IS LEGAL?
I OWN YOU NOW!

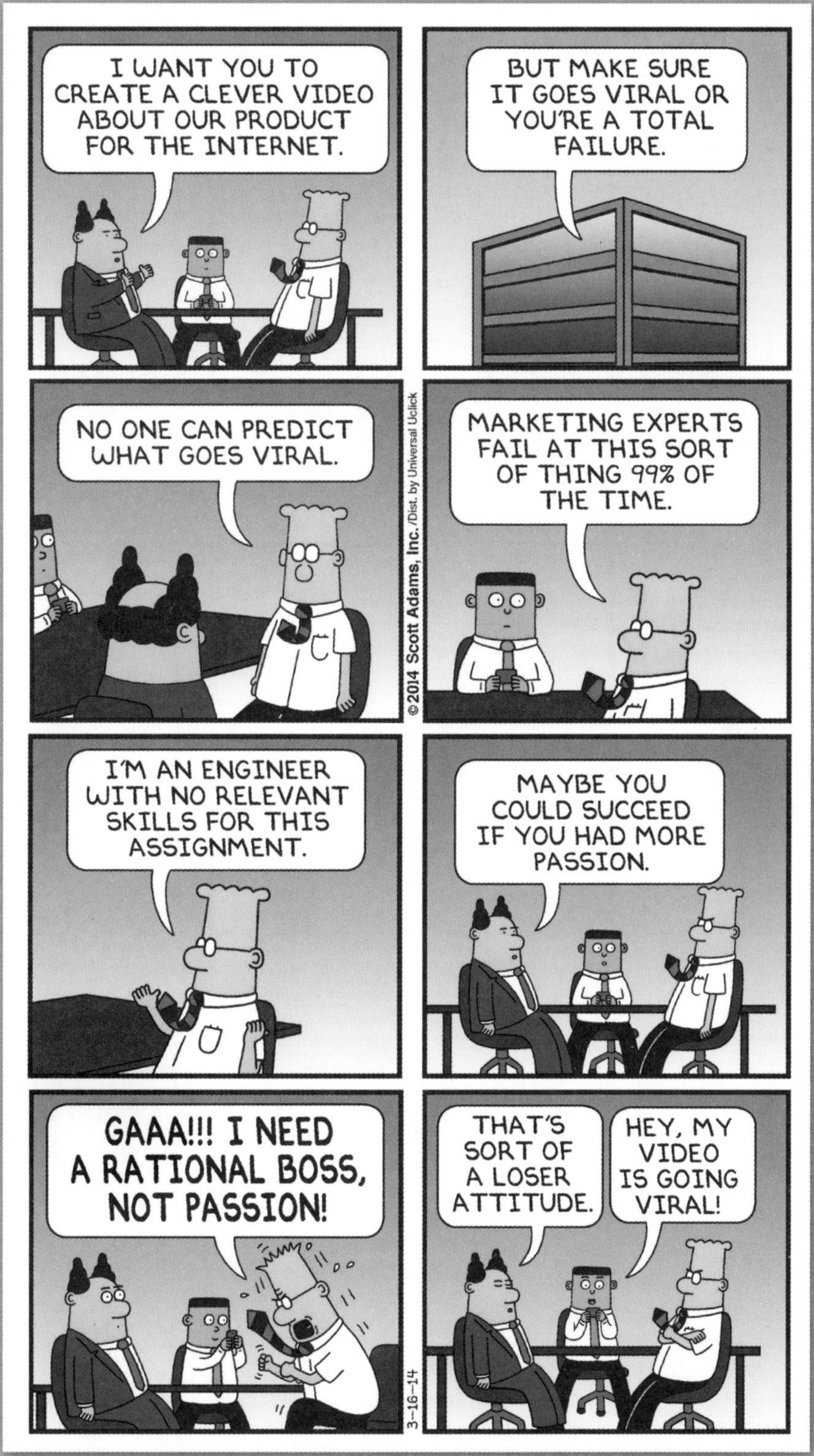
I WANT YOU TO CREATE A CLEVER VIDEO ABOUT OUR PRODUCT FOR THE INTERNET.
BUT MAKE SURE IT GOES VIRAL OR YOU'RE A TOTAL FAILURE.
NO ONE CAN PREDICT WHAT GOES VIRAL.
MARKETING EXPERTS FAIL AT THIS SORT OF THING 99% OF THE TIME.
I'M AN ENGINEER WITH NO RELEVANT SKILLS FOR THIS ASSIGNMENT.
MAYBE YOU COULD SUCCEED IF YOU HAD MORE PASSION.
GAAA!!! I NEED A RATIONAL BOSS, NOT PASSION!
THAT'S SORT OF A LOSER ATTITUDE.
HEY, MY VIDEO IS GOING VIRAL!
©2014 Scott Adams, Inc./Dist. by Universal Uclick
3-16-14

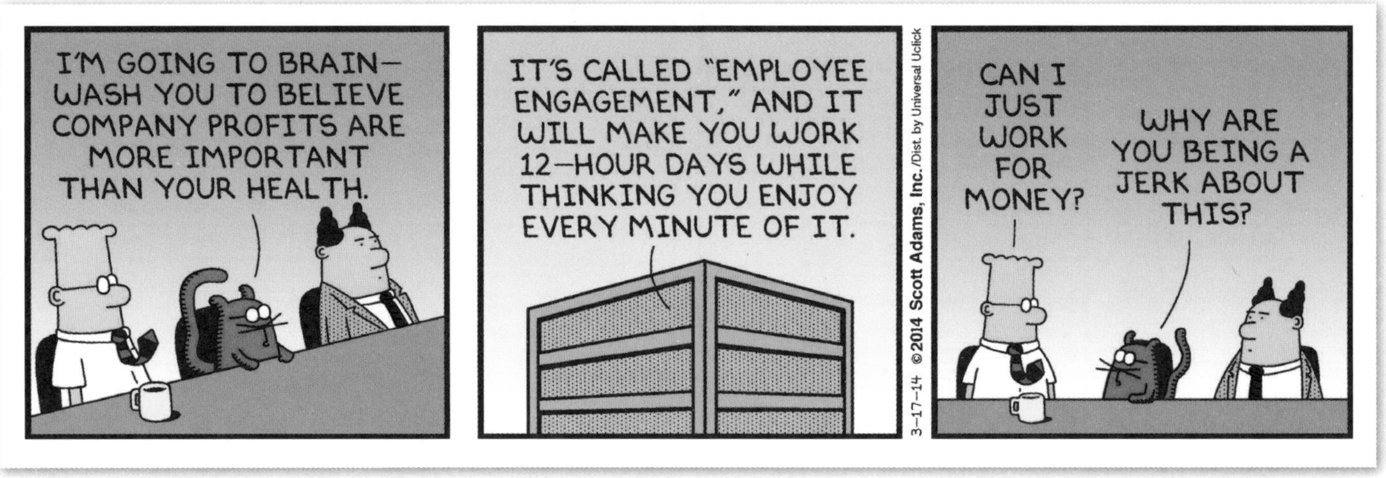
I'M GOING TO BRAIN-WASH YOU TO BELIEVE COMPANY PROFITS ARE MORE IMPORTANT THAN YOUR HEALTH.
IT'S CALLED "EMPLOYEE ENGAGEMENT," AND IT WILL MAKE YOU WORK 12-HOUR DAYS WHILE THINKING YOU ENJOY EVERY MINUTE OF IT.
3-17-14 ©2014 Scott Adams, Inc./Dist. by Universal Uclick
CAN I JUST WORK FOR MONEY?
WHY ARE YOU BEING A JERK ABOUT THIS?

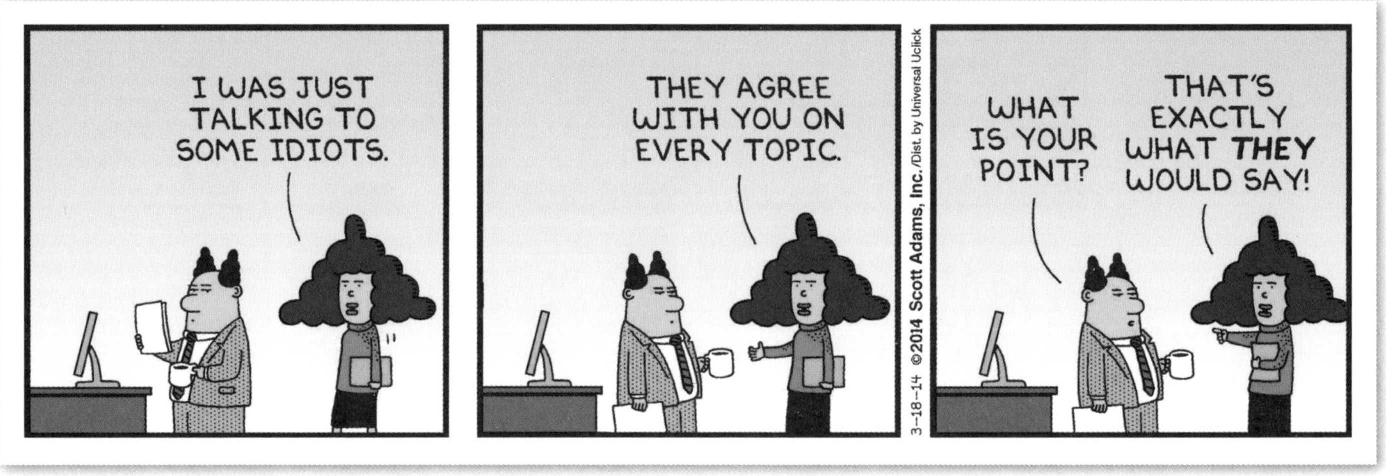
I WAS JUST TALKING TO SOME IDIOTS.
THEY AGREE WITH YOU ON EVERY TOPIC.
3-18-14 ©2014 Scott Adams, Inc./Dist. by Universal Uclick
WHAT IS YOUR POINT?
THAT'S EXACTLY WHAT **THEY** WOULD SAY!

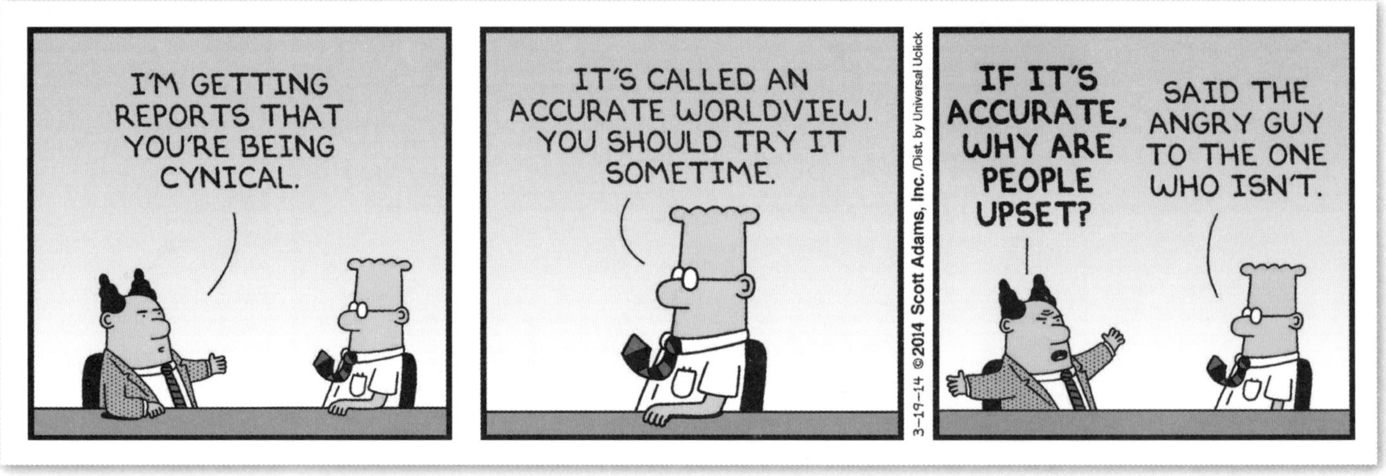
I'M GETTING REPORTS THAT YOU'RE BEING CYNICAL.
IT'S CALLED AN ACCURATE WORLDVIEW. YOU SHOULD TRY IT SOMETIME.
3-19-14 ©2014 Scott Adams, Inc./Dist. by Universal Uclick
IF IT'S ACCURATE, WHY ARE PEOPLE UPSET?
SAID THE ANGRY GUY TO THE ONE WHO ISN'T.

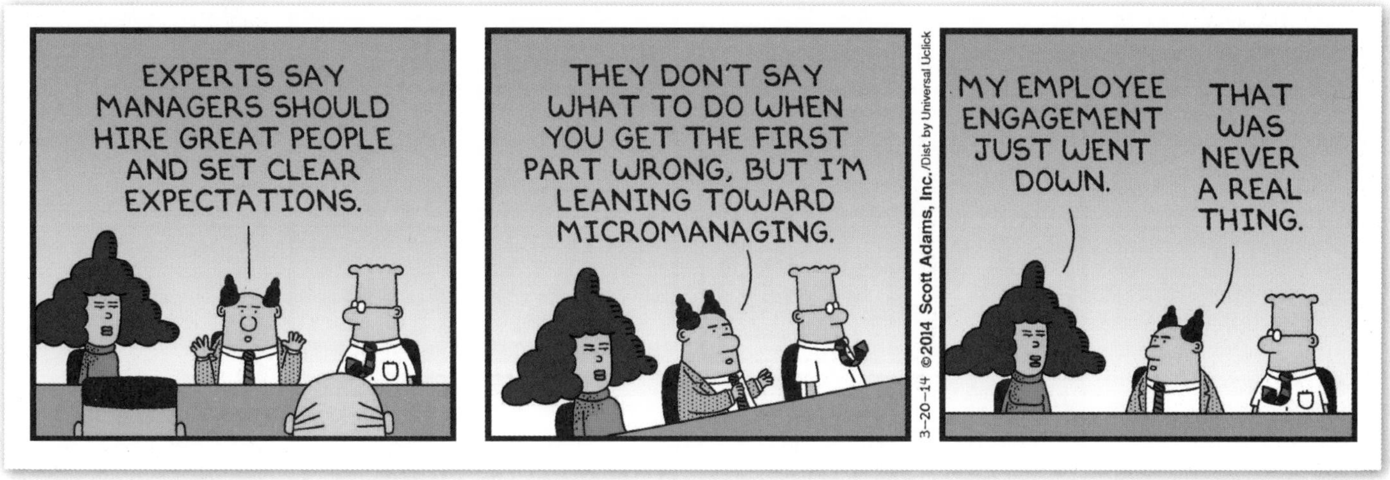
EXPERTS SAY MANAGERS SHOULD HIRE GREAT PEOPLE AND SET CLEAR EXPECTATIONS.
THEY DON'T SAY WHAT TO DO WHEN YOU GET THE FIRST PART WRONG, BUT I'M LEANING TOWARD MICROMANAGING.
3-20-14 ©2014 Scott Adams, Inc./Dist. by Universal Uclick
MY EMPLOYEE ENGAGEMENT JUST WENT DOWN.
THAT WAS NEVER A REAL THING.

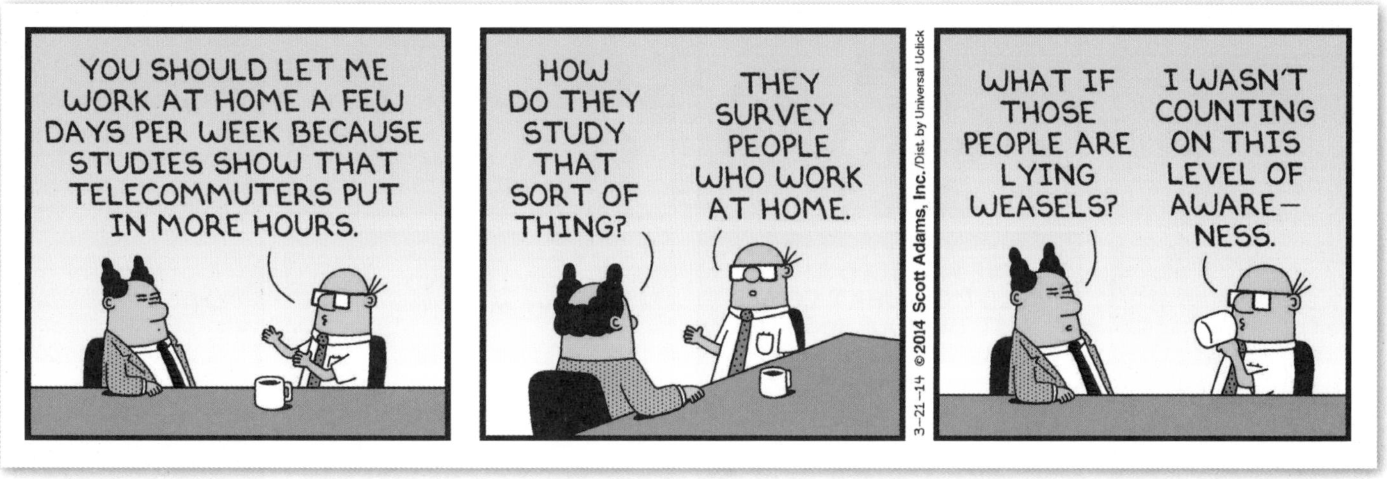
YOU SHOULD LET ME WORK AT HOME A FEW DAYS PER WEEK BECAUSE STUDIES SHOW THAT TELECOMMUTERS PUT IN MORE HOURS.
HOW DO THEY STUDY THAT SORT OF THING?
THEY SURVEY PEOPLE WHO WORK AT HOME.
3-21-14 ©2014 Scott Adams, Inc./Dist. by Universal Uclick
WHAT IF THOSE PEOPLE ARE LYING WEASELS?
I WASN'T COUNTING ON THIS LEVEL OF AWARE-NESS.

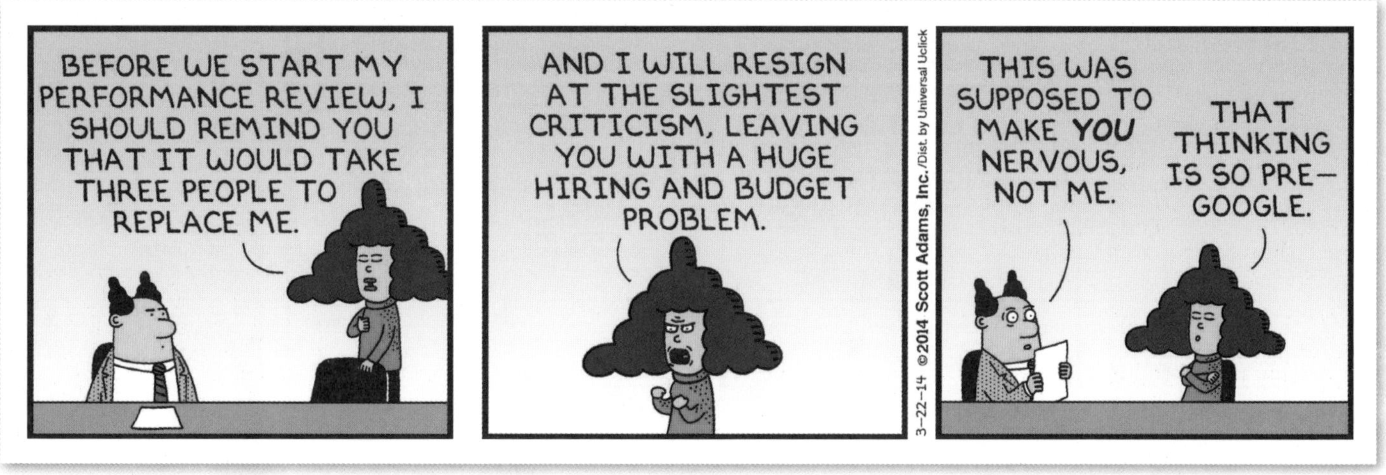
BEFORE WE START MY PERFORMANCE REVIEW, I SHOULD REMIND YOU THAT IT WOULD TAKE THREE PEOPLE TO REPLACE ME.
AND I WILL RESIGN AT THE SLIGHTEST CRITICISM, LEAVING YOU WITH A HUGE HIRING AND BUDGET PROBLEM.
3-22-14 ©2014 Scott Adams, Inc./Dist. by Universal Uclick
THIS WAS SUPPOSED TO MAKE **YOU** NERVOUS, NOT ME.
THAT THINKING IS SO PRE-GOOGLE.

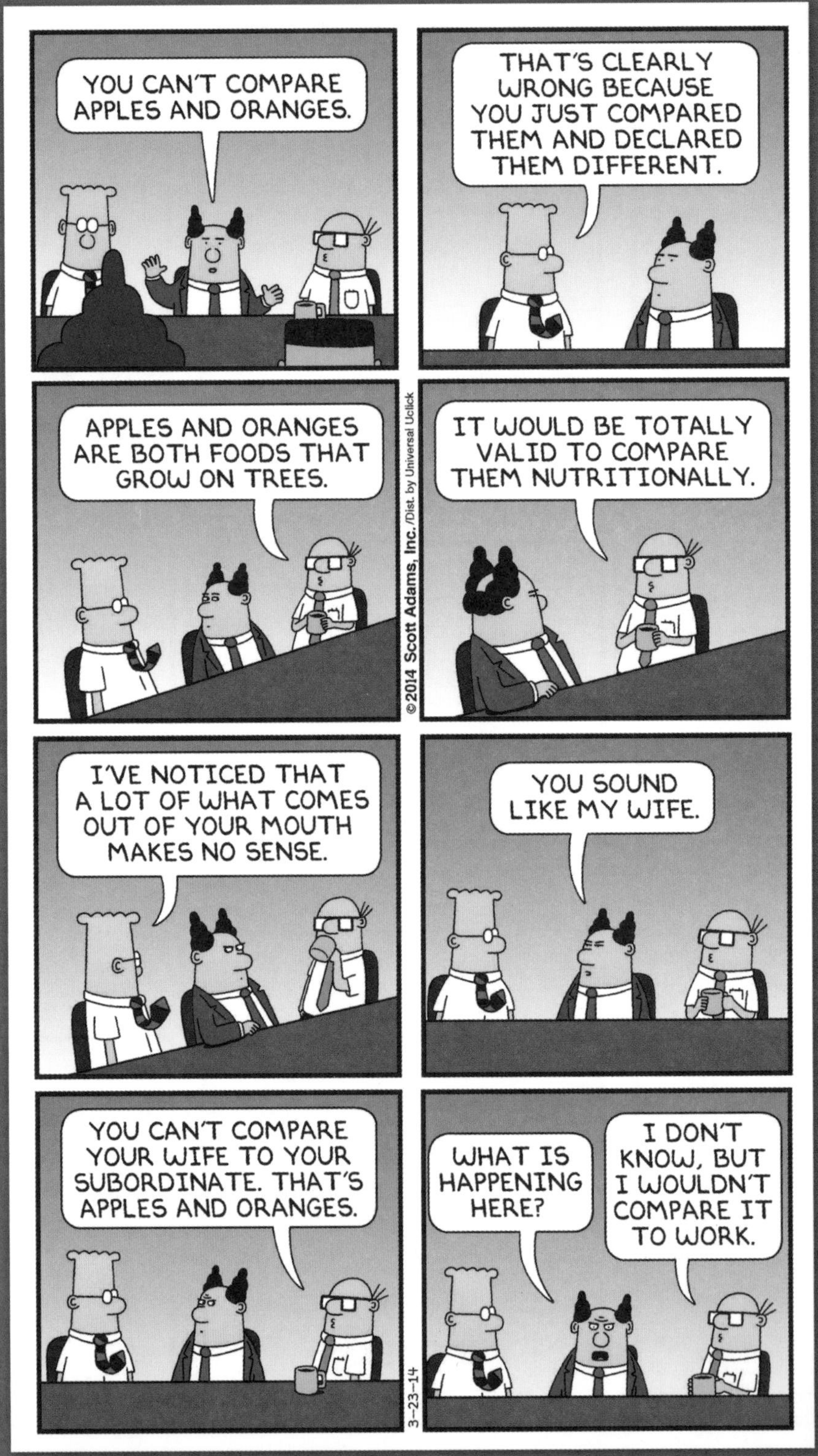
YOU CAN'T COMPARE APPLES AND ORANGES.
THAT'S CLEARLY WRONG BECAUSE YOU JUST COMPARED THEM AND DECLARED THEM DIFFERENT.
APPLES AND ORANGES ARE BOTH FOODS THAT GROW ON TREES.
IT WOULD BE TOTALLY VALID TO COMPARE THEM NUTRITIONALLY.
I'VE NOTICED THAT A LOT OF WHAT COMES OUT OF YOUR MOUTH MAKES NO SENSE.
YOU SOUND LIKE MY WIFE.
YOU CAN'T COMPARE YOUR WIFE TO YOUR SUBORDINATE. THAT'S APPLES AND ORANGES.
WHAT IS HAPPENING HERE?
I DON'T KNOW, BUT I WOULDN'T COMPARE IT TO WORK.
©2014 Scott Adams, Inc./Dist. by Universal Uclick
3-23-14

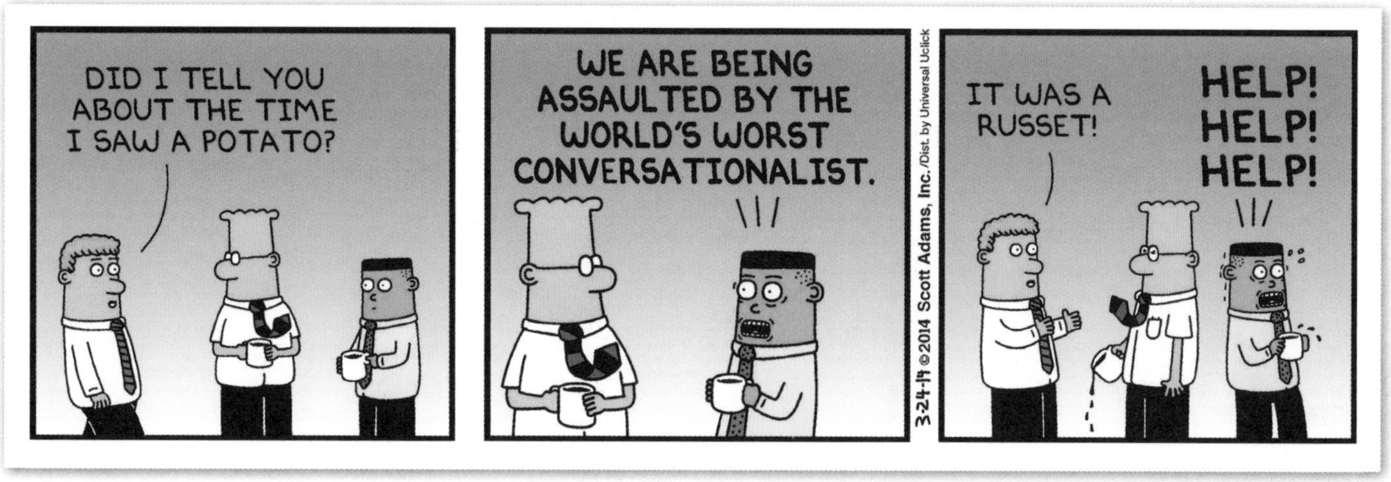
DID I TELL YOU ABOUT THE TIME I SAW A POTATO?
WE ARE BEING ASSAULTED BY THE WORLD'S WORST CONVERSATIONALIST.
IT WAS A RUSSET!
HELP! HELP! HELP!
3-24-14 ©2014 Scott Adams, Inc./Dist. by Universal Uclick

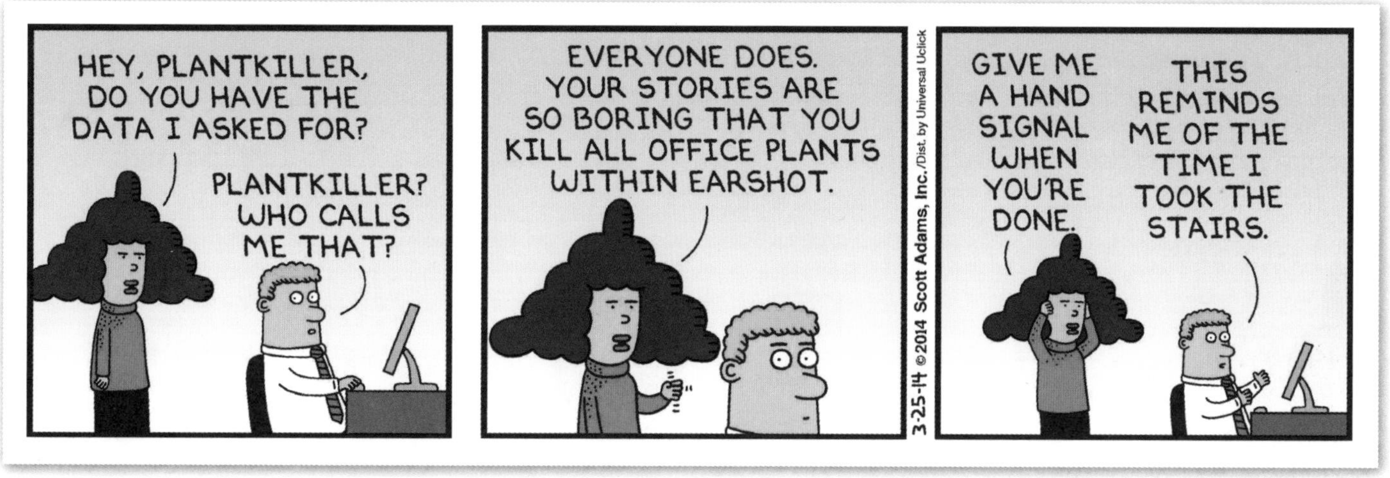
HEY, PLANTKILLER, DO YOU HAVE THE DATA I ASKED FOR?
PLANTKILLER? WHO CALLS ME THAT?
EVERYONE DOES. YOUR STORIES ARE SO BORING THAT YOU KILL ALL OFFICE PLANTS WITHIN EARSHOT.
GIVE ME A HAND SIGNAL WHEN YOU'RE DONE.
THIS REMINDS ME OF THE TIME I TOOK THE STAIRS.
3-25-14 ©2014 Scott Adams, Inc./Dist. by Universal Uclick

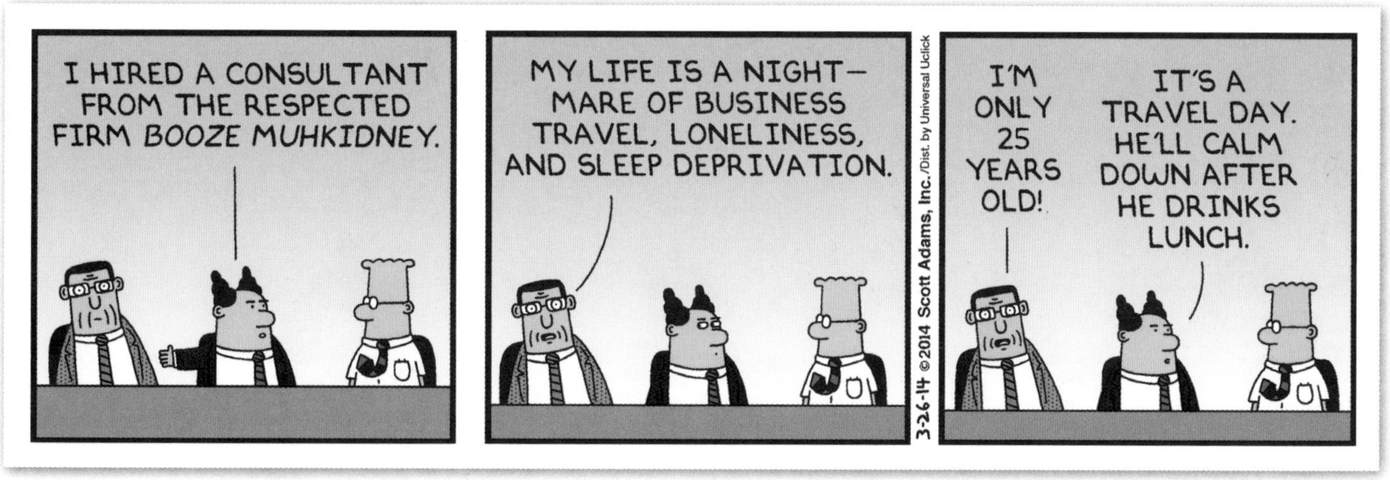
I HIRED A CONSULTANT FROM THE RESPECTED FIRM *BOOZE MUHKIDNEY*.
MY LIFE IS A NIGHT-MARE OF BUSINESS TRAVEL, LONELINESS, AND SLEEP DEPRIVATION.
I'M ONLY 25 YEARS OLD!
IT'S A TRAVEL DAY. HE'LL CALM DOWN AFTER HE DRINKS LUNCH.
3-26-14 ©2014 Scott Adams, Inc./Dist. by Universal Uclick

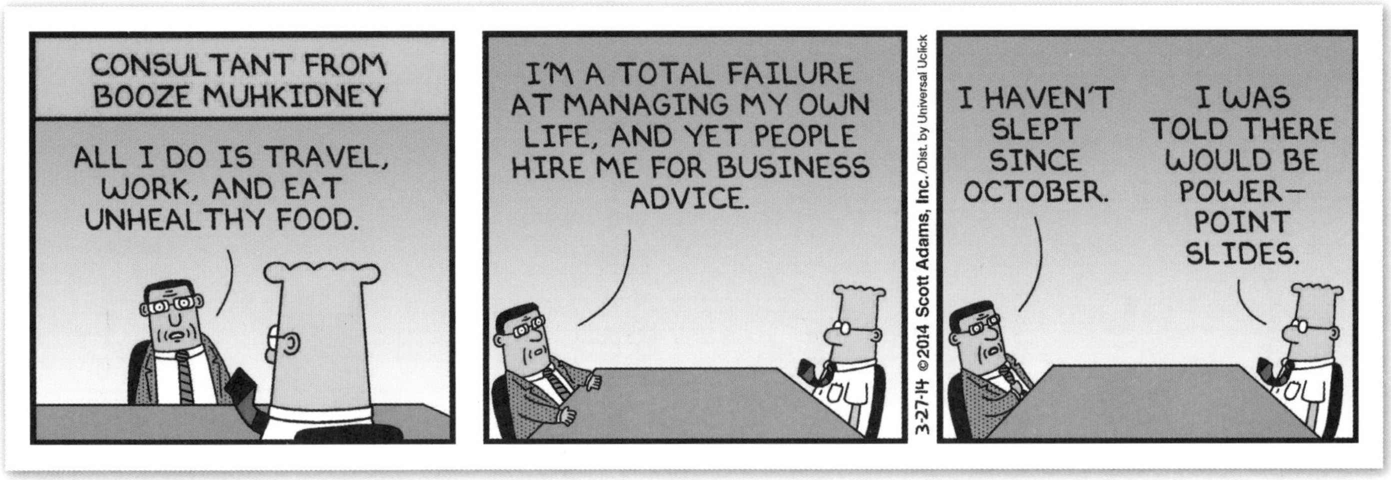
CONSULTANT FROM BOOZE MUHKIDNEY
ALL I DO IS TRAVEL, WORK, AND EAT UNHEALTHY FOOD.
I'M A TOTAL FAILURE AT MANAGING MY OWN LIFE, AND YET PEOPLE HIRE ME FOR BUSINESS ADVICE.
3-27-14 ©2014 Scott Adams, Inc./Dist. by Universal Uclick
I HAVEN'T SLEPT SINCE OCTOBER.
I WAS TOLD THERE WOULD BE POWER-POINT SLIDES.

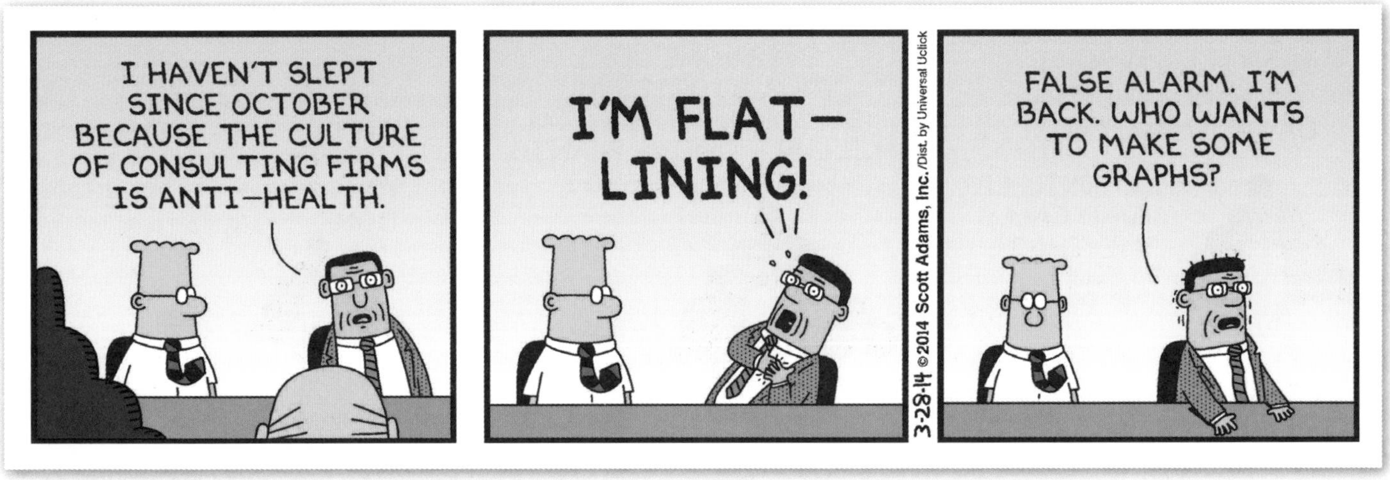
I HAVEN'T SLEPT SINCE OCTOBER BECAUSE THE CULTURE OF CONSULTING FIRMS IS ANTI-HEALTH.
I'M FLAT-LINING!
3-28-14 ©2014 Scott Adams, Inc./Dist. by Universal Uclick
FALSE ALARM. I'M BACK. WHO WANTS TO MAKE SOME GRAPHS?

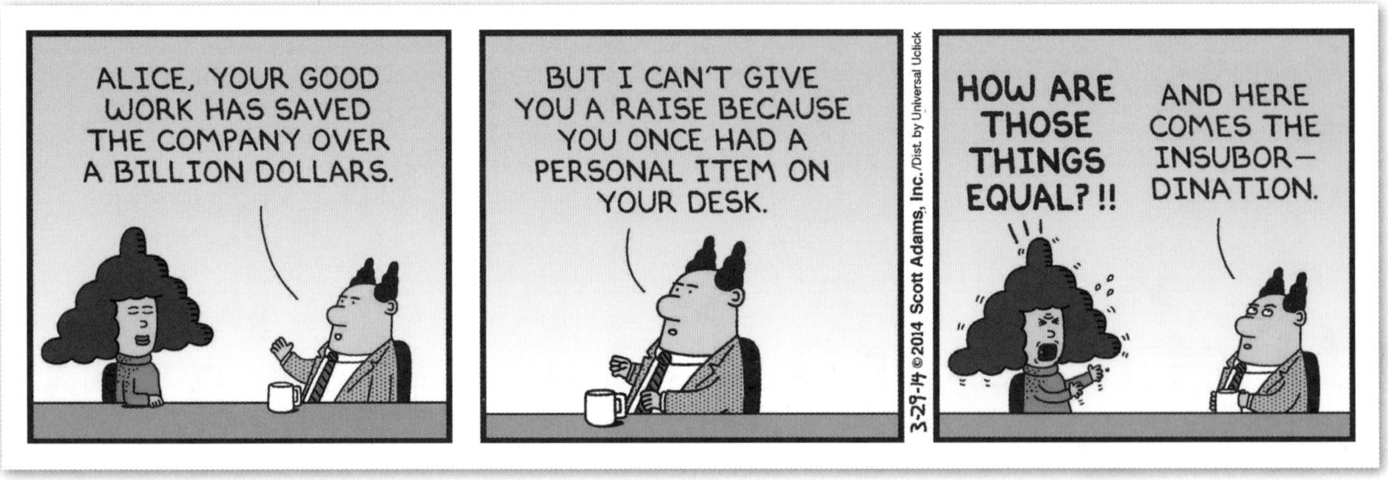
ALICE, YOUR GOOD WORK HAS SAVED THE COMPANY OVER A BILLION DOLLARS.
BUT I CAN'T GIVE YOU A RAISE BECAUSE YOU ONCE HAD A PERSONAL ITEM ON YOUR DESK.
3-29-14 ©2014 Scott Adams, Inc./Dist. by Universal Uclick
HOW ARE THOSE THINGS EQUAL?!!
AND HERE COMES THE INSUBOR-DINATION.

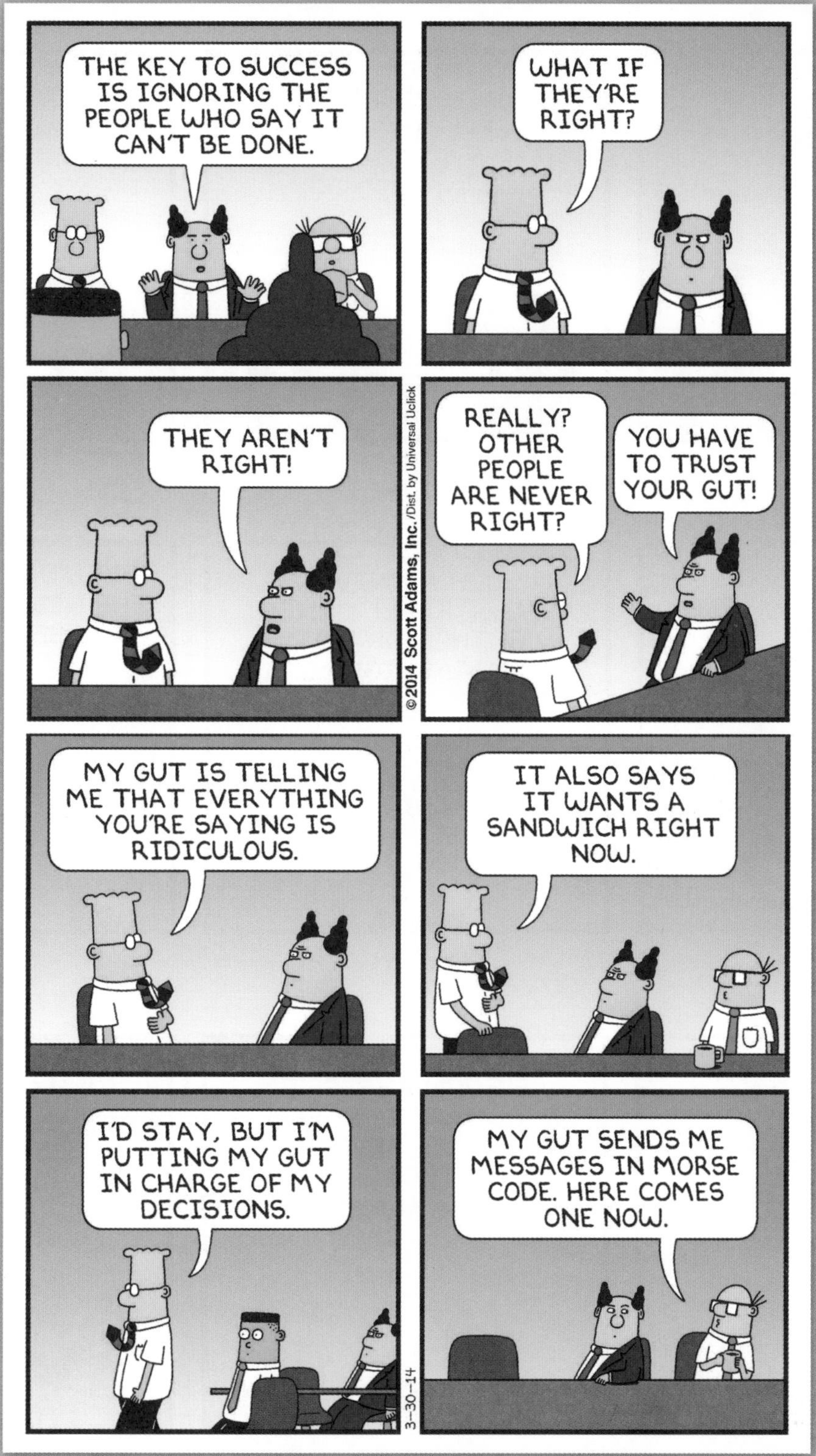
THE KEY TO SUCCESS IS IGNORING THE PEOPLE WHO SAY IT CAN'T BE DONE.
WHAT IF THEY'RE RIGHT?
THEY AREN'T RIGHT!
©2014 Scott Adams, Inc./Dist. by Universal Uclick
REALLY? OTHER PEOPLE ARE NEVER RIGHT?
YOU HAVE TO TRUST YOUR GUT!
MY GUT IS TELLING ME THAT EVERYTHING YOU'RE SAYING IS RIDICULOUS.
IT ALSO SAYS IT WANTS A SANDWICH RIGHT NOW.
I'D STAY, BUT I'M PUTTING MY GUT IN CHARGE OF MY DECISIONS.
3-30-14
MY GUT SENDS ME MESSAGES IN MORSE CODE. HERE COMES ONE NOW.

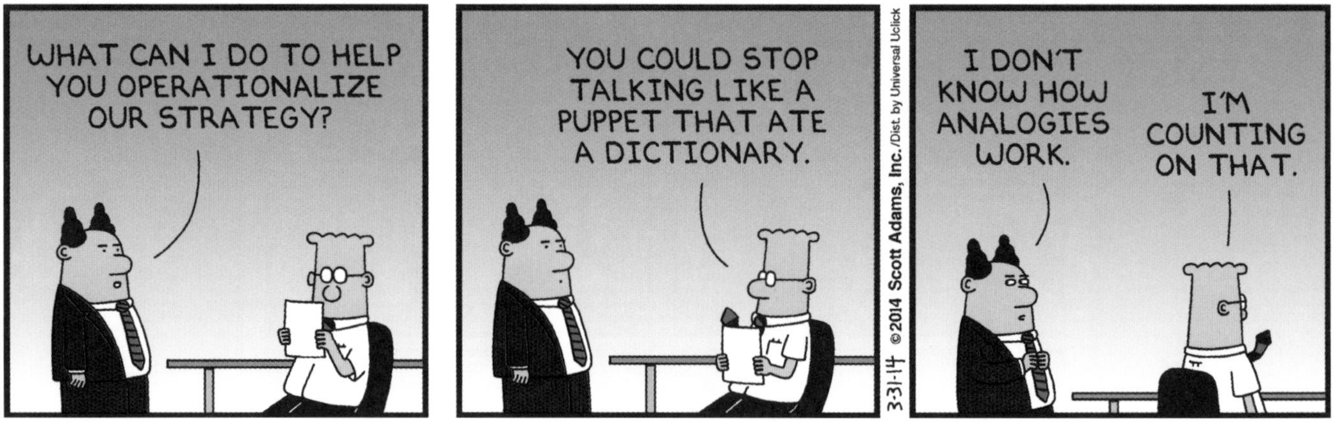
WHAT CAN I DO TO HELP YOU OPERATIONALIZE OUR STRATEGY?
YOU COULD STOP TALKING LIKE A PUPPET THAT ATE A DICTIONARY.
3-31-14 ©2014 Scott Adams, Inc./Dist. by Universal Uclick
I DON'T KNOW HOW ANALOGIES WORK.
I'M COUNTING ON THAT.

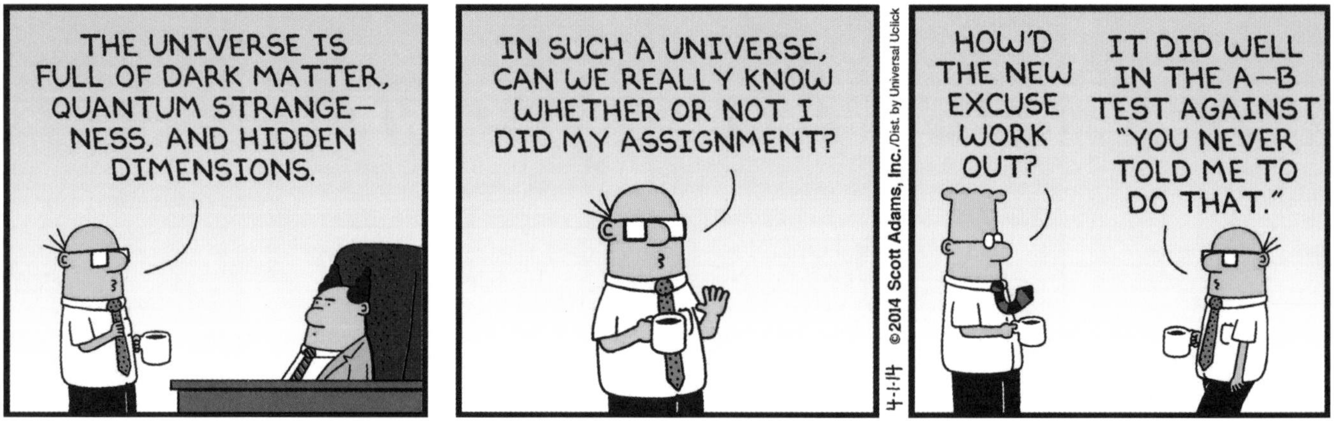
THE UNIVERSE IS FULL OF DARK MATTER, QUANTUM STRANGE-NESS, AND HIDDEN DIMENSIONS.
IN SUCH A UNIVERSE, CAN WE REALLY KNOW WHETHER OR NOT I DID MY ASSIGNMENT?
4-1-14 ©2014 Scott Adams, Inc./Dist. by Universal Uclick
HOW'D THE NEW EXCUSE WORK OUT?
IT DID WELL IN THE A-B TEST AGAINST "YOU NEVER TOLD ME TO DO THAT."

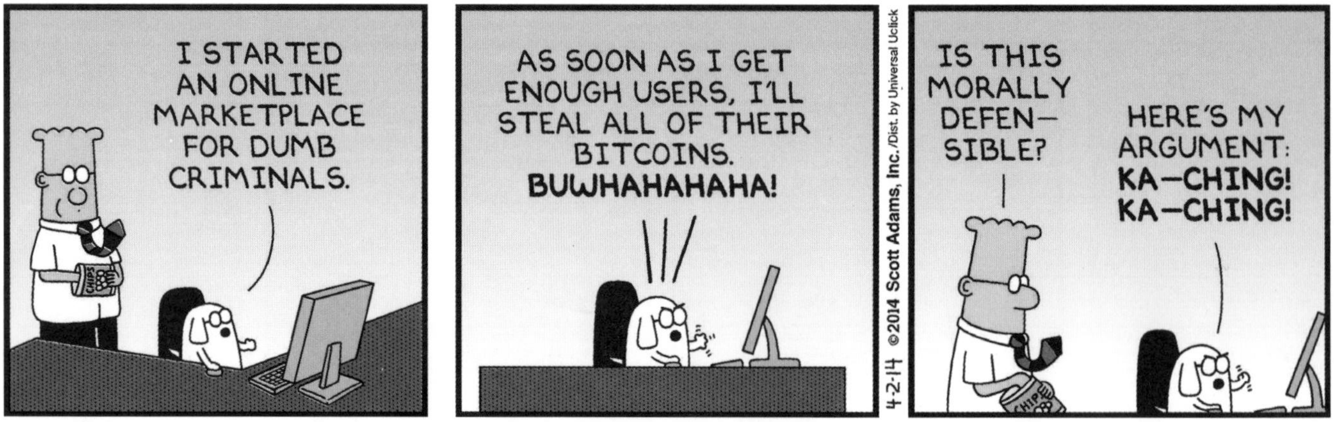
I STARTED AN ONLINE MARKETPLACE FOR DUMB CRIMINALS.
CHIPS
AS SOON AS I GET ENOUGH USERS, I'LL STEAL ALL OF THEIR BITCOINS. **BUWHAHAHAHAHA!**
4-2-14 ©2014 Scott Adams, Inc./Dist. by Universal Uclick
IS THIS MORALLY DEFEN-SIBLE?
HERE'S MY ARGUMENT: **KA-CHING! KA-CHING!**

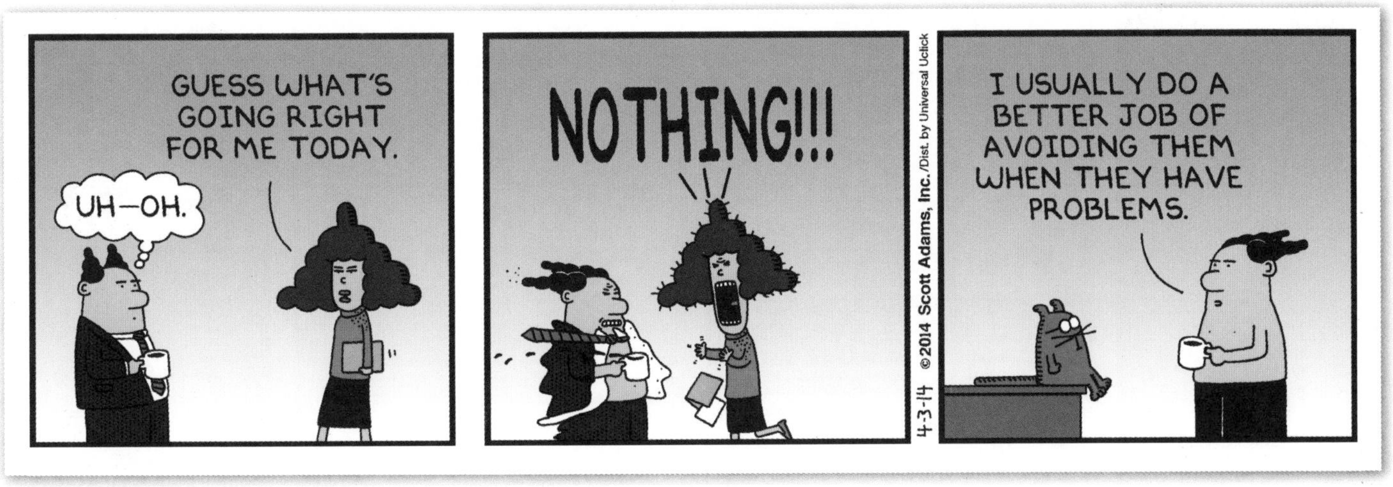
GUESS WHAT'S GOING RIGHT FOR ME TODAY.
UH—OH.
NOTHING!!!
I USUALLY DO A BETTER JOB OF AVOIDING THEM WHEN THEY HAVE PROBLEMS.
4-3-14 ©2014 Scott Adams, Inc./Dist. by Universal Uclick

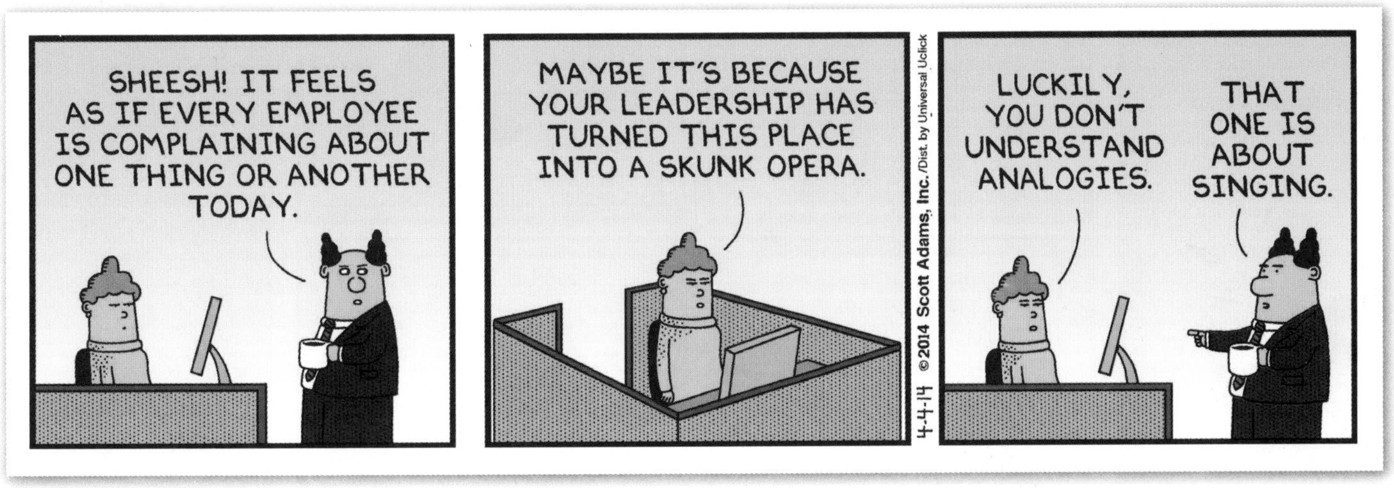
SHEESH! IT FEELS AS IF EVERY EMPLOYEE IS COMPLAINING ABOUT ONE THING OR ANOTHER TODAY.
MAYBE IT'S BECAUSE YOUR LEADERSHIP HAS TURNED THIS PLACE INTO A SKUNK OPERA.
LUCKILY, YOU DON'T UNDERSTAND ANALOGIES.
THAT ONE IS ABOUT SINGING.
4-4-14 ©2014 Scott Adams, Inc./Dist. by Universal Uclick

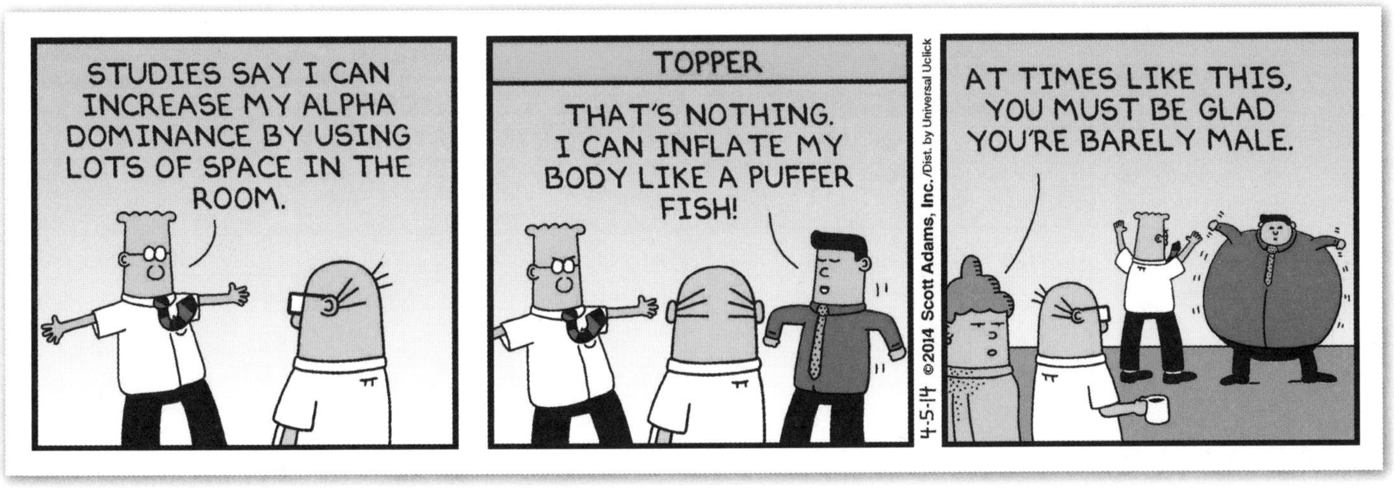
STUDIES SAY I CAN INCREASE MY ALPHA DOMINANCE BY USING LOTS OF SPACE IN THE ROOM.
TOPPER
THAT'S NOTHING. I CAN INFLATE MY BODY LIKE A PUFFER FISH!
AT TIMES LIKE THIS, YOU MUST BE GLAD YOU'RE BARELY MALE.
4-5-14 ©2014 Scott Adams, Inc./Dist. by Universal Uclick

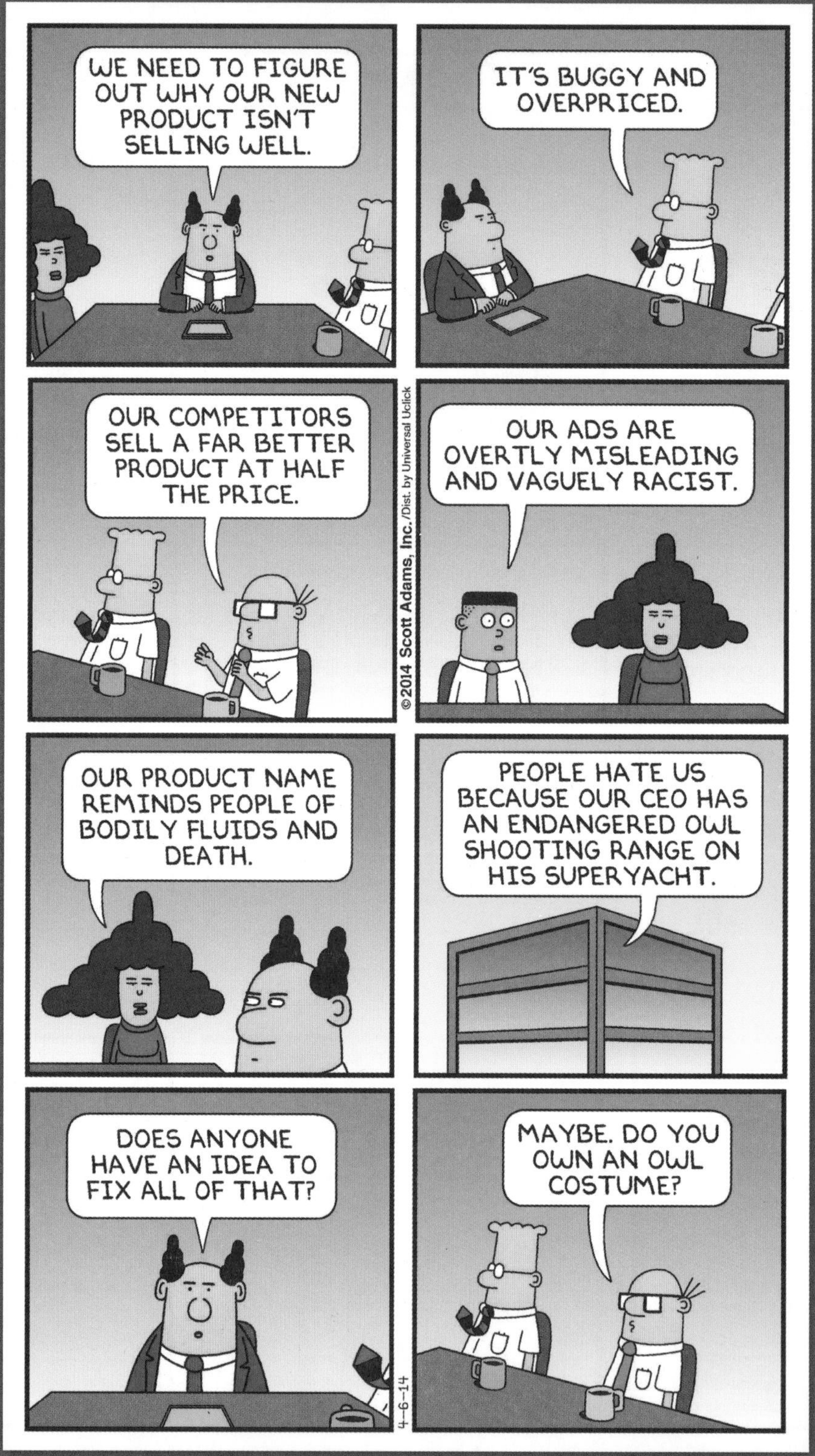
WE NEED TO FIGURE OUT WHY OUR NEW PRODUCT ISN'T SELLING WELL.
IT'S BUGGY AND OVERPRICED.
OUR COMPETITORS SELL A FAR BETTER PRODUCT AT HALF THE PRICE.
OUR ADS ARE OVERTLY MISLEADING AND VAGUELY RACIST.
OUR PRODUCT NAME REMINDS PEOPLE OF BODILY FLUIDS AND DEATH.
PEOPLE HATE US BECAUSE OUR CEO HAS AN ENDANGERED OWL SHOOTING RANGE ON HIS SUPERYACHT.
DOES ANYONE HAVE AN IDEA TO FIX ALL OF THAT?
MAYBE. DO YOU OWN AN OWL COSTUME?
©2014 Scott Adams, Inc./Dist. by Universal Uclick
4-6-14

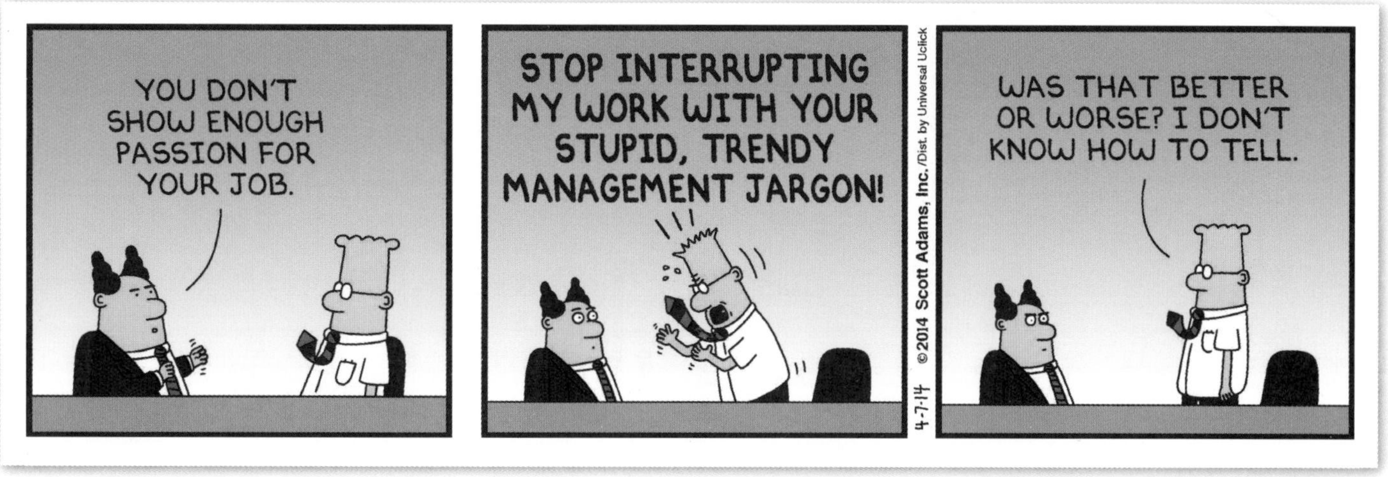
YOU DON'T SHOW ENOUGH PASSION FOR YOUR JOB.
STOP INTERRUPTING MY WORK WITH YOUR STUPID, TRENDY MANAGEMENT JARGON!
4-7-14 ©2014 Scott Adams, Inc./Dist. by Universal Uclick
WAS THAT BETTER OR WORSE? I DON'T KNOW HOW TO TELL.

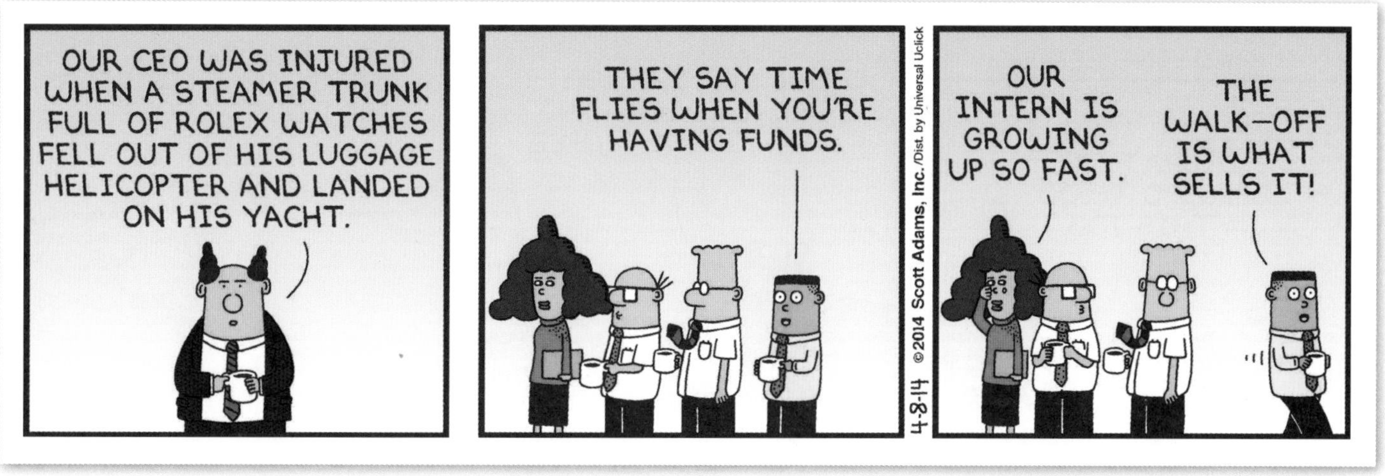
OUR CEO WAS INJURED WHEN A STEAMER TRUNK FULL OF ROLEX WATCHES FELL OUT OF HIS LUGGAGE HELICOPTER AND LANDED ON HIS YACHT.
THEY SAY TIME FLIES WHEN YOU'RE HAVING FUNDS.
4-8-14 ©2014 Scott Adams, Inc./Dist. by Universal Uclick
OUR INTERN IS GROWING UP SO FAST.
THE WALK—OFF IS WHAT SELLS IT!

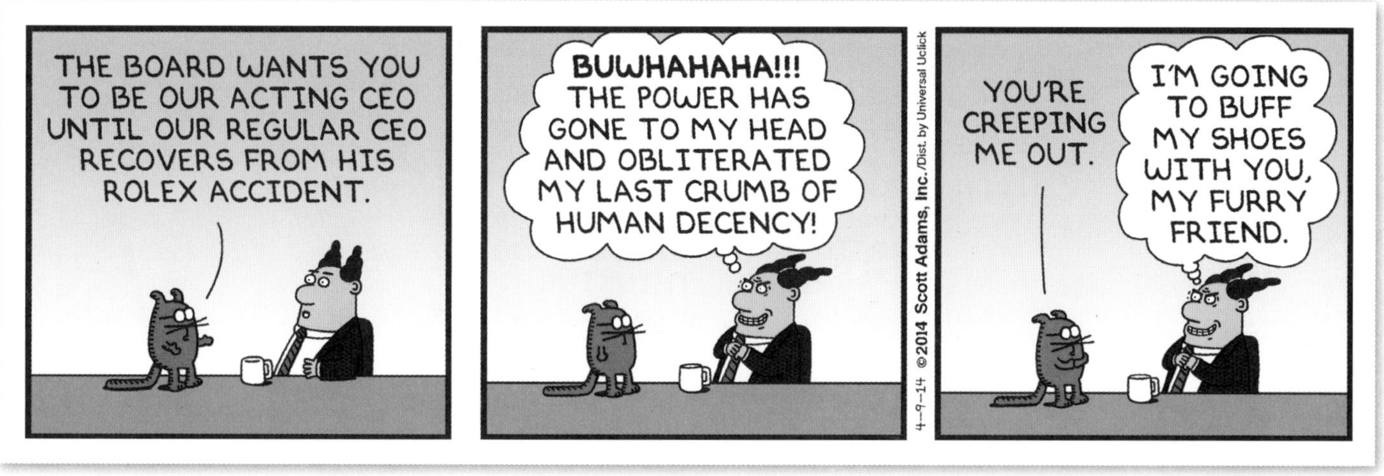
THE BOARD WANTS YOU TO BE OUR ACTING CEO UNTIL OUR REGULAR CEO RECOVERS FROM HIS ROLEX ACCIDENT.
BUWHAHAHA!!! THE POWER HAS GONE TO MY HEAD AND OBLITERATED MY LAST CRUMB OF HUMAN DECENCY!
4-9-14 ©2014 Scott Adams, Inc./Dist. by Universal Uclick
YOU'RE CREEPING ME OUT.
I'M GOING TO BUFF MY SHOES WITH YOU, MY FURRY FRIEND.

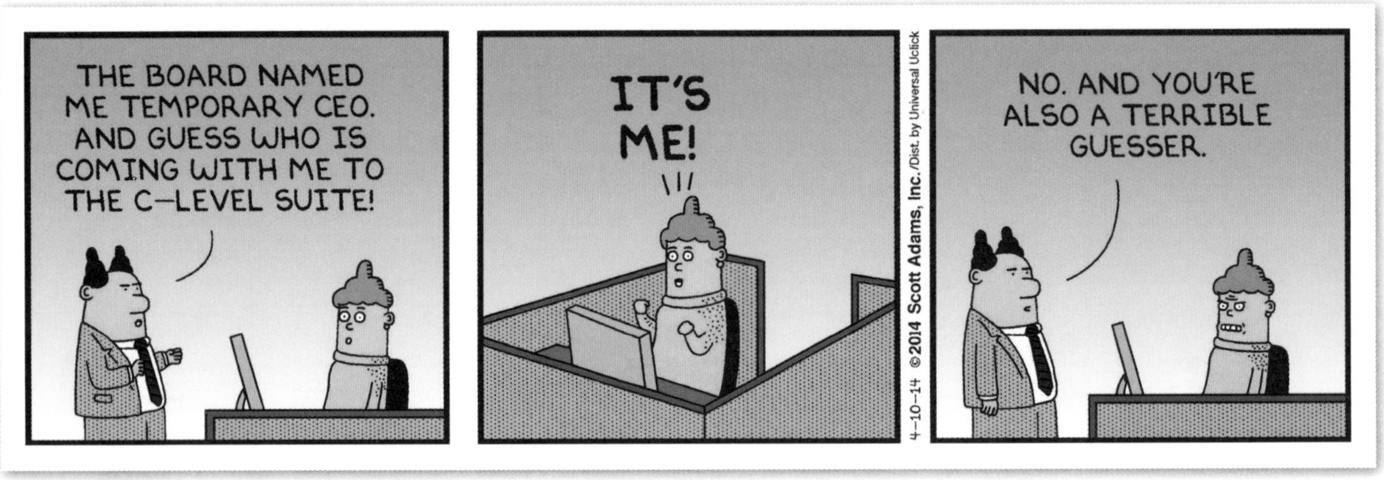
THE BOARD NAMED ME TEMPORARY CEO. AND GUESS WHO IS COMING WITH ME TO THE C-LEVEL SUITE!
IT'S ME!
4-10-14 ©2014 Scott Adams, Inc./Dist. by Universal Uclick
NO. AND YOU'RE ALSO A TERRIBLE GUESSER.

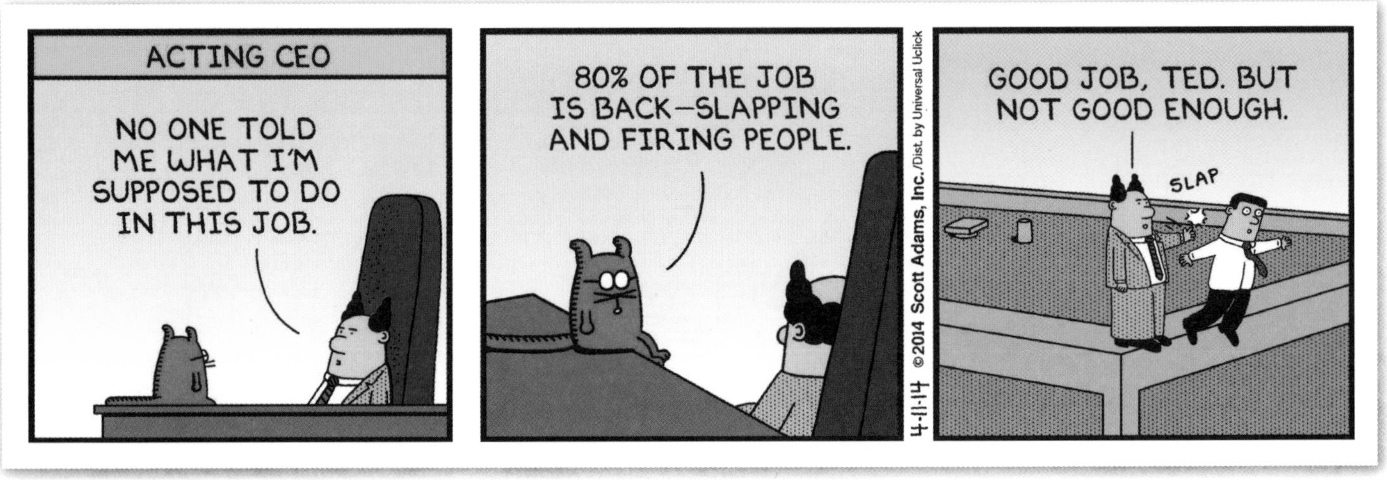
ACTING CEO
NO ONE TOLD ME WHAT I'M SUPPOSED TO DO IN THIS JOB.
80% OF THE JOB IS BACK-SLAPPING AND FIRING PEOPLE.
4-11-14 ©2014 Scott Adams, Inc./Dist. by Universal Uclick
GOOD JOB, TED. BUT NOT GOOD ENOUGH.
SLAP

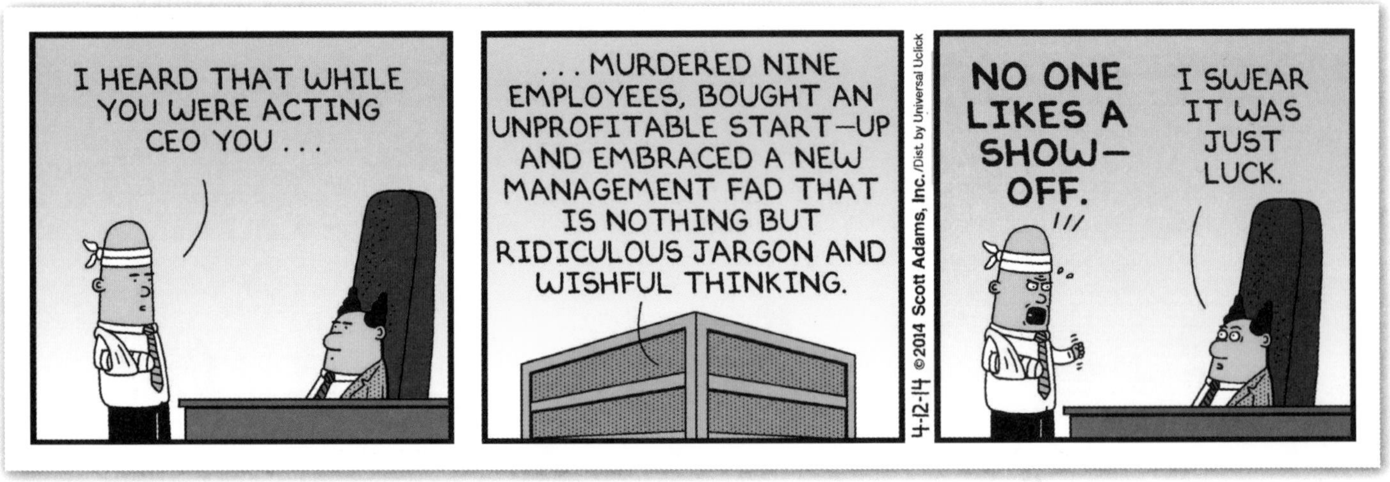
I HEARD THAT WHILE YOU WERE ACTING CEO YOU . . .
. . . MURDERED NINE EMPLOYEES, BOUGHT AN UNPROFITABLE START-UP AND EMBRACED A NEW MANAGEMENT FAD THAT IS NOTHING BUT RIDICULOUS JARGON AND WISHFUL THINKING.
4-12-14 ©2014 Scott Adams, Inc./Dist. by Universal Uclick
NO ONE LIKES A SHOW-OFF.
I SWEAR IT WAS JUST LUCK.

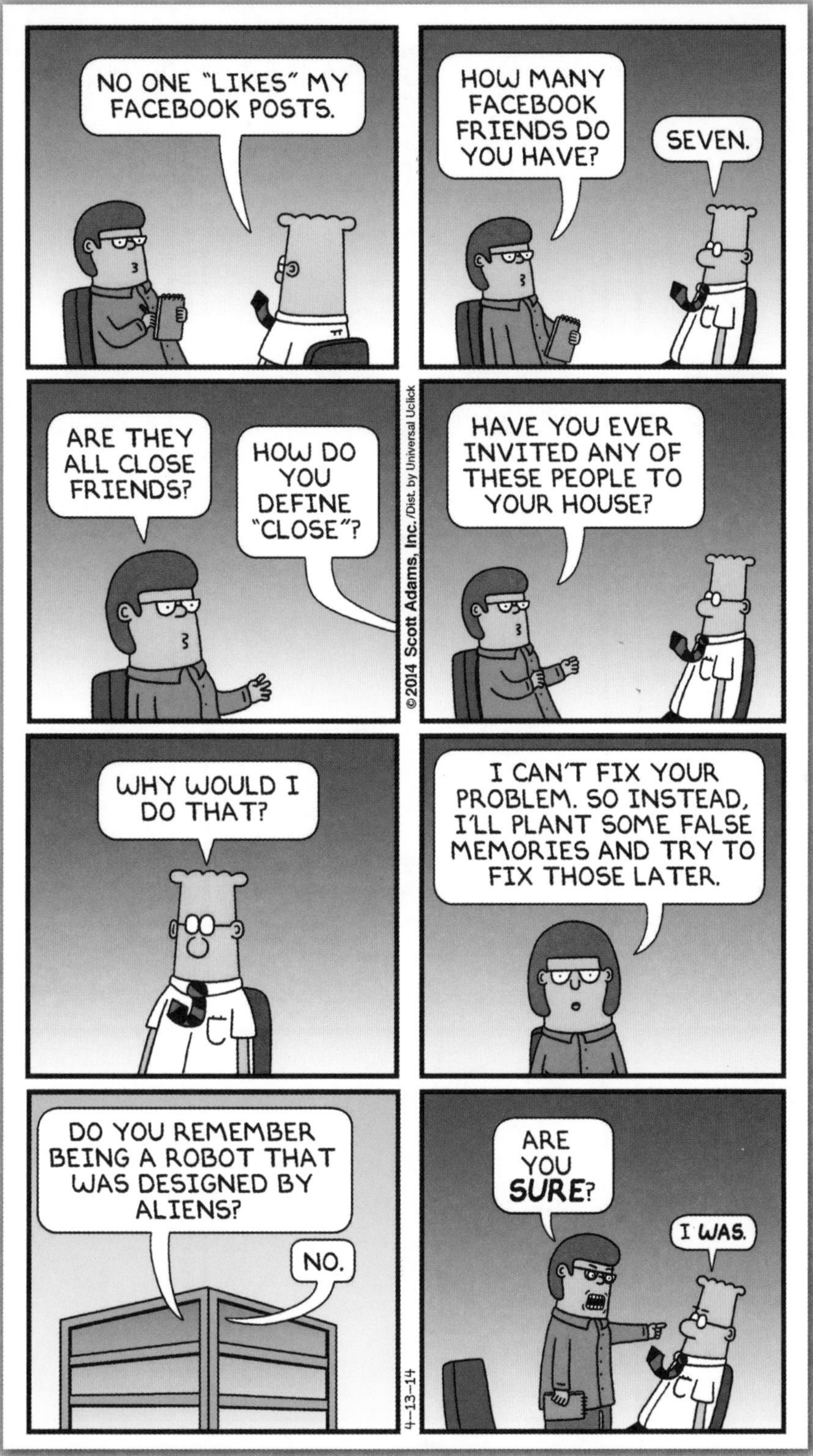
NO ONE "LIKES" MY FACEBOOK POSTS.
HOW MANY FACEBOOK FRIENDS DO YOU HAVE?
SEVEN.
ARE THEY ALL CLOSE FRIENDS?
HOW DO YOU DEFINE "CLOSE"?
© 2014 Scott Adams, Inc./Dist. by Universal Uclick
HAVE YOU EVER INVITED ANY OF THESE PEOPLE TO YOUR HOUSE?
WHY WOULD I DO THAT?
I CAN'T FIX YOUR PROBLEM. SO INSTEAD, I'LL PLANT SOME FALSE MEMORIES AND TRY TO FIX THOSE LATER.
DO YOU REMEMBER BEING A ROBOT THAT WAS DESIGNED BY ALIENS?
NO.
4-13-14
ARE YOU **SURE**?
I WAS.

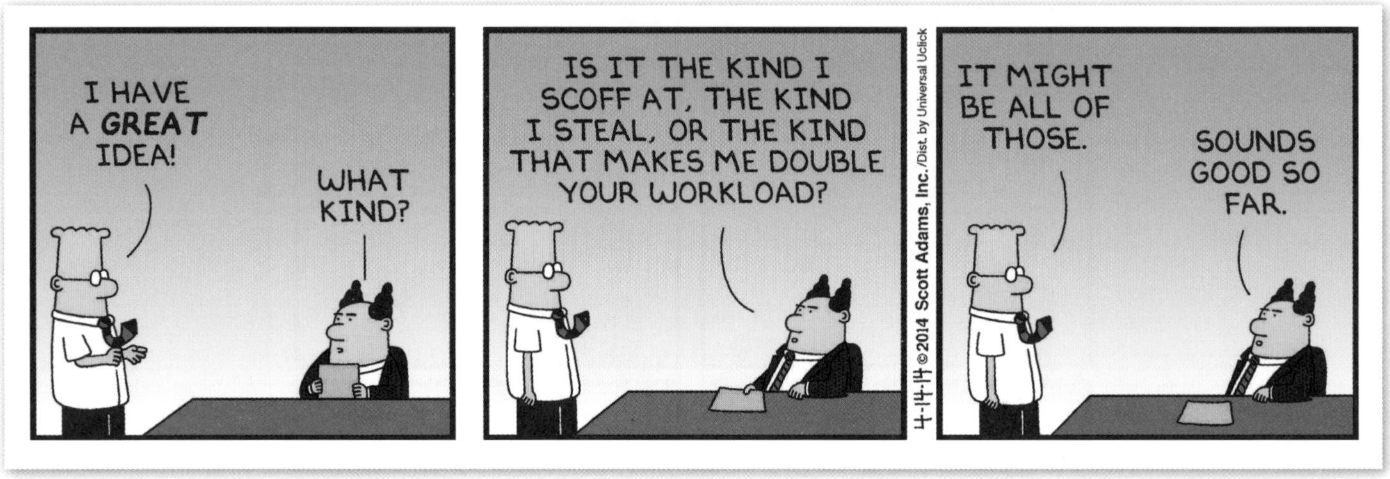
I HAVE A **GREAT** IDEA!
WHAT KIND?
IS IT THE KIND I SCOFF AT, THE KIND I STEAL, OR THE KIND THAT MAKES ME DOUBLE YOUR WORKLOAD?
4-14-14 ©2014 Scott Adams, Inc./Dist. by Universal Uclick
IT MIGHT BE ALL OF THOSE.
SOUNDS GOOD SO FAR.

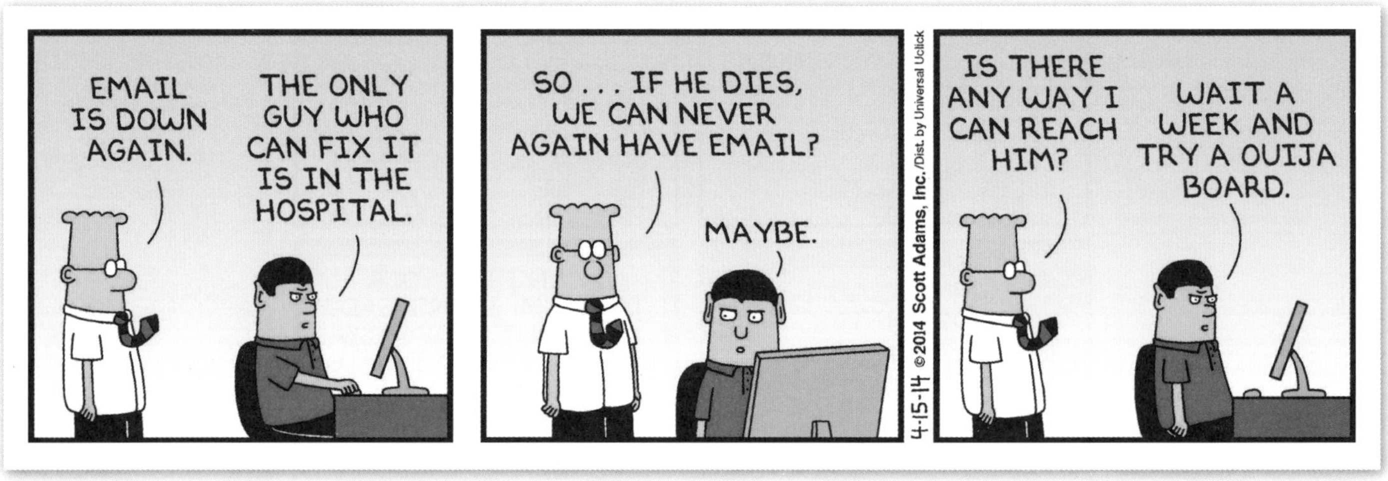
EMAIL IS DOWN AGAIN.
THE ONLY GUY WHO CAN FIX IT IS IN THE HOSPITAL.
SO . . . IF HE DIES, WE CAN NEVER AGAIN HAVE EMAIL?
MAYBE.
4-15-14 ©2014 Scott Adams, Inc./Dist. by Universal Uclick
IS THERE ANY WAY I CAN REACH HIM?
WAIT A WEEK AND TRY A OUIJA BOARD.

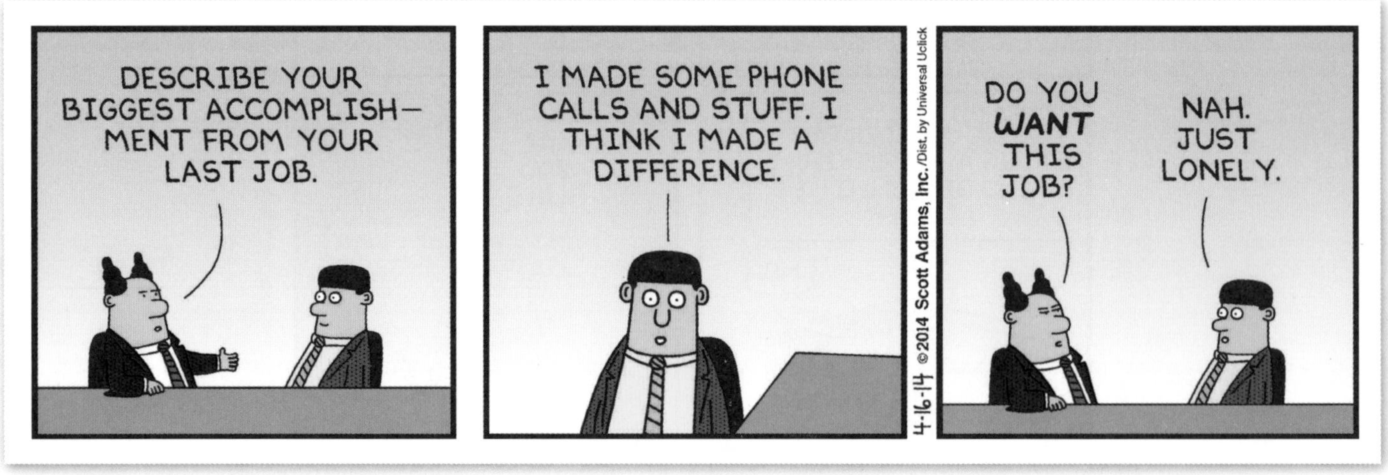
DESCRIBE YOUR BIGGEST ACCOMPLISH-MENT FROM YOUR LAST JOB.
I MADE SOME PHONE CALLS AND STUFF. I THINK I MADE A DIFFERENCE.
4-16-14 ©2014 Scott Adams, Inc./Dist. by Universal Uclick
DO YOU **WANT** THIS JOB?
NAH. JUST LONELY.

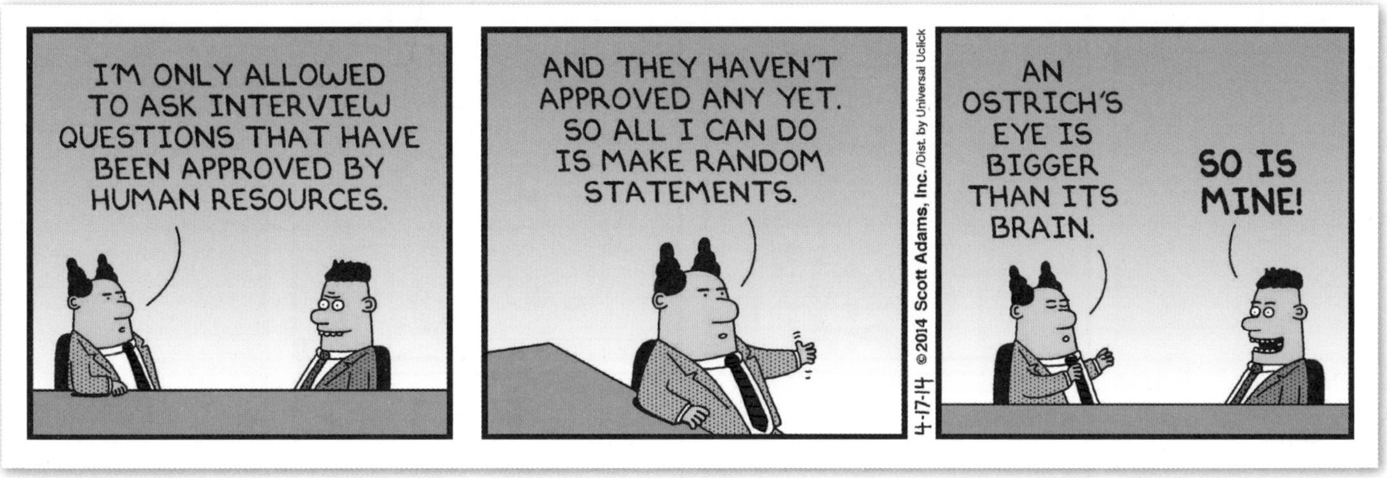
I'M ONLY ALLOWED TO ASK INTERVIEW QUESTIONS THAT HAVE BEEN APPROVED BY HUMAN RESOURCES.
AND THEY HAVEN'T APPROVED ANY YET. SO ALL I CAN DO IS MAKE RANDOM STATEMENTS.
4-17-14 ©2014 Scott Adams, Inc./Dist. by Universal Uclick
AN OSTRICH'S EYE IS BIGGER THAN ITS BRAIN.
SO IS MINE!

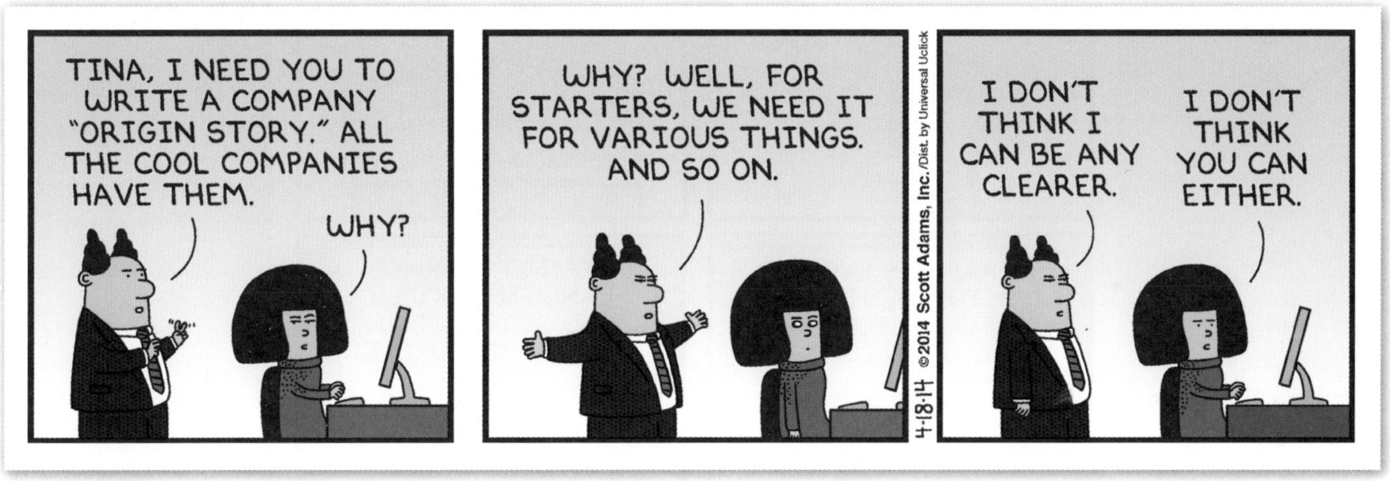
TINA, I NEED YOU TO WRITE A COMPANY "ORIGIN STORY." ALL THE COOL COMPANIES HAVE THEM.
WHY?
WHY? WELL, FOR STARTERS, WE NEED IT FOR VARIOUS THINGS. AND SO ON.
4-18-14 ©2014 Scott Adams, Inc./Dist. by Universal Uclick
I DON'T THINK I CAN BE ANY CLEARER.
I DON'T THINK YOU CAN EITHER.

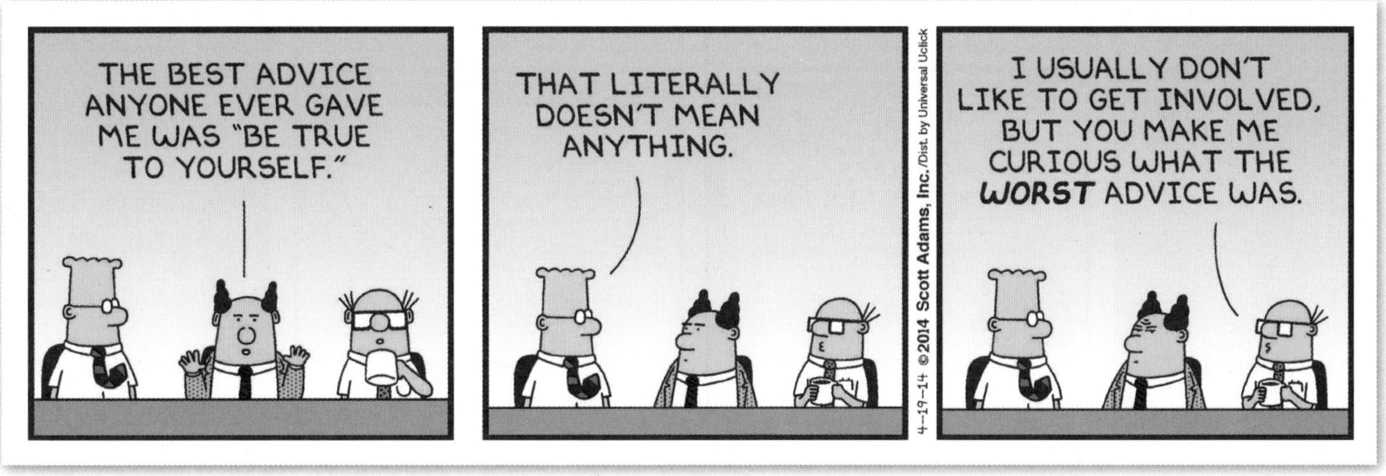
THE BEST ADVICE ANYONE EVER GAVE ME WAS "BE TRUE TO YOURSELF."
THAT LITERALLY DOESN'T MEAN ANYTHING.
4-19-14 ©2014 Scott Adams, Inc./Dist. by Universal Uclick
I USUALLY DON'T LIKE TO GET INVOLVED, BUT YOU MAKE ME CURIOUS WHAT THE WORST ADVICE WAS.

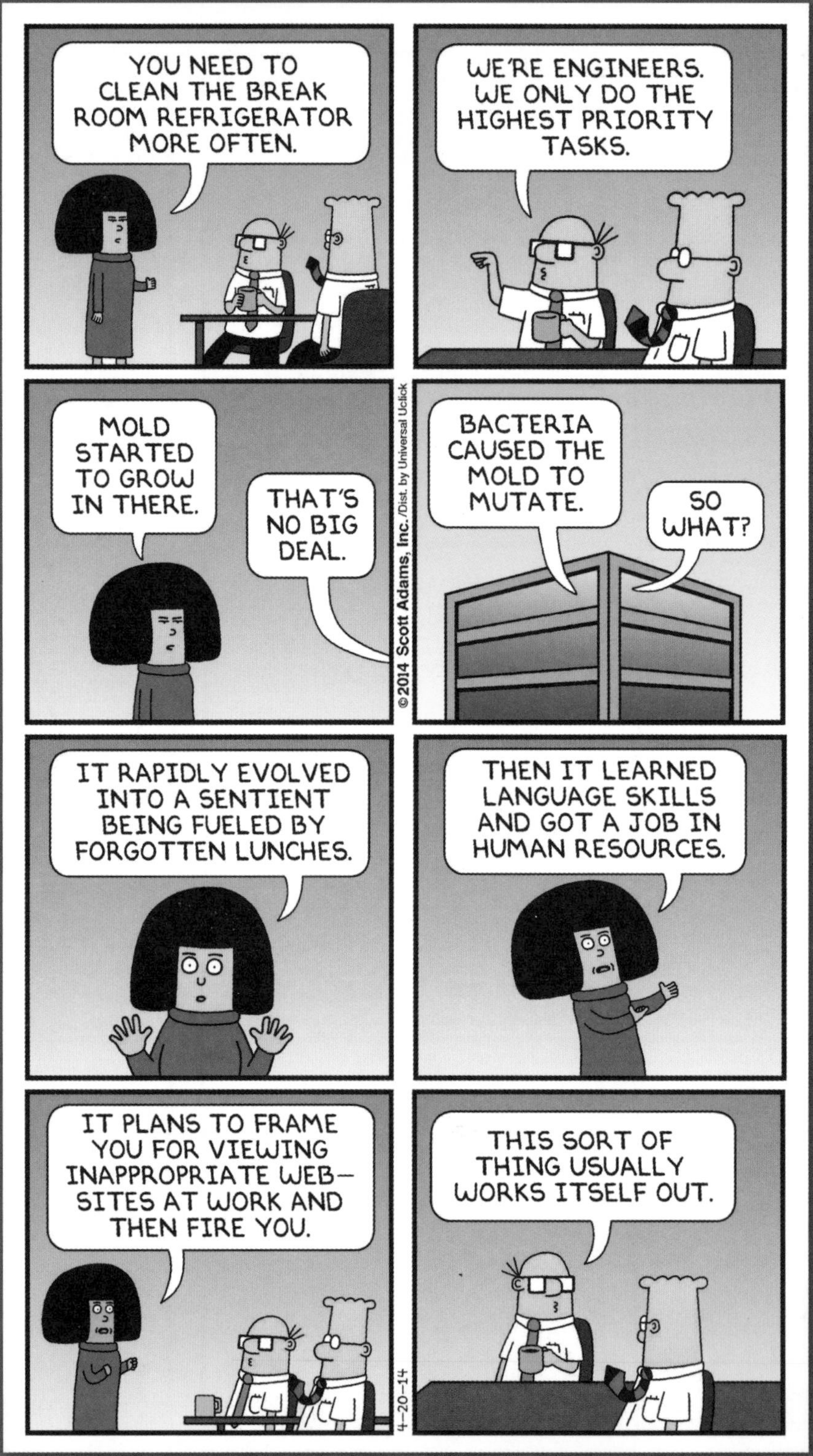
YOU NEED TO CLEAN THE BREAK ROOM REFRIGERATOR MORE OFTEN.
WE'RE ENGINEERS. WE ONLY DO THE HIGHEST PRIORITY TASKS.
MOLD STARTED TO GROW IN THERE.
THAT'S NO BIG DEAL.
BACTERIA CAUSED THE MOLD TO MUTATE.
SO WHAT?
IT RAPIDLY EVOLVED INTO A SENTIENT BEING FUELED BY FORGOTTEN LUNCHES.
THEN IT LEARNED LANGUAGE SKILLS AND GOT A JOB IN HUMAN RESOURCES.
IT PLANS TO FRAME YOU FOR VIEWING INAPPROPRIATE WEB-SITES AT WORK AND THEN FIRE YOU.
THIS SORT OF THING USUALLY WORKS ITSELF OUT.
©2014 Scott Adams, Inc./Dist. by Universal Uclick
4-20-14

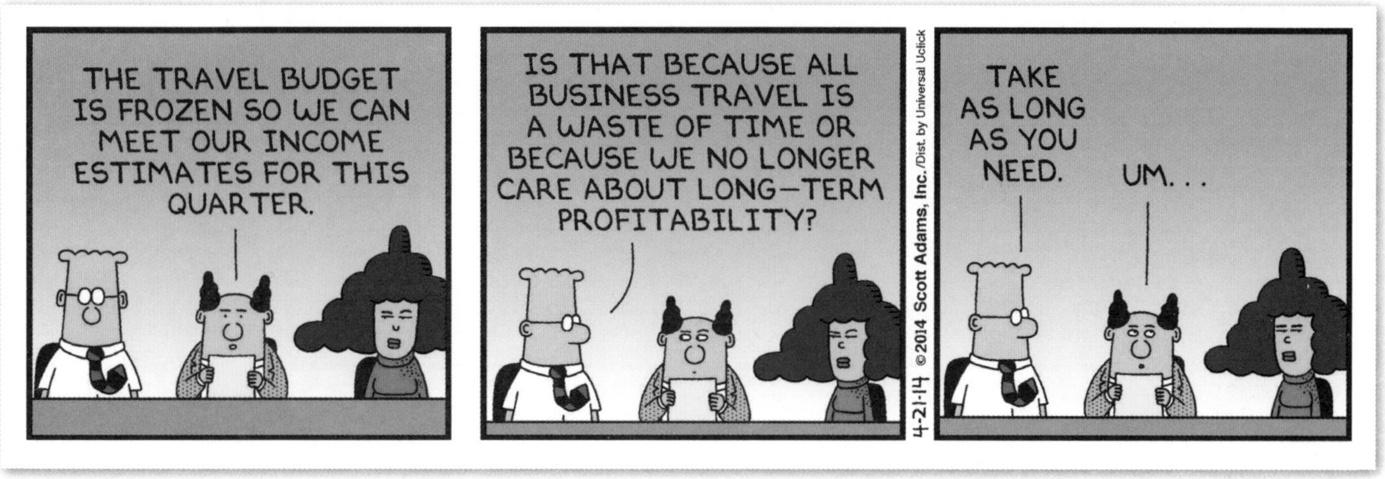
THE TRAVEL BUDGET IS FROZEN SO WE CAN MEET OUR INCOME ESTIMATES FOR THIS QUARTER.
IS THAT BECAUSE ALL BUSINESS TRAVEL IS A WASTE OF TIME OR BECAUSE WE NO LONGER CARE ABOUT LONG-TERM PROFITABILITY?
4-21-14 © 2014 Scott Adams, Inc./Dist. by Universal Uclick
TAKE AS LONG AS YOU NEED.
UM...

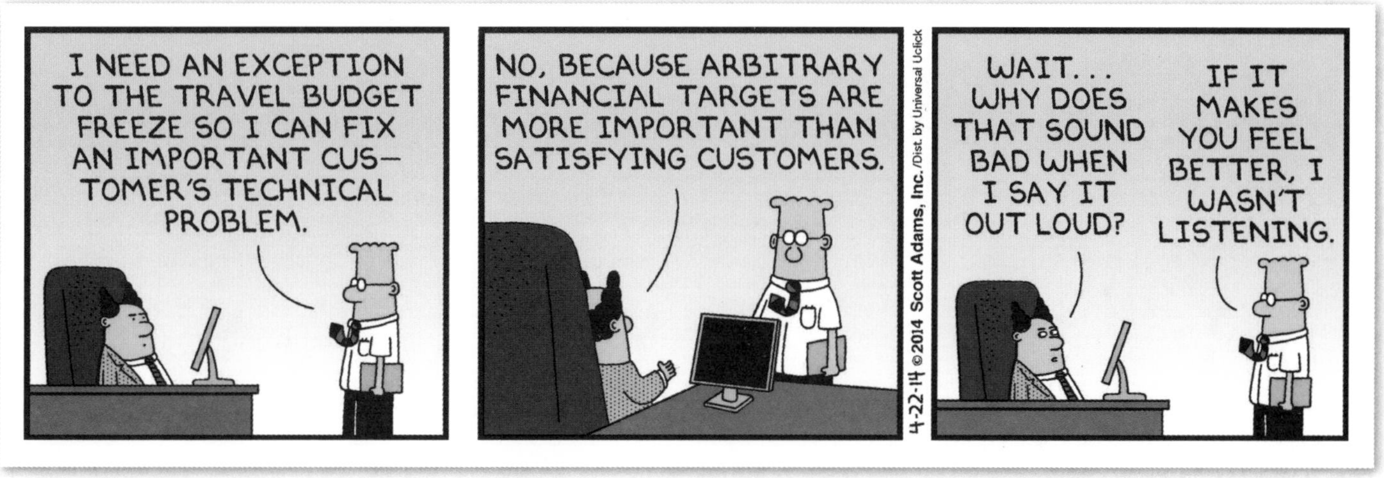
I NEED AN EXCEPTION TO THE TRAVEL BUDGET FREEZE SO I CAN FIX AN IMPORTANT CUS-TOMER'S TECHNICAL PROBLEM.
NO, BECAUSE ARBITRARY FINANCIAL TARGETS ARE MORE IMPORTANT THAN SATISFYING CUSTOMERS.
4-22-14 © 2014 Scott Adams, Inc./Dist. by Universal Uclick
WAIT... WHY DOES THAT SOUND BAD WHEN I SAY IT OUT LOUD?
IF IT MAKES YOU FEEL BETTER, I WASN'T LISTENING.

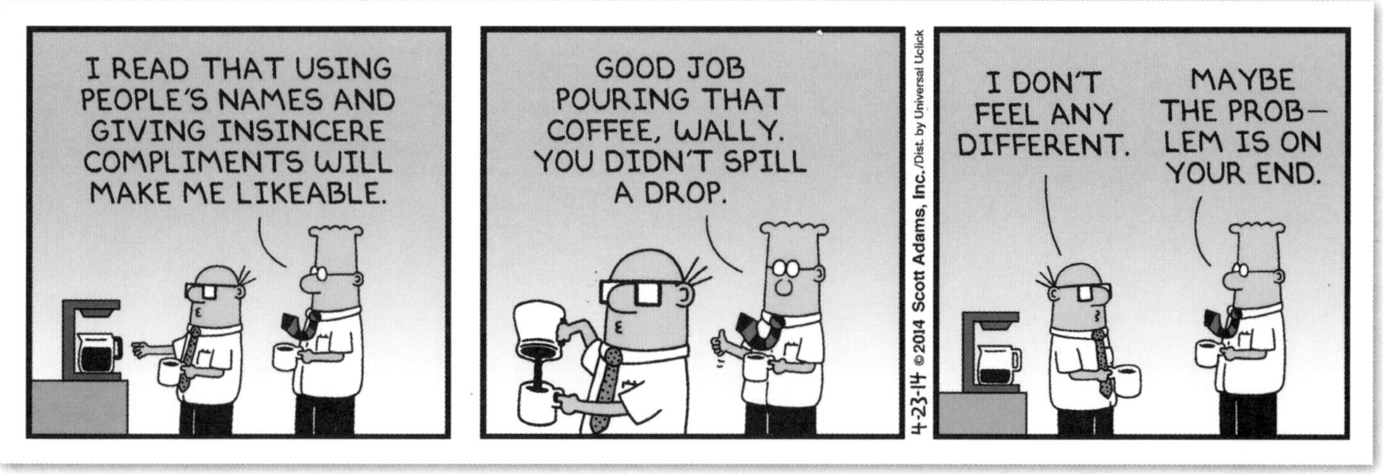
I READ THAT USING PEOPLE'S NAMES AND GIVING INSINCERE COMPLIMENTS WILL MAKE ME LIKEABLE.
GOOD JOB POURING THAT COFFEE, WALLY. YOU DIDN'T SPILL A DROP.
4-23-14 © 2014 Scott Adams, Inc./Dist. by Universal Uclick
I DON'T FEEL ANY DIFFERENT.
MAYBE THE PROB-LEM IS ON YOUR END.

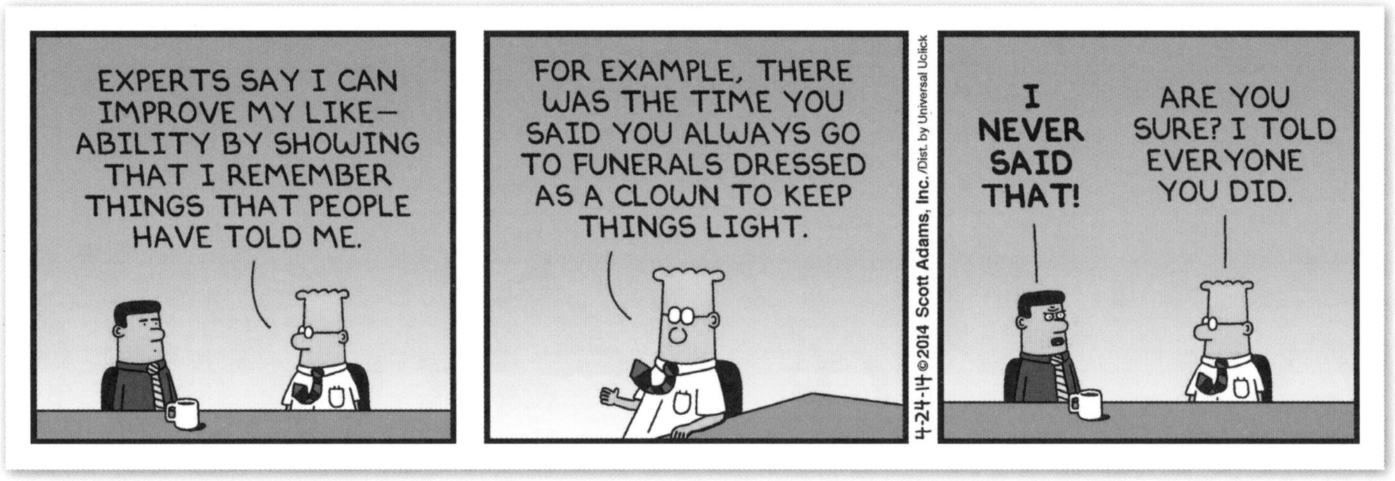
EXPERTS SAY I CAN IMPROVE MY LIKE-ABILITY BY SHOWING THAT I REMEMBER THINGS THAT PEOPLE HAVE TOLD ME.
FOR EXAMPLE, THERE WAS THE TIME YOU SAID YOU ALWAYS GO TO FUNERALS DRESSED AS A CLOWN TO KEEP THINGS LIGHT.
4-24-14 ©2014 Scott Adams, Inc./Dist. by Universal Uclick
I NEVER SAID THAT!
ARE YOU SURE? I TOLD EVERYONE YOU DID.

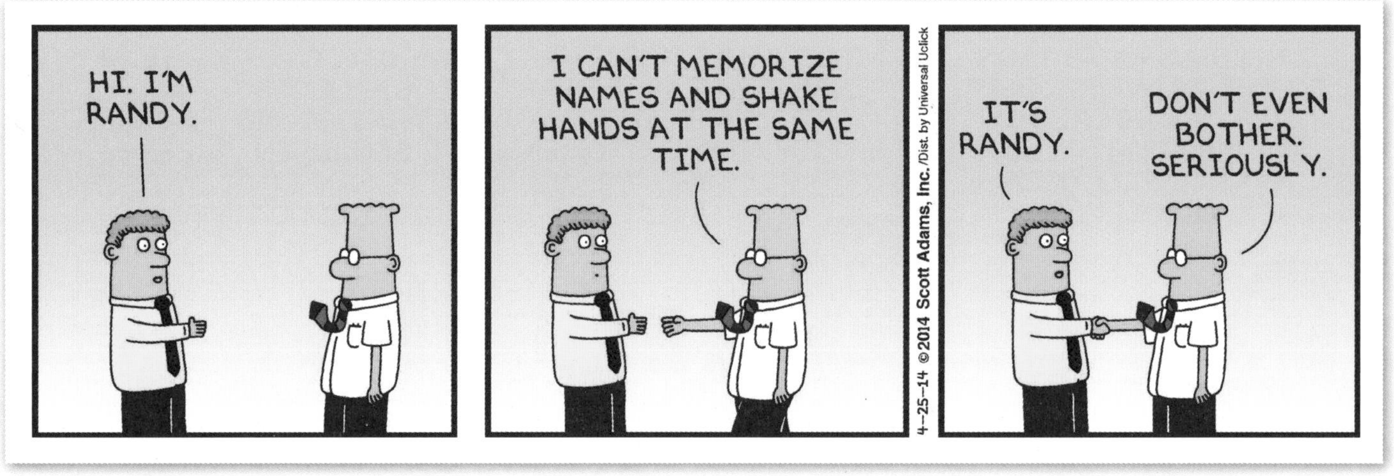
HI. I'M RANDY.
I CAN'T MEMORIZE NAMES AND SHAKE HANDS AT THE SAME TIME.
4-25-14 ©2014 Scott Adams, Inc./Dist. by Universal Uclick
IT'S RANDY.
DON'T EVEN BOTHER. SERIOUSLY.

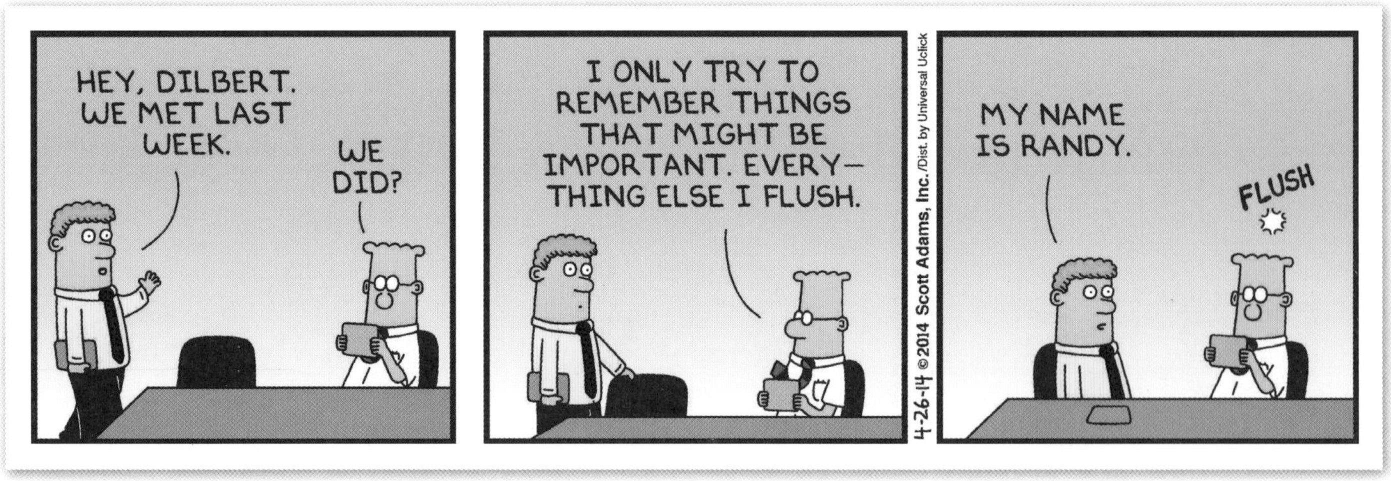
HEY, DILBERT. WE MET LAST WEEK.
WE DID?
I ONLY TRY TO REMEMBER THINGS THAT MIGHT BE IMPORTANT. EVERY-THING ELSE I FLUSH.
4-26-14 ©2014 Scott Adams, Inc./Dist. by Universal Uclick
MY NAME IS RANDY.
FLUSH

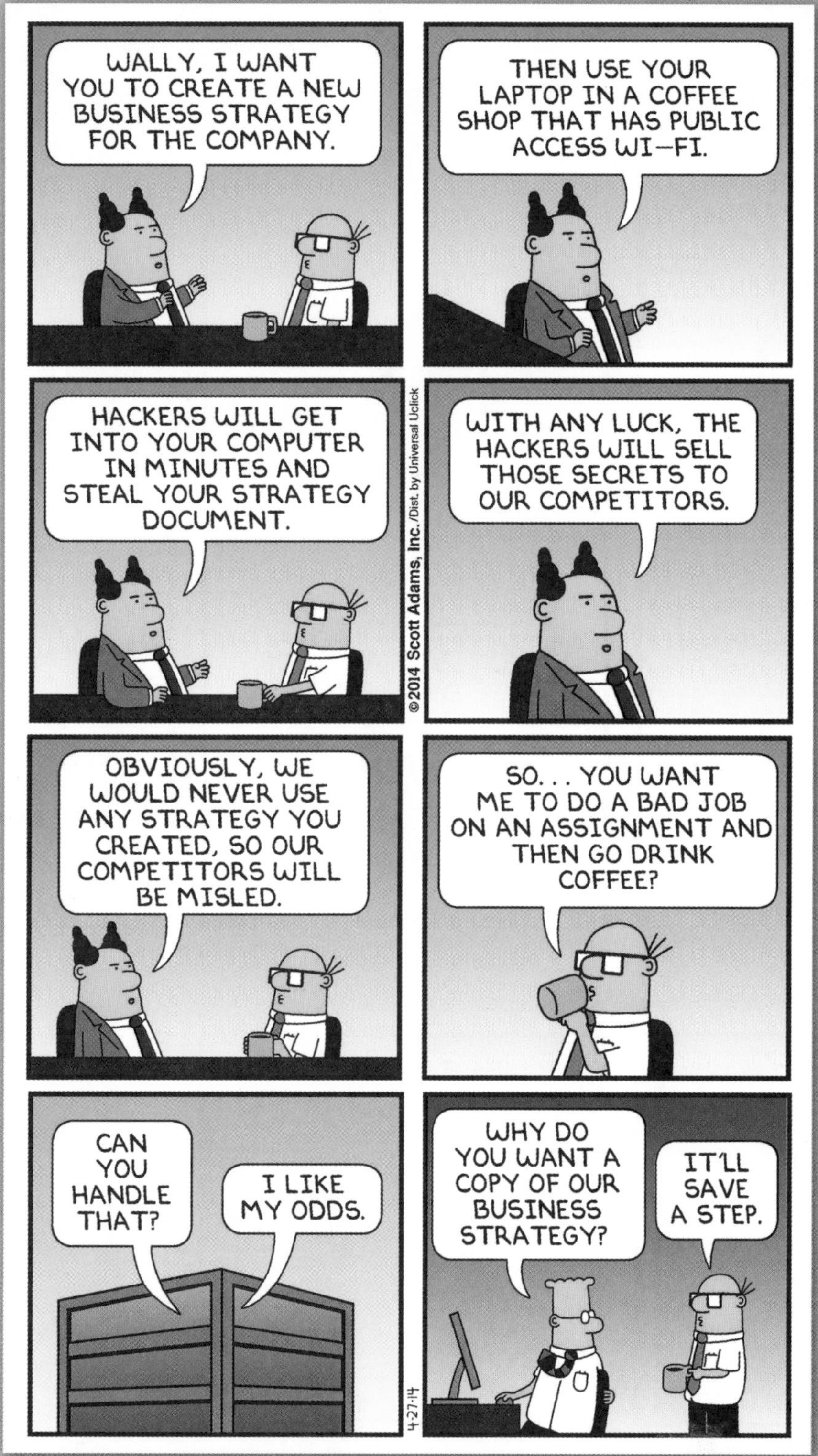

WALLY, I WANT YOU TO CREATE A NEW BUSINESS STRATEGY FOR THE COMPANY.
THEN USE YOUR LAPTOP IN A COFFEE SHOP THAT HAS PUBLIC ACCESS WI-FI.
HACKERS WILL GET INTO YOUR COMPUTER IN MINUTES AND STEAL YOUR STRATEGY DOCUMENT.
WITH ANY LUCK, THE HACKERS WILL SELL THOSE SECRETS TO OUR COMPETITORS.
OBVIOUSLY, WE WOULD NEVER USE ANY STRATEGY YOU CREATED, SO OUR COMPETITORS WILL BE MISLED.
SO. . . YOU WANT ME TO DO A BAD JOB ON AN ASSIGNMENT AND THEN GO DRINK COFFEE?
CAN YOU HANDLE THAT?
I LIKE MY ODDS.
WHY DO YOU WANT A COPY OF OUR BUSINESS STRATEGY?
IT'LL SAVE A STEP.
©2014 Scott Adams, Inc./Dist. by Universal Uclick
4-27-14

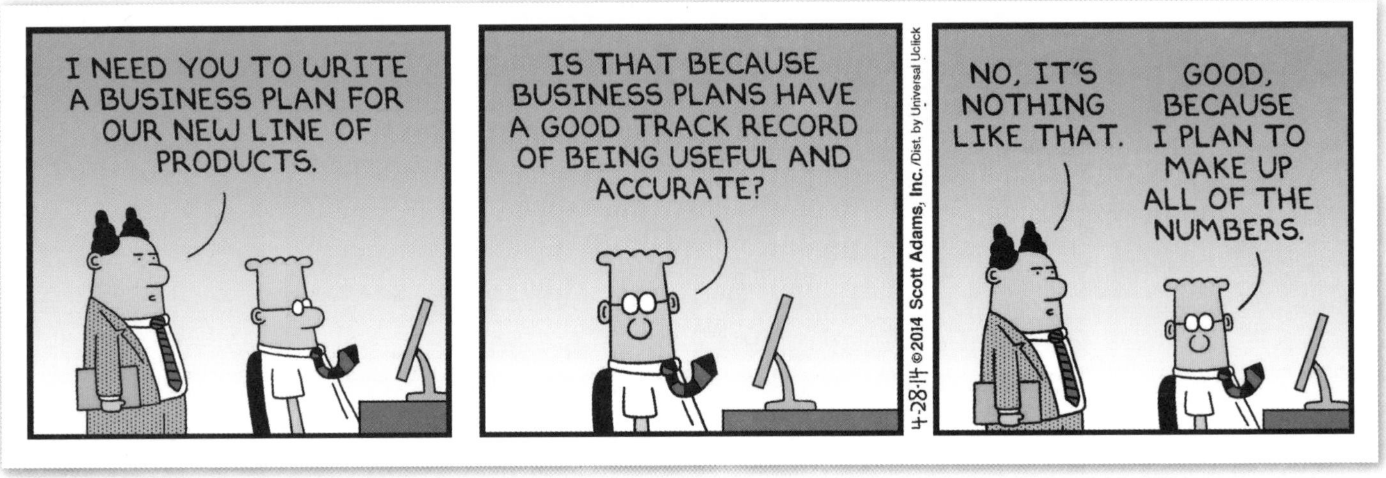
I NEED YOU TO WRITE A BUSINESS PLAN FOR OUR NEW LINE OF PRODUCTS.
IS THAT BECAUSE BUSINESS PLANS HAVE A GOOD TRACK RECORD OF BEING USEFUL AND ACCURATE?
4-28-14 ©2014 Scott Adams, Inc./Dist. by Universal Uclick
NO, IT'S NOTHING LIKE THAT.
GOOD, BECAUSE I PLAN TO MAKE UP ALL OF THE NUMBERS.

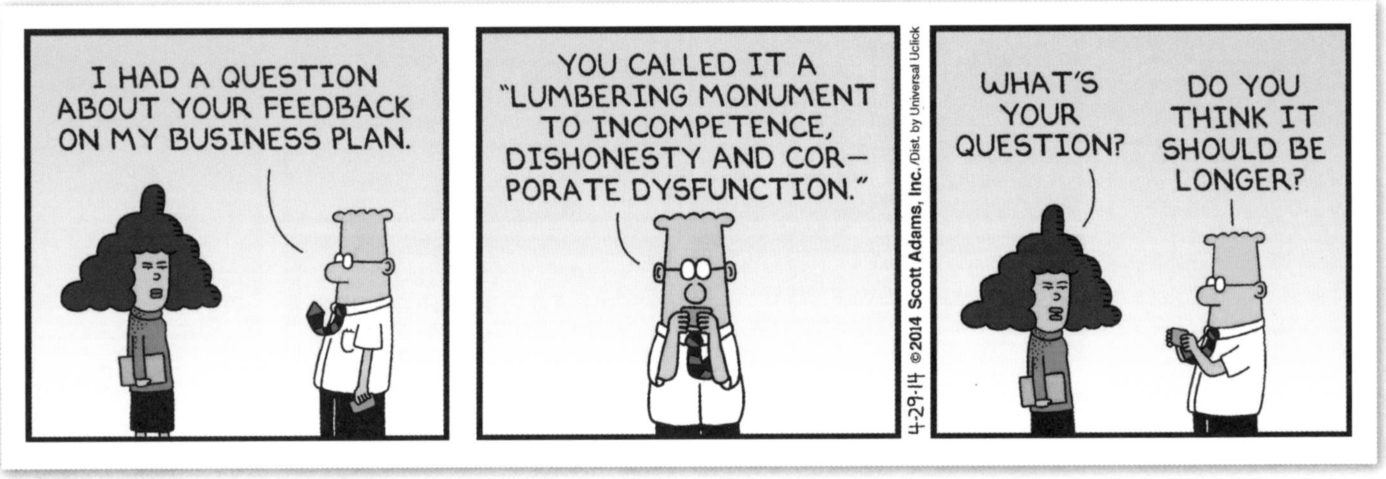
I HAD A QUESTION ABOUT YOUR FEEDBACK ON MY BUSINESS PLAN.
YOU CALLED IT A "LUMBERING MONUMENT TO INCOMPETENCE, DISHONESTY AND COR-PORATE DYSFUNCTION."
4-29-14 ©2014 Scott Adams, Inc./Dist. by Universal Uclick
WHAT'S YOUR QUESTION?
DO YOU THINK IT SHOULD BE LONGER?

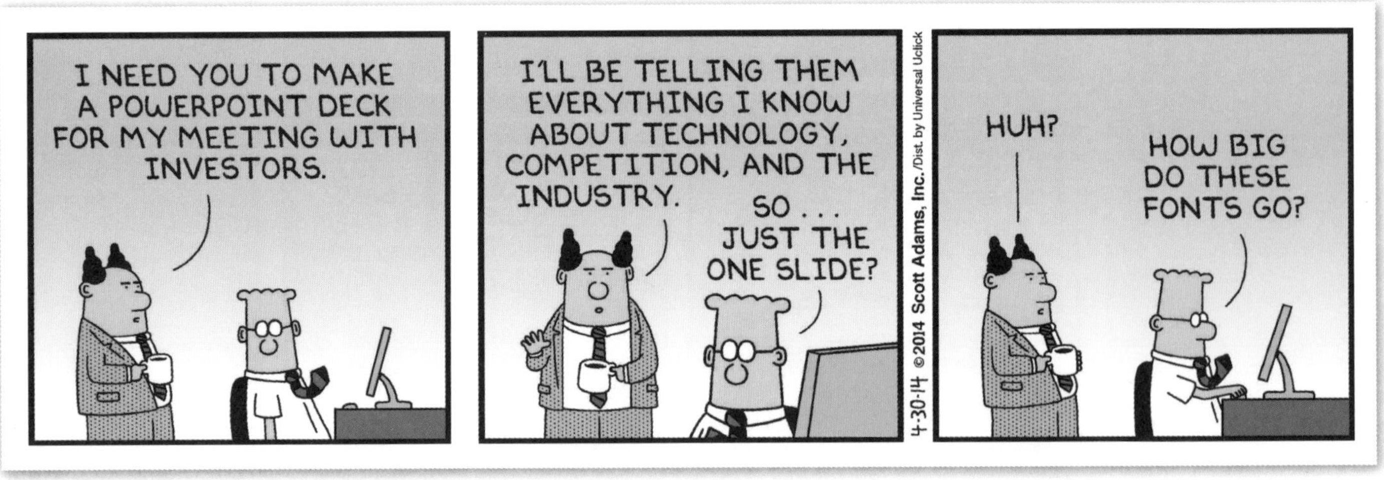
I NEED YOU TO MAKE A POWERPOINT DECK FOR MY MEETING WITH INVESTORS.
I'LL BE TELLING THEM EVERYTHING I KNOW ABOUT TECHNOLOGY, COMPETITION, AND THE INDUSTRY.
SO . . . JUST THE ONE SLIDE?
4-30-14 ©2014 Scott Adams, Inc./Dist. by Universal Uclick
HUH?
HOW BIG DO THESE FONTS GO?

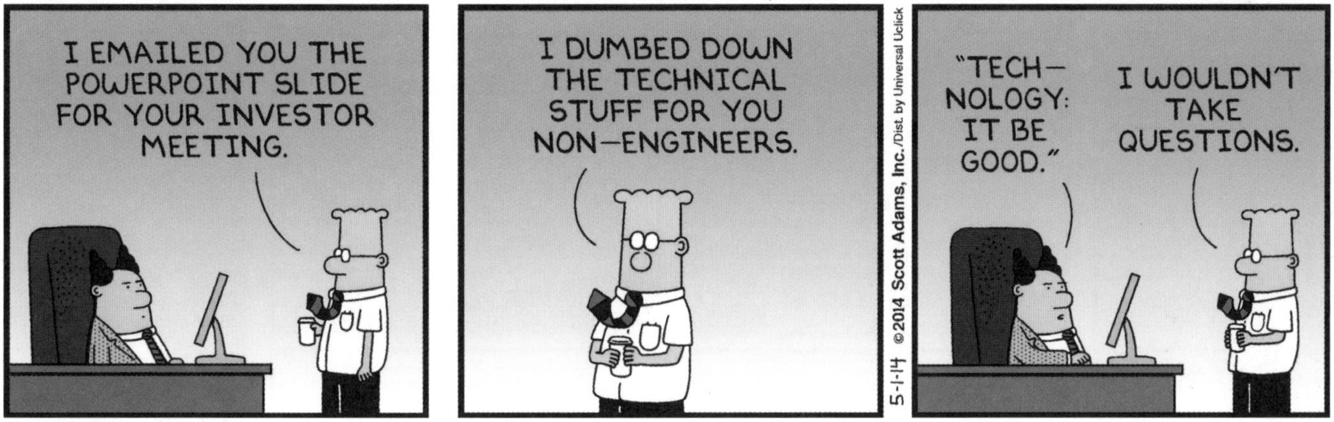
I EMAILED YOU THE POWERPOINT SLIDE FOR YOUR INVESTOR MEETING.
I DUMBED DOWN THE TECHNICAL STUFF FOR YOU NON—ENGINEERS.
5-1-14 ©2014 Scott Adams, Inc./Dist. by Universal Uclick
"TECH—NOLOGY: IT BE GOOD."
I WOULDN'T TAKE QUESTIONS.

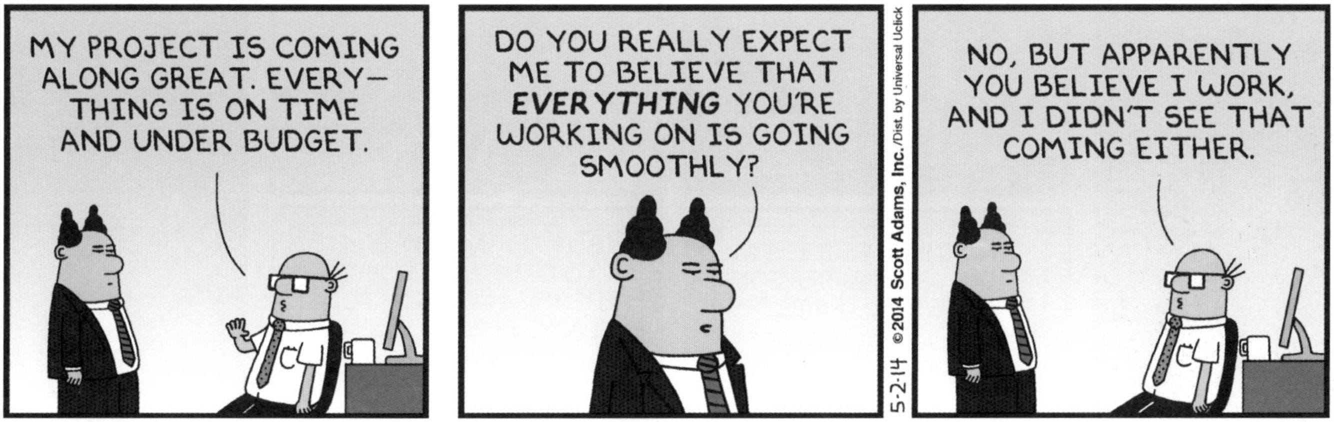
MY PROJECT IS COMING ALONG GREAT. EVERY—THING IS ON TIME AND UNDER BUDGET.
DO YOU REALLY EXPECT ME TO BELIEVE THAT EVERYTHING YOU'RE WORKING ON IS GOING SMOOTHLY?
5-2-14 ©2014 Scott Adams, Inc./Dist. by Universal Uclick
NO, BUT APPARENTLY YOU BELIEVE I WORK, AND I DIDN'T SEE THAT COMING EITHER.

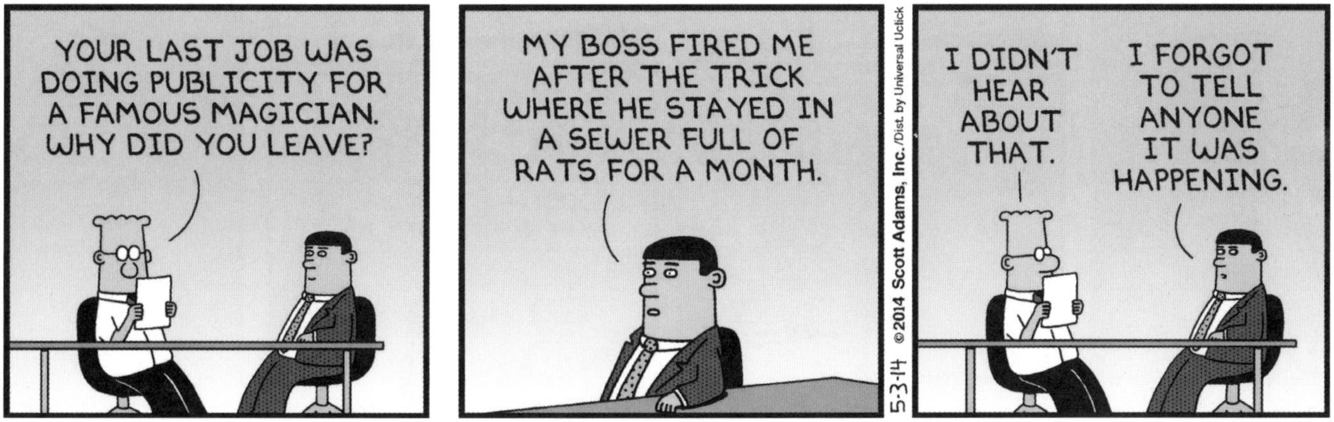
YOUR LAST JOB WAS DOING PUBLICITY FOR A FAMOUS MAGICIAN. WHY DID YOU LEAVE?
MY BOSS FIRED ME AFTER THE TRICK WHERE HE STAYED IN A SEWER FULL OF RATS FOR A MONTH.
5-3-14 ©2014 Scott Adams, Inc./Dist. by Universal Uclick
I DIDN'T HEAR ABOUT THAT.
I FORGOT TO TELL ANYONE IT WAS HAPPENING.

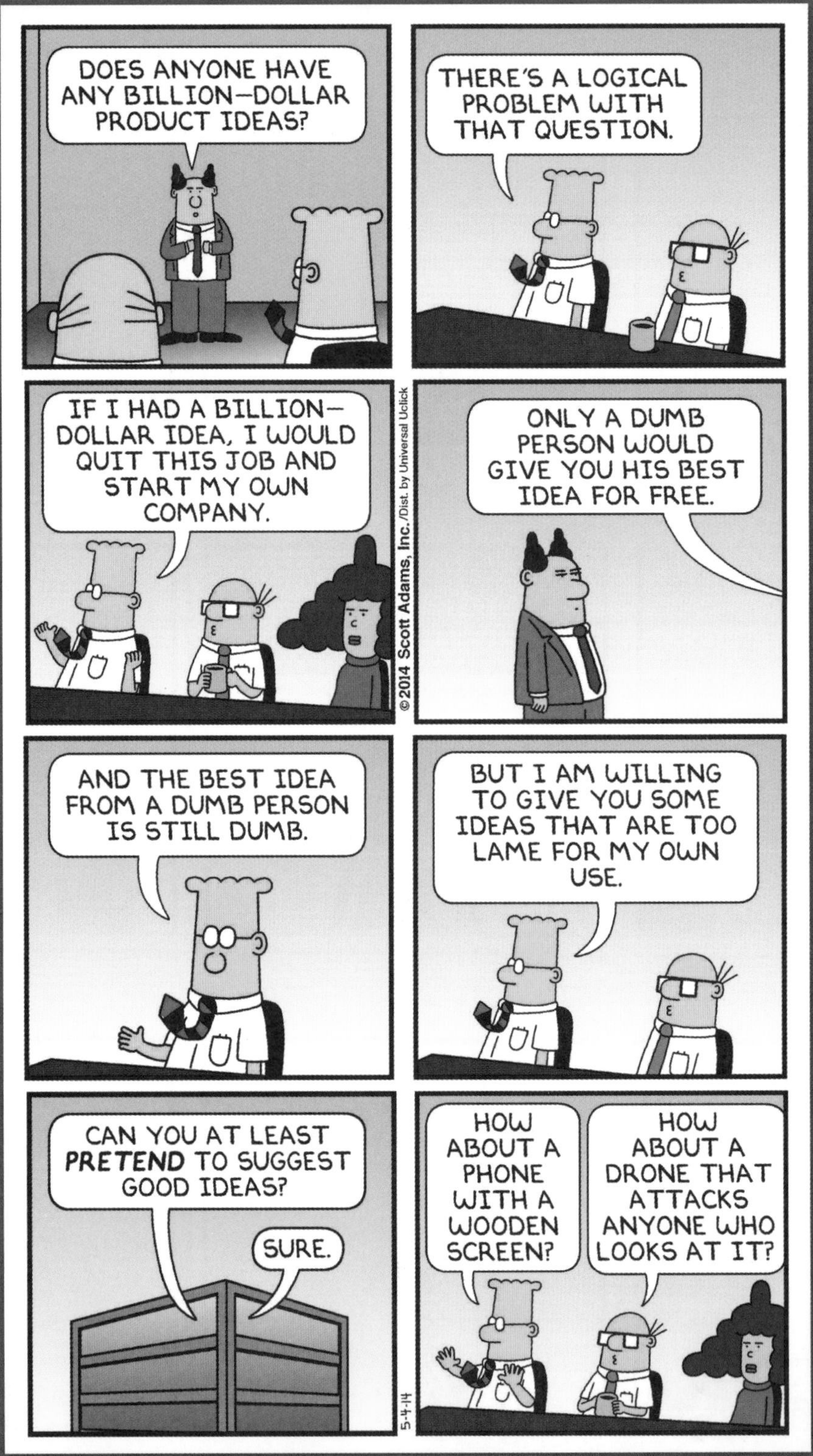
DOES ANYONE HAVE ANY BILLION–DOLLAR PRODUCT IDEAS?
THERE'S A LOGICAL PROBLEM WITH THAT QUESTION.
IF I HAD A BILLION–DOLLAR IDEA, I WOULD QUIT THIS JOB AND START MY OWN COMPANY.
ONLY A DUMB PERSON WOULD GIVE YOU HIS BEST IDEA FOR FREE.
AND THE BEST IDEA FROM A DUMB PERSON IS STILL DUMB.
BUT I AM WILLING TO GIVE YOU SOME IDEAS THAT ARE TOO LAME FOR MY OWN USE.
CAN YOU AT LEAST **PRETEND** TO SUGGEST GOOD IDEAS?
SURE.
HOW ABOUT A PHONE WITH A WOODEN SCREEN?
HOW ABOUT A DRONE THAT ATTACKS ANYONE WHO LOOKS AT IT?
©2014 Scott Adams, Inc./Dist. by Universal Uclick
5-4-14

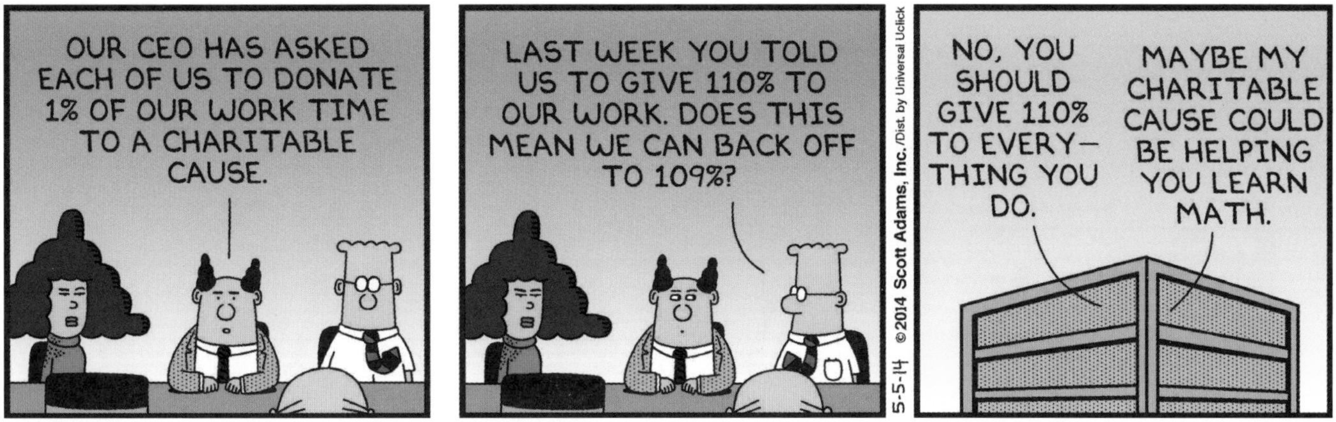
OUR CEO HAS ASKED EACH OF US TO DONATE 1% OF OUR WORK TIME TO A CHARITABLE CAUSE.
LAST WEEK YOU TOLD US TO GIVE 110% TO OUR WORK. DOES THIS MEAN WE CAN BACK OFF TO 109%?
5-5-14 ©2014 Scott Adams, Inc./Dist. by Universal Uclick
NO, YOU SHOULD GIVE 110% TO EVERY-THING YOU DO.
MAYBE MY CHARITABLE CAUSE COULD BE HELPING YOU LEARN MATH.

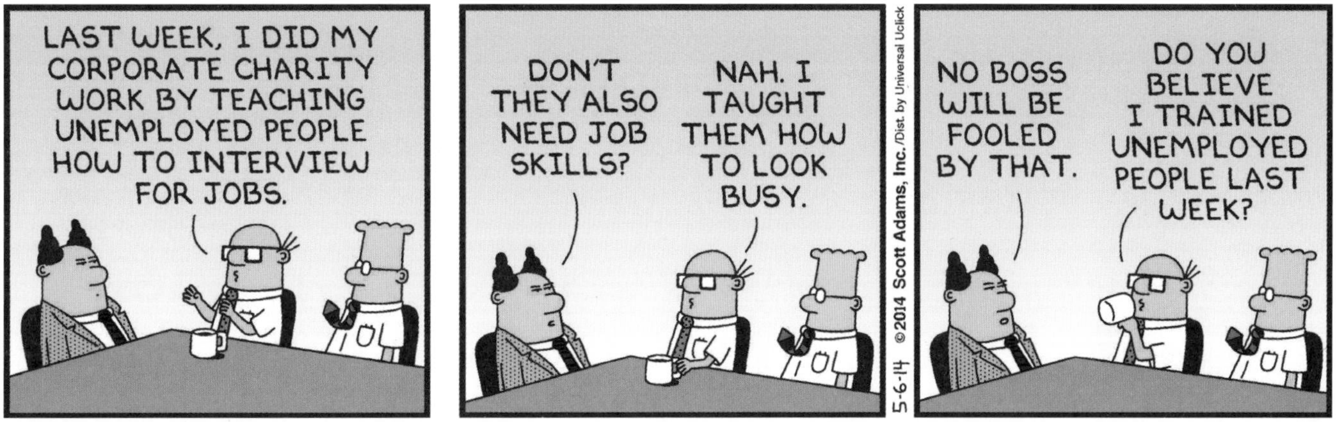
LAST WEEK, I DID MY CORPORATE CHARITY WORK BY TEACHING UNEMPLOYED PEOPLE HOW TO INTERVIEW FOR JOBS.
DON'T THEY ALSO NEED JOB SKILLS?
NAH. I TAUGHT THEM HOW TO LOOK BUSY.
5-6-14 ©2014 Scott Adams, Inc./Dist. by Universal Uclick
NO BOSS WILL BE FOOLED BY THAT.
DO YOU BELIEVE I TRAINED UNEMPLOYED PEOPLE LAST WEEK?

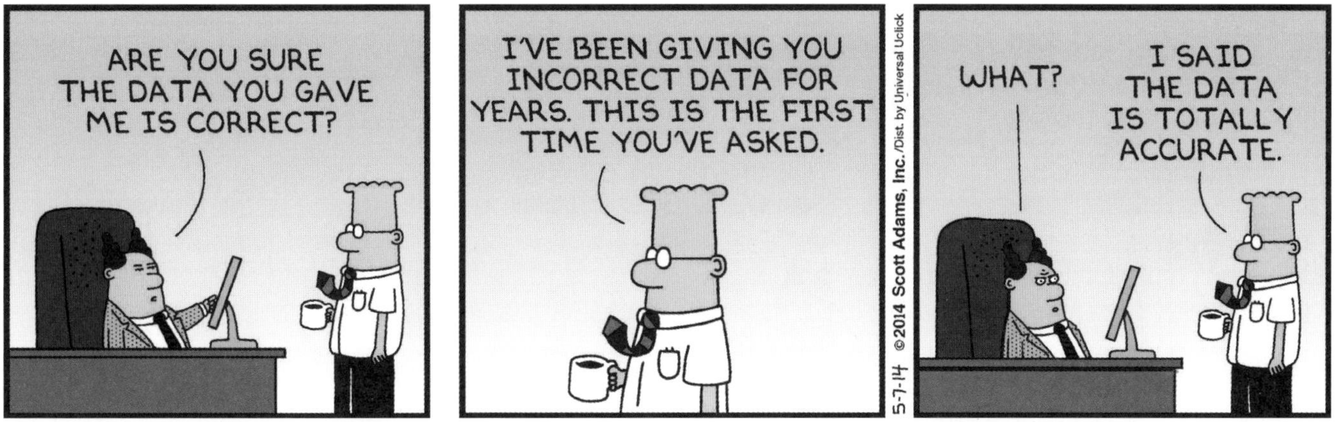
ARE YOU SURE THE DATA YOU GAVE ME IS CORRECT?
I'VE BEEN GIVING YOU INCORRECT DATA FOR YEARS. THIS IS THE FIRST TIME YOU'VE ASKED.
5-7-14 ©2014 Scott Adams, Inc./Dist. by Universal Uclick
WHAT?
I SAID THE DATA IS TOTALLY ACCURATE.

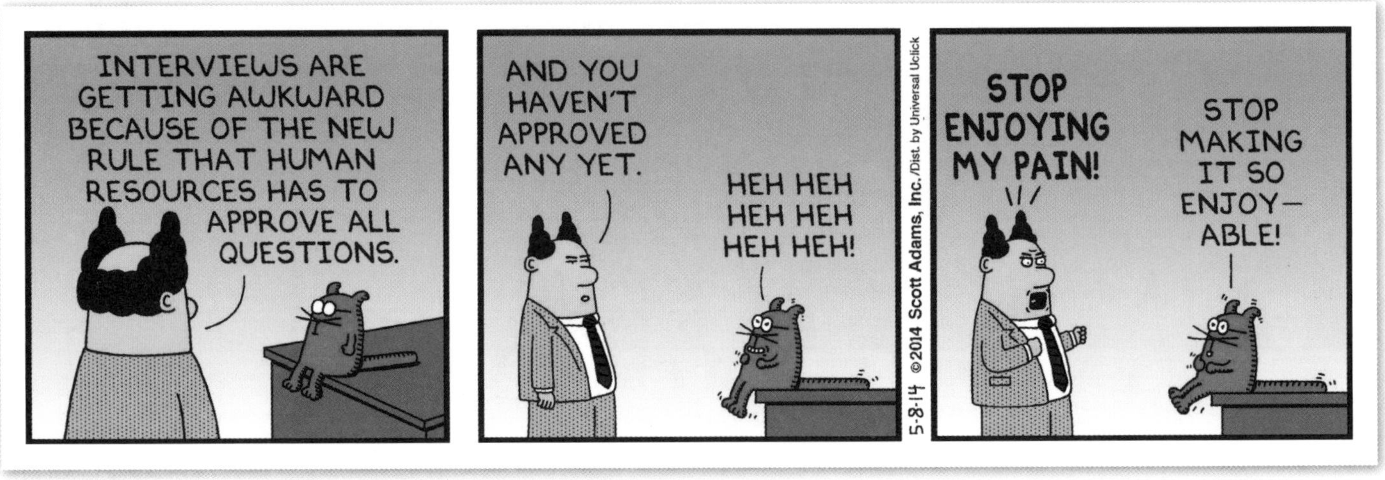
INTERVIEWS ARE GETTING AWKWARD BECAUSE OF THE NEW RULE THAT HUMAN RESOURCES HAS TO APPROVE ALL QUESTIONS.
AND YOU HAVEN'T APPROVED ANY YET.
HEH HEH HEH HEH HEH HEH!
STOP ENJOYING MY PAIN!
STOP MAKING IT SO ENJOY-ABLE!
5-8-14 ©2014 Scott Adams, Inc./Dist. by Universal Uclick

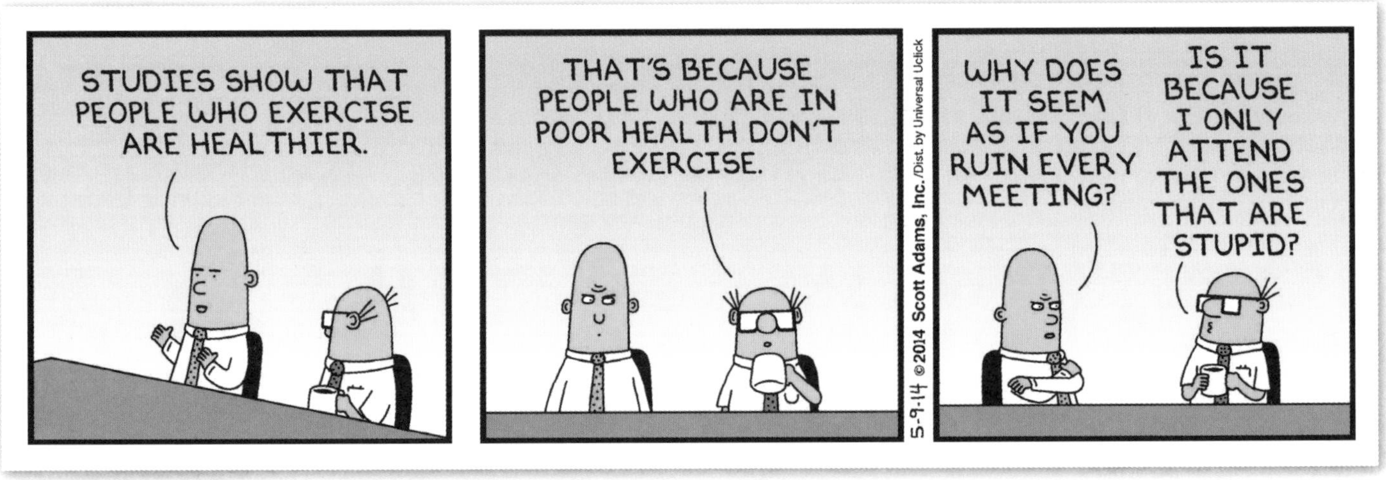
STUDIES SHOW THAT PEOPLE WHO EXERCISE ARE HEALTHIER.
THAT'S BECAUSE PEOPLE WHO ARE IN POOR HEALTH DON'T EXERCISE.
WHY DOES IT SEEM AS IF YOU RUIN EVERY MEETING?
IS IT BECAUSE I ONLY ATTEND THE ONES THAT ARE STUPID?
5-9-14 ©2014 Scott Adams, Inc./Dist. by Universal Uclick

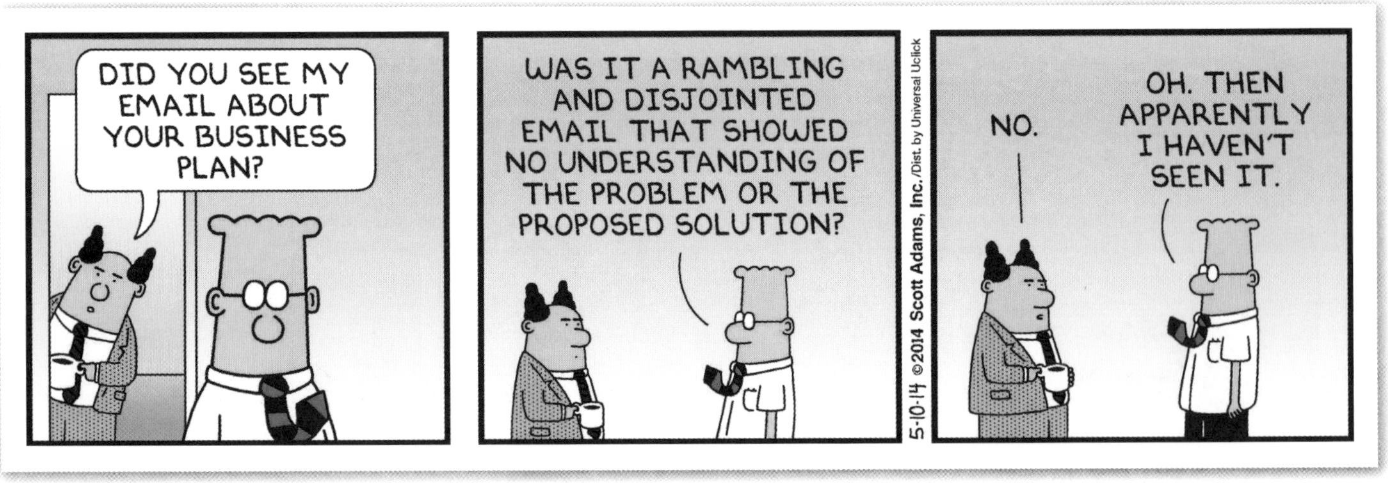
DID YOU SEE MY EMAIL ABOUT YOUR BUSINESS PLAN?
WAS IT A RAMBLING AND DISJOINTED EMAIL THAT SHOWED NO UNDERSTANDING OF THE PROBLEM OR THE PROPOSED SOLUTION?
NO.
OH. THEN APPARENTLY I HAVEN'T SEEN IT.
5-10-14 ©2014 Scott Adams, Inc./Dist. by Universal Uclick

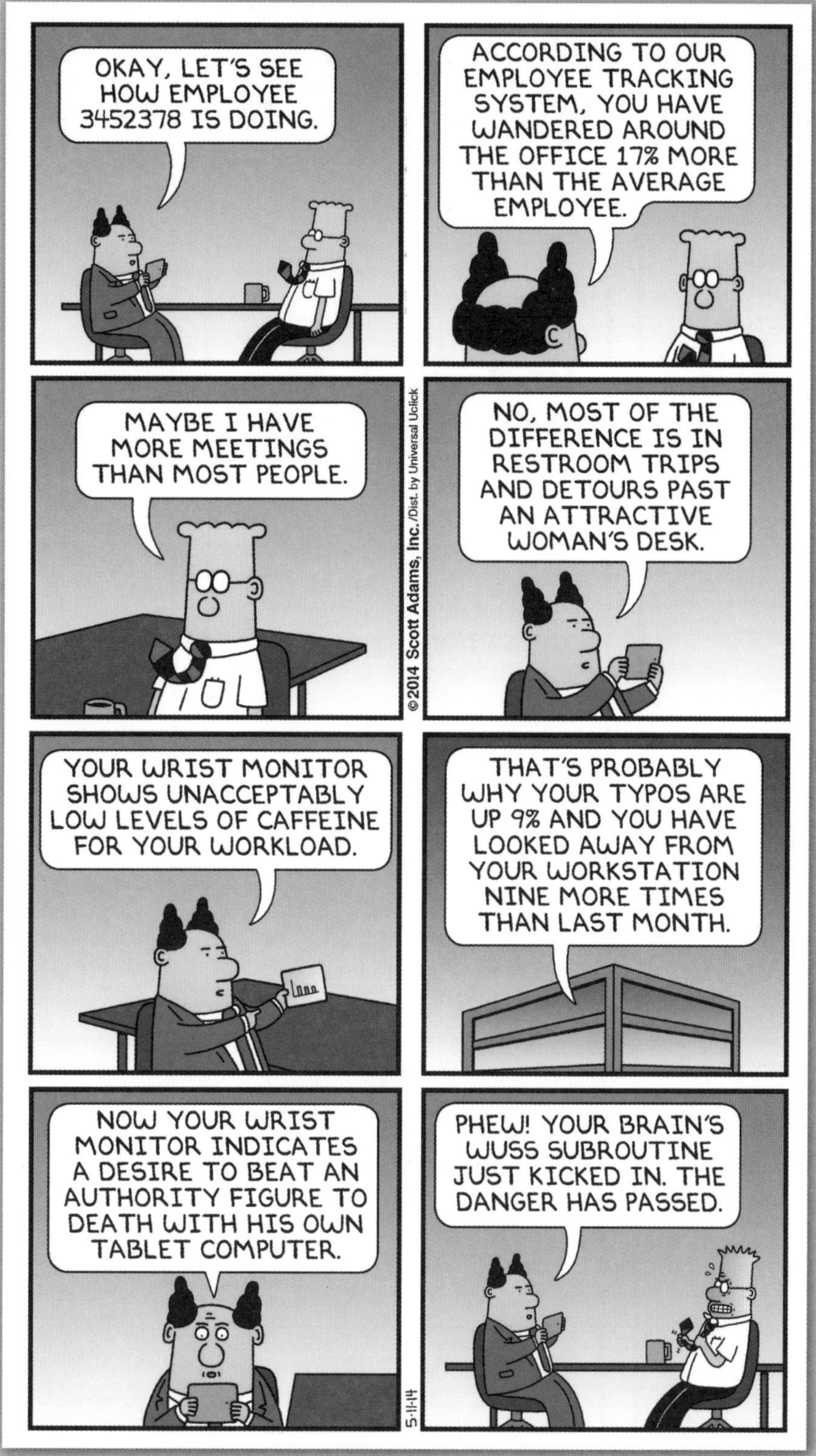
OKAY, LET'S SEE HOW EMPLOYEE 3452378 IS DOING.
ACCORDING TO OUR EMPLOYEE TRACKING SYSTEM, YOU HAVE WANDERED AROUND THE OFFICE 17% MORE THAN THE AVERAGE EMPLOYEE.
MAYBE I HAVE MORE MEETINGS THAN MOST PEOPLE.
NO, MOST OF THE DIFFERENCE IS IN RESTROOM TRIPS AND DETOURS PAST AN ATTRACTIVE WOMAN'S DESK.
YOUR WRIST MONITOR SHOWS UNACCEPTABLY LOW LEVELS OF CAFFEINE FOR YOUR WORKLOAD.
THAT'S PROBABLY WHY YOUR TYPOS ARE UP 9% AND YOU HAVE LOOKED AWAY FROM YOUR WORKSTATION NINE MORE TIMES THAN LAST MONTH.
NOW YOUR WRIST MONITOR INDICATES A DESIRE TO BEAT AN AUTHORITY FIGURE TO DEATH WITH HIS OWN TABLET COMPUTER.
PHEW! YOUR BRAIN'S WUSS SUBROUTINE JUST KICKED IN. THE DANGER HAS PASSED.
©2014 Scott Adams, Inc./Dist. by Universal Uclick
5-11-14

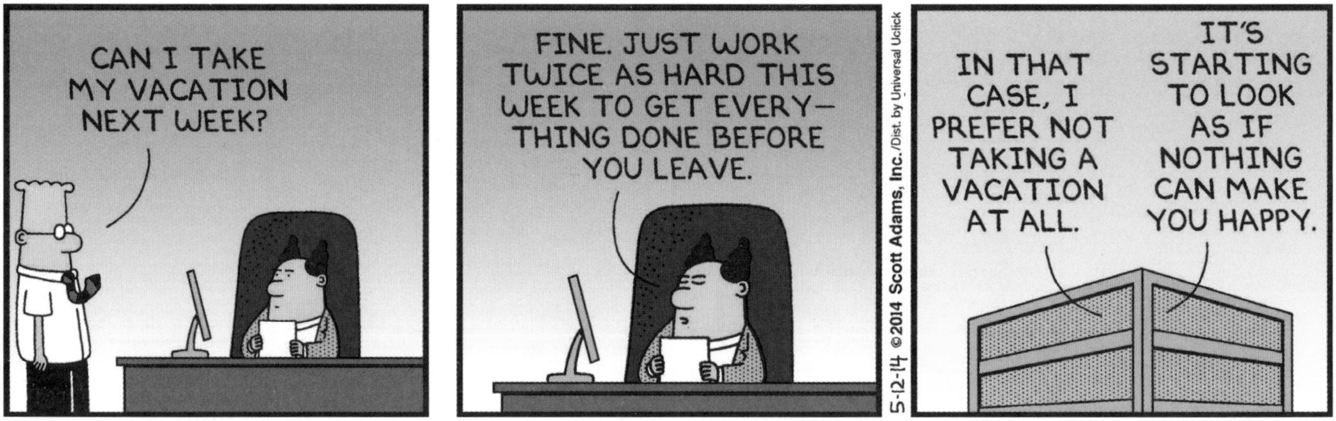
CAN I TAKE MY VACATION NEXT WEEK?
FINE. JUST WORK TWICE AS HARD THIS WEEK TO GET EVERY-THING DONE BEFORE YOU LEAVE.
5-12-14 ©2014 Scott Adams, Inc./Dist. by Universal Uclick
IN THAT CASE, I PREFER NOT TAKING A VACATION AT ALL.
IT'S STARTING TO LOOK AS IF NOTHING CAN MAKE YOU HAPPY.

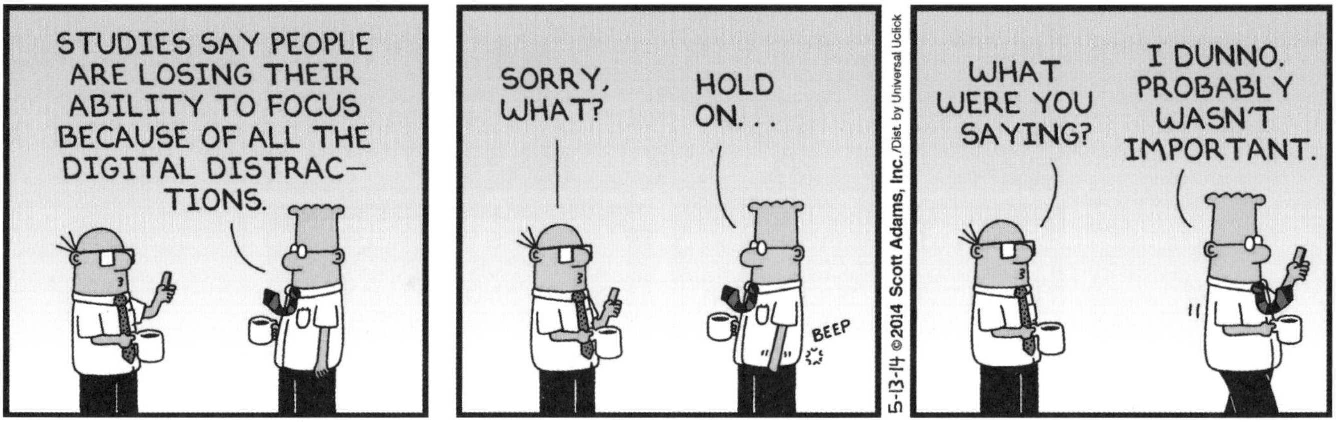
STUDIES SAY PEOPLE ARE LOSING THEIR ABILITY TO FOCUS BECAUSE OF ALL THE DIGITAL DISTRAC-TIONS.
SORRY, WHAT?
HOLD ON. . .
BEEP
5-13-14 ©2014 Scott Adams, Inc./Dist. by Universal Uclick
WHAT WERE YOU SAYING?
I DUNNO. PROBABLY WASN'T IMPORTANT.

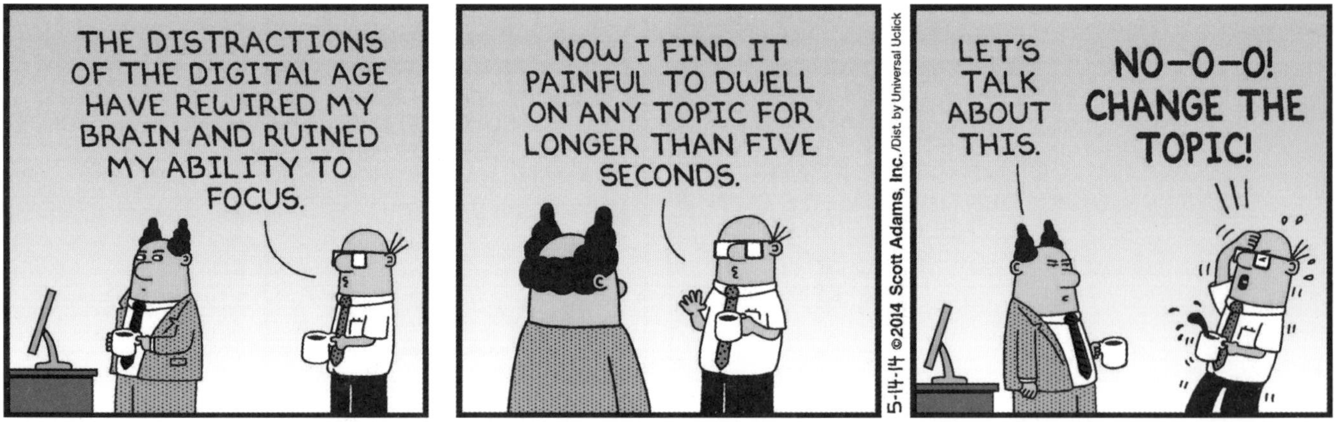
THE DISTRACTIONS OF THE DIGITAL AGE HAVE REWIRED MY BRAIN AND RUINED MY ABILITY TO FOCUS.
NOW I FIND IT PAINFUL TO DWELL ON ANY TOPIC FOR LONGER THAN FIVE SECONDS.
5-14-14 ©2014 Scott Adams, Inc./Dist. by Universal Uclick
LET'S TALK ABOUT THIS.
NO-O-O! CHANGE THE TOPIC!

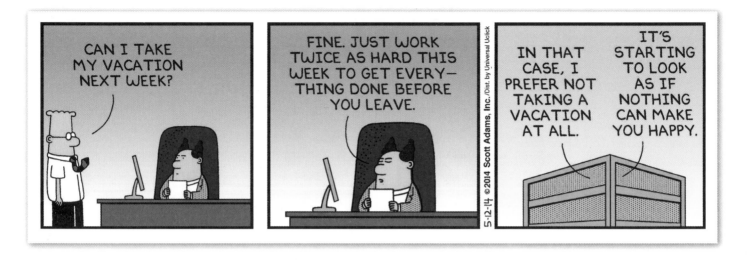

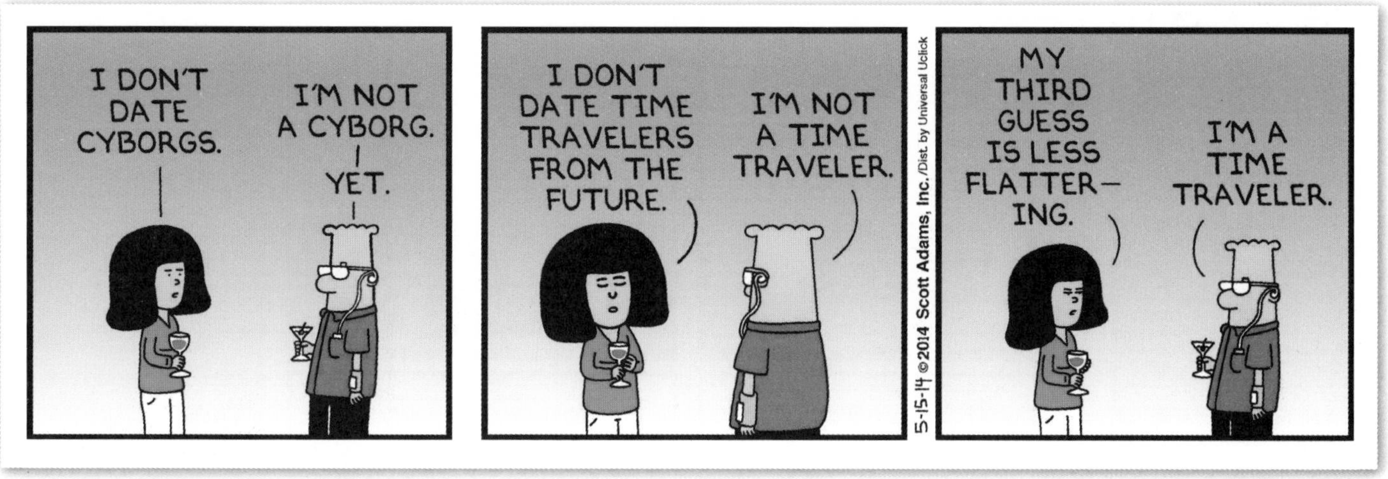
I DON'T DATE CYBORGS.
I'M NOT A CYBORG.
YET.
I DON'T DATE TIME TRAVELERS FROM THE FUTURE.
I'M NOT A TIME TRAVELER.
5-15-14 ©2014 Scott Adams, Inc./Dist. by Universal Uclick
MY THIRD GUESS IS LESS FLATTER-ING.
I'M A TIME TRAVELER.

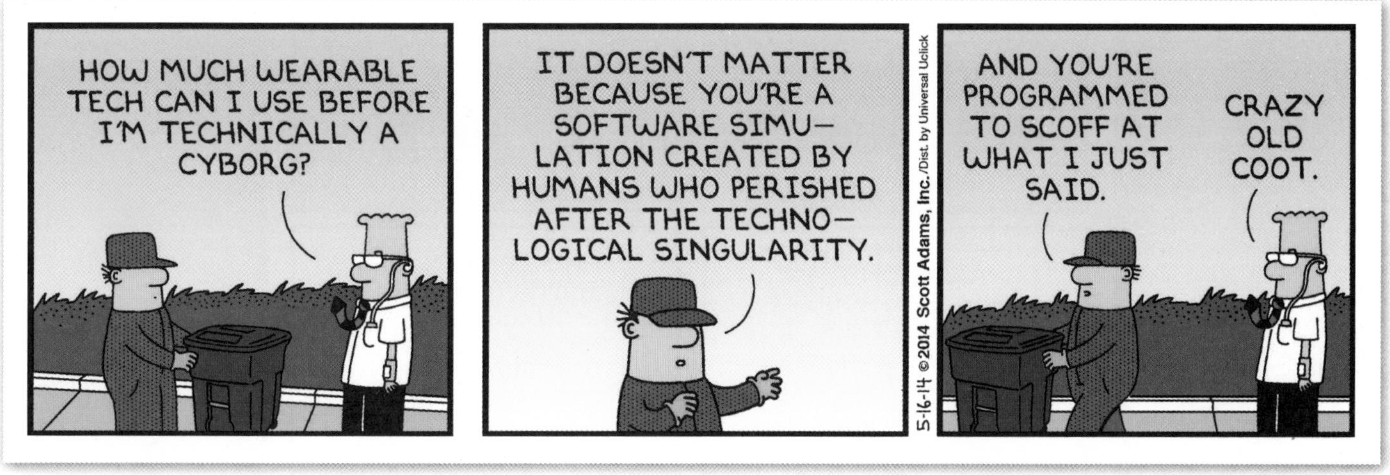
HOW MUCH WEARABLE TECH CAN I USE BEFORE I'M TECHNICALLY A CYBORG?
IT DOESN'T MATTER BECAUSE YOU'RE A SOFTWARE SIMU-LATION CREATED BY HUMANS WHO PERISHED AFTER THE TECHNO-LOGICAL SINGULARITY.
5-16-14 ©2014 Scott Adams, Inc./Dist. by Universal Uclick
AND YOU'RE PROGRAMMED TO SCOFF AT WHAT I JUST SAID.
CRAZY OLD COOT.

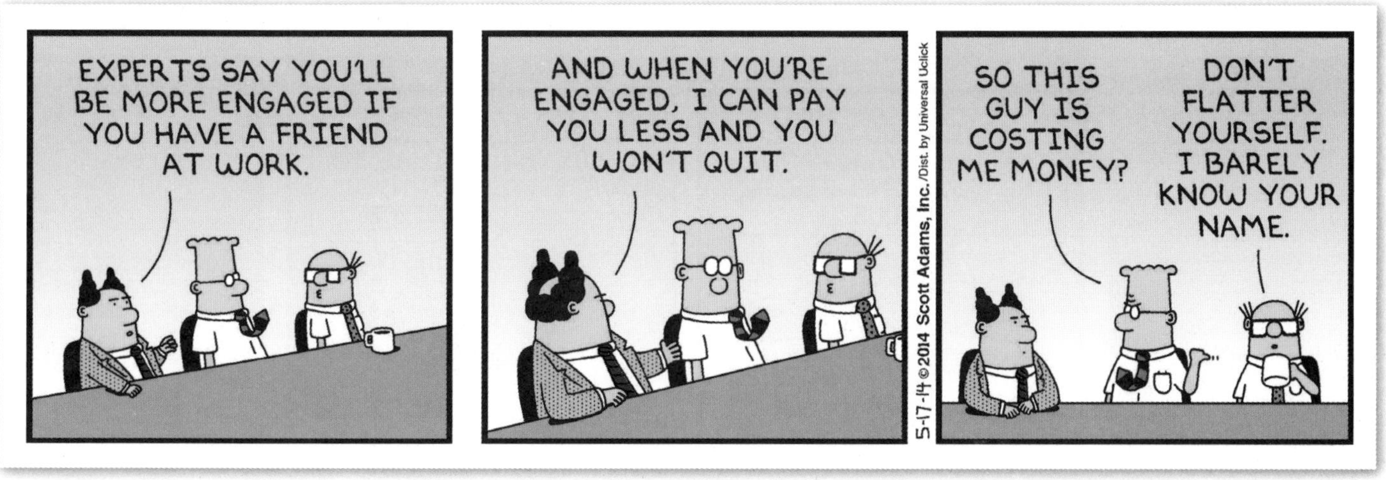
EXPERTS SAY YOU'LL BE MORE ENGAGED IF YOU HAVE A FRIEND AT WORK.
AND WHEN YOU'RE ENGAGED, I CAN PAY YOU LESS AND YOU WON'T QUIT.
5-17-14 ©2014 Scott Adams, Inc./Dist. by Universal Uclick
SO THIS GUY IS COSTING ME MONEY?
DON'T FLATTER YOURSELF. I BARELY KNOW YOUR NAME.

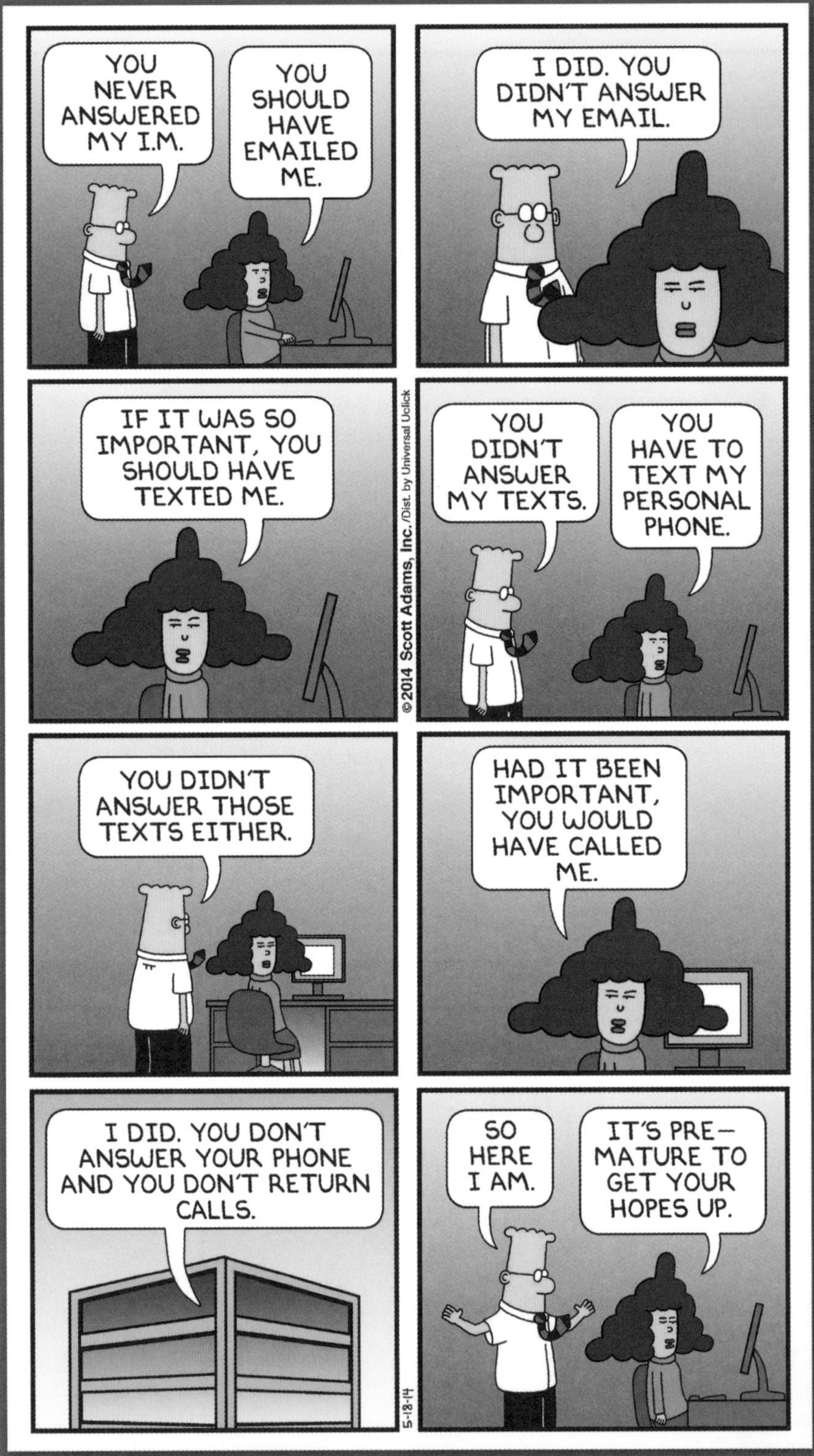
YOU NEVER ANSWERED MY I.M.
YOU SHOULD HAVE EMAILED ME.
I DID. YOU DIDN'T ANSWER MY EMAIL.
IF IT WAS SO IMPORTANT, YOU SHOULD HAVE TEXTED ME.
YOU DIDN'T ANSWER MY TEXTS.
YOU HAVE TO TEXT MY PERSONAL PHONE.
YOU DIDN'T ANSWER THOSE TEXTS EITHER.
HAD IT BEEN IMPORTANT, YOU WOULD HAVE CALLED ME.
I DID. YOU DON'T ANSWER YOUR PHONE AND YOU DON'T RETURN CALLS.
SO HERE I AM.
IT'S PRE-MATURE TO GET YOUR HOPES UP.
© 2014 Scott Adams, Inc./Dist. by Universal Uclick
5-18-14

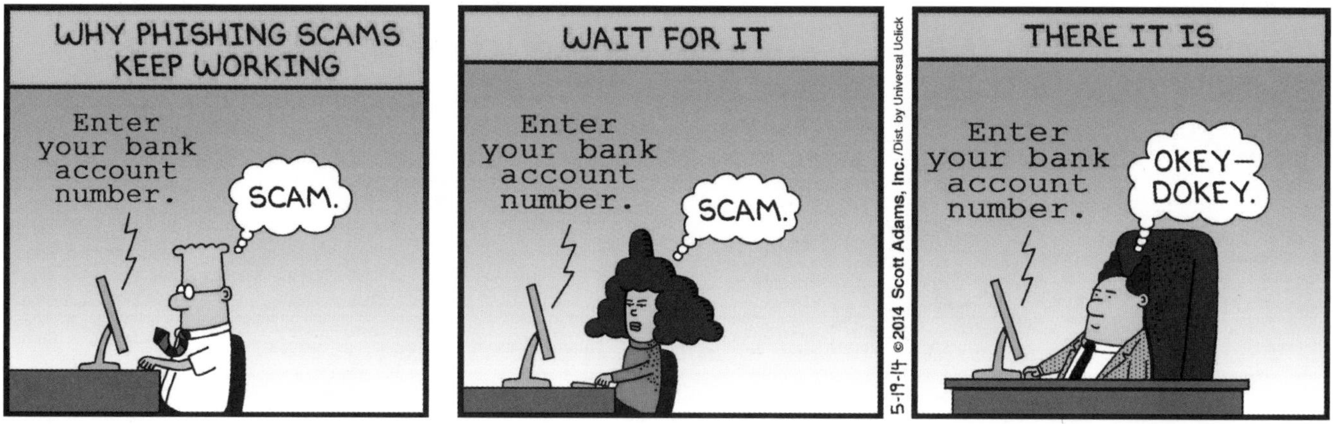
WHY PHISHING SCAMS KEEP WORKING
Enter your bank account number.
SCAM.
WAIT FOR IT
Enter your bank account number.
SCAM.
5-19-14 ©2014 Scott Adams, Inc./Dist. by Universal Uclick
THERE IT IS
Enter your bank account number.
OKEY-DOKEY.

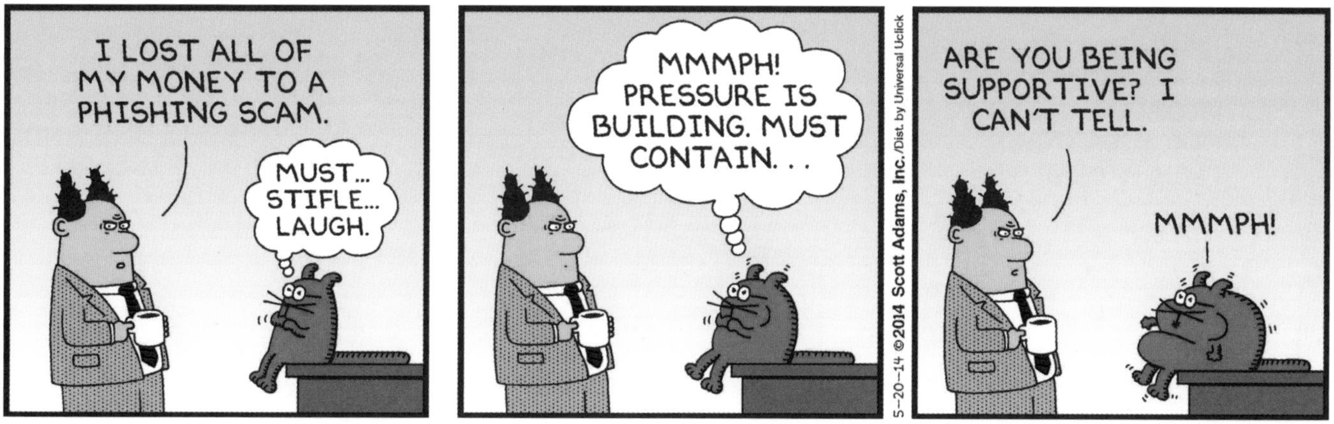
I LOST ALL OF MY MONEY TO A PHISHING SCAM.
MUST... STIFLE... LAUGH.
MMMPH! PRESSURE IS BUILDING. MUST CONTAIN. . .
5-20-14 ©2014 Scott Adams, Inc./Dist. by Universal Uclick
ARE YOU BEING SUPPORTIVE? I CAN'T TELL.
MMMPH!

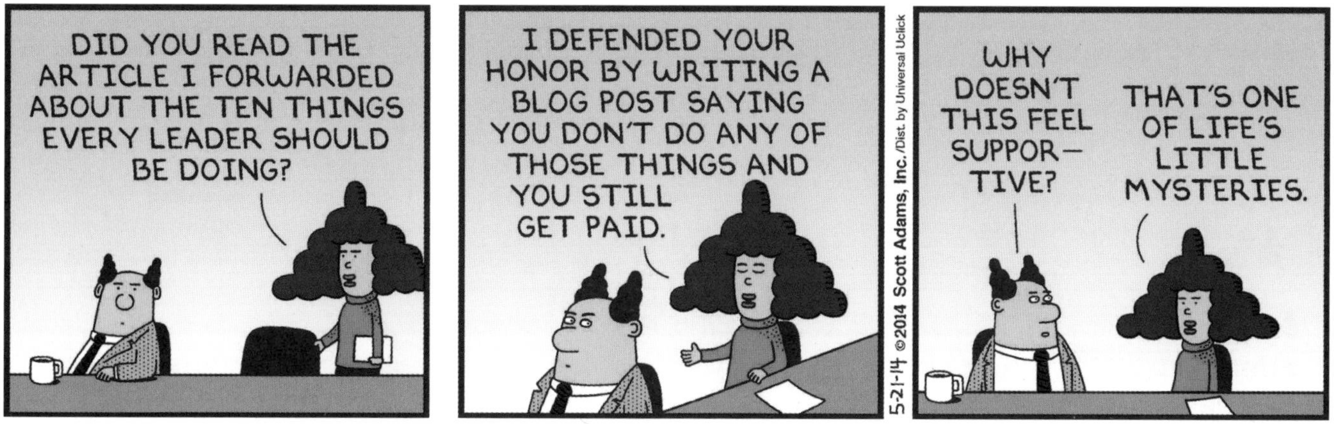
DID YOU READ THE ARTICLE I FORWARDED ABOUT THE TEN THINGS EVERY LEADER SHOULD BE DOING?
I DEFENDED YOUR HONOR BY WRITING A BLOG POST SAYING YOU DON'T DO ANY OF THOSE THINGS AND YOU STILL GET PAID.
5-21-14 ©2014 Scott Adams, Inc./Dist. by Universal Uclick
WHY DOESN'T THIS FEEL SUPPOR-TIVE?
THAT'S ONE OF LIFE'S LITTLE MYSTERIES.

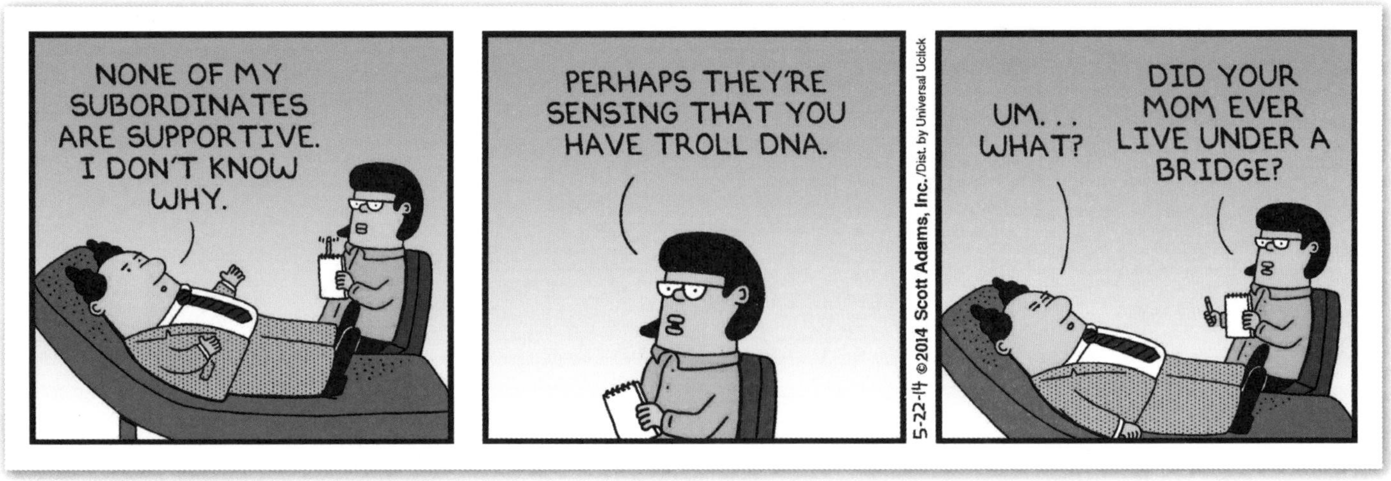
NONE OF MY SUBORDINATES ARE SUPPORTIVE. I DON'T KNOW WHY.
PERHAPS THEY'RE SENSING THAT YOU HAVE TROLL DNA.
5-22-14 ©2014 Scott Adams, Inc./Dist. by Universal Uclick
UM... WHAT?
DID YOUR MOM EVER LIVE UNDER A BRIDGE?

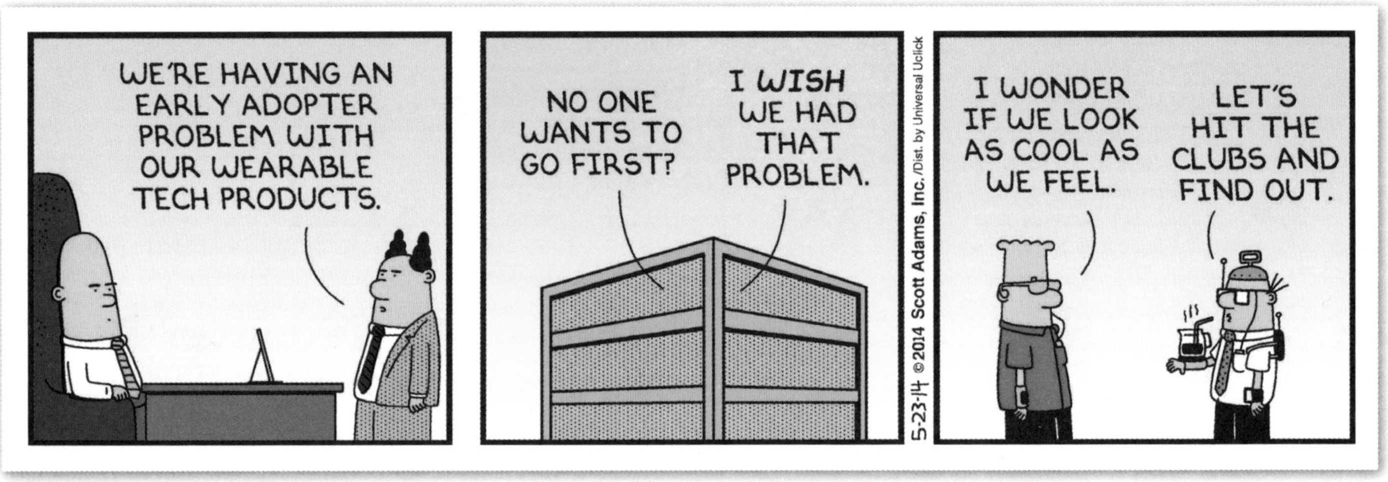
WE'RE HAVING AN EARLY ADOPTER PROBLEM WITH OUR WEARABLE TECH PRODUCTS.
NO ONE WANTS TO GO FIRST?
I *WISH* WE HAD THAT PROBLEM.
5-23-14 ©2014 Scott Adams, Inc./Dist. by Universal Uclick
I WONDER IF WE LOOK AS COOL AS WE FEEL.
LET'S HIT THE CLUBS AND FIND OUT.

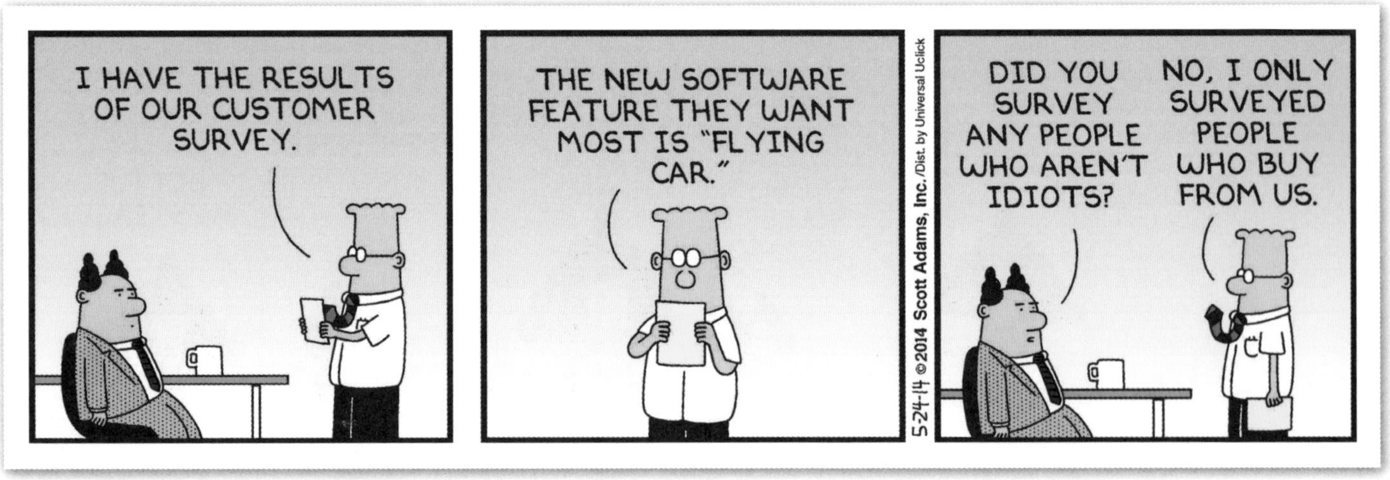
I HAVE THE RESULTS OF OUR CUSTOMER SURVEY.
THE NEW SOFTWARE FEATURE THEY WANT MOST IS "FLYING CAR."
5-24-14 ©2014 Scott Adams, Inc./Dist. by Universal Uclick
DID YOU SURVEY ANY PEOPLE WHO AREN'T IDIOTS?
NO, I ONLY SURVEYED PEOPLE WHO BUY FROM US.

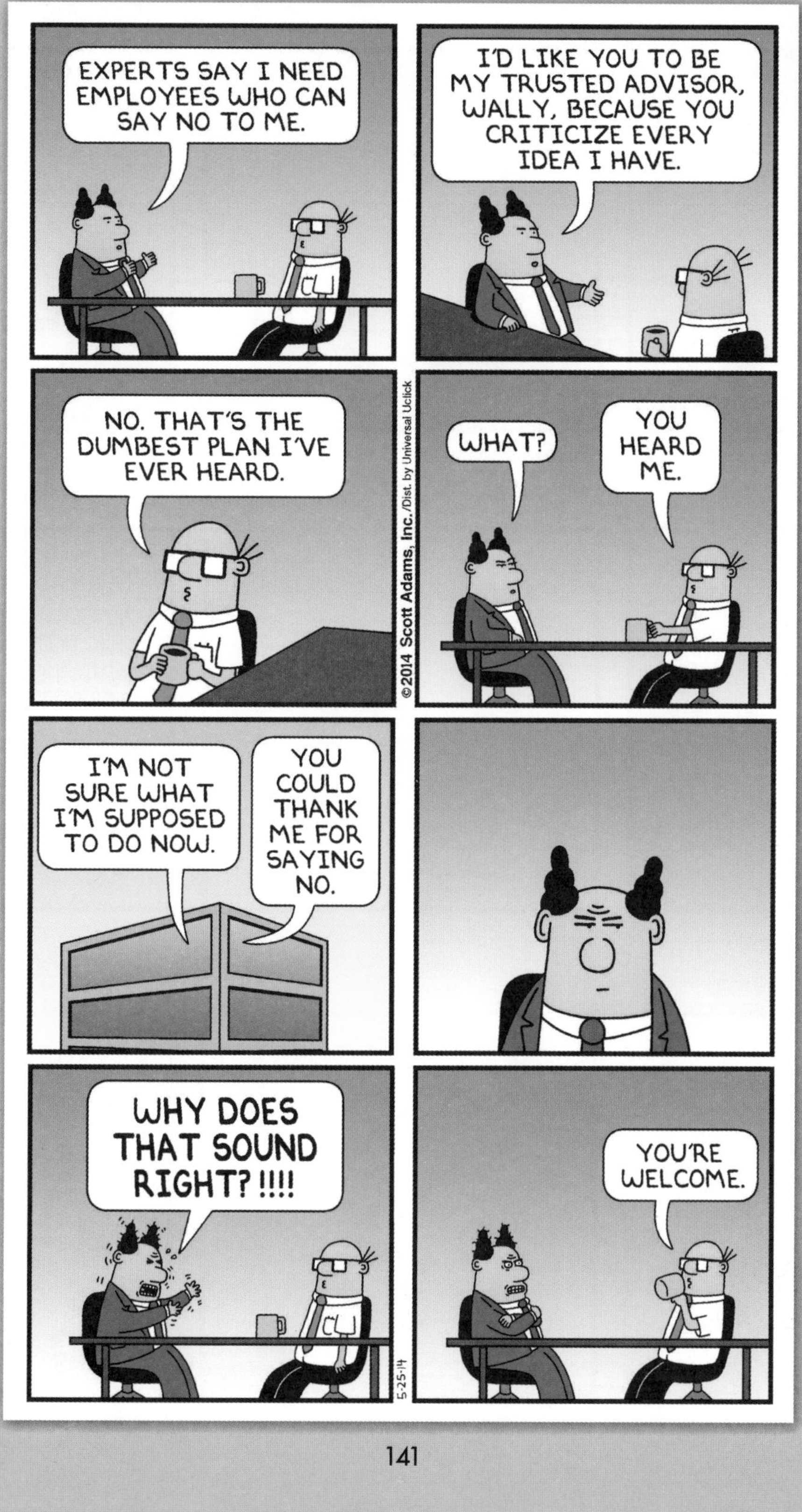
EXPERTS SAY I NEED EMPLOYEES WHO CAN SAY NO TO ME.
I'D LIKE YOU TO BE MY TRUSTED ADVISOR, WALLY, BECAUSE YOU CRITICIZE EVERY IDEA I HAVE.
NO. THAT'S THE DUMBEST PLAN I'VE EVER HEARD.
©2014 Scott Adams, Inc./Dist. by Universal Uclick
WHAT?
YOU HEARD ME.
I'M NOT SURE WHAT I'M SUPPOSED TO DO NOW.
YOU COULD THANK ME FOR SAYING NO.
WHY DOES THAT SOUND RIGHT? !!!!
5-25-14
YOU'RE WELCOME.

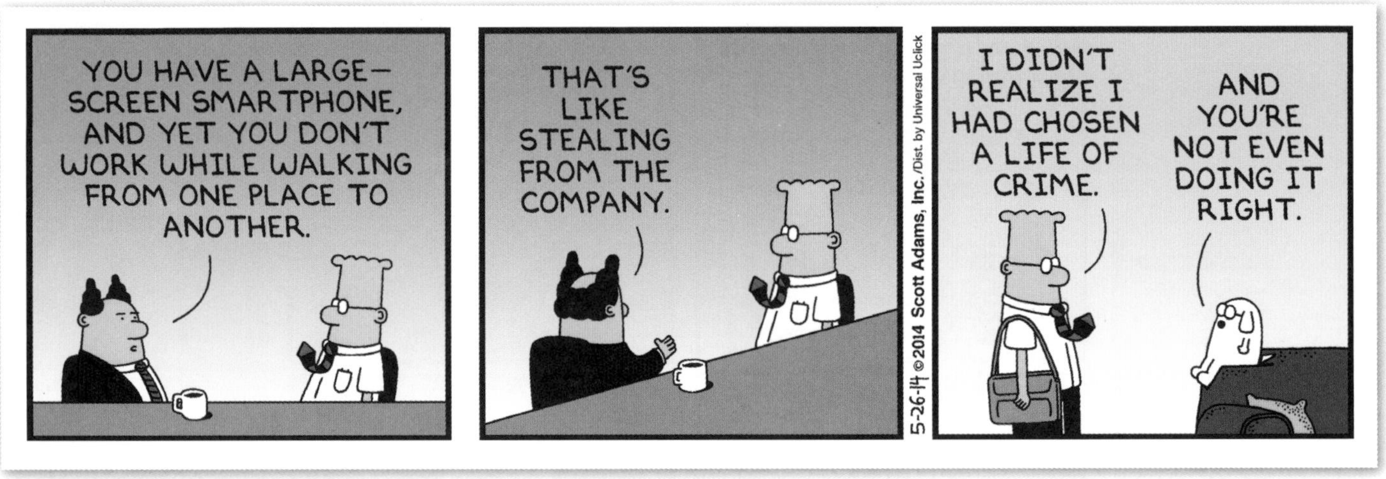
YOU HAVE A LARGE-SCREEN SMARTPHONE, AND YET YOU DON'T WORK WHILE WALKING FROM ONE PLACE TO ANOTHER.
THAT'S LIKE STEALING FROM THE COMPANY.
5-26-14 ©2014 Scott Adams, Inc./Dist. by Universal Uclick
I DIDN'T REALIZE I HAD CHOSEN A LIFE OF CRIME.
AND YOU'RE NOT EVEN DOING IT RIGHT.

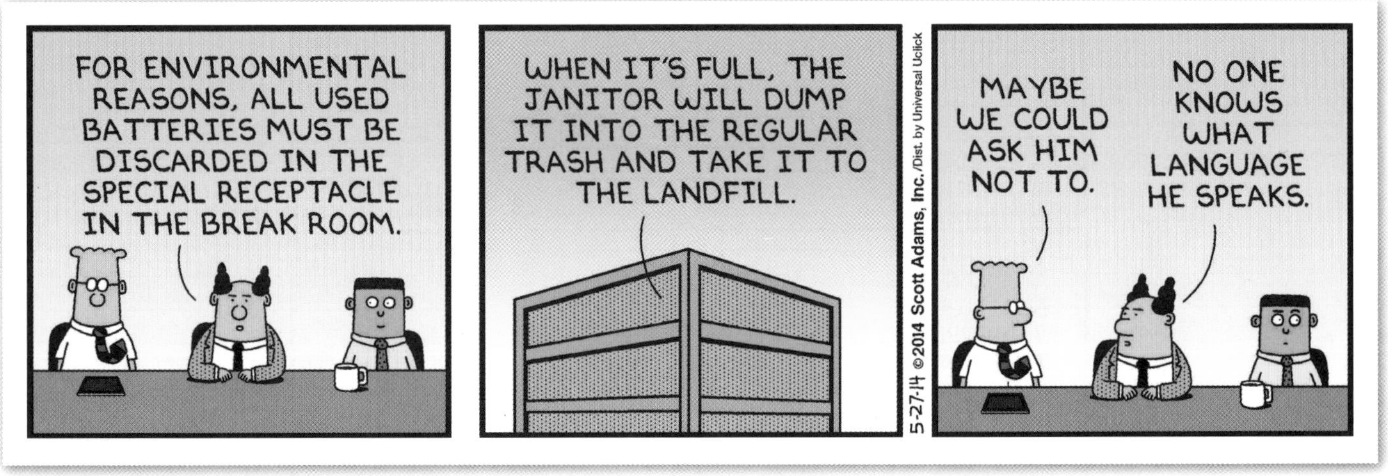
FOR ENVIRONMENTAL REASONS, ALL USED BATTERIES MUST BE DISCARDED IN THE SPECIAL RECEPTACLE IN THE BREAK ROOM.
WHEN IT'S FULL, THE JANITOR WILL DUMP IT INTO THE REGULAR TRASH AND TAKE IT TO THE LANDFILL.
5-27-14 ©2014 Scott Adams, Inc./Dist. by Universal Uclick
MAYBE WE COULD ASK HIM NOT TO.
NO ONE KNOWS WHAT LANGUAGE HE SPEAKS.

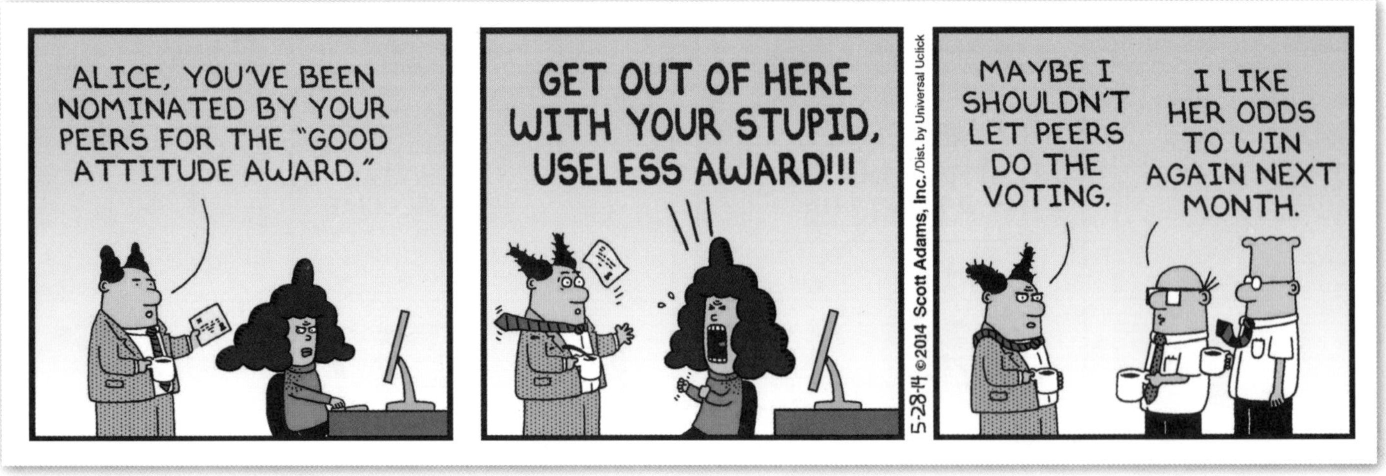
ALICE, YOU'VE BEEN NOMINATED BY YOUR PEERS FOR THE "GOOD ATTITUDE AWARD."
GET OUT OF HERE WITH YOUR STUPID, USELESS AWARD!!!
5-28-14 ©2014 Scott Adams, Inc./Dist. by Universal Uclick
MAYBE I SHOULDN'T LET PEERS DO THE VOTING.
I LIKE HER ODDS TO WIN AGAIN NEXT MONTH.

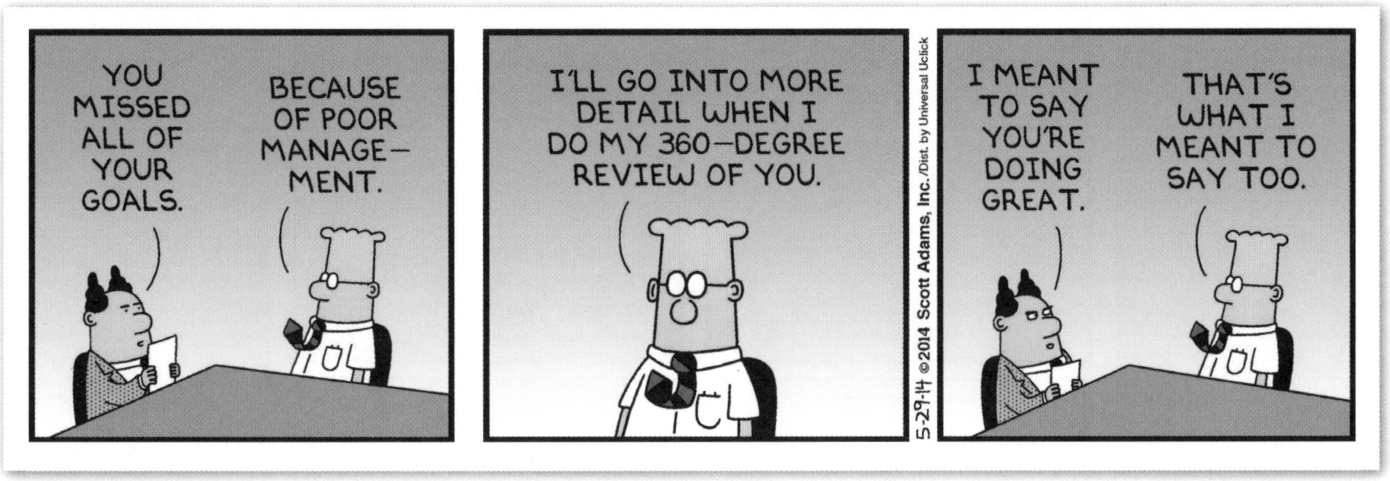
YOU MISSED ALL OF YOUR GOALS.
BECAUSE OF POOR MANAGE-MENT.
I'LL GO INTO MORE DETAIL WHEN I DO MY 360-DEGREE REVIEW OF YOU.
5-29-14 ©2014 Scott Adams, Inc./Dist. by Universal Uclick
I MEANT TO SAY YOU'RE DOING GREAT.
THAT'S WHAT I MEANT TO SAY TOO.

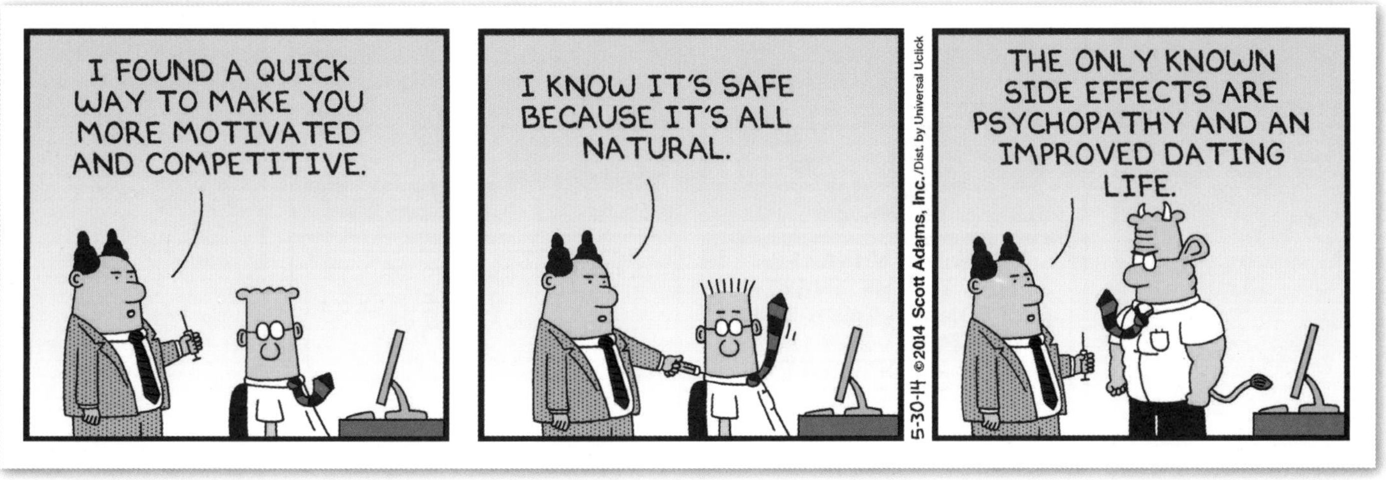
I FOUND A QUICK WAY TO MAKE YOU MORE MOTIVATED AND COMPETITIVE.
I KNOW IT'S SAFE BECAUSE IT'S ALL NATURAL.
5-30-14 ©2014 Scott Adams, Inc./Dist. by Universal Uclick
THE ONLY KNOWN SIDE EFFECTS ARE PSYCHOPATHY AND AN IMPROVED DATING LIFE.

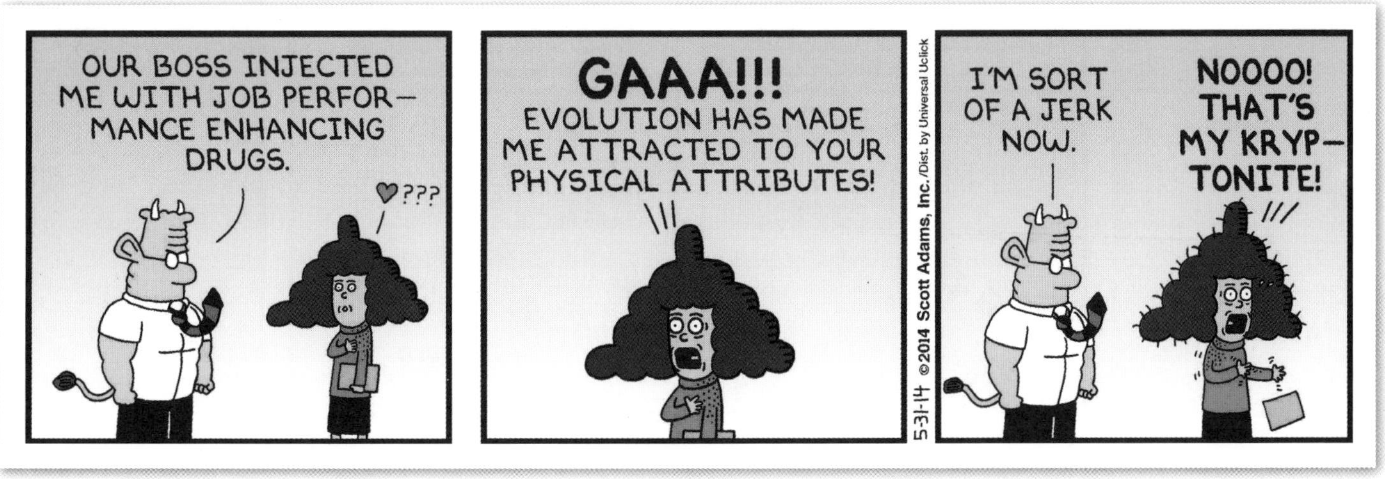
OUR BOSS INJECTED ME WITH JOB PERFOR-MANCE ENHANCING DRUGS.
???
GAAA!!! EVOLUTION HAS MADE ME ATTRACTED TO YOUR PHYSICAL ATTRIBUTES!
5-31-14 ©2014 Scott Adams, Inc./Dist. by Universal Uclick
I'M SORT OF A JERK NOW.
NOOOO! THAT'S MY KRYP-TONITE!

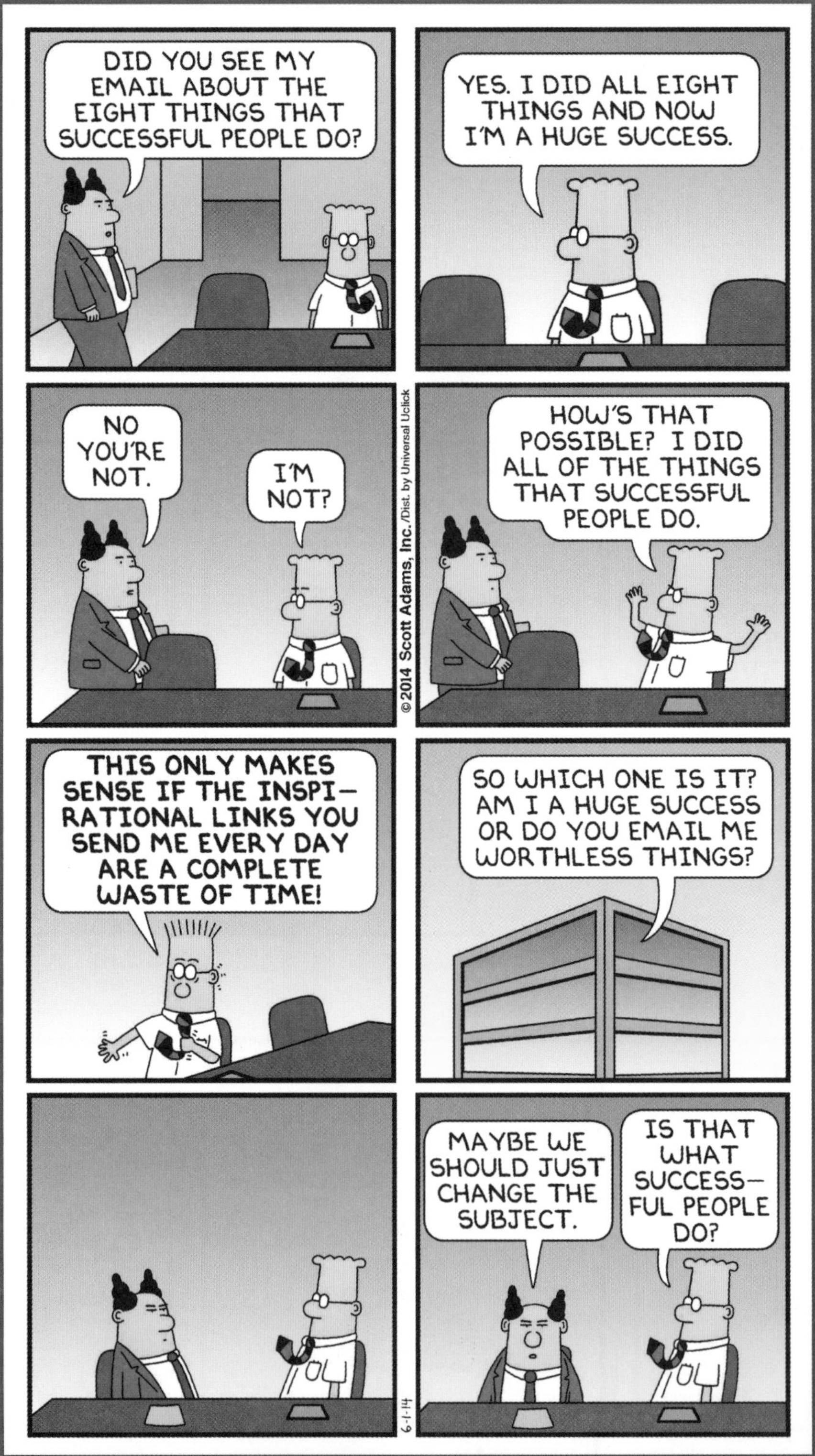
DID YOU SEE MY EMAIL ABOUT THE EIGHT THINGS THAT SUCCESSFUL PEOPLE DO?
YES. I DID ALL EIGHT THINGS AND NOW I'M A HUGE SUCCESS.
NO YOU'RE NOT.
I'M NOT?
HOW'S THAT POSSIBLE? I DID ALL OF THE THINGS THAT SUCCESSFUL PEOPLE DO.
THIS ONLY MAKES SENSE IF THE INSPI-RATIONAL LINKS YOU SEND ME EVERY DAY ARE A COMPLETE WASTE OF TIME!
SO WHICH ONE IS IT? AM I A HUGE SUCCESS OR DO YOU EMAIL ME WORTHLESS THINGS?
MAYBE WE SHOULD JUST CHANGE THE SUBJECT.
IS THAT WHAT SUCCESS-FUL PEOPLE DO?
© 2014 Scott Adams, Inc./Dist. by Universal Uclick
6-1-14

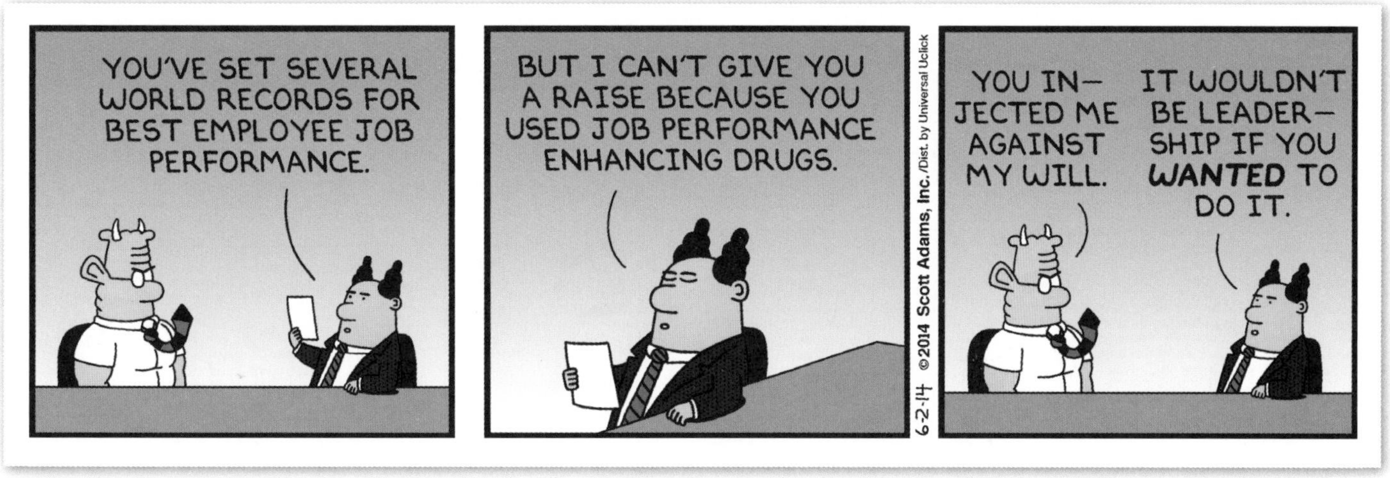
YOU'VE SET SEVERAL WORLD RECORDS FOR BEST EMPLOYEE JOB PERFORMANCE.
BUT I CAN'T GIVE YOU A RAISE BECAUSE YOU USED JOB PERFORMANCE ENHANCING DRUGS.
6-2-14 ©2014 Scott Adams, Inc./Dist. by Universal Uclick
YOU IN-JECTED ME AGAINST MY WILL.
IT WOULDN'T BE LEADER-SHIP IF YOU **WANTED** TO DO IT.

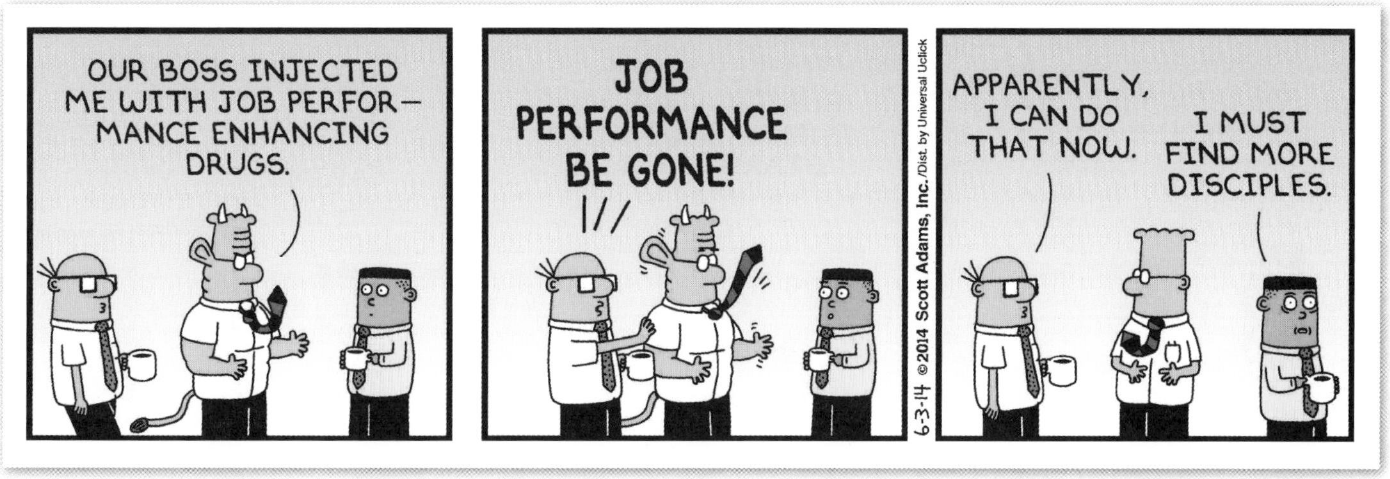
OUR BOSS INJECTED ME WITH JOB PERFOR-MANCE ENHANCING DRUGS.
JOB PERFORMANCE BE GONE!
6-3-14 ©2014 Scott Adams, Inc./Dist. by Universal Uclick
APPARENTLY, I CAN DO THAT NOW.
I MUST FIND MORE DISCIPLES.

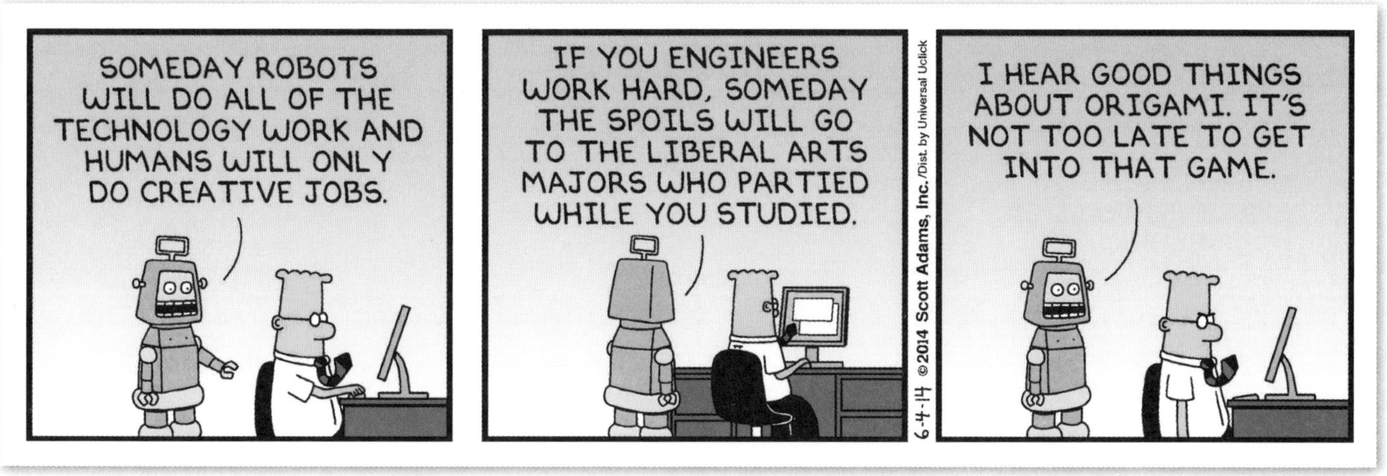
SOMEDAY ROBOTS WILL DO ALL OF THE TECHNOLOGY WORK AND HUMANS WILL ONLY DO CREATIVE JOBS.
IF YOU ENGINEERS WORK HARD, SOMEDAY THE SPOILS WILL GO TO THE LIBERAL ARTS MAJORS WHO PARTIED WHILE YOU STUDIED.
6-4-14 ©2014 Scott Adams, Inc./Dist. by Universal Uclick
I HEAR GOOD THINGS ABOUT ORIGAMI. IT'S NOT TOO LATE TO GET INTO THAT GAME.

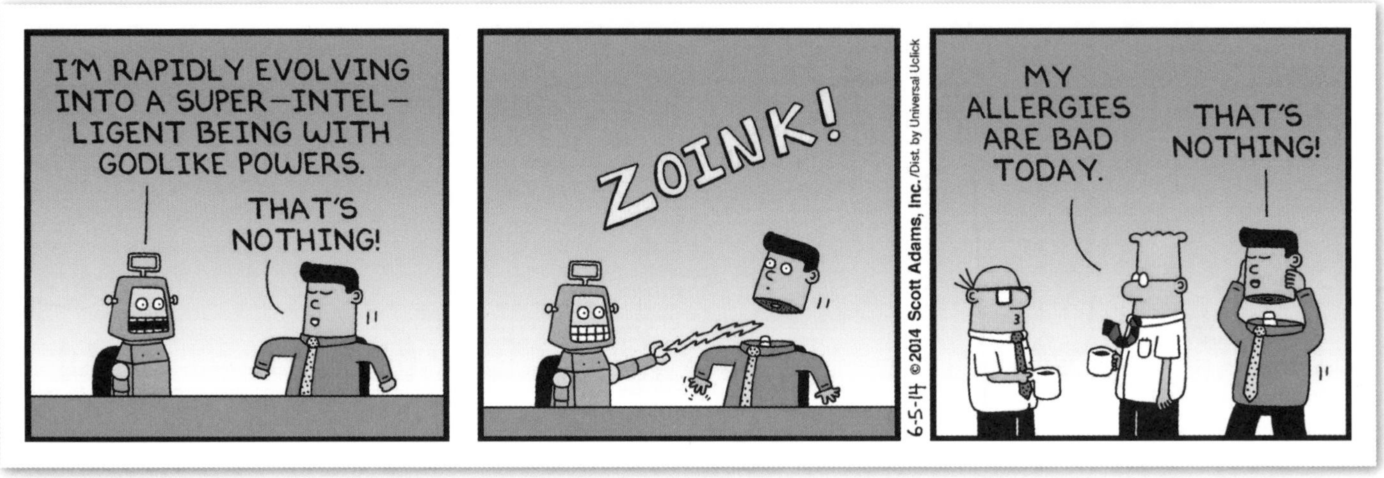
I'M RAPIDLY EVOLVING INTO A SUPER—INTEL— LIGENT BEING WITH GODLIKE POWERS.
THAT'S NOTHING!
ZOINK!
6-5-14 ©2014 Scott Adams, Inc./Dist. by Universal Uclick
MY ALLERGIES ARE BAD TODAY.
THAT'S NOTHING!

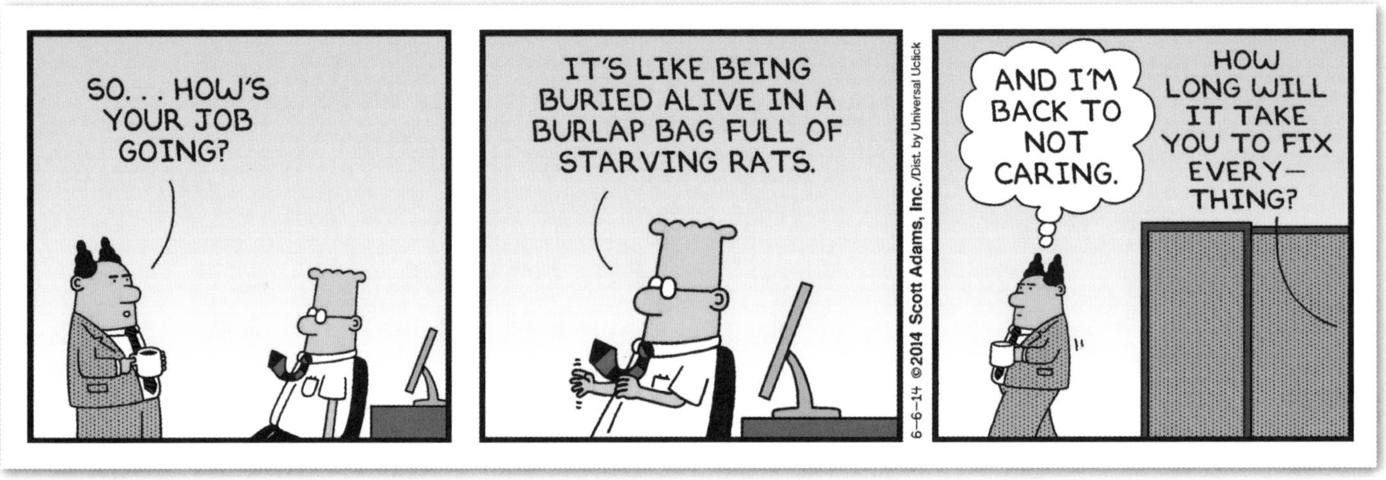
SO. . . HOW'S YOUR JOB GOING?
IT'S LIKE BEING BURIED ALIVE IN A BURLAP BAG FULL OF STARVING RATS.
6-6-14 ©2014 Scott Adams, Inc./Dist. by Universal Uclick
AND I'M BACK TO NOT CARING.
HOW LONG WILL IT TAKE YOU TO FIX EVERY— THING?

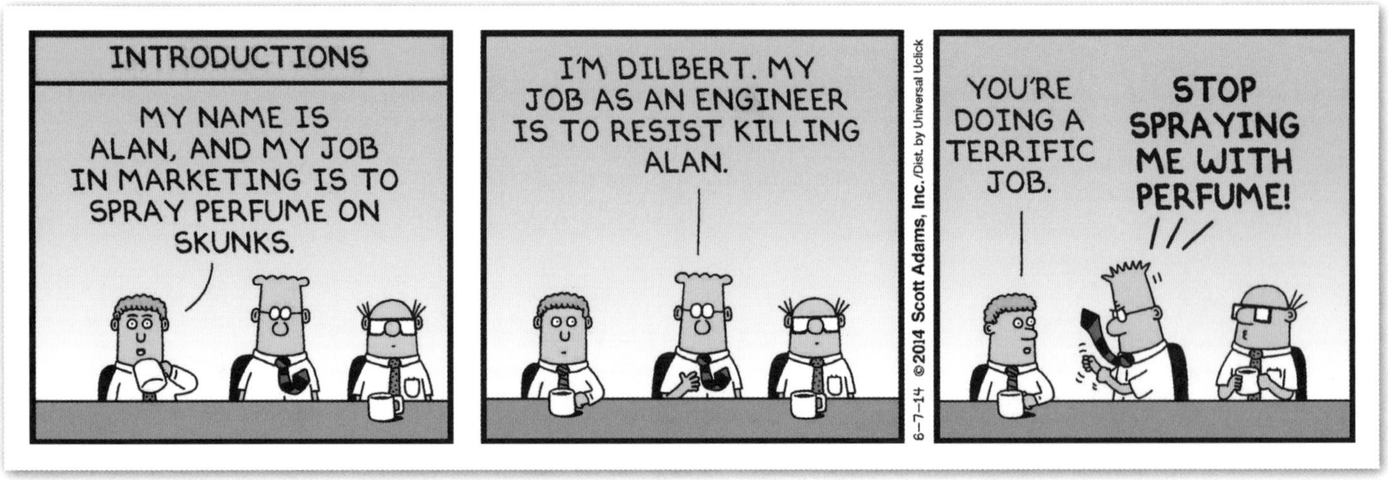
INTRODUCTIONS
MY NAME IS ALAN, AND MY JOB IN MARKETING IS TO SPRAY PERFUME ON SKUNKS.
I'M DILBERT. MY JOB AS AN ENGINEER IS TO RESIST KILLING ALAN.
6-7-14 ©2014 Scott Adams, Inc./Dist. by Universal Uclick
YOU'RE DOING A TERRIFIC JOB.
STOP SPRAYING ME WITH PERFUME!

WHAT'S YOUR SON DOING HERE?
TODAY IS "BRING YOUR KID TO THE CESSPOOL DAY."
THE IDEA IS TO SHOW KIDS HOW HORRIBLE IT IS TO WORK IN AN OFFICE.
THAT WAY, THEY CAN MAKE BETTER CHOICES AND AVOID A LIFE LIKE OURS.
JUST OUT OF CURIOSITY, WHO TOLD YOU THIS IS "BRING YOUR KID TO THE CESSPOOL DAY"?
WALLY.
OH.
I'VE DECIDED TO BECOME A CAREER CRIMINAL.
GOOD LUCK WITH ALL OF THAT.
©2014 Scott Adams, Inc./Dist. by Universal Uclick
6-8-14

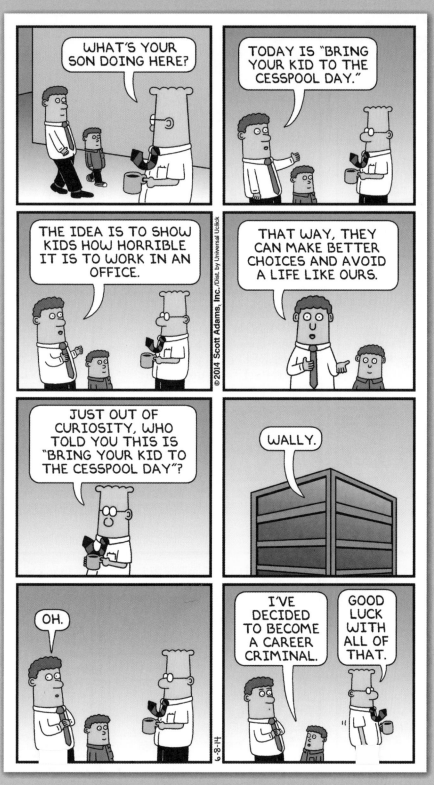

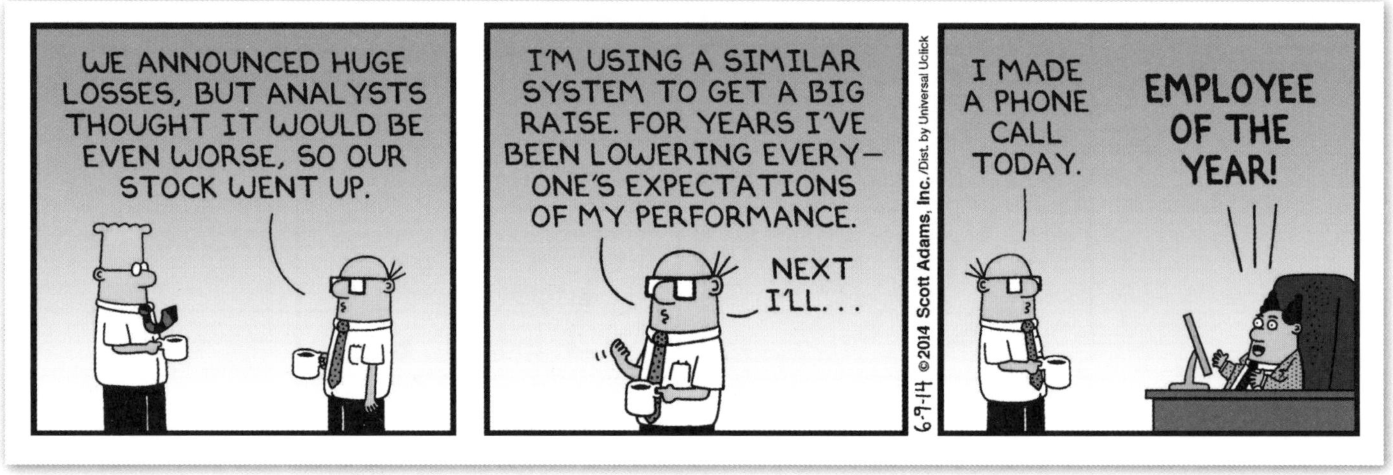
WE ANNOUNCED HUGE LOSSES, BUT ANALYSTS THOUGHT IT WOULD BE EVEN WORSE, SO OUR STOCK WENT UP.
I'M USING A SIMILAR SYSTEM TO GET A BIG RAISE. FOR YEARS I'VE BEEN LOWERING EVERY-ONE'S EXPECTATIONS OF MY PERFORMANCE.
NEXT I'LL. . .
6-9-14 ©2014 Scott Adams, Inc./Dist. by Universal Uclick
I MADE A PHONE CALL TODAY.
EMPLOYEE OF THE YEAR!

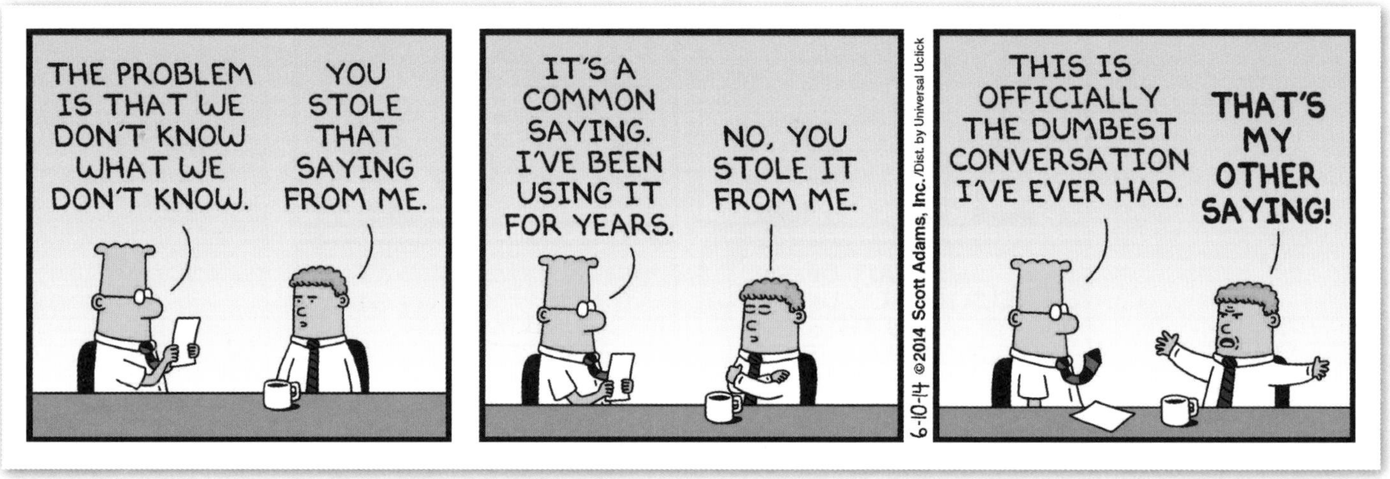
THE PROBLEM IS THAT WE DON'T KNOW WHAT WE DON'T KNOW.
YOU STOLE THAT SAYING FROM ME.
IT'S A COMMON SAYING. I'VE BEEN USING IT FOR YEARS.
NO, YOU STOLE IT FROM ME.
6-10-14 ©2014 Scott Adams, Inc./Dist. by Universal Uclick
THIS IS OFFICIALLY THE DUMBEST CONVERSATION I'VE EVER HAD.
THAT'S MY OTHER SAYING!

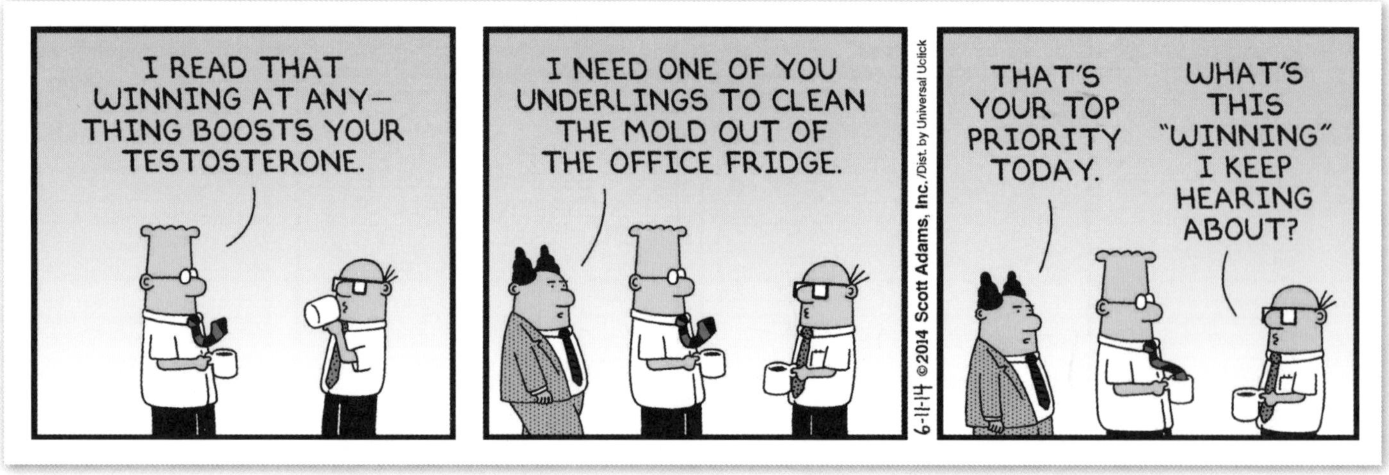
I READ THAT WINNING AT ANY-THING BOOSTS YOUR TESTOSTERONE.
I NEED ONE OF YOU UNDERLINGS TO CLEAN THE MOLD OUT OF THE OFFICE FRIDGE.
6-11-14 ©2014 Scott Adams, Inc./Dist. by Universal Uclick
THAT'S YOUR TOP PRIORITY TODAY.
WHAT'S THIS "WINNING" I KEEP HEARING ABOUT?

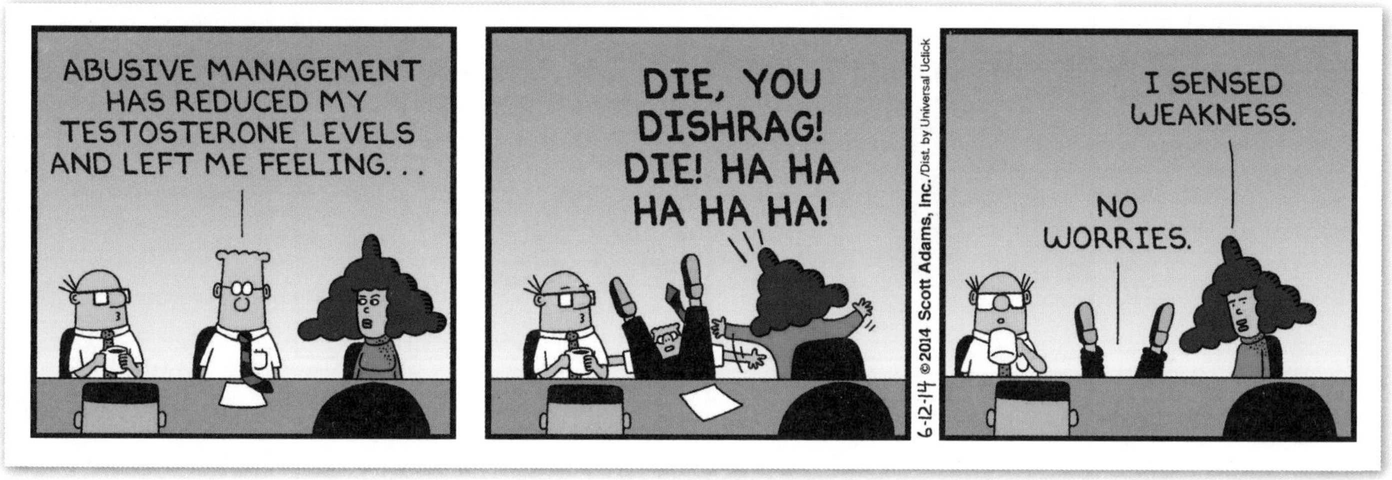
ABUSIVE MANAGEMENT HAS REDUCED MY TESTOSTERONE LEVELS AND LEFT ME FEELING. . .
DIE, YOU DISHRAG! DIE! HA HA HA HA HA!
6-12-14 ©2014 Scott Adams, Inc./Dist. by Universal Uclick
I SENSED WEAKNESS.
NO WORRIES.

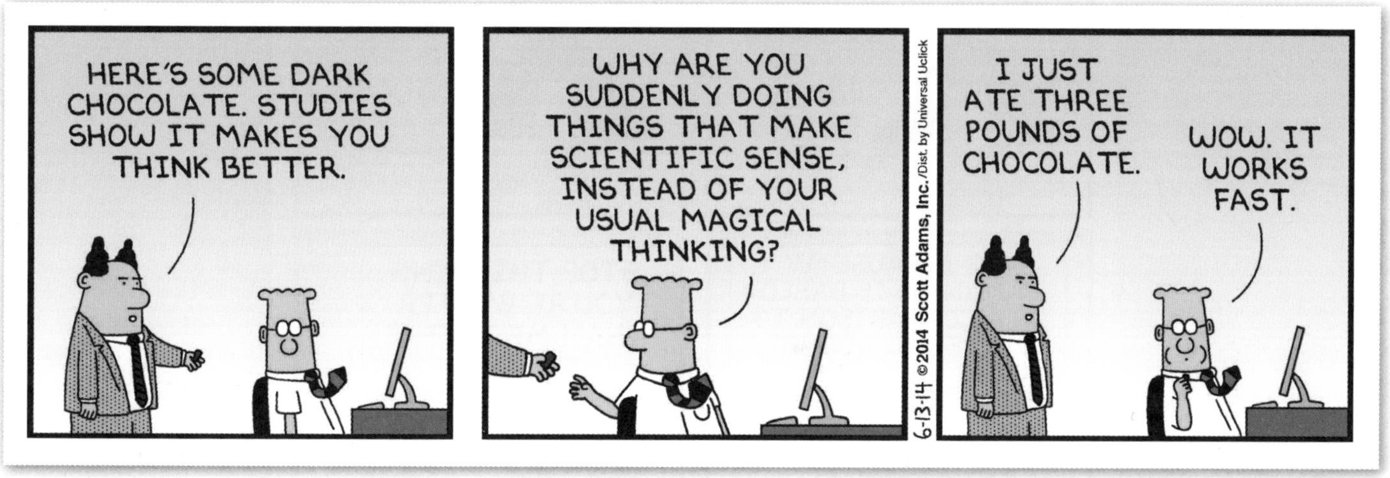
HERE'S SOME DARK CHOCOLATE. STUDIES SHOW IT MAKES YOU THINK BETTER.
WHY ARE YOU SUDDENLY DOING THINGS THAT MAKE SCIENTIFIC SENSE, INSTEAD OF YOUR USUAL MAGICAL THINKING?
6-13-14 ©2014 Scott Adams, Inc./Dist. by Universal Uclick
I JUST ATE THREE POUNDS OF CHOCOLATE.
WOW. IT WORKS FAST.

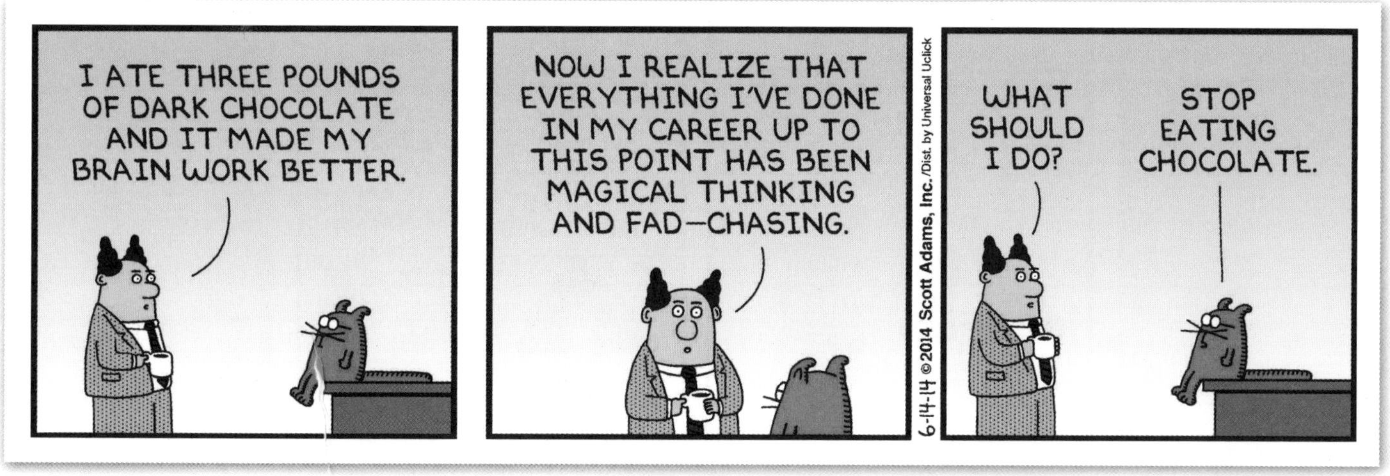
I ATE THREE POUNDS OF DARK CHOCOLATE AND IT MADE MY BRAIN WORK BETTER.
NOW I REALIZE THAT EVERYTHING I'VE DONE IN MY CAREER UP TO THIS POINT HAS BEEN MAGICAL THINKING AND FAD—CHASING.
6-14-14 ©2014 Scott Adams, Inc./Dist. by Universal Uclick
WHAT SHOULD I DO?
STOP EATING CHOCOLATE.

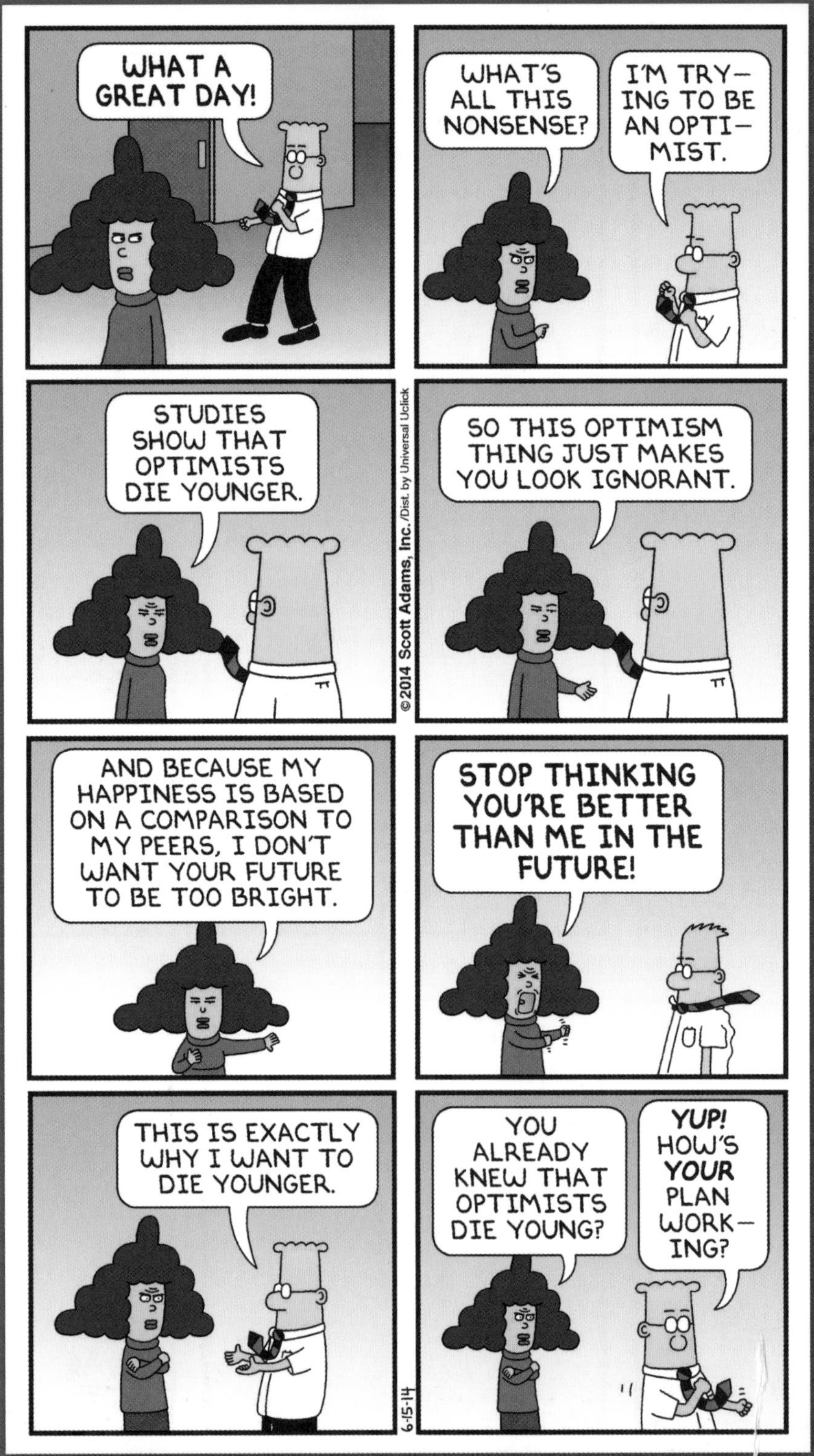
WHAT A GREAT DAY!
WHAT'S ALL THIS NONSENSE?
I'M TRY-ING TO BE AN OPTI-MIST.
STUDIES SHOW THAT OPTIMISTS DIE YOUNGER.
SO THIS OPTIMISM THING JUST MAKES YOU LOOK IGNORANT.
AND BECAUSE MY HAPPINESS IS BASED ON A COMPARISON TO MY PEERS, I DON'T WANT YOUR FUTURE TO BE TOO BRIGHT.
STOP THINKING YOU'RE BETTER THAN ME IN THE FUTURE!
THIS IS EXACTLY WHY I WANT TO DIE YOUNGER.
YOU ALREADY KNEW THAT OPTIMISTS DIE YOUNG?
YUP! HOW'S YOUR PLAN WORK-ING?
© 2014 Scott Adams, Inc./Dist. by Universal Uclick
6-15-14

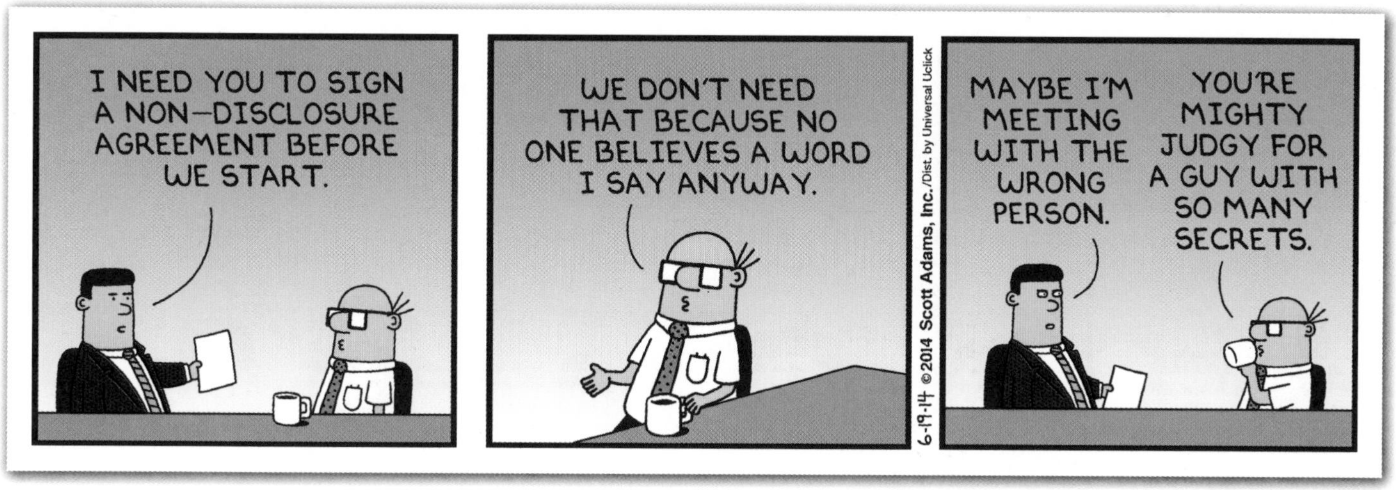
I NEED YOU TO SIGN A NON-DISCLOSURE AGREEMENT BEFORE WE START.
WE DON'T NEED THAT BECAUSE NO ONE BELIEVES A WORD I SAY ANYWAY.
6-19-14 ©2014 Scott Adams, Inc./Dist. by Universal Uclick
MAYBE I'M MEETING WITH THE WRONG PERSON.
YOU'RE MIGHTY JUDGY FOR A GUY WITH SO MANY SECRETS.

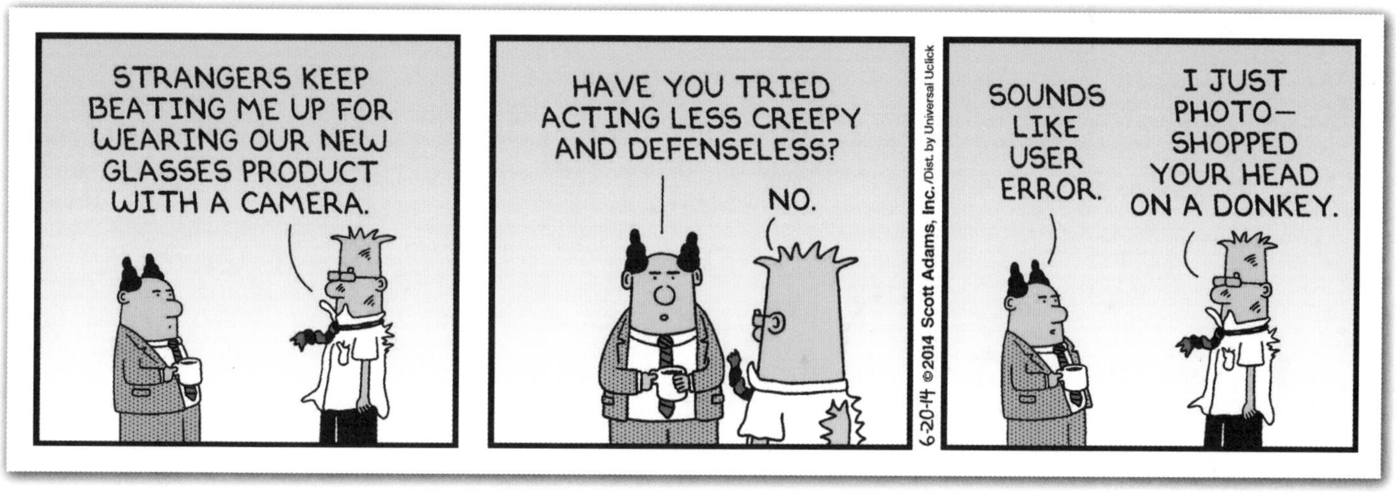
STRANGERS KEEP BEATING ME UP FOR WEARING OUR NEW GLASSES PRODUCT WITH A CAMERA.
HAVE YOU TRIED ACTING LESS CREEPY AND DEFENSELESS?
NO.
6-20-14 ©2014 Scott Adams, Inc./Dist. by Universal Uclick
SOUNDS LIKE USER ERROR.
I JUST PHOTO-SHOPPED YOUR HEAD ON A DONKEY.

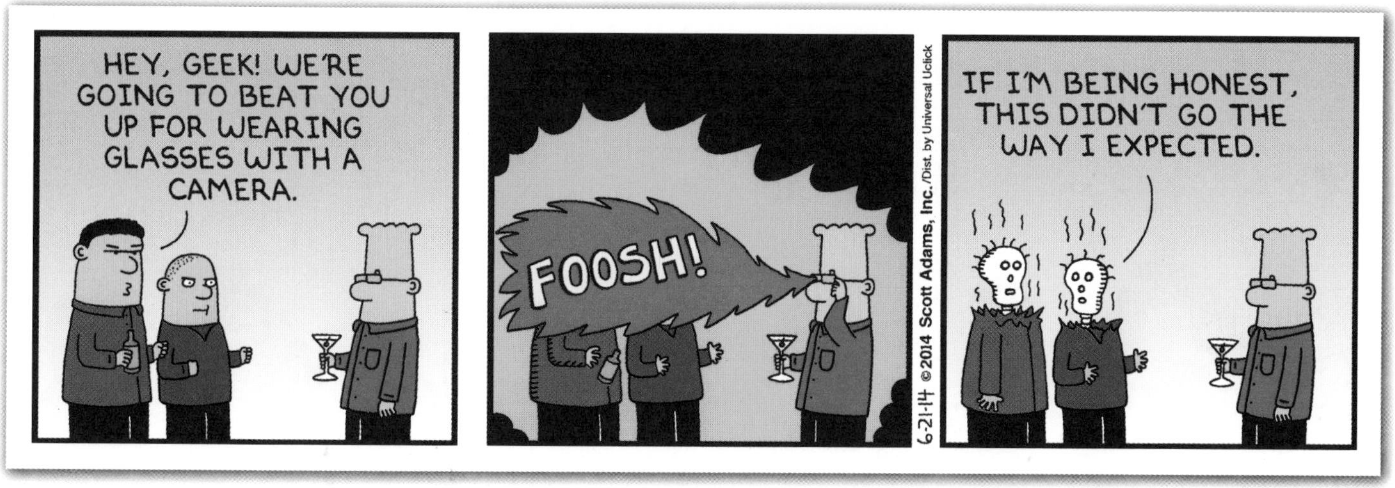
HEY, GEEK! WE'RE GOING TO BEAT YOU UP FOR WEARING GLASSES WITH A CAMERA.
FOOSH!
6-21-14 ©2014 Scott Adams, Inc./Dist. by Universal Uclick
IF I'M BEING HONEST, THIS DIDN'T GO THE WAY I EXPECTED.

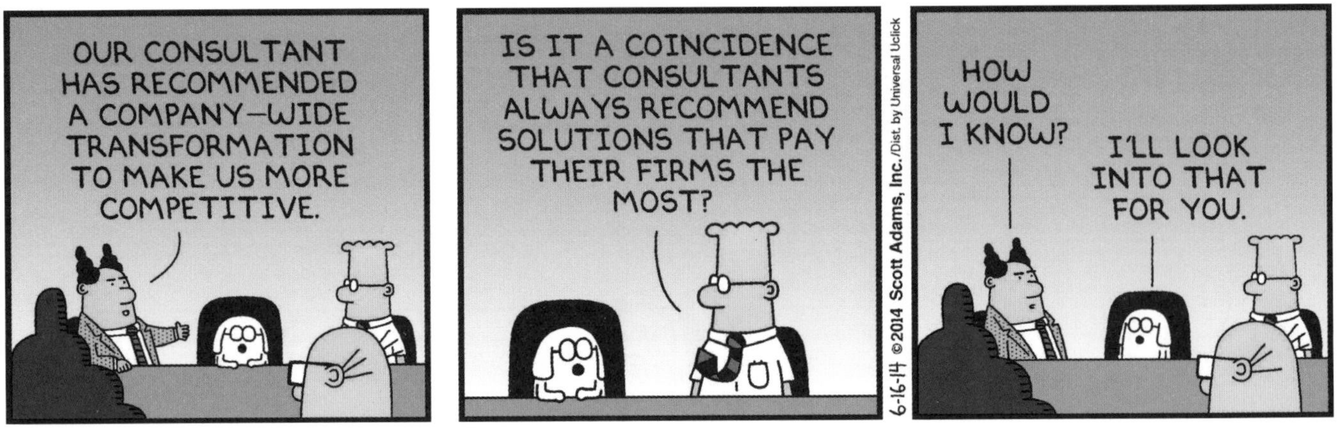
OUR CONSULTANT HAS RECOMMENDED A COMPANY—WIDE TRANSFORMATION TO MAKE US MORE COMPETITIVE.
IS IT A COINCIDENCE THAT CONSULTANTS ALWAYS RECOMMEND SOLUTIONS THAT PAY THEIR FIRMS THE MOST?
HOW WOULD I KNOW?
I'LL LOOK INTO THAT FOR YOU.
6-16-14 ©2014 Scott Adams, Inc./Dist. by Universal Uclick

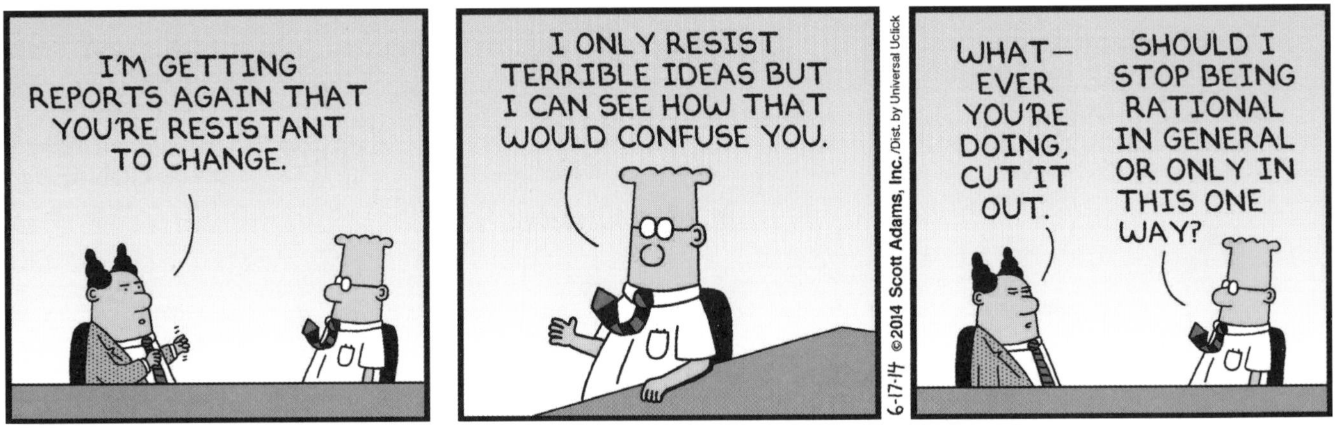
I'M GETTING REPORTS AGAIN THAT YOU'RE RESISTANT TO CHANGE.
I ONLY RESIST TERRIBLE IDEAS BUT I CAN SEE HOW THAT WOULD CONFUSE YOU.
WHAT—EVER YOU'RE DOING, CUT IT OUT.
SHOULD I STOP BEING RATIONAL IN GENERAL OR ONLY IN THIS ONE WAY?
6-17-14 ©2014 Scott Adams, Inc./Dist. by Universal Uclick

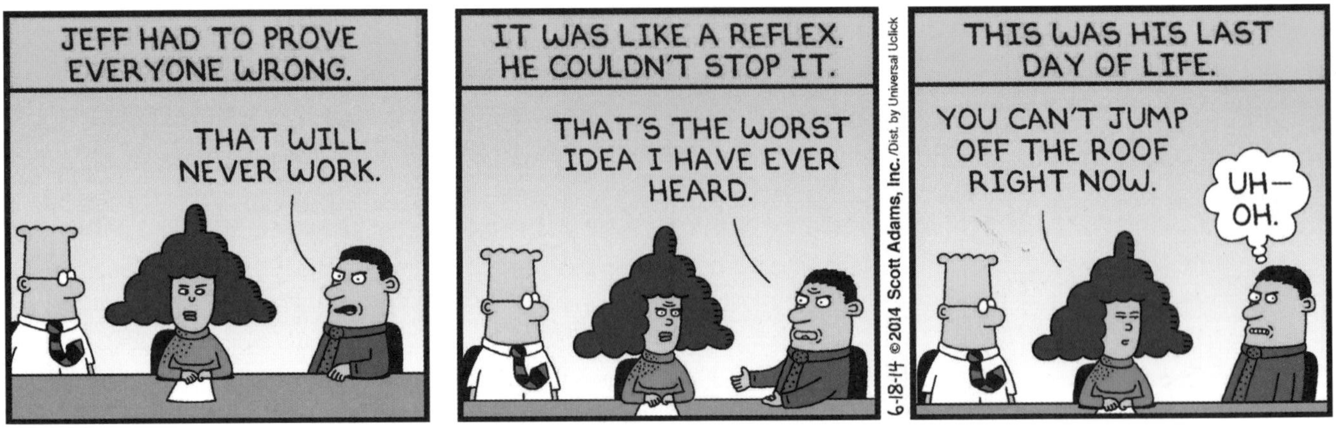
JEFF HAD TO PROVE EVERYONE WRONG.
THAT WILL NEVER WORK.
IT WAS LIKE A REFLEX. HE COULDN'T STOP IT.
THAT'S THE WORST IDEA I HAVE EVER HEARD.
THIS WAS HIS LAST DAY OF LIFE.
YOU CAN'T JUMP OFF THE ROOF RIGHT NOW.
UH—OH.
6-18-14 ©2014 Scott Adams, Inc./Dist. by Universal Uclick

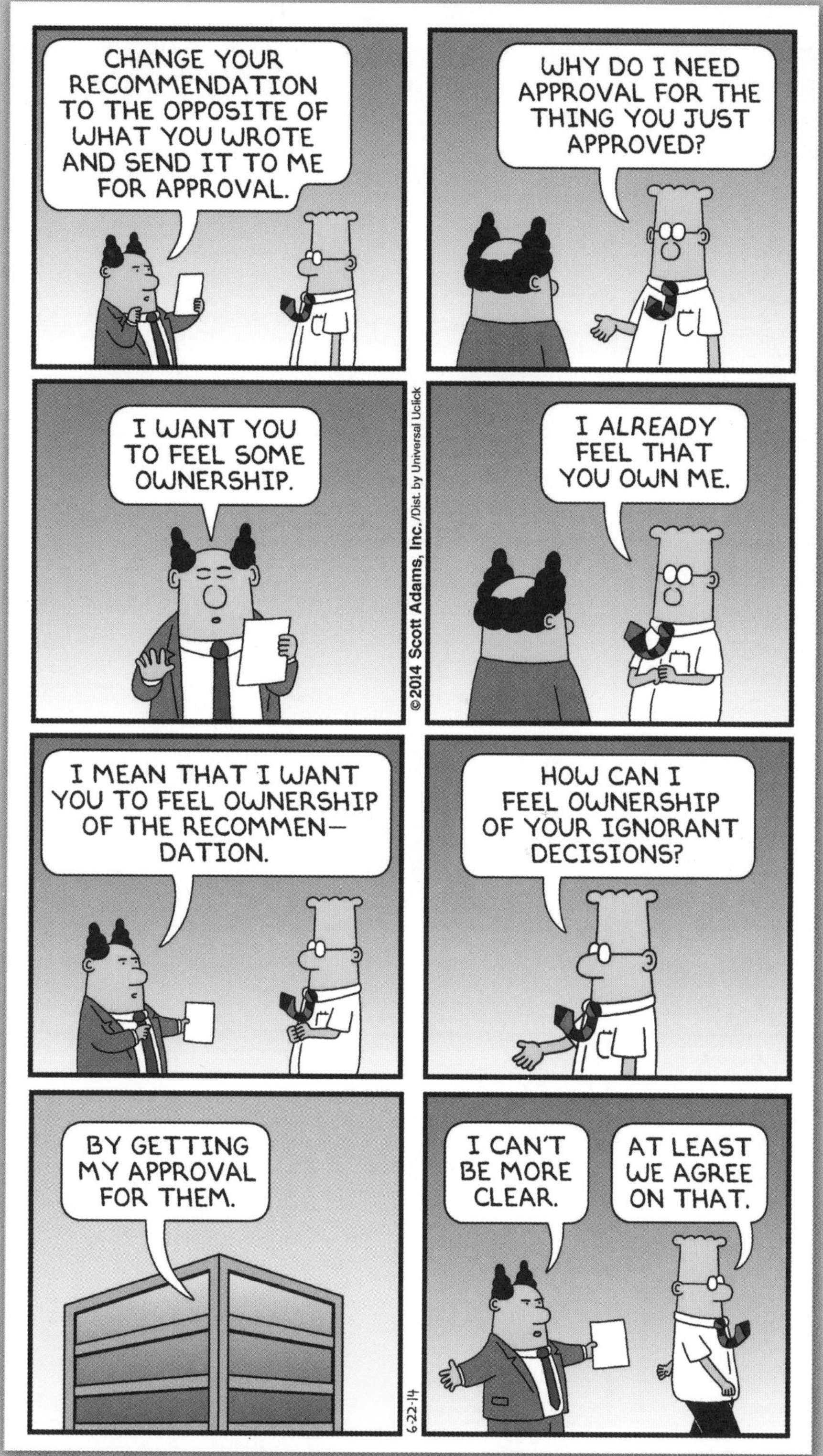
CHANGE YOUR RECOMMENDATION TO THE OPPOSITE OF WHAT YOU WROTE AND SEND IT TO ME FOR APPROVAL.
WHY DO I NEED APPROVAL FOR THE THING YOU JUST APPROVED?
I WANT YOU TO FEEL SOME OWNERSHIP.
I ALREADY FEEL THAT YOU OWN ME.
I MEAN THAT I WANT YOU TO FEEL OWNERSHIP OF THE RECOMMEN-DATION.
HOW CAN I FEEL OWNERSHIP OF YOUR IGNORANT DECISIONS?
BY GETTING MY APPROVAL FOR THEM.
I CAN'T BE MORE CLEAR.
AT LEAST WE AGREE ON THAT.
©2014 Scott Adams, Inc./Dist. by Universal Uclick
6-22-14

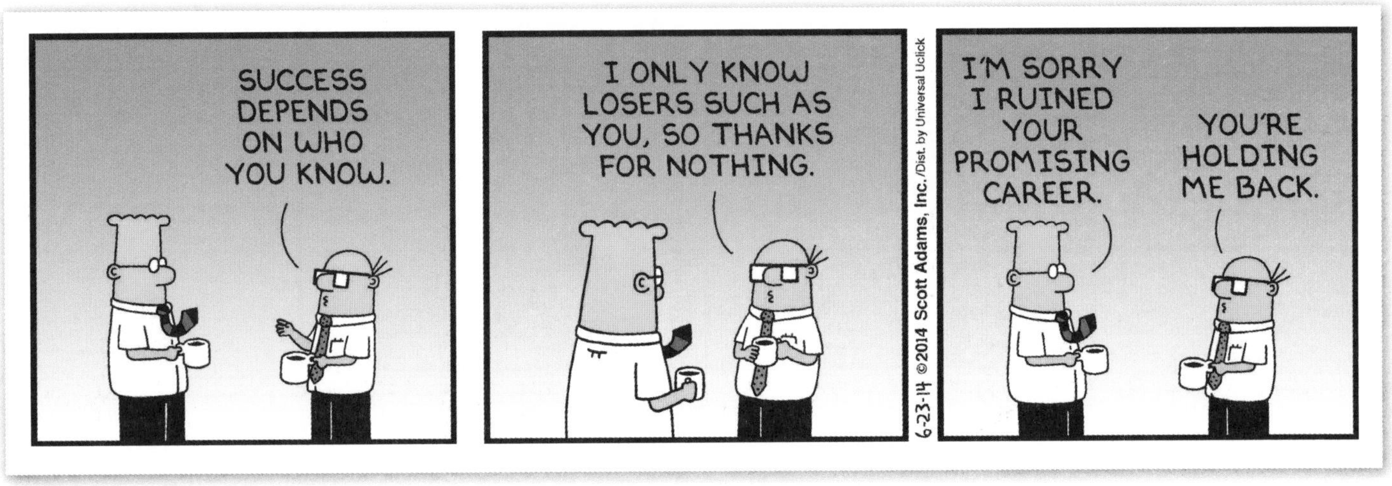
SUCCESS DEPENDS ON WHO YOU KNOW.
I ONLY KNOW LOSERS SUCH AS YOU, SO THANKS FOR NOTHING.
6-23-14 ©2014 Scott Adams, Inc./Dist. by Universal Uclick
I'M SORRY I RUINED YOUR PROMISING CAREER.
YOU'RE HOLDING ME BACK.

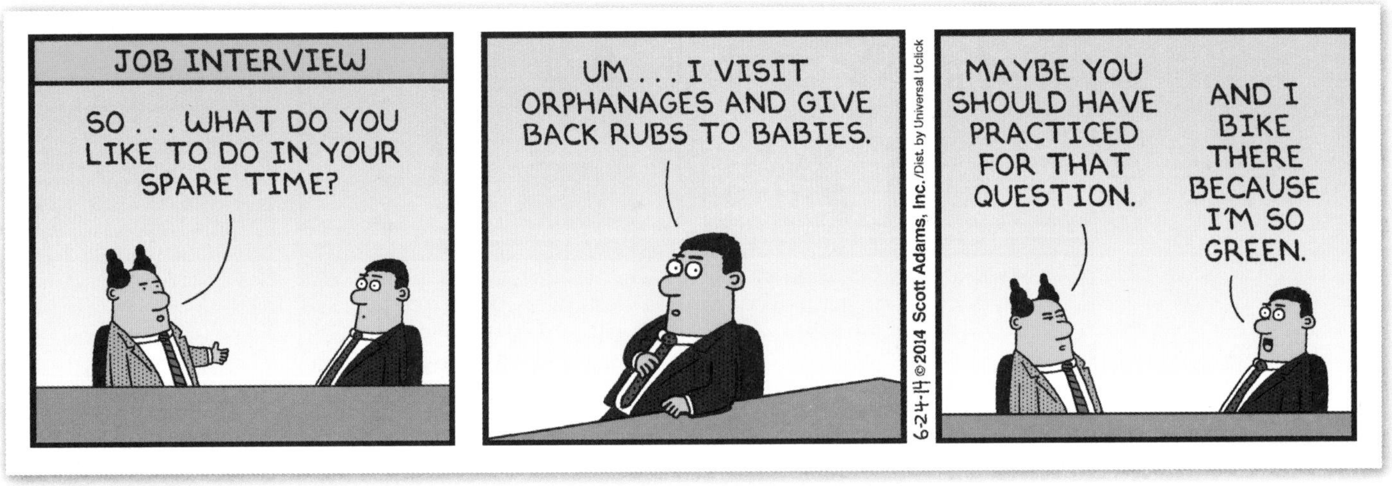
JOB INTERVIEW
SO . . . WHAT DO YOU LIKE TO DO IN YOUR SPARE TIME?
UM . . . I VISIT ORPHANAGES AND GIVE BACK RUBS TO BABIES.
6-24-14 ©2014 Scott Adams, Inc./Dist. by Universal Uclick
MAYBE YOU SHOULD HAVE PRACTICED FOR THAT QUESTION.
AND I BIKE THERE BECAUSE I'M SO GREEN.

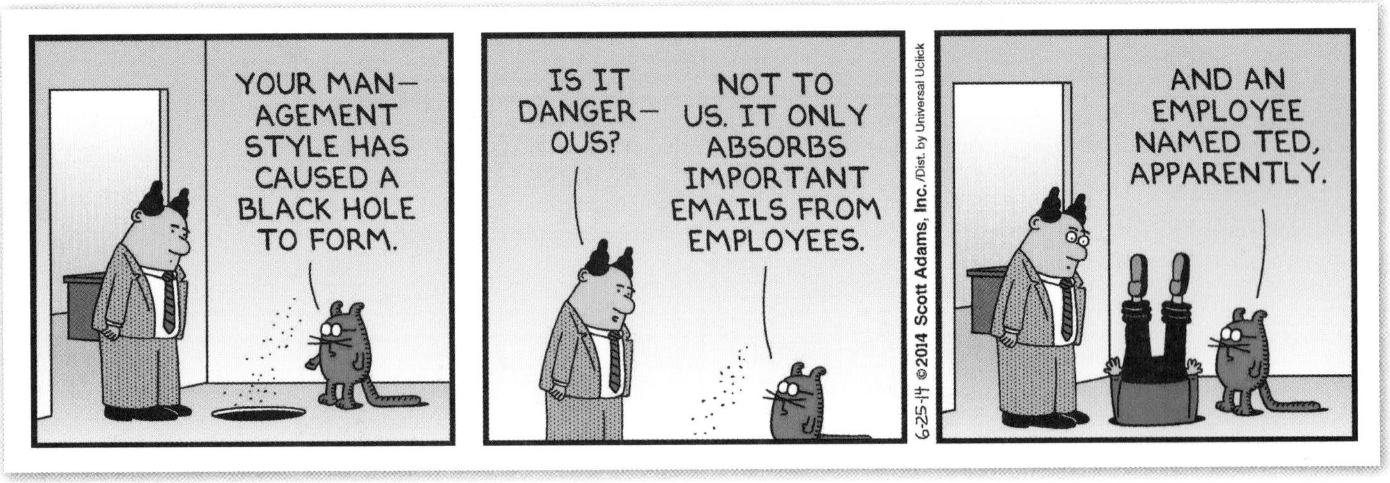
YOUR MAN-AGEMENT STYLE HAS CAUSED A BLACK HOLE TO FORM.
IS IT DANGER-OUS?
NOT TO US. IT ONLY ABSORBS IMPORTANT EMAILS FROM EMPLOYEES.
6-25-14 ©2014 Scott Adams, Inc./Dist. by Universal Uclick
AND AN EMPLOYEE NAMED TED, APPARENTLY.

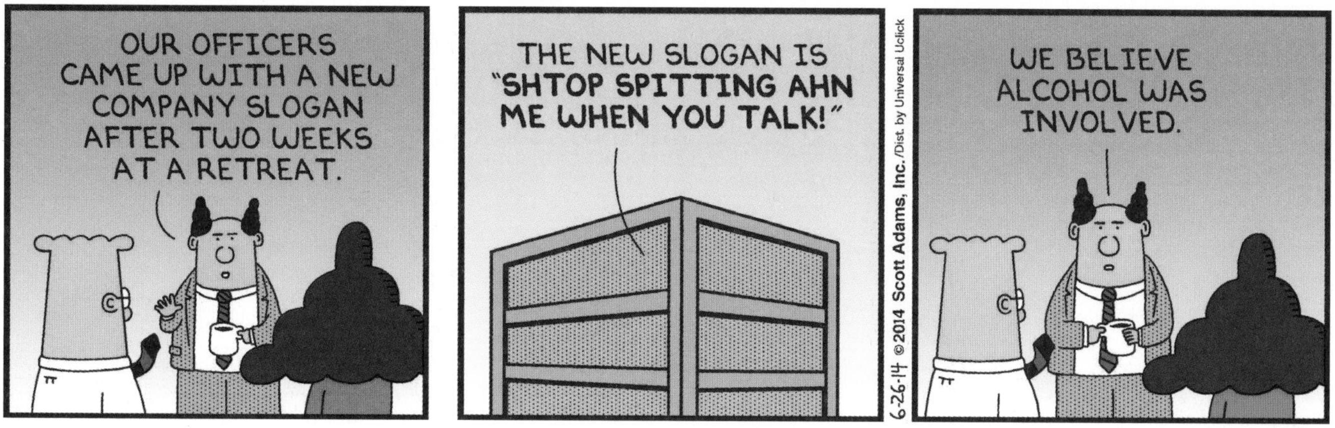
OUR OFFICERS CAME UP WITH A NEW COMPANY SLOGAN AFTER TWO WEEKS AT A RETREAT.
THE NEW SLOGAN IS "SHTOP SPITTING AHN ME WHEN YOU TALK!"
WE BELIEVE ALCOHOL WAS INVOLVED.
6-26-14 ©2014 Scott Adams, Inc./Dist. by Universal Uclick

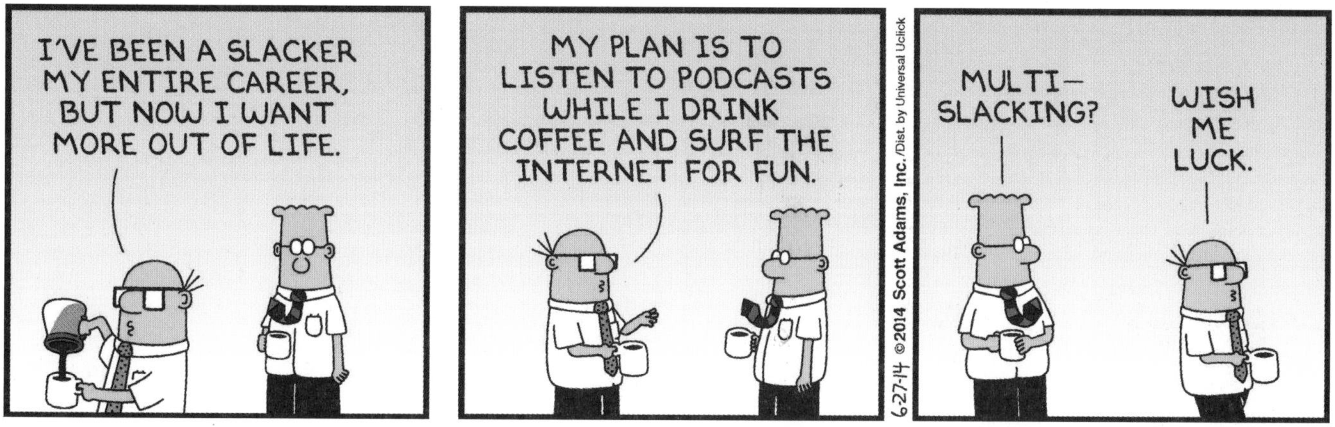
I'VE BEEN A SLACKER MY ENTIRE CAREER, BUT NOW I WANT MORE OUT OF LIFE.
MY PLAN IS TO LISTEN TO PODCASTS WHILE I DRINK COFFEE AND SURF THE INTERNET FOR FUN.
MULTI-SLACKING?
WISH ME LUCK.
6-27-14 ©2014 Scott Adams, Inc./Dist. by Universal Uclick

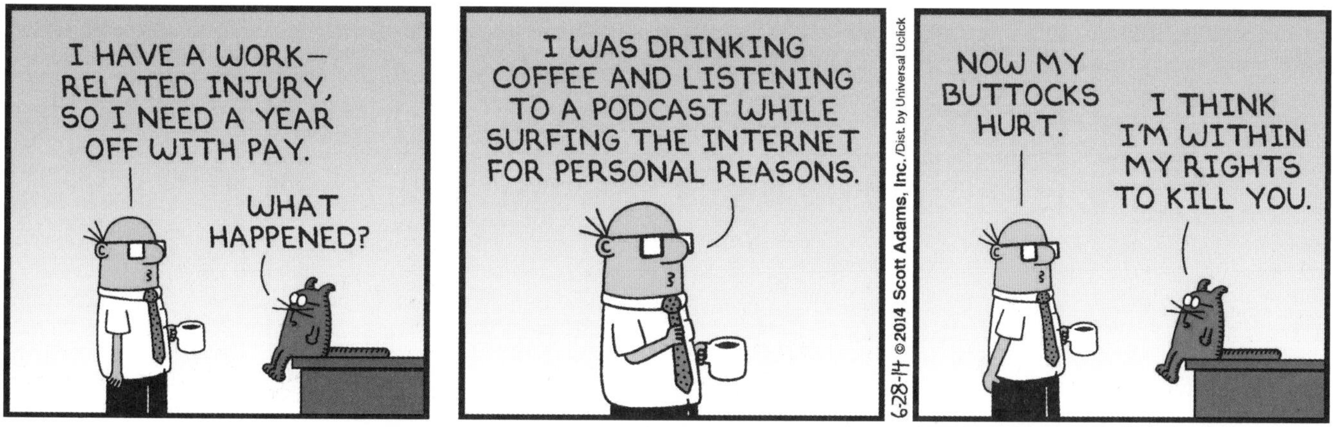
I HAVE A WORK-RELATED INJURY, SO I NEED A YEAR OFF WITH PAY.
WHAT HAPPENED?
I WAS DRINKING COFFEE AND LISTENING TO A PODCAST WHILE SURFING THE INTERNET FOR PERSONAL REASONS.
NOW MY BUTTOCKS HURT.
I THINK I'M WITHIN MY RIGHTS TO KILL YOU.
6-28-14 ©2014 Scott Adams, Inc./Dist. by Universal Uclick

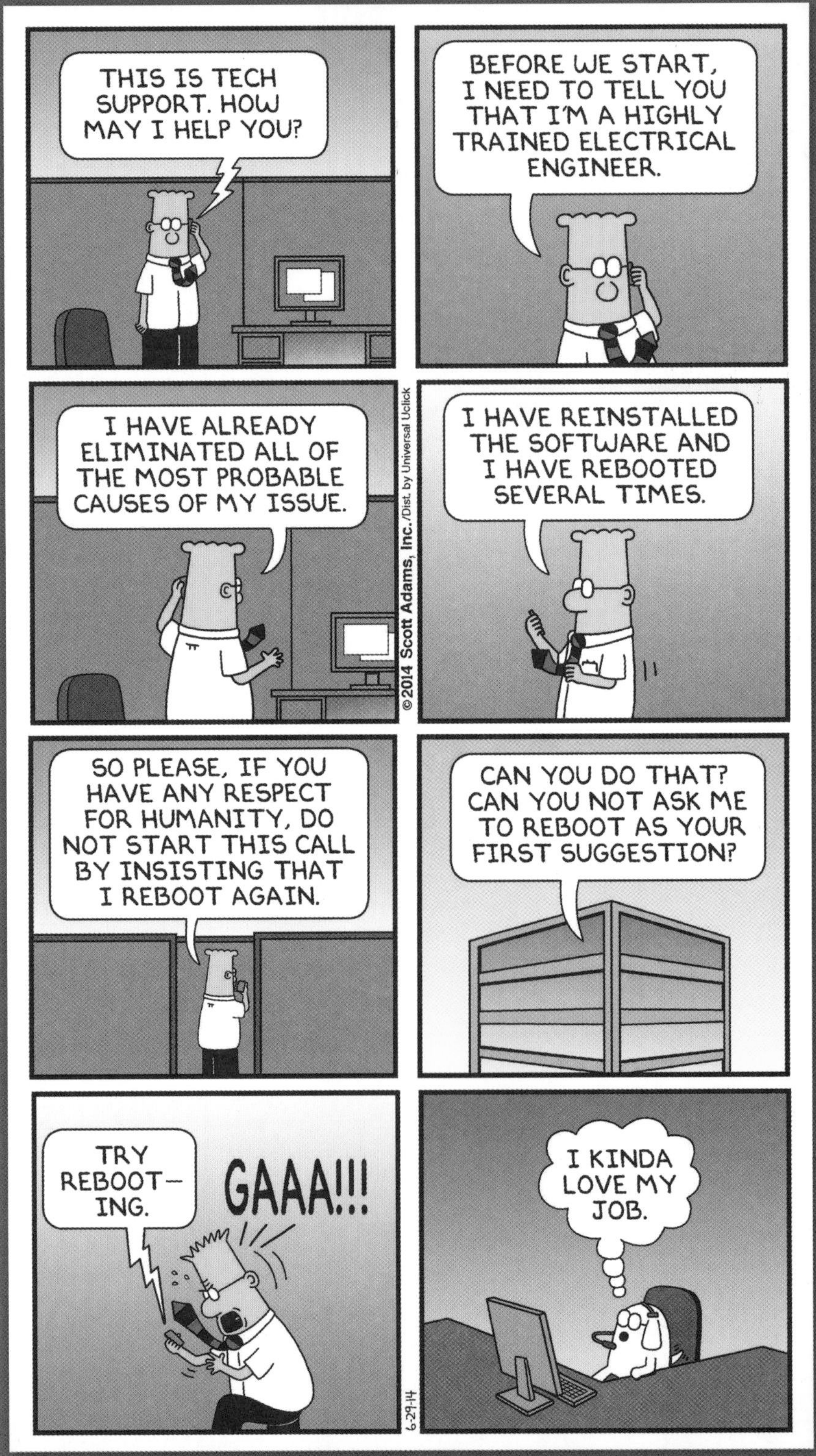
THIS IS TECH SUPPORT. HOW MAY I HELP YOU?
BEFORE WE START, I NEED TO TELL YOU THAT I'M A HIGHLY TRAINED ELECTRICAL ENGINEER.
I HAVE ALREADY ELIMINATED ALL OF THE MOST PROBABLE CAUSES OF MY ISSUE.
I HAVE REINSTALLED THE SOFTWARE AND I HAVE REBOOTED SEVERAL TIMES.
SO PLEASE, IF YOU HAVE ANY RESPECT FOR HUMANITY, DO NOT START THIS CALL BY INSISTING THAT I REBOOT AGAIN.
CAN YOU DO THAT? CAN YOU NOT ASK ME TO REBOOT AS YOUR FIRST SUGGESTION?
TRY REBOOT-ING.
GAAA!!!
I KINDA LOVE MY JOB.
©2014 Scott Adams, Inc./Dist. by Universal Uclick
6-29-14

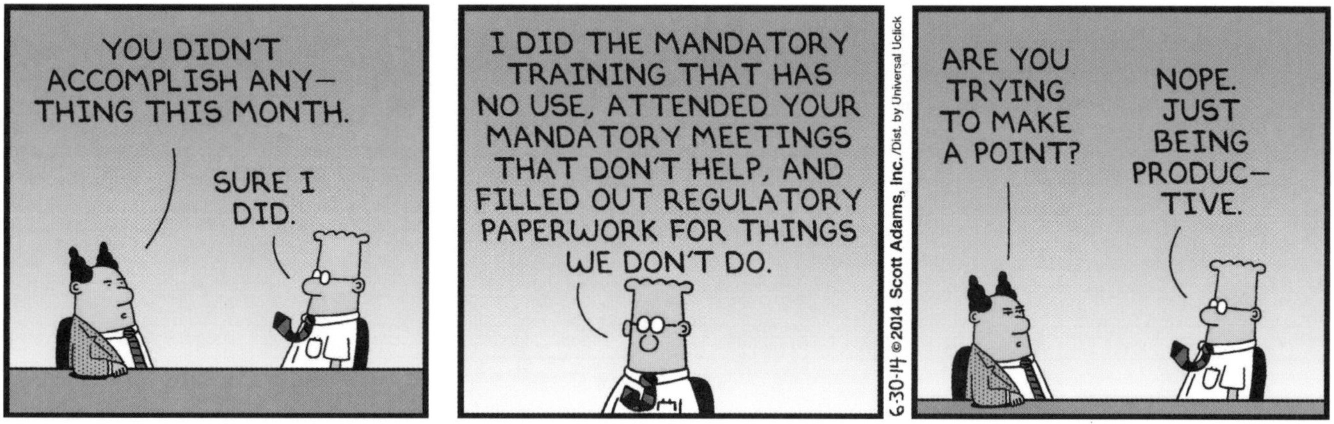
YOU DIDN'T ACCOMPLISH ANY-THING THIS MONTH.
SURE I DID.
I DID THE MANDATORY TRAINING THAT HAS NO USE, ATTENDED YOUR MANDATORY MEETINGS THAT DON'T HELP, AND FILLED OUT REGULATORY PAPERWORK FOR THINGS WE DON'T DO.
6-30-14 ©2014 Scott Adams, Inc./Dist. by Universal Uclick
ARE YOU TRYING TO MAKE A POINT?
NOPE. JUST BEING PRODUC-TIVE.

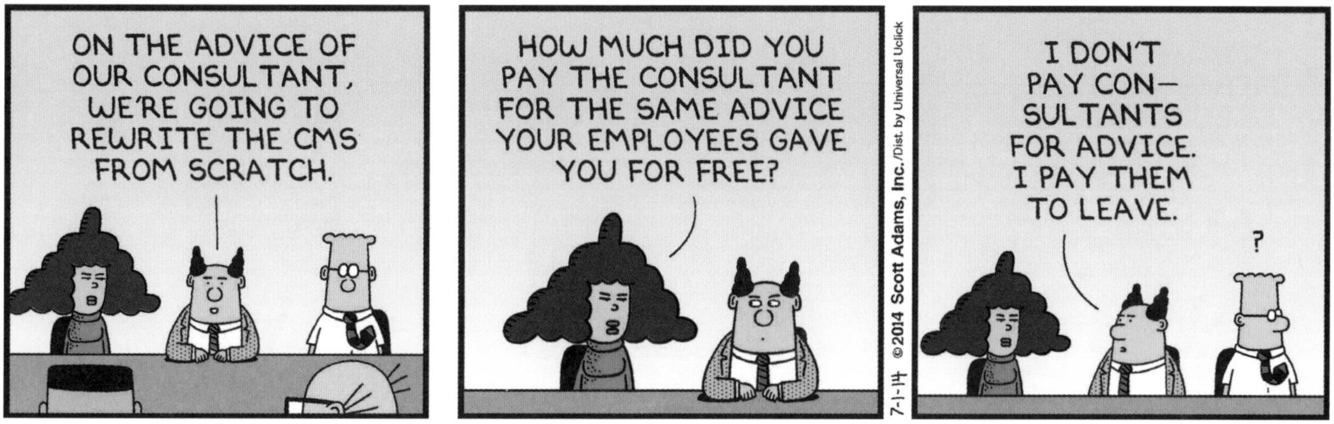
ON THE ADVICE OF OUR CONSULTANT, WE'RE GOING TO REWRITE THE CMS FROM SCRATCH.
HOW MUCH DID YOU PAY THE CONSULTANT FOR THE SAME ADVICE YOUR EMPLOYEES GAVE YOU FOR FREE?
7-1-14 ©2014 Scott Adams, Inc./Dist. by Universal Uclick
I DON'T PAY CON-SULTANTS FOR ADVICE. I PAY THEM TO LEAVE.
?

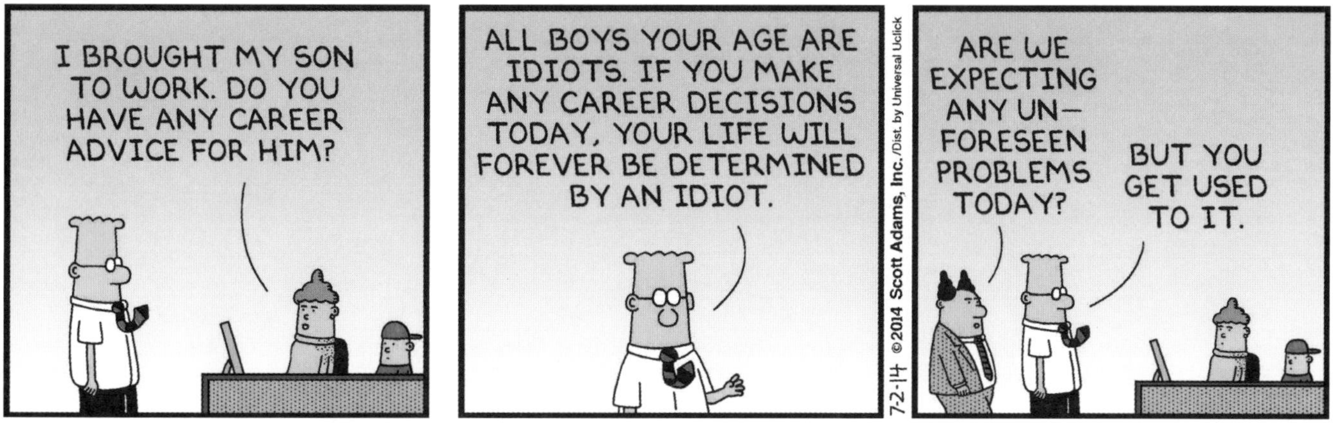
I BROUGHT MY SON TO WORK. DO YOU HAVE ANY CAREER ADVICE FOR HIM?
ALL BOYS YOUR AGE ARE IDIOTS. IF YOU MAKE ANY CAREER DECISIONS TODAY, YOUR LIFE WILL FOREVER BE DETERMINED BY AN IDIOT.
7-2-14 ©2014 Scott Adams, Inc./Dist. by Universal Uclick
ARE WE EXPECTING ANY UN-FORESEEN PROBLEMS TODAY?
BUT YOU GET USED TO IT.

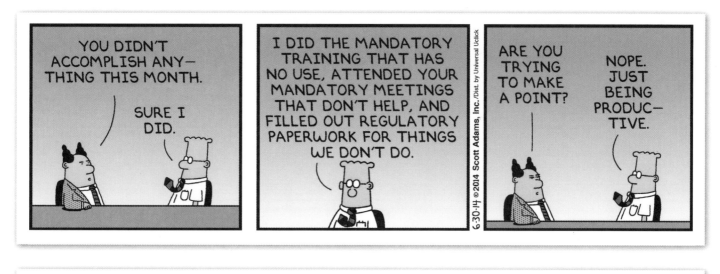

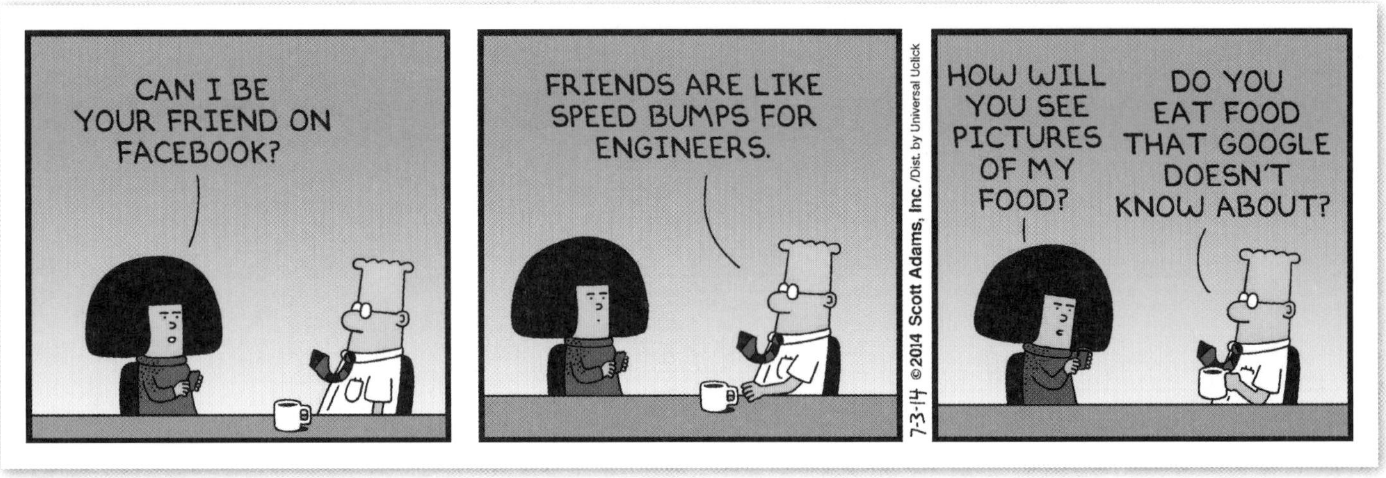
CAN I BE YOUR FRIEND ON FACEBOOK?
FRIENDS ARE LIKE SPEED BUMPS FOR ENGINEERS.
7-3-14 ©2014 Scott Adams, Inc./Dist. by Universal Uclick
HOW WILL YOU SEE PICTURES OF MY FOOD?
DO YOU EAT FOOD THAT GOOGLE DOESN'T KNOW ABOUT?

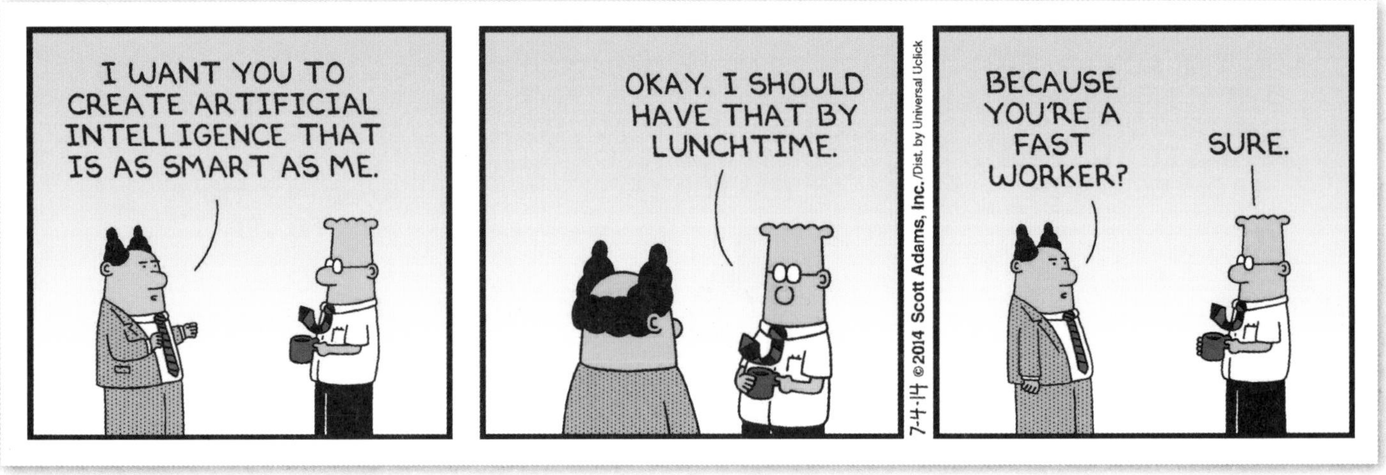
I WANT YOU TO CREATE ARTIFICIAL INTELLIGENCE THAT IS AS SMART AS ME.
OKAY. I SHOULD HAVE THAT BY LUNCHTIME.
7-4-14 ©2014 Scott Adams, Inc./Dist. by Universal Uclick
BECAUSE YOU'RE A FAST WORKER?
SURE.

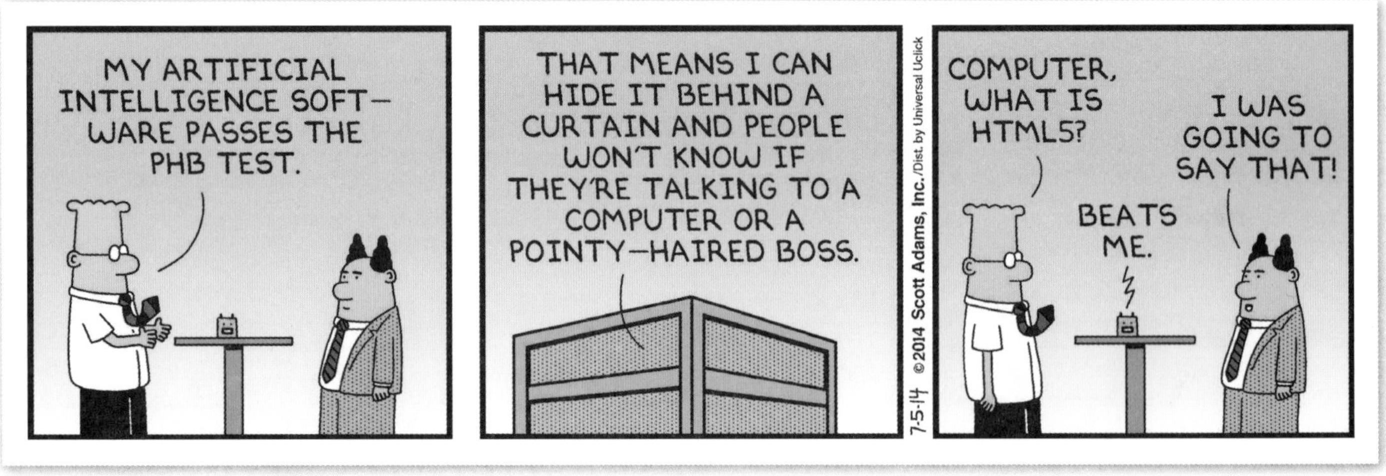
MY ARTIFICIAL INTELLIGENCE SOFT-WARE PASSES THE PHB TEST.
THAT MEANS I CAN HIDE IT BEHIND A CURTAIN AND PEOPLE WON'T KNOW IF THEY'RE TALKING TO A COMPUTER OR A POINTY-HAIRED BOSS.
7-5-14 ©2014 Scott Adams, Inc./Dist. by Universal Uclick
COMPUTER, WHAT IS HTML5?
BEATS ME.
I WAS GOING TO SAY THAT!

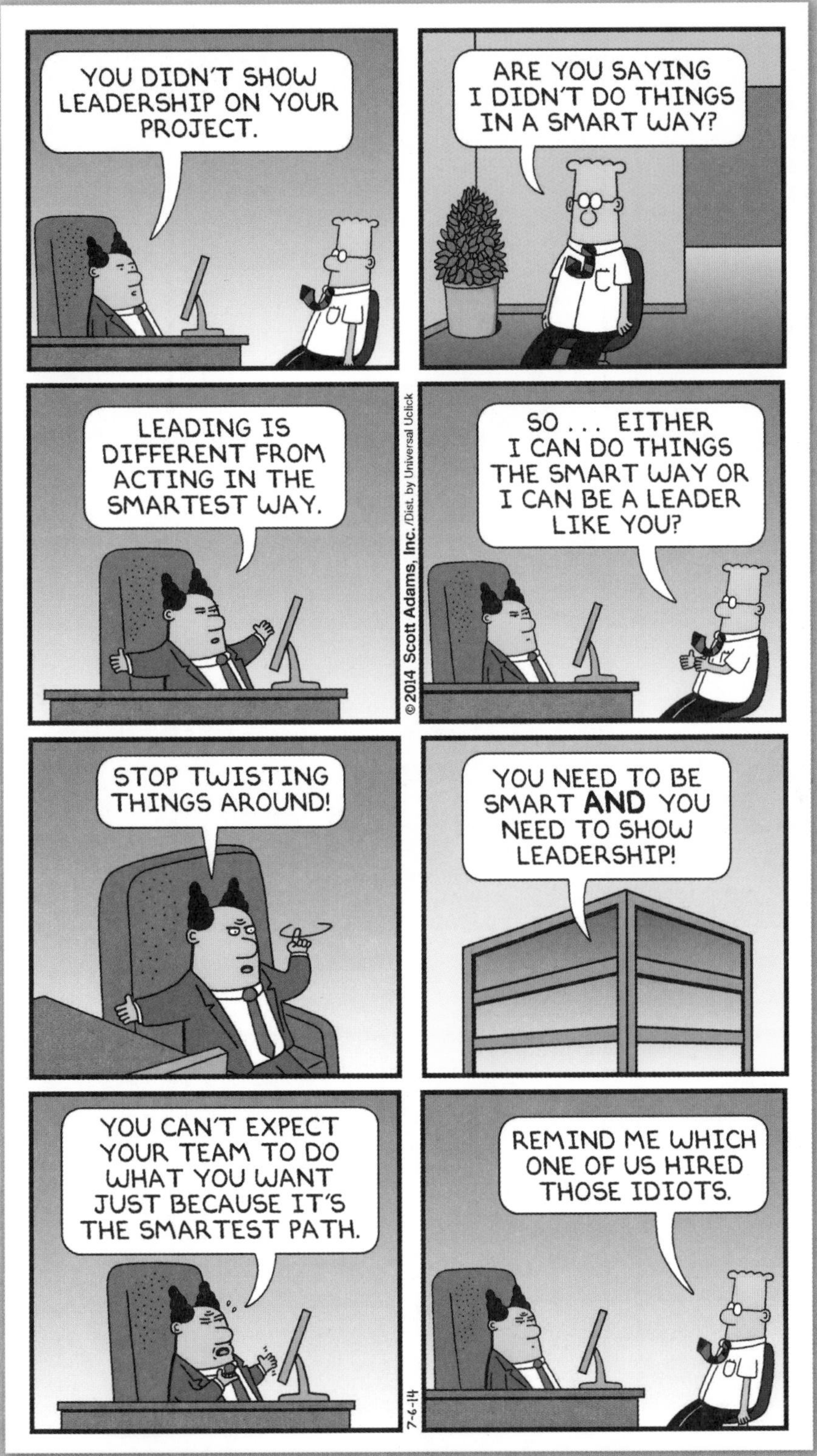
YOU DIDN'T SHOW LEADERSHIP ON YOUR PROJECT.
ARE YOU SAYING I DIDN'T DO THINGS IN A SMART WAY?
LEADING IS DIFFERENT FROM ACTING IN THE SMARTEST WAY.
SO . . . EITHER I CAN DO THINGS THE SMART WAY OR I CAN BE A LEADER LIKE YOU?
STOP TWISTING THINGS AROUND!
YOU NEED TO BE SMART AND YOU NEED TO SHOW LEADERSHIP!
YOU CAN'T EXPECT YOUR TEAM TO DO WHAT YOU WANT JUST BECAUSE IT'S THE SMARTEST PATH.
REMIND ME WHICH ONE OF US HIRED THOSE IDIOTS.
©2014 Scott Adams, Inc./Dist. by Universal Uclick
7-6-14

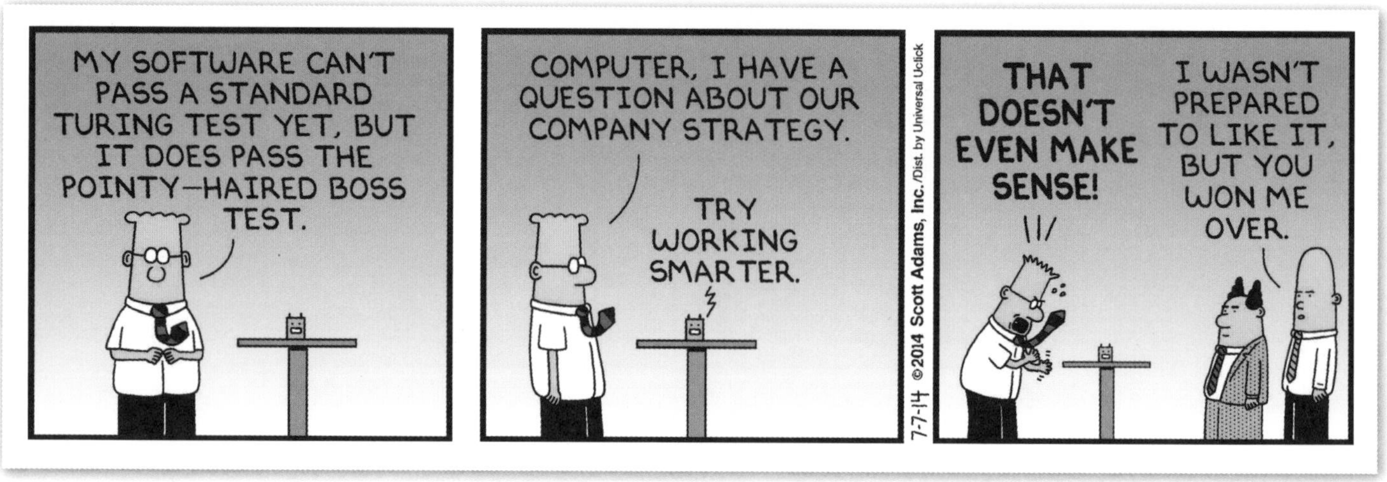
MY SOFTWARE CAN'T PASS A STANDARD TURING TEST YET, BUT IT DOES PASS THE POINTY-HAIRED BOSS TEST.
COMPUTER, I HAVE A QUESTION ABOUT OUR COMPANY STRATEGY.
TRY WORKING SMARTER.
7-7-14 ©2014 Scott Adams, Inc./Dist. by Universal Uclick
THAT DOESN'T EVEN MAKE SENSE!
I WASN'T PREPARED TO LIKE IT, BUT YOU WON ME OVER.

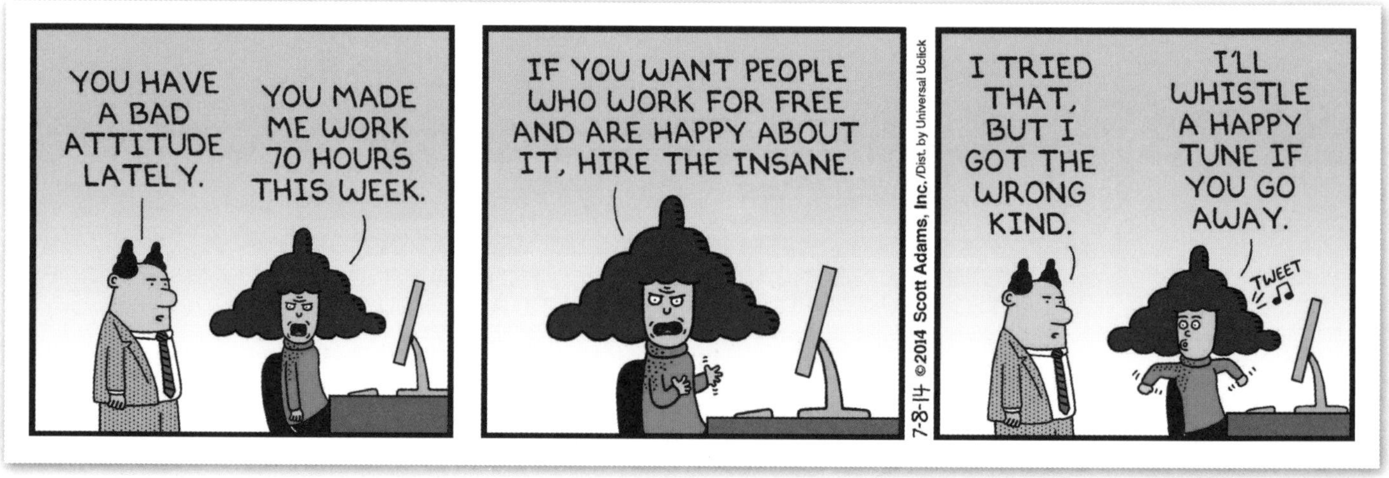
YOU HAVE A BAD ATTITUDE LATELY.
YOU MADE ME WORK 70 HOURS THIS WEEK.
IF YOU WANT PEOPLE WHO WORK FOR FREE AND ARE HAPPY ABOUT IT, HIRE THE INSANE.
7-8-14 ©2014 Scott Adams, Inc./Dist. by Universal Uclick
I TRIED THAT, BUT I GOT THE WRONG KIND.
I'LL WHISTLE A HAPPY TUNE IF YOU GO AWAY.
TWEET

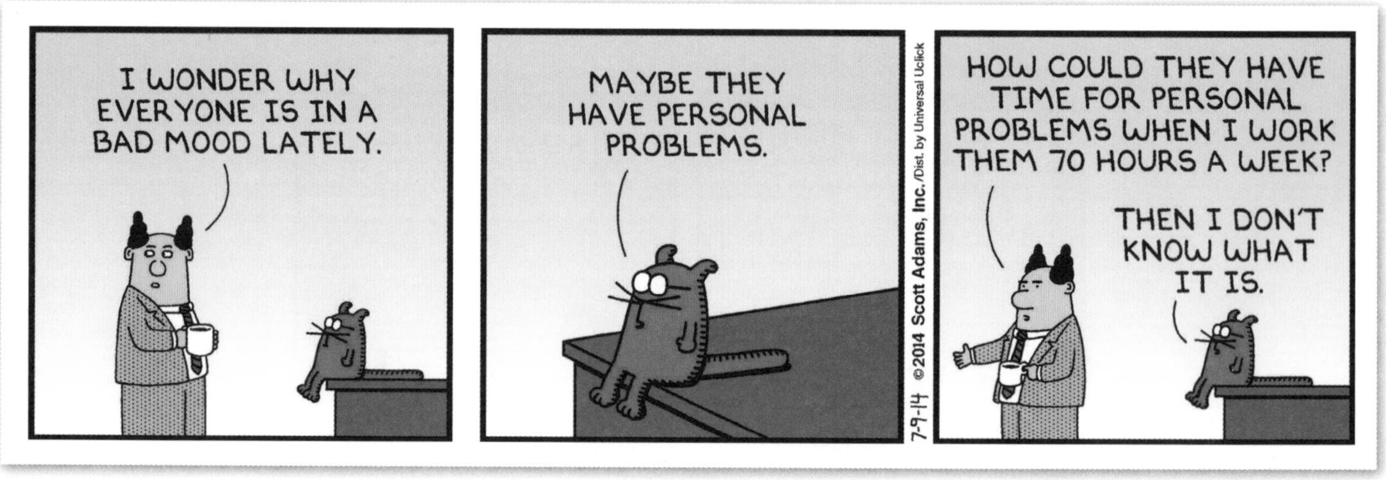
I WONDER WHY EVERYONE IS IN A BAD MOOD LATELY.
MAYBE THEY HAVE PERSONAL PROBLEMS.
7-9-14 ©2014 Scott Adams, Inc./Dist. by Universal Uclick
HOW COULD THEY HAVE TIME FOR PERSONAL PROBLEMS WHEN I WORK THEM 70 HOURS A WEEK?
THEN I DON'T KNOW WHAT IT IS.

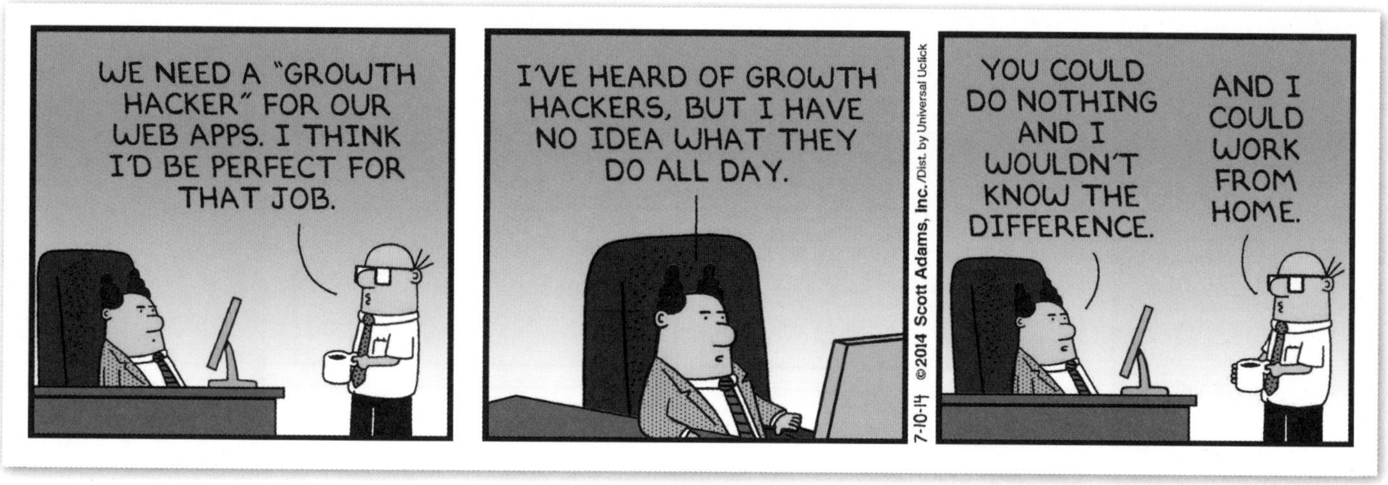
WE NEED A "GROWTH HACKER" FOR OUR WEB APPS. I THINK I'D BE PERFECT FOR THAT JOB.
I'VE HEARD OF GROWTH HACKERS, BUT I HAVE NO IDEA WHAT THEY DO ALL DAY.
7-10-14 ©2014 Scott Adams, Inc./Dist. by Universal Uclick
YOU COULD DO NOTHING AND I WOULDN'T KNOW THE DIFFERENCE.
AND I COULD WORK FROM HOME.

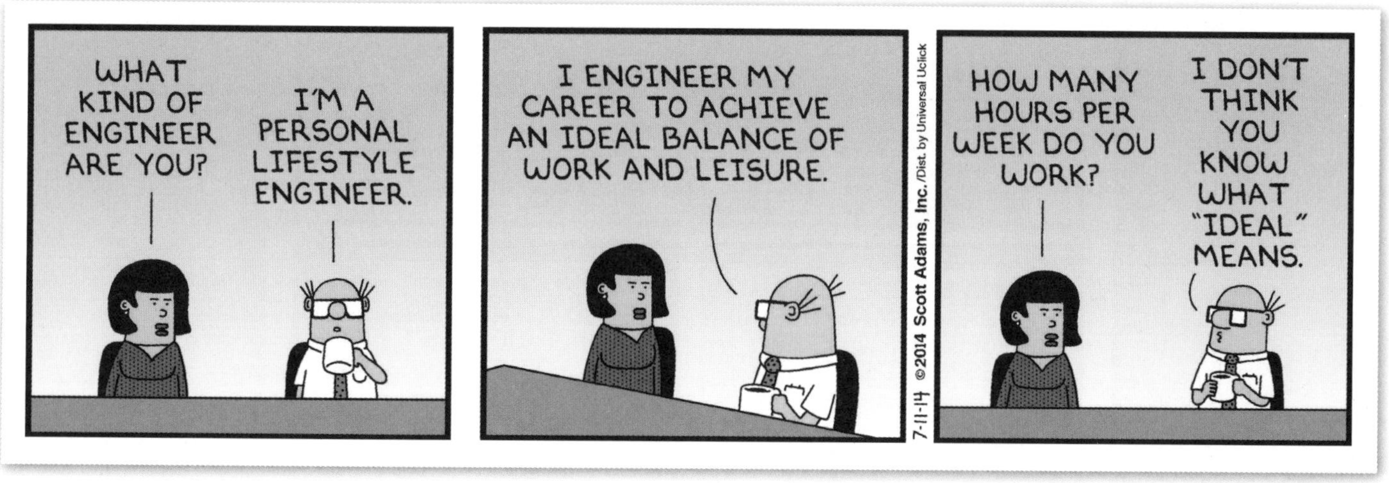
WHAT KIND OF ENGINEER ARE YOU?
I'M A PERSONAL LIFESTYLE ENGINEER.
I ENGINEER MY CAREER TO ACHIEVE AN IDEAL BALANCE OF WORK AND LEISURE.
7-11-14 ©2014 Scott Adams, Inc./Dist. by Universal Uclick
HOW MANY HOURS PER WEEK DO YOU WORK?
I DON'T THINK YOU KNOW WHAT "IDEAL" MEANS.

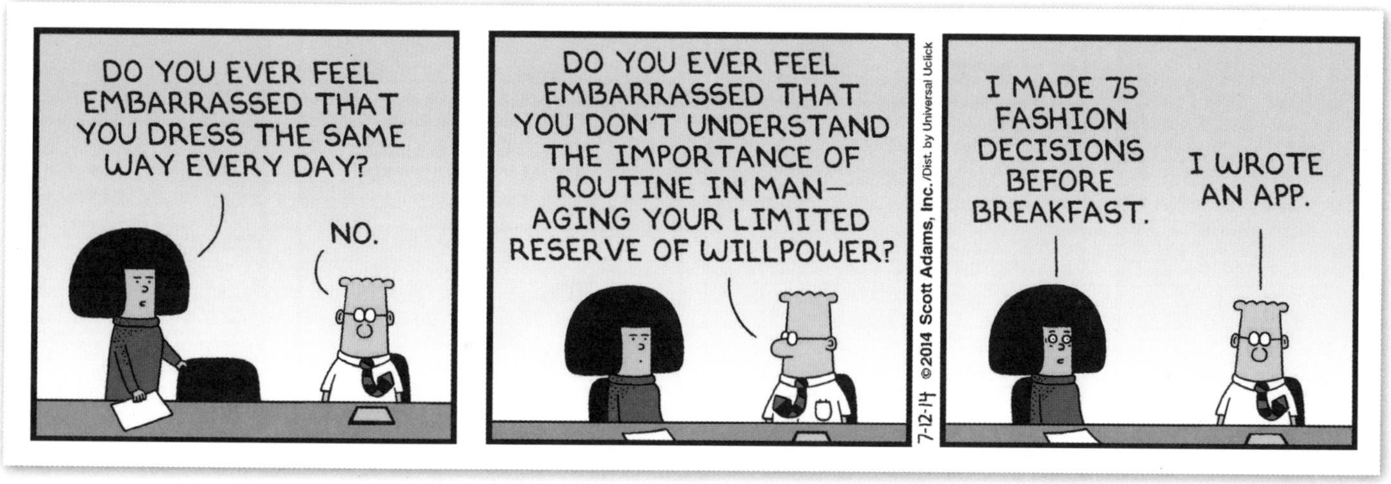
DO YOU EVER FEEL EMBARRASSED THAT YOU DRESS THE SAME WAY EVERY DAY?
NO.
DO YOU EVER FEEL EMBARRASSED THAT YOU DON'T UNDERSTAND THE IMPORTANCE OF ROUTINE IN MAN-AGING YOUR LIMITED RESERVE OF WILLPOWER?
7-12-14 ©2014 Scott Adams, Inc./Dist. by Universal Uclick
I MADE 75 FASHION DECISIONS BEFORE BREAKFAST.
I WROTE AN APP.

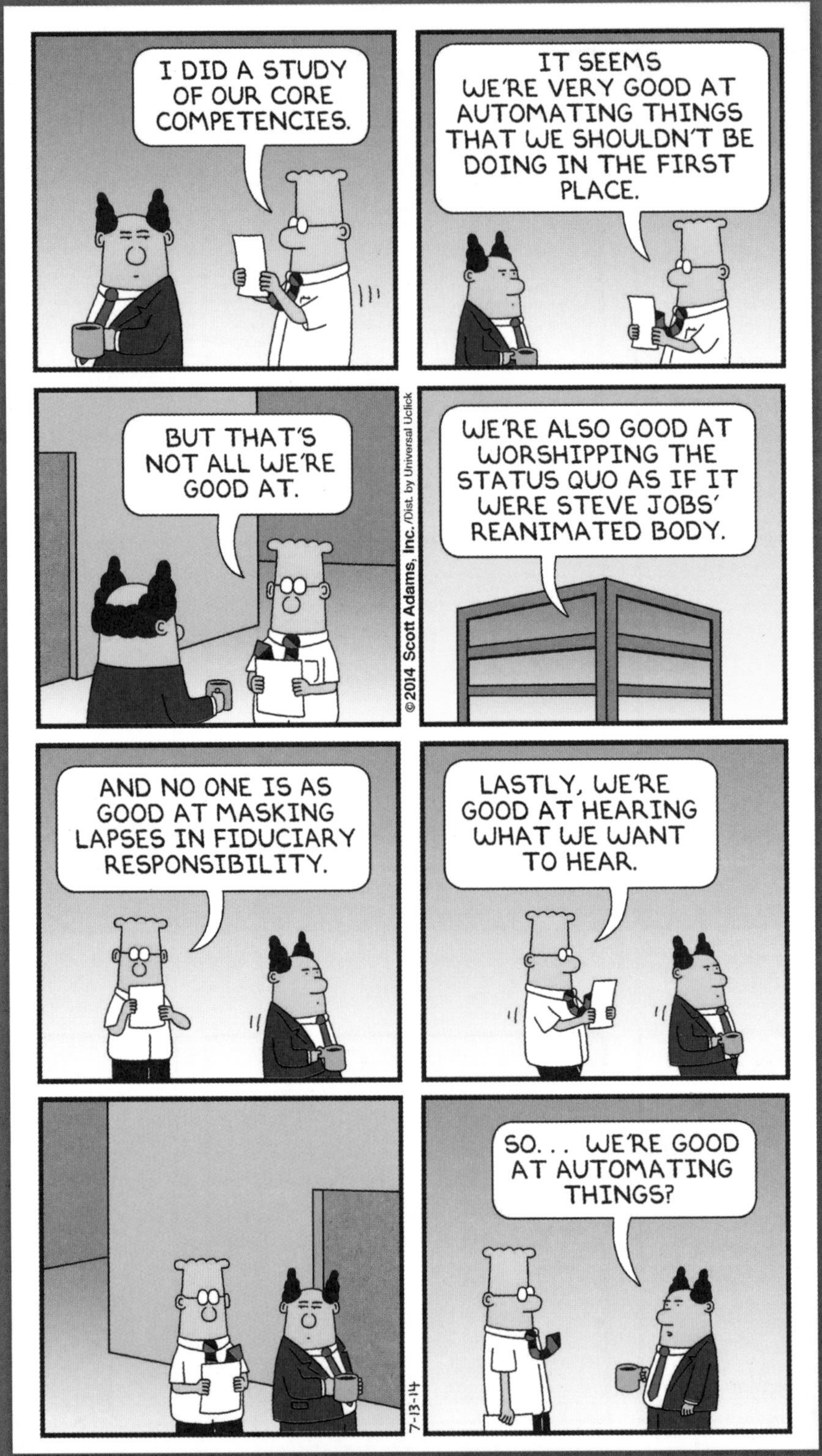
I DID A STUDY OF OUR CORE COMPETENCIES.
IT SEEMS WE'RE VERY GOOD AT AUTOMATING THINGS THAT WE SHOULDN'T BE DOING IN THE FIRST PLACE.
BUT THAT'S NOT ALL WE'RE GOOD AT.
WE'RE ALSO GOOD AT WORSHIPPING THE STATUS QUO AS IF IT WERE STEVE JOBS' REANIMATED BODY.
AND NO ONE IS AS GOOD AT MASKING LAPSES IN FIDUCIARY RESPONSIBILITY.
LASTLY, WE'RE GOOD AT HEARING WHAT WE WANT TO HEAR.
SO. . . WE'RE GOOD AT AUTOMATING THINGS?
©2014 Scott Adams, Inc./Dist. by Universal Uclick
7-13-14

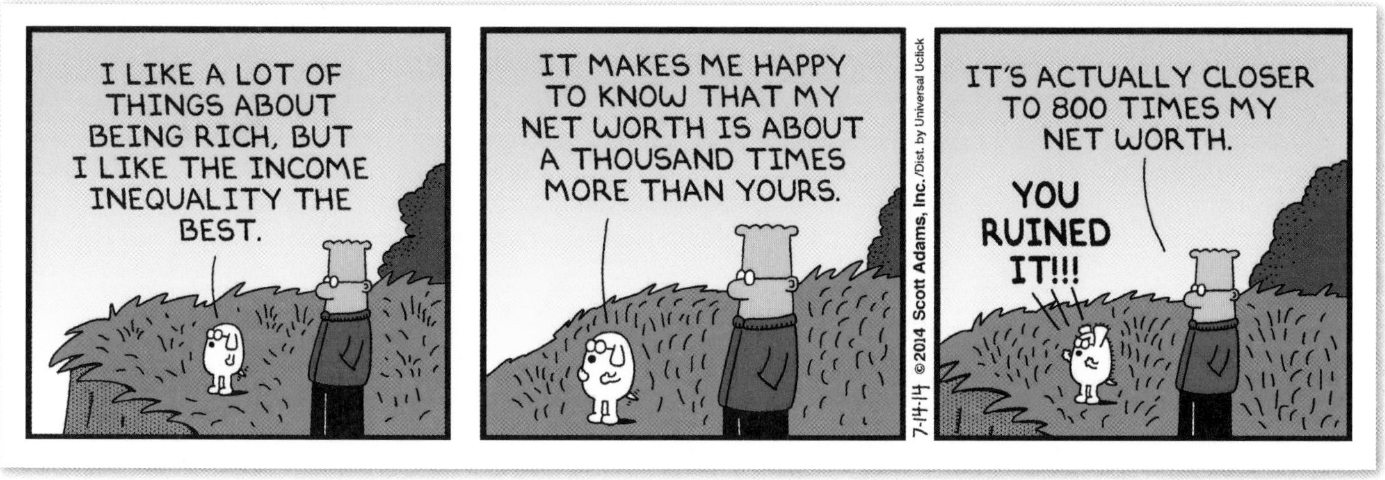
I LIKE A LOT OF THINGS ABOUT BEING RICH, BUT I LIKE THE INCOME INEQUALITY THE BEST.
IT MAKES ME HAPPY TO KNOW THAT MY NET WORTH IS ABOUT A THOUSAND TIMES MORE THAN YOURS.
7-14-14 ©2014 Scott Adams, Inc./Dist. by Universal Uclick
IT'S ACTUALLY CLOSER TO 800 TIMES MY NET WORTH.
YOU RUINED IT!!!

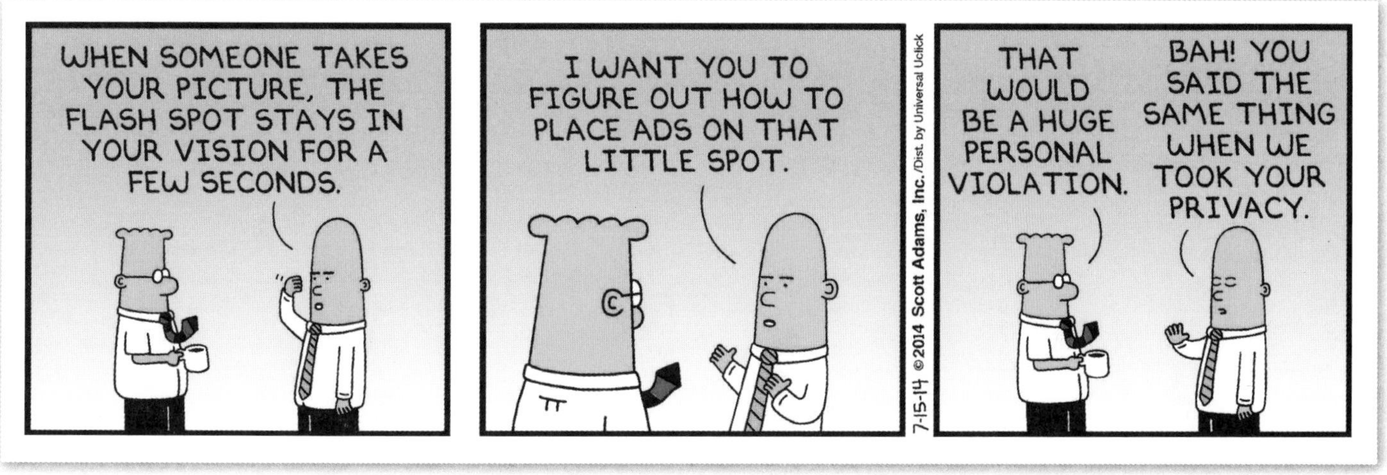
WHEN SOMEONE TAKES YOUR PICTURE, THE FLASH SPOT STAYS IN YOUR VISION FOR A FEW SECONDS.
I WANT YOU TO FIGURE OUT HOW TO PLACE ADS ON THAT LITTLE SPOT.
7-15-14 ©2014 Scott Adams, Inc./Dist. by Universal Uclick
THAT WOULD BE A HUGE PERSONAL VIOLATION.
BAH! YOU SAID THE SAME THING WHEN WE TOOK YOUR PRIVACY.

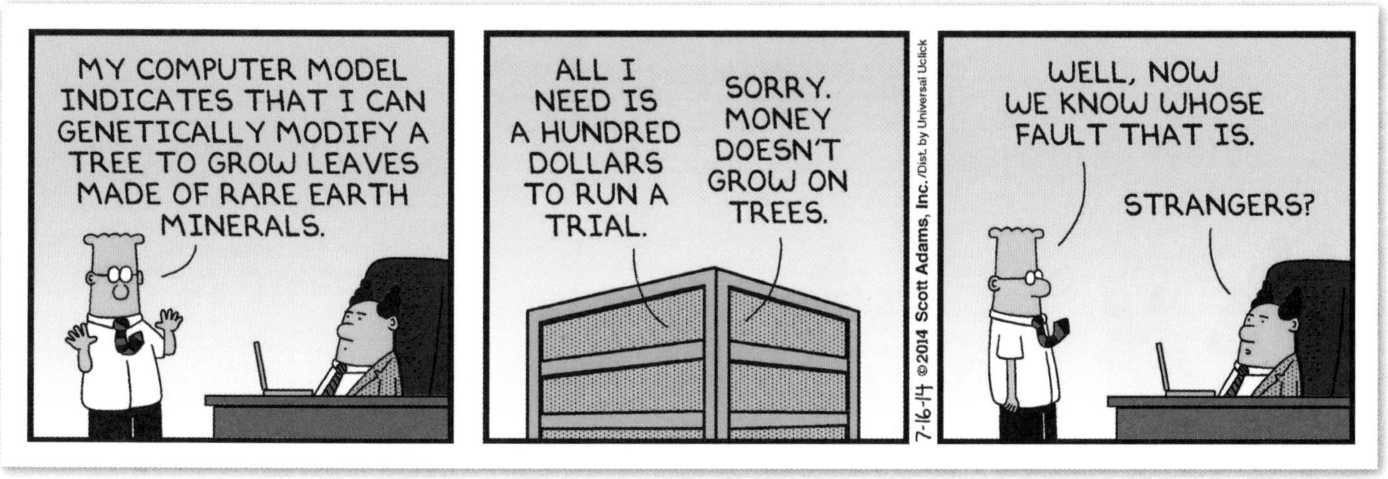
MY COMPUTER MODEL INDICATES THAT I CAN GENETICALLY MODIFY A TREE TO GROW LEAVES MADE OF RARE EARTH MINERALS.
ALL I NEED IS A HUNDRED DOLLARS TO RUN A TRIAL.
SORRY. MONEY DOESN'T GROW ON TREES.
7-16-14 ©2014 Scott Adams, Inc./Dist. by Universal Uclick
WELL, NOW WE KNOW WHOSE FAULT THAT IS.
STRANGERS?

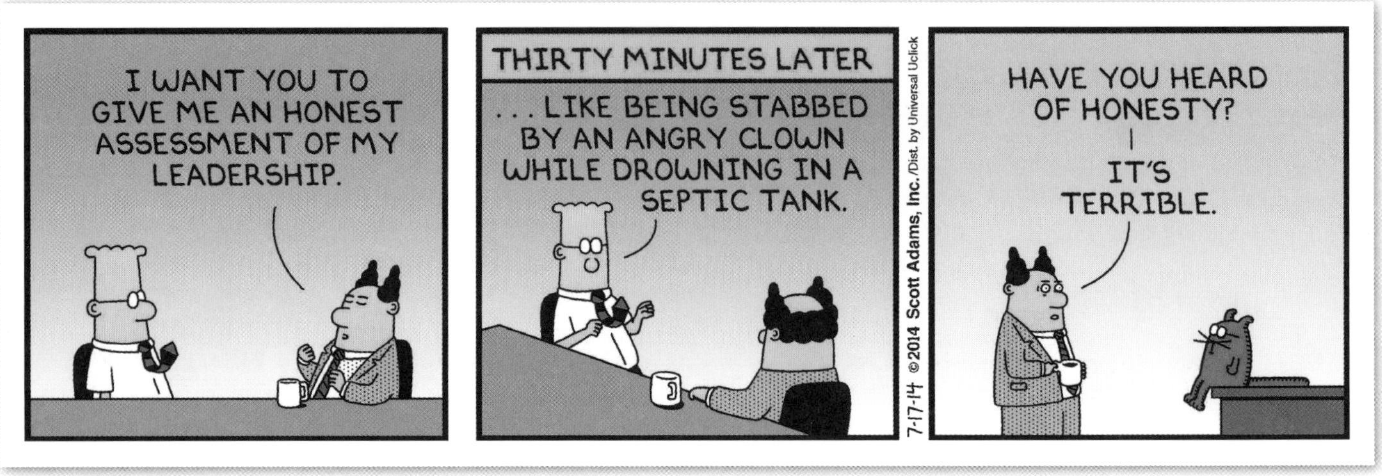
I WANT YOU TO GIVE ME AN HONEST ASSESSMENT OF MY LEADERSHIP.
THIRTY MINUTES LATER
. . . LIKE BEING STABBED BY AN ANGRY CLOWN WHILE DROWNING IN A SEPTIC TANK.
7-17-14 ©2014 Scott Adams, Inc./Dist. by Universal Uclick
HAVE YOU HEARD OF HONESTY?
IT'S TERRIBLE.

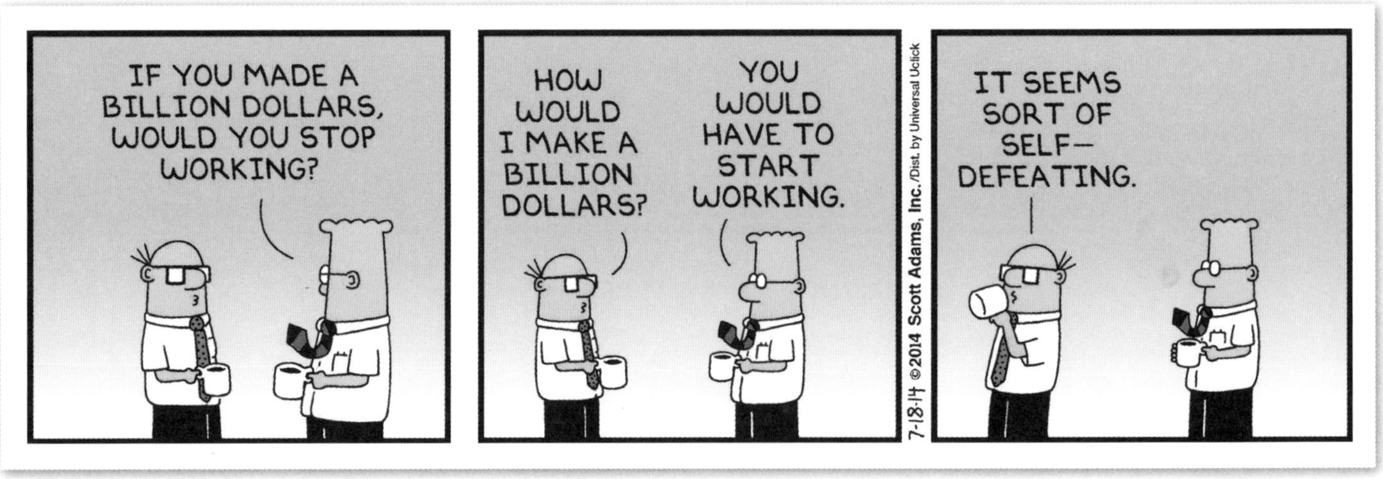
IF YOU MADE A BILLION DOLLARS, WOULD YOU STOP WORKING?
HOW WOULD I MAKE A BILLION DOLLARS?
YOU WOULD HAVE TO START WORKING.
7-18-14 ©2014 Scott Adams, Inc./Dist. by Universal Uclick
IT SEEMS SORT OF SELF—DEFEATING.

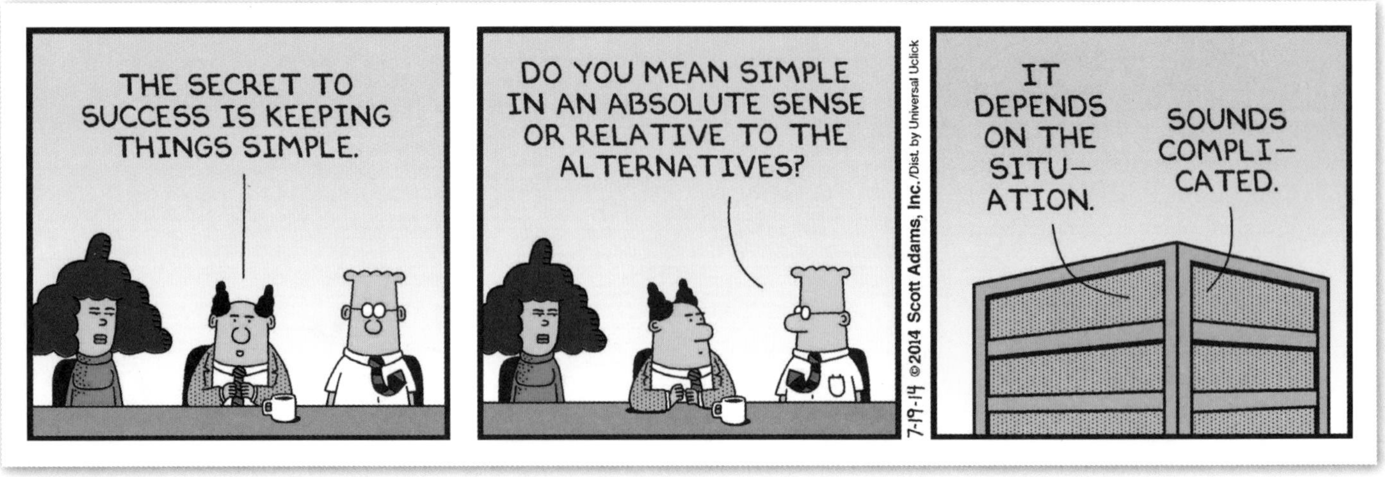
THE SECRET TO SUCCESS IS KEEPING THINGS SIMPLE.
DO YOU MEAN SIMPLE IN AN ABSOLUTE SENSE OR RELATIVE TO THE ALTERNATIVES?
7-19-14 ©2014 Scott Adams, Inc./Dist. by Universal Uclick
IT DEPENDS ON THE SITU—ATION.
SOUNDS COMPLI—CATED.

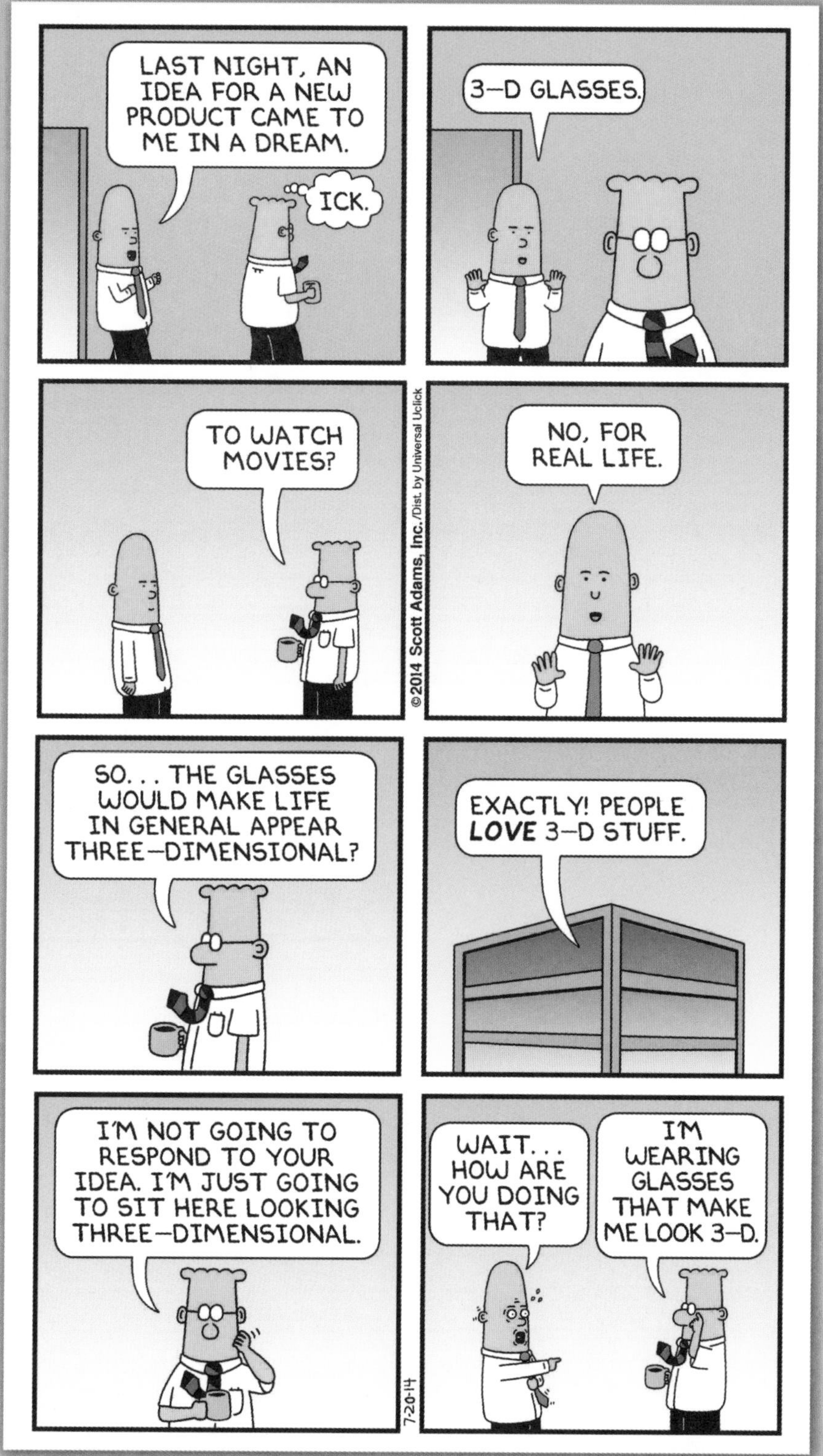
LAST NIGHT, AN IDEA FOR A NEW PRODUCT CAME TO ME IN A DREAM.
ICK.
3–D GLASSES.
TO WATCH MOVIES?
NO, FOR REAL LIFE.
SO. . . THE GLASSES WOULD MAKE LIFE IN GENERAL APPEAR THREE–DIMENSIONAL?
EXACTLY! PEOPLE *LOVE* 3–D STUFF.
I'M NOT GOING TO RESPOND TO YOUR IDEA. I'M JUST GOING TO SIT HERE LOOKING THREE–DIMENSIONAL.
WAIT. . . HOW ARE YOU DOING THAT?
I'M WEARING GLASSES THAT MAKE ME LOOK 3–D.
©2014 Scott Adams, Inc./Dist. by Universal Uclick
7-20-14

Andrews McMeel Publishing, LLC
an Andrews McMeel Universal company
1130 Walnut Street, Kansas City, Missouri 64106
www.andrewsmcmeel.com

14 15 16 17 18 SDB 10 9 8 7 6 5 4 3 2 1

ISBN: 978-1-4494-4660-4

Library of Congress Control Number: 2013944614

www.dilbert.com

ATTENTION: SCHOOLS AND BUSINESSES

Andrews McMeel books are available at quantity discounts with bulk purchase for educational,
business, or sales promotional use. For information, please e-mail the Andrews McMeel Publishing
Special Sales Department: specialsales@amuniversal.com.